dBASE DIALECTS SOFTWARE ENGINEERING, VOLUME 1

T. DAVID MILLICAN
DATABASE SOFTWARE CONSULTANTS

with a Foreword by dBASE creator C. Wayne Ratliff

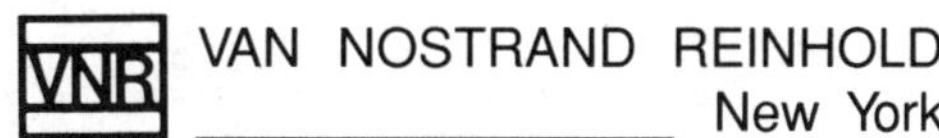
VAN NOSTRAND REINHOLD
New York

All large collections of highly technical information, such as the collection of information in this book, contain errors which will continue to be discovered as the information is used over a period of time. Although this book has been subjected to extensive quality control measures, it is certain that some errors remain. Therefore, *you use the information in this book at your risk.*

You may reduce your risk by buying the book's companion diskette or semiannual supplements (see Appendix A). These products contain continuously updated lists of identified errors in the book's information.

Library of Congress Catalog Card Number 90-12633
ISBN 0-442-00254-8

Printed in the United States of America

Van Nostrand Reinhold
115 Fifth Avenue
New York, New York 10003

Van Nostrand Reinhold International Company Limited
11 New Fetter Lane
London EC4P 4EE, England

Van Nostrand Reinhold
102 Dodds Street
South Melbourne 3205, Victoria, Australia

Nelson Canada
1120 Birchmount Road
Scarborough, Ontario M1K 5G4, Canada

16 15 14 13 12 11 10 9 8 7 6 5 4 3 2 1

Library of Congress Cataloging-in-Publication Data

Millican, T. David
dBASE dialects software engineering, volume 1 / by T. David Millican
608 p. 23.5 cm.
Includes index.
ISBN 0-442-00254-8
1. Software engineering. 2. Data base management—Computer programs
I. Title.
QA76.758.M55 1991
005.75'65—dc20 90-12633
CIP

A BARD PRODUCTIONS BOOK

Text Design: Gayle Smith Advertising Design
Typesetting: T. David Millican
Production: Gayle Smith Advertising Design

Dedication

This book is lovingly dedicated to Maude Eileen Cardwell, Ph.D., a true servant of mankind and as fine a person as you could ever hope to meet.

About the Author

Since 1970, T. David Millican has combined determination and zest in his pursuit of multidisciplinary expertise across the fields of computer sciences. In the world of academia, he earned a math & computers B.S. from Stanford University, and completed graduate work in the computer sciences at Stanford, the University of Hawaii, and the University of Texas at Austin. He has performed extensive original research into elementary function computation, but his main career focus is the optimization of the software engineering process.

Mr. Millican has worked in small, medium, and large R&D companies in Silicon Valley and in Texas, including such firms as Ford Aerospace and IBM. His work has spanned the gamut of scientific and business systems analysis and computer programming for both technical and nontechnical end-users. This broad background has led him to promote the "canonical" approach, wherein one can find breathtakingly elegant solutions to computing problems which are 10, 100, or 1,000 times faster for both human and computer.

During most of the 1980s, Mr. Millican provided microcomputer consulting services to the business and scientific communities. In addition to his consulting work, the author has written articles and product reviews for *InfoWorld, Data Based Advisor,* and *Programmer's Update.* In the late 1980s, he moved into software publishing with the release of a line of productivity products for dBASE dialect programmers. As Publisher and Chief Software Designer at Database Software Consultants, he produces docusoftware™ products which maximize programmer productivity by giving equal attention to text and software in design and implementation.

Apart from computer activities, he sings, plays acoustic and electric guitars, and hikes in the Texas Hill Country. He is an active community volunteer, essayist, and lyricist, and has published a book of song lyrics.

Quick Contents

Part I Fundamental Concepts and the dBASE Language

Part II The World of dBASE Dialects

Part III Building Blocks for Standard and Custom dBASE Applications

Part IV dBASE Software Engineering Techniques of General Application

Reference Material

Contents

Part II The World of dBASE Dialects

Part III Building Blocks for Standard and Custom dBASE Applications

Part IV dBASE Software Engineering Techniques of General Application

Reference Material

Source Code Listings

Tables

Foreword

When I wrote Vulcan, the first dBASE dialect, back in 1978, I had never heard of "dBASE" — a term coined in 1980 — and I certainly didn't consider my one-of-a-kind language product to be a "dialect," although it was based in part on an earlier program called JPLDIS. However, JPLDIS ran on UNIVAC mainframes with hard-copy terminals, whereas Vulcan ran on CP/M microcomputers with screens, so the computing environments were quite different.

In 1980, Ashton-Tate began marketing Vulcan as "dBASE II," and since then an entire industry of products and services has developed to support the users of dBASE dialects. These dialects are now offered by many different vendors, and there is a vast array of horizontal and vertical market software to assist dBASE dialect programmers and end-users, not to mention books, magazines, and consulting services!

Faced with the proliferation of continually changing aids, dBASE dialect programmers need ongoing answers to two central questions:

Which are the best dialects and tools to select?

What is the wisest way to use the selected dialects and tools?

This uniquely authoritative book and its semiannual supplements will give you an enormous amount of help in answering these two questions, both now and in the future. *dBASE Dialects Software Engineering* answers the needs of dBASE dialect programmers in a great variety of situations, and for this reason I am sure that many other people will do as I have done, and add this indispensable reference work to their collections.

C. Wayne Ratliff

Preface

What gets me up in the morning, ready to work with dBASE dialects all day long? You guessed it, the neighbor's dog.

But after the cannon-like vocalizations of this nearby beast have propelled me into motion, what keeps me going is the thought that I can learn something which will help you and me to have more fun, to write "better" programs, and to take less time to write those programs. You know what fun is, and "less time" is pretty clear, too. You and your users, clients, and employers will decide — hopefully harmoniously — on the definition of "better."

I was astonished when I discovered during the 1970s that better ideas in computing are often better not by *percents,* but by *factors.* In some occupations, such as steelmaking, management would be ecstatic to receive an idea which could improve the efficiency of a given task by 10% or 50%, but a better programming tool or procedure may be better by 10X or 50X, which is 1,000% or 5,000%. *Best of all, a better tool or procedure may eliminate some tasks entirely!*

This book represents an effort by me and my many helpers to bring you comprehensive information about the kind of dBASE dialects, tools, and services which are available to make your programming more fun and productive, and about the procedures and techniques that make the tools get the work done in a New York minute and not a South Sea summer.

Keeping the Book Up-to-Date: Semiannual Supplements

Most of the conceptual material in this book is relatively free of aging, and much of the information on dialects will continue to be accurate, even after the dialects have been updated to new versions. For example, future versions of Clipper are sure to offer the "-V" compilation switch, or its equivalent.

Nevertheless, new versions of the dialects tend to solve or eliminate the programming problems associated with earlier dialects, and to offer new possibilities for software development. Consequently, I intend to issue a new edition of this book every two or three years in the foreseeable future.

Some readers will be adequately served by a new book edition every two or three years, whereas other readers need more frequent updates. To help keep you informed about the most important dBASE dialect developments, I will publish *A Supplement to dBASE Dialects Software Engineering, Volume 1,* every six months, starting around June 1991. See Appendix A for ordering information.

The Companion Diskette

This book uses approximately 37 command files of about 69,000 bytes, approximately 13 template files of about 16,000 bytes, and several small databases which exercise the book's demonstration programs. The companion diskette contains all of these files, plus several text files generated by the demonstration programs running under various dialects.

There is so much to say in a book of this type that almost no space has been devoted to sample screens. Instead, you are directed to run each demonstration program, which is listed with an explanation that may be only partially comprehensible if you do not execute the demonstration code.

Consequently, if you wish to receive the benefits of the demonstrations, the alternatives are for you or your agent to type the source code and templates into your computer, or for you to acquire the companion diskette. In practice, it is difficult to type source code without introducing errors, and this typing is always time-consuming.

Since the companion diskette is an essential study aid for this book, I have priced it at a fraction of the book's cost in order to make the diskette very accessible. Appendix A explains how to order the companion diskette. Order this diskette today, so that you will have it the first time you need it!

How to Get Error Information

This book has been subjected to extensive quality control measures, utilizing in part the services of the leading dBASE dialect vendors and the superb members of the book's Expert Panel! Nevertheless, many errors are sure to remain in a book which includes such a large volume of highly technical material. As these errors are identified, they will be documented on the companion diskette and in each *Supplement*. (I would very much appreciate receiving your comments and specific, constructive criticisms. Write to me directly at the address in Appendix A.)

Professional Development

Volumes 1 and 2 of *dBASE Dialects Software Engineering*, along with the semi-annual *Supplements* and the companion diskettes, give you a fairly comprehensive set of text and programming tools to support your career development as a dBASE dialect programmer. In particular, I have used a conceptual approach which is designed to *empower* you to integrate and extend all of the material in this book to the limits of your continuously evolving abilities ...

Acknowledgments

The book that you hold in your hands has a depth, breadth, and accuracy which could not have been achieved without the assistance of leading vendors of dBASE dialects, as well as the assistance of leading experts in the field. I'd like to thank the following vendor representatives for providing information or products, and for arranging or performing the technical review of dialect-specific material in the book.

Ms. Pam Allen, Director of Corporate Communications, WordTech Systems.

Ms. Nannette Jenk, Marketing Assistant, Fox Software.

Ms. Barbara Katzoff, Nantucket Corporation.

Mr. Thomas Leylan, Senior Systems Analyst, Nantucket Corporation.

Mr. Dave Micek, dBASE IV Product Manager, Ashton-Tate.

Ms. Allen Mireles, Marketing Specialist, Fox Software.

Mr. Craig Ogg, Senior Systems Analyst, Nantucket Corporation.

Ms. Traci Owens, Corporate Communications, Ashton-Tate.

Ms. Gloria Pfeif, Manager of Training and Developer Services, Fox Software.

Mr. Robert Pirani, Manager of Technical Support, WordTech Systems.

Ms. Liz Sidnam-Wright, Manager of Public Relations for Database Products, Ashton-Tate.

Also, without listing them, I'd like to thank the various vendor representatives who have kept me supplied with review copies of the dialect products over the years. Without these review copies, I would never have been able to develop the expertise that makes this book possible.

This book was written on two microcomputers which were provided to me by their manufacturers for evaluation purposes. Special thanks to Brian K. Fawkes of Dell Computer Corporation for the loan of a Dell System 200 and to John Pope and Tom Irby of CompuAdd Corporation for the loan of a CompuAdd 325. The great speed of the CompuAdd 325 was essential in the timely production of this very large and complex book.

Rebecca M. Lasher, the talented Head Librarian and Bibliographer at the Mathematical and Computer Sciences Library at Stanford University, designed and executed the DIALOG search strategy which extracted dBASE-related books from the electronic form of *Books in Print* for Appendix F. Glenn Claudi-Magnussen developed an IBM ASCII extension for the PostScript driver in Borland International's Sprint product, which was used to edit and typeset the book. He graciously donated this extension to Sprint users by placing it on CompuServe, where the indispensable volunteer Andrew Morrow answered my countless questions about Sprint. (I am grateful to Borland International for providing a review copy of this very powerful word processor; however, Sprint has been frozen at version 1.01 for years and this version is quite buggy.)

The Expert Panel

I have had significant experience with a number of dialects — my commercial software products support Clipper, dBASE III PLUS, and FoxBASE+, with support under development for other dialects — but no single person could have in-depth experience with *all* of the major dialects. Fortunately, a *group* of persons, such as those represented on the Expert Panel, *can* have such expertise.

Five leading dBASE experts and one generalist served on the Expert Panel. Each expert brought to the project a very high level of expertise in one or more dBASE dialects and helped to ensure proper and accurate coverage of each major dialect.

The generalist, Mr. Christopher von Schweinitz, served in two unique ways. As the only Expert Panelist living in my community, Christopher acted as both an alpha tester and a beta tester for the book text and code. Second, Christopher's feedback helped me make this book more accessible to novice and intermediate dBASE dialect programmers.

You may be as intrigued as I am by the following information: each Expert Panelist submitted a large number of corrections and suggestions which were incorporated into the book. However, there was very little overlap in the submissions!

Following is a list of the Expert Panelists, with a brief description of their roles. **Please note that contact information for virtually all companies mentioned in this book is listed in Appendix I on page 457.**

Dr. John Bauman, M.D. John is a physician on active duty with the U.S. Army in San Antonio, Texas. John is also a rather clever FoxBASE+ programmer who is known to many through his articles in *Data Based Advisor* magazine.

Dr. Mark Leavitt, Ph.D., M.D. Mark is a practicing physician and Clipper developer with a doctorate in electrical engineering. You can contact him about his medically oriented applications at 9155 SW Barnes Road, Suite 333, Portland, OR 97225, (503) 292-0768.

Mr. Christopher von Schweinitz. Christopher is on the lead programming team at OmniQuest Software, Incorporated, in Austin, Texas. He has worked in dBASE environments in the past and now develops groupware with C, C libraries, and Novell networks.

Ms. Monique Verrier. Monique is a coauthor of the long-running "Quicksilver/dBXL Programming" column in *Data Based Advisor* magazine. She offers consulting services through Creative Software of Santa Rosa, California.

Mr. Randy Wallin. Randy is a coauthor of the book *dBASE Power: Building and Using Programming Tools* (Olympia, Freeland, and Wallin 1988). He offers consulting services for dBASE IV, FoxPro, and other dialects through COB System Designs in Jupiter, Florida.

Mr. Craig Yellick. Craig is the owner of Yellick Computing and a partner in Alto Microcomputer, Incorporated, in Edina, Minnesota. He has published a number of text-based and/or code-based productivity products for Clipper programmers. (See page 454.) Craig is the only Expert Panelist whose feedback resulted in a major reorganization and improvement of the book's strategy and tactics. A special tip of the hat to the man from the Snow Belt!

In addition, dBASE consultant Andy Pergiel tested some of the code in this book. Andy may be reached in Austin, Texas, at (512) 323-9771.

I stand on the shoulders of giants.
Sir Isaac Newton, 1642–1727

The new techniques do *work — they* do *double the productivity of the average programmer, increase the reliability of his code by an order of magnitude, and decrease the difficulty of maintenance by a factor of two to ten.*
Edward Yourdon, *Managing the Structured Techniques*, 1979a, p. 4

Nothing Runs Like The Fox.
Fox Software slogan

The Path to the Stars suddenly forms in our view.
Holding each hand, we go mind in mind
to a destiny made from the Dream of the World:
to the New World we dreamed with our breathless world-dream,
breathless dream.
"New World World-Dream," T.D.M., 1988

Part I

Fundamental Concepts and the dBASE Language

The three chapters in Part I deal with the necessary preliminaries of our subject and the book. This book contains many databases of dBASE-related text information and a number of organizational principles which are meant to give you answers as rapidly as possible. For that reason, there is more than usual to say about "How to Use This Book."

We also survey the basic concepts of structured systems analysis, structured programming, and other "structured" concepts, referring the reader to the literature for more information. We will witness the almost unlimited power of the "canonical approach," and use it to discover and develop software engineering technologies based on the layer concept, the macro concept, the subroutine concept, the library concept, and the data-driven concept.

Then we take a programmer's tour of the essential facilities of the dBASE language and development environment. Although some recommendations appear in this survey, the basic purpose of the tour is to provide factual information rather than advice — most of the rest of the book concentrates on "how-to."

Chapter 1

Introduction

This chapter introduces the basic philosophy of the book and explains its various information resources and how they are structured. You will also find information on the book's optional companion diskette and semiannual *Supplements.*

Audience and Prerequisites

If you are a manager or other nonprogramming professional, this book will put you in a position to better understand and/or manage dBASE programming efforts. Since you read for fundamental concepts like "do's and don't's" while skipping the technical details, a modest familiarity with electronic data processing is sufficient preparation. Chapters 12, 13, and 14 are nontechnical and especially relevant.

Otherwise, I assume that you have some programming experience, but this experience doesn't have to be extensive, as long as you have a firm grasp on basic concepts like file I/O (input/output) and tree-structured directories. Since the "primary" dBASE dialects execute under the MS-DOS operating system, all examples are given for MS-DOS dialects,[1] and I further assume that you are familiar with MS-DOS basics like filename and pathname conventions.

However, an effort has been made to exhibit sensitivity to the needs of mainframe and minicomputer programmers who are moving into the microcomputer world. This effort takes the form of especially explicit information and instructions for MS-DOS.

I further assume that every reader has access to the manuals of one or more of the dBASE dialects. If not, there are a number of books which present the basic language information. (See Appendix F on page 435.)

Teachers

If you plan to teach a course or seminar based in whole or in part on this book, you should have a good familiarity with at least one of the dBASE dialects. I recommend that you also have some (not necessarily formal) background in software engineering concepts; Edward Yourdon's book *Managing the Structured*

---

1. Most examples will work with all dBASE dialects. For our purposes, IBM PC-DOS is equivalent to MS-DOS.

Techniques (Yourdon 1979a) is an excellent, compact, and very accessible source of these concepts.

To prepare students to properly utilize the techniques and tools in the book, I recommend that you emphasize the "canonical" approach explained in Chapter 2.

What to Expect from the Book

This book offers a comprehensive treatment of dBASE tools and techniques which you can exploit to increase your programming productivity by up to 50% to 1,000%, depending on your experience and skill level and your budget for tools. Here, the term *programming productivity* refers to the time you take to program from specifications. It does not include the time required to develop specifications or train users. For example, if you become 100% faster in coding from specifications, your overall job productivity might increase by 50%.

The use of the word *exploit* in the previous paragraph is quite deliberate, because this book has much more information in it than would usually be relevant to any one person. Some of the techniques and tools will *not* be appropriate for you, and some of the demonstrated *uses* of these tools and techniques will not be appropriate for you — *without modification*.

For example, I may show you three menu-making methods sorted in increasing order of programmer time needed and user appeal delivered. If you always go for the quickest programming time, then use the first method and ignore the others. If you always go for the best-looking menu, then use the third method and ignore the others. If you match your effort to the importance of the program, then you will of course study the spectrum of alternatives and look at the trade-offs between the alternatives.

Sometimes half of what I say will make sense to you for your situation and the other half won't fit at all. In that case, ignore the half that doesn't fit and put in the missing ingredient whose identity *you* know. The point is not which of us is more correct, but rather, how our ideas can be combined to make your job faster and more fun!

If you'd like to see some specific examples of productivity gains for programmers in different situations, look at Appendix D on page 429. This appendix discusses four programmers at three different levels of experience.

Why a Book on Several Dialects Instead of One Dialect?

If you look at the dBASE books in print which are listed in Appendix F on page 435, you will notice that these books almost without exception treat a single dialect. A book which covers the spectrum of dialects is definitely more work for the author and would seem to be more work for the reader, so why write it or read it?

Most people who work with one dBASE dialect over a period of time find that they eventually have the opportunity or requirement to maintain or develop applications for other dBASE dialects. People move into different dialects when they change jobs, and consultants find that supporting more dialects increases their income.

There is also the challenge of porting an application from one dialect to another. As an example, many programmers have been called upon to modify dBASE III PLUS applications to run under Clipper.

In some cases, an application must operate under more than one dialect. All of the dialects have bugs, and one way that you can protect yourself and your users, clients, and employers from the disastrous consequences of a bug which you can't fix is to write your application to execute under at least two dialects. There are many issues and options which apply to porting an application from one dialect to another, or to writing it so it can execute under more than one dialect.

Even if you use one dialect exclusively, you will benefit from knowing the strengths and weaknesses of your dialect relative to the others. In many cases, you will discover a labor-saving feature in another dialect and will incorporate that feature into your dialect via a subroutine!

Finally, *there are many techniques which work under all dialects.* For example, the decision about whether to split a name into a first-name field and a last-name field is a design decision which has very little dependency on the dialect used.

Similarly, there are many tools which support several dialects. Therefore, this book treats tools and techniques in the context of software engineering in general and in the specific context of dBASE dialects!

The Philosophy of This Book

If you say that the average professional typist works at 60 words per minute, then you may find that the very fastest typists deliver 2 or 3 times this speed, but you will never find a typist who delivers 10 times the standard speed, nor will you find a 1,000% difference in productivity between workers in most professions. Yet the first example in Appendix D, which describes the programming productivity of identical twins Jeb and Ed, shows us that one programmer may be 10 times more productive than his or her counterpart.

The philosophy of this book is to tell you *what fast programmers do that makes them fast.* In the next chapter, we'll meet the *canonical approach* and related concepts, and the rest of the book will be an application of these concepts to dBASE dialect software engineering.

But the canonical approach is about much more than programmer speed during initial development. It is also about program speed, user empowerment, and the speed and reliability with which the program may be modified during its period of use.

The canonical approach is also about alternatives. You cannot know if your choice was a good one or a bad one if you don't know the alternatives.

Finally, the canonical approach is about understanding. Do you understand the implications and consequences of your programming choices for the user? For the maintenance programmer? What if the application must be ported to another dialect? What if the application must be multiple-user? Will the application have a large or small user population, a long or short lifetime, a flexible or inflexible budget, or a flexible or inflexible schedule?

Will it be difficult or easy to support the users? Do they need bomb-proof applications, or is down-and-dirty appropriate, because the users are sophisticated, or because the data is not critical, or because there are many programs that the users *must* have at the earliest possible time?

At current levels of programmer productivity, the global demand for custom applications cannot be met. My interpretation of the canonical approach stresses the *minimum* use of programmer and computing resources to produce a *satisfactory* result.[2] If your choice is to write one application this year which has a fancier interface than your in-house users require, or to write two *satisfactory* applications, then I advocate that you write two applications.

This book supports your decision-making process by showing you alternatives whenever feasible, and by constantly striving to refer you to all other known sources of products, services, and concepts. You will find many lists and discussions of the advantages and disadvantages of recommended approaches and competing alternatives.

The Default Dialect

This book attempts to give explicit support for the dBASE dialects vended by Ashton-Tate, Fox Software, WordTech Systems, and Nantucket, and implicit support for all other dialects. When examples are shown which are not identified as dialect-specific, assume that the dialect is dBASE III PLUS.

With an installed base of over 2.5 million copies, dBASE III PLUS is the de facto standard in the marketplace. While our main interest is naturally in the more recent and powerful dialects, *dBASE III PLUS is essentially the common subset of all the dialects.*

This "common subset" feature is important for two reasons. First, many dBASE programmers must convert programs from one dialect to another or write programs which will execute under more than one dialect. These programmers need to know what commands are common to the dialects they use. Second, a rapid path to understanding any dialect is to ascertain its relationship to the standard core of features in dBASE III PLUS.

For these reasons, I often use the dBASE III PLUS dialect as a reference point when I discuss other dialects. However, generally speaking, I compare each dialect to each other dialect for which the comparison is useful and relevant.

Remark. When FoxBASE+ is referenced without a version number, assume version 2.1. When Clipper is referenced without a version number, assume the Summer '87 version, which is also called version 4.0.

2. The definition of "satisfactory" is of course made by you and your users, clients, and employers.

The Organization of Volumes 1 and 2

dBASE Dialects Software Engineering is published in two volumes. Parts I to IV are in Volume 1 and Parts V to VIII are in Volume 2.

Part I covers the topic of how to use the book and then reviews fundamental concepts of software engineering and surveys the dBASE programming language and development environment. Part II compares the major and minor dBASE dialects to each other and introduces the world of dBASE-related products and services. In this part of the book, you meet each dialect and learn the wide range of reasons for selecting dBASE dialects to develop database-oriented application programs for microcomputers and minicomputers.

Part III takes you into some of the core material of the book, namely, the building block concept and its application to dBASE dialects through libraries of subroutines and fill-in-the-blanks source code templates. The book's library of templates is presented in a way which demonstrates some provocative concepts and benefits of standardization. These concepts and benefits will be yours from now on.

Part IV, "dBASE Software Engineering Techniques of General Application," and Part V, "dBASE Software Engineering Techniques of Specific Application," present a fairly comprehensive collection of solutions to intermediate and advanced single-user dBASE programming problems. Part IV presents techniques which you will probably use in most of your programs, whereas Part V presents techniques to handle data processing problems which are restricted to certain kinds of applications. For example, the techniques for handling mailing addresses will be used only in programs which process mailing addresses.

Part VI deals with the increasingly important topic of programming applications to share resources on a network. Even after you thoroughly understand single-user programming, there is a whole new set of concepts and techniques to learn in order to understand the objectives and pitfalls of multiple-user programming. This part first gives you the necessary conceptual background and then shows you what must be done and how to automate (most of) the process of making applications network-ready.

When you code small sample programs in a programming class or in a course of self-guided study, there is no greater context for the code that you generate. Once the code works correctly on a few sample test cases, you abandon it.

However, when you develop programs which will be used for "serious" information processing, there are many other considerations. Part VII shows you dBASE debugging facilities and gives you ways to handle the differences between the hardware/software configuration of your computer and those of your users. We also investigate testing and validation tactics and strategies and their implications for you and your users.

High technology consists of the sophisticated use of tools. While most of this book is devoted to dBASE language technique, Part VIII covers more than 100 commercial tools for dBASE programmers. In addition to product information, explanations and recommendations for use appear for several products, notably R&R Relational Report Writer from Concentric Data Systems.

The Companion Products and Resources of This Book

This section describes the companion products for the book and the various information resources which are incorporated into the pages of Volume 1.

1. **Diskette of Source Code, Test Databases, and Errata.** The companion diskette contains the command files and templates listed in this book, as well as some small test databases which exercise the book's demonstration programs. The companion diskette also has several text files generated by the demonstration programs running under various dialects, and it lists all known errors in the book.[3] Appendix A tells you how to order this inexpensive and indispensable study aid.

2. **The Semiannual Supplements.** Despite the pace of developments in the dBASE world, it is not feasible to produce updated editions of the book more often than every two or three years, and some of you cannot wait that long for updated information. Therefore, I will publish a supplement to the book every six months, starting six months after the publication of Volume 1.

   Remark. *dBASE Dialects Software Engineering, Volume 1,* is published by Van Nostrand Reinhold and may be purchased in bookstores or from Van Nostrand Reinhold. In contrast, the companion diskette and the semiannual supplements are published by Database Software Consultants and must be purchased according to the procedures in Appendix A.

3. **Tables of Contents.** In the front of the book you will find four lists of text items with page numbers. The first table lists the chapters and appendixes in the book for your quick reference. The second list is a conventional table of contents. The third list, "Source Code Listings," and the fourth list, "Tables," contain approximately 170 titled listings and tables.

4. **Names and Descriptions of Included Utility Files.** The book includes a number of templates and utilities. To assist your exploitation of these utilities, their names are listed and their functions are summarized in Appendix B, "Names and Descriptions of Templates and Listings," on page 423.

5. **Lists of dBASE-Related Information.** Several appendixes list dBASE-related information.

   Appendix F on page 435 lists all the dBASE books in the authoritative *Books in Print* as of May 1990. Several dozen titles on database theory, software engineering, and systems analysis are listed for further reading.

   Appendix G on page 449 lists six kinds of information sources: user groups, dBASE-related periodicals, electronic bulletin boards, consulting services, training directories, and courseware.

---

3. Please report all errors to me in writing at the address in Appendix A.

To discover the vendor of a product which you read about in this book, look at Appendix H, "Alphabetic List of dBASE-Related Products," on page 455. You can find contact information for the service providers and product vendors in this book by looking at Appendix I, "Alphabetic List of dBASE-Related Vendors," on page 457.

The product listings do not have any reviews or descriptions, because this information is given in the text where the product is referenced. If you see a product in the list, and you would like to know what the book has to say about the product, then look up the product by name in the Index to discover the page numbers on which the product is referenced.

6. **Glossary.** A glossary appears on page 461. It defines some microcomputer terminology which may be unfamiliar to minicomputer and mainframe programmers. Some terminology is specific to dBASE dialects, and there is some discrepancy between dBASE and mainframe database terms. Again, the Glossary helps you keep it all straight.

7. **Citations and References.** Whenever possible, the book gives you one or more references for further information. Immediately preceding the Index you will find the list of references, alphabetized by the author's last name. Citations in the text point you to items in the list of references.

   Citations appear in two forms, according to whether a page number or range of page numbers is included in the citation. For example, "(Bauman 1989b)" points you to the reference for John Bauman's article, "DBFs on the Fly," in the August 1989 issue of *Data Based Advisor*. (The "b" in "1989b" indicates the second Bauman reference from 1989.) If I want to show the page number or a range of page numbers, the reference is "(Bauman 1989b: 128)" or "(Bauman 1989b: 128–134)."

8. **Index of Terms, Product References, Routines and Templates.** A key requirement for a book of this type is a comprehensive, well-structured index. Depending on the information you seek, you may benefit more from the table of contents, table of source code listings, or table of tables than the Index. In addition to the usual entries which you would expect, the Index contains the names of products, vendors, subroutines, and templates which appear in the book.

   To look up a template by its position in the book, use the table of source code listings in the front of the book — if the word "template" appears in the title of a listing, then the listing is a template. Look up named templates under "Templates" in the index and look up named and unnamed templates by topical area under "templates" in the index.

   Files of various types appear in the index under the name of the file type and/or under the index heading "files." Look up files such as .BAT files and .EXE files before the "A" entries in the Index.

You will find useful groups of references under the following main headings in the Index: books in print, cautions (10 entries), concept, Directories, environmental identification, Examples (13 entries), files, index files, information sources, keyboard facilities, locking, maximum, menus, new features of interest to programmers, pick lists, prices, Recommendations (76 entries), Remarks (20 entries), Rules (10 entries), specifications (57 entries), Templates (22 entries), templates (56 entries), and Warnings. In addition, there are dozens of listings under the name of each major dialect and obvious headings like "software" and "parameters."

How to Find Recommendations and Software Engineering Principles in This Book

In some cases, I start with a basic engineering principle and then give an explanation and examples. At other times, I present problems and solutions and make recommendations as appropriate when presenting the solutions.

With this organizational strategy, the recommendations and citations of principles are somewhat dispersed and cannot be accessed just by turning from one page to the next. However, the book gives you two kinds of index tools to help you locate this information.

First, you can consult the table of tables in the front of the book to see which tables contain general software engineering information. Second, you can look under the following terms in the Index: cautions, Examples, menus, new features of interest to programmers, pick lists, Recommendations, Rules, Templates, templates, and warnings. Third, you can examine Appendix E, "Coding Standards for dBASE Dialects," on page 431.

Typographic and Notational Conventions

No special font is used for code fragments or keywords which appear in paragraphs. Instead, code is capitalized, as in SET TALK ON; quoted, as in "SET Talk ON"; or displayed, as in

SET Talk ON

Listings of source code or source code templates are presented in the following format. Note that each named listing appears in the table of source code listings at the front of the book.

Listing 1.1 Sample Code Listing

```
* File = Sample1.PRG.
SET CONSOLE ON
?  "This file is Sample1.PRG."
* End of Sample1.PRG.
```

I use the universal angle-bracket and square-bracket notation. Items in angle brackets are descriptions of contents which are to replace the angle-bracketed item in actual use. For example, the syntax to open a dBASE database file without options is

USE <.DBF file name>

To open the Accounts.DBF database without options, you code

USE Accounts

Square brackets are used for optional text. For example, one multiple-user form of the USE command is

USE <.DBF file name> [EXCLUSIVE]

This means that the two alternative forms of the syntax are

USE <.DBF file name>

and

USE <.DBF file name> EXCLUSIVE

A different form of alternation is described with the vertical rule "|". For example, you can import foreign file formats into properly structured databases with this syntax.

APPEND FROM <text file> TYPE DELIMITED | SDF

The two supported forms are

APPEND FROM <text file> TYPE DELIMITED

and

APPEND FROM <text file> TYPE SDF

For keystrokes, the following notation is used. When I want you to stroke the key which is labeled "Enter" and typically referred to as the enter key, the carriage return key, or just "carriage return," then I write ENTER. When I want you to depress the Control key, usually labeled "Ctrl," and stroke a second key such as "W" while the Control key is depressed, then I write CONTROL-W. The "direction" keys are specified as Home, End, PageDown, PageUp, UpArrow, DownArrow, LeftArrow, and RightArrow; the "Escape" key is specified as ESCAPE.

Chapter 2

Fundamental Concepts: Structure and the Canonical Approach

This chapter reviews fundamental concepts in software engineering. We look at what must happen before, during, and after coding in order to increase the likelihood of acceptable results. We then meet some concepts of quality control and product optimization.

Systems Analysis

Extremely simple or small programs that you use for yourself may not need any written description of functionality. The program name alone may be enough to help you remember what the program does.

At the other extreme, very large programs that are used by large numbers of people can be successfully implemented only if great attention is given to planning and quality control at all phases of the project. *Systems analysis* is the name given in the jargon for the part of the process that produces a description or *specification* for an information processing system which has both a human and a software component.

Classical systems analysis tends to produce monolithic specifications which may be poor communication devices between users and programmer/analysts. Yet, the entire purpose of the specification is to ensure (1) that the customer gets what he or she orders, and (2) that what the customer *requests* and what the customer *wants* are actually the same thing!

Structured Systems Analysis

Structured systems analysis organizes the information acquired during the analysis of an existing or proposed information processing system into a tree structure. This inherently modular approach is very accessible to both users and programmers.

For example, the mail tellers at a bank may perform a three-step process to handle mail deposits:

1. Open and screen mail deposits.
2. Prepare magnetic tape of deposit information.
3. Post magnetic tape information to the central computer.

Whenever you and the bank client need to discuss the mail deposit system, you can immediately narrow your concern to one of the three areas. Each of the three high-level tasks is broken down further into subtasks. For example, the first task, "Open and screen mail deposits," may be more precisely defined as follows.

1. If an envelope is not marked "Mail Deposit," return it to the mail room for rerouting.
2. Open the envelope.
3. If the contents are not in order, return them to the mailer with an explanation.
4. Feed the checks through the magnetic reader.

In a monolithic specification, the procedure for checking whether the contents are in order appears, say, on page 57. The description of this procedure is a collection of details in a collection of details, which tends to overwhelm everyone. In a structured specification, this procedure is seen as the third component of the first high-level process, which is easy to understand for both client and analyst.

Every group of people which is involved with information processing evolves its own terminology. In practice, usage is inconsistent among group members, so you can see the challenge for outside analysts to understand a group's special language. When practicing structured systems analysis, you will literally develop a dictionary of special terms. This dictionary is called by a title which you have probably heard before: *data dictionary*.

The data dictionary also contains definitions of the data elements which are processed in the system. For example, if phone numbers are stored, you specify the amount of space for each number and the phone number formats which are supported. During analysis, you or your client may wonder, "Does the phone number format allow extensions to be stored?" Such questions are answered by consulting the data dictionary.

The tree-structured description of the system is supplemented by *data-flow diagrams*. Such diagrams show sources and destinations for information, the processing performed on the information, and the way that information flows between the sources, processes, and destinations. In the context of our bank example, the highest-level data-flow diagram has one source (customers who mail in deposits), three processes (open deposit envelopes, make magnetic tape, post magnetic tape), and one destination (the central computer's customer accounts database).

Just as with the written descriptions, data-flow diagrams follow the tree structure. A data-flow diagram for the first process (open deposit envelopes) would itself have one source (customers who mail in deposits), four processes (sort, open, qualify, and feed), and three destinations (mail room, customer, and magnetic reader).

How Much Structure?

Microcomputer software which fully supports structured systems analysis has historically cost thousands of dollars, although prices are bound to decline over time. However, you can do a lot without specialty software.

Data dictionaries can be constructed with standard text editors without much problem; as you add new entries to the dictionary, you insert them in alphabetic order. This means that you don't need any sort. Alternatively, you can store the data dictionary in a database in order to maintain and report the data with database techniques.

The descriptions of processes (which are organized according to the tree structure of the system) can be easily implemented in word processors which have automatic numbering of lists. Without this facility, you will have to forgo the numbering of lists or else renumber lists as you insert, delete, or rearrange items. Alternatively, you can use the memo facility of dBASE dialects to store and manage this process-description information.

The data-flow diagrams can be drawn by hand, but this is slow and incompatible with frequent revisions. Implementing the data-flow diagrams with the character graphics of your word processor is not much better. Drawing these diagrams automatically is one slick trick that makes the systems analysis software cost so much (in addition to the limited market size).

The larger and more complex the project, the more necessary it will be to take formal, slow approaches to each step, generating a list of process descriptions, a data dictionary, and a collection of data-flow diagrams, all of which must be comprehensive and constantly updated. When you write a program of any size for someone else, I feel that it is necessary to have a written description of some sort upon which you both agree. You will determine the scope and nature of the description according to your experience and judgment.

When you write a nontrivial program for yourself, open a new file in your word processor and enter a plan before you start coding. Again, this doesn't have to be fancy or long, but it can help you see pitfalls before you fall into them, and it can help you spend the minimum possible amount of time in implementation. With a plan or checklist, you do things in the correct order and don't forget any necessary steps. The concept here is that "an ounce of prevention is worth a pound of cure." (See the systems analysis titles in Appendix F for more information.)

Structured Programming

The main idea in structured programming is to perform standard tasks in standard ways which offer superior benefits. This is a theme which we will see throughout the book.

Structured programming offers a set of guidelines for both the implementation and design of computer programs. We'll look first at the structure of the programming code inside program units, and then we'll look at the structure of the application in terms of the number of and relationships between program units.

Code Constructs in Structured Programming

Let's define a *proper program* as one which has no unreachable code, no infinite loops, one entrance point, and one exit point. It is known that any proper program can be written with these three procedure structures (Bohm and Jacopini 1966):

1. **Sequence.** The sequence structure is simply an ordered list of statements, executed one after another.
2. **Alternatives.** This is the familiar "IF ... THEN ... ELSE" programming construct ("IF ... ENDIF" in dBASE dialects).
3. **Repetition.** This is the "loop" construct in which a sequence of statements is executed while a logical expression remains true. In dBASE dialects, this is the "DO WHILE ... ENDDO" structure.

In practice, one also needs a subprogram construct in order to allow a large program to be decomposed into a set of sequences. dBASE dialects offer three kinds of subprogram units: command files, procedures, and user-defined functions, all of which are introduced in Chapter 3.

Top-Down Analysis and Iterative Refinement

Many books and magazine articles have been written about the top-down approach to structured computer programming, so we won't go into the concept here in detail.[1] Furthermore, the basic concept is easy to state and grasp (although its wise application is another matter altogether).

In the beginning of this chapter, we used an outline approach in a systems analysis example. This outline approach *is* the top-down approach. When it is applied to software engineering, there is a correspondence between procedures and outline items. In terms of the example starting on page 13, you might have procedures named OpenMail, MakeTape, and PostTape to implement each of the three steps.

The procedure MakeTape might have to perform the following three steps: (1) format the tape, (2) write the tape, and (3) rewind the tape. Following the top-down approach, you might have MakeTape call the three procedures FormatTp, WriteTp, and RewindTp, in order to deliver each listed service. These three procedures would call other procedures as necessary, and the process would terminate with procedures that do not call other (user-defined) procedures.

The top-down approach contrasts with the bottom-up approach, in which you determine the most elementary services that you will need. You write procedures to perform those elementary services and call those procedures from what we'll call level 1 procedures for the sake of discussion. Then level 2 procedures call the level 1 procedures, level 3 procedures call the level 2 procedures, and so on, until a top-level procedure implements the application.

1. See the software engineering titles in Appendix F or virtually any college-level programming textbook for more information.

In some structured theories, one rigorously avoids the bottom-up approach, but in practice, a programmer must often use *some* of the bottom-up approach. A program's specification and source code are often a product of a refinement process that shifts back and forth between a bottom-up and a top-down view.

In the jargon, this process is called *iterative refinement*, and it may involve only the top-down approach, only the bottom-up approach, or a combination of the two. The specification and source code of an application are developed in stages. The understanding developed in each stage is used to choose the refinements which are introduced on the next stage. This process is repeated, that is, *iterated,* until a satisfactory result is obtained (or until programming resources are exhausted).

The Structure and Relationships of Program Units

In the structured approach, each subprogram is a proper program with a precisely defined task. The design and documentation of a program unit indicates (1) the assumptions that the unit makes about the data it receives, (2) the processing that is performed, and (3) the conditions which can be assumed if the entry assumptions are true. (We'll explore these issues in detail in Chapter 20, "Design of dBASE Dialect Subroutines." Also see Appendix E on page 431 for a coding standard which addresses these and other coding issues.)

Summary

To summarize, the structured programming approach leads you to perform standard tasks in standard ways which offer superior benefits. Your program units have no unreachable code, no infinite loops, one entrance point, and one exit point. Each unit has a well-defined task, and the documentation and design of the unit show clearly what the unit expects and what you can expect from the unit when you use it properly.

Software Engineering and the Product Life Cycle

With a written description, or *specification,* you can begin to implement the information system. Programmers tend to think of an information system as consisting of program code alone, so that implementation becomes a two-phase process: write a lot of code, and then train the user.

However, our bias in this book is to attend to all of the human patterns which are related to the information system. With this bias, we see that there are many aspects of an information system besides the initial writing of program code. These other aspects include, but are not limited to, the following: the system's specification, documentation for the programmer, printed documentation for the user, online help, quality control and production procedures for staff, and the evolution of the software as user wish lists are implemented.

This perspective furnishes us with another definition of software engineering: the design, implementation, and maintenance of all aspects of a computer-based information system. How can the software and the documentation be matched to each other? What facts and procedures must the competent user understand? How do you handle the training of staff members over time as people come and go? How do you modify the software to give a new requested feature to the user without causing a chain reaction of unwanted changes? How do you keep management in touch with the management requirements of the information system, when managers come and go over time? How do you coordinate the updating of printed documentation and online help when software features change?

A general-purpose computer program is typically used for between one year and ten years; the length of time during which the program is used is called the *product life cycle*. Advances in computer software and hardware, or changes in business or personal circumstances, limit the life cycle of a particular program, which will eventually be discontinued or replaced.

However, during its life cycle, a program, that is, an information system, must typically be modified to one extent or another. One of the main challenges of software engineering is to design systems that can be safely and cheaply modified.

It is *safe* to modify an application if its results are correct after the modifications are performed. Although there are many concepts in software engineering, *correctness* is probably the most important of all.

The importance of correctness cannot be overstated. If results are not correct, then why compute them at all? Part of the value system which this book promotes is that the primary objective of an information system is to produce correct results — all other goals are secondary.

Remark. Computer software is used to control nuclear reactors, advanced aircraft and seacraft, factories, payrolls, and business decisions, to name but a few applications. Incorrect software can cause the failure of careers and companies and sudden or early death for living creatures. For example, omission of one hyphen from one programming statement caused the 1962 space probe, U.S. Mariner I, to go off course, at a loss of $18 million! (Wallace et al. 1980: 486)

The number and range of factors which are potentially related to the operation of any given computer-based information system resist classification. A *thorough* treatment of these factors for a standard application like a mailing list would take hundreds of pages, and our space requirements (not to mention your patience!) mean that such detail is not for us. However, to the maximum extent which is feasible, we will try to bear these additional factors in mind in each situation. For the record, let me say that software engineering is a bottomless subject, and that what I reveal is always the tip of the iceberg; for further reading, see the lists of systems analysis and software engineering titles in Appendix F (page 435).

Information Structures

The computer component of a computer-based information system consists of bit patterns (assuming that the computer is digital). These bit patterns are interpreted either as instructions or as data upon which the instructions operate. The instructions are structured (perhaps poorly) into units which are called *procedure structures* in the jargon. By analogy, the data is arranged in *data structures*.

Together, procedure structures and data structures comprise the *information structures* of the software component of an information system. **A large portion of this book is devoted to explanations of recommended information structures for dBASE dialects.**

The Structured Techniques

As computer scientists gained experience over the years, it became obvious that the way in which the data and code of programs were structured made an enormous difference to every aspect of the software: how easy its insides were for the programmer to understand, how easy its outsides were for the user to understand, how fast it was, and how much storage was used by the code and the data.

Eventually, computer scientists of broad interdisciplinary skills and vision realized that the idea of looking for good structures among the possibilities applied to the whole process of software development and usage. I think of Edward Yourdon as the primary advocate of the application of the structured techniques to the entire software problem, and, as such, he is in my mind the founder of modern software engineering.

Yourdon has a series of books on software engineering written alone or in collaboration with others. He also has his own press, Yourdon Press, which publishes in the software engineering area.

I believe that his most accessible book is *Managing the Structured Techniques* (Yourdon 1979a), now in its fourth edition! Here you will find a succinct and very useful exhibition of the structured techniques applied to the gamut of software engineering activities.

Another accessible and useful book is *Structured Walkthroughs* (Yourdon 1979b), also in its fourth edition. "Walkthrough" is a technology which you can practice alone, although its real power shines in group situations. This technique comprises a structured review of program code, typically in its "first draft," before it enters testing. This technique is another application of the fundamental concept, "An ounce of prevention is worth a pound of cure."

The "Superprogrammer" Phenomenon

In the late 1960s, a research team led by Harold Sackman (Sackman et al. 1968) constructed a now-famous experiment to assess the value of online versus batch programming. Several professional programmers were given the same programming assignments; half worked on CRT terminals and half with punch cards.

As often happens in science, Sackman's team made an unexpected discovery, which Edward Yourdon calls the "superprogrammer" phenomenon. This phenomenon, which has nothing to do with the online versus batch issue, tells us an astonishing and unusual fact about programmer productivity.

What will happen if you assemble a large group of programmers at comparable skill levels and give them the same programming assignment?[2] You will find that, despite the equivalence of backgrounds, the fastest programmers will be 5 to 10 times faster than the average programmer, and perhaps 100 times faster than the slowest programmers!

You might predict that the programs produced by the fastest programmers would be sloppy and slow. In fact, their programs will typically run 5 to 10 times faster than the code of the average programmer. Not coincidentally, the faster programs typically have 2 to 5 times fewer code lines than the typical program.

So if you measure programmer productivity by a combination of programmer speed and program speed, then *the fastest individuals in a large test group are 25 to 100 times more productive than the typical programmer. How do they do it?*

Remark on canonical information structures. If there is one thing that I want you to take from this book, it is the answer to that question: *canonical information structures.* This discovery is of the utmost importance to you personally, because canonical techniques can be *learned.*

No matter what your skill level is, you can always increase your productivity still further by deepening your understanding of canonical approaches.

Canonical Information Structures

Researchers and practitioners have realized for some time that there is typically a range of solutions for a given information processing problem. Furthermore, *the better solutions may be dozens or hundreds of times faster and more economical of storage than other solutions.*

We naturally wonder how we may find the better solutions. That is, we ask, "What are the best information structures for this problem?" These structure questions are inherently mathematical in nature, and mathematicians have been dealing with structure concepts for centuries. In the Middle Ages, researchers borrowed the term *canonical* from the Roman Catholic church to denote structures that were "best" or "ultimate" in some sense.

In this day and age, we understand explicitly that the laws of physics and the laws of governments are quite different, but in medieval times, this distinction did not exist. The church issued *canons,* in which both physical and social reality were defined. Hence, we have the term *canonical* to denote the "true" representation.

---

2. This programming "experiment" is verified thousands of times annually in computer science courses around the world.

Canonical approaches in software engineering have almost miraculous results. Let's see what "almost miraculous" means in terms of commercial software products.

Canonical Proof, Canonical Pudding

We say that the "proof of the pudding is in the eating," and the consequences of following or not following the canonical approach to software engineering can be seen in any comparative review of at least 5 competing products where performance measurements (benchmarks) are published. Look at the speed with which the products perform a standard task on identical files. Providing that the group of products is large enough, you will typically see variations from the slowest to the fastest of up to 500% to 1,000% or more.

For example, in the December 1984 *Software Digest Ratings Newsletter* (Software Digest 1984), there are several benchmarks on 14 "Integrated Productivity Programs." Over a sample of about 10 benchmarks, I found the gap in speed between the fastest and slowest products to range from a low of 860% to a staggering high of 52,300%. The fastest program on each benchmark was roughly 1,000% faster than the average program.

Bear in mind that these are all complex commercial software packages written by computing professionals. Even in this arena, we still see the vast differences which distinguish canonical approaches from noncanonical approaches.

Fortunately, canonical approaches can be *learned*. This book does not try to develop a comprehensive theory of canonical approaches in software engineering. Instead, the canonical approach is taught by implicit and explicit examples.

For example, the programming philosophy and techniques in this chapter and in Parts III through VII of the book are all products of canonical thinking. The other parts of the book present information which supports the canonical approach to software development, under which you consider a spectrum of alternatives in the search for a canonical solution.

At this time, let's take a look at some concrete examples. We'll then attempt a comprehensive listing of the various dBASE software engineering tools and techniques which are outcomes of canonical thinking.

A First Example: Now You See It, Now You Don't

As a first example of the canonical approach, examine the following program fragment and measure how long it takes you to determine what this code does.

```
USE Sales
T = 0
DO WHILE (.NOT. EOF())
   T = T + Sales->Received
ENDDO
? T
USE
```

This fragment appears to display the total sales in the Sales database. However, if the Sales database has no records, the fragment displays "0" and otherwise the value of the Received field in record 1 of Sales is repeatedly added to T. Let's try again.

```
USE Sales
T = 0
DO WHILE (.NOT. EOF())
   T = T + Sales->Received
   SKIP
ENDDO
? T
USE
```

After a little study, you can see that this fragment displays the sum of the Received field in the Sales database. However, you can surely decipher the following version of the same code in less time, and with less likelihood of missing a bug.

```
USE Sales
TotalSales = 0
DO WHILE (.NOT. EOF())
   TotalSales = TotalSales + Sales->Received
   SKIP
ENDDO
?  "Total sales:", TotalSales
USE
```

The variable "T" was renamed to the self-describing "TotalSales", and the total sales figure is labeled as such when it is displayed.

Recommendation on descriptive names. Choose names for procedures, variables, and other programming objects which are as descriptive as possible, within the length limit of 8 or 10 characters per name. In dBASE dialects, it is possible to write code which is largely self-explanatory. Using identifiers which are as descriptive as possible is one of the most fundamental of all canonical techniques.

One final enhancement to this code fragment will make it truly canonical. We exploit one of the several dBASE commands which can be used to replace DO WHILE loops, as the following code demonstrates.

```
USE Sales
SUM Received TO TotalSales
?  "Total sales:", TotalSales
USE
```

The final version of this code can be comprehended almost literally at a glance, whereas the other versions require study. Note that if we weren't alert, we would miss the bug in the first version. This demonstrates another problem with source code which is not canonical. In addition to being longer and more time-consuming to decipher, the correctness of such code is also more difficult to verify by inspection.

A Second Example: Cutting the Gordian Knot of Details

Now let's look at a more complex example, where we are presented with a maze of technical details that make it difficult to find a solution which we can understand, explain, and defend. This example was chosen to show how we can use canonical thinking to select the superior alternative or alternatives from a collection of alternatives.

Imagine that we are writing an application which has to understand the placement of lines on flat surfaces. This means that we have to pick one of several possible representations of a line to use in our program. Since we don't remember our geometry too well, we ask our friend Mason, the math whiz, for some help.

Mason says that our application requires us to answer the following three questions about any line in the database:

1. What is the *slope* of the line?
2. Where does the line cross the x-axis, that is, what is the *x-intercept?*
3. Where does the line cross the y-axis, that is, what is the *y-intercept?*

Mason gives us some possible representations of the line. He says that there are two design issues. First, how much storage is taken by each representation of a line? Second, how much work is it to compute the three characteristics of interest from the numbers which define a line in its computer representation?

In order to address these issues, we list in Table 2.1 the *slope, x-intercept,* and *y-intercept* after each possible representation. In the table, "x" and "y" represent variables and uppercase letters represent numeric constants.

Table 2.1 Alternative Representations and Characteristics of Lines

	Representation	Slope	x-intercept	y-intercept	Memvars	Divisions
1.	A*x + B*y + C = 0	–A/B	–C/A	–C/B	3	3
2.	D*x + E*y = F	–D/E	F/D	F/E	3	3
3.	G*x = H*y + I	G/H	I/G	–I/H	3	3
4.	x = J*y + K	1/J	K	–K/J	2	2
5.	y = L*x + M	L	–M/L	M	2	1
6.	y/N + x/P = 1	–N/P	P	N	2	1

Mason tells us to look through the choices. We notice that the first three representations use three database fields to represent a line and require us to perform three divisions to compute the three required characteristics. The last three forms require only two database fields to represent a line. The fourth form gives us the three required data items with two divisions, whereas the last two forms use only one division to produce the three items.

Now we see that the fifth and sixth forms require the same amount of computer storage and computation, and that no other form requires either less storage *or* less computation. From the viewpoint of storage and speed, *both* of these two forms are canonical.

However, the fifth representation involves one multiplication and one addition, whereas the sixth representation involves two divisions and one addition, so the fifth form is easier to understand. Since the fifth and sixth forms are otherwise equally preferred, we choose the fifth form over all the others.

In summary, the fifth form is the most canonical when we consider all three factors of storage, speed of execution, and ease of understanding. The fifth form's representation is simple, and two of the three required characteristics are available by inspection without computation.[3] Table 2.2 lists the characteristics of canonical structures.

Remark on selecting the canonical form. The choice of the fifth form for our program will lead to code which is easier to understand than code based on the other forms. Furthermore, this code will execute faster because the canonical form minimizes computation!

Table 2.2 Characteristics of Canonical Structures

1. There may be one or more canonical representations.
2. Canonical representations permit you to answer as many questions as possible about the characteristics of the structure by *inspection*, that is, *by just looking at the representation*.
3. Canonical representations tend to make it easy to determine the characteristics which cannot be determined by inspection.

A Third Example: Cleaning Up a Loop

Now let's look at a standard information processing task and see what benefits are available from the canonical approach. We are given a database with the following structure.

Table 2.3 Structure of Ranks.DBF

Field	Field Name	Type	Width	Dec
1	SCORE	Numeric	5	0
2	SPREAD	Numeric	5	0

3. A note to the mathematically inclined: to avoid excessive complication in this example, we assume that we don't have to represent lines like x = 2, because the fifth form cannot represent such lines. With this qualification, notice that canonical thinking led us to the standard slope-intercept form of the line which you see in all the textbooks!

This database has records consisting of two fields named SCORE and SPREAD. Both fields are numeric and store unsigned integers of up to five digits and signed integers of up to four digits.

The scores are stored in increasing numeric order, so that the SCORE in record i is greater than or equal to the SCORE in record i – 1, and there are at least two records. The assignment is to calculate the SPREAD field as the difference between the current SCORE and the previous SCORE. Let's look at a typical solution to that task in the dBASE programming language as shown in Listing 2.1.

Listing 2.1 A Noncanonical Form of a Common Loop

```
* File = SpreadsN.PRG.  A typical (noncanonical) approach.
* Entry condition assumed: Ranks.DBF has at least 2 records.
* Exit condition: define Score[I] and Spread[I] as the values of the fields
* Score and Spread in record I, for I = 1, 2, ..., RecCount().  Then
* Spread[I] = Score[I] - Score[I-1], for I = 2, 3, ..., RecCount().

PRIVATE LastScore

USE Ranks
DO WHILE (.NOT. EOF())

   IF (RecNo() = 1)
      REPLACE Spread WITH 0
      LastScore = Score
   ELSE
      REPLACE Spread WITH Score - LastScore
      LastScore = Score
   ENDIF

   SKIP
ENDDO (.NOT. EOF())

USE

* End of SpreadsN.PRG.
```

The USE statement opens the database file Ranks.DBF, and the WHILE loop processes records as long as there are any to process. The SKIP verb advances the record pointer to the next record, and the EOF() built-in function tests the record pointer to see if it is pointing to the end-of-file marker. The IF statement tests whether the current record is the first record, record 1. The REPLACE statement is used to change the values of database fields, whereas the usual assignment statement is used to change the values of memory variables, as in "LastScore = Score".

The USE statement at the end of SpreadsN.PRG closes the database. A RETURN statement is optional after the USE, because RETURN is automatically generated if end-of-file is encountered in program code files.

What is wrong with this approach? The IF statement is performed *each time through the loop,* even though the first alternative is only taken once, the first time through the loop. SpreadsC.PRG in Listing 2.2 shows a canonical form of the loop.

We have added three lines to the loop initialization, but we have removed five lines from the loop, which will dramatically increase the speed of the loop. The processing in the loop is much more straightforward, and that is a very important advantage for the human programmer. Next to parameter-passing problems, errors in loop logic probably cause programmers more grief than any other kind of

Listing 2.2 A Canonical Form of a Common Loop

```
* File = SpreadsC.PRG.  A canonical approach.
* Entry condition assumed: database has at least 2 records.
* Exit condition: define Score [I] and Spread[I] and the values of the fields
* Score and Spread in record I, for I = 1, 2, ..., RecCount().  Then
* Spread[I] = Score[I] - Score[I-1], for I = 2, 3, ..., RecCount().
PRIVATE LastScore
USE RANKS
REPLACE Spread WITH 0
LastScore = Score
SKIP  && Since the database has at least 2 records, the REPLACE and SKIP work.
DO WHILE (.NOT. EOF())
   REPLACE Spread WITH Score - LastScore
   LastScore = Score
   SKIP
ENDDO (.NOT. EOF())
USE
* End of SpreadsC.PRG.
```

standard error. Clear and simple loop contents support correct programming, whereas complex contents endanger correctness.

The typical benefits achieved with the canonical approach are listed in the following table. Note that these benefits apply to high-level languages, which are closer to human processes than to machine processes. The benefits of the canonical approach would have to be restated in the context of assembly language and C programming.

Table 2.4 Typical Benefits of the Canonical Approach

1. The total amount of source code is *usually* reduced.
2. The total amount of object code is *almost always* reduced.
3. The intellectual complexity of the code is *always* reduced.
4. For the computer: execution speed increases *typically* range from modest to dramatic.
5. For the human: implementation speed increases *typically* range from pleasant to startling!

The Role of Patterns in the Canonical Approach

As you gained experience in programming, you began to notice more and more patterns in your code and in your work. In the case of dBASE dialects, you noticed simple things first, like the fact that every IF must be matched with its own ENDIF. Later you realized that you dealt with larger patterns in your code, such as open file/process file data/close file or the even more general pattern, input data/process data/output data.

Of course, information structures are patterns, and there are some very provocative discoveries to be made when we analyze the patterns in programs and in programming with the canonical approach. In particular, we are about to discover six concepts: the layer concept, the macro concept, the subroutine concept, the library concept, the data-driven concept, and the code-object concept. **The intelligent and aggressive application of these and related concepts is crucial if the programming profession is to have any hope of meeting the global demand for new software.**

The Layer Concept

The layer concept is what some writers would call a *meta-concept,* because it is so fundamental and powerful that you could start with the layer concept and then develop virtually all of the other concepts in this book. A *layer* is a collection of one or more program units which make the computer you *have* look like the computer you *want*.

For example, computer hardware understands instructions which consist of a series of binary ones and zeroes. However, early programmers wanted a computer which understood instructions written with a human-readable alphabet. An *assembler* is a layer which makes the binary computer you have look like a computer which processes alphabetic instructions.

Just as quickly, the first programmers realized that they wanted much more than a computer which would understand alphabetic forms of symbolic commands. The need to manage data on media such as magnetic tape led to the desire to have a computer which had instructions for the management of files and the associated input and output processes.

Programmers developed a second layer called an *operating system* to fit between the binary hardware and the symbolic assembler. With these two layers in place, programmers coded for a machine which understood (1) alphabetic instructions for low-level hardware control and (2) low-level file management instructions to control data at the file level.

The next layer consists of higher-level languages, which offer high-level file management and support for the storage and processing of several types of data. Languages at this level give you a computer which looks like a mathematical entity: it understands numbers and arithmetic, alphabets and sorting, and records and files. Most higher-level languages, such as PASCAL, FORTRAN, and dBASE dialects, resemble a combination of English and mathematical notation.

When we write dBASE programs over a period of time, we eventually notice many ways in which the layer concept can be applied to reduce the duration and complexity of the programming process, while simultaneously elevating the quality and speed of the programs produced. In the remainder of this chapter, we'll look at the *macro* concept, the *subroutine* concept, the *library* concept, the *data-driven* concept, and the *code-object* concept. These core concepts reflect some of the most powerful, accessible, and useful advances in the computing profession to date!

The Macro Concept

The macro concept was hard to miss for early assembly language programmers, who noticed that there were many repetitions of fixed code fragments in their programs. For example, a pattern like[4]

```
          STA M+1
          STB M+2
          STX M+3
          STY M+4
```

might occur repeatedly in a program. Why not abbreviate this four-line fixed fragment as, say, an object called STABXY? Then, every instance of the four-line pattern could be represented with the object name STABXY.

These objects are called *macros* in the jargon. In this example, STABXY is the name of a macro. The macro name must appear in source code in a way that distinguishes the macro from other named objects. For example, you might represent the STABXY macro like this:

```
          STABXY()
```

The expansion of the object name into the code it represents adds another step to the translation process. This expansion might be done manually with a text editor, which would tend to use a great deal of programmer time. However, the expansion can be done automatically with a tool which is generically called a *preprocessor*.

A preprocessor can be used to generate input for the translator software, an assembler in this example. Without abbreviations, translation is a two-step process: (1) prepare source code, and (2) have the translator produce object code from the source code. When abbreviations are expanded with a preprocessor, there is a three-step translation process: (1) prepare source code with abbreviations, (2) preprocess the source code to expand all macros, and (3) have the translator produce object code.

Some translators have a built-in preprocessor to expand macros without the need for a separate preprocessor. This approach is usually the best one for the programmer. The same two-step translation process then works for source code with macros and for source code without macros. (Macro assemblers and the dBASE dialect Clipper 5.0 have built-in preprocessors.)

dBASE Macros

Macros are implemented internally in dBASE dialects, so dBASE code with macro references does not need a separate preprocessing step (unless you want multiple-line macros or substitutable parameters). The ampersand is used as a

4. Following a typical assembly language convention, I list commands starting in column 11.

prefix to identify a symbol as a macro reference. For example, if you initialized a PUBLIC memvar named ShowTime as in

ShowTime = "? Time(),Date()"

then you could write

&ShowTime

throughout your application as an abbreviation for "? Time(),Date()". See page 47 for a list of rules for dBASE dialect macros.

The Macro with Substitutable Parameters

We can now return to our assembly language example with a new twist. Let's say that we notice many occurrences of the pattern

```
STA <identifier>+1
STB <identifier>+2
```

Two instances of the pattern might be

```
STA StackTop+1
STB StackTop+2
```

and

```
STA E+1
STB E+2
```

In this example, we see that the pattern has one parameter and could be written as

```
STA <Parameter1>+1
STB <Parameter1>+2
```

For a particular macro assembler, we might abbreviate the code

```
STA StackTop+1
STB StackTop+2
STA E+1
STB E+2
```

as the following, where the first three lines are the macro definition, and the last two lines are the two references to the defined macro:

```
DEFMACRO  SaveAB(Offset)
          STA Offset+1
ENDDEF    STB Offset+2
          SaveAB(StackTop)
          SaveAB(E)
```

You will have noticed the similarity between macros with substitutable parameters and subroutines with parameters. The main difference is that each reference to a macro with N lines causes N lines of source code to be inserted. In contrast, each reference to a subroutine uses only R lines of source code, where R is 1 for higher-level languages and is usually greater than 1 for assembly language.

The dBASE dialects do not support macros with parameters. However, in Part III we'll see that something very similar to parameterized macros can be easily implemented with a text editor, to our tremendous advantage!

The Subroutine Concept

The macro concept is independent of which programming language we use, since we can use a preprocessor to implement macros for us. Yet, as we have just seen, the use of macros to abbreviate patterns saves labor, but not any source code — the amount of source code is the same whether we write out the macros ourselves or have them expanded automatically.

In contrast, a repetitive pattern which is implemented as a subroutine is written once for all references. For example, when I want my user to read something onscreen and give a keystroke to indicate that the material has been read, I code "DO WaitOnC", which calls a 21-line procedure with no parameters. If I have 10 uses for WaitOnC in an application, then I add 31 lines of source code: 10 lines for each occurrence of "DO WaitOnC" and a 21-line definition of "WaitOnC". In contrast, with the macro approach, I would have a 21-line definition of the macro which would *not* become part of the source code, but the 10 references would constitute 210 lines of source code.

In this case, it is obviously far more canonical to use the subroutine approach with its 31 lines of source code. Such code saves 179 lines over the macro approach and leads to code which is far easier to read and verify. (As a side issue, you'd have to use a preprocessor to get multiple-line macros for a dBASE dialect.)

How to Construct Subroutines

When you design your application with the top-down approach, the design itself tends to dictate the subroutines which are used in the top-level routine and the routines it calls. However, there are typically a variety of options for implementing the other routines.

The design of subroutines which reflect the canonical approach requires considerable judgment and even intuition, but the basic goals are clear. The resulting code should be efficient and easy to understand, verify, and modify.

For every application, there is a subroutine design which will minimize the total amount of source code in the application. Minimizing the amount of source code in an application is a prime imperative when we think in canonical terms because short programs that do the same job as long programs are almost always much easier to understand and they typically run much more rapidly.

Psychological Considerations

Certain psychological considerations in subroutine design may lead to longer-than-minimum-size programs. For example, programmers tend to partition tasks in ways that reflect human conceptualizations. Humans will think about subroutines to open files, process files, and close files. Yet the shortest-source-code design might use routines that combine opening and processing in a way that is not intuitive for humans.

It is important to design your information structures so that they may be understood easily. *Since our number-one goal must always be to develop correct programs, information structures must usually reflect human biases to a certain extent.* For example, when programmers make fast execution a higher priority than correctness, they tailor the application to machine logic and not to human logic. The result is often a buggy and hard-to-maintain application which is delivered late or which is never finished.

> **Recommendation on correctness versus execution speed.** When you want a fast application, write one first that is correct. Then see where it is slow and improve the algorithms in the slow sections.

Another psychological consideration is that there are many conventions and traditions which have evolved among computer programmers. It is inevitable, and to a certain extent desirable, to have subroutine designs adhere to traditional conventions. *But please remember to keep your common sense with you at all times!*

Correctness and Programmer Productivity

The overriding goal of all programming is to produce correct results; the canonical approach to subroutine design is particularly important because this approach increases the likelihood of writing correct code. Subroutines which are well written and documented can be debugged and collected into libraries for reuse. When you use such debugged routines in new applications, you reduce your programming time *and* increase your likelihood of producing correct code!

> **Recommendation on library subroutines.** Generally speaking, the ideal is to have the vast majority of an application's work done by library routines, so that the part of the application which is outside the library has minimum size and consists primarily of calls to library routines.

The Library Concept

If you are thinking canonically, you will want to design subroutines that can be used in many applications. This will sometimes lead you to make a subroutine more general than you would otherwise. *When in doubt, make it general.*

As you identify reuseable subroutines, you will collect them together in a set that is generically called a *library*, regardless of the specific implementation of the set of subroutines. When you design a subroutine which you will put into the library, you will want to consider the grouping of services in the routine.

For example, if you design a routine to provide both service A and service B, then you should be confident that programmers will always want both services, or else when they call the routine, you should give them a way to select A only, B only, or both A and B.

When we contemplate the question of how the limited number of programmers in the world can meet an insatiable demand for programs, the library concept appears as possibly the main hope. For example, the dBASE language contains the SORT and INDEX verbs, which give the dBASE programmer access to a library (collection) of prewritten routines that save days or weeks of coding on each database application.

Each dBASE dialect programmer can extend the dBASE language by developing libraries of source and/or object code which can dramatically reduce the intellectual complexity and amount of nonlibrary code in an application. For example, Arthur Fuller's ArtFul.LIB for the Clipper dialect contains a very high-level function called THE_USUAL(), which handles an entire style of application!

> **Remark on using subroutine libraries.** Libraries that *you* write permit you to capture *your* intelligence and recycle *your* labor. In time, your productivity with dBASE dialects should increase 200% to 1,000% or more over its initial level.
>
> However, libraries that *others* write permit you to capture *their* intelligence and to recycle *their* labor! Even if you are relatively inexperienced and quite incapable of *designing* a professional library, you can *use* the code of master programmers by buying their libraries.

Through a combination of your library routines and professional library routines, you can increase your productivity to perhaps 5,000% of its initial level. Although there are some costs to libraries (in addition to their purchase prices) which must be thoroughly understood in order for intelligent implementation decisions to be made, the benefits of libraries are overwhelming and irresistible.

How Much Advantage?

If you increase your programming productivity by 1,000%, you will code in 1 hour what used to take you *10 hours*. If you increase your programming productivity by 5,000%, you will code in 1 hour what used to take you *50 hours*.

This does *not* mean that you will produce finished applications 50 times faster, because we are only looking at the coding and debugging stages of the development process. Library use typically has little or no bearing on the amount of time taken for specifications development, user documentation, and user training.

References

For more information on the library concept, see the book *Dynamics of Clipper* (Fuller 1989) and the 30-page *Building Source Code Libraries* (Yellick 1989a). The Yellick monograph also details a coding standard which addresses variable naming and uppercase/lowercase conventions.

The Data-Driven Concept

A concept which is closely related to the subroutine concept is the *data-driven* concept. Let's explore this concept through some examples.

When we need to send control codes to a printer in our applications, we could write the control codes directly into the application. However, in some cases, we would have to write the same control codes over and over. If we found a mistake in the control codes we were using to signal, say, 6 lines per inch, then it might be difficult for us to find every place in our source code where we were asking for 6 lines per inch. Any location in the source code that we missed and failed to update would constitute a bug.

This is an example of the *data-duplication* problem which arises in so many contexts, particularly in database applications. As a way around it — that is, as a way to store the control codes in only one location — we can store these codes in files in the C:\Batch\ directory. The filename will indicate the control function, and the extension will represent the printer. Thus, C:\Batch\6LPI.o92 and C:\Batch\12CPI.o92 might hold the control codes for 6 lines per inch and 12 characters per inch on an Okidata 92 printer.

Storing the control codes in only one place is a first application of the data-driven concept, which has a second application in the following example of a report routine. The first RUN command in the routine sends an initialization string to the printer before printing starts, and the second RUN command sends a deinitialization string after printing finishes.

```
* File = Report.PRG.
  ...
RUN COPY C:\Batch\6LPI.o92 + C:\Batch\12CPI.o92 PRN:
  ...
RUN COPY C:\Batch\8LPI.o92 + C:\Batch\17CPI.o92 PRN:
* End of Report.PRG.
```

In this example, the control strings for an Okidata 92 printer are stored in files matching the filespec C:\Batch*.o92. If the report is sent to another printer at a future time, the above four occurrences of "o92" would have to be changed to the code of the new printer, say, "LJ2":

```
* File = Report.PRG.
  ...
RUN COPY C:\Batch\6LPI.LJ2 + C:\Batch\12CPI.LJ2 PRN:
  ...
RUN COPY C:\Batch\8LPI.LJ2 + C:\Batch\17CPI.LJ2 PRN:
* End of Report.PRG.
```

The First Level of the Data-Driven Concept

In practicing the first level of the data-driven concept, you use an identifier instead of a constant whenever the constant appears more than once in a program to represent the same attribute of the data being processed, as in:

```
* File = Report.PRG.
PRIVATE PrinterExt
PrinterExt =  "LJ2"
  ...
RUN COPY C:\Batch\6LPI.&PrinterExt + C:\Batch\12CPI.&PrinterExt PRN:
  ...
RUN COPY C:\Batch\8LPI.&PrinterExt + C:\Batch\17CPI.&PrinterExt PRN:
* End of Report.PRG.
```

Notice that there is now only one line of code to change when we change printers.[5] Although we change only one line of source code, we must create the four new files 6LPI.LJ2, 12CPI.LJ2, 8LPI.LJ2, and 17CPI.LJ2 in the C:\Batch\ directory. These files are of course available at all times to all applications.

The Second Level of the Data-Driven Concept

Notice that the source code still depends on the printer being used. When the printer is changed to one which requires different control codes than the printer it replaces, the statement that assigns a value to the PrinterExt memvar must be updated. It is possible to move the data to which PrinterExt is assigned from the source code to a disk file, with the result that this data is read at execution time:

```
* File = Report.PRG.
PRIVATE PrinterExt
RESTORE FROM Printer ADDITIVE && Printer.MEM contains a value for PrinterExt.
  ...
RUN COPY C:\Batch\6LPI.&PrinterExt + C:\Batch\12CPI.&PrinterExt PRN:
  ...
RUN COPY C:\Batch\8LPI.&PrinterExt + C:\Batch\17CPI.&PrinterExt PRN:
* End of Report.PRG.
```

5. In practice, PrinterExt would be a PUBLIC variable or a PRIVATE memvar defined and assigned in the top-level routine, so that PrinterExt would be known throughout the application.

The Data-Driven Rules

The data-driven approach has enormous benefits which you might not expect from the simple way in which it can be stated. Programs are easier to read, verify, and update when they follow the first rule in Table 2.5. If programs follow the second rule in the table, then you can adapt them to a variety of external conditions by updating their configuration data rather than their code!

Table 2.5 The Two Rules of the Data-Driven Approach

Data-driven rule on duplicated constant data in source code. Assign data to an identifier and use the identifier instead of constant data whenever the constant data would appear more than once with the same meaning, would be likely to be changed in the future, or would not be obvious in its meaning.

Data-driven rule on separating source code from data. If constant data appears in source code, and that data might be changed at a later date, then remove the data to disk files and read it at execution time.

Bret Oliver of Quicktek Corporation has developed Schooner, "an open architectured, data driven, integrated, interactive, object oriented CASE tool which lets one design, document and run an application without generating code, while being able to call Clipper, C, and assembly code from anywhere in the system." At the time of writing, he was seeking a publisher for a book adaptation of the Schooner manual, to be called *Data Driven Systems.* You can buy the Schooner manual for $50, and you can read an excerpt from *Data Driven Systems* in the Summer/Fall 1990 issue of *Ashton-Tate Update Developer* (Oliver 1990).

The Code-Object Concept

If we want our dBASE code to include references to macros with parameters, then we must run the source code through a preprocessor before using it. However, subroutine support must be built into a computer language, because it cannot be added with a preprocessor. Similarly, support for so-called *Object Oriented Programming,* or *OOP,* must be built in.

At the time of writing, Clipper 5.0 from Nantucket was the only dBASE dialect to support OOP (in a limited way). OOP is an extension to the subroutine and library concepts which seeks to simplify the construction of subroutines which are extensions or fragments of existing subroutines.

OOP is an extremely powerful and sophisticated technique. I believe that intermediate programmers can make elegant use of OOP if they use it in a limited, simple, and straightforward way, particularly if well-constructed examples are imitated. I also believe that you must be both experienced and gifted to use OOP in a way which is both elegant and extensive, assuming that you create all of your own objects.

However, as is the case with commercial subroutine libraries, you can benefit from the objects developed by other people, no matter what your experience level is, providing that such objects are well-constructed and documented and are used carefully.

Recommendation on OOP. If you are a beginning to intermediate programmer, avoid OOP or else use it sparingly, with great care, after much study and experimentation.

Superprogramming and You

One of the objectives of this book is to pump you full of the secrets of the superprogrammers. By reading this chapter so far, you know that structure alternatives are crucially important in software engineering. You know that the canonical approach can help you find alternatives which, if not *best,* are at least *better*. You have seen one meaty example in the "before" and "after" versions of a typical loop.

The advancement of your skills now requires two different efforts. First, use the ideas that you just read about *structure alternatives* and *the canonical approach* to seek a deeper understanding of the trade-offs involved in the programming choices that you make. Second, study the other programming and design examples in this book to broaden your repertoire of techniques.

Chapter 3

Overview of the dBASE Language and Development Environment

The dBASE dialects typically provide both a stored-program mode, in which you execute previously prepared program code stored in files, and an interpretive mode, where commands are executed as you type them. Thus, a dBASE dialect usually provides an entire development environment in addition to the programming language.

In this chapter we take a programmer's tour of the dBASE programming language and development environment, with a concentration on what I call *major dialects* from the four dBASE vendors which have the top market shares: Ashton-Tate, Fox Software, Nantucket Corporation, and WordTech Systems. These companies publish the single-user and multiple-user dialect products listed on page 103.

My intention is to introduce the main features of the dBASE language and development environment from a programmer's perspective, with discussions of dialect differences as appropriate and occasional comparisons to other programming languages. Although this chapter is mandatory reading for beginners, intermediate and advanced programmers should at least skim for material which is unfamiliar to them. Since there are many tables and discussions to explain differences in dialects, there is bound to be new information for everyone.

> **Remark.** Although this chapter contains a few recommendations, its mission is to introduce the major programming-related features of dBASE dialects. This chapter is not meant to teach you dBASE software engineering. The rest of the book deals with dBASE dialect software engineering issues.

Interpreting, Pseudocompiling, and Compiling

There are three main themes in the translation of the human-readable form of a program to the underlying binary language of the hardware, and dBASE dialects employ all three methods. These themes are *interpretation, pseudocompilation* (also called *tokenization*), and *compilation*. Table 3.1 shows a chart of dialects and translation methods.

Table 3.1 dBASE Dialects and Code Translation Methods

Clipper	Compiled.
dBASE II	Interpreted.
dBASE III	Interpreted, with manual pseudocompilation.
dBASE III PLUS	Interpreted, with manual pseudocompilation.
dBASE IV	Automatic pseudocompilation for procedures not manually pseudocompiled.
dBXL	Interpreted.
FoxBASE+	Automatic pseudocompilation for procedures not manually pseudocompiled.
FoxPro	Automatic pseudocompilation for procedures not manually pseudocompiled.
Quicksilver	Compiled.

Interpretation

When a source program is interpreted, its statements are translated one by one at execution time. The advantage of this approach is that you can edit a program file and then execute it immediately. The disadvantage is that translation is done over and over as the program executes, instead of only once, as with compiled programs.

The execution time environment consists of DOS, the interpreter, and the application's code and data files. Before we can understand pseudocompiling and compiling, we need to understand the concepts of tokens and tokenization.

The Concepts of Tokens and Tokenization

There is a generic technique in the translation of source code to lower-level languages, which is called *tokenization* in the jargon, in reference to the production of *tokens*. dBASE vendors often use the terms *pseudocompilation* or even *compilation* as synonyms for *tokenization*.

A token is a data structure which we can think of in dBASE terms as a database record with a small number of fields. When your source code is translated into tokens, each syntactic element is represented by one token. For example, the assignment statement "X = 5" would be represented by three tokens, one for "X", one for "=", and one for "5".

If these tokens were stored in a dBASE database, they would comprise three consecutive records. Such a database might have a structure like that shown in Table 3.2.

The Tokens->ID_Number field holds the code number for the token. This code depends on the language and the tokenization scheme. For example, the "=" character (when it occurs as a syntactic element and not inside a character string constant) might be a code 1. There is no Tokens->Data value for this token.

Table 3.2 Tokens.DBF, a Data Structure for Source Code Tokens

Field	Field Name	Type	Width	Dec
1	ID_Number	Numeric	3	
2	Data	Character	254	

In contrast, the token that represents one of your identifiers called "X" will have Tokens->ID_Number equal to the "user identifier" code, and Tokens->Data will be "X".

For an example, let's assume that our dBASE language has identifiers, constants, and the assignment, IF/ENDIF, and DO/WITH statements. We can assign each of the fixed syntactic elements in this language a code for Tokens->ID_Number as shown in Table 3.3.

Table 3.3 Token Types for a dBASE Language Subset

1. = (as the assignment operator)
2. ,
3. <user identifier>
4. <constant>
5. IF
6. ENDIF
7. DO
8. WITH
9. PARAMETERS

In this toy language, we would translate the statements "X = 1023" and "DO Proc1 WITH X" as shown in Table 3.4.

Table 3.4 A Sample Tokenization

Token	ID_Number	Data
X	3	X
=	1	
1023	4	1023
DO	7	
Proc1	3	Proc1
WITH	8	
X	3	X

Tokens are not generally stored in a simple list, as we have shown in Table 3.4, although the tokens are produced and processed in the order shown. There is a varying amount of sophistication in the way that the tokens are structured, according to the handling of loops, expressions, subroutine calls, and so on. The final structure of tokens is intermediate between source code and machine code, and therefore it is called *intermediate code.*

For example, the FoxBASE+ dialect from Fox Software produces the intermediate code for the source code file Proc1.PRG[1] in RAM when "DO Proc1" is executed and the corresponding intermediate code file Proc1.FOX is not found. A FoxBASE+ utility called FoxPcomp.EXE is used to make Proc1.FOX from Proc1.PRG. In contrast, FoxPro and Ashton-Tate's dBASE IV will make the intermediate code file automatically from the .PRG file if the intermediate code file is not found at execution time.

Compilation in MS-DOS

Compilation in MS-DOS is usually a two-step process that includes a link stage as well as a compile stage. First, you make — that is, *compile* — .OBJ files from source code files using a program called a *compiler.*

Second, you use a program called a *linker* to combine your .OBJ (object code) files with .LIB (library) files to make an .EXE file or a .COM file. The compiler vendor usually supplies one or more .LIB files and perhaps one or more .OBJ files as well.

Three types of files are executable under MS-DOS. Batch files have an extension of .BAT and are equivalent in function to UNIX scripts. They contain text-based DOS commands like DIR and TIME, and commands to execute .BAT, .COM, or .EXE files. Executable files produced by linking have extensions of .COM or .EXE. Unlike .COM files, the .EXE files can have overlays.

Linking produces either a single executable file or a single executable file with overlay files. Overlay files are used when the size of a single executable file would otherwise be too large to fit into available RAM. This technology permits an application to be run in a smaller amount of RAM than would be required to hold the entire application. For example, with overlays, it might be possible to run an application with 700K of object code in 400K of RAM.

Remark. There is sometimes confusion about which programmer-created dBASE files are combined into the executable file and any overlay files of a compiled application. Only source code in .PRG and possibly .FMT files is compiled; all other dBASE files contain data and not code, and there is no translation issue for data files in this context. (You may have to translate the format of data files when you move data from one platform to another, such as a port from an ASCII microcomputer to an EBCDIC mainframe.)

The advantage of compilation is that the translation is done once to prepare the object code, which then can be executed repeatedly with no translation delay.[2] In theory, compiled applications can run 10 or 100 times faster than interpreted applications, although a five-fold increase is more typical in practice.

---

1. Source code files with .PRG extensions are called *command files.*
2. In the section on packaging below, we will see that the difference between compilers and tokenizers is in how they package the executable code. The packaging method influences load time, but not execution speed.

The disadvantage in working with a compiler is that it tends to be much slower and more complicated than working with an interpreter. For example, Clipper makes .OBJ files from .PRG files quite rapidly, but the linking step tends to be quite time-consuming. In rough terms, an application that compiles in a second may take a minute to link with the linker provided with Clipper 4.0. Minimum link times with this linker tend to be half a minute to a minute, even on fast machines — unless there is a RAM disk big enough to hold the linker, its libraries, and the .EXE file being made!

Linking is faster under the scheme of Clipper 5.0. However, the edit-compile-link-execute cycle of compilers is inevitably slower than the edit-execute cycle of interpreters. In addition, it is more resource-intensive, because you have the additional .OBJ, .LIB, and .EXE files to store on your disk. Finally, compilers are more complex to operate, as you have not only additional processing steps, but also a host of design and debugging issues associated with the extra steps.

In return for the trouble of dealing with .OBJ and .LIB files, compilers, and linkers, you have the ability to customize your runtime environment in many ways which are not possible when you use interpreters and runtimes, which are executable programs that cannot be modified. In particular, you can produce an executable file with Clipper which is smaller than the combination of the .FOX file of a FoxBASE+ application plus the FoxBASE+ runtime.

> **Remark. The Summer '87 version of Clipper is supported by a product called NoLink from Next Wave Software, which eliminates the link step, and a product called dCLIP from Donnay Software Designs, which offers a Clipper "dot prompt."**[3] However, in the absence of such a product, you must wait for compilation *and* linkage before you can test changes to a source code file. When you compile and link applications, it often takes up to 10 times longer to fix a bug and test the fix than when you interpret applications. Expert Panelist Craig Yellick reports Clipper 4.0 link times under 10 seconds, but he uses a 386-based PC with a 2 MB RAM disk and a fast third-party linker.

Compilation in dBASE Dialects

At the time of writing, Ashton-Tate and Fox Software have not shipped their announced dBASE compilers. Nantucket offers the leading dBASE compiler, Clipper, while WordTech Systems competes with its Quicksilver compiler and compatible dBXL interpreter. In 1989, newcomer Sophco shipped its FORCE compiler, which is an innovative product with few users relative to the other dialects.

Nantucket provides no interpreter for its Clipper dialect, whereas WordTech provides the dBXL interpreter and the Quicksilver compiler as companion products. dBXL recognizes some commands that Quicksilver does not support, but if you don't use these commands, you can develop and debug your Quicksilver

3. These products are reviewed in Part VIII of Volume 2.

applications in the interpreted environment of dBXL. (See "Between Friends" (Feldheim 1990) for a list of seven differences between dBXL and Quicksilver.)

You may then compile your debugged dBXL application under Quicksilver, presumably without difficulty. In contrast, Clipper programmers have to debug without an interpreter (although NoLink and dCLIP tend to remove this difference for Clipper programmers who use them).

Pseudocompilation in dBASE Dialects

The dBASE dialects implement several different pseudocompilation services. The *first* service gives you a utility to pseudocompile the source files. In providing the *second* service, the dialect looks for the pseudocompiled form of .PRG and .FMT files and creates the pseudocompiled form in RAM. However, this tokenized code is not written to disk, so the pseudocompilation occurs repeatedly.

In the *third* service, the pseudocompiled code is written to a disk file in the current MS-DOS directory if the pseudocompiled disk file is not found. In the *fourth* service, the pseudocompiled code is written to a disk file in the same MS-DOS directory as the source code file if the pseudocompiled disk file is not found.

In the *fifth* service, the dates of last modification of the source and pseudocompiled files are compared, and the pseudocompiled file is made again if it is older than the source file. To date, only the dBASE IV and FoxPro dialects offer this service; they have the SET DEVELOPMENT ON/OFF command to control whether the service is performed.

The following table shows the level of pseudocompilation services from different dialects. The service numbers correspond to the hierarchy just described.

Table 3.5 Level of Pseudocompilation Services

Dialect	Level of Service	Pseudocompiler and Linker
dBASE III PLUS	1	dBC.COM with dBL.COM.
FoxBASE+	1 and 2	FoxPcomp.EXE with FoxBind.EXE.
dBASE IV	1, 3, and 5	Built-in COMPILE command or Build.COM with DBlink.EXE.
FoxPro	1, 4, and 5	Built-in COMPILE command with FoxBind.EXE.

With dBASE III PLUS, source code files are translated by dBC.COM to files with a .PRG extension. You cannot tell from the .PRG extension on a file if it is in source code or intermediate code form. Individual intermediate code .PRG files are combined into one .PRG file with dBL.COM. The linkage step is optional.

FoxBASE+ takes a more commonsense approach in which Menu.PRG is translated to Menu.FOX, so you can manage your files much more easily. In contrast to dBASE III PLUS, you link your source code files into one procedure file with FoxBind.EXE, and then pseudocompile the one procedure file with FoxPcomp.EXE, assuming that your application has no more routines than the maximum number which can be stored in a procedure file. Notice that dBASE III PLUS links intermediate code files, whereas FoxBASE+ links source code files.

If FoxBASE+ does not find Menu.FOX when you "DO Menu", then it will make the equivalent of Menu.FOX in RAM and execute the .FOX form. The temporary .FOX form is not written to disk because FoxPcomp.EXE performs error-checking and optimizations that are not done for on-the-fly translation.

The smarter products dBASE IV and FoxPro are able to create the pseudocompiled file if it does not exist. In addition, these products will pseudocompile the source file as needed if the statement SET DEVELOPMENT ON has been executed. dBASE IV and FoxPro translate .PRG files to .DBO files and .FPX files, respectively.

A dBASE compiler will produce an .EXE file from your source code files, so the translation issues involved with compilers seem to be entirely different from the translation issues associated with interpreters. However, there is more similarity than difference, as we'll see in the next section.

Packaging: .EXE Files or Separate Runtimes?

A dBASE dialect which can immediately execute a command that you enter from the keyboard is implemented in a product with two components: a component to execute stored programs and a component to execute commands which are entered interactively. When the vendor offers the part which executes stored programs as a separate product, this product is called a *runtime*.

An intermediate code file such as Proc1.FOX can be executed by the FoxBASE+ interpreter or its runtime; that is, the execution time environment for an intermediate code file contains the data files of the application plus one of the following sets of files: (1) the intermediate code file plus the interpreter and the operating system, or (2) the intermediate code file plus the runtime and the operating system.

If the number of subroutines in your dBASE application does not exceed the maximum number of procedures permitted in one procedure file, then you can combine all of your source code files into one procedure file. If your dialect has a tokenization utility, then this procedure file can be converted to its intermediate code form, so your application can be distributed as one file which can be executed either by the interpreter or by the interpreter's runtime, if such a runtime is available.

This approach requires a minimum of two files, not counting operating system files and data files. It is the first of two standard dBASE packaging methods, and it is supported by the dBASE interpreters which offer tokenization.

The second packaging scheme offered by MS-DOS language products combines the runtime environment and the intermediate code file into a single .EXE file. In programming languages like PASCAL, which force you to declare a fixed size and type for all of your identifiers and which prohibit self-modifying code constructs like the dBASE macro, the intermediate code can be translated to literal machine code that is directly executed by the hardware.

The dBASE dialects (except FORCE — see page 186) permit so much flexibility in the execution time behavior of the program that dBASE intermediate code usually cannot be reduced to machine code. *When an interpreter executes a tokenized file, that file is data to the interpreter. When a runtime executes a tokenized file, that file is data to the runtime.*

When a dBASE application is compiled into an .EXE file, part of the .EXE file holds the intermediate code which is data to the runtime that is packaged into the .EXE file. The dBASE compilers (except FORCE) use the same execution method as the interpreters which provide a separate runtime; the distinction is whether the runtime is combined with the intermediate code files to make a single file, or whether the runtime is in one or more files which are separate from the intermediate code files at execution time.

dBASE File Types

MS-DOS versions of dBASE dialects categorize the numerous types of dBASE files via the file extension. Identical or equivalent schemes are used for non-DOS dialects.

In addition to data files and files of source code, some of the dialects also have translated forms of the source code files. Table 3.6 shows both the native and translated forms of source code files for the dialects which have this distinction. The dialects which recognize each extension are indicated in a list of codes, as shown in the legend below the table.

This list is not exhaustive. For example, FoxPro uses the extensions .FV, .GEN, .INC, and .COD for code generation purposes, .ERR for COMPILE errors, and .DOC and .ACT for FoxDoc reports. FoxPro also allows you to specify different extensions for a variety of file types using the Config.FX file.

Expert Panelist Dr. John Bauman observes that FoxBASE+ and FoxPro support .NDX index files by automatically converting them to .IDX indexes. For example, if your dBASE III PLUS program has the command "USE Receipts INDEX In_Date", but In_Date.NDX is found and In_Date.IDX is not found, then when that program is executed under a Fox dialect, In_Date.IDX will be built.[4]

Procedure Structures

The term *procedure structures* is used as in Chapter 2 to describe the code structures in a programming language. As we will see below, dBASE dialects support procedure structures called *procedures* and *procedure files*.

---

4. There is a qualification: FoxBASE+ and FoxPro expect to find that In_Date.NDX is in a Fox format if the line "INDEX = NDX" appears in the configuration file.

Table 3.6 dBASE Dialect File Types, Including Translated Files

Description	File Type	Translated Form	Dialects
External Binary Routines	.BIN		All
Backup File	.BAK		All
Backup, Memo File	.TBK		4P
Catalog File	.CAT		+4
Database File	.DBF		All
Database Text (Memo) File	.DBT		All
Database Text (Memo) File	.FPT		P
Format File	.FMT		3+QX
Format File	.PRG	.EXE	C
Format File	.FMT	.FMX	F
Format File	.FMT	.FMO	4
Format File	.FMT	.PRX	P
Report Form	.FRM		All
Report Form	.FRX		P
Report Form	.FRM	.FRO	4
Label Form	.LBL		All
Label Form	.LBL	.LBO	4
Label Form	.LBX		P
Keyboard Macro File	.FKY		P
Keyboard Macro File	.KEY		4
Memory Variable File	.MEM		All
Index Data File	.NDX		C3+4QX
Index Data File	.NTX		C
Index Data File	.IDX		FP
Index Data File	.MDX		4
Printer Driver File	.PR2		4
Command File	.PRG	.EXE	CQ
Command File	.PRG		3X
Command File	.PRG	.PRG	+
Command File	.PRG	.DBO	4
Command File	.PRG	.FOX	F
Command File	.PRG	.FXP	P
dBASE/SQL Command File	.PRS		4
Query File	.QRY	.QBO	4
ASCII Text File	.TXT		All
View File	.VUE		+4P
Label View	.LBV		P
Report View	.FRV		P
Window File	.WIN		4P

Legend:
C = Clipper 4.0, 3 = dBASE III, + = dBASE III PLUS, 4 = dBASE IV,
F = FoxBASE+, P = FoxPro, Q = Quicksilver, X = dBXL.

Macros

dBASE is often said to be a fourth-generation language, or 4GL, for short. Much of this claim rests on the so-called macro facility of the language (which implements self-modifying code).

Any variable with a character type can be used as a macro. The syntax is

&<variable>

as in

&Command

In dBASE III PLUS, you can assign "SET COLOR TO B/W,G/B,BG" to the variable Command, and then enter "&Command" at the interactive prompt. When you do, the dBASE colors will be set to B/W,G/B,BG. Similarly, you can use "&Command" as a command in a program, with the same result.

Other dialects may be more restrictive about the placement of macros. For example, the Clipper dialect only lets you use macro substitution for *parts* of commands, not entire commands, as in the following code. (The macros are terminated with periods, according to Nantucket's recommendation.)

```
Colors =  "B/W,G/B,BG"
SET COLOR TO &Colors.
DB =  "Members"
Index1 =  "Date_In"
USE &DB. INDEX &Index1.
```

There are a number of ways in which macros can simplify coding tasks. We will see some of these techniques later in the book.

Macros can also be very confusing. The primary question is often "Do I need to write '&Command' or just 'Command'?" For example, you can code

SEEK "&Name"

but surely it is better to use the equivalent and much simpler

SEEK Name

Table 3.7 on page 48 shows some rules for dBASE dialect macros.

Branching

The dBASE language includes the IF, IF ELSE, and CASE statements to handle branching. The syntax for IF and IF ELSE is

```
IF <logical expression>
   <one or more statements>
ENDIF
IF <logical expression>
   <one or more statements>
ELSE
   <one or more statements>
ENDIF
```

If the logical expression is true, the first list of statements is executed. If the expression in the IF ELSE is false, the second list of statements is executed.

The CASE statement has this syntax:

```
DO CASE
   CASE <logical expression>
      <one or more statements>
   CASE <logical expression>
      <one or more statements>
   .
   .
   .
   [OTHERWISE
      <one or more statements>]
ENDCASE
```

The logical expressions are evaluated in order. If one of them is true, then its corresponding statements are executed, after which control passes to the statement following ENDCASE. If none of the expressions is true, and the OTHERWISE clause is present, then the statements between OTHERWISE and ENDCASE are performed. **Note that at most *one* of the CASE or OTHERWISE alternatives is performed.**

> **Recommendation on Clipper's IF/ELSEIF construct.** Clipper offers an alternative to the CASE construct in its IF/ELSEIF/ENDIF statement. I recommend that you always use CASE. I believe that CASE is much more canonical; furthermore, it is dialect-independent and comprehensible to any dBASE dialect programmer.

Looping

The dBASE III PLUS programming language provides only a generic WHILE loop. There is no equivalent of PASCAL's "REPEAT ... UNTIL <expression>", FORTRAN's "DO I = M,N,D", or BASIC's "FOR ... NEXT". These other forms must be simulated with the dBASE WHILE loop, whose syntax is

```
DO WHILE <logical expression>
   <statement(s)>
ENDDO
```

Table 3.7 Rules for dBASE Dialect Macros

1. A variable to be used as a macro has type CHARACTER. For example, if memvar ShowTime is to be used as a macro, then TYPE("ShowTime") = "C" after ShowTime is defined.
2. dBASE macros can be used to abbreviate an entire command or part of a command. Unlike assembler macros, dBASE macros cannot abbreviate more than one command. Macros must be defined before they are referenced.
3. To insert the macro's text into your source code, write an ampersand immediately before the macro name, as in

   &TimeDate

4. If a macro abbreviates one command, then the macro reference &TimeDate appears on a line by itself. If a macro abbreviates part of a command, then the macro reference appears in place of the part of the command which it abbreviates. For example, if Name = "Mr. Ed", then

   ? 'My name is &Name'

   would abbreviate

   ? "My name is Mr. Ed"

5. If the macro name is *not* followed by a blank or end-of-line, then it is either optional or required that the macro name be terminated by a period, depending on the dialect and other factors. For example, if Name = "Mr. Ed", then

   ? "My name is &Name"

   and

   ? "My name is &Name."

   are equivalent as abbreviations for

   ? "My name is Mr. Ed"

   In contrast,

   ? "My name is &Name.."

   abbreviates

   ? "My name is Mr. Ed."

6. In some dialects, a macro can be referenced without the initial ampersand, for a performance improvement. For example, Clipper would permit "SET COLOR TO (Colors)" as a faster-executing alternative to "SET COLOR TO &Colors." See your dialect's manual for more information. (In many uses, the speed of macro expansion versus the speed of character memvar expansion is not an issue. However, the speed of macro expansion may very well be an issue for macro references inside DO WHILE loops.)
7. Clipper users are advised to terminate all macros with a period. Users of other dialects may also wish to follow this rule, particularly if there is the possibility that the code will be compiled under Clipper.

However, Clipper, dBXL, FoxPro, and Quicksilver provide an iterative loop which is very similar to that of FORTRAN in its capabilities. The syntax is

```
FOR <memvar> = <expN1> TO <expN2> [STEP <expN3>]
   <statements>
NEXT
```

FoxPro also permits you to substitute "ENDFOR" for "NEXT".

Program Units

Source code is structured into routines which are stored in individual .PRG files; .PRG files which include collections of routines; and user-defined functions, or UDFs, in the dialects which support UDFs. The second type of structure is called a *procedure file*. Procedure files may contain procedures, which are used exactly like command files; some dialects also permit UDFs to appear in procedure files.

Source Code Format

The following information applies to all subroutine types: command files, procedures, and UDFs. Command and procedure files have extensions of .PRG. FoxBASE+ and FoxPro permit command files to be used optionally as UDFs; otherwise, a collection of procedures and/or functions is stored in a procedure file.

Like FORTRAN and unlike PASCAL, dBASE has a line orientation for its statements. At most one statement can appear on a line. If "&&" is found on a line, then the two ampersands and any characters following them are ignored.

Statements are continued with the semicolon character. Statements can be continued onto an arbitrary number of lines, but the total number of characters per statement must not exceed the dialect's limit. dBASE III PLUS supports up to 254 characters per statement, and dBASE IV and FoxPro handle up to 1,024 characters per statement.

Blank lines are ignored. *Insert them freely to improve the readability of your source code.*

Any line starting with an asterisk is ignored as a comment line. The asterisk may optionally be preceded by any combination of tab and blank characters.

Any text following double ampersands on a line is ignored, including the ampersands. Some dialects ignore any text following ELSE, ENDIF, ENDCASE, and ENDDO, but the practice of putting comments following these keywords may cause problems with some tools and dialects. However, there won't be any problem if such comments are preceded with double ampersands.

dBASE Subroutine Types and Calling Conventions

Subroutines provide two types of abbreviation services in a programming language, according to whether the subroutines have parameters. A subroutine without parameters acts as a simple abbreviation for the statements in the subroutine. At the place in your code where you would otherwise write the statements which comprise the subroutine, you instead place a *reference* to the subroutine.

The dBASE language offers three types of subroutines: command files, procedures, and user-defined functions. A command file or procedure file without arguments is referenced with the syntax "DO <command filename>" and a UDF without arguments is referenced with the syntax "<UDF name>()". For example, Proc1 is referenced as "DO Proc1" when Proc1 is a procedure or command file, and it is referenced as "Proc1()" when it is a UDF.

A dBASE subroutine with parameters is an abbreviation for a more complex list of statements. The code in a subroutine looks the same as the code which it replaces, with the exception that some of the identifiers have different names, and some expressions in the original code are replaced by identifiers in the subroutine code. The identifiers and expressions in the code which the subroutine reference will replace are called *arguments* and the corresponding identifiers in the subroutine are called *parameters*.

Identifiers which are used as parameters appear in a PARAMETERS statement. The initial value of these identifiers is provided by *arguments,* which are listed after the WITH keyword in a procedure or command file reference, or inside parentheses in a UDF reference, as in "DO Proc1 WITH Name" or "Proc1(Name)". The process of providing arguments to a subroutine in a subroutine reference is called *passing arguments* or *passing parameters*.

An explicit example will make this information easier to understand. Examine the following three command files. In Test.PRG, the memvar Name is the argument in the statement "DO Proc1 WITH Name"; it provides the initial value for the parameter P1 in Proc1.PRG. Similarly, the memvar Name is the argument in the statement "DO Proc2 WITH Name"; it provides the initial value for the parameter P1 in Proc2.PRG.

```
*********************************** File = Test.PRG.  Called from dot prompt.

Name =  'Amy'
DO Proc1 WITH Name
?  "Name =  ", Name

Name =  'Amy'
DO Proc2 WITH Name
?  "Name =  ", Name

* End of Test.PRG.

*********************************************************** File = Proc1.PRG.
PARAMETERS P1
?  "On entry to Proc1, parameter P1 =", P1
* End of Proc1.PRG.

*********************************************************** File = Proc2.PRG.
PARAMETERS P1
?  "On entry to Proc2, parameter P1 =", P1
P1 =  "Jill"
* End of Proc2.PRG.
```

When we "DO Test", Test.PRG will call Proc1 and then Proc2. Here is the output. Notice that the command file Proc2.PRG *changed* the value of the memvar argument in the calling routine, Test.PRG.

```
On entry to Proc1, parameter P1 = Amy
Name = Amy
On entry to Proc2, parameter P1 = Amy
Name = Jill
```

Before we can conveniently give a UDF example, we need to investigate the two varieties of parameter passing used by dBASE dialects.

Parameter Passing: Reference versus Value

Arguments may be passed in two ways, called *passing by reference* and *passing by value*. The argument Name in the preceding example is passed by reference to Proc1 and to Proc2, which means that any changes to its corresponding parameter P1 will be reflected in the argument. Arguments which are passed by value cannot be changed.

For example, if Name were passed by value to Proc2, then Name would be "Amy" both before and after the call to Proc2. You always pass arguments by reference to dBASE command files and procedures. No major dialect offers you any language-level alternative, such as SET PASSBYREFERENCE ON. However, Table 3.8 lists three techniques which you can use to protect memvars from being changed when you only want to provide their *values* to subroutines.

Table 3.8 Alternatives to Passing by Value

1. **Use a temporary variable.** Assign the value of Name to a PRIVATE variable like ArgValue, which has one use: to appear after the WITH keyword in place of Name — for example, "ArgValue = Name" followed by "DO Proc1 WITH ArgValue".
2. **Pass an expression.** This generic technique works in all programming languages with which I am familiar. Instead of coding "DO Proc2 WITH Name", code "DO Proc2 WITH (Name)". In the second form, you pass an *expression* whose *value* is the same as that of Name. The memvar Name cannot be changed because it hasn't been passed.
3. **Use a temporary memvar in the subroutine.** The *recommended* way to protect a memvar argument from being changed by a subroutine is to assign the corresponding parameter to a memvar which is PRIVATE to the subroutine, on entry to the subroutine. This is the only reference to the parameter in the subroutine.

Now say that we write the following dBASE IV test program and UDF.

```
*************************************************************   PROCEDURE Test3
PROCEDURE Test3
Name =  "Amy"
? Proc3(Name)
?  "Name =",Name
RETURN
*************************************************************   PROCEDURE Test3

*************************************************************   PROCEDURE Proc3
FUNCTION Proc3
PARAMETERS P1
?  "On entry to Proc3, parameter P1 =", P1
P1 =  "Jill"
RETURN P1
*************************************************************   PROCEDURE Proc3
```

Here is the output from "DO Test3". In this case, Name is passed by *value* to UDF Proc3(), so when its corresponding parameter P1 changes, Name does *not* change.

```
On entry to Proc3, parameter P1 = Amy
Jill
Name = Amy
```

Virtually all dBASE programmers know that arguments are passed by reference to command files and procedures, but many do not realize that dialects which support user-defined functions typically pass arguments by value to functions, as shown in Table 3.9.

Clipper lets you have it your way with the @ prefix. In the UDF reference "? ShowIt(X)", the memvar X is passed by value and cannot be changed by the UDF ShowIt(). In the UDF reference "? ShowIt(@X)", X is passed by reference and *can* be changed by the UDF ShowIt()! (In contrast, if X is a Clipper array, then "? ShowIt(X)" passes X by reference; "? ShowIt(X[1])" passes array element X[1] by value.)

Table 3.9 Passing UDF Arguments by Value or Reference in dBASE Dialects

Dialect	Passed by Value or Reference
Clipper	Either
dBASE III	No UDFs
dBASE III PLUS	No UDFs
DBASE IV	Value
dBXL	Value
FoxBASE+	Reference
FoxPro	Either
Quicksilver	Value

FoxBASE+ only knows that a subroutine is a function when the RETURN statement is encountered. If the RETURN statement is followed by an expression, then the subroutine is a function, and otherwise it is not. Therefore, arguments are always passed by reference.

In contrast, FoxPro 1.01 provides the command

```
SET UDFPARMS TO VALUE | REFERENCE
```

to control the passing of arguments by value or reference to UDFs. UDF arguments are passed by value as the default. (FoxPro 1.0 does not have this command.)

Multiple Arguments

Multiple arguments are separated by commas, as in “DO Proc4 WITH A,B,C”. These arguments are associated with parameters in the command file by one-to-one correspondence to names in the PARAMETERS statement of the command file, which must be the first statement.

Clipper permits you to pass 0 to N arguments to subroutines with N parameters — that is, with N identifiers listed in the PARAMETERS statement. You cannot skip arguments; you must pass the first argument, or the first two arguments, or the first three arguments, and so on. You test the number of arguments passed with the built-in function PCOUNT().

FoxPro permits you to pass 1 to N arguments to subroutines with N parameters. Test the number of arguments passed with the built-in function PARAMETERS().

> **Rule on memvars as arguments.** You cannot create a memvar by using it as an argument. It is insufficient to declare a memvar to be PRIVATE or PUBLIC before using it as an argument. You must assign a memvar a value before using it as an argument.

Blanks in PARAMETERS lists in dBASE III PLUS are a known problem, as follows. (In other dialects, feel free to use blanks and semicolons as appropriate to improve the readability of PARAMETERS statements.)

> **Recommendation on PARAMETERS lists in dBASE III PLUS.** dBASE III PLUS tends to get confused by blanks in the PARAMETERS list. List the parameter names separated by commas, with no embedded blanks. Do not use the semicolon to continue a long PARAMETERS line.

.PRG Command Files

Although dBASE permits you to store a set of subroutines in one file (called a *procedure file*), dBASE also supports the FORTRAN approach of storing one routine to a file. These files, called *command files,* have .PRG extensions. (FORMAT files, which are presented on page 90, are a special type of source code file with a .FMT extension.)

Command files are text files which contain a list of dBASE statements. If a PARAMETERS statement occurs, it must be the first (executable) statement. Many programmers wonder if a RETURN statement is required as the last statement in the command file.

Rule on the RETURN statement in command files. Control will return to the calling routine when the end of the command file is encountered, so you may code RETURN as the last statement at your option.

Procedure Files

Several routines can be combined into one procedure file by concatenating the source code lines and separating each routine with a line of the form

PROCEDURE <filename of former .PRG file>

or, in all major dialects except dBASE III PLUS,

FUNCTION <name of UDF or filename of former .PRG file>

You must then tell dBASE where to find the procedures, and this is done with the syntax

SET PROCEDURE TO [<pathname>]<filename>[.<extension>]

except in Clipper 4.0, which is limited to

SET PROCEDURE TO <procedure filename>[.<extension>]

However, Clipper compiles all procedures which it finds in any command file that it compiles. If FoxPro finds PROCEDURE or FUNCTION definitions in a command file that it executes, those procedures and functions will be available while that command file is executing.

In some situations, a RETURN statement is required as the last statement in a procedure or a UDF in a procedure file.

Rule on the RETURN statement in UDFs and procedures. The RETURN statement is the mechanism which allows UDFs to pass their function value back to the calling routine. In all dialects, a UDF must contain at least one statement of the form "RETURN <expression>". This rule applies to a UDF in a procedure file and to a UDF stored by itself in a .PRG file.

dBASE IV UDFs, like all UDFs, must end with a statement of the form "RETURN <expression>". However, unlike other dialects, dBASE IV requires procedures to end with a RETURN statement.

Note that interpreted dBASE dialects do not permit references to more than one procedure file in SET PROCEDURE TO. To overcome this limitation, you must combine procedure files into one file, if possible.

Procedure files have the .PRG command file extension by default. However, you are free to name your own procedure files with the .PRC extension, in which case you reference them with the syntax

SET PROCEDURE TO <procedure filename>.PRC

The distinction between a procedure and a UDF in a procedure file is blurred by different interpretations in different dialects. In Clipper, dBASE IV, dBXL, and Quicksilver, you must use the FUNCTION keyword to define UDFs in procedure files. dBASE III and dBASE III PLUS do not offer UDFs.

In FoxBASE+ and FoxPro, you can use the form "RETURN <expression>" anywhere that a RETURN statement is permitted; if a subroutine exits with the form "RETURN <expression>", then it is used as a UDF and otherwise it is not used as a UDF. In FoxPro, you may use FUNCTION as a synonym for PROCEDURE; use of the FUNCTION keyword does not imply or require all of the RETURN statements in the subroutine to be of the form "RETURN <expression>".

Compiled Procedure Files versus Interpreted Procedure Files

Procedure files have very different uses in Clipper and Quicksilver as opposed to the dBASE interpreters. For example, in dBASE III PLUS, you could have procedure files Version1.PRG and Version2.PRG; on entry to an application which uses them, you could give the user (or yourself) a choice of using the debugged Version1.PRG or the beta-test Version2.PRG with "SET PROCEDURE TO Version1" or "SET PROCEDURE TO Version2".

Now say that you have a library of accounts receivable subroutines in AR.PRG and a library of accounts payable subroutines in AP.PRG; your accounts receivable module contains the statement "SET PROCEDURE TO AR", and your accounts payable module contains the statement "SET PROCEDURE TO AP". In a compiler, *both* procedure files become part of the executable code — hence, they must not contain any procedures with the same names. In contrast, at any given time during the execution of an interpreted application, (1) the procedures in AR are defined and those in AP are not, (2) the procedures in AP are defined and those in AR are not, or (3) neither the procedures in AP nor those in AR are defined! In the interpreted application, procedures in AP and AR can have the same names.

In interpreters, you can change the set of routines which defines your application at any time during execution with the SET PATH TO and SET PROCEDURE TO statements. These two statements define lists of files which are searched when a referenced routine is not found in the current directory.

Note a big difference between SET PATH TO, which permits a *list* of directories to appear, and SET PROCEDURE TO, which permits only *one* procedure file to appear. At most one procedure file will be searched at any one time.

In contrast, Clipper and Quicksilver use the SET PROCEDURE TO command as a compiler "include" directive. For example, when Clipper encounters the command "SET PROCEDURE TO Version1" while compiling Main.PRG, then all of the procedures in Version1.PRG are compiled and added to Main.OBJ.

Remark on compiled versus interpreted procedure files. An interpreted application includes the subroutines in *at most one* procedure file at any given time during execution. The subroutines which are included are determined by the last SET PROCEDURE TO statement that was executed, if any.

A compiled application includes *all* of the subroutines referenced in *all* of the SET PROCEDURE TO statements in the application.

For example, if Version1.PRG and Version2.PRG contain procedures with the same names, then the presence of both "SET PROCEDURE TO Version1" and "SET PROCEDURE TO Version2" in the same Clipper application will cause a link time "duplicate name" error for each routine found in both Version1.PRG and Version2.PRG.

A Quicksilver Quirk

There is the following additional consideration in Quicksilver compilation. This compiler does not place the names of procedures in its symbol table at compile time, so that compile time references to these procedures cause Quicksilver to look for a command file!

For example, say that the command "SET PROCEDURE TO Version1" is compiled, Version1.PRG contains procedure V1Proc1, and you are compiling with the -A option. Although the code for V1Proc1 and any other procedure in Version1.PRG will be added to the executable file, V1Proc1 does *not* appear in the compiler's symbol table.

When Quicksilver compiles the statement "DO V1Proc1", it looks for V1Proc1.PRG and gives you a warning message if V1Proc1.PRG is not found. This warning message does not indicate a problem with your code. You can suppress all compiler warning messages by compiling with the -W option.

A worse problem occurs when V1Proc1.PRG is found. Its name and code are added to the object file, which means that this file contains two subroutines with the same name, namely, a command file named V1Proc1 and a procedure named V1Proc1.

Procedure Name Lengths

In DOS, command filenames are limited to eight characters, but in theory there is no limit on the length of a procedure name. In fact, the dialects support a variety of maximum lengths for procedure names, as shown in Table 3.10.

Most of the dialects later than dBASE III PLUS give the programmer the ability to augment the collection of built-in functions with UDFs. In most cases, UDFs are a convenience in that procedures can be used as well. For example, our program might need to calculate the logarithm of X to the base B, so we could write LogBaseB.PRG to accept three arguments, as in form 1 below, or we could write a UDF called LogBaseB to accept two arguments, as in form 2 below:

1. DO LogBaseB WITH <number>, <base>, <result>
2. LogBaseB(<number>, <base>)

Table 3.10 Maximum Procedure Name Lengths by Dialect

Dialect	Length
Clipper	10
dBASE III PLUS	8
DBASE IV	8
dbXL	8
FoxBASE+	8 documented, 9 supported
FoxPro	8
Quicksilver	8

Here are examples of the difference in the use of LogBaseB as a procedure or a UDF.

Listing 3.1 Example of a User-Defined Function versus a Procedure

```
* LogBaseB as a procedure or command file:
PRIVATE Answer
Answer = 0
DO LogBaseB WITH 5,2,Answer
? Answer

* LogBaseB as a UDF:
? LogBaseB(5,2)
```

Which form would you rather use? UDFs shine in situations where we want a subroutine to return a single value to the calling routine.

It clearly requires less text to write "LogBaseB(5,2)" than to write "DO LogBaseB WITH 5,2,Answer". In fact, Clipper permits "<subroutine>(<argument list>)" as an alternative to "DO <subroutine> WITH <argument list>".

While it is convenient to use a UDF in many cases where you would otherwise use a command file or procedure, in some situations you do not have the option of using a command file or procedure. There are at least two important commands which can be significantly enhanced by the use of UDFs.

In dialects which support both UDFs and the VALID clause of the @ GET statement, you can use a UDF reference in the VALID clause, to obtain virtually unlimited error checking and validation. It is sometimes very convenient to use a UDF as the key expression in "INDEX ON <key expression> TO <file>", although, to date, only Clipper, dBXL, and Quicksilver permit key expressions to be defined by UDFs.

In fact, at the time of writing, these three dialects are the only major ones that permit any command to appear in a UDF and that permit a UDF to appear anywhere a reference to a built-in function may appear. FoxPro permits any command to appear in a UDF, but there are restrictions on where UDF references may appear; in particular, UDFs may not appear in index expressions. dBASE IV places restrictions on commands which may appear in UDFs and on where UDF references may occur.

MS-DOS and dBASE Searches for Data Files and Code Files

When DOS cannot find a referenced executable file in the current directory, it searches for this file in a list of directories contained in a DOS environment variable named PATH. For example, if you store the external commands of DOS in C:\DOS and DOS utility programs in C:\UTIL, then your AutoExec.BAT file would contain a line like

PATH=C:\DOS;C:\PATH

This facility allows you to type the names of external DOS commands at the DOS prompt without specifying the pathname of the command file. For example, with the above SET PATH command, you can enter "XCOPY" at the DOS prompt instead of "C:\DOS\XCOPY".

If you request DOS to open a *data* file and you specify only a file name and not a path, then DOS usually looks for the file only in the current directory. However, the APPEND command in DOS versions 3.3 and higher permits you to list directories as you would with SET PATH to define a set of directories to be searched for data files.

dBASE supports a similar path concept through the "SET PATH TO <directory list>" command. For example, if dBASE executes "USE Accounts" either interactively or in a program, it looks for Accounts.DBF in the current DOS directory and in the list of directories specified in the dBASE SET PATH TO statement.

dBASE interpreters make no distinction between requests for executable and data files. For example, if a dBASE interpreter executes "DO AcctMenu", it looks for AcctMenu.PRG (or the tokenized form of AcctMenu.PRG) in the current DOS directory or in the directories specified in SET PATH TO.

In contrast, Clipper and Quicksilver expect all of your source code files to be in the same directory at compile time. At execution time, all source code files have been translated into one .EXE file and possibly one or more overlay files. This means that SET PATH TO is used only for data file searches in Clipper and Quicksilver programs.[5]

A related dBASE command, not supported by Clipper or Quicksilver,[6] is

SET DEFAULT TO <drive letter>

When this command has *not* been executed, and dBASE needs a file which is referenced by file name without drive and path qualification, then it looks first in the current directory on the current DOS drive. For example, if the current DOS directory is C:\Accounts, dBASE will look for Receipts.DBF in C:\Accounts when it

5. dBXL and Quicksilver implement the SET DBF and SET NDX commands to specify the directories where .DBF and .NDX files are stored.

6. FoxPro supports the extended form SET DEFAULT TO <pathname>.

executes the command "USE Receipts", assuming no SET DEFAULT TO command has been executed.

If "SET DEFAULT TO <current DOS drive>" has been executed, dBASE again looks for files referenced only by file name in the current DOS directory. Otherwise, the current DOS directory on the drive in the SET DEFAULT TO command is searched *instead of* the current DOS directory on the current DOS drive.

If a file referenced only by file name is not in the current DOS directory on the current dBASE drive, then the directories in the dBASE path are searched. Thus, the SET DEFAULT TO command extends the capability of the SET PATH TO command.

If you are like me, you can easily understand the SET PATH TO command, because it is so similar to the MS-DOS PATH command. However, I find that the SET DEFAULT TO command presents too many options, so I make the following recommendation.

Recommendation on SET DEFAULT TO. Use SET PATH TO instead of SET DEFAULT TO. In that case, the current DOS drive and current dBASE drive will always be the same.

Data Attributes and the Symbol Table

In this section we look at how data is represented in dBASE dialects. We'll see which attributes dBASE associates with various data objects in your source code, and we'll see how you define data objects and control their attributes.

Data Representation Options and Attributes

dBASE data is stored in *constants* and in three kinds of *variables: database fields, parameters,* and *memory variables* (called *memvars* in dBASE terminology). Various *attributes* are associated with dBASE constants and variables.

Constants, memvars, and parameters have the attributes of *type* and *length*. Possible types are *character, date, logical,* and *numeric*. Dates are stored in 8 bytes, logical data is stored in 1 byte, and the number of bytes used by a character or numeric constant varies. Memvars and parameters have an additional attribute called *scope,* whose value is PRIVATE or PUBLIC.[7]

Database fields also have the attributes of type and length. In addition to the types mentioned in the preceding paragraph, fields may have the *memo* type; memo fields can hold large amounts of character data. Numeric fields have an additional attribute called *decimals,* which consists of the number of digits to the right of the decimal point. Numeric fields must be of type F or N, for hexadecimal or decimal arithmetic, as discussed in the subsection "Float and Numeric Variables and Expressions," starting on page 65.

7. dBASE has a second scope feature: database commands may include a SCOPE clause. The two scope features have the same name by coincidence and are not otherwise related.

The Symbol Table

Any language processor (such as a compiler, interpreter, or linker) has an internal data structure called a *symbol table,* which is used to manage named code and data objects in programs. dBASE dialects use a symbol table during execution to manage an application's identifiers. Table 3.11 lists *some* of the data which the execution-time symbol table may store on each identifier.

Table 3.11 Symbol Table Structure in dBASE Dialects

1. The name of the identifier (up to 10 characters).
2. The type of the identifier.
3. Whether the identifier is a database field, a parameter, or a memvar.
4. Whether the scope of memvar identifiers is PUBLIC or PRIVATE.
5. The subroutine in which the identifier was created.
6. The data which is currently assigned to a parameter or a memvar. (Technically speaking, the symbol table typically contains the RAM *address* where the data may be found, and not the data itself.)

Defining dBASE Data Objects

The names and types of database fields are defined when a database is created or its structure is modified with the interactive MODIFY STRUCTURE command. The fields and their types become known to your application when you open a database with commands like USE, COPY TO, and APPEND FROM.

When a memvar appears as the target of an assignment statement, and the memvar does not appear in the symbol table, it is entered in the symbol table with the PRIVATE scope and the type of the value which is assigned to it. When a memvar appears in a PUBLIC or PRIVATE statement, and that variable has not been assigned a value, it is entered in the symbol table with the specified scope. The memvar may or may not receive a value subsequently; its default initial value is logical .F. (References to memvars which are not in the symbol table are treated as references to .F.)

Rule on PRIVATE and PUBLIC statements. If you want to list an identifier in a PRIVATE or PUBLIC statement, then do so *before* you assign data to the memvar which the identifier represents — for example, "PRIVATE X" followed by "X = 5", *not* "X = 5" followed by "PRIVATE X".

A parameter is defined in a PARAMETERS statement. Parameters are associated with arguments listed after the WITH keyword, or inside the parentheses of a UDF reference, as follows: on entry to a subroutine with a PARAMETERS statement, the initial value and type of the first parameter is the same as the value and type of the first argument, the initial value and type of the second parameter is the same as the value and type of the second argument, and so on.

Some dBASE dialects require that the number of arguments in the subroutine reference and the number of parameters in the PARAMETERS statement of the subroutine be the same. In these dialects, a parameter always has data associated with its symbol table entry.

The FoxPro and Clipper dialects permit you to pass fewer arguments than parameters. In these dialects, a parameter may be entered into the symbol table because of its presence in a PARAMETERS statement even though there is no value associated with the parameter.

Data Types for dBASE Dialects

Data types for dBASE dialects are shown in the following table. (The Recital dialect for minicomputers offers several types not shown below. See page 183 for a list of extra field types in Recital.)

Table 3.12 dBASE Data Types with Lengths in Bytes

Field Letter	Data Type and Length
C	Character fields, length 1 to 254 (32K in Clipper).
N/A	Character memvars, length 1 to 254 (64K in Clipper, FoxPro).
D	Date, length 8.
F	Float, length 1 to 20. (dBASE IV, FoxPro only.)
L	Logical, length 1.
M	Memo, variable length limited only by disk space and the memo editor, except 64K in Clipper and dBASE IV.
N	Numeric, length 1 to 19 (20 in dBASE IV, FoxPro).

All data types except Float are supported by all dialects. dBASE IV and FoxPro also support Float. See the subsubsection "Float versus Numeric Types" on page 65.

Identifier Formation: Rules and Conventions

If a procedure or data structure has a name, that name identifies the structure to dBASE and thus the name is called an *identifier*. The dBASE standard permits identifiers of 1 to 10 characters. The first character must be alphabetic, except in Clipper and FoxPro, which permit the underscore as the first character. (dBASE IV reserves the underscore as the starting character of predefined system memvars. FoxPro *uses* the underscore as the starting character of its system memvars, but it does not *reserve* this character for this purpose.) The remaining characters can be alphabetic, numeric, or the underscore.

Recommendation on variable-name spellings. Use a mixture of uppercase and lowercase letters in identifiers to make the meaning clearer. For example, write "FileIndex" and not "fileindex" or "FILEINDEX".

If you have the characters to spare, use the letter denoting the type of the variable (if it has a fixed type) as the last letter of the variable's name. For example, "FileIndexN" and "IndexN" would be numeric memvars and "IndexC" or "Index_C" would be character memvars.

Coding Conventions

Generally speaking, there are many rules, like those governing indentation and the use of uppercase and lowercase letters in variable names, which are associated with the appearance and structure of source code. This book presents a fairly comprehensive coding standard for dBASE dialects in Appendix E, starting on page 431. That appendix also gives references to coding standards which you can find in other books.

Data Types and Expressions

In this section, we look at the basic capabilities of variables with character, date, logical, numeric, and memo types. Then we see how these variables may be combined in expressions.

Character Variables and Expressions

There are two dialect-dependent issues for character memvars. The first issue is the maximum number of characters permitted and the second issue is whether all 256 bit patterns may be represented in an 8-bit character, or just non-null characters.

FoxPro permits up to 64K characters in a memvar, Clipper permits up to 32K in a memvar, and the other major dialects, including dBASE IV, support up to 254 characters in a memvar. FoxPro, Clipper, and dBASE IV permit the null character, CHR(0), to occur in character memvars, whereas the other major dialects permit only non-null characters in character memvars.

In those dialects, you may include a CHR(0) character in a character expression. However, this means that the first null character in the expression is taken as the end of the string. For example, "?? CHR(27) + CHR(0) + CHR(65)" would have the same effect as "?? CHR(27)" in these dialects.

Character string constants are enclosed in single or double quotes. In the following example, A, B, C, and D have the same value. The built-in functions deliver the values indicated in the comments. The memvar Compare has the value "True". (Remember that double ampersands are used to mark the beginning of a comment in dBASE source code.)

Listing 3.2 Examples of Character Functions and Expressions

```
A = "Excellent Adventure"
B = 'Excellent Adventure'
C = "Excellent" + ' Adventure'
D = "Excellent" + SPACE(1) + 'Adventure'

I = AT("x",A)       && I = 2, the position of the first "x"
J = AT("X",A)       && J = 0 to denote that "X" was not found.
L = LEN(A)          && L = 19, the length of A.

S = SUBSTR(A,6,4)  && = "lent", the 4 characters starting in the 6th character.

Lower = LOWER(A)   && = "excellent adventure"
Upper = UPPER(A)   && = "EXCELLENT ADVENTURE"

Compare = IIF("a" < "b", "True", "False")  && = "True"
```

Date Variables and Expressions

A date takes 8 bytes as a database variable, where it is stored in the character format YYYYMMDD — for example, "17760704" for July 4, 1776. The date format can be converted to and from the character format with the built-in functions DtoC(<date value>) and CtoD(<character form of date>). The built-in function DATE() returns the current date in the computer system, which is today's date if the system is properly maintained.

With the "American" setting of SET DATE, date constants can be represented in any dialect by enclosing the month/day/year form of the date in quotes, and applying the "character-to-date" function CtoD(), as in CtoD("7/4/76"), CtoD("7/4/1776"), or CtoD("07/04/1776"). dBASE IV and FoxPro permit the equivalent forms {"7/4/76"}, {"7/4/1776"}, or {"07/04/1776"}. The twentieth century is assumed if no century is specified.

The SET DATE command can be used to define the date format to one that corresponds to the convention in your country. For example, if you SET CENTURY ON and SET DATE GERMAN and today is December 31, 1991, then "? Date()" shows "31.12.1999".

In the following listing, Date_C, Date1_C, and Compare are character variables, One_N is numeric, and the other variables have the date type. Although Date_D and Date1_D always have the same values irrespective of the setting of SET CENTURY, Date_C and Date1_C are the same or different according to whether CENTURY is set OFF or ON.

Listing 3.3 Examples of Date Functions and Expressions

```
Date_C  =  "07/04/1776"   && July 4, 1776 in character format.
Date_C  =  "07/4/1776"    && July 4, 1776 in character format.
Date_C  =  "7/4/1776"     && July 4, 1776 in character format.
Date_C  =  "7/4/76"       && July 4, 1976 in character format.
Date_C  =  "07/04/76"     && July 4, 1976 in character format.
                                     && Date_D has the date type.
Date_D  = CtoD(Date_C)   && July 4, 1976 in date format.
Year_N  = YEAR(Date_D)   && = 1976
Month_N = MONTH(Date_D)  && = 7
```

```
SET CENTURY OFF
Date1_C = DtoC(Date_D)        && Date1_C = Date_C =   "07/04/76"
SET CENTURY ON
Date1_C = DtoC(Date_D)        && Date_C # Date1_C: Date1_C =   "07/04/1976"
Date1_D = CtoD(Date1_C)       && July 4, 1976 in date format, same as Date_D.
Today   = DATE()
Tomorrow= DATE() + 1          && Add one day to today's date.
***************************** Subtract two dates for number of days between:
One_N    = Tomorrow - Today  && = 1
Compare = IIF(Today < Tomorrow,   "True",   "False")  && =  "True"
```

Logical Variables and Expressions

Logical variables have either a true or false value, represented by the dBASE logical constants .T. and .F., respectively. The usual use of logical variables or expressions is in IF, CASE, and WHILE statements, as shown in Listing 3.4.

Listing 3.4 Examples of Logical Expressions and Flow of Control

```
IF (Due_Date > DATE())
   ?  "Member is current."
ELSE
   ?  "Member is not current."
ENDIF
DO CASE
   CASE (MemberType = 1)
      Label =  "Regular Membership"
   CASE (MemberType = 2)
      Label =  "Reduced Income Membership"
   CASE (MemberType = 3)
      Label =  "Life Membership"
   OTHERWISE
      Label =  "Nonmember"
ENDCASE
******************************************************* WHILE LOOP, form 1:
Continue_L = .T.
Pointer    = 1
Whole      =  "  Some text with blanks in it."
DO WHILE Continue_L
   Continue_L = (SUBSTR(Whole,Pointer,1) =  "  ") .AND. (Pointer < LEN(Whole))
   Pointer    = Pointer + 1
ENDDO
******************************************************* WHILE LOOP, form 2:
Pointer    = 1
Whole      =  "  Some text with blanks in it."
DO WHILE (SUBSTR(Whole,Pointer,1) =  "  ") .AND. (Pointer < LEN(Whole))
   Pointer    = Pointer + 1
ENDDO
```

The two loops are equivalent in results, although the first loop requires an extra memvar to be in the symbol table, namely, Continue_L.

Rule. The form "IF (Continue_L = .T.)" is *not* allowed; use "IF Continue_L" instead.

Logical expressions can be formed by connecting logical expressions with .AND. or .OR.; you can negate a logical expression with .NOT. For example, "DO WHILE (.NOT. Found_L)" repeats a loop until Found_L becomes true.

Float and Numeric Variables and Expressions

Database numeric and float variables are stored in character form. When you define database numeric variables, you specify a *width* of 1 to 19 or 20 and a *decimals* value of 0 to the value of *width*. The *decimals* value represents the number of digits stored to the right of the decimal point in the character representation.

If the numeric value is very large or very small, it may be stored in scientific notation, as in "2E+06" to represent "$2*10^6$". If the number is not stored in scientific notation, then it appears in an optionally signed integer or fixed decimal representation. Table 3.13 shows the range of numeric and float variables in different dialects.

Unsigned integers of K digits total need a width of K and a decimals of 0. For example, if we say as a notational convenience that "N,4,0" represents a numeric type of width 4 and 0 decimals, then a variable with this type can represent the unsigned integers 0, 1, ..., 9999. Note that signed integers of K digits total need a width of K + 1 and a decimals of 0. A variable of type N,4,0 can represent the signed integers –999, –998, ..., –1, 0, +1, ..., +999.

Rational numbers of M digits before the decimal and L digits after the decimal need a decimals of L and a width of M + L + 1 if there is no sign and M + L + 2 if there is a sign. For example, a variable of type N,4,1 can store the signed values –9.9, –9.8, ..., –0.1, 0, +0.1, ..., +9.9, or the unsigned values 0, 0.1, ..., 99.9.

Table 3.13 Range of Numeric and Float Variables

Dialect	Type	Smallest	Largest
Clipper 4.0	Numeric	10^{-19}	10^{+18}
Clipper 5.0	Numeric	10^{-308}	10^{+308}
dBASE III PLUS	Numeric	10^{-307}	10^{+99}
DBASE IV	Numeric	$.1*10^{-307}$	$.9*10^{+308}$
DBASE IV	Float	$.1*10^{-307}$	$.9*10^{+308}$
dBXL	Numeric	10^{-307}	10^{+308}
FoxBASE+	Numeric	10^{-100}	10^{+98}
FoxPro	Numeric	10^{-307}	10^{+308}
FoxPro	Float	10^{-307}	10^{+308}
Quicksilver	Numeric	Undocumented	Undocumented

Float versus Numeric Types

Numeric and float variables are represented in character form when they are displayed, with the number of decimal places shown controlled by the third argument in the built-in function STR(<value to show>,<width>,<decimal places>) or the command SET DECIMALS TO <decimal places>. When numeric or float values are stored in fields, the representation is again in character form, according to the definition of the field.

However, for purposes of calculation, numbers are represented internally in the format

Sign * (Base**Exponent) * Mantissa

where Sign is +1 or –1, Base is 10 or 16, Exponent is an integer with a range which depends on the dialect and the base, and Mantissa is a fraction between 1/10 inclusive and 1 exclusive if Base = 10, or between 1/16 inclusive and 1 if Base = 16. The amount of accuracy carried in the mantissa, which represents the amount of accuracy in the entire number, is also dependent on the dialect.

The representation is called *hexadecimal* when Base = 16 and *decimal* when Base = 10. Decimal arithmetic — that is, arithmetic on numbers in the decimal format — is best for calculations which involve money. Hexadecimal arithmetic is best for most other kinds of calculations.

The following table shows the association of the field types N and F with hexadecimal and decimal arithmetic in the different dialects.

Table 3.14 Meaning of Types N and F in Different Dialects

Dialect	Type	Arithmetic
Clipper	N	Hexadecimal
dBASE III	N	Hexadecimal
dBASE III PLUS	N	Hexadecimal
DBASE IV	F	Hexadecimal
DBASE IV	N	Decimal
dBXL	N	Hexadecimal
FoxBASE+	N	Hexadecimal
FoxPro	F	Hexadecimal
FoxPro	N	Decimal
Quicksilver	N	Hexadecimal

The most common problem which is solved by the new N type is summing monetary amounts. When a great many dollar amounts are added together with the old N type, the result is often off by a few cents. This is due to the loss of accuracy when amounts are converted back and forth between base 10 and base 16. When such amounts are stored in the new N format, the sum is always exact, assuming that its absolute value is less than about one thousand trillion dollars.

Recommendation on type N in dBASE IV and FoxPro. Always use type N for storing monetary amounts.

Recommendation on type F in dBASE IV and FoxPro. Use type F fields in applications which perform a lot of arithmetic on values with a large number of decimal places.

Comparison of Numbers

When dBASE III PLUS compares two nonzero numbers, it rounds each one to (approximately) 13 decimal digits. For example, the expression 1/3 + 1/3 + 1/3 compares equal to 1, even though, due to round-off error, the value of this expression is actually a tiny bit smaller than 1. dBXL rounds values to 11 digits before comparing them.

Operations and Precedence

Addition, subtraction, multiplication, division, and exponentiation are represented as X + Y, X – Y, X*Y, X/Y, and X**Y or X^Y. Parentheses can (and should) be used to indicate precedence of operations. For example, 20 + (30/10) = 23, but (20 + 30)/10 = 5.

Exponentiation has precedence over multiplication and division, so that A*B^C = A*(B^C) and A^B/C = (A^B)/C. Multiplication and division have precedence over addition and subtraction, so that A/B – C*D = (A/B) – (C*D) and A/B + C*D = (A/B) + (C*D).

Built-In Numeric Functions

dBASE III PLUS contains built-in functions to calculate absolute values, the integer part of a number, the greater or lesser of two values, X MOD Y, X rounded to the nearest integer, square roots, and logarithms and exponents to the base e. Other dialects have additional numerically oriented built-in functions.

Memo Fields

In dBASE terminology, identifiers which represent values stored in databases are called *fields*. In dBASE dialects, only fields can have the memo type.

Memo contents are stored in a separate file with a .DBT extension, except in FoxPro, which reads the .DBT form of memo files, but which creates memo files with a different internal organization and a .FPT extension. For example, if the database Accounts.DBF has one or more memo fields, then Accounts.DBT is opened every time that Accounts.DBF is opened. A 10-byte field in the database record holds a pointer to a block number in the memo file.

During full-screen editing, the usual inverse video box holds the word "memo". When the cursor is in such a box, pressing CONTROL-PageDown invokes the built-in editor (or user-installed editor) for full-screen editing of the memo contents as a text file. In fact, a temporary text file *is* created; after the memo contents are edited in this temporary file, its contents are copied back into the .DBT (memo) file. **Most dialects do *not* reuse space in the memo file, so the only way to reclaim unused space in such dialects is to re-create the .DBF file with the PACK, APPEND FROM, or COPY TO commands.**

Clipper Memo Extensions

Clipper offers the functions MemoEdit(), MemoLine(), MemoRead(), MemoTran(), and MemoWrit() to support the processing of memo fields and character memvars, which can be of length 64K and 32K, respectively, in Clipper 4.0. You can move data from a character memvar to a memo with REPLACE, and if the memo data is less than 32K in length, you can move the memo data to a character memvar by assignment: "<Character memvar> = <memo name>".

MemoEdit() supports browsing or editing character data in windows. MemoRead() and MemoWrit() move data between character variables and disk files. MemoLine() and MemoTran() are used to process character data as *lines*. The character functions AT(), LEN(), SUBSTR(), LEFT(), and RIGHT() can also be applied to memo fields. Listing 3.5 shows a simple routine to browse files of up to 32K in length.

Listing 3.5 TextBrow.PRG—Browse a Text File in Clipper

```
* File = TextBrow.PRG.  Called from several .PRG to allow the user to browse
* the contents of text file of up to 32K.
*******************************************************************************
* Dialects: Clipper only.
*******************************************************************************
* Input parameters:
* First parameter: name of file to be browsed.
*******************************************************************************

PARAMETERS FileName

IF FILE(FileName)
   Temp =  Replicate(SPACE(1), 80)
   @ 23,0 GET Temp
   Temp =  "      PageUp for previous screen, PageDown for next screen,    " + ;
        "ESCAPE to exit.        "
   @ 24,0 GET Temp
   CLEAR GETS
   SET CURSOR OFF
   MemoEdit( MemoRead(FileName), 0,0, 22,79, .F. )
   SET CURSOR ON
ELSE
   ?  "I'm sorry.  I would like to present the file &FileName for browsing, but I"
   ?  "can't find it."

   DO WaitOnC
ENDIF

* End of TextBrow.PRG.
```

dBASE IV Memo Extensions

As in Clipper, the character functions AT(), LEN(), SUBSTR(), LEFT(), and RIGHT() can be applied to memo fields. The APPEND MEMO and COPY MEMO commands let you move data between files and memo fields. The SET WINDOW OF MEMO TO command associates a previously defined window with a memo field. The memo contents can be edited in this window during APPEND, BROWSE, and EDIT operations. MEMLINES() and MLINE() are used to display the memo contents in word-wrapped form.

dBXL and Quicksilver Memo Extensions

These WordTech dialects offer "STORE MEMO <field> TO ARRAY <name>" and its companion command "REPLACE MEMO <field> WITH ARRAY <name>" to move line-oriented text data between memo fields and arrays. One line of text is stored in each array element; the number of lines in such a memo field is MLCOUNT(<memo field>). The built-in function MEMOLINE() returns specified lines from a line-oriented memo field.

FoxPro Memo Extensions

FoxPro supports all the memo extensions of dBASE IV, but it goes beyond dBASE IV in treating all character data the same. Therefore, if a FoxPro command or function can be used on memo data, it can be used on character data, and vice versa.

While dBASE IV permits character memvars to be no longer than 254 characters, and Clipper character memvars are limited to 32K characters, FoxPro permits character memvars of up to 64K characters in length; as in dBASE IV, FoxPro memo fields can be any length. Memo fields with up to 64K bytes of data can be copied to character memvars, and memvars of any length can be copied to memo fields.

Data Structures

Like all general-purpose programming languages, dBASE permits variable values to be stored in files, but there is explicit support for unstructured files (.MEM extensions) and structured files (.DBF extensions). The dialects which are newer than dBASE III PLUS also usually support arrays of memory variables.

However, unlike a traditional general-purpose programming language, dBASE has structure concepts that normally are provided by the programmer with custom code. These include *formats,* which permit you to determine the onscreen appearance of a database record; *filters,* which permit you to restrict your view of the database to records which meet a given condition; and *indexes,* which permit you to retrieve database records in the order you need (not necessarily storage order).

Moreover, you can generate mailing labels and columnar reports with standard facilities. Label files with .LBL extensions (.LBX in FoxPro) hold the data which defines label sizes and contents in terms of database fields. One label is printed for each database record.

Report definitions are stored in .FRM files (.FRX in FoxPro) and are invoked with the REPORT FORM command. This command causes one line of data to be printed for each database record, except in dBASE IV and FoxPro, which offer much more flexibility than the other dialects, with truly powerful report generation capabilities comparable to those of R&R Relational Report Writer from Concentric Data Systems.

.DBF Database Files

A nonempty dBASE database file is conceptually a collection of records, numbered 1 to RecCount(). Each record consists of a delete byte, which has the value of a blank or asterisk, and the fields defined by the database's creator. The delete byte is an asterisk if the record is marked for deletion and is blank otherwise. Each field has a name and one of the data types described earlier in this chapter.

dBASE interpreters permit you to create databases with the syntax "CREATE <database name>"; this command gives you a spreadsheet-like screen on which to define fields. You can update these definitions at a later time with the MODIFY STRUCTURE command.

Clipper users can create databases with dBASE III PLUS or dBXL, or they can use a utility provided with Clipper called DBU. Quicksilver users have the interpreter dBXL as a companion product and can create databases and modify database structures with dBXL.

dBASE dialects typically support at least 128 fields, as shown in Table 3.15. The database is physically implemented as a header followed by the records in the order 1, 2, 3, and so on. The header stores the field definitions and file information such as the date of last update. The records consist of a delete byte followed by data for the first field, data for the second field, and so on.

Table 3.15 Maximum Number of Fields per Database

Dialect	Field Limit
Clipper	1,024
dBASE III	128
dBASE III PLUS	128
DBASE IV	255
dbXL	128 if COMPATIBLE is SET ON
dbXL	512 if COMPATIBLE is SET OFF
FoxBASE+	128
FoxPro	255
Quicksilver	128 if COMPATIBLE is SET ON
Quicksilver	512 if COMPATIBLE is SET OFF

During processing, an entity called the *record pointer* points to the beginning-of-file mark (BOF() is true), a specific record numbered 1 to RecCount() (RecNo() = <the record number>), or the end-of-file mark (EOF() is true). The SET DELETED ON/OFF command controls whether database records with delete marks will be processed by database commands.

When a database with at least one record is opened, and SET DELETED OFF is the last SET DELETED command to be executed, then record 1 becomes the current record — that is, the record pointer points to record 1 and RecNo() = 1. If SET DELETED ON is the last SET DELETED command to be executed, then the record pointer first points to the nondeleted record with the lowest record number, if any.

If there are no nondeleted records, then the record pointer points to the end-of-file mark, and EOF() becomes true.

When a database exists, it is opened for use with the command

USE <database name> [ALIAS <ALIAS name>]
[INDEX <index file list>] [EXCLUSIVE]

If no ALIAS clause appears, the ALIAS is the same as the filename of the database, exclusive of extension. For example, the following database files all have the ALIAS of "Accounts", but the database files are, respectively, Accounts.DBF, Accounts.JAN, and January.DBF.

USE Accounts
USE Accounts.JAN
USE January ALIAS Accounts

Once the USE command opens a database, a great many commands in the dBASE language can be used to manipulate or query the database in one way or another. For example, the PACK command is used to physically remove records that are marked for deletion. A record is marked for deletion with the DELETE command or by stroking CONTROL-U during full-screen editing. The delete mark can be reset with the RECALL command.

You can open an index file for a database at the same time as the database if you use the INDEX clause in the USE command. For example, if Receipts.DBF has an index file named Date_In.NDX, then "USE Receipts INDEX Date_In" opens Receipts with the Date_In index controlling the order in which the records from Receipts are retrieved.

In a network environment, you usually SET EXCLUSIVE OFF in order to open database files in shared mode by default. You can open a database for exclusive use with the EXCLUSIVE clause, which we will explore in detail in Volume 2.

Work Areas

When you read or write a file with a conventional programming language, you refer to the file name (directly or indirectly) in each input/output (I/O) command. Indeed, dBASE dialects which offer byte-level access to files use commands and functions that require the file "handle" to be specified for each I/O.

In contrast, dBASE dialects implement a file mode concept for processing database files. Generally speaking, I/O commands do not refer to database files. Rather, you select an "area" in which you open a database file. Thereafter, all database commands refer to the database in the currently selected area.

This is an appropriate approach for dBASE dialects, and it results in programs which are simpler for the human to read and write. FoxPro and dBASE IV permit you the option of including a database ALIAS in a function like RecCount() — RecCount() refers to the currently selected database and RecCount(<ALIAS>) refers to the open database of the specified ALIAS. Clipper 4.0 uses the syntax

<ALIAS> -> (RecCount())

Clipper permits you to open databases in any of 254 predefined "areas," sometimes called "work areas." The number of databases which Clipper can open depends on the DOS version; for MS-DOS 3.1 or higher, 255 total files may be open, and work-arounds are available for earlier versions.

Recommendation on how to open more files in MS-DOS 2.x. There are several ways to work around the limit on the maximum number of open files in versions of MS-DOS prior to version 3.1. See your public BBSs, speak to your DOS experts, or contact Gibson Research for "Steve's TSR Offer #1." (The best solution may be to upgrade yourself and your users to MS-DOS 3.1 or higher, if that is feasible.)

FoxPro permits you to open up to 25 databases simultaneously in work areas 1 to 25. You can refer to the first 10 work areas as A, B, ..., J.

The other major dialects permit up to 10 databases to be open simultaneously in any of 10 areas. If no database is open in an area, then the area must be referenced by numbers, as in 1, 2, 3, ..., 10, or with letters, as in A, B, C, ..., J. Once a database is open in an area, it can be referenced by the ALIAS of a database — *which I strongly recommend.* Clipper programmers must reference databases in areas 11 through 254 with the number of the area or the ALIAS of the database open in the area, the latter of which is recommended.

Areas are chosen with the syntax

SELECT <number, letter, or ALIAS>

as in SELECT 1, SELECT J, or SELECT Accounts.

The ALIAS, or work area, is used to qualify references to variables in databases open in other work areas. For example, if March.DBF and April.DBF are open in areas 1 and 2, and both contain a field named StartDate, then you reference the StartDate field in March.DBF with 1->StartDate, A->StartDate, or March->StartDate (which is strongly recommended when feasible). Similarly, you reference StartDate in April.DBF with 2->StartDate, B->StartDate, or April->StartDate.

If the current work area is area 1, then the abbreviation for 1->StartDate is just "StartDate" with no prefix.

SELECT 0

Most dialects after dBASE III PLUS have the SELECT 0 command, which selects the available area of lowest number. dBASE IV requires SELECT SELECT(), which is more logical but nonstandard. The dBASE III PLUS dialect does not have this incredibly useful — and strongly recommended — command, but SELECT 0 can be simulated with the command file in Listing 3.6, which should work in most or all dialects.

Listing 3.6 Select0.PRG—SELECT 0 for dBASE III PLUS

```
* File = Select0.PRG.  Implements the SELECT 0 command in dBASE III Plus.
*   "DO SELECT0" can be used in Clipper & FoxBASE+ applications transparently as
* substitute for  "SELECT 0".
*********************************************************************
* The only state change is possibly to the SELECT area.
* On entry, any area is SELECTed.  If there is no open area, all files are
* closed and a CANCEL or QUIT is issued.  Otherwise, the available
* area with the lowest number is SELECTed on exit.

PUBLIC CLIPPER,FOX

IF (CLIPPER .OR. FOX)
   SELECT 0
ELSE
   PRIVATE I,Ichar
   I = 1
   DO WHILE (I <= 10)
      Ichar = LTRIM(STR( I ))
      SELECT &Ichar
      IF ("" = DBF())
    RETURN
      ENDIF
      I = I + 1
   ENDDO && WHILE (I <= upper bound)
   ?  "All SELECT areas are in use, yet another is needed."
   ?  "Copy or print this screen and notify your programmer."
   DO WaitOnC
   CLOSE ALL
   CANCEL
ENDIF
* End of Select0.PRG.
```

Commands for Databases

There is a collection of commands, central to dBASE, which operate on database files. These commands, some of which are shown in Table 3.16, simplify the retrieval and/or updating of existing records and the creation of new records.

For example, the SKIP command moves the record pointer according to this syntax:

SKIP [<expN>]

If no expression appears, "SKIP +1" is assumed and the record pointer advances to the next record in index or storage order, depending on whether an index is in place. SKIP –1 returns to the previous record.

Most Commonly Used Database Commands and Functions

Table 3.16 lists the most commonly used database commands and functions. In many cases, use of the appropriate command or function will collapse many lines of code into one line. Bear in mind the distinction between commands and functions: commands act upon the database in some way, whereas functions return one piece of information about a database.

Table 3.16 Commonly Used Database Commands and Functions

ALIAS()	ALIAS of a work area.
APPEND	Interactively adds records to the end of the database file and prompts user to enter field values.
APPEND BLANK	Adds a blank record to the end of the database file.
APPEND FROM	Adds records from the source database file to the end of the target database file.
AVERAGE	Computes the average of numeric fields.
BOF()	True when record pointer is moved before the first record (by SKIP with a negative argument). Companion to EOF().
BROWSE	With EDIT, one of the two most important commands in dBASE. Gives a tabular view of data in a database file. Fields are listed across the screen and records are listed down.
CLOSE DATABASES	Closes all database, index, format, and memo files.
COUNT	Counts the number of records in any current index which meet any SET DELETE and SET FILTER conditions in place.
COPY STRUCTURE	Copies the structure of the current database to a new, empty database.
COPY TO	Copies selected records and fields to a new database.
COPY TO <file> STRUCTURE EXTENDED	Copies the field definitions of the current database into a "structure extended" database. The field definitions can be then be manipulated by program code.
CREATE	Interactively specifies field definitions for a database.
CREATE FROM	Companion command to COPY TO <file> STRUCTURE EXTENDED. Creates a database from the field definitions in a structure extended file.
DELETE	Sets the delete byte in a record to signify later physical removal of the record by the PACK command. Inverse of RECALL.
DELETED()	True if the current record is marked for deletion.
DISPLAY	Lists selected fields from selected records, one screen at a time. A screen is displayed, and the user must then stroke a key to see the next screen. Companion to LIST.
EOF()	True when the record pointer is moved after the last record (by SKIP with a positive argument). Companion to BOF().
FIELD()	Name of field; FIELD(1) is the name of the first field. Clipper uses FieldName().
FOUND()	True if the last CONTINUE, FIND, LOCATE, or SEEK command was successful (but not as reliable as EOF() in dBASE III PLUS and FoxBASE+, Kalman 1989: 217).
INDEX ON	Creates an index file for the current database.

LIST	Lists selected fields from selected records. Companion to DISPLAY.
PACK	Physically removes records which are marked for deletion.
RECALL	Sets the delete byte of a record to "don't remove."
RECCOUNT()	or RecCount(). Number of records in a database.
RECNO()	or RecNo(). Current value of record pointer.
SET AUTOSAVE	In FoxPro and dBASE IV, writes database record updates to disk as soon as possible.
SET DELETED	A companion command to SET FILTER. When ON, records marked for deletion are not accessed by other commands. This condition applies in addition to any filter.
SET FIELDS	Limits the view of the database to the specified fields.
SET FILTER	Specifies a logical condition which each record must meet in order to be accessed by other commands.
SET RELATION TO	Relates one "parent" database to one or more "child" databases so that when the record pointer moves in the parent database, the record pointer also moves in the child databases.
SKIP	Moves the record pointer forward or backward in the currently selected database.
SORT	Produces a second database with records in order by a specified key.
SUM	Adds the numeric fields in the specified records and displays the results, optionally storing them to memvars.
TOTAL ON	Adds the numeric fields in the specified records and stores the results in a second database.
USE	Opens a database with optional index files, an ALIAS, and the EXCLUSIVE option.
ZAP	Resets the record counter for a database so that dBASE sees it as having no records.

ALIAS Qualification of Database Commands and UDFs

FoxPro and dBASE IV permit database functions to include the ALIAS of a work area as an argument. For example, RecCount() is the number of records in the currently selected work area, but RecCount("Members") is the number of records in the currently open database with the ALIAS "Members", which is not necessarily in the currently selected work area.

Clipper uses the rather awkward syntax Members->(RecCount()). The remaining major dialects require you to select a database's work area in order to retrieve information about the database.

As a very nice compensation for its awkward syntax, Clipper permits its users to apply ALIAS-qualification to UDFs! In the example in Listing 3.7, we need to print a line reading "Order: <order number>" followed by a line reading "Customer: <customer name>"; we are given indexed databases Orders and Customer and the keys Order_Num and CustomerID to search into these two databases. The Clipper

UDF Retrieve, in combination with ALIAS-qualification, permits this code to be very canonical.

Listing 3.7 Canonical Code via ALIAS-Qualification of a Clipper UDF

```
* Assume that the current work area is 7 and that Receipts.DBF is open there.
?  "Order:  "     + Orders   ->( Retrieve( Order_Num,     "Number" ) )
?  "Customer:  " + Customer->( Retrieve( CustomerID,     "Name"    ) )
* Work area 7 is selected and Receipts.DBF is open there.
*****************************************************************  Retrieve
FUNCTION Retrieve
* This UDF doesn't know whether it will be compiled with the convention of
* using the memvar when a memvar and field have the same name, versus
* using the field when a memvar and field have the same name.  Therefore, we
* must specify fields and memvars explicitly.
PARAMETERS Key,FieldName
PRIVATE Alias_C
Alias_C = ALIAS()
SEEK M->Key  && It is possible that the current database has a field named Key.
RETURN (IIF(FOUND(), &Alias_C. -> &FieldName.,   "missing data"))
*****************************************************************  Retrieve
```

The Scope Construct

Many of the commands in Table 3.16 take a scope, which specifies the range of records on which the command is to operate. For example, "COPY NEXT 1 TO EraseMe" causes the current record to be copied to a new database with the same structure as the current database. The command "LIST REST" causes the fields in the remaining records in the database to be listed.

The intelligent use of the scope construct is important to the canonical way of thinking. You can often avoid programming loops with the right combination of database command and scope. The scope construct variations are shown in Table 3.17.

Table 3.17 Scope Construct Variations

ALL	Acts on all records meeting the current SET DELETED and filter conditions, which are also in the current index, if any.
NEXT <expN>	Acts on the number of records specified by the numeric expression, starting with the current record as record 1. Advances in index order if an index is in place, or in storage order otherwise.
RECORD <expN>	Acts on the specified record.
REST	Acts on the remainder of the records in the index if an index is in use, or on the remainder of the records in storage order if no index is in use. The current record is included.

The FOR and WHILE Constructs

The database commands which accept a scope generally also support a FOR or WHILE clause. The syntax of the clauses is "FOR <expL>" or "WHILE <expL>", where the logical expression should reference at least one field in the database being processed. The FOR clause is used to process all records in the scope which meet the FOR condition. The WHILE clause is used to process all records in the scope which meet the WHILE condition, starting with the first record in the scope and continuing until the WHILE condition is false.

Note that if SET DELETED ON and/or SET FILTER TO <expL> have been executed, records which have been marked for deletion and/or for which <expL> is false are already excluded from our view of the database. Restrictions of scope, FOR, or WHILE clauses apply *in addition* to these other restrictions.

Say that you have a database MailAddr.DBF with an index on the State field. To list all records for New Mexico, which are coded "NM" in the State field, you could use the following code.

Listing 3.8 Example of WHILE Clause

```
USE MailAddr INDEX State
SEEK  "NM"
LIST WHILE State =  "NM"
```

You could achieve the same result without using the index.

Listing 3.9 Example of FOR Clause

```
USE MailAddr
LIST FOR State =  "NM"
```

Generally speaking, the order in which New Mexico records will be reported by the LIST FOR command is different from the order reported by the LIST WHILE command with the index file in place. The LIST FOR command in this example presents the records in storage order,[8] but the LIST WHILE command may present the selected records in any order, depending on the dialect; some dialects will preserve storage order in an index with equal keys. You can force these two orders to be the same by creating the State index with "INDEX ON UPPER(State) + STR(RecNo(),6) TO State" instead of the usual "INDEX ON UPPER(State) TO State".

> **Remark.** For a large database, the LIST WHILE command usually produces the data *much* faster than the LIST FOR command (although this is not guaranteed, as Expert Panelist Dr. Mark Leavitt observes). In the first case, we access all the New Mexico records, plus one more record, and then we stop. With LIST FOR, we access every record in the database!

8. It would present the records in index order if an index were in place.

Recommendation on FOR and WHILE clauses. Whenever possible, replace DO WHILE loops with single database commands which are qualified with a scope clause and a FOR or WHILE clause. Whenever possible, use COUNT for counting, SUM for adding, LIST for listing, and so on.

Indexes

Since indexing, sorting, and retrieval are among the most important topics to dBASE dialect programmers, we devote an entire chapter to these topics later in the book. (See Chapter 23 on page 381.) Here, we take a first look at indexing.

Index files are a central dBASE feature. They permit you to view the records in your databases as if they were stored in date order, customer number order, or whatever order you wish, instead of the actual storage order. Index files also support very rapid retrieval of records through the FIND and SEEK commands; a record is specified by key for so-called *random retrieval.* (In contrast, the LOCATE command permits random retrieval without an index file, but may be extremely slow.)

In dBASE IV, you can mark fields in the database as TAGs. Each TAG is an index key with an associated index which is stored in a "production" index file with an .MDX extension. .MDX index files are like .DBT files in that they are opened automatically when the associated .DBF file is opened. They are unlike all other index files in dBASE dialects, in that *other index files must be explicitly created and opened.*

If a database is open in the current work area, you can create an index file for the database with the syntax

INDEX ON <expression> TO <index filename>

By convention, you supply a filename only for the index file and the dialect provides a dialect-specific extension. For example, the statement "INDEX ON Name TO Name" in dBASE III PLUS causes the creation of an index file called "Name.NDX".

The <expression> must reference at least one field of the database; be of type character, date, or numeric; and have a length no greater than the maximum index expression length permitted by the dialect. In both dBASE and generic terminology, the result of evaluating this expression for a given record is called the *key*; the key must have a length no greater than the maximum key length permitted by the dialect.

Most dialects assign an extension to index files which is unique to the dialect. dBASE III PLUS, FoxBASE+, and Clipper use .NDX, .IDX, and .NTX extensions, respectively, for index files; see the table of dBASE file types on page 45. Table 3.18 shows the maximum number of indexes per work area and the maximum number of bytes in a key.

The order in which the database is retrieved is determined by the index expression. For example, if your index expression is the last-name field in your database, then your database will be processed in last-name order when the last-name index is open.

Table 3.18 Maximums for Index Files and Keys

Dialect	Indexes per Work Area	Bytes per Key
Clipper	15	250
dBASE III PLUS	7	100
DBASE IV	517	100
dbXL	7	100
FoxBASE+	7	100
FoxPro 1.0	25	100
Quicksilver	7	100

Once an index exists, it can be associated with its database file in two ways. The first way is to reference the file in the USE command, following the syntax

USE <database> INDEX <list of index filenames>

Either a single index filename or a comma-separated list of index filenames may follow the INDEX keyword. As field values change in the database, all the listed indexes are updated, but the retrieval order is (initially) determined by the first index in the list.

The second way to associate one or more index files with a database is to open the database with a USE command and then use the syntax

SET INDEX TO <list of index filenames>

If more than one index file is associated with a database file, then the index which is used for retrieval purposes, the so-called *master index,* is initially the first index in the list. Any index in the list can be selected by ordinal to be the master index with the syntax

SET ORDER TO <ordinal of index in list>

For example, if "SET INDEX TO Surname,ZIP" was issued, and was then followed by "SET ORDER TO 2", then the ZIP index would be the master index.

The command "SET ORDER TO 0" causes all of the indexes to be maintained as usual, but the access order becomes storage order. Expert Panelist Dr. John Bauman points out that SET ORDER TO 0 is important when you REPLACE a key field. For example, assume that Members.DBF and one index file are open and that the index is on Members->Name. Consider the REPLACE command

REPLACE Name WITH "Smith" FOR Name = "Jones"

If the first Jones record found is record 57, the REPLACE command (1) changes the Name field to "Smith" in record 57 in Members.DBF, and (2) changes the key value for record 57 in the index file to "Smith". The next record in index order has Name >= "Smith"; in fact, all subsequent records have Name >= "Smith"; record 57 is the only "Jones" record which is changed, even if there are many records with Name = "Jones".

If you SET ORDER TO 0 and then REPLACE, the index or indexes will be updated as desired, and all the records will be replaced that you expect to be replaced.

Unique Keys

If SET UNIQUE ON is the last SET UNIQUE statement to have been executed, then an INDEX command will index a record only if the record has a key that is not in the index already. Some dialects also permit you to add the keyword UNIQUE to an INDEX command to cause keys in the index file to be unique.

Unique indexes can be used to determine the number of different values in a field. For example, in a database with a character field called "State", you can open the database and INDEX ON UPPER(STATE) UNIQUE. The COUNT command tells you how many states are represented in your database, and the LIST STATE command shows you the represented states in alphabetic order.

Filters

One of the most useful and frequently used dBASE facilities is the *filter,* which restricts your view of the database to consist only of records which meet the filter criterion. The syntax is

SET FILTER TO <logical expression>

The logical expression must reference at least one field in the database. For example, in a mailing list database with a STATE field,

SET FILTER TO STATE = "TX"

would limit your view of the database to the Texas records as long as that filter is in place.

The SET FILTER command does not advance the record pointer to the first record meeting the filter. The current record may or may not meet the filter. Move to the first record meeting the filter with GOTO TOP. Use the SKIP command to move the record pointer forward through the records.

Move to the last record meeting the filter with GOTO BOTTOM. Then use the "SKIP –1" command to move the record pointer backward through the records.

Filtered Indexes

FoxBASE+ 2.1 and FoxPro support the concept of filters combined with the concept of indexes. If indexes are not made UNIQUE, there is normally one key stored in the index file for each record in the database. Then the only way in which there can be fewer records in the index file than in the database is when records are appended to the database when the index file is not open — normally a bad bug.

In many situations, it is desirable to have an index on a subset of records of interest. For example, say that you have a mailing list database that contains fields for last name and organization. You usually have the name of a person and not an organization, but some records have nonblank organization fields. You would like to view or report the records with nonblank organization fields in alphabetic order by organization name.

You could of course have the usual index on the organization field for the entire database, but that would be very wasteful of disk space. You can't use the UNIQUE option to cause only one record with a blank organization field to be represented in the index file, because you mail to multiple recipients at some organizations.

The elegant solution is provided by FoxBASE+ and FoxPro with the syntax

```
INDEX ON <expression> TO <filename> [FOR <expL>]
```

The logical expression is the same as a filter expression; it must reference at least one field of the database. A record is included in the index if it meets the FOR condition, that is, if the logical expression is .T. for that record.

Assume that the organization names in the previous example are stored in a field called "Org". Then the problem would be solved with

```
INDEX ON UPPER(Org) TO Org FOR "" # TRIM(Org)
```

This INDEX command builds an index for the records with nonblank Org fields. The index ignores uppercase/lowercase distinctions in organization names.

Clipper remark. Expert Panelist Craig Yellick reports that this capability is available for Clipper via a utility called SubNtx() by Skip Moon. "Skip and his wonderful utility can be reached on CompuServe/NanForum."

.MEM Memory Variable Files

Collections of memory variables can be stored in memory variable files with .MEM extensions using the SAVE TO command. These memvars can be retrieved with the RESTORE FROM command, whose syntax is

```
RESTORE FROM <memory variable file> [ADDITIVE]
```

If the ADDITIVE keyword appears, the memvars and their values which are stored in the memory variable file are added to the symbol table. Otherwise, all entries are removed from the symbol table prior to storing the memvars from the .MEM file. The PUBLIC/PRIVATE attribute of memvars is saved in the .MEM file, and this attribute is restored when the memvar is entered into the symbol table by the RESTORE command.

This is an important facility, but, sadly, it is crippled by a lack of control over the variables which are included in the .MEM file. This major design flaw in dBASE is due to the fact that the syntax

SAVE <memvar list> TO <filename>

is *not* supported, even in dBASE IV 1.0 and FoxPro 1.0.

This deficit would be of much less consequence if identifiers could be as long as one needed them to be in order to describe the identifier usage, or if dBASE supported tree-structured groups of memvars, as does PASCAL. For example, in PASCAL, we can define a group of variables that specify printer page characteristics to be held in a structure called PrinterPage. This structure might contain the numeric variables TopMargin, LeftMargin, and BottomMargin. We can save the variables in the PrinterPage structure to a disk file by referencing only the identifier PrinterPage, and not its constituent memory variables.

At the time of writing, only Clipper 5.0 supports these structures, so in the other dialects we currently cannot code a statement like

SAVE PrinterPage TO Printer.DAT

Since the limit on identifier length is 10 characters, we cannot use memory variable names like PrinterPageTopMargin; if so, we could code

SAVE ALL LIKE PrinterPage* TO Printer.DAT

To use this technique with current dialects, we have to abbreviate TopMargin, LeftMargin, and BottomMargin to 10 characters *minus* the number of characters which we use to implement a hopefully unique prefix for the three memvars. As if the limitation to 10 characters weren't severe enough already!

Well, what if we use the names PagTmargin, PagLmargin, and PagBmargin? These names conform to the 10-character limit, so that we can code

SAVE ALL LIKE Pag* TO Printer.DAT

We still have trouble, because we will write into Printer.DAT memvars such as PageCount, Page_L, and PageNumber. When Printer.DAT is restored, unwanted memvars are restored along with the desired memvars, which can cause some very subtle (read maddening) bugs!

Even if one of these techniques were to work, it would put a constraint on our choices of identifier names which has nothing to do with the goal of writing self-documenting code. Rather, the constraint is imposed by a deficit of the programming language. To accommodate this deficit by placing additional and perhaps ineffective limitations on top of the 10-character limitation on identifier names is to me not sensible; in my view, this approach is like the tail wagging the dog.

Countermeasure for No List Support

You can use so-called wildcard patterns when specifying the variables to be saved. For example, to save all variables which start with "ZZ", you would code "SAVE ALL LIKE ZZ* TO <filename>".

Let's assume that you need to save the values of PRIVATE variables TopMargin, LeftMargin, and BottMargin to ABC.MEM when you exit a routine; you also need to restore the values when you enter. The following code will check for the existence of the file ABC.MEM and restore the values of TopMargin, LeftMargin, and BottMargin, if the file is found. Otherwise, the values of TopMargin, Left-Margin, and BottMargin are taken from assignment statements. Then, before exit, the values are saved in "coded" form in ABC.MEM.

Listing 3.10 Simulating a "SAVE <memvar list>" Command

```
* File = Save_ABC.PRG.  Demonstrates a simulation of  "SAVE <memvar list>".
*****************************************************************************
* Dialects: All.
*****************************************************************************
PRIVATE BottMargin, LeftMargin, TopMargin
*************************** Part of the initialization code for this routine.
PRIVATE ALL LIKE PrintPage*
IF FILE("ABC.MEM")
   RESTORE FROM ABC ADDITIVE
   BottMargin = PrintPage1
   LeftMargin = PrintPage2
   TopMargin  = PrintPage3
ELSE
   BottMargin = <initial value>
   LeftMargin = <initial value>
   TopMargin  = <initial value>
ENDIF
**************************** End of the initialization code for this routine.

<main part of routine with no QUIT or RETURN statements>

*************************** Save BottMargin, LeftMargin, TopMargin to ABC.MEM:
PrintPage1 = BottMargin
PrintPage2 = LeftMargin
PrintPage3 = TopMargin
SAVE ALL LIKE PrintPage* TO ABC
RELEASE ALL LIKE PrintPage*
* End of Save_ABC.PRG.
```

Arrays of Memory Variables

In the beginning, dBASE designers and users may have thought, "Who needs memvar arrays in forms other than the .DBF file?" Indeed, the .DBF file *is* an ordered set of data, and on the conceptual level, it is the same as an array.

In practice, there are a number of important differences between memvars and fields, and it is convenient to have arrays of memvars at one's disposal. Dialects subsequent to dBASE III PLUS generally support arrays of memvars.

Unfortunately, vendors have made different syntax choices for arrays. Array elements may be referenced inside parentheses, as in MemberCode(2), or inside square brackets, as in MemberCode[2]. Array sizes are declared with DIMENSION or DECLARE. Each dialect offers a different maximum number of array elements, and there is wide variation in the number of dimensions which an array may have, as you can see in the following table.

Table 3.19 dBASE Dialect Array Specifications

Dialect	Defining Keyword	Bracket Type	Number of Dimensions	Maximum Number of Elements
Clipper	DECLARE	[ ]	1	4,096
dBASE III	N/A	N/A	N/A	N/A
dBASE III PLUS	N/A	N/A	N/A	N/A
DBASE IV	DECLARE	()	1 or 2	1,023
dbXL	DIMENSION	[ ]	1 to 255	255
FoxBASE+	DIMENSION	()	1 or 2	3,600
FoxPro	DIMENSION or DECLARE	() or [ ]	1 or 2	3,600
Quicksilver	DIMENSION or DECLARE	[ ]	1 to 255	4,000

dBASE arrays are unity-indexed; that is, the minimum subscript value in each dimension is 1. If an array is sized with the statement

```
DECLARE MemberCode[4]
```

then you may reference MemberCode[1], MemberCode[2], MemberCode[3], and MemberCode[4]. The bracket type used to define the array size with a DECLARE or DIMENSION statement is also used in array references. If an array is defined as

```
DIMENSION MemberCode(4)
```

then its elements are referenced as MemberCode(1), MemberCode(2), MemberCode(3), and MemberCode(4).

Some dialects offer the commands APPEND FROM ARRAY, COPY TO ARRAY, GATHER, and SCATTER to transfer data between arrays and database records. See your dialect's reference manual for more information.

Array or User-Defined Function?

When you are examining dBASE code, you must sometimes know the dialect in order to interpret the code correctly. In the dBASE dialects that use parentheses for array references, you cannot distinguish array references from references to user-defined functions. For example, you may see the command "?Data(5)" in a listing. If this code is written in a dialect which uses square brackets for array references, then Data() is a user-defined function; otherwise Data() may be *either* an array *or* a user-defined function.

Labels and Reports

In another distinct departure from traditional programming languages, dBASE dialects provide built-in support for printing mailing labels and columnar reports. The data structures which define labels and reports are called *forms*.

dBASE interpreters give you the following forms commands. Label forms are created and modified with the CREATE LABEL and MODIFY LABEL commands and are stored in files with .LBL extensions (.LBX in FoxPro). Report forms are created and modified with the CREATE REPORT and MODIFY REPORT commands and are stored in files with .FRM extensions (.FRX in FoxPro).

Clipper users can create forms with dBASE III PLUS or dBXL, or they can use a utility provided with Clipper called RL. Quicksilver users have the interpreter dBXL as a companion product and can create and modify forms with dBXL (or dBASE III PLUS).

You print labels or reports with the LABEL FORM and REPORT FORM commands. Output can be directed to one, two, or three of the destinations of screen, printer, and file. For more information, see the LABEL FORM, REPORT FORM, SET CONSOLE, SET ALTERNATE, and CLOSE ALTERNATE commands in your dBASE dialect manual.

Input/Output

The standard dBASE programming language offers a rich set of facilities for full-screen I/O and the manipulation of .DBF files. Through its ALTERNATE file facility, it does a good job of writing text files. However, only Clipper and FoxPro offer facilities which permit you to read text files in a straightforward fashion.

Text File Input

Clipper and FoxPro have low-level functions to read (or write) files byte by byte; FoxPro also offers low-level functions to read (or write) text files by line. The other dBASE dialects have no concept of reading text files byte by byte, as in PASCAL, or line by line, as in FORTRAN. Instead, you must import the text file into a database with a structure like the following one:

Table 3.20 Structure of TextData.DBF

Field	Field Name	Type	Width	Dec
1	Rec	Character	150	

This database has one field per record. The field is named Rec, short for *record*. You may adjust the length of Rec, as necessary, to match the length of the data you wish to import. Having the length of Rec any longer than the longest line you wish to import wastes time and memory.

If you wish to retrieve information from a file named Dir.TXT, use the following sequence:

```
USE TextData
ZAP  && After ZAP, the next record to be appended is record 1.
APPEND FROM Dir.TXT TYPE SDF
```

Line 1 in Dir.TXT is now stored in record 1 of the TextData database, line 2 in record 2, and so on. If lines are shorter than LEN(Rec), they are padded out with blanks. Lines longer than LEN(Rec) are truncated.

Byte-Level Input in Clipper and FoxPro

Clipper and FoxPro provide low-level file handling with a group of commands which start with the letter "F", as in FOPEN, FCLOSE, and so on. These commands can be used to read a text file (or any other file) byte by byte.

Input of One Variable

The ACCEPT and INPUT commands can be used to solicit a single value from the user. A dBASE programmer will sometimes use the full-screen commands (@ GET with READ) to solicit a single value, but these commands are typically used to solicit many values on one screen.

The syntax of the ACCEPT command is

ACCEPT [<character expression>] TO <memvar>

Any character expression provided after the ACCEPT verb is used as a prompt for the user. The data entered is treated as character data and the user strokes ENTER to terminate the string.

The syntax of the INPUT command is the same as for the ACCEPT command, even though this command is more general:

INPUT [<character expression>] TO <memvar>

With this command, the data type of the memvar is set by the data type of the entry. For example, the response "9" versus 9 gives the memvar either a character or numeric value, respectively.

The WAIT command accepts a single keystroke as optional input to a character variable. Its syntax is

WAIT [<character type data>] [TO <memvar>]

Output of One or More Variables

Output in dBASE dialects is very easy. There are several variations of the syntax:

```
TEXT
   <one or more lines of text>
ENDTEXT
? <memvar expression>
? <memvar expression>, ..., <memvar expression>
?? <memvar expression>
?? <memvar expression>, ..., <memvar expression>
* Use ??? to send data directly to the printer in dBASE IV or FoxPro:
??? <memvar expression>
??? <memvar expression>, ..., <memvar expression>
```

The TEXT and ENDTEXT keywords can be used to bracket lines of text which are displayed to the screen. In dBASE III PLUS, the bracketed text may not contain any line which starts with "END".

The double question mark is used to output the data with no initial line feed/carriage return. Otherwise, the line feed/carriage return pair is sent before the data. One blank is inserted between list items.

To list two character variables with a space between them, use the form "? A, B". To list two character variables with no space between them, use the form "? A + B".

You can select one, two, or three different destinations for output. The destinations available are the screen, the printer, and a (text) file. If SET CONSOLE ON is the last SET CONSOLE command to be executed, then data is shown onscreen. If SET CONSOLE OFF is the last SET CONSOLE command to be executed, then data is not shown onscreen.

If SET PRINT ON is the last SET PRINT command to be executed, then data is printed. If SET PRINT OFF is the last SET PRINT command to be executed, then data is not printed.

Three commands are required to output to a text file, because we must provide the name of a target file. First, we name the file with

SET ALTERNATE TO <filename>

Then we enable or disable output to this file with SET ALTERNATE ON and SET ALTERNATE OFF, respectively. The file is closed with CLOSE ALTERNATE.

FoxBASE+, FoxPro, and Quicksilver offer the command SET PRINTER TO <filename> as an alternative to SET ALTERNATE TO <filename>. You then enable or disable file output with SET PRINT ON and SET PRINT OFF and you close the file with SET PRINTER TO. You must also SET PRINT OFF unless you want subsequent output to go to the standard MS-DOS print device PRN:.

Full-Screen I/O

Here is an introduction to full-screen input/output in dBASE. This is a very important topic, as the full-screen I/O facilities are used to implement the user interface of dBASE applications. Chapters 21 and 22 in Part IV deal with full-screen I/O and the user interface, and related topics are discussed as appropriate throughout the book.

One of the most obvious departures of dBASE from conventional programming languages is its built-in support of full-screen editing of sets of variables. You can freely mix fields and memvars in such sets, although there is special support for sets of variables that correspond to the fields of a database.

Full-screen editing is implemented with one @ GET or one @ SAY GET statement for each variable whose value is to be edited, plus a READ statement to invoke editing of the set. The @ GET and @ SAY GET commands specify a screen coordinate in the form

<row>, <column>

The @ GET command has the syntax

@ <row>, <column> GET <variable> <options>

At the indicated coordinates, the variable's value will be displayed in the currently defined inverse video colors. Any options given control the appearance and/or validation of the value of the variable.

To display information, including a variable's values, there is a corresponding @ SAY command with the syntax

@ <row>, <column> SAY <character expression>
<display options>

This command displays the given expression at the given screen coordinates. You may customize the format in which the data is displayed with a PICTURE clause.

A third variant combines the SAY and the GET to produce a prompt or description of each variable to be edited. Its syntax is

@ <row>, <column> SAY <character expression>
GET <memvar or field> <options>

Screen coordinates are (0,0) at the top left hand corner of the screen. In its most common display mode, the MS-DOS screen has 25 rows and 80 columns, so the coordinates of the lower right hand corner are (24,79). Row R and column C are located at coordinates (R,C).

As @ GET or @ SAY GET commands are encountered, their screen coordinates, prompt (if any), and options are recorded in a first-in first-out (FIFO) list. *When a READ statement is executed following one or more such commands, then all prompts are displayed and editing starts with the first variable in the list.* The user moves from variable to variable by stroking ENTER or the UpArrow or DownArrow keys. To move to the next variable on the list, the user strokes ENTER or DownArrow. To move to the previous variable on the list, the user strokes UpArrow.

The READ SAVE Command

After the user finishes editing the screen of data displayed by the READ command, the FIFO list of read-only and read-write text and screen locations is empty. The READ SAVE command is used to traverse the list without removing any of its items. If no FORMAT file is open, then it is an error to execute a READ command which immediately follows a READ command.

However, a READ command which follows a READ SAVE command causes the previous data-entry screen to be displayed again. Read-only text is the same, but read-write text reflects any changes made during the previous READ, or between the READ and the READ SAVE commands.

A typical application of READ SAVE is to display data again for editing after it fails a validation check. In Listing 3.11, the data is displayed and edited with READ SAVE. Then a validation check is made and, if necessary, the data is edited repeatedly until it is correct. The CLEAR GETS command is used to empty the FIFO list if the data is correct.

Listing 3.11 Example of READ SAVE

```
************************************************ Validation without READ SAVE:
Valid_L = .F.
DO WHILE (.NOT. Valid_L)
   <series of @ GET, @ SAY, and @ SAY GET statements>
   READ
   IF (<data OK>)
      Valid_L = .T.
   ELSE
      @ <unused location> SAY <error message>
   ENDIF
ENDDO

*************************************************** Validation with READ SAVE:
<series of @ GET, @ SAY, and @ SAY GET statements>
READ SAVE
Valid_L = .F.
DO WHILE (.NOT. Valid_L)
   IF (<data OK>)
      CLEAR GETS
      Valid_L = .T.
   ELSE
      @ <unused location> SAY <error message>
      READ SAVE
   ENDIF
ENDDO
```

As an extension to READ SAVE, Clipper 5.0 gives you explicit control over the FIFO list associated with a group of @ SAY GET statements — you can save and restore these lists as you wish. See Rick Spence's "Nested READS the Smart Way" column in the September issue of *Data Based Advisor* (Spence 1990: 52–55).

FORMAT Files

A text file which contains only @ GET, @ SAY, or @ SAY/GET statements, in which the @ GET statements reference the fields from a single database, can be used as a FORMAT file. A FORMAT (.FMT) file is usually given the same filename as its corresponding database, so People.DBF would have a FORMAT file named People.FMT. The FORMAT file is used to position the database fields onscreen at desired locations for editing, with deliberately chosen labels.

In dBASE, FORMAT files are optional, since there is a default built-in format which is used if there is no FORMAT file. This format lists the fields down the screen, with at most one field per line. The first 10 characters on the line list the field name, left justified, followed by a blank and the field value, which will wrap onto multiple lines as necessary to show all of the data. Data from date, numeric, and logical fields always fits on one line, but data from character fields may extend over more than one line.

This default format, while very convenient, does allow you to edit very many fields on the screen at one time and is not very attractive. Most programmers therefore write command files or FORMAT files with @ SAY/GET statements activated by READ or EDIT.

FORMAT files are a little tricky to use in the dialects which support both READ and EDIT, because FORMAT files are used in a modal fashion, as follows. dBASE could conceivably implement the syntax "READ FORMAT <FORMAT filename>" or "EDIT FORMAT <FORMAT filename>" to edit a database record with the format defined in the FORMAT file. Instead, it uses "SET FORMAT TO <FORMAT filename>" to determine which FORMAT file will be used for the next READ or EDIT statement.

> **Rules on FORMAT files.** Open a FORMAT file with "SET FORMAT TO <FORMAT filename>" and close the file with "SET FORMAT TO". To edit a database record with the data-entry form defined by a particular FORMAT file, open the FORMAT file and then use the READ or EDIT command. In Clipper and Quicksilver, you must use the READ command, because the EDIT command is not implemented.

In practice, you will often open a FORMAT file in the statement before each READ or EDIT which is to invoke the FORMAT file and close the file in the following statement, in order to avoid the pitfall in the following code:

```
USE Members.DBF
SET FORMAT TO Members.FMT
EDIT
CLEAR
Name = SPACE(10)
@ 1,1 SAY  "Your name:" GET Name
READ
```

The EDIT statement will cause the first record in Members.DBF to be edited according to the data-entry form defined by Members.FMT. Then the screen will be cleared, and "Your name:" will be displayed near the upper left corner, followed by 10 space characters in the currently defined "enhanced" background color. You might expect that the READ statement would GET the value of the Name memvar; instead, the action is equivalent to the following code:

```
USE Members.DBF
SET FORMAT TO Members.FMT
EDIT
CLEAR
EDIT
```

Recommendation on FORMAT files. In a dialect which implements the EDIT command, follow these steps to edit a database record with the data-entry form defined by a particular FORMAT file: in three consecutive statements, (1) open the FORMAT file, (2) EDIT, and (3) close the FORMAT file. If your Clipper program must execute under a dialect which supports the EDIT command, then to edit a database record with the data-entry form defined by a particular FORMAT file, (1) open the FORMAT file, (2) READ, and (3) close the FORMAT file.

If your Clipper program will not be executed under a dialect which supports the EDIT command, then I recommend that you do not use FORMAT files, because in Clipper, FORMAT files are simply crippled command files that can only contain @ SAY/GET statements. Instead, write command files and use commands like SET COLOR TO and IF/ENDIF to improve the user interface of the data-entry form.

The major dialects other than Clipper support multiple-page FORMAT files which can show your data on two or more screens. The user employs PageDown and PageUp to move between screens belonging to the same record. You insert a READ command after every group of @ commands which you want to display on one screen, except for the last group.

Now what if you would like the services of a multiple-page FORMAT file in your Clipper program, or in a program which must run under both Clipper and other dialects? Expert Panelist Dr. John Bauman has written a nice article in *Data Based Advisor* magazine to tell you how to simulate multiple-page FORMAT files with a dialect-independent technique (Bauman 1989a).

Foreign File Import/Export

The Ashton-Tate dBASE dialects offer import and export facilities that are not usually duplicated in other dialects. dBASE III PLUS can convert PFS data files to its .DBF format with the IMPORT command, whose syntax is

IMPORT FROM <file name> TYPE PFS

In addition, the conversion process generates a FORMAT file and a VIEW file.

The EXPORT command is the output counterpart of the IMPORT command. Its syntax is

EXPORT TO <file name> TYPE PFS

dBASE IV imports dBASE II files, Ashton-Tate Framework II files, PFS files, Ashton-Tate Rapidfile databases, and Lotus 1-2-3 version 2.x .WK1 files. It exports all these file types except .WK1 files.

Built-In Functions

Each dialect provides many functions which the programmer can reference without defining, because they are built into the language. I use the common term *built-in* to reference such functions.

The dBASE built-in functions are divided broadly into the categories in Table 3.21. In each category, I list the more important functions. (The manuals of most dBASE dialects have similar categorized lists, with the exception that the lists in manuals are much longer, because they cover all the commands and functions, not just the ones which are most frequently used.)

Table 3.21 Most Important Built-In Functions

1. **Date manipulation and query.**

CtoD	Converts date data to character form.
DATE	Computer's idea of today's date.
DtoC	Converts character form of date data to date form.
TIME	Computer's idea of the current time.

2. **Character manipulation and query.**

AT	Returns position of substring in string.
LEFT	Leftmost characters of a string.
LEN	Length of a character string.
LOWER	Converts to lowercase.
REPLICATE	Repeats string a specified number of times.
RIGHT	Rightmost characters of a string.
SPACE	Replicates blanks.
STUFF	Replaces a portion of a string.
SUBSTR	Selects a substring of specified length starting at a specified position.
TRIM	Removes trailing blanks.
UPPER	Converts to uppercase.

3. **Input and output.**

InKey	Records most recent key pressed.
ReadKey	Keystroke used to exit full-screen editing.
TRANSFORM	Converts typed value according to PICTURE or template.

4. **Numerical manipulation and query.**

ABS	Absolute value.
EXP	Exponentiation to the base e.
INT	The integer part of a numeric value.

LOG	The logarithm to the base e.
MAX	The larger of two values.
MIN	The smaller of two values.
MOD	Modular arithmetic.
SQRT	Square root.

5. **Specialized tests and system information.**

BOF	Beginning-of-file.
COL	Current column of onscreen cursor.
DELETED	Deletes status of current record.
DISKSPACE	The number of unused bytes on disk.
EOF	End-of-file.
FIELD	Names of database fields.
FILE	Existence of file.
GetEnv	Retrieves value of DOS environment variable. (GetE in Clipper.)
IIF	Immediate IF.
ISCOLOR	Is user's monitor connected to a color card?
RecCount	Number of records in a database.
RecNo	Number of currently selected record (value of record pointer).
ROW	Current row of onscreen cursor.
TYPE	Determines the type of an expression.

6. **Type conversion.**

ASC	Returns the numeric form of an ASCII byte (8 bits), given its character form. Example: ASC("A") = 65.
CHR	Returns the character form of an ASCII byte (8 bits), given its numeric form. Example: CHR(65) = "A".
CtoD	Converts date data to character form.
DtoC	Converts character form of date data to date form.
INT	The integer part of a numeric value.
STR	Converts number to string with specified length and decimal places.
TRANSFORM	Converts data to string formatted according to your PICTURE.

Trapping Errors and Processing Events

The dBASE language offers a set of "ON" commands which associate actions with events which may occur (1) at any time during the execution of the application or (2) during so-called *wait states*. ON commands have a syntax which is identical to or similar to "ON <event> <command>", where <event> is a keyword. The form "ON <event>" cancels the previous action associated with the <event> and specifies that the default action is now to be taken when the named event occurs. When your application starts, default actions are associated with all events.

For example, when your application starts, ERROR events such as "file not found" invoke the dBASE dialect's critical error handler, which produces the prompt "Cancel, Ignore, or Suspend?" or its equivalent. If your application specifies "ON ERROR QUIT" when it begins, then an error condition which would otherwise invoke the critical error handler causes the application to QUIT instead.

Using terminology which is fairly generic, I'll call the condition which causes the action specified in the ON command to be the *ON-condition* and I'll call the action which is specified by the ON command the *ON-unit*. If the ON command specifies an action other than calling a subroutine, then the ON-unit is just the one command given in the ON statement. Otherwise, the ON-unit is the subroutine which is called. For example, in the statement "ON ERROR DO Handler", the Handler routine is the ON-unit for ON ERROR.

The ON-unit is usually a subroutine. Inside such ON-units, the RETRY verb is used to execute again the command that caused the event. Otherwise, the RETURN verb is used to cause execution to proceed, if possible, with the command following the command that caused the event.

ON-Commands for dBASE Dialects

There are two tables of ON-commands for the various dialects. Table 3.22 shows which events are implemented by which dialects, and Table 3.23 explains the events.

Table 3.22 ON-Commands for dBASE Dialects

Command	Dialects
ON ERROR	All except Clipper
ON ESCAPE	All except Clipper
ON EVENT	dBXL, Quicksilver
ON KEY	All except Clipper
ON NETERROR	dBXL, Quicksilver
ON PAGE	FoxPro, dBASE IV
ON PAD	FoxPro, dBASE IV
ON READERROR	FoxPro, dBASE IV
ON SELECTION PAD	FoxPro, dBASE IV
ON SELECTION POPUP	FoxPro, dBASE IV
SET KEY	Clipper, dBXL, Quicksilver

The commands ON PAD, ON SELECTION PAD, and ON SELECTION POPUP are associated with menu-building facilities in dBASE IV and FoxPro. As such, they are in a special category of event-processing commands and are treated in detail in the menu-building chapter, Chapter 22. The other event-processing commands are described in Table 3.23.

Table 3.23 ON-Events for dBASE Dialects

ERROR	This event occurs at execution time whenever the dBASE dialect encounters a problem which it cannot handle, such as a syntax error in interpreted code, or a missing file. The ON ERROR command is the only way that some dialects have to detect network events such as attempts to lock files which have already been locked by another user. You can use the built-in functions ERROR() and MESSAGE() to get the text and number of the last error message. You can process error conditions with the built-in functions LINENO(), PROCNAME(), PROGRAM(), and SYS(16), which are not found in all dialects; see your dialect's manual for details.
ESCAPE	This event occurs when the user strokes the ESCAPE key, *except* during full-screen editing, when the ESCAPE key is used to exit and discard changes to database data.
EVENT	This impressively general facility in dBXL and Quicksilver permits you to define any logical expression as an event. You can implement modem communications via the special form "SET EVENT TO FILE <filename>", which is used to access two utilities provided by WordTech.
KEY	There are several varieties of the ON KEY statement. dBASE III PLUS, dBASE IV, dBXL, FoxBASE+, FoxPro, and Quicksilver implement the syntax "ON KEY <command>", in which case the KEY event is any keypress (except Shift, Alt, Ctrl, Num Lock, Scroll Lock, or Pause). dBASE IV, dBXL, FoxBASE+, FoxPro, and Quicksilver implement a second form with the syntax "ON KEY <key identification> <command>" to specify an ON-unit for a *specific* keystroke. FoxBASE+ and FoxPro use the syntax "ON KEY = <key code> <command>" to define keystroke events which can occur only during the execution of READ statements. Clipper uses the syntax "SET KEY <key code> TO <subroutine>" to define keystroke events which occur only during wait states. dBXL and Quicksilver use this syntax to define keystroke events which can occur at any time!
NETERROR	dBXL and Quicksilver provide a special service for developers of multiple-user applications. Whereas dBASE IV and FoxPro process network errors just like any other critical error (either the critical error handler or your ON-unit is invoked), dBXL and Quicksilver give you ON NETERROR to trap errors which are specific to the multiple-user environment.
PAGE	FoxPro and dBASE IV implement the wonderful ON PAGE command, which is used for printing tasks such as easy programming of page headers and footers in printed output. The syntax is "ON PAGE AT LINE <line number> <command>". ON PAGE is used in combination with the commands PRINTJOB and ENDPRINTJOB.
READERROR	FoxPro and dBASE IV execute any defined READERROR ON-unit when a data-entry error occurs during full-screen editing, such as an invalid date, or data which lies outside the limits defined in a RANGE clause.

On-Demand Processing versus Wait-State Processing

There is an important difference between conditions which can be caused by the user at any time and conditions which can be caused only during a wait state, that is, during commands which cause the program to pause while it waits for input from the user. During a wait state, the user's keystrokes are used for entering and editing data onscreen. In this situation, the ON-condition is a specified keystroke, such as F8 or ALT-E.

Any dialect can detect such a keystroke and respond immediately. In contrast, when a dialect must detect keystrokes which can happen at any time, it is usually not able to respond immediately. For example, if you code "ON KEY F8 QUIT",[9] then your application may continue processing for a noticeable (and perhaps problematically lengthy) period of time after the F8 key is pressed. In contrast, when you code "ON KEY F8 DO UserHelp" and the user presses F8 during editing, the UserHelp routine is immediately executed.

Recommendation on ON-commands. Read all of the documentation which your dialect provides on the ON-commands you want to use. Then, test the event detection and handling under a variety of operating conditions in order to ascertain the correspondence between the expected and actual behavior of your application. Note whether any events occur which are supposed to be detected but which are not detected. Note the rapidity of response to detected events. Modify your application and/or documentation as appropriate, according to your findings.

Debugging Facilities

Part VII in Volume 2 contains a great deal of material on debugging techniques for the various dialects. By way of introduction, here is a brief survey.

Dialects subsequent to dBASE III, including dBASE III PLUS and FoxBASE+, contain several kinds of debugging support. In the interpretive environments, a program error leads to a prompt like "Cancel, Ignore, or Suspend?" The programmer can Suspend and issue any desired commands from the interpreter's prompt. The programmer eventually enters either CANCEL or RESUME, according to whether the problem requires a restart.

dBXL adds the "Fix" option to the list of "Cancel, Ignore, or Suspend?" Choosing this option causes the dBXL editor to display the file in which the error was located, with the cursor positioned at the offending line.

In addition, in many dialects, you can "SET DOHISTORY TO <number of statements to record>" and then SET DOHISTORY ON. When you suspend or finish normally, you can view the last statements that were executed with the LIST DOHISTORY command.

9. This syntax is legal for some dialects and not others.

If you SET STEP ON, dBASE will single-step through your code, prompting you after each statement for a keystroke to continue, cancel, or suspend. If you SET ECHO ON, then the source code of each statement will be displayed on the screen as the statement is executed.

When you SET TALK ON, values which are calculated are also shown onscreen. For example, if the statement "X = 3" is performed, a carriage return, line feed, and "3" are sent to the screen, so that the screen scrolls up by one line, and the character "3" appears by itself on the last line.

If you SET STATUS ON, you can monitor the current database and record, the delete status of the current record, and other information in a status line, which is shown in inverse video on line 22. You can alternatively SET SCOREBOARD ON to display a subset of the information shown by SET STATUS ON on the top line of the screen.

FoxPro delivers a text-based window environment where you can use windows for various testing purposes. One window might show the program's output, another might show the source code as the program executes, and still another window might show the value of selected expressions.

On a VGA screen, you can use FoxPro in a mode which shows 50 lines by 80 characters. In that mode, there is room for a "full-sized" screen of 25 lines by 80 characters, plus other tiled windows. You do not have to overlap these windows to use them simultaneously.

There are more things in heaven and earth, Horatio,
Than are dreamt of in your philosophy.
William Shakespeare, *Hamlet*, Act 1, Scene 5

"*What an interesting dialect,*" *said Mad Hatter to the Queen.*
"*But, no, that is what I would not* ever *want to mean.*"
(overheard in dWonderland)

Some of us use dBASE IV to develop real *applications.*
Ashton-Tate dLAB member Candy Price, 1990, p. 126

Perhaps of all the creations of man
language is the most astonishing.
Giles Lytton Strachey, 1880–1932

Part II

The World of dBASE Dialects

Part II introduces the history of dBASE dialects and then surveys each major dialect from a programmer's perspective. Although Part VIII in Volume 2 will deal with the world of support products for dBASE dialect programmers in comprehensive detail, you'll find an introduction to this world of products and services in Part II.

There is one table on page 103 which you may find to be of particular interest. This table lists the many hardware platforms for which one or more dBASE dialects is currently available.

Chapter 4

The History and Performance of dBASE Dialects

In the 1970s, before the microcomputer era, most programmers didn't associate the term *database* with an interpreted environment where commands like dBASE's USE, BROWSE, and LIST could permit the easy examination and updating of data in files. To most, *database* was just another term for *data file*.

However, many programmers who had had some experience writing applications which created, maintained, and reported data in files realized that there was a common core to data-based applications, whose files consisted of a list of records and whose records consisted of a list of fields. The first central, canonical idea was to separate — as much as possible — the *structure* of the records from the code that processed the data.

This is an example of the data-driven concept we met in Chapter 2. In contrast to the conventional approach of storing the structure of the data in a *program* file, we store the structure information separately in a *data* file.

The structure information for a data file could be stored in a related file; for example, we might store data in Receipts.DAT and store the structure for Receipts.DAT in a file like Receipts.STR. However, the dBASE approach is to store the structure of the data and the data itself in the same .DBF file. (The initial bytes of the file comprise the *header,* which contains the structure; the data records follow.)

Armed with that key data structure, designers could augment it with related data structures like indexes and report definition files. On the processing side, an unlimited number of commands could be developed to process these data structures.

JPL and Vulcan

Using the kernel idea of getting the structure of database files out of program code and into the file itself, a Mr. Jeb Long created a simple DBMS (database management system) on a mainframe computer at Pasadena, California's, Jet Propulsion Library in the middle 1970s. Wayne Ratliff, a JPL systems designer, developed a similar system for CP/M microcomputers, dubbed it Vulcan, and began selling it in 1979.[1]

Ashton-Tate

In 1980, a software distributor named George Tate formed the now-famous Ashton-Tate, which began selling Vulcan as dBASE II.[2] Over the years, Ashton-Tate brought out dBASE II for MS-DOS, dBASE III, dBASE III Developer's Edition, dBASE III PLUS, and dBASE IV.

Other Vendors

In the early 1980s, Nantucket and WordTech began to release versions of compiler or compiler-like translators for the dBASE language. WordTech also had its interpreter, dBXL. Fox Software had an in-between approach, with a tokenizer and an interpreter which would automatically tokenize files that had not previously been tokenized.[3]

Fox Software brought dBASE to the Macintosh and the XENIX operating system.[4] The Recital Corporation brought its Recital super-clone, laden with extensions, to VAX VMS and VAX UNIX.

By 1990, dBASE dialects may already constitute the most common programming environment. During the 1990s, the dBASE environment will be available for MS-DOS, MS-Windows, the Macintosh, XENIX, VAX VMS, UNIX, and other operating systems running on personal computers, workstations, minicomputers, and mainframes. Table 4.1 lists operating systems or hardware platforms for which a dBASE dialect is available at the time of writing.

There are four major vendors in the world of dBASE dialects — Ashton-Tate, Fox Software, Nantucket, and WordTech Systems; the dialects of each vendor are covered in a separate chapter in this part of the book. A fifth chapter covers the dialects from other vendors.

Dialects whose names start with "Fox" come from Fox Software, those which start with "dBASE" are from Ashton-Tate, and "dBXL" and "Quicksilver" dialects are from WordTech. The dialects whose names start with "dBFast" are from Gen Soft Development Corporation (who purchased those products from Bumblebee Software in November 1990), and Nantucket publishes Clipper and McMax. dBMAN V is from Versasoft Corporation, Recital is from the Recital Corporation, Vulcan and Emerald Bay are from Ratliff Software Productions, and FORCE is from Sophco. dBXL and Quicksilver are Japanese-language versions of dBXL and Quicksilver which use a 2-byte Kanji character set.

---

1. Some of this history is taken from *dBASE for Professionals, with dBASE IV* (Dunlop 1989).
2. There was no Ashton and no dBASE I.
3. See the Glossary for the definition of "tokenize" and many other terms used in this book.
4. Ashton-Tate's dBASE MAC was *not* dBASE III on a Macintosh.

Table 4.1
Operating Systems and Servers with Available dBASE Dialects or Front Ends

Operating Systems	dBASE Dialects
80386-based MS-DOS PCs	FoxBASE+/386
AIX	dBMAN V
Ashton-Tate/MS-SQLserver	dBXL/SQL
AT&T 3Bx/UNIX	Recital
Atari ST	dBMAN V
Commodore Amiga	dBMAN V
Emerald Bay	Vulcan
IBM System 36/38	dBASE Direct/36, dBASE Direct/38
ISC 386/ix	Quicksilver/UNIX
LIFELAN & NEXOS	dBXL/Kanji, Quicksilver/Kanji
Macintosh PCs	dBFast/PLUS/Mac, FoxBASE+/Mac, McMax
Macintosh Networks	FoxBASE+/Mac Multi-User
MicroVAX/VMS	Recital
MS-Windows	dBFAST/PLUS/Windows
Novell Netware SQL	dBXL/SQL
OS/2 EE	dBXL/SQL
PC/MS-DOS	Clipper, dBASE III PLUS, dBASE IV, dBFAST/PLUS, dBMAN V, dBXL, FORCE, FoxBASE+, FoxPro, Quicksilver
PC Networks	Clipper, dBASE III PLUS, dBASE IV, dBXL/LAN, dBMAN V, FoxBASE+/LAN, FoxPro/LAN, Quicksilver
SCO XENIX	dBMAN V, FoxBASE Multi-User
SCO XENIX 386	Quicksilver/UNIX
SUN 3	Recital
SUN 386	Recital
UNIX	dBMAN V
VAX/VMS	Recital
VAX/UNIX	Recital

The Performance of dBASE Dialects

When you select a dBASE dialect, you naturally want it to run your programs at a fairly high speed. The execution speed of a product or application is called by the technical term *performance*.

Performance is measured by structured speed tests called *benchmarks*. The set of benchmarks which is used can favor one product over another, so some care must be taken in order to draw supportable conclusions from a set of benchmarks. Your applications will usually depend on some features of your dBASE dialect and not on others, so the benchmarks in a given set may or may not reflect the kind of processing done by one of your applications.[5]

Therefore, the performance issues involved when you select a dialect for a particular application may be different from those involved when you pick a dialect in which you will write most or all of your applications. For this kind of choice, you would probably be best served by a large set of benchmarks which covers a large number of dialects.

Fortunately, such a set of benchmarks was published in the April 1989 issue of *Data Based Advisor* magazine for the following dialects: Clipper, dBASE III PLUS, dBASE IV, dBMAN, dBXL, FoxBASE+, FoxBASE+/386, and Quicksilver (Goley 1989a). In April of 1990, benchmarks appeared for FORCE, FoxPro, Clipper, dBASE III PLUS, and dBASE IV (Streich and Kalman 1990).

The 1989 MS-DOS benchmarks, as a set, showed FoxBASE+ 2.10 and Clipper 4.0 to be in the fastest category of performance, followed by dBMAN 5.1 and dBASE IV 1.0 in the second fastest category, with dBXL 1.2 and Quicksilver 1.2c far back in the slowest category.[6] On the set of benchmarks, FoxBASE+ 2.10 was 1.33 times faster than Clipper 4.0 without a math coprocessor and 1.37 times faster with a math coprocessor.

The April 1989 issue of *Data Based Advisor* compares the two Macintosh dialects, FoxBASE+/MAC from Fox Software, and McMax from Nantucket (Goley 1989b). On the set of benchmarks that was used, FoxBASE+/MAC was 4.2 times faster than McMax!

FoxPro wins or ties 25 of 43 benchmarks in the 1990 competition. It is dramatically faster than dBASE IV on most benchmarks, and at worst is comparable in speed. FoxPro 1.0 is generally faster or comparable to Clipper 4.0, but Clipper wins 7 of the 43 benchmarks. FORCE 1.02 wins 10 benchmarks, and dBASE III PLUS 1.1 and dBASE IV 1.0 don't win any benchmarks.

Correctness and a Recommended Dialect

If results are not correct, we may as well not bother to compute them in the first place. On the one hand, we are the ones who create the bugs in our source code, and, in theory, we can fix those bugs. On the other hand, any large software program has many bugs, and programs like FoxPro and dBASE IV are very large indeed. Sometimes the bug your application manifests results from a defect in the dialect product you use, and not from a defect in your code.

When you find improper performance of your application as a result of a vendor bug, you may be able to change your code so as to work around the bug. When this is not possible, you have a problem that can be very serious, depending on the bug and the application.

5. For example, although FoxBASE+ is usually at least as fast as Clipper 4.0, I run one of my reports in Clipper because Clipper is 3.9 times faster in this particular instance.
6. At the time of writing, the current versions were dBXL 1.3R and Quicksilver 1.3R. In June 1990, Wordtech Systems announced Arago dBXL and Arago Quicksilver for shipment early in 1991, claiming that these new versions would be faster than FoxPro.

Your options are severely limited. You can port your application to another dialect. A port is normally a great deal of work — unless you anticipate vendor bugs and write your application to a common dialect.[7] (In some cases, you can use a source code translator which converts source code from one dialect to another. Buzzwords International offers several such translators.)

You can rewrite your application in C or PASCAL, using one of the libraries for those languages that provide subroutines to duplicate dBASE facilities. This is arduous and again places you at the mercy of the bugs in the compilers and the libraries you use.

You can petition the vendor to give you a personal bug fix update to handle the particular problem that you encountered. When a vendor is small, this is feasible, but the major vendors are too large for this kind of service. (No vendor guarantees such service, but my research indicates that Fox Software and WordTech Systems have often provided it.)

You can urge the vendor to release a bug fix update as soon as possible. After you have reported the bug with sufficient information to allow the vendor to duplicate the problem, then — unless you are fortunate enough to get a personal bug fix update — you have little choice but to wait for the new release.

Your users, clients, and employers may not care very much about the distinction between your bug and a vendor bug, so if you have a choice, you will want to use a dialect from a vendor who tends to release stable software and who releases frequent bug fix updates. Let's distinguish *feature* updates from *bug fix* updates.

Examples of bug fix updates are versions 1.2b and 1.2c of WordTech's dBXL, which updated version 1.2. WordTech responded to bug reports by updating their version 1.2 product with fixes. They did not add new features in these releases — they fixed bugs for the programmers and their users who desperately needed those fixes.

A *feature* release is usually identified by a change in version number or product name, such as the change from dBASE III to dBASE III PLUS, or the change from FoxBASE+ 2.0 to FoxBASE+ 2.1. Generally speaking, new code (yours, mine, or theirs) means new bugs. A feature release may or may not fix reported bugs in the previous version, so it comes with its own set of bugs, new and old.

In recent years, WordTech has had the best performance in frequency of bug fix updates, followed by Fox Software. Nantucket let more than two years elapse between Clipper 4.0 and Clipper 5.0, and Ashton-Tate has not updated dBASE III PLUS since 1986, even though dBASE IV is not meant to replace dBASE III PLUS on microcomputers with modest amounts of RAM and disk capacity.

The question of stability is much less straightforward, except in the case of Ashton-Tate, whose dBASE III PLUS 1.1 and dBASE IV 1.0 have numerous problems; see the following remark. The users of dialects from Fox Software, Nantucket, and WordTech seem to think that their dialects have satisfactory stability.

---

7. I don't recommend that you always do this, but I do recommend that you always consider it.

Remark on dBASE IV anomalies. See the Ashton-Tate area on CompuServe (GO ASHTON) for lists of what Ashton-Tate calls "anomalies" for dBASE IV 1.0. dBASE IV 1.1 was released as this book went to press amid many published accolades, but this version must prove itself over a period of time to a skeptical market. In a talk in Austin, Texas, on September 4, 1990, Ashton-Tate dLAB member Tony Lima estimated that dBASE IV is 90% to 95% compatible with dBASE III PLUS; in contrast, I believe that FoxPro is nearly 100% compatible with FoxBASE+. There are simple dBASE III PLUS programs which dBASE IV 1.1 will not execute correctly.

Recommendation on which dialect to use. In my opinion,[8] Fox Software has the best overall record when one considers features, stability, frequency of updates, and performance. I recommend that you use either the most current or the next-to-last release, according to which you trust the most — or which you need the most!

In the next five chapters, we look at each of the major dialects in turn, using the following format to present each major dialect. A product summary shows whether the product is a nontokenizing interpreter, a tokenizing interpreter, a pseudo-compiler, or a compiler, and what the system requirements are. We then look at the release history and list some of the new features in each release. Each dialect is compared to the dialect or dialects with which it competes on the basis of compatibility, programming power, and performance.

Thus, dBXL 1.3, Clipper, and FoxBASE+ are compared to dBASE III PLUS, and dBXL/LAN and multiple-user FoxBASE+ are compared to multiple-user dBASE III PLUS. Similarly, FoxPro is compared to dBASE IV and FoxPro/LAN is compared to multiple-user dBASE IV. As a companion product to dBXL, Quicksilver's compatibility is examined with respect to dBXL and dBXL/LAN.

8. This opinion is held by several leading dBASE dialect experts.

Chapter 5

Ashton-Tate dBASE Dialects

Ashton-Tate created and made popular the "dBASE" way of computing. Since 1980, it has released dBASE II for CP/M (1980), dBASE II for MS-DOS, dBASE III (1985), dBASE III PLUS (1986), and dBASE IV (1988).

dBASE Dialect Products and Prices

Here is a list of dBASE dialect products from Ashton-Tate with their prices.

Table 5.1 Ashton-Tate dBASE Dialect Products and Prices

Price	Product
N/A	dBASE III
N/A	dBASE III Developer's Edition
$ 695	dBASE III PLUS (includes single-user and multiple-user versions)
$ 250	dBASE III PLUS Single-User Runtime (five licenses)
N/A	dBASE III PLUS Multiple-User Runtime
$ 995	dBASE III LAN Pack (five users)
$ 795	dBASE IV
$1,295	dBASE IV Developer's Edition
	dBASE IV Single-User Runtime (in dBASE IV Developer's Edition)
	dBASE IV Multiple-User Runtime (in dBASE IV Developer's Edition)
$ 995	dBASE IV LAN Pack (five users)
$1,695	dBASE Direct/36
$2,995	dBASE Direct/38

dBASE III and dBASE III Developer's Edition are no longer being sold by Ashton-Tate. dBASE III was available for the TI PC, a computer with marginal compatibility with other MS-DOS machines. All dialects listed above which are still being sold are for MS-DOS computers only, except for the dBASE Direct products for IBM minicomputers and mainframes.

dBASE III PLUS applications which are tokenized and linked with the DBC.COM and DBL.COM utilities can be executed with either dBASE III PLUS or with its runtime. When you distribute a tokenized application to users who don't have dBASE III PLUS, you must provide each user with a copy of the dBASE III PLUS runtime. These copies are available in packages of five.

Multiple-user dBASE III PLUS applications cannot be distributed with a runtime. Such applications require the network version of dBASE III PLUS.

The dBASE III PLUS package includes the multiple-user form of dBASE III PLUS, which initially supports one network user. More users can be added with the dBASE III PLUS LAN Pack, as explained on page 115.

The dBASE IV Developer's Edition includes a runtime which works for both single-user and multiple-user applications. You may distribute tokenized dBASE IV applications (.DBO files prepared with the COMPILE command or BUILD facility) with copies of the dBASE IV runtime. Although the dBASE III PLUS runtime pricing requires you to pay Ashton-Tate a royalty for each runtime that you give to a user, owners of the dBASE IV Developer's Edition can distribute the dBASE IV runtime to their users without royalty payments.

The Developer's Edition of dBASE IV includes the following components which are not found in the Standard Edition.

Table 5.2 Extra Components of the dBASE IV Developer's Edition

1. Runtime software with a license for unlimited distribution at no extra cost.
2. A windowing debugger.
3. A BUILD utility to collapse an application's code into a single .DBO file.
4. A code generator with a template language.
5. Two extra LAN keys, permitting three simultaneous users of multiple-user dBASE IV with the components of the dBASE IV Developer's Edition.
6. Extra programmer documentation to cover the additional components.

Editions of dBASE III PLUS are available for American English, British English, Chinese, Danish, Dutch, Finnish, French, German, Greek, Hangul, Italian, Japanese, Norwegian, Portuguese, Spanish, Swedish, and Taiwanese. dBASE IV is available for American English, British English, French, German, and Spanish; in September of 1990, an Arabic version was in development.

dBASE II

dBASE II is such an old dialect that we won't spend much time on it in this book. However, don't be too shocked if you find some dBASE II applications still being used by co-workers or clients. If an application performs a task in a satisfactory manner, and the application runs on hardware which continues to function properly, there is little, if any, reason to replace either the hardware or the software.

I know a consultant who is maintaining a dBASE II application on CP/M equipment with 8-inch floppy diskette drives. This shows us that a dialect such as dBASE III PLUS, with 2.5 million installed copies, will be with us for a very long time. (This same consultant maintains a dBASE III PLUS multiple-user application at a site where the client does not want to upgrade to any newer dialect.)

See Table 2-7, "dBASE Compatibility with Operating Systems," in the *Advanced Programmer's Guide* (Castro, Hanson, and Rettig 1985: 29) for a listing of versions of dBASE II which were released for CP/M-80, CP/M-86, Concurrent CP/M, Concurrent DOS, PC-DOS, MS-DOS, TurboDOS, MP/M-II, MP/M-86, DPC/OS, MMOST, 3-COM Ethernet, PC-NET, and UNIX System V on AT&T 3Bx computers. Note that Ashton-Tate no longer sells any version of dBASE II.

dBASE III

dBASE III was a major upgrade to dBASE II and a product which was much more appealing to programmers than the severely limited dBASE II. After its initial release in the middle of 1984, it went to version 1.1 in November of 1984 and to the "Developer's Release," 1.2, in August of 1985 (Castro, Hanson, and Rettig 1985: 665).

According to the *Advanced Programmer's Guide* (Castro, Hanson, and Rettig 1985: 666), "version 1.1 consists primarily of [bug] fixes." The SET DATE TO command appeared, and the copy protection scheme was changed (but not dropped).

Version 1.2, the "Developer's Release," was an intermediate feature update while Ashton-Tate was on the way to a truly usable product in dBASE III PLUS.[1] This version introduced the immensely useful command line history feature, the SUSPEND debugging facility, and error and key trapping via ON ERROR, ON ESCAPE, and ON KEY. The SET ORDER command appeared, which permitted programmers to change the active index file without closing and reopening indexes, as well as interface functions to MS-DOS (DISKSPACE(), GETENV(), ISCOLOR(), OS()), the immediate if function IIF(), and the PICTURE-formatting power of TRANSFORM().

With the approaching new century in mind, SET CENTURY controlled whether the date type displayed the last two digits of the year, or all four digits, as in "1/1/99" versus "1/1/1999". For the first time, we saw the double ampersand comment facility, which everyone now takes for granted.

Single-User dBASE III PLUS

As of the time of writing, dBASE III PLUS has been at version 1.1 since 1986, although a bug fix upgrade has been promised. Version 1.0 came out in November of 1985.

You may run single-user dBASE III PLUS on your workstation on a network by loading it from your local drive. In this mode of operation, you will be the only one with access to your files, and you will only be able to access files which physically reside on your computer. (Multiple-User dBASE III PLUS is treated in the next section.)

1. This praise for dBASE III PLUS refers to its features and not its implementation, which, as of version 1.1, still contained important flaws such as unstable indexes.

Classification

dBASE III PLUS, like dBASE II and dBASE III PLUS, is a nontokenizing interpreter which executes command files, which are text files that have an extension of .PRG by default. dBASE III PLUS includes the DBC.COM and DBL.COM utilities which create and link tokenized command files, and dBASE III PLUS will execute files in either the ASCII source code form that you see when you edit the files, or in the tokenized form prepared with the DBC tokenizer and optionally linked with the DBL linker. (The DBC tokenizer is sometimes called a pseudocompiler. Unfortunately, both input and output files to the DBC tokenizer have the .PRG extension, which is a blatant violation of the canonical approach.)

System Requirements

According to the *Getting Started* booklet in the dBASE III PLUS documentation, the hardware and software requirements are as follows:

1. IBM PC-DOS 2.0 or higher, or MS-DOS 2.1 or higher.
2. 256K RAM for DOS 2.x or 384K for DOS 3.x.
3. One of the following: (1) one hard drive and one diskette drive, (2) two diskette drives (360K or greater), or (3) access to a network drive on which single-user dBASE III PLUS is installed.

New Features of Interest to Programmers

Here is a summary of new features in this release which are of particular interest to programmers. Features which do not appear here may have been excluded due to space considerations, or because they are oriented to users who don't write source code. I have made an attempt to list short items, or those which are of particular importance, near the beginning of the list.

New Scope Option

The REST option appears for the first time. This scope means "the current record and all records to the end of the file, accessed in storage order or index order according to whether an index is active."

New Numeric Functions

The functions ABS(), MAX(), MIN(), and MOD() appear, to compute absolute value, greater of two values, lesser of two values, and the least residue of a modular division, respectively. For example, when changing from 24-hour to 12-hour time, we might make calculations like MOD(11,12) = 11, MOD(12,12) = 0, and MOD(13,12) = 1.

Numeric memvars are now compared to a precision of only 13 decimal digits, instead of the full 15.9 digits represented internally. For example, in dBASE III, (2.51 – .51 = 2) is false but it is true in dBASE III PLUS.

System Information Functions

The DOS-specific GETENV() function[2] retrieves the value of the specified DOS environment variable. The OS() function returns the name of the current operating system, including its version number. You can discover the amount of free space on a disk with DiskSpace(). The IsColor() function tells you if the monitor card is a color card, but dBASE III PLUS does not know if a monochrome monitor is attached to the color card.

Debugging Features

If SET ESCAPE ON has been executed, dBASE III PLUS gives you a choice to "Cancel, Ignore or Suspend?" when you stroke the ESCAPE key. If you suspend, you can enter commands at the dot prompt as usual; enter RESUME to start again or CANCEL to terminate the application. When you deliver the application to your users, you SET ESCAPE OFF (which does not affect the use of the ESCAPE key to exit full-screen editing without saving the changed items).

You can SET DOHISTORY ON to record a specified number of the most recently executed commands in a list which you can review with the LIST/DISPLAY HISTORY command. The length of the list is set by the SET HISTORY TO statement (or an entry in CONFIG.DB).

The Keystroke-Level Interface

You can set the size of the type-ahead buffer with SET TYPEAHEAD TO, and you can discard any keystrokes in this buffer with the CLEAR TYPEAHEAD command. Following a READ command, you can test ReadKey() to determine the keystroke that was used to exit the READ command. The InKey() function returns the next-to-use character in the type-ahead buffer, if the buffer contains at least one character.

The ON ESCAPE and ON KEY = <key> commands cause programmed actions to take place when the ESCAPE key or another specified key is stroked. The actions taken usually conclude with a RETURN or RETRY command.

Indexes with Unique Keys

When an index is built (using the INDEX ON command) and SET UNIQUE ON has been executed, or the UNIQUE keyword has been added to the INDEX ON command, then a record's key and record number will be entered into the index file

---

2. GetE() in Clipper.

only if the record's key is not already in the index. Say that you have a database with a FAMILY field, and that all records have FAMILY as "Smith" or "Jones". When you SET UNIQUE OFF and INDEX ON FAMILY, then all records in the database will be represented in the index; when you INDEX ON FAMILY UNIQUE, then the index will have two records: the first Smith record and the first Jones record. (Hint: Using INDEX ON <fieldname> TO EraseMe UNIQUE followed by USE EraseMe and COUNT is an easy way to discover how many unique values exist in a given field in a database!)

Multiple-Page FORMAT Files

Many databases have too many fields to handle on one screen, but formerly FORMAT files could only show one screen for each database record.[3] Now each screen in a FORMAT file, except the last, is followed by READ.[4] If you are building the FORMAT file by hand, remember that the file does *not* end with a READ statement!

Horizontal Scrolling

The new @S function, which you can use in the FUNCTION or PICTURE clauses of @ GET statements, permits you to solicit items from the user which may consist of more keystrokes than the editing window can display.

Assembly Language Interface

Up to five .BIN files, which can be created via assembly language or C, can be loaded simultaneously. They are executed with the CALL verb (which contrasts with the DO verb).

Database Commands and Functions

When you open a database with multiple indexes, the first index in the list is the active index, that is, the index which determines the order of access. The other indexes are maintained, but are not used otherwise. The SET ORDER TO command specifies which, if any, of the listed indexes is to be active. The command SET ORDER TO 0 specifies that all indexes are to be maintained, but that the database is to be accessed in storage order.[5]

A library subroutine can manipulate the index files in a work area through the NDX() function. If three index files are open (out of the maximum of seven) in the currently selected work area, then the names of the index files are NDX(1), NDX(2),

---

3. This limitation still occurs in other dialects, including Clipper 4.0.
4. FORMAT files could formerly contain only @ SAY GET statements, but now the READ statement is allowed.
5. In contrast, SET INDEX TO closes the currently open index file or files.

and NDX(3); NDX(4), NDX(5), NDX(6) and NDX(7) all return null strings. (Null strings are represented as "" and have length 0.)

The name of the database in the current work area is DBF(), and its fieldnames are FIELD(1), FIELD(2), and so on. LUPDATE() tells you when the database file was last updated, but you can't tell the difference between an update to the structure and an update to the data records with this function.

You no longer have to GO BOTTOM to discover the number of records in a database, which is reported in RecCount(). You no longer have to test EOF() to determine the success of a FIND, SEEK, or LOCATE command, as success is reported in the more natural FOUND(). Unfortunately, the FOUND() method is not as reliable as the EOF() method, because you must test FOUND() *immediately* after the FIND, SEEK, or LOCATE command.

Furthermore, David Kalman reports, "FOUND() does not always work properly in dBASE III PLUS and FoxBASE+. Instead, you should use EOF() to test for the end-of-file. If EOF() is true, the FIND did not succeed" (Kalman 1989: 217).

Disk Management Aids

The amount of free space on the default dBASE disk[6] is given by DiskSpace(). There is no function that tells you the size of a file, but you can calculate the size of the data part of a .DBF file with the RecCount() function, which tells you the number of records in the .DBF file, and the RecSize() function, which tells you the size of each record in bytes. By using the FIELD() function, you can determine the number of fields in the database; the size of the .DBF file is given by the formula

34 + 32*<number of fields> + RecSize()*RecCount()

By knowing the amount of space free on the disk and the size of your databases, you can enable or disable certain operations according to whether sufficient disk space is available.

Data-Entry Screen Tool

dBASE III PLUS contains a utility to develop data-entry forms for the screen. This utility, whose dBASE III equivalent was an external program, is accessed via the CREATE/MODIFY SCREEN command in dBASE III PLUS. The screen is built from references to fields from the currently active database and can include special effects such as double-line and single-line boxes. Labels and edit windows for GET statements appear onscreen in the same locations where your user will see them in your application. You can associate PICTURE specifications with GET and SAY data without this information cluttering the screen (as it did in the predecessor utility).

---

6. Set by default, by SET DEFAULT TO, or by DEFAULT = <disk> in Config.DB.

The screen definition is held in a file with a .SCR extension, which is not an executable file; CREATE/MODIFY SCREEN uses the .SCR file to generate an executable file with a .FMT extension. This file is called a FORMAT file, which is a special variety of command file that contains only @ SAY/GET commands and possibly one or more READ commands. You can use this file in two ways:

1. DO <file>.FMT followed by READ. This permits the user to edit the current record in the currently selected database.
2. SET FORMAT TO <file> followed by EDIT <scope>. This form permits the user to edit the records in the currently selected database which are defined by the scope. (To limit access to the current record, use a scope of "RECORD RecNo()".)

A large number of competing commercial products are available. These so-called *screen generators* usually handle menus also. See Part VIII in Volume 2.

Saving and Restoring the Database Environment

In writing a subroutine for a library, it is often necessary to save some information about the computing environment on entry and to restore some aspects of the computing environment at exit. The new view facility saves and restores such information for the database part of the dBASE environment.

The CREATE VIEW FROM ENVIRONMENT command creates a file with a default .VUE extension that contains the following information for each open database, as well as information on any relations set with SET RELATION TO in the currently selected work area.

1. Work area.
2. Name of database file.
3. Names of all index files.
4. The active field list.
5. Name of any open FORMAT file.
6. Definition of any active filter.

The command SET VIEW TO <file> causes the database environment which is defined in the view file to be re-created.

Multiple-User dBASE III PLUS

You may run single-user dBASE III PLUS on your workstation on a network by loading it from your local drive. In this mode of operation, you will be the only one with access to your files, and you will only be able to access files which physically reside on your computer.

The network setup for dBASE locates a component called the dBASE Administrator on the file server in a shared directory. An access program called ACCESS is used on each workstation to access the Administrator and to load dBASE III PLUS into the RAM memory at the workstation.

Remark. This is *not* client-server architecture; it's just loading an executable file from a shared directory on a network.

System Requirements

When you run dBASE III PLUS on the IBM PC network, each workstation requires

1. An IBM PC, IBM XT, IBM AT, or 100% compatible PC.
2. 384K RAM, but 512K RAM is recommended.
3. One floppy drive.
4. One hard drive.
5. IBM PC-DOS 3.1 or higher.
6. IBM PC Network Program 1.0 or higher.

When you run dBASE III PLUS on the Novell network, each workstation requires

1. An IBM PC, IBM XT, IBM AT, 100% compatible PC, or any other PC supported by Novell.
2. 384K RAM.
3. One floppy drive.
4. One hard drive.
5. MS-DOS 3.1 or higher.
6. Novell Advanced Netware/86 1.01 or higher.

Remark. These requirements are for the workstation. The computer acting as the server where the Administrator will be installed must have 640K RAM.

Each copy of dBASE III PLUS contains the diskettes and documentation needed to install the network version; hence, there is no separate network version. In addition to the Administrator software, each copy of dBASE III PLUS contains a *single* copy of the ACCESS program.

For copy protection and for network identification purposes, each copy of the ACCESS program is unique. In order to test your multiple-user dBASE III PLUS applications in situations where two users are competing for a resource that only one of them may have, you must have at least *two* copies of the ACCESS program.

Additional copies of the ACCESS program are sold in groups of five in a product called the dBASE III PLUS LAN Pack. At the time of writing, these Packs cost $995. Contrast this pricing with that of multiple-user FoxBASE+ or FoxPro/LAN, where the software is installed on the server and then is available to everyone with read permission to the shared directory containing multiple-user FoxBASE+ or FoxPro/LAN.

Remark on testing dBASE III PLUS LAN applications. In particular, note that you cannot fully test your multiple-user dBASE III PLUS applications without buying a LAN Pack, or otherwise having the use of a second ACCESS diskette.

New Features of Interest to Programmers

Part VI of this book deals with multiple-user programming of dBASE dialects for networks. Here we note only that dBASE III PLUS supports both *implicit locking* and *explicit locking*.

Following is an example of explicit locking. If the USE Members statement is successful, then we attempt to place a lock on the file to prevent anyone from appending records while we count. If the attempt to lock is successful, we count the records and release the lock. Otherwise, we call the Panic routine.

Listing 5.1 Example of dBASE III PLUS Explicit Locking

```
USE Members
IF FLOCK()
   COUNT TO MemberTot
   UNLOCK
ELSE
   DO Panic
ENDIF
```

Next is the same example, with implicit locking in use. When an error is encountered which would otherwise cause the "Cancel, Ignore, or Suspend?" message to appear, the ErrUnit subroutine is called by dBASE III PLUS. The ErrUnit subroutine has a CASE statement that tests the values of ERROR() and/or MESSAGE(), which give the error number and error message text. In ErrUnit, you may code RETRY to cause the statement which raised the error condition to be executed again.

Listing 5.2 Example of dBASE III PLUS Automatic Locking

```
ON ERROR DO ErrUnit

USE Members
COUNT TO MemberTot
```

In the example above, either dBASE III PLUS opens Members.DBF successfully, or else control passes to the ErrUnit subroutine. dBASE III PLUS then attempts to lock the file Members.DBF when the COUNT command is encountered. If the lock is granted, the COUNT command is executed and the file is unlocked. If the lock is not granted, control passes to ErrUnit, which might respond with RETRY, QUIT, or RETURN TO MASTER. (For more information, see Part VI in Volume 2.)

Single-User dBASE IV

dBASE IV is a tokenizing interpreter; .PRG command files are translated to a tokenized form with a .DBO extension. When dBASE IV executes the statement "DO Proc", it searches for Proc.DBO in the current directory and in the dBASE PATH list. If a PROCEDURE file is in use, it is also searched for a procedure named Proc. Proc.DBO is executed if found; otherwise, dBASE IV looks for Proc.PRG in the current directory and in the dBASE PATH list.

If Proc.PRG is found, then it is tokenized and stored in Proc.DBO. You may produce .DBO files with the COMPILE command.

> **Remark on dBASE IV COMPILEs and subdirectories.** I note sadly that — unlike FoxPro — versions 1.0 and 1.1 of dBASE IV store Proc.DBO in the current subdirectory even if Proc.PRG is *not* in the current directory. As a consequence, you may have different versions of Proc.DBO in numerous subdirectories.
>
> For example, say that Proc.PRG is stored in \DB\Util and that Proc.DBO does not exist in any subdirectory. If you are logged into \App1, you SET PATH TO \DB\Util, and you execute Proc, dBASE IV will produce Proc.DBO in \App1. If you then log into \App2, SET PATH TO \DB\Util, and execute Proc, dBASE IV will produce Proc.DBO in \App2. FoxPro avoids these problems by always storing Proc.DBO in the same directory as Proc.PRG.

If you execute SET DEVELOPMENT ON, then the time/date stamps of corresponding .PRG and .DBO files will be compared. The .DBO files which are older than their corresponding .PRG files will be updated.

System Requirements

According to the booklet *Getting Started with dBASE IV*, which is included with the dBASE IV product, the hardware and software requirements are as follows:

1. IBM PC-DOS 2.0 or higher, or Compaq DOS 3.31.
2. 640K RAM.
3. One of the following: (1) one diskette drive (360K or greater) and one hard drive with 5 MB free, or (2) access to a network drive on which single-user dBASE IV is installed.

New Features of Interest to Programmers

Here is a summary of new features in this release which are of particular interest to programmers. Features which do not appear here may have been excluded due to space considerations, or due to an orientation to users who don't write source code. I have made an attempt to list items which are short or are of particular importance near the beginning of the list.

Basic Structural Changes

Here is a summary of basic structural changes.

1. The maximum number of fields is now 255, up from the limit of 128 in dBASE III PLUS. dBASE IV now implements both hexadecimal and decimal arithmetic through the new F and N data types. (The old N type for hexadecimal arithmetic is the same as the new F type. The new N type, which is far more appropriate for calculations with money, uses decimal arithmetic.)
2. Source code commands can now be up to 1,024 characters in length, up from the dBASE III PLUS limit of 254 characters. This new length tends to remove the problem of not knowing how many clauses one can add to REPLACE commands.
3. Procedure files can now contain up to 963 procedures per file, up from the previous limit of 32. The previous limit was too small to permit general-purpose libraries to be implemented with the procedure file facility. You may have performance or memory problems if you put hundreds of procedures in a procedure file, but this is now possible.
4. User-defined functions now appear. These functions can be referenced in any dBASE expression, but there are many dBASE IV commands which cannot be used in user-defined functions 1.0; version 1.1 has many fewer restrictions.
5. Multiple child relations may now be set with the SET RELATION TO command.
6. Up to 35 keyboard macros may be defined. These macros insert text into the type-ahead buffer for use by dBASE IV at the dot prompt or in programs.
7. There are 22 new commands and functions that support the programming of various styles of menus. Ten new commands support up to 20 user-defined windows.
8. Unity-indexed arrays — arrays with minimum subscript values of 1 — are now implemented. They can have either one or two dimensions, with a maximum of 1,170 elements per array.
9. You can now open a maximum of 99 files of all types, up from the severe limit of 15 files in dBASE III PLUS. The maximum number of open database files is still 10, but you can now have up to 10 open index files per database, up from the previous limit of 7 indexes.
10. When you define a field for a database, you can specify that field as a TAG, which means that an index on that field is built and maintained automatically by dBASE IV. All such indexes are stored in a file with an .MDX extension, which can contain up to 47 indexes.

11. If no TAGs are defined, no .MDX file is created. Otherwise, the .MDX file is opened when the .DBF file is opened. For example, if any fields in Members.DBF are defined as TAGs, then Members.MDX must be found when Members.DBF is opened.
12. If you should choose to use the built-in editor, you will find that it supports up to 32,000 source code lines. The built-in editor in dBASE III PLUS could properly handle files only if they had fewer than 4,097 bytes.
13. There is basically no comparison between the reporting facilities in dBASE IV and those in dBASE III PLUS. The dBASE IV report generator has borrowed heavily from the splendid R&R Relational Report Writer from Concentric Data Systems and offers a great deal of new power.
14. Other new components are QBE, with a maximum of eight joined files, and SQL, which is known to be unreliable in version 1.0. There is an applications generator with its own template language and a transaction processing facility with rollback. The AUTOSAVE feature can force updated record data to be written to disk as soon as possible.
15. dBASE IV offers two new facilities to help you control the appearance of printed output: *printer drivers* and *system memvars*. Up to four printer drivers may be installed. Each driver may specify control codes for boldface, underscore, and so on.
16. A new type of memvar appears, called a *system memvar*. These memvars have names which start with an underscore. They are used to store information, such as the left and right margins, which dBASE IV uses when printing. Printer drivers may override some system memvar values.

dBASE Environment Preservation and Restoration

In dBASE III PLUS and dBASE IV, the command CREATE VIEW FROM ENVIRONMENT saves all of the database part of the environment for possible later restoration. dBASE IV offers the very important SET() function to return the ON/OFF or integer values of the various SET commands. For example, you can write a subroutine which saves the status of SET DELETED on entry in a memvar, executes SET DELETED OFF for its own purposes, and then restores the former status of SET DELETED on exit.

Remark on the importance of SET() in supporting reusable code. This feature has very great significance for developing libraries of reusable code and for implementing subroutines which require as little information as possible to be passed in PARAMETERS or PUBLIC variables.

ALIAS Support in Functions

In dBASE III PLUS, if you wanted information from a database, you had to select the area in which the database was open in order to invoke functions like RecCount(). In dBASE IV, you may code RecCount("Members") to get the number of records in the currently opened database with ALIAS "Members", whether or not Members is currently selected.

Number-Crunching Features

Although dBASE III PLUS offered logarithmic and exponential functions, there were no trigonometric functions. dBASE IV adds inverse and regular trigonometric functions, degree-to-radian conversion, least and greatest integer, a pseudorandom number generator, financial functions for future or present values and payments, and statistical functions such as standard deviation through the CALCULATE command.

The delicious CALCULATE command delivers statistics on a database using only one pass. This command can be used to replace some fairly complex DO WHILE loops.

Date Delimiters

Date constants are now implemented. In dBASE III PLUS, you represent the date January 1, 2000, as CTOD("1/1/2000"), but dBASE IV permits {1/1/2000}.

Memo Handling

A dozen new or enhanced commands make memos much more functional in dBASE IV than they were in dBASE III PLUS. For example, the search and extraction functions AT(), SUBSTR(), LEFT(), and RIGHT() can now be used on memo fields. You can also control some aspects of the memory management of memo data and you can define a window in which memo data will appear for viewing and/or editing.

Foreign File Format Support

dBASE IV can read and write files in the formats of PFS, Lotus 1-2-3 (.WKS and .WK1 files), Framework II, Multiplan, dBASE II, and Rapidfile. dBASE IV still implements the dBASE III PLUS options of the DIF format and SDF and delimited ASCII files. (Contrast FoxPro, which only imports SDF and delimited ASCII files.)

International Support

There are nine functions to support the formats for dates and monetary amounts which are used in various countries. In some cases, you specify the country by name, and in other cases, you specify a character, such as the currency character ("$" in the United States).

Printer Control

In addition to the new system memvars and printer drivers, dBASE IV offers the ??? command to send data directly to the printer. Character strings can now include the null character, CHR(0), so there is no longer any restriction on what control strings can be sent to printers, or what files can be built with SET ALTERNATE ON.

The PRINTJOB facility is used to print a specified number of copies of a report or other document using the initialization and deinitialization strings defined in system memvars, along with other facilities, such as control over pauses between pages. After PRINTJOB is executed, built-in counter variables track the line number and page number being printed, in order to support the ON PAGE command, with the syntax

ON PAGE AT LINE <line number> <command>

This command is used to automatically branch to a specified subroutine after the specified line is printed on the current page. These facilities permit you to print page headers and footers in a very convenient manner.

PICTUREs and Enumerated Types

There is a new set of PICTURE functions which you can use to control the alignment of data items that are shorter than the space allotted to display them. You can now cause data to be right justified, left justified, or centered in @ GET statements or output statements which use the TRANSFORM() function.

dBASE IV provides support for PASCAL's enumerated types in an interesting way, namely, through the "M" function character. For example,

@ GET Members->MembType FUNCTION "M A,B,C"

permits the user to select one of the values A, B, or C for MembType. As the user presses the space bar, the values A, B, and C appear; a value is selected by stroking the ENTER key.

In some cases, dBASE III PLUS would display or store numeric data in scientific notation, according to its own internal rules. In dBASE IV, you can specify scientific notation with the PICTURE function "^" (the caret character).

SELECT()

Other dialects, such as Clipper and FoxBASE+, give you the SELECT 0 command to select the available work area of lowest number. The SELECT() function of dBASE IV returns the number of the available work area of lowest number, so its equivalent of SELECT 0 is SELECT SELECT().

Multiple-User dBASE IV

You may run single-user dBASE IV on your workstation on a network by loading it from your local drive. In this mode of operation, you will be the only one with access to your files; you will only be able to access files which physically reside on your computer.

The network setup for dBASE IV locates multiple-user dBASE IV on the file server in a shared directory. An access program called ACCESS is used on each workstation to access multiple-user dBASE IV and to load it into the RAM memory at the workstation.

Remark. This is *not* client-server architecture; it's just loading an executable file from a shared directory on a network.

The number of users who are permitted simultaneous access to multiple-user dBASE IV is controlled by the Access Control Program. A minimum of one user is always permitted. To add more users, you can use System Disk #1 or the ACCESS diskette from any previous version of dBASE or the ACCESS diskette from any copy of dBASE IV. The Developer's Edition of dBASE IV permits at least three simultaneous accesses, and a LAN Pack grants another five accesses.

System Requirements

Ashton-Tate supports dBASE IV for the following networks:

1. IBM PC Network.
2. IBM Token-Ring Network.
3. Novell Network.
4. Ungermann-Bass Network.
5. 3Com 3+ Network.

When you run dBASE IV on a network, each workstation requires

1. An IBM PC, IBM XT, IBM AT, or 100% compatible PC.
2. 640K RAM.
3. IBM PC-DOS 3.1 or higher.
4. The workstation component of the network operating system in use.

When you run dBASE IV on a network, the file server requires

1. An IBM PC, IBM XT, IBM AT, or 100% compatible PC.
2. 640K RAM.
3. One floppy drive.
4. One hard drive with 5 MB free (3.5 MB if you don't install Developer Edition files).
5. IBM PC-DOS 3.1 or higher.
6. The file server component of the network operating system in use.

New Features of Interest to Programmers

There are several new multiple-user features of interest to programmers.

Automatic Handing of Resource Contention

The vendor claim is that dBASE IV can run unaltered dBASE III PLUS programs as multiple-user programs. Although this may be true, few programmers would be satisfied with the behavior of unaltered applications in multiple-user mode.

This claim is based on the automatic file and record locking facilities and the SET REPROCESS TO <count> command. Automatic locking means that you don't have to code locking and unlocking statements. The SET REPROCESS command determines the number of times which dBASE IV will automatically retry a failed resource request, with a maximum count of 32,000!

However, you as the programmer would like to control the duration of retry attempts by the number of seconds, not the number of retry attempts. Furthermore, you would want the unavailable resource to be requested no more often than twice per second — why flood the network with dozens or hundreds of requests per second?

Network Screen Refresh

In network usage, dBASE IV is able to update my view of record 1 in the Members database if you have changed the data in this record after I have displayed the record on my screen. One the one hand, you want to minimize the delay between the time when one user changes data and the time when other users see the changed data on their screens.

On the other hand, the network will run slower if you are constantly checking screens to see if they need updating. dBASE IV provides the SET REFRESH command to control the refresh delay and consequent load on the network.

Record Lock Holder Identification

dBASE IV offers a facility to record the time and date when a lock was placed on a record and to optionally record who placed the lock, assuming that dBASE IV is run on a LAN which requires workstation identification. This facility requires you to add a special field, _dBASElock, to the databases which are to be processed with this service. The special field is added with the CONVERT command.

You can then determine if a record has been changed since you last read it with the CHANGE() function. If you unsuccessfully attempt to lock a record with RLOCK() or lock a file with FLOCK(), you can determine who has the lock and when they placed this lock by calling the LkSys() function.

dBASE DIRECT Products

dBASE DIRECT products connect dBASE III PLUS users to IBM System 36 and System 38 minicomputers, the IBM AS/400, and IBM mainframes which use 3270 terminals. dBASE DIRECT for the 3270 permits you to access data in DB2, IMS, and VSAM files, and to communicate with FORTRAN and COBOL applications on the mainframe.

You execute the dBASE DIRECT Connectivity Control Center on your PC to log onto the host and transfer data into dBASE III PLUS databases. Contact Customer Service at Ashton-Tate for more information.

Chapter 6

Fox Software dBASE Dialects

While Ashton-Tate is famous for its size and the number of its installed units, Fox Software is famous as a firm staffed with a number of talented computer scientists who turn out products of sparkling speed and very high compatibility with the Ashton-Tate dialects. Fox Software has two important dBASE dialect products, dBASE III PLUS–compatible FoxBASE+ and the dBASE IV–compatible FoxPro.

Fox Software Dialect Products and Prices

Here is a list of dBASE dialect products from Fox Software with prices, followed by a list of related products from The Santa Cruz Operation.

Table 6.1 Fox Software Dialect Products and Prices

Price	Product
$ 395	FoxBASE+ 2.1
$ 495	FoxBASE+/MAC 2.0
$ 300	FoxBASE+/MAC Unlimited Runtime
$ 695	FoxBASE+/MAC Multi-User
$ 500	FoxBASE+/MAC Multi-User Unlimited Runtime
$ 500	FoxBASE+ 2.1 Single-User Unlimited Runtime
$ 595	FoxBASE+/LAN 2.1
$ 700	FoxBASE+/LAN 2.1 Unlimited Runtime
$ 595	FoxBASE+/386
$ 500	FoxBASE+/386 Unlimited Runtime
$ 795	FoxPro
$ 500	FoxPro Unlimited Runtime
$1,095	FoxPro/LAN

FoxBASE+ and FoxPro are available in English, French, German, and Spanish. Fox Software also licenses part of its product line to The Santa Cruz Operation, as shown in the following table.

Table 6.2
Fox-Related Products Separately Licensed to The Santa Cruz Operation

Price	Product
$795	SCO FoxBASE Multi-User for XENIX
$995	SCO FoxBASE Multi-User for XENIX/386

FoxBASE+ for XENIX requires the SCO XENIX operating system, and FoxBASE+/MAC runs on the Macintosh computers. The other products listed require MS-DOS. The SCO products are purchased from The Santa Cruz Operation or a distributor, not from Fox Software.

FoxPro is the current dialect and the last version of FoxBASE+ released was 2.1. Unlike dBASE IV, which does not replace dBASE III PLUS due to the much greater hardware requirements of dBASE IV, FoxPro has similar hardware requirements and is meant to replace FoxBASE+.

The FoxBASE+ runtime package is available in a single-user or multiple-user version. The multiple-user version will execute both single-user and multiple-user programs, so there is no need to have both runtimes. The FoxPro runtime executes both single-user and multiple-user code.

According to the vendor, FoxBASE+/386 is two or three times faster than FoxBASE+ 2.1 on the same 80386-based PC.

Single-User FoxBASE+

The last version of FoxBASE+ to be released before FoxPro replaced it was version 2.1. Versions 2.0 and 2.1 were the last significant releases.

When we looked at the Ashton-Tate dialects, we considered how the dialect had evolved compared to the version it replaced. With the Fox Software dialects, we must also consider how the dialect compares to the Ashton-Tate dialect with which it is supposed to be compatible.

Classification

FoxBASE+ is an interpreter with automatic tokenization. A utility called FoxPcomp is included to make tokenized files (with the .FOX extension) from .PRG files. If the tokenized form of a command file or a procedure file is not found, then the tokenized form is produced in RAM. Unlike dBASE IV and FoxPro, FoxBASE+ will not write the automatically tokenized file to disk.

The tokenized files (.FOX files) can be executed by the FoxBASE+ interpreter or by its runtime, which is available separately. Unlike dBASE III PLUS, which only offers a single-user runtime, the FoxBASE+ runtime is available in single-user and multiple-user versions, as is FoxBASE+ itself.

System Requirements

The system requirements for single-user FoxBASE+ are as follows:

1. PC/MS-DOS 2.0 or higher.
2. As documented, 360K free bytes of RAM for FoxBASE+ versions 2.0 and 2.1, but a Fox Software representative stated that the requirement is 390K free bytes.
3. One of the following: (1) one hard drive and one diskette drive, or (2) access to a network drive on which single-user FoxBASE+ is installed.

Compatibility with dBASE III PLUS

Versions 2.x of FoxBASE+ have a very high compatibility with dBASE III PLUS. In marked contrast to Clipper, FoxBASE+ implements virtually all of the commands in dBASE III PLUS and almost always executes these commands as dBASE III PLUS does. Table 6.3 lists dBASE III PLUS features which are not implemented in FoxBASE+, and Table 6.4 lists some known differences between dBASE III PLUS and FoxBASE+.

Table 6.3 dBASE III PLUS Features Not Implemented in FoxBASE+

1. APPEND FROM command does not support the .DIF, .SYLK, and .WKS file formats.
2. CATALOG commands (CREATE/MODIFY/SET CATALOG, SET TITLE).
3. COPY command does not support the .DIF, .SYLK, and .WKS file formats.
4. CREATE/MODIFY/SET QUERY.
5. CREATE/MODIFY/SET SCREEN.
6. EXPORT.
7. IMPORT.

FoxBASE+ 2.0 Features Not in dBASE III PLUS

FoxBASE+ offers a number of extensions to the dBASE III PLUS standard. Here is a partial list.

1. **EMS memory support.** Up to 64K of LIM EMS memory will be used, if available. Using EMS memory does not reduce the amount of RAM that FoxBASE+ needs to load. (Contrast FoxPro, which reduces free RAM required by 40K when EMS is available.)
2. **More memory variables.** Up to 3,600 memvars may be simultaneously defined.

Table 6.4 Behavior Differences between dBASE III PLUS and FoxBASE+ 2.0

1. **More open files.** The agonizing limit of only 16 open files in dBASE III PLUS increases to 48 files, which removes a barrier to the use of subroutines. Due to this limit, dBASE III PLUS programmers sometimes had to write large command files without the benefit of subroutines.
2. **Configuration files.** FoxBASE+ uses a configuration file called Config.FX if it finds it. If not, FoxBASE+ looks for Config.DB and uses that file if found.
3. **Index files.** The .IDX index files of FoxBASE+ use a different index file format from the .NDX index files of dBASE III PLUS. When FoxBASE+ needs an index file and only finds the .NDX dBASE III PLUS form available, it automatically makes the .IDX form. If you still need your FoxBASE+ indexes to have the .NDX extension, you can add the line INDEX = NDX in Config.FX.
4. **The FOX PUBLIC variable.** If you declare a PUBLIC memvar called FOX, then this variable will be set to .T. automatically when you execute under FoxBASE+. Since dBASE dialects see uninitialized memvars as .F., other dialects will consider FOX to be .F. The construct "IF FOX/ELSE/ENDIF" allows you to isolate dialect-dependent code when your code is to execute under multiple dialects.

   Remark. The PUBLIC memvar FOX is .T. for both FoxBASE+ and FoxPro. To distinguish FoxBASE+ from FoxPro, define PUBLIC memvars

   1. FoxBASE_L = ("FOXBASE" $ UPPER(VERSION())) and
   2. FoxPro_L = ("FOXPRO" $ UPPER(VERSION())).
5. **Editing difference.** Consider an @ GET data-entry window of one line by three or more characters to get a numeric value. If the initial value in the window is 0, which will be right justified, and you stroke "1" followed by PageDown when the cursor enters the window, then FoxBASE+ removes the spaces between the "1" and the "0" to make "10" and treats your entry as 10. dBASE III PLUS treats this entry as 1.
6. **.BIN file arguments.** dBASE III PLUS permits you to pass either a memvar or a parameter to a .BIN file via the CALL statement. FoxBASE+ does not support passing a parameter; in FoxBASE+ the syntax of CALL is

   CALL <.BIN file name> [WITH <memvar which is not a parameter>]
7. **Parameters versus memvars.** Consider a procedure where an identifier is declared both in a PARAMETERS statement and in a PRIVATE statement. Is a reference to such an identifier a reference to a parameter or a memvar? In dBASE III PLUS, the reference is to the parameter, whereas FoxBASE+ uses the memvar in such cases.

3. **SELECT 0.** This variant of the SELECT command causes the next available work area to be selected. When you use this form of SELECT to get new areas, you are free of the necessity of managing the relation of work areas and open databases. Once a database is open, you select its work area with SELECT <ALIAS>.

4. **User-defined functions.** Procedures or command files may include an expression after the RETURN verb. Such a syntax change converts a procedure to a function.
5. **Validation during READ.** The VALID clause appears, which is universally considered to be crucial by contemporary standards. This clause, when added to an @ GET statement, permits you to require the user to enter data which is valid by your definition, before the user can leave the @ GET. A logical expression or a user-defined function may be used for the validation.
6. **Screen control.** The SAVE SCREEN and RESTORE SCREEN commands appear which are so crucial to contemporary programming. These commands support dialogs and windows.
7. **Hot key facility.** This facility permits you to associate an action with a particular user keystroke. For example, the statement "ON KEY = 315 DO UserHelp", when placed before a READ statement, will permit your users to receive your custom-designed help information, as implemented in the UserHelp subroutine, when they press F1. UserHelp would begin with a SAVE SCREEN and end with a RESTORE SCREEN command.
8. **Keyboard control.** You can clear the type-ahead buffer with CLEAR TYPEAHEAD and you can store characters into this buffer with KEYBOARD <expression>. You can retrieve the next character in the buffer with InKey().
9. **Timed delays.** You can control the amount of time which your program will wait for a keystroke by supplying an argument to InKey().
10. **The "==" operator.** This relational operator for character string comparisons, also found in Clipper and FoxPro, works the same as "=" with SET EXACT ON.
11. **Read-only browsing.** The BROWSE command is incredibly powerful in its ability to let you see potentially any field data in any record, depending on what options are used. However, the dBASE III PLUS BROWSE command also permits you to change any data that you can see, which eliminates BROWSE from use as a read-only tool — in that dialect. FoxBASE+ introduces the NOMODIFY clause to make BROWSE read-only by your option!
12. **Disk buffering control.** The FLUSH command permits you to write all buffered disk data to the disk. After data is changed programmatically or via full-screen editing, it is buffered and is not necessarily written to disk until a later time. Buffered data is held in the volatile memory of a computer, so that a power failure or a number of other conditions will prevent the data from ever moving from transient buffer storage to permanent disk storage.
13. **Memvar arrays.** Unity-indexed arrays with one or two dimensions and up to 3,600 elements are implemented. Initialize an entire array with the syntax "STORE <expression> to <array name>" or "<array name> = <expression>". You can copy field data for a record back and forth between

the record and an array with the "SCATTER TO <array name>" and "GATHER FROM <array name>" commands.

14. **More procedures per file.** This version of FoxBASE+ supports up to 128 procedures per procedure file, in contrast to the 32 procedures of dBASE III PLUS. The included FoxBind utility can gather all of the .PRG files in a directory into one procedure file, so that you can distribute the software component of your FoxBASE+ application in one .PRG file or in one .FOX file.[1]
15. **Status information.** The SET ODOMETER command determines how often the onscreen reports from SET TALK ON are updated. You can use SET TALK ON and SET ODOMETER to implement a nice status-reporting facility for indexing progress. If you execute SET TALK ON and SET ODOMETER TO 100 before the index command, a report of the number of records indexed appears onscreen and is updated every time another 100 records are indexed.
16. **Multiple related children.** This version of FoxBASE+ introduces the ADDITIVE keyword for the SET RELATION command. The new keyword lets you relate one database to more than one other database. This facility can significantly reduce programming effort when multiple databases are related with one-to-one or many-to-one relationships, but it is of little or no help when the relationships are one-to-many.
17. **Tokenizer enhancements.** You can now specify the directory into which the tokenizer utility, FoxPcomp, will store the .FOX files it makes. An encryption facility permits you to produce .FOX files which cannot be disassembled.
18. **Prompted pick lists.** There is a prompted pick list facility which is programmed in a way which is analogous to painting the screen with a series of @ SAY/GET statements and then "activating" the GETs with READ. Here, you paint the screen with @ PROMPT statements and activate with the "MENU TO <memvar>" statement. An option lets you associate a one-line message with each item; this message is displayed at the location specified by "SET MESSAGE TO <screen line>" as the bar cursor is moved through the PROMPT items with the arrow keys. The ordinal of the selected item is returned to <memvar> by the MENU TO statement.[2]
19. **System information.** A variety of system information is provided by 18 options of the SYS() function. The SYS() options are listed in Table 6.6 on page 132, which shows FoxBASE+ 2.1 features not in dBASE III PLUS.
20. **Print spooling.** The "SET PRINT TO <file name>" command permits you to send print data to a file for later printing.
21. **Work area references.** You can obtain information about open databases in unselected work areas by specifying the database's work area number in references to the built-in functions ALIAS(), BOF(), DBF(), DELETED(),

1. You still need LABEL FORM, REPORT FORM, index, and database files.
2. If the first item is selected, 1 is returned; if the second item is selected, 2 is returned; and so on.

EOF(), FCOUNT(), FIELD(), FOUND(), NDX(), RECCOUNT(), RECNO(), and RECSIZE().

22. **Character-form date indexes.** The character form of a date returned by DTOC(<date>) is only suitable for ordering data by month, day, and year (assuming the American date format). The form DTOC(<date>,1) returns the format YYYYMMDD as in DTOC(DATE(),1) = "19900514". (Note that DTOC(<date>,1) returns the same value as the built-in function DTOS(<date>), which appears in Clipper and other dialects.)
23. **Edit 64K files.** The built-in (MODIFY COMMAND) editor handles files of up to 64K in size, in contrast to the 4K limit of dBASE III PLUS.

FoxBASE+ 2.1 Features Not in dBASE III PLUS

The following extensions to the dBASE III PLUS standard are new to version 2.1:

1. **View enhancements.** The FoxBASE+ 2.1 VIEW file includes the information in Table 6.5.

Table 6.5 FoxBASE+ 2.1 VIEW File Contents

1. All database, index, alternate, and FORMAT files currently open in all 10 work areas.
2. All fields contained in the SET FIELDS list.
3. All relations established with SET RELATION TO.
4. All filters for open databases.
5. The current function key settings.
6. ON ESCAPE and ON KEY settings.
7. The DEFAULT, PATH, and PROCEDURE settings.
8. If the ALL keyword is specified, all ON/OFF switch settings are saved.

Remark on the ability of the FoxBASE+ CREATE VIEW command to save SETtings. *There is a most significant enhancement in the CREATE VIEW FROM ENVIRONMENT command,* which is that the settings of the SET <option> ON/OFF commands can be saved as part of the environment with the ALL keyword! This gives even stronger support for structured programming and library development. A routine can CREATE VIEW <view file> FROM ENVIRONMENT ALL at entry, close and open databases and modify settings as needed, and then SET VIEW TO <view file> on exit to restore the environment.

2. **System information.** Many different kinds of system information can be retrieved with the SYS() function, as shown in Table 6.6. The SYS() function always returns a character value. **The SYS() options 18, 2000, 2001, 2002, and 2003 are new to version 2.1, but the other options are also implemented in FoxBASE+ 2.0.**

Table 6.6
System Information Available through the FoxBASE+ SYS() Function

1. SYS(0) returns the name and number of your workstation on the network.
2. SYS(1) returns the system date as a number in character form.
3. SYS(2) returns the number of seconds elapsed since midnight as a character string.
4. SYS(3) creates a filename which is guaranteed to be unique.
5. SYS(5) returns the current default disk, as set by SET DEFAULT TO.
6. SYS(6) returns the device or fully qualified file name set by SET PRINT TO.
7. SYS(7) returns the name of the current FORMAT file.
8. SYS(9) returns your FoxBASE+ serial number.
9. SYS(12) returns the remaining available memory in bytes. (Note: To see how much memory remains to run applications with the RUN command, RUN CHKDSK.)
10. SYS(13) returns the status of the printer as "READY" or "OFFLINE".
11. SYS(14,<index file ordinal>) returns the index expression of the indicated index file in the list of open index files for the current database.
12. SYS(16,<lexical level>) returns the names of the current procedure, the procedure that called it, the procedure that called the caller of the current procedure, and so on.
13. SYS(17) returns the processor in use as "8086/88", "80286", or "80386".
14. SYS(18) returns the name of the field being edited in a READ, for use in a help routine called by the ON KEY facility during a READ.
15. SYS(100) returns the current setting of SET CONSOLE.
16. SYS(101) returns the current setting of SET DEVICE.
17. SYS(102) returns the current setting of SET PRINT.
18. SYS(103) returns the current setting of SET TALK.
19. SYS(2000,<wildcard file name pattern> [,1]) returns the first file name which matches the pattern if the third argument is *not* specified; otherwise, the *next* file name matching the pattern is returned.
20. **SYS(2001,<SET option name>) returns the current setting of a specified SET command. For example, SYS(2001,"DELETED") returns "ON" or "OFF", according to whether the last SET DELETED statement was SET DELETED ON or SET DELETED OFF.**
21. **SYS(2001,<SET option name>,1) returns the alternate file name or message line, according to whether the SET option is SET ALTERNATE TO or SET MESSAGE TO. SYS(2001,"ALTERNATE") and SYS(2001, "MESSAGE") return "ON" or "OFF".**
22. SYS(2002) turns the cursor off and SYS(2002,1) turns it on.
23. **SYS(2003) returns the name of the currently selected DOS directory on the current DOS drive.**

3. **Validation.** Formerly, if a user pressed ENTER or DownArrow to pass through a GET statement, the VALID clause was *not* executed. Version 2.1 always executes the VALID clause.

4. **Macintosh-type menus.** In this famous interface, as implemented in FoxBASE+, a list of choices appears across the top screen row; a bar cursor manipulated with arrow keys selects a choice. When a top-line option is highlighted with the bar cursor, a boxed list of choices appears under the top line. Arrow keys move the bar cursor up and down the boxed list, which is continued onto multiple screens if necessary. This facility is implemented with arrays which store the top-line and pick list choices, and with the MENU BAR, MENU, and READ MENU BAR commands.
5. **Popup menus.** You can define an array of up to 128 character strings with a maximum length of 50 characters each to represent the choices in a list. The choices are presented in a box which lists them in order, from the top toward the bottom of the screen. The location at which the box is displayed is controlled by the @ <row>,<column> MENU command, which can be used for display purposes only, if you wish. More commonly, you will then use the READ MENU command to have the user pick one of the list items.
6. **Filtered indexes.** Consider a Members database containing information on individual and corporate members of an organization; the company name, if any, is stored in the Company field. It may be the case that only 1% of the records are corporate, that is, have a nonblank Company field. When you print reports on the corporate members, you need to present the company names in alphabetical order, but if you index on the Company field, you will have an index file which is 100 times bigger than it has to be, and which contains a vast number of blanks before the first corporate record. The UNIQUE option would eliminate all but one of the records with blank Company fields from the index, but it would also eliminate records with the same company name. The following command creates an index which only indexes records with nonblank Company fields:

   ```
   INDEX ON Company TO Company FOR ("" # TRIM(Company))
   ```

7. **Softseek searches.** Suppose that you want to print all addresses in your database with ZIP codes of "50000" or greater. However, how do you find the first record with a ZIP code of "50000" or greater? If you SEEK "50000" and there is no record with that ZIP code, then the record pointer moves to the end of the file. Version 2.1 gives you the RecNo(0) call to return the number of the record which has the largest key less than the key you sought. To find the first record with a ZIP code greater than "50000", when there is no record with that ZIP code, SEEK "50000", GOTO RecNo(0), and SKIP.
8. **FORMAT file enhancements.** The SET COLOR TO and CLEAR commands may now appear in FORMAT files. FORMAT files can now reference fields in databases related with the SET RELATION TO command.

FoxBASE+/LAN

The network version of FoxBASE+ is called FoxBASE+/LAN. There are two important differences between FoxBASE+/LAN and the dBASE III PLUS Administrator, which is the multiple-user dBASE III PLUS. First, while the Administrator is included with dBASE III PLUS, FoxBASE+/LAN is a different product from FoxBASE+.

Second, you must purchase dBASE III PLUS LAN Packs in order to enable users to load multiple-user dBASE III PLUS. In contrast, once FoxBASE+/LAN is installed on the network, anyone with read permission to the shared directory where it is installed can load it.

At the time of writing, the cost of FoxBASE+/LAN is less than the cost of a single dBASE III PLUS or dBASE IV LAN Pack, which adds users at a current cost of at least $200 per user. This means that it may be thousands of dollars cheaper to install multiple-user FoxBASE+ than to install multiple-user dBASE III PLUS or dBASE IV. In addition, there is no administrative overhead to manage ACCESS diskettes, to inventory LAN Packs, and to counsel users with access problems.

System Requirements

FoxBASE+/LAN runs on any NetBIOS network, including networks costing less than $200 per node, like LANtastic and The Invisible Network. Each workstation on the network which will access FoxBASE+/LAN needs the following:

1. PC/MS-DOS 3.1 or higher.
2. As documented, 360K free bytes of RAM after loading DOS and the workstation component of the network operating system, but a Fox Software representative stated that the correct specification is 390K free RAM.

No local hard disks or diskette drives are required.

Compatibility with Multiple-User dBASE III PLUS

The following dBASE III PLUS features are not implemented in FoxBASE+/LAN. *In addition, you must not use dBASE III PLUS and FoxBASE+/LAN to access the same databases at the same time.*

1. File encryption.
2. Access control features of the dBASE III PLUS PROTECT facility.
3. The LIST USERS and DISPLAY USERS commands.

FoxBASE+/LAN also offers the following enhancements to the multiple-user dBASE III PLUS standard:

1. **Less locking.** FoxBASE+/LAN performs less locking than dBASE III PLUS. For example, in dBASE III PLUS, an APPEND BLANK command requires a file lock, but FoxBASE+/LAN only locks the database header.

2. **Unique file name generation.** When you need a temporary file in a single-user situation, EraseMe.DBF works fine, but in a multiple-user situation, more than one user may try to use EraseMe.DBF concurrently. The SYS(3) function is guaranteed to deliver a unique filename to help you in such situations. You can form a unique database file name with the expresion SYS(3) + ".DBF".
3. **Workstation identification.** The SYS(0) function returns the name and number of your workstation on the network, assuming that the LAN used requires workstation identification.
4. **Novell network printer support.** The SET PRINTER command has several options to support control of printers on Novell networks.

FoxPro

At the time of writing, FoxPro, a FoxPro runtime, and FoxPro/LAN have been released, and a XENIX version, an .EXE compiler, and a client-server version are in development. FoxPro is a tokenizing interpreter which is analogous to FoxBASE+ in a number of ways.

For example, FoxBASE+ was designed to run almost 100% of dBASE III PLUS programs without modification, at a *much* higher speed than dBASE III PLUS. FoxPro was designed to run almost 100% of dBASE IV programs without modification, at a *much* higher speed than dBASE IV.

Although FoxBASE+ offers a number of very useful capabilities not found in dBASE III PLUS, in some ways even the initial release of FoxPro goes so far beyond dBASE IV that it appears to be positioned against the successor to dBASE IV, and not just dBASE IV. I base this statement largely on the *event-driven, full-paradigm windows* of this very provocative dialect, which we will discuss below. (To be fair to Ashton-Tate, we must note that some important dBASE IV features, such as .MDX files and transaction processing with rollback, are missing from FoxPro 1.0.)

Whereas dBASE IV compiles command and procedure files into .DBO files, FoxPro produces .FXP files from .PRG files and .PRX files from .FMT files. When dBASE IV 1.0 executes DO MENU, and MENU.PRG is found, but MENU.DBO is not found, dBASE IV automatically creates MENU.DBO in the current directory, *even if MENU.PRG is* not *in the current directory! FoxPro stores a compiled file in the directory which contains its source file.*

If SET DEVELOPMENT is ON, both FoxPro and dBASE IV will compare the dates of compiled and source files. If a compiled file is older than its source file, the compiled file is created again.

System Requirements

The system requirements for single-user FoxPro are the same as for single-user FoxBASE+, as follows:

1. PC/MS-DOS 2.0 or higher.

2. As documented under "EMS Support" in Chapter 7 of the FoxPro manual, 400K free bytes of RAM after loading DOS and all TSRs, but a Fox Software representative stated that the correct specification is 420K free RAM.
3. One of the following: (1) one hard drive with at least 1 MB free and one diskette drive, or (2) access to a network drive on which single-user FoxBASE+ is installed. FoxPro uses less than 1 MB of disk space if you don't install some of the options.

Special Video and Memory Management Support

FoxPro offers special support for expanded memory and extended video modes. Whereas FoxBASE+ would use up to 64K of available EMS memory, FoxPro uses *all* available LIM 4.0 EMS memory. Needless to say, making more memory available to FoxPro will increase its speed and processing capabilities. (Note that there are utilities which make your garden variety extended memory appear as LIM 4.0 EMS memory to your software.)

FoxPro will automatically detect the video text mode you are using; modes include but are not limited to resolutions of 25 (lines) by 80 (rows), 43 by 80, 50 by 80, 60 by 80, and 28 by 132. Select the video text mode you want, using software from the maker of your video adapter card, and then execute FoxPro.

The Command Window and the Output Window

When you install and start FoxPro, you will see a mostly empty screen with a top-line menu bar a la Macintosh and a window with a border which is labeled "Command". The other major dialects do not distinguish onscreen between the source of commands and the output from the commands, but in FoxPro you enter commands in the Command Window and the results from the commands appear on the full screen, which *is* the Output Window. Output text scrolls underneath the Command Window.

FoxPro's Event-Driven Windowing Interface

The interpretive dBASE dialects like to present themselves as two products in one. Users who do not program can use the menu interface — often called a *non-procedural* interface — of each product to manage their data. For example, dBASE III PLUS offers the Assistant, FoxBASE+ has FoxCentral, dBASE IV offers the Control Center, and FoxPro offers a Macintosh-type menu interface with windows.

Programming-level users of dBASE dialects are unlikely to use the Assistant or FoxCentral and are somewhat unlikely to use the Control Center. This occurs because applications which are programmed in dBASE III PLUS, FoxBASE+, or dBASE IV control their own "look and feel" — the appearance of the built-in menu interface may be a design issue, but it is not a programming issue. For example, the look and feel of a dBASE IV application need not bear any resemblance to the look and feel of the Control Center.

In contrast, the look and feel of a FoxPro application is typically influenced by the look and feel of FoxPro. Although you can hide built-in facilities from users of your FoxPro applications, in many cases it will be appropriate to enable some or all of these built-in facilities for those users.

Of course, there is nothing magical about an onscreen window — it's just some text surrounded by a border of some sort. Windows can *look* very flashy when you control the color of the border, the interior, whether there is a shadow, and, if so, whether the shadow is translucent. But the flashiest windows quickly become irritating if they do not really help the user.

FoxPro windows come alive in an *event-driven* environment. When you use the interpreter or an application which has not limited or hidden any features, you can popup any defined window at any time, subject to memory constraints, of course — at a certain point, you will have opened too many windows and FoxPro will complain.

For example, say that you are using the built-in hard disk manager, Filer. Suddenly, you remember that you must meet with Mary Smith before the end of the month. So you popup the built-in Calender Window and check your appointments and diary entries for the remaining times and dates this month. You select a date and a time and then popup the built-in editor to write Mary a note. You popup the Print Window under the Files Menu, and select the Editor Window you just left as the print source. You then close the Print Window, the Editor Window, and the Calender Window, and — you are back to Filer!

An Integrated Environment with Implemented Windowing Paradigms

The objective of FoxPro's designers is clearly to provide an integrated environment for both the programmer and the end-user that will serve both for most of their computing needs. If a facility is not built in and must be accessed from another DOS program, you can now use the RUN command to execute programs of almost any size. If you or your users use a standard set of programs accessed through the RUN command, you can build a little menu program to RUN the selected programs with the correct amount of free RAM. (It is desirable to specify the minimum amount of free RAM required in order to save and restore the FoxPro environment more quickly.)

The top-line FoxPro menu offers seven choices: the System Menu, the File Menu, the Edit Menu, the Database Menu, the Record Menu, the Program Menu, and the Window Menu, from left to right. Of these, the File Menu, the Edit Menu, the Database Menu, the Record Menu, and the Window Menu comprise the typical nonprocedural interface that gives a nonprogramming user some processing capability that would otherwise require a program.

The Program Menu serves developers and shows another aspect of FoxPro's integration. This menu contains DO, CANCEL, RESUME, ECHO, STEP, TALK, COMPILE, FoxView, FoxDoc, and FoxGraph, which gives menu-driven access to familiar features and three external utilities. (FoxView and FoxDoc are bundled with FoxPro, but the excellent FoxGraph program is sold separately.)

Windowing Paradigms

Certain paradigms of the windowing environment became well established during the 1980s, and FoxPro implements several of them. Windows can be overlapped, moved, resized, scrolled, colored, opened, and closed. They can be activated by moving the cursor to the window to be activated; if a window to be activated is partially or completely hidden behind other windows, it is brought forward to appear on top of the windows which concealed it before its activation. You can ZOOM a window to fill the screen and ZOOM back to the window's original size. (The amount of data that you can see in a full-screen BROWSE in an extended video mode is *very* impressive.)

Many of the keyboard options have mouse equivalents, because FoxPro supports both the mouse and the keyboard as input devices. One mouse option without a keyboard equivalent is the following. If an application has not blocked this feature, a user can use a mouse to move in any order through the fields in a series of GETs during full-screen editing. (See the vendor documentation for the READ command.)

One of the most important windowing paradigms is to extract information from one window, save this information in a temporary storage area, and then insert this information into another window. In Macintosh and FoxPro terminology, this process is called "cutting and pasting with the clipboard."

FoxPro dialog boxes are fully engineered with several state-of-the-art interface features. *Check boxes* take a blank to indicate that the item is not chosen, or an "X" to choose the item. *Radio buttons* are similar to check boxes, except that they are used for lists of mutually exclusive items; like buttons on a car radio, only one can be selected at a time.

A FoxPro dialog box can contain inverse video edit windows of the same type as those created by @ GET with READ. *Text buttons* identify choices which cause an immediate action. Two standard text buttons are "OK" and "Cancel"; text buttons can also bring up a further dialog in its own box.

Dialog boxes have a facility called *popup controls* to handle the selection of one item, such as a disk drive, from a list of possible choices. When the popup is selected, a boxed pick list appears from which you make your choice.

Alternatively, a list of choices may be displayed inside the dialog box as a *scrollable list*. Dialog boxes have double-line borders; scrollable lists have single-line borders on three sides and a *scroll bar* on the fourth side.

The System Menu

Several windowing paradigms are implemented on the System Menu, which offers programmers and end-users alike some very useful facilities. These facilities are always available if they are not blocked and if sufficient memory is free.

The Capture option permits you to define a rectangular area onscreen which is then copied to the clipboard. The Paste option on the Edit Menu inserts the text at the cursor. For example, you can cut a syntax description from a Help Window and paste it into your source code or the Command Window; there it can be edited as necessary prior to execution.

The Macros option of the System Menu permits you to assign strings of characters to single keystrokes. For example, you could define key F9 to enter "Sam" at the cursor, or today's date, or any other text. Approximately 250 keystrokes — for example, F9, CONTROL-F9, or ALT-F9 — are available to store up to 1,024 characters each. Each macro has a name of up to 20 characters. Macros are grouped into sets and are managed as sets.

> **Remark.** Fox Software claims that FoxPro's macro facility will enable you to make the FoxPro editor behave like the editor that you now use. This is true only if your editor uses single keystroke combinations for all commands, and if the keystrokes used are ones which FoxPro can use for macros. For example, in my editor, ESCAPE-J moves the cursor to a new line which has the same indentation as the current line. If AutoIndent is selected under editor "Preferences", I can stroke END-ENTER to get the same effect in FoxPro.
>
> However, a FoxPro macro is an abbreviation for *one* keystroke, and ESCAPE-J has two keystrokes. Furthermore, the ESCAPE key cannot be used for a FoxPro macro. FoxPro macros offer one-to-one or one-to-many mappings of keystrokes to keystrokes, but to make one editor respond to the commands of another editor, one generally requires many-to-many mappings.
>
> The macro facility in an editor like Brief is a full programming language. Such editors have the power to map many keystrokes to many keystrokes.

The System Menu accesses a quite serviceable hard disk manager called Filer (although only the name of the current directory is shown, and not the complete path). This could be a boon for cross-platform development — you might have a lovely hard disk manager for DOS 3.x, but how about DOS 4.x, LANs, and XENIX? And of course, end-users who would never be able to manage their own files properly with DOS or XENIX commands can handle Filer with only a little training.

The Calculator and Calender/Diary options of the System Menu are self-explanatory. Wouldn't it be nice if users of your database applications could have a calender and calculator that they could popup without the costs and crashes associated with TSR programs like Sidekick? When you develop with FoxPro, these facilities are automatically available.

The ASCII chart is a reference for programmers that lists for each ASCII character the decimal number of the character, the hexadecimal number, the IBM PC 8-bit ASCII graphic for the character, the usual text reference (^K for CONTROL-K), and the three-letter code for control characters (NUL, SOH, etc.). The only missing column is one for the names of the printing characters. (Did you know that "^" is a caret and "/" is a virgule? Note that the companion diskette contains an ASCII table in a file called ASCII.REF.)

There is a splendid and very clever facility for creating special effects like boxes in your text files, which is accessed via the Special Characters option of the System Menu. Say that you want to insert a special character like an umlauted vowel or a double vertical rule. Popup the Special Characters Window, put the cursor on the desired character, and stroke ESCAPE or the space bar or double-click your mouse. The Special Characters Window is closed, and the selected character is inserted at the cursor in the original window!

Debug and Trace Windows

FoxPro offers a full source-code-level debugging facility which is admirably presented in its windowing environment. A Debug Window permits you to monitor the value of expressions as your application executes. You may mark an expression as a breakpoint, which will trigger a Suspend when the expression changes value.

A Trace Window shows you the lines of source code as they execute. You may mark a source code line as a breakpoint, in which case a Suspend is triggered when control passes to the code on the marked line.

Although the Debug and Trace Windows may be moved and resized, debugging will be difficult to manage in the text mode of 25 rows by 80 columns. It is much nicer to have 43 or more lines, so that the top 25 rows can be used for program output and the remaining onscreen space can be used for the Debug Window and Trace Window. (Pressing SHIFT-CONTROL-ALT will temporarily remove the Debug Window and/or the Trace Window, so you can see the underlying output.)

Compatibility with dBASE IV and FoxBASE+

The first comment is that FoxPro usually executes FoxBASE+ programs without modification, so that dBASE III PLUS programs which executed under FoxBASE+ will execute under FoxPro.[3] On the other hand, dBASE IV 1.0 does *not* execute all dBASE III PLUS programs without modification; something as simple as a dBASE III PLUS @ GET command may require modification for dBASE IV.

Compared to dBASE III PLUS and FoxBASE+, dBASE IV and FoxPro are far more full featured, and a comparison of features is much more complex. For example, FoxPro offers the SET COMPATIBLE ON/OFF command to determine whether some commands will work as in dBASE IV.

The command SET COMPATIBLE ON is equivalent to SET COMPATIBLE DB4; SET COMPATIBLE OFF is equivalent to SET COMPATIBLE FOXPLUS. According to the SET COMPATIBLE table in Appendix A in FoxPro's *Release Notes and Installation Instructions*, the features in Table 6.7 are affected by SET COMPATIBLE; Table 6.8 lists the dBASE IV features which are not implemented in FoxPro 1.0.

---

3. One problem is that SET HEADING ON affects commands which were not formerly affected.

Table 6.7 FoxPro Features Affected by SET COMPATIBLE

1. @ SAY and the ASCII BELL character, CHR(7).
2. All file processing commands with a drive reference.
3. ACTIVATE SCREEN.
4. ACTIVATE WINDOW.
5. APPEND MEMO.
6. GO or GOTO with TALK ON.
7. MENUs and POPUPs.
8. PLAY MACRO.
9. READ with a VALID clause on a GET.
10. READ with a numeric PICTURE clause on a GET.
11. READ commands which are nested.
12. RUN command and the placement of the screen cursor.
13. RUN command and screen scrolling when STATUS ON.
14. SET COLOR TO and screen line 24.
15. SET FIELDS.
16. SET MESSAGE.
17. STORE for array initialization.
18. SUM and SET DECIMALS.
19. INKEY() and codes for HOME and SHIFT-HOME.
20. LASTKEY() and codes for HOME and SHIFT-HOME.
21. LIKE() and trailing blanks.
22. SELECT(). Highest unused work area or the current work area.
23. SYS(2001,"COLOR"). ON/OFF or a color specification.
24. TRANSFORM() with a numeric PICTURE clause.

According to the FoxPro *User's Guide,* FoxPro has over 200 commands and functions not found in FoxBASE+, over 140 commands and functions not found in dBASE IV, and over 90 commands and functions not found in either FoxBASE+ or dBASE IV. Here are some of the differences and enhancements.

Data Structure Differences and Enhancements

FoxPro character memvars can be up to 64K in length, quite unlike the 254-character limit for FoxBASE+ and dBASE IV. Like dBASE IV but unlike FoxBASE+, FoxPro character fields and memvars can contain CHR(0). FoxPro implements the curly brace notation for date constants: {1/1/99} versus CtoD("1/1/99"), which is required in FoxBASE+. FoxPro and dBASE IV implement both hexadecimal and decimal arithmetic through the F (hexadecimal) and N (decimal) field types, whereas the N type in FoxBASE+ implemented hexadecimal arithmetic.

Table 6.8 dBASE IV Features Not Implemented in FoxPro 1.0

1. APPEND FROM command does not support the .DIF, .SYLK, and .WKS file formats.
2. CATALOG commands (CREATE/MODIFY/SET CATALOG, SET TITLE).
3. COPY command does not support the .DIF, .SYLK, and .WKS file formats.
4. CREATE/MODIFY/SET QUERY.
5. CREATE/MODIFY/SET SCREEN.
6. EXPORT.
7. IMPORT.
8. LOOKUP().
9. **.MDX files (multiple index files).**
10. Printer drivers.
11. QBE commands.
12. **SET SKIP TO.**
13. SQL commands.
14. Transaction processing via BEGIN TRANSACTION, END TRANSACTION, and ROLLBACK.

dBASE IV and FoxPro support up to 255 fields per database. (Like dBASE III PLUS, both dialects are limited to 4,000 characters per record, 100 characters per index key, and 254 characters per character field.) FoxPro permits up to 3,600 elements per array versus the 1,170 permitted by dBASE IV.

FoxPro permits about 250 different macro keys to be defined, in contrast to the dBASE IV limit of 35. dBASE IV can show a maximum of 20 windows onscreen, but FoxPro is limited only by memory. The maximum number of procedures per procedure file is similar, at 963 for dBASE IV and 1,170 for FoxPro — but — FoxPro permits any source code file to contain procedures; simply define your procedures with the PROCEDURE keyword. When FoxPro reads the source code file, it also reads any procedures in the file!

Remark on nested READs in FoxPro. FoxPro can support up to four nested READ statements. No major dialect other than Clipper 5.0 has the ability to nest READ statements without an add-on product.

In both dBASE IV and FoxPro, source code commands can be up to 1,024 characters in length, up from the dBASE III PLUS limit of 254 characters. This new length tends to remove the problem of not knowing how many clauses one can add to REPLACE commands.

In FoxPro, user-defined functions (UDFs) may contain any FoxPro command, but there are many dBASE IV commands which cannot be placed in dBASE IV UDFs. Neither dialect has yet reached the Clipper standard of permitting references to UDFs to appear anywhere that a reference to a built-in function may appear. References to FoxPro UDFs can occur only in STORE and assignment statements, REPLACE statements, control statements such as DO WHILE and IF, print statements (?, ??, and ???), DISPLAY, LIST, @ GET with VALID/DEFAULT/WHEN, @ SAY <expression>, BROWSE VALID/DEFAULT/WHEN, AVERAGE, SUM,

RETURN, SCHEME, and label and report definitions. In particular, note the absence of INDEX ON from this list: UDFs are not permitted in index expressions.

There are 27 new commands and functions to support the programming of various styles of menus, which is 5 more commands than in dBASE IV. There are 19 new commands (versus 10 in dBASE IV) to support a number of windows which is limited only by memory, in contrast to the 20 user-defined windows in dBASE IV 1.0.

As in dBASE IV, you can now open a maximum of 99 files of all types, up from the limit of 48 files in FoxBASE+. Relative to dBASE IV, the maximum number of open database files increases from 10 to 25, the maximum number of open index files increases from 10 to 25, and the maximum number of open indexes per database increases from 10 to 25.

The built-in FoxPro editor can handle very large files. It has a number of features to support both the line-by-line orientation of source code and the paragraph orientation of documentation.

There is basically no comparison between the reporting facilities in FoxPro and those in dBASE III PLUS and FoxBASE+. The FoxPro report generator has borrowed heavily from the splendid R&R Relational Report Writer from Concentric Data Systems and offers a great deal of new power.

Other Differences

FoxPro 1.0 does *not* implement QBE and SQL, which are found in dBASE IV. As with dBASE IV Developer's Edition, there is an applications generator with its own template language, and the AUTOSAVE feature can force updated record data to be written to disk as soon as possible. Unlike dBASE IV, there is *no* transaction processing facility with rollback.

While FoxPro 1.0 implements the system memvars of dBASE IV, it lacks printer drivers.

Variable-Length Argument Lists

When a PARAMETERS statement in a subroutine contains N identifiers, most dialects require you to pass N arguments to the subroutine. FoxPro permits you to pass from 1 to N arguments — contrast this with Clipper, which permits 0 to N arguments. The FoxPro PARAMETERS() function returns the number of arguments passed. (Clipper's equivalent function is PCOUNT().)

Low-Level File I/O

FoxPro contains a set of functions which support the reading and writing of files in units of bytes, records, or blocks. In this context, a record is a "line" in a text file. The first line in a text file starts with the first byte of the file and extends up to and including a carriage return/line feed pair, CR/LF (CHR(13) + CHR(10)). Subsequent lines consist of text between and not including a CR/LF pair and up to and including the next CR/LF pair.

You may define a block size in number of bytes. In particular, you can use a block size of 1 to read or write 1 byte at a time, as you would in a PASCAL text filter program. However, FoxPro 1.0 executes such code at an unacceptably slow rate, so you must do your own buffering at the source code level.

dBASE Programming: Environment Preservation and Restoration

In FoxPro and dBASE IV, the command CREATE VIEW FROM ENVIRONMENT saves all of the database part of the environment for possible later restoration. While FoxPro retains the FoxBASE+ SYS(2001) built-in function to get the ON/OFF or integer values of the various SET commands, FoxPro also implements the more natural SET() function of dBASE IV.

dBASE Development: Environment Preservation and Restoration

A contemporary paradigm is automatic restoration of an application's computing environment when the application is entered after being exited. When a text editor follows this paradigm, it presents you with the same onscreen view when you start again: the same files are open for editing, and the cursor is positioned at the same place in the same file that you were editing when you stopped.

Fortunately, FoxPro implements this paradigm, because its development environment may be complex, with many open windows and open files. When you QUIT, environment information is automatically saved in FoxUser.DBF, which is used to set up the environment when FoxPro starts.

ALIAS Support in Functions

In dBASE III PLUS, if you wanted information from a database, you had to select the area in which the database was open in order to invoke functions like RecCount(). In FoxBASE+, you can use the form RecCount(<work area number>). In dBASE IV and FoxPro, you may code RecCount("Members") to get the number of records in the currently opened database with ALIAS "Members", whether or not Members is currently selected.

Number-Crunching Features

Although dBASE III PLUS and FoxBASE+ offered logarithmic and exponential functions, there were no trigonometric functions. dBASE IV and FoxPro add inverse and regular trigonometric functions, degree-to-radian conversion, least and greatest integer, a pseudorandom number generator, financial functions for future or present values and payments, and statistical functions such as standard deviation through the CALCULATE command.

The wonderful CALCULATE command delivers statistics on a database using only one pass. This command can be used to replace some fairly complex DO WHILE loops.

Memo Handling

A dozen new or enhanced commands make memos much more functional in FoxPro than they were in FoxBASE+ and dBASE III PLUS. For example, the search and extraction functions AT(), SUBSTR(), LEFT(), and RIGHT() can now be used on memo fields. You can copy any memo expression into a memo field and copy memo fields of arbitrary size between databases with the command

REPLACE <memo name 1> WITH <memo expression>

You can copy memo fields of up to 64K into a FoxPro memvar by an assignment statement of the form <character memvar> = <memo expression>.

No major dBASE dialect yet offers the substring pseudofunction found in PL/I, which permits you to replace a part of a string which is indicated by a substring expression. Say that you wish to replace 5 bytes starting at byte 1,000 in a memo or character string. You *cannot* use the syntax

SUBSTR(<identifier>,1000,5) = <new data>

Instead, you must use code like one of the following:

```
<identifier> = SUBSTR(<identifier>,1,999) + <new data> + ;
          SUBSTR(<identifier>,1005)
<identifier> = STUFF(<identifier>,1000,5,<new data>)
```

If <identifier> has a million bytes of data, you will make the computer copy a million bytes of data in order to change 5 bytes of the one million!

Foreign File Format Support

FoxPro lacks almost all of the foreign file format support offered by dBASE IV, which can read and write files in the DIF format and in the formats of PFS, Lotus 1-2-3 (.WKS and .WK1 files), Framework II, Multiplan, dBASE II, and Rapidfile. FoxPro only supports SDF and delimited ASCII files.

International Support

FoxPro offers all nine dBASE IV functions which support the formats for dates and monetary amounts that are used in various countries.

Printer Control

Printer drivers like those in dBASE IV will presumably appear in a version of FoxPro subsequent to version 1.0. FoxPro offers all other dBASE IV print control facilities, including PRINTJOB/ENDPRINTJOB, ON PAGE, and system memvars.

Pictures and Enumerated Types

FoxPro offers all of the dBASE IV PICTURE and function options for formatted input/output. These include a new set of PICTURE functions which you can use to control the alignment of data items that are shorter than the space allotted to display them. You can now cause data to be right justified, left justified, or centered in @ GET statements or output statements which use the TRANSFORM() function.

Both FoxPro and dBASE IV now provide support for PASCAL's enumerated types through the "M" function character. Both dialects let you specify scientific notation with the PICTURE function "^" (the caret character).

The FoxPro BROWSE: A One-Man Band

There are two types of views of database records in dBASE dialects, the EDIT view and the BROWSE view. The EDIT view, when used without a FORMAT file, shows a field name and a field value on each screen line. Although the field names may not be changed, the field values may be updated.

The EDIT view displays fields from the currently selected record.[4] In contrast, the BROWSE view is tabular, with records as rows and field values as columns. The BROWSE view shows several records on the same screen, but typically only a small subset of the fields in a database may be displayed on any given BROWSE screen.

FoxPro offers some delightful innovations to these fundamental facilities. You can switch back and forth between the EDIT and BROWSE views with a single keystroke! Don't want to choose? Then use the BROWSE/EDIT view!

The BROWSE/EDIT view splits the BROWSE Window vertically. The left part of the window shows the BROWSE view as it did before, but the right part of the BROWSE Window shows an EDIT view of one or more records, depending on the number of rows in the BROWSE Window and the number of fields in the database being used.

Notice that the EDIT/BROWSE view gives us *summary* data in the left part of the window, and *detail* data in the right part of the window. This kind of hat trick seems magical at first, but later seems both routine and indispensable.

---

4. The fields which are displayed can be limited with the "SET FIELDS TO <field list>" command.

Field Control

You can interactively rearrange the order of fields which are displayed in the BROWSE view, or you may engage in a "field picker dialog" in order to point and shoot at the fields which you want to display. This dialog is an alternative to typing a list of field names, as is required in dBASE III PLUS and FoxBASE+.

FoxPro users can also define calculated fields. Say that you have a database with a field called COST and a field called SALES_TAX. You can define a calculated field called TOTAL to show the sum of COST and SALES_TAX. If you change the value of COST or SALES_TAX while you BROWSE, the TOTAL field will immediately reflect the change.

It may take you 5 to 10 minutes to get all of your BROWSE options set up to your satisfaction. Naturally, you don't want to repeat all that work the next time you need that view. When you exit a BROWSE, FoxPro saves the view in FoxUser.DBF, using the ALIAS of the open database as identification for the set of BROWSE options. To BROWSE again with that same view, just choose BROWSE from the menus or enter BROWSE LAST in the Command Window. Alternatively, you can permanently save the view as a named PREFERENCE.

For example, you might save a view as a PREFERENCE called MY_VIEW. To use that view again, you enter BROWSE PREFERENCE MY_VIEW in the Command Window.

Field Protection

The old-style BROWSE view could be dangerous without the NOMODIFY clause,[5] because if you could *see* a field value, then you could *change* that value. For example, when you BROWSE the employee database, you may want to show the employee name onscreen for reference only, yet you may wish to let other fields be edited. Your former BROWSE choice was (1) to show the Name field and risk the possibility of an accidental change, or (2) not to show the Name field. As usual, when the built-in command runs out of power, you write a lot of code that could be avoided with a more powerful command.

In FoxPro, you can exercise extensive BROWSE control at the field level. For *each* selected field, you can specify a maximum displayed width for the field and whether the field can be be updated. When the field is updated, you can force the new value to be validated as with the VALID clause in @ GET, which means that validation can vary from a simple logical expression to a UDF.

If you do not wish to set the maximum display width for each field individually, you can specify a maximum width which is to apply to all selected fields. When you BROWSE, you can disable the option to add records, delete records, edit records, or access the BROWSE command's powerful menu. For further protection, you can also specify the set of database records that you want to BROWSE.

---

5. BROWSE NOMODIFY is not implemented in dBASE III PLUS.

In summary, the FoxPro BROWSE command provides you with many powerful ways to examine and update selected data in your database files while still protecting your data from unwanted changes. One interesting programming option allows you to develop and maintain a complex BROWSE command — which can contain up to 1,024 characters — with the nonprocedural interface and the PREFERENCE facility. Then your program code simply reads "BROWSE <options> PREFERENCE <preference name>", where <options> are restricted to a scope and a list of single keywords such as NOMODIFY and NOAPPEND.

FoxPro/LAN

The network version of FoxPro is called FoxPro/LAN. There are two important differences between FoxPro/LAN and the dBASE IV Administrator, which is the multiple-user dBASE IV. First, although the Administrator is included with dBASE IV and the Administrator and two extra LAN keys are included with the dBASE IV Developer's Edition, FoxPro/LAN is a different product from FoxPro.

Second, you must purchase dBASE IV LAN Packs in order to enable extra users to load multiple-user dBASE IV. In contrast, once FoxPro/LAN is installed on the network, anyone with read permission to the shared directory where it is installed can load it.

At the time of writing, the cost of FoxPro/LAN is $100 more than the cost of a single dBASE III PLUS or dBASE IV LAN Pack, which adds users at a current cost of at least $200 per user. This means that it may be thousands of dollars cheaper to install multiple-user FoxPro than to install multiple-user dBASE III PLUS or dBASE IV. In addition, there is no administrative overhead to manage ACCESS diskettes, to inventory LAN Packs, and to counsel users with access problems.

A Caution on FoxPro/LAN Documentation

At the time of writing, Fox Software distributed FoxPro/LAN with the single-user manual titled *FoxPro Commands and Functions* and a much smaller manual titled *FoxPro FoxPro/LAN*. Be sure to look in the smaller document for information on multiple-user commands.

System Requirements

FoxPro/LAN runs on any NetBIOS-compatible network, including networks costing less than $200 per node, such as LANtastic and The Invisible Network, as well as more expensive, higher-performance networks such as 3Com 3+ Network, Banyan Vines, IBM PC Network, Novell Advanced Netware 1.02 or higher, Novell Netware 286, and Novell Netware 386. Each workstation on the network which will access FoxPro/LAN needs the following:

1. PC/MS-DOS 3.1 or higher.

2. 480K free RAM, after loading DOS and the workstation component of the network operating system, or 440K free RAM with LIM 4.0 EMS memory. (In contrast, single-user FoxPro requires 420K free RAM and multiple-user FoxBASE+ requires 390K free RAM.)

No local hard disks or diskette drives are required. However, Fox Software recommends that each workstation have a hard disk and/or expanded memory which is compatible with the LIM 4.0 standard.

NetBIOS and DOS SHARE Compatibility

Sometimes NetBIOS compatibility will be incorporated into the network operating system so that NetBIOS services are always available. In other cases, the vendor of the network operating system provides a separate NetBIOS module which must be loaded into RAM in order to enable NetBIOS services. If a NetBIOS module is provided separately, then it must be loaded before FoxPro.

FoxPro/LAN will operate either with or without the DOS SHARE command being loaded. You must load SHARE if it is required by your network operating system.

Table 6.9
dBASE IV Multiple-User Features Not Implemented in FoxPro/LAN 1.01

1. Transaction processing and recovery. Version 1.01 does not support BEGIN TRANSACTION, END TRANSACTION, and ROLLBACK.
2. The network-oriented dBASE IV functions ACCESS(), CHANGE(), COMPLETED(), ISMARKED(), LKSYS(), ROLLBACK(), and USER().
3. File encryption. FoxPro supports encryption of program files through the ENCRYPT option of the COMPILE command, but it does not encrypt data files with an equivalent of the dBASE IV SET ENCRYPTION ON facility.
4. Access control features of the dBASE IV PROTECT facility.
5. The LIST USERS and DISPLAY USERS commands.

Compatibility with Multiple-User dBASE IV

Table 6.9 lists dBASE IV features which are not implemented in FoxPro/LAN. *In addition, you must not use dBASE IV and FoxPro/LAN to access the same databases at the same time.*

FoxPro/LAN also offers the following enhancements to the multiple-user dBASE IV standard:

1. **No locking of command files.** FoxPro permits the following: if SHARE is not loaded, then you can suspend a command file which is being executed, execute MODIFY COMMAND on the file, and resume execution. dBASE IV opens the command file in exclusive mode, which means that you

cannot suspend, edit, and resume — you must cancel, edit, and start the application again.

2. **Unique file name generation.** When you need a temporary file in a single-user situation, EraseMe.DBF works fine, but in a multiple-user situation, more than one user may try to use EraseMe.DBF concurrently. The SYS(3) function is guaranteed to deliver a unique filename to help you in such situations.

Commands Supported Differently

Workstation identification is handled differently. The FoxPro SYS(0) function returns the name and number of your workstation on the network. dBASE IV has the USER() function for this purpose.

Chapter 7

Nantucket dBASE Dialects

The Nantucket Corporation offers a dBASE compiler called Clipper for MS-DOS computers and a dBASE compiler called McMax for the Macintosh. Clipper and Quicksilver from WordTech Systems are the leading dBASE compilers. Recall from Chapter 3 that an MS-DOS dBASE compiler produces .OBJ files which are combined by a linker into one .EXE file and zero or more overlay files.[1]

Here is a table listing Nantucket products and prices. Clipper Tools One is a subroutine library for Clipper. The remainder of this chapter is devoted to the Clipper product for MS-DOS.

Table 7.1 Nantucket Products and Prices

Price	Product
$695	Clipper 4.0
$795	Clipper 5.0
$195	Clipper Tools One
$295	McMax

Clipper 4.0 is available in a French-language edition. In September 1990, French, Portuguese, and Spanish editions of Clipper 5.0 were in development.

When to Consider Clipper

In many cases, your employers or clients will have Clipper programs for you to maintain or write, and you won't be able to substitute another dialect. If you anticipate working with dBASE dialects for an extended period of time, it is quite likely that you will work with Clipper at some point, and you may choose to learn Clipper now in order to be prepared later.

You may study Clipper because you are curious, or because you want to see if Clipper extensions give you any ideas about subroutines that you can write for your own dialect, in order to improve its power and your productivity. You may want to use Clipper because you must produce compiled applications which can fit on a 360K disk, and the Fox dialect runtimes take one 360K diskette by themselves.

1. Remember that .FRM and .LBL files are data files and, as such, will not be included in the .EXE file.

Clipper offers special opportunities for developers who wish to produce commercial-quality database applications with unique extensions. Most of the leading subroutine libraries for dBASE dialects are available in the Clipper dialect, and many of these libraries are available *only* for the Clipper dialect.

In addition, multiple-user Clipper applications require only an MS-DOS 3.1 compatible network; NetBIOS is *not* required. Thus, you can test your multiple-user Clipper applications on a single computer running QuarterDeck's multi-tasking environment DESQview.

> **Recommendation on when to consider Clipper.** If you have a professional need to learn Clipper, or a strong personal interest, then I urge you to exploit Clipper for everything that it can give you. *Otherwise, I recommend that you avoid the Clipper dialect in preference to Fox software dialects.*

Consider that dBASE III PLUS (and by implication, the other interpretive dialects) is famous for its long learning curve, which is traditionally called the "dBASE Wall." Even if you are expert in an interpreted dialect like dBASE IV or FoxBASE+, you still face the "Clipper Wall" when you begin to work with Clipper. In addition to dealing with the low level of compatibility and the subtleties of some of the differences between Clipper and other dBASE dialects, you face the multitude of issues involved with linking .OBJ and .LIB files to make .EXE files!

If you are a Clipper developer who uses one or more Clipper libraries, then you must master Clipper and each library you select. Furthermore, there are a number of maintenance pitfalls for applications which rely on subroutine libraries, which we will explore under the heading "Maintenance Pitfalls of Subroutine Libraries" on page 218.

There is no question that Clipper offers some significant advantages over the other dialects. However, as we will see in this chapter, Clipper offers barriers to development which just do not exist in FoxBASE+ and FoxPro. FoxPro 1.0 implements or supports (through other commands) almost all of the programming commands and options of Clipper and goes very far beyond Clipper in many respects.[2] See, for example, the three-part series "FoxPro for Clipperheads" by the renowned dBASE dialect expert Tom Rettig (Rettig 1990a, 1990b, 1990c). And consider the following quote from Expert Panelist and Clipper authority Craig Yellick, under the heading, "Commands and Functions Supported Differently," in *Wonderful Differences: dBASE & Clipper* (Yellick 1990: 25).

> *This is a topic that can never be completely covered. Since the internal workings of dBASE and Clipper are wildly different and come from two separate companies, there are bound to be subtle differences in many commands and functions, even the ones which appear to be identical.*

2. The promised compiler for FoxPro will offer programmers the option of linking .OBJ files produced by other languages.

The Packaging Issue

If users must run your dBASE dialect application from a single 360K diskette, or on systems with less than 360K free RAM, then you will not be able to use a runtime for FoxBASE+ or FoxPro, and using Clipper is one of a small number of your options. However, by now, most business users have either 512K or 640K RAM and hard disks on their PCs. In fact, most database users need hard disks, because their database files are too large to store on floppy diskettes.

This means that dBASE dialect programmers can assume that almost all of their applications will always be run from a hard disk on a PC with at least 512K RAM. In that case, a user types a few keystrokes at the DOS prompt or selects a choice on a DOS-level menu, and the application is executed.

The user cannot tell what happens behind the scenes to produce the main menu, so the only issues for the user are the speed of execution and the size of disk files. Generally speaking, the FoxBASE+ runtime will load and execute a dBASE program in a .FOX file roughly as fast as that same program will execute in a Clipper-prepared .EXE file.[3] However, the size of the .FOX file and the runtime will probably exceed the size of the .EXE file.

Now consider a hard disk with 10 dBASE applications, prepared as either 10 .FOX files or 10 .EXE files made by Clipper. In this case, the combined size of the 10 .FOX files and the FoxBASE+ runtime will be *much* smaller than the combined size of the 10 .EXE files. Clipper developers need a *lot* of disk space if they keep their Clipper-prepared utilities in .EXE form!

Nantucket likes to point out that Clipper costs less than a copy of FoxBASE+ plus the cost of the associated runtime with an unlimited distribution license. At the time of writing, Clipper costs $695;[4] Clipper plus the interactive environment dCLIP from Donnay Software Designs costs $895; single-user FoxBASE+ and its runtime cost $895; multiple-user FoxBASE+ and its runtime cost $1,295; single-user FoxPro and its runtime cost $1,295; and both Ashton-Tate and Fox Software have announced but not delivered .EXE compilers for dBASE IV and FoxPro, respectively.

Table 7.2 summarizes these recommendations.

The Clipper Community

This chapter would be incomplete without a reference to the community of Clipper users. Using Clipper wisely requires a great deal of special knowledge which Clipper programmers seem eager to share with each other. Once you master certain programming techniques and selected libraries, you can develop some very powerful programs very quickly. Clipper users who have learned how to exploit this dialect and its libraries often find this dialect to be compelling.

3. There are some dramatic exceptions: one of my reports, which stores cross-tab results from one database into a second database, runs about four times faster under Clipper 4.0 than under FoxBASE+ 2.0.

4. Clipper 5.0 costs $795.

Table 7.2 When to Consider Learning and/or Using Clipper

1. Clipper use is a nonnegotiable requirement of your employer or client.
2. You want to develop a dBASE application which requires the services of a subroutine library which is available only for the Clipper dialect.
3. The Clipper version of some of your dialect-independent code is significantly faster than that same code executed under another dialect.
4. You want to test multiple-user dBASE applications on one PC.
5. You will be working with dBASE dialects for many years, and you anticipate an employer or client requirement, or a business opportunity.
6. You are curious about Clipper.
7. You have a fast computer with a RAM disk of at least 2 MB, or you have an alternative to linking, such as dCLIP or NoLink (from Next Wave Software).
8. Your computer has a big hard disk with lots of free space, or you have linker alternatives like dCLIP or NoLink.
9. You must distribute ready-to-run dBASE dialect applications on one 360K diskette.
10. Your dBASE dialect applications must execute on PCs with less than 360K free RAM.
11. You want to see how Clipper's extensions and philosophy might be applied to your favorite dialect in order to improve your productivity and increase your fun!
12. You understand the issues involved with compiling to .OBJ files and linking .OBJ files and .LIB files into .EXE files.

For example, the *Database Directory 1990* from *Data Based Advisor* magazine lists about 60 Clipper user groups. That source lists almost no other user groups which are devoted to a specific dBASE dialect. I consider the large number of Clipper groups to be quite extraordinary!

If you do not have a Clipper group in your community, you can still participate in perhaps the most elite Clipper forum of all, the Nantucket Forum on the CompuServe information service. In addition, you can often find Clipper programmers through local BBSs.

Introduction to Clipper

For most of its lifetime, Clipper has offered its users the traditional edit-compile-link-execute cycle as an alternative to the edit-execute development cycle of the Ashton-Tate and Fox Software dialects. Moreover, the Clipper dialect had limited compatibility with the dBASE III PLUS standard, so that it was difficult to write programs which could be tested under an interpreter and then compiled with Clipper once they were debugged.

> *For a long time Nantucket has been trying to compete with C. They think of Clipper as a more productive version of C. They think that's why people like them. They think people like them for themselves, as Clipper, not as a Dbase product. No. If they think they can take programmers away from Dbase, they're mistaken.* (Green 1990)

While Nantucket seems to have no intent to produce a Clipper interpreter, third parties have responded to an obvious market opportunity. The NoLink product from Next Wave Software eliminates the link step from the Clipper development cycle, which becomes edit-compile-execute.

Link times tend to be the bottleneck in the Clipper development cycle. When one links with the Plink86 linker provided with Clipper, compile times are insignificant in comparison with link times. (Linkers from Microsoft and Borland International are faster or much faster than Plink86.)

However, Donnay Software Designs provides dCLIP, an interactive environment for Clipper. dCLIP is even more powerful and convenient than NoLink and removes many of the barriers that Clipper development has presented to first-time users and to users of interpreted dialects.

Remark. Since NoLink and dCLIP are *not* Nantucket products, they cannot be expected to support Clipper as completely as companion products produced by Nantucket. If Nantucket ever produces an equivalent of NoLink or dCLIP at a reasonable price, then, on principle, I would recommend the Nantucket products over third-party products.

System Requirements

The system requirements are the same for computers on which Clipper programs are developed and those upon which they are executed, as follows.

1. PC/MS-DOS 2.0 or greater for single-user applications.
2. PC/MS-DOS 3.1 or greater for multiple-user applications.
3. 256K RAM.
4. A diskette drive.
5. A hard disk.

Clipper applications can use any 8087, 80287, or 80387 math coprocessor which is installed. In practice, you will typically want to develop Clipper applications on an 80386-based PC with a fast hard disk, 640K RAM, and at least 1 MB of extended memory.

Compatibility with dBASE III PLUS

The dBASE III PLUS commands and functions in Table 7.3 are not implemented in Clipper. In many cases, the service offered by the missing command or function can be provided by a Clipper command which is not found in dBASE III PLUS or one of the Clipper utilities. In this section, we will look at what a dBASE III PLUS programmer loses in Clipper, as well as which lost services can be recovered and which cannot be recovered. Subsequently, we'll examine what extra features Clipper offers to users of other dialects.

Table 7.3
dBASE III PLUS Commands and Functions Not Implemented in Clipper 4.0

1. APPEND.
2. APPEND FROM command does not support the .DIF, .SYLK, and .WKS file formats.
3. ASSIST.
4. BROWSE.
5. CHANGE, a synonym for EDIT.
6. CLEAR FIELDS.
7. COPY command does not support the .DIF, .SYLK, and .WKS file formats.
8. QS
9. CREATE. In dBASE III PLUS, this command gives the user a data-entry form on which to enter the structure information for a new database file. In Clipper, this command's syntax is CREATE <filename>, which causes an empty structure extended file to be created.
10. CREATE CATALOG, LABEL, REPORT, QUERY, SCREEN, VIEW.
11. DISPLAY HISTORY, MEMORY, STATUS, STRUCTURE, USERS.
12. EDIT.
13. ERROR().
14. EXPORT.
15. GETENV(). (Clipper uses the spelling GETE().)
16. HELP.
17. IMPORT.
18. INSERT.
19. LIST HISTORY, MEMORY, STATUS, STRUCTURE, USERS.
20. LOGOUT.
21. MESSAGE().
22. MODIFY CATALOG, COMMAND, LABEL, QUERY, REPORT, SCREEN, STRUCTURE, VIEW.
23. ON ERROR, ESCAPE, KEY.
24. RESUME.
25. RETRY.
26. RETURN TO MASTER.
27. SET.
28. SET CARRY, CATALOG.
29. SET COLOR ON/OFF.
30. SET DEBUG, DOHISTORY, ECHO, ENCRYPTION, FIELDS, HEADING, HELP, HISTORY, MEMOWIDTH, MENU, SAFETY, STATUS, STEP, TALK, TITLE, VIEW.

When Clipper provides the equivalent service of one of the missing commands or functions listed in Table 7.3, it does so with a command or function not found in dBASE III PLUS, or with a Clipper utility. Two of the four Clipper utility programs are of interest in this context.

The DBU Utility

The DBU utility included with Clipper implements a portion of the environment of the interpretive dialects. This utility, **whose source code is provided,** gives you the following services.

Table 7.4 Services of the Clipper DBU Utility

1. Creates or modifies a database structure.
2. Creates an index file in Clipper's .NTX format.
3. Opens an existing database file.
4. Opens an existing index file.
5. Sets a filter.
6. Sets a relation between two open databases in the current view.
7. Controls which fields are part of the view.
8. Saves the current environment in a view file with a .VEW extension.
9. Opens a view file.
10. Saves the view file with a .VEW extension.
11. Database services:
    a. Appends records into the currently selected database.
    b. Browses a database.
    c. Copies the current database to another file.
    d. Edits a database record.
    e. Packs the current database.
    f. ZAPs the current database.
12. Move services:
    a. GOTO a specified record.
    b. LOCATE a record by matching an expression of its fields to a given value.
    c. SEEK a record by its key value in the current index file.
    d. SKIP to the next record.
13. RUN a DOS command. (Return to DBU by typing EXIT at the DOS prompt.)

The RL Utility

The RL utility permits you to create and modify .FRM and .LBL files. Clipper will also process the .FRM and .LBL files made by other dialects.

Now that we have seen what the DBU and RL utilities offer, we can see which of the missing dBASE III PLUS commands and functions can be simulated by one of these utilities. *Remember that both of these utilities come with Clipper source code, so you can incorporate them into your Clipper applications if you wish.*

dBASE III PLUS Commands Simulated via DBU or RL

When we examine the list of unimplemented dBASE III PLUS commands and functions, we see that DBU implements, in whole or in part, the APPEND, ASSIST, BROWSE, CHANGE, CLEAR FIELDS, CREATE, CREATE VIEW, DISPLAY STRUCTURE, EDIT, MODIFY STRUCTURE, and MODIFY VIEW commands. The RL utility implements CREATE LABEL, CREATE REPORT, LIST STRUCTURE, MODIFY LABEL, and MODIFY REPORT.

dBASE III PLUS Commands Simulated via a Millican or Straley Routine

See page 333 for a listing of EditCl.PRG, a Millican routine to simulate the EDIT command in Clipper. *Programming in Clipper, Second Edition,* by Steve Straley, a former senior support engineer at Nantucket, lists Clipper code to simulate the following dBASE III PLUS commands (Straley 1988: 837–870).

Table 7.5 Straley Routines to Simulate dBASE III PLUS Commands in Clipper

BROWSE
CREATE STRUCTURE
EDIT
DISPLAY STRUCTURE
RETURN TO MASTER

Debugging Facilities

The dBASE III PLUS debugging commands DISPLAY HISTORY, LIST HISTORY, SET DOHISTORY, SET DEBUG, SET ECHO, and SET HISTORY TO have no direct counterpart in Clipper, which provides a Debug.OBJ module which you can link to your applications to provide a debugging facility accessed via the ALT-D keystroke. When you have paused to enter the debugger, you can examine memory variable values; check database and index status; set and modify "watch" expressions; and so on. The GO command in the debugger is the equivalent of RESUME in dBASE III PLUS, and GO (Single Step) is the equivalent of SET STEP ON in dBASE III PLUS.

Missing dBASE III PLUS Features Handled in Other Ways

Now let's see how some of the dBASE III PLUS commands and functions which are not implemented in Clipper may be handled in other ways.

External Low-Level Routines

dBASE III PLUS supports low-level code in the .BIN format with the LOAD and CALL statements. Clipper supports low-level code in the .OBJ format, so that this code must be linked when the .EXE file is made. Therefore, the LOAD command does not appear. The CALL command is used to invoke the low-level routines in both dialects.

Interpreter-Related Commands

The LOGOUT command terminates the interpreter and is therefore not applicable to a compiled application.

The catalog facility in dBASE III PLUS helps interactive users group related databases, indexes, and so on. It is not relevant to compiled applications. The catalog commands include CREATE CATALOG, MODIFY CATALOG, SET CATALOG, and SET TITLE.

Text File and Memo Editing

Although Clipper does not implement dBASE III PLUS's MODIFY COMMAND, it does have a powerful MemoEdit() function which can be used for full-screen editing of character memvars and fields and memo fields. The MemoRead() and MemoWrit() functions can be used to move text between files and memo fields, so any text file less than 64K may be created and/or edited with these functions. See TextBrow.PRG in Listing 3.5 on page 68 for an example of the power and easy use of these functions.

Missing dBASE III PLUS Features Which Can Be Coded in Clipper

So far we have seen which of the missing dBASE III PLUS commands and functions can be replaced by the DBU and RL utilities and the Clipper debugger. The remaining commands and functions can be duplicated in Clipper source code, in assembly language or C, or not at all. (Assembly language and C routines can be linked to Clipper applications through Clipper's EXTEND system.)

The following commands can be implemented in a more or less straightforward way in Clipper source code: CREATE QUERY, HELP, INSERT, MODIFY QUERY, SET CARRY, SET COLOR ON/OFF, SET HEADING, SET HELP, SET MEMOWIDTH, and SET MENU. Several other commands can be implemented in theory, although in practice the labor may be prohibitive: CREATE SCREEN, ERROR(), EXPORT, IMPORT, MESSAGE(), MODIFY SCREEN, RETRY, SET ENCRYPTION, SET SAFETY, SET STATUS, and SET TALK.

These missing dBASE III PLUS commands can only be *fully* implemented with low-level code accessed via the CALL command, if they can be implemented at all: DISPLAY STATUS, DISPLAY USERS, LIST STATUS, LIST USERS, ON ERROR, ON ESCAPE, and ON KEY.

Note that many missing commands are provided by Nantucket's Clipper Tools One subroutine library or by third-party products. Some third-party products are available without charge on BBSs.

Other Differences in Common Features

Here are some of the differences between the features that Clipper and dBASE III PLUS have in common.

Macros

dBASE dialects implement self-modifying code through the macro facility: a character memvar is treated as code if it is preceded by an ampersand and placed in the source code where code is expected. Interpreters such as dBASE III PLUS generally permit all of a command or any portion of it to be contained in a macro. Clipper permits macros to represent data or the individual components of a command, but not an entire command.

Macro Termination

dBASE III PLUS only requires a period to terminate a macro reference when the macro reference is not followed by an end-of-line or punctuation character, except the period. For example,

```
?  "Thank you, &Name, for using the HAL 9000."
?  "Is &Name your first name?"
?  "Hello, &Name..  You can call me HAL."
?  "I think of you as &Name.1."
```

If Name = "Dave", these statements produce the same text as these statements:

```
?  "Thank you, Dave, for using the HAL 9000."
?  "Is Dave your first name?"
?  "Hello, Dave.  You can call me HAL."
?  "I think of you as Dave1."
```

In Clipper, you are advised to code the macro references as follows, so that the macro reference always terminates with a period.

```
?  "Thank you, &Name., for using the HAL 9000."
?  "Is &Name. your first name?"
?  "Hello, &Name..  You can call me HAL."
?  "I think of you as &Name.1."
```

PROCEDURE Files

Procedure files have a different significance in interpreted and compiled dialects. In dBASE III PLUS, the SET PROCEDURE statement selects different subroutine libraries to be used — one at a time — at execution time, but Clipper treats the SET

PROCEDURE command as a compiler "include" directive. *All* referenced PROCEDURE files become part of the application. See the discussion starting on page 54 for more information.

FORMAT Files

FORMAT files are not supported in the same way as in dBASE III PLUS. First, they must have a .PRG extension, not the .FMT extension used by the other dialects. Second, you cannot invoke full-screen editing (based on a FORMAT file) with the currently selected database record by using the EDIT command, which is not found in Clipper — you must use the READ command. Third, Clipper FORMAT files cannot have a READ statement, so you cannot implement multiple-page data-entry screens except by a laborious alternative. See the *Data Based Advisor* article "SuperFMT: A Better Format File" (Bauman 1989a).

Keystroke Processing

The SET KEY TO Clipper command replaces *some* of the capabilities of SET ESCAPE, ON KEY, and ON ESCAPE. The biggest difference is that Clipper only acts on keystrokes defined in SET KEY TO when your application is in a situation that Nantucket labels a "wait state." The following commands create wait states: ACCEPT, INPUT, MENU TO, READ, and WAIT.

Clipper Enhancements

Clipper offers many significant enhancements to the dBASE III PLUS standard and, at the time of writing, some features not found in any other major dialect, such as the ability to include any command in a user-defined function. Let's look at some of the enhancements.

Procedure and Data Structure Enhancements

Here are some enhancements to the procedure and data structures used by dBASE III PLUS.

User-Defined Functions

dBASE III PLUS does not support UDFs, and most dialects which do support UDFs place a number of restrictions on the definition and use of these functions. Clipper permits you to reference a UDF anywhere a built-in function may be referenced, and Clipper UDFs can include any Clipper command.

Remark on UDF limitations. At the time of writing, Clipper and dBXL/Quicksilver are the only major dBASE dialects which permit you to reference a user-defined function anywhere a built-in function may be referenced.

Database, Field, and Memvar Extensions

Clipper databases can have up to 1,024 fields, in comparison to the 128 fields of dBASE III PLUS. Clipper character fields can be up to 32K in length, and memo fields can contain up to 64K characters. In dBASE III PLUS, character memvars are limited to 254 bytes in length, but Clipper implements character memvars of up to 64K bytes in length. Unlike dBASE III PLUS, Clipper permits CHR(0) characters in character and memo data.

Clipper 4.0 supports unity-indexed arrays with one subscript. Arrays can have up to 4,096 elements, and an array element can be up to 64K in size. Clipper 5.0 supports two-dimensional arrays which can contain array elements.

File-Handling Extensions

Under dBASE III PLUS you are limited to a maximum of 15 open files, whereas Clipper permits up to 255 open files under DOS 3.3 or later.[5] dBASE III PLUS limits you to 10 open database files, but under DOS 3.3, Clipper permits up to 255 databases to be open in up to 255 work areas!

In contrast to the dBASE III PLUS limit of 7 open indexes per database, Clipper permits up to 15 open indexes per database. Although Clipper can use the .NDX files of dBASE III PLUS if you link in the NDX.OBJ module provided, its native .NTX index files are faster and smaller.

Like FoxBASE+ 2.1, Clipper implements the ADDITIVE clause for the SET RELATION command. You may establish up to eight relations for a database under Clipper.

Expanded Memory Variable Capacities

dBASE III PLUS permits a maximum of 256 memory variables to be defined at one time, although the amount of memory allocated to the variables may be set in the configuration file, Config.DB, at 1K to 31K, with the default being 6K. Clipper permits up to 2,048 memvars to be defined at once.

The "V" component of a DOS environment variable named CLIPPER controls the amount of memory that Clipper allocates to memvars. This environment variable replaces the configuration file facility of dBASE III PLUS but is able to specify only six parameters.

Expanded Character Memvar and Memo Field Capabilities

Clipper provides a powerful set of commands and functions to process text in memvars and memo fields. You can copy character memvars into memos with the syntax REPLACE <memo> WITH <memvar>. Memo data can be copied to a

5. Patches are available for earlier versions of DOS which permit these earlier versions to open up to 255 files. Check your freeware and shareware BBSs.

memvar by assignment: <memvar> = <memo>, after which all the usual string functions such as AT(), STUFF(), and SUBSTR() may be applied! Memo data may be retrieved for reports on a line-by-line basis, with words wrapping at the line length which you set. Before you start retrieving lines of a given maximum length, you can determine how many such lines can be retrieved.

An Iterative Loop Construct

Clipper offers a standard iterative loop construct, FOR/NEXT, as a replacement for DO WHILE for loops that iterate on a numeric counter. See page 49 for the syntax.

Light Bar Menus and Pick Lists

Clipper implements light bar menus with @ PROMPT and MENU TO, and unboxed pick lists for arrays are implemented with the ACHOICE() function (Array CHOICES). Boxes are drawn with the @ TO command. In dBASE III PLUS, you can implement a simple pick list with BROWSE, but Clipper gives you the DBEDIT() function for browsing databases.

RETURN from a Block of Code

In some interpretations of structured programming for dBASE, the RETURN statement is only used in functions, and there, only as the last statement; command files and procedures have a RETURN statement, if one is desired or required, only as their last statement. However, coding a RETURN statement in the middle of a routine *may* be preferable to making its logic much more complex with the introduction of one or more logical memvars or other coding changes.

The RETURN statement allows you to escape from a block of code which is implemented as a subroutine. In Clipper, the BREAK command permits you to escape from a block of code which is preceded with a BEGIN SEQUENCE statement and followed by an END statement. When BREAK is executed, control passes to the statement following END, if any. If the END statement is the last statement in the main routine, then BREAK is equivalent to QUIT, assuming that the application has not made a recursive call to the main routine.

> **Remark.** Some Clipper programmers try to simulate RETURN TO MASTER with a call to the main routine. For example, in an application whose top-level routine is Main.PRG, they will have DO MAIN statements.
>
> **Recommendation on simulating RETURN TO MAIN with DO <procedure>.** Recursion consists of calling a routine which has already been called, from which return has not yet been made. Examples are DO TREE in TREE.PRG or DO MAIN anywhere in an application whose top-level routine is MAIN.PRG. *I strongly recommend that you do not simulate RETURN TO MASTER with recursion.* Use recursion only for recursive algorithms (which are wonderful for processing tree-structured data).

Syntactical and Semantic Enhancements

Here are some Clipper enhancements to dBASE III PLUS syntax and semantics.

Parameter-Passing Enhancements

Most programming languages require you to pass arguments which are identical in type and number to their corresponding parameters. dBASE dialects do not have this restriction on type, since there is no way to specify a type (Character, Date, etc.) for identifiers in PARAMETERS statements; however, most dialects require the same number of arguments and parameters.

Clipper permits you to pass 0 to N arguments to a routine with N parameters.[6] You can test for the number and type of arguments with the PCOUNT() and TYPE() functions.

When arguments are *passed by reference,* any changes to the corresponding parameter are reflected in the argument after the routine returns to its caller. When arguments are *passed by value,* changes are not reflected in the argument. Arguments in the list following the WITH keyword are always passed by reference.

Arguments to functions are passed by value, with two exceptions. Arrays are always passed by reference, as are arguments preceded with "@". Note that array elements can only be passed by value. For example, if X is an array, then it is passed by reference in YOUR_UDF(X), but the element X[1] is passed by value in MY_UDF(X[1]). The form MY_UDF(@X[1]) is not allowed.

EXTERNAL Routines

Say that you have written an accounting application whose receipts and disbursements facilities are so similar that in many cases you have the same code handle both receipts and disbursements with a macro. You define a memvar AcctType as either "Receipts" or "Disburs" and your dual-purpose code has references to &AcctType, as in "DO &AcctType.".

Clipper and the linker do not know that your application will call either the Receipts or the Disburs subroutines with the "DO &AcctType." statement. To ensure that these routines are included in the .EXE file, you may compile and link them separately or simply include the statement "EXTERNAL Receipts,Disburs" in your code.

6. Contrast this to FoxPro, which requires you to pass 1 to N arguments.

Chapter 8

WordTech Systems dBASE Dialects

Nantucket does not have an interpreter for the Clipper dialect and seems to have no interest in producing one. Although Ashton-Tate and Fox Software announced .EXE compilers in the 1980s, neither company has delivered an .EXE compiler at the time of writing.

In contrast, WordTech has offered the dBXL interpreter and the Quicksilver compiler for years.[1] The WordTech dialects also have some interesting extensions over the other dialects, including built-in graphics!

Here is a table listing WordTech products and prices.

Table 8.1 WordTech Products and Prices

Price	Product
$249	dBXL 1.3R (shipped 8/17/90)
$599	dBXL/LAN 1.3R (shipped 8/17/90)
	dBXL/Kanji (for LIFELAN, NEXOS)
$259	Networker Plus
$599	Quicksilver 1.3R (shipped 8/17/90)
$ 79	Quicksilver 1.3 MS-DOS Libraries
	Quicksilver/Kanji (for LIFELAN, NEXOS)
$795	Quicksilver/SQL
$995	Quicksilver/UNIX (for SCO XENIX 386, ISC 386/ix)
$199	WorkFast

Unless otherwise indicated, the above products are for the IBM PC-DOS or MS-DOS operating systems. The Japanese versions of dBXL and Quicksilver use the 2-byte Kanji character set and execute under the LIFELAN and NEXOS operating systems. The OEM for these versions is the Japanese computer company Kobe.

The software and documentation of dBXL is available in Danish, Dutch, English, French, German, Italian, Japanese, Norwegian, Spanish and Swedish. The Quicksilver software is available in the above languages, but the documentation is only available in English.

Versions 1.3 of dBXL, dBXL/LAN, and Quicksilver were released on or about March 15, 1989, and versions 1.3R began shipping on August 17, 1990. The 1.3R versions include R&R Relational Report Writer from Concentric Data Systems; Quicksilver 1.3R also includes the R&R Code Generator. WordTech has announced

1. The compiler was once called dBCOMPILER.

the dBASE IV-compatible Arago updates to dBXL and Quicksilver and expects to ship them in late 1990.

Networker Plus and dBXL/LAN are network products whose network requirements will be discussed in the section below dealing with dBXL/LAN. WorkFast is a diskette which contains several documents and utilities to assist your development of dBXL and Quicksilver programs. Document files tell you the most frequently asked technical questions about Quicksilver and how to program a user-defined function (UDF) in C. Utilities include bar-cursor menus, keyboard status detectors, trigonometric routines, and simulators for BROWSE, EDIT, and APPEND.

dBXL/SQL is a family of dBXL implementations which act as front ends for various SQL database servers. WordTech sells implementations to support Novell Netware SQL, IBM OS/2 EE, Ashton-Tate/Microsoft SQLserver, and Gupta SQL-Base; Oracle Corporation sells a version for Oracle RDBMS.

Single-User dBXL

dBXL 1.3 is a replacement for dBASE III PLUS. According to WordTech, dBASE III PLUS programs should execute under dBXL with little or no change.

System Requirements

Here are the system requirements for dBXL 1.3:

1. PC/MS-DOS 2.1 or higher.
2. 430K free RAM.
3. One of the following: (1) two diskette drives, or (2) access to a network drive on which single-user dBXL 1.3 is installed.

dBXL can use up to 64K of EMS memory. Use of EMS memory can reduce the RAM needed in the lower 640K by up to 64K. (Contrast dBXL to FoxPro, which can use all available EMS memory.)

Compatibility with dBASE III PLUS

Although dBXL 1.3 is a variant of the dBASE III PLUS dialect, and not the current-generation dBASE IV/FoxPro dialect, the design of dBXL was sufficiently innovative to influence dBASE IV and FoxPro. For example, dBXL offers a RUN command that can store on disk an image of most of the RAM used by dBXL to let you execute DOS programs almost as large as those you can run from the DOS prompt (SET SWAPPING ON). Now let's look at missing features, features that are handled differently, and enhancements; the following table shows dBASE III PLUS features not in dBXL 1.3.

Table 8.2 dBASE III PLUS Commands Not Implemented in dBXL 1.3

1. CATALOG commands (CREATE/MODIFY/SET CATALOG, SET TITLE).
2. CREATE/MODIFY/SET SCREEN.
3. CREATE/MODIFY/SET VIEW.
4. EXPORT to the PFS file formats.
5. IMPORT from the PFS file formats.
6. SET HELP/MENU/TITLE.

Note in particular that dBXL *does* implement all of the TYPE options of the dBASE III PLUS APPEND FROM and COPY TO commands to handle the DIF, SYLK, and .WKS file formats. Here are some known differences between dBASE III PLUS and dBXL.

Table 8.3 Behavior Differences between dBASE III PLUS and dBXL 1.3

1. **Configuration files.** dBXL uses a configuration file called Config.XL if it finds it. If not, dBXL uses default values for configuration parameters.
2. **The Fix option.** dBXL adds the choice "Fix" to the list "Cancel, Ignore, Suspend?" which greets the user of an application which encounters a problem that generates an error message. When you choose the Fix option, the command file which caused the error is edited with the built-in editor and the cursor is positioned to the problematic code in the source file.
3. **Views.** Although CREATE VIEW and MODIFY VIEW are not implemented, they are supported through the commands "CREATE VIEW <view file> FROM ENVIRONMENT" and "SET VIEW TO <view file>".

dBXL Enhancements

dBXL offers a number of extensions to the dBASE III PLUS standard. Some of these extensions are not found in *any* other major dialect, such as dBXL's graphics facilities, which are covered separately in the next subsection.

1. **Configuring the dBXL prompt.** dBXL offers a prompt facility equivalent to the one in MS-DOS. In particular, the DOS prompt "pg", which is so commonly used to show the currently selected drive and directory, can be used as the dBXL prompt. In addition to standard MS-DOS prompt characters like $d for date and $t for time, dBXL offers $a to show the ALIAS of the currently selected database, $i to show the filename of the master index, $w to show the active work area, and $v to show the dBXL version number. This facility, accessed dynamically with the SET PROMPT TO command, instead of statically in the configuration file, is a dramatic improvement over the prompt facility in all other major dialects. The dBXL prompt can

be defined to keep you constantly informed of the current DOS directory, which is absolutely essential information.[2]

2. **EMS memory support.** Up to 64K of LIM EMS memory will be used, if available. Using EMS memory reduces the free RAM dBXL needs in the lower 640K.
3. **More open files.** While dBASE III PLUS limits you to only 16 open files, dBXL permits a maximum of the number of files in the FILES statement in CONFIG.SYS minus 9. For example, if you specify FILES=50, then you can open up to 41 files in dBXL, subject to the following limitations on each file type: 10 database files, 7 index files per database, 1 FORMAT file per database, 1 query file per database, 1 procedure file, 1 function file, 1 alternate file, and *25 program files*. Unlike dBASE III PLUS programmers, dBXL programmers never have to worry about whether they will exceed the open file limit if they write a subroutine to help shorten a command file.
4. **More fields.** dBXL increases the dBASE III PLUS limit of 128 fields per database to 512 fields per database.
5. **Memvar arrays.** dBXL arrays may be defined with either the DECLARE or the DIMENSION keywords, which support coding for multiple dialects. Although these unity-indexed arrays are rather limited in size at a maximum of 254 elements, any number of subscripts which is compatible with the limit of 254 elements is supported. The REPLACE MEMO and STORE MEMO commands permit you to move line-oriented text between memo fields and one-dimensional arrays. You may initialize an entire array with the syntax "STORE <expression> to <array name>" or "<array name> = <expression>".
6. **Descending character-key indexes via DESCEND().** When you index on a character key, as in "INDEX ON <character expression> TO <file>", the keys in the index file will be in ascending order: first keys starting with A, then B, C, and so on. To get *descending* order, as in Z, Y, ..., A, use "INDEX ON DESCEND(<character expression>) TO <file>". To use this trick with numeric and date data, use the DtoS() and STR() functions to convert the data to character format, as in "INDEX ON DESCEND(STR(Category,3) + DtoS(BirthDate)) TO <file>". (DESCEND() is also available in Clipper.)
7. **User-defined functions.** dBXL implements UDFs through a mechanism similar to the PROCEDURE facility. Up to 32 user-defined functions may be grouped into a .PRG file called a UDF file; to make the UDFs in a particular UDF file available to your application, code "SET UDF TO <UDF file name>". Inside the UDF file, use the command "FUNCTION <UDF name>" to start each function definition, and follow the RETURN keyword with the function value to return. Arguments to UDFs are passed by value, in contrast to arguments to procedures and command files, which are

2. The provision of this DOS-equivalent but unique-to-dBASE-dialects prompt feature reflects a design principle of courtesy. You don't have to be Einstein to incorporate courtesy into your designs, and it can really mean a lot to the user.

passed by reference. *UDFs may include any dBXL command and may appear anywhere that a built-in function may appear!*

8. **Validation during READ.** The VALID clause appears, which is universally considered to be crucial by contemporary dBASE dialect standards. This clause, when added to an @ GET statement, permits you to require the user to enter data which is valid by your definition, before the user can leave the @ GET. A logical expression or a user-defined function may be used for the validation.
9. **Read-only browsing.** The BROWSE command is incredibly powerful in its ability to let you see potentially any field data in any record, depending on what options are used. However, the dBASE III PLUS BROWSE command also permits you to change any data that you can see, which eliminates BROWSE from use as a read-only tool — in that dialect. dBXL implements the NOMODIFY clause to make BROWSE read-only by your option!
10. **Extra configuration options.** Here is a list of dBXL configuration facilities which are not available in dBASE III PLUS:
    a. **Clear.** Sets the dBXL prompt to appear at either the top or the bottom of the screen after a CLEAR command.
    b. **Comment.** Sets whether dBXL code following "*\" or "&&\" is executed.
    c. **Goodbye.** Sets whether the dBXL signoff message appears when you QUIT.
    d. **GraphPrint.** Sets the printer for graphics output to Epson FX, IBM, Okidata, or HP LaserJet and controls other aspects of printing graphics.
    e. **Logo.** Sets whether the dBXL logo is to appear when you execute dBXL.
    f. **WildCards.** Sets whether a program can use file-matching patterns containing "*" and "?" where otherwise there would be a reference to a specific file.
    g. **xVars.** Sets whether the dBXL environmental variables will be created when dBXL starts.
11. **dBXL environmental variables.** These memory variables belong to a special class of PUBLIC memvars which have "X" as the first character of their names; they are different from DOS environment variables, whose values can be retrieved with GETENV(). If the line "XVARS = ON" appears in Config.XL, then dBXL creates from 4 to 34 dBXL environmental variables, as follows:
    a. **xCurrDir.** The directory from which you started dBXL, in the format <drive>:\<directory>\ ... \<directory>\.
    b. **xDrive.** The first character of xCurrDir.
    c. **xArg00.** The first argument following "dBXL" on the DOS command line, if any. For example, xArg00 = "Receipts" if you entered "dBXL Receipts" at the DOS prompt. Command line arguments are separated by blanks.

d. **xArgC.** The number of tokens following dBXL on the DOS command line. If you entered "dBXL Receipts" at the DOS prompt, then xArgC = 1.

e. **xArg<n>.** The memvars xArg01, xArg02, ..., xArg30, which hold up to 30 additional command line arguments, as needed.

12. **Environment identification.** If the line "XVARS = ON" appears in Config.XL, then you can detect whether your code runs under dBXL with the following template:

```
IF (TYPE("xDrive") =  "C")
   <statements for only dBXL>
ELSE
   <statements for dialects other than dBXL>
ENDIF
```

13. **Hiding dBXL code in comments.** dBXL gives you an interesting alternative to the preceding template when you only need to isolate dBXL-specific code. When the line "COMMENT = ON" appears in Config.XL, then code following "*\" or "&&\", which would otherwise be treated as a comment, is executed instead!

14. **AutoMem variables.** The CLEAR AUTOMEM command, or USE with the AUTOMEM option, permits you to create a set of memvars which have the same names as the fields in the currently selected database. APPEND AUTOMEM appends a blank record and copies the values of the AUTOMEM memvars into the fields of the same names. REPLACE AUTOMEM copies the values of the AUTOMEM memvars into the fields of the same names in the current record, and both CLEAR AUTOMEM and STORE AUTOMEM copy the non-memo field values into the AUTOMEM memvars of the same names.

15. **Memo handling.** When memo data consists of line-oriented text, you can use STORE MEMO <memo name> TO ARRAY <array name> to transfer up to 254 lines to array elements; the inverse command is REPLACE MEMO <memo name> WITH ARRAY <array name>.

16. **Window support.** Using dBXL windows involves a four-step process. You first define the window with WSET WINDOW, which means that you name it and specify its size, location, border, and colors. You then select the window with WSELECT, analogous to selecting an open database in a work area. When you activate the window with WUSE, subsequent commands that write to the screen show text in the window, until you close the window with WCLOSE. You can define up to 99 windows and manipulate them with the 16 windowing commands WABANDON, WCLOSE, WCOPY, WDISPLAY, WDISPLAY STATUS, WMOVE, WRELEASE, WRESTORE, WSAVE, WSELECT, WSET FRAME, WSET SIZE, WSET TITLE, WSET WINDOW, WSET WINFILE, and WUSE.[3]

3. Expert Panelist Monique Verrier comments, "True windows. The implementation is great!"

17. **The help facility.** The SET HELP ON/OFF command is replaced by the far more capable SET USERHELP ON/OFF and SET USERHELP TO commands. These commands permit you to construct customized help information, disable the F1 "help" key if needed, and show help information in a dBXL window.
18. **Trapping errors and processing events.** In addition to the ON ERROR, ON ESCAPE, and ON KEY commands implemented in dBASE III PLUS, dBXL offers ON EVENT, SET EVENT, and SET KEY TO. The difference between SET KEY and ON KEY is that SET KEY will detect a keystroke at all times, but ON KEY will not detect a keystroke during a "waiting" command, such as READ, WAIT, or ACCEPT. ON EVENT is a very general event-processing facility used with the command SET EVENT TO <logical expression>. When the logical expression becomes true, the event occurs, and the command defined by ON EVENT <command> is executed.
19. **Keyboard control.** You can clear the type-ahead buffer with CLEAR TYPEAHEAD and you can store characters into this buffer with KEYBOARD <expression>. You can retrieve the next character in the buffer with InKey().
20. **CD at the dBXL prompt.** In the other major dialects, you gain access to a DOS command like CD with the run command: RUN CD. dBXL has the courtesy to implement the CD DOS command as a dBXL command.[4] You can use CD without an argument to show the current DOS directory.
21. **Disk buffering control.** The FLUSH command permits you to write all buffered disk data to the disk. After data is changed programmatically or through full-screen editing, it is buffered and is not necessarily written to disk until a later time. Because buffered data is held in the volatile memory of a computer, a power failure or a number of other conditions will prevent the data from ever moving from transient buffer storage to permanent disk storage.

    Remark. WordTech commits one of the cardinal sins of software design by tying two distinct services to a single command: the second service of FLUSH is writing all buffers associated with databases other than the currently selected database to disk, *after which those other buffers are released*. When you select the other databases, the buffers are allocated again, and the record and index data is loaded from disk — again.

22. **Multiple related children.** This version of dBXL implements the ADDITIVE keyword for the SET RELATION command. The new keyword lets you relate one database to more than one other database. This facility can significantly reduce programming effort when multiple databases are related with one-to-one or many-to-one relationships, but is of little or no help when the relationships are one-to-many. (See the SET SKIP command of dBASE IV.)

---

4. In my view, courtesy is an essential principle in design. In this context, it would be most courteous to have *all* of the most common DOS commands available with DOS syntax at the interpreter prompt.

23. **Prompted pick lists of files.** In many cases, you can code a "?" where a file name would normally appear. dBXL will present a boxed moving-bar pick list of files from which you choose.
24. **Systems programming support.** The DOSINT command calls the specified DOS interrupt routine and passes register data back and forth between dBXL memvars. WordTech gives you CheckCom.BIN and GetCom.BIN, which you may use with the syntax SET EVENT TO FILE <CheckCom | GetCom> to implement modem communications.[5] The "OUT <byte>, <port>" command sends the given data byte to the specified output port; its counterpart is IN(<port>), which receives a data byte on the specified input port. Built-in functions HtoI() and ItoH() implement hexadecimal-decimal conversions, and BITSET() lets you examine individual bits in data.
25. **Editor extensions.** The dBXL built-in editor, accessed via MODIFY COMMAND, is a fairly general-purpose text editor which permits you to control wordwrap, onscreen margins, and page breaks. Special commands for programmers include ALT-E, which executes the current line (what a great way to check syntax!), and ALT-R, which restores the current line to the status it had before you edited it.

dBXL Graphics Features

No other major dialect offers built-in graphics capability. Without this capability, you must use a separate graphics package when you produce onscreen and printed graphics at the pixel level. (As an alternative, you may sometimes be able to use character graphics to display very simple data.)

dBXL offers a reasonable selection of six graph types: pie, step, line, bar, scatter, and linear-regression. Unfortunately, each of these six graph types is limited to 40 data points. This is large enough for typical uses of pie, step, line, and bar graphs, but may be moderately limiting for linear-regression graphs. It may be extremely limiting for scatter graphs.

With syntax analogous to the syntax which handles report and label forms, dBXL offers CREATE GRAPH, MODIFY GRAPH, and GRAPH FORM. Graph files have a .GRF extension. Since the data sets which are graphed are so small, the .GRF file holds the most recently used data for the graph as well as the graph format.

GRAPH FORM permits you to write a graph to a file in the popular .IMG and .PCX formats, which are widely supported. .IMG files are used in the GEM operating environment, which is home for the industry-standard desktop publishing program, Ventura Publisher;[6] .PCX files are used by PC Paintbrush from Zsoft and PageMaker from Aldus.

RESTORE GRAPH will display graphics images in the .IMG and .PCX formats, in addition to the "native" .BIT format of dBXL. Since the only work done by this command is to display an already prepared image, execution is rapid.

5. A WordTech representative commented: "These are intended as sample programs. We have yet to see anyone use them to implement modem communications."
6. A Windows version was released in September 1990.

There is support for Epson FX, IBM, Okidata, or HP LaserJet printers through the "SET GRAPHPRINT TO <option>" command. You may set the default destination for graphics output with the GraphPrint parameter in the configuration file. SET GRAPHPRINT also permits you to control the size, orientation, and page position of the printed graph.

The Quicksilver Compiler and Single-User Programming

The Quicksilver compiler, a companion product to dBXL, is designed to produce .EXE forms of dBXL programs which will run under DOS without dBXL. Single-user Quicksilver applications require only DOS, unlike multiple-user Quicksilver applications, which sometimes require the Networker Plus product, as explained in the next section, "The Quicksilver Compiler and Multiple-User Programming."

System Requirements

Here are the system requirements for Quicksilver 1.3 on the development PC:

1. PC/MS-DOS 3.1 or higher.
2. 300K free RAM.
3. One of the following: (1) one diskette drive and one hard drive, or (2) access to a network drive on which Quicksilver is installed.

Here are the system requirements for Quicksilver 1.3 on the user's PC:

1. PC/MS-DOS 3.1 or higher for multiple-user applications.
2. PC/MS-DOS 2.0 or higher for single-user applications.
3. A screen which is 100% IBM PC compatible, or which is driven by the MS-DOS ANSI.SYS screen driver.
4. 315K free RAM, or more, depending on .EXE size.
5. One of the following: (1) one diskette drive (in practice, a hard drive is also required), or (2) access to a network drive on which a Quicksilver application is installed.

Operation Summary

Program preparation is more complex under Quicksilver than under Clipper. Program files are tokenized with DB3C.EXE, which WordTech calls a "compiler." Source files whose file names are of the form "<filename>.PRG" are tokenized into files whose file names are of the form "@<filename>.PRG" or "#<filename>.PRG", depending on whether the debugger will be used with the tokenized files.

Remark. This dreadful convention goes completely against the canonical philosophy espoused in this book and causes a number of problems. First, when filenames are eight characters long, either the first or last character of the filename is discarded to make room for the at-sign, according to a command line argument for DB3C.EXE. This means that AcctMenu.PRG is tokenized to either @AcctMen.PRG or @cctMenu.PRG. The canonical appproach is to change the extension and preserve the filename, as in dBASE IV, where AcctMenu.PRG is tokenized into AcctMenu.DBO.

Programmers don't like the at-sign cluttering up their filenames, and so @cctMenu.PRG tends to get renamed to AcctMenu.PRG, which must be stored in a different directory from the *source* file, AcctMenu.PRG. This strategy increases the amount of time a programmer spends on file and directory management. Also, the filename no longer tells you if AcctMenu.PRG is a source file or a tokenized file.

Recommendation on filenames for Quicksilver top-level routines. Use filenames for Quicksilver top-level routines which are one to seven characters in length. In that case, <filename>.PRG is the source code form and @<filename>.PRG is the translated form.

The utility DB3L.EXE, called a "linker" by WordTech, combines one or more tokenized files with code providing a runtime environment for Quicksilver and produces three files with the same filename and extensions of .EXE, .OVL, and .DBC. The runtime environment is implemented in the .EXE and .OVL files, which are fixed in size at about 130K. The .DBC file, which holds all of the tokenized code of the application, may be as large as 32 MB, according to WordTech.

Example. DB3L.EXE would process @AcctMen.PRG to produce AcctMen.EXE, AcctMen.OVL, and AcctMen.DBC. AcctMen.DBC contains all of the tokenized code from AcctMenu.PRG. The tokenized form is executed by entering AcctMen at the DOS prompt in the directory where AcctMen.EXE is stored.

If the application is being debugged with the debugger, then you work with the .DBC form during testing. If the application is sufficiently rapid, you may leave it in this form.

Otherwise, an additional step, performed with the QS.EXE utility, is used to convert the .DBC file to one or more .OBJ files, which are then linked to Quicksilver libraries with standard linkers like Microsoft's LINK.EXE, which is included with MS-DOS, or PLINK86plus.[7] For example, AcctMen.DBC may be translated into AcctMen.OBJ, AcctM00.OBJ, and AcctM01.OBJ.

In most cases, the final result of linking the .OBJ files (holding your code in .OBJ form) and .LIB files (holding the Quicksilver runtime environment) is a single .EXE file. Of course, if your linker supports overlays, then it may produce an .EXE file and one or more overlay files.

For example, if AcctMen.OBJ, AcctM00.OBJ, and AcctM01.OBJ were linked with the appropriate .LIB file or files without overlays, the linker would create only the AcctMenu.EXE file. If one overlay file were specified, then the linker might create both AcctMenu.EXE and an overlay file called AcctMenu.OVL.

7. Formerly from Sage, now being marketed by POLYTRON.

Automatic versus Manual Memory Management

The 32 MB limit on the size of .DBC files suggests that you could build Quicksilver applications of virtually arbitrary size, but you are still subject to the limitations on the number of open files, the number of memory variables, and so on. It is more relevant to note that using the .DBC form gives you the option of letting Quicksilver handle memory management problems which would require the manual construction of overlays if you were to use the .OBJ form.

Assume that you start with a small Quicksilver application to which you gradually add more and more code, and that you have R kilobytes of RAM in each computer on which the application executes, where R is between 256 and 640. Initially, you can execute either the .DBC form or the .OBJ form linked into an .EXE file without overlays. When the application grows beyond a certain size, your options become to use the .DBC form or to design overlays for an .EXE file.

Compatibility with dBXL

Quicksilver is a companion product to dBXL and not a stand-alone compiler like Clipper, whose vendor offers no interpretive environment for the Clipper dialect. Therefore, while we compared Clipper to dBASE III PLUS, we will compare Quicksilver to dBXL.

An additional consideration is that Quicksilver is also a companion product to the multiple-user dBXL/LAN. There is only one version of Quicksilver, which supports both single-user and multiple-user applications.

The ideal situation would be for Quicksilver to compile all dBXL programs without modification of source code to produce applications whose behavior is identical under both dBXL and Quicksilver, except for faster speed under Quicksilver. This ideal situation is not quite achieved with versions 1.3 of dBXL and Quicksilver, so let's look at the differences. (Also see "Between Friends" (Feldheim 1990) for a discussion of seven differences between dBXL and Quicksilver.)

There are four commands and one function which Quicksilver offers in addition to those found in dBXL, as shown in Table 8.4. Quicksilver also includes several utilities, which are shown in Table 8.5.

Unlike Clipper, Quicksilver does not include a utility to create and maintain .FRM (report form) and .LBL (label form) files. However, unlike Clipper, Quicksilver's vendor offers an interpretive environment for its compiler, namely, dBXL. The (reasonable) assumption seems to be that everyone who has Quicksilver also has either dBXL or dBASE III PLUS.

In fact, the Quicksilver manual says that you may create label and report "files in advance, using dBASE III Plus." Of course, dBXL can also create .FRM and .LBL files.

Note that Quicksilver 1.3R includes R&R Relational Report Writer *plus* the R&R Code Generator to generate report code. The latter product enables you to avoid report and label forms.

Table 8.4 Quicksilver Extensions to dBXL 1.3

1. **CCALL.** This command is used to call external routines written in C or assembly language. Notice that the dBXL CALL command requires the .BIN file format, but routines called with CCALL are prepared in .OBJ format and linked into the .EXE file.
2. **CREATE <blank structure extended file>.** In dBXL, the CREATE command initiates a dialog for the user to define the fields of a new database. In Quicksilver (and Clipper), the CREATE command makes a blank structure extended file. The APPEND and REPLACE commands are used to enter the field definitions in this structure extended file. Then a database with the desired field structure is constructed with "CREATE <database file> FROM <structure extended file>".
3. **Environmental variables.** Quicksilver supports the following additional environmental variables: xColor, xNative, xPrintOn, xPrintBusy, and xQuicks.
4. **ON KEY.** Quicksilver supports scan codes in addition to the key specifications supported by dBXL.
5. **SET CURSORMOVE ON/OFF.** For faster screen displays, you can leave the cursor in the upper left hand corner of the screen when you write to the screen.
6. **SET EDITOR TO <editor program file name>.** This command permits you to specify an editor to be used for memo field editing.
7. **SET GRAPHPRINT TO.** Quicksilver also supports the HP Plotter.
8. **SINKEY().** This function is a variant of INKEY().

Table 8.5 Quicksilver Utilities Included by WordTech

1. **BuildWin.EXE.** This utility binds your window files with .SCN extensions into a single .WIN file. The application is directed to look for window definitions in the .WIN file using WSET WINFILE TO <file name>.
2. **CheckCom.BIN.** This file is used as in dBXL, with the same syntax: SET EVENT TO FILE CheckCom. Its paired command is ON EVENT CALL GetCom to reference the utility GetCom.BIN. CheckCom and GetCom can be used to implement background or foreground modem communications.
3. **GetCom.BIN.** See **CheckCom.BIN** in this table.
4. **Juggle.COM.** According to the Quicksilver manual, this alternative to overlays should only be employed if you do not have access to a linker which handles overlays. Quicksilver does not include a DOS linker; WordTech directs users to the Link.EXE linker included with PC/MS-DOS, which does *not* support overlays. (In contrast, Clipper includes a special version of the Plink86 linker, which *does* handle overlays.)
5. **ModiScn.EXE.** This utility creates and modifies window definitions stored in .SCN files.
6. **ModiGrf.EXE.** This utility is an alternative to the CREATE/MODIFY GRAPH commands in dBXL.
7. **QuickS.EXE.** This utility can automate part of the object code preparation process for simple applications.
8. **Split.EXE.** This utility permits you to break one file into pieces that can be rejoined with the /B option of the DOS COPY command. You might use this utility to distribute a file larger than 360K on 360K diskettes.

There are many dBXL commands which are missing from Quicksilver. I have listed them in Table 8.6 in categories according to my estimate of the likelihood of their relevance and the possible degree of their impact on your programming efforts.

Table 8.6 dBXL 1.3 Commands Not Implemented in Quicksilver

1. **Missing commands usually of little or no consequence.** APPEND (interactive form), ASSIST, CREATE (interactive form), DOS, HELP, INSERT (interactive form), INTRO, MODIFY COMMAND, MODIFY FILE, MODIFY STRUCTURE, and the following SET commands: DEBUG, PROMPT, and SAFETY.
2. **Debugging commands handled by the debugger.** SET ECHO, SET DOHISTORY, SET TALK, and SET STEP. The services of these commands are replaced by the services of the debugger, but not necessarily in an equivalent fashion.
3. **Missing commands occasionally of consequence.** CREATE/MODIFY GRAPH, CREATE/MODIFY LABEL, CREATE/MODIFY QUERY, CREATE/MODIFY REPORT, and the SET commands CARRY, ODOMETER, STATUS, and TALK. The status line displayed by the SET STATUS command is useful in some situations for providing status information to users. SET TALK ON in combination with SET ODOMETER TO <interval> is useful for reporting progress information during indexing. You may sometimes wish to give your users the ability to create and maintain graphs, labels, queries, and reports.
4. **Missing commands of potentially large consequence.** BROWSE, CHANGE, DISPLAY STATUS, EDIT, LIST STATUS, RESTORE STATUS, SAVE STATUS, SET HEADING, and SET SCOREBOARD. SAVE STATUS permits you to save the status of the ON/OFF commands to a file; RESTORE STATUS restores those settings. Facilities like this are of great importance in writing subroutines for libraries or other reuse. With DISPLAY/LIST STATUS, you can capture the status report with an ALTERNATE file, and then parse the file to recover the open files, indexes, ON/OFF settings, and other aspects of the application's environment. BROWSE, CHANGE, and EDIT are central dBASE dialect commands of great utility. SET HEADING ON causes field headings to be automatically constructed for the LIST command. Both the SET STATUS and SET SCOREBOARD commands control the onscreen display of important status information, such as the current record number and whether editing is done in "insert" mode or not.

The Quicksilver Compiler and Multiple-User Programming

The multiple-user commands and functions in Quicksilver are ignored when an application uses them in a single-user environment. The Quicksilver 1.3 documentation states that a Quicksilver application believes that it is in single-user mode unless it detects that Networker Plus has been loaded, but this is false.

Quicksilver supports file and record locking and the opening of .DBF files in exclusive mode. It does not support electronic mail, the identification of users who hold specified resources, the exchange of screen images, and so on. However, these services are offered by a companion product from WordTech called Networker Plus.

Networker Plus

WordTech offers the Networker Plus product to add a layer of standard network services to any application. In particular, multiple-user dBXL/LAN and Quicksilver applications can be enhanced with Networker Plus, but Networker Plus is not required in order to perform file and record locking or to open files in exclusive mode.

Networker Plus offers several levels of service. When the LAN.COM component of Networker Plus is loaded as a TSR, you may execute a number of Networker Plus utility functions at the DOS prompt. When the LAN.COM and DIALOG.COM components are both loaded, then a user of any application may access functions in DIALOG.COM with a specified keystroke. When a Quicksilver or dBXL program is loaded after LAN.COM, the program can execute a special set of built-in commands and functions to receive the services of Networker Plus. For example, the dBXL/Quicksilver workstation-identification function WhoHasIt() becomes active when Networker Plus is loaded.

System Requirements

Here are the system requirements for workstations which execute multiple-user applications prepared with Quicksilver 1.3:

1. PC/MS-DOS 3.1 or higher.
2. If you use Networker Plus, a NetBIOS-compatible network is required to enable Networker Plus's communications, task sending, and screen transmission features; otherwise NetBIOS compatibility is not required.
3. Enough free RAM to load the following: DOS, the workstation component of the network operating system, Networker Plus (if needed), and the .EXE file made by Quicksilver.
4. One of the following: (1) one diskette drive and one hard drive, or (2) access to a network drive on which the Quicksilver application is installed.

Multiple-user Quicksilver applications which require only file and record locking do not require Networker Plus. When Networker Plus is used, one copy serves the entire network; contrast this to the LAN Pack schemes of dBASE III PLUS and dBASE IV, which entail a per-user cost. If needed, the copy of Networker Plus can be installed in a shared directory on a network server.

Compatibility with Multiple-User dBASE III PLUS

With a few exceptions, Quicksilver uses the dBASE III PLUS syntax for multiple-user commands and functions. However, as a nice extension to simplify the preparation of multiple-user applications and the conversion of single-user applications to multiple-user applications, network errors are handled by "ON NETERROR <command>", while dBASE III PLUS handles all errors with "ON ERROR <command>" (or its built-in error handler, when no ON ERROR command has been executed).

The SET AUTOLOCK ON command, also an extension, causes records to be locked automatically by certain commands. Under some conditions, use of this command may remove the necessity of coding IF RLOCK() statements in your application (although we will see in the networking material in Volume 2 that automatic locking in programs is *not* typically satisfactory).

Under most conditions, multiple-user Quicksilver applications coexist peacefully with multiple-user dBASE III PLUS applications, because both products use the same low-level locking mechanisms. However, Quicksilver cannot identify dBASE III PLUS users (unless those users have loaded Networker Plus), and under some conditions, a Quicksilver program will not detect changes made to files by dBASE III PLUS applications.

Quicksilver includes the NetError.PRG utility, meant to be referenced in the command "ON NETERROR DO NetError". This utility, which you may modify as appropriate to fit your situation, provides the user with several options in the event of resource contention — that is, when the user wants a file or record which is temporarily locked by someone else. A window opens and the user chooses from a pick list the options of trying the resource request again, going to the top menu via RETURN TO MASTER,[8] sending a message to another user (assuming Networker Plus is loaded), or changing the count in SET RETRY TO <count>.

Extensions for the Network

We have seen the extension ON NETERROR just above. The SET PRINTER TO command has options to send the output to a printer or spooler on the network server, instead of to the local printer.

Some files are opened for read-only access in the multiple-user environment, whereas they would be opened for read-write access in the single-user environment. An example is the source file for APPEND FROM, which enables concurrent appending from the same file by different users.

When your program requests a record or file which is unavailable, you usually want to know which user has the resource that you need. Quicksilver lets you query the resource usage of other users; you may list open files and the mode in which they are open, list the workstations which have the files open, and so on. User identification features permit you to determine (1) the number of Networker

8. Your application must be coded so that it supports such an option.

Plus users online, (2) a workstation's unique identifier, and (3) whether a particular workstation has Networker Plus currently loaded.

Networker Plus — which can be used with applications other than Quicksilver — supports message exchange between terminals (e-mail), the exchange of entire screens between terminals, distributed processing, a set of 16 on/off flags whose values are set at each Networker Plus workstation, and the listing of users currently online. The distributed processing facility is fairly provocative, but its hardware and procedural requirements are too complex for most network installations.

This facility permits you to send a task to be performed at a workstation that is online and waiting to perform a task. The specified task, when sent, is executed as if it had been entered at the DOS prompt at the target workstation!

In particular, you can run Quicksilver programs — at times that you can schedule — if the programs do not require any user input. Examples would be standard reports, batch updates using the UPDATE command, and sort and indexing operations, but watch your disk space!

Chapter 9

The Recital/4GL dBASE Dialect for UNIX Platforms and VAX VMS

Since September 1988, the Recital Corporation has been shipping the Recital/4GL dBASE dialect for Digital Equipment Corporation (DEC) VAX minicomputers. The Recital dialect is extremely ambitious, as 60% of it is said to consist of extensions to dBASE III PLUS (Adams 1989). Here is an introduction to the family of dBASE products from the Recital Corporation, which are now also available on a variety of UNIX platforms.

Introduction to Products

In addition to the Recital interpreter, which is called Recital/4GL, there are several companion products. Some of these products support the relationship of the Recital development environment to the PC development environment, and others extend the functionality of the Recital environment for end-users. These products are described in Table 9.1.

Since Recital runs on multiple-user computers, it is inherently a multiple-user product. This distinguishes it from the PC-based dBASE dialects we have looked at so far. Note that the multiple-user versions of these other dialects operate in a LAN environment, whose hardware configuration is rather different from that of a multiple-user minicomputer.

Prices and System Requirements

Table 9.2 lists the prices of various Recital products. The prices for the MicroVAX/VAX series depend on the CPU and not on the number of users. If you are the only person in your organization who needs Recital/4GL and its support products, you can get a single-user license to run Recital products only at your workstation.

Recital/4GL and its support products are available for the VMS operating system on MicroVAX and VAX series computers from Digital Equipment Corporation (DEC). Recital/4GL is available for a variety of UNIX platforms, as shown in Table 9.3. In contrast to VAX pricing, UNIX pricing is based on the number of users. At the time of writing, one user cost $995, 2 to 4 users cost $1,500, 5 to 9 cost $3,400, 10 to 19 cost $6,800, 40 to 49 cost $19,600, and 90 to 99 cost $40,600.

Table 9.1 Recital Corporation Products

Recital/4GL	This is the Recital interpreter. Its price is based on the computer, and not on the number of users.
Recital/Encryptor	This product encrypts and links your files for distribution.
Recital/RMS bridge	This product gives you transparent access to RMS indexed sequential files.
Recital/2020 bridge	This product permits you to import and export data in the 2020 spreadsheet format which is commonly used on VAX computers.
Recital/PCServer	This conversion facility permits you to import dBASE data and code files from MS-DOS and translate them to native file formats on the Recital computer.
Recital/Library	Routines in this library give C, FORTRAN, and COBOL programs access to Recital databases.
Recital Office Automation	This program implements diary, mail, phonebook, and other database functions. It includes a link to word processing, spreadsheet, and user-developed applications.

Table 9.2 Recital Corporation Prices

Product	MicroVAX/VAX CPU License	VAX Station One User
Recital/4GL	$4,500 to $70,000	$1,500
Recital/Encryptor	$1,000 to $14,000	$ 300
Recital/RMS bridge	$1,350 to $21,000	$ 300
Recital/2020 bridge	$ 500 to $ 1,500	$ 300
Recital/PCServer	$ 600	$ 300
Recital/Library	$ 500 to $ 1,500	$ 300
Recital Office Automation	$1,000 to $ 2,000	$ 300

Recital/4GL Compatibility

According to Adams (Adams 1989: 52), Recital contains all of the features in Clipper 4.0, FoxBASE+ 2.10, dBASE III PLUS 1.1, and dBXL/Quicksilver 1.3, except dBXL's windows and graphics. The evident strategy here is to support the migration to minicomputers of unmodified dBASE III PLUS and Clipper programs. dBXL/Quicksilver programs without window commands will also port without changes, except for those changes that are connected with the operating system.

Table 9.3 UNIX Platforms for Recital/4GL

Computer	UNIX Implementation
386	386/IX System V.3.2 SCO XENIX System V.2.3 SCO UNIX System V.3.2 AT&T UNIX/386 System V.3.2
ACORN R140	BSD 4.3
AT&T 3B series	UNIX System V.3.2
BULL XPS 100	UNIX System V.2
IBM PS/2 (386 models)	AIX 1.1
IBM RT/PC	AIX 1.1
ICL DRS 300	UNIX System V.2
ICL DRS 400	UNIX System V.3.2
Intergraph 3000	CLIX
MIPS	UNIX System V.3.2
NCR Tower (400, 600)	UNIX System V.2.1
Unisys 5000	UNIX System V.2.1
Unisys 6000	UNIX System V.3.2
VAX series	ULTRIX 2.0, ULTRIX 3.0

One Australian Recital user reports porting the SBT commercial accounting package, with over 100,000 lines of dBASE III PLUS source code, to VAX/VMS Recital/4GL in one day (Strickler 1989). The same user ported a 40,000-line dBASE III PLUS application with only one problem: the application used a DOS file called T&D.PRG, whose name was illegal under VMS, and the file name and references to it had to be changed.

Recital/4GL Enhancements

Table 9.4 shows the field types which Recital/4GL adds to the dBASE language. Database structures include 25 characters for a field description, which implements a first level of data dictionary support in this dBASE dialect. This field description can be toggled on and off in EDIT, APPEND, QUERY, and INSERT.

Table 9.4 Recital's Extra Field Types

Type	Description
R	4-byte floating point
F	8-byte floating point
I	4-byte integer
S	2-byte integer
B	1-byte integer
P	Packed decimal (VAX/VMS only)
Q	Quadword (VAX/VMS only)

The screen painter has a data dictionary for each screen definition. The following data and settings are recorded for each onscreen field: action, source, content, type, width, decimal, PICTURE, range, help, relation, lookup, validation, error, calculated, recalculate, must enter, and read-only.

During full-screen editing, pressing the help key, F1, causes a calculator to popup when the cursor is on a numeric field. Pressing F1 on a date field triggers a popup calender.

You may have up to 255 fields per database, 20 indexes per database, and a (gasp!) unlimited number of memory variables and elements per array. You are still limited to 10 open databases and 254 characters in a character memvar.

Recital includes a free-format report writer with its own report definition language, RDL. Although this report writer is not in a class with R&R Relational Report Writer, it goes far beyond the capabilities of REPORT FORM and saves time over equivalent dBASE-language coding.

The mechanism for implementing recovery in transaction processing is very robust. Since Recital operates on multiple-user operating systems, it has special support for multiple-user applications at the source code level and "behind the scenes."

Chapter 10

dBASE Dialects from Other Vendors

There are several dBASE dialects which have not been able to achieve the status of dialect products from the four major vendors, Ashton-Tate, Fox Software, Nantucket Corporation, and WordTech Systems. Some of these products are relatively new, whereas others have been marketed for years. Because the current number of programmers using these products is small relative to the other dialects, I will not give much detail on any of these products.

Nonetheless, they deserve mention. A product may have a small installed base, yet still be influential or of high quality. Furthermore, some of these products may later reach total unit sales comparable to the sales of dialects from the four major vendors.

Emerald Bay from Ratliff Software Productions

Yes, this is *the* Ratliff in the dBASE world, C. Wayne Ratliff,[1] whose California company is Ratliff Software Productions Incorporated, sometimes refered to as RSPI. Here is a table describing some of their products.

Table 10.1 dBASE Products from Ratliff Software Productions

Emerald Bay	The server component of a client-server database.
Vulcan	A dBASE-compatible front-end to Emerald Bay.
Liaison	A Lotus 1-2-3 add-in which is a front-end to Emerald Bay.
C Toolkit	A product to access Emerald Bay services through C programs.
PASCAL Toolkit	A product to access Emerald Bay services through PASCAL programs.

Each front-end and toolkit includes a copy of the Emerald Bay engine. The engine is also sold separately at three price points, depending on the number of users supported. The QuarterDeck Corporation's DESQview environment is supported by these products, so you may operate a Vulcan-developed application in one DESQview window and a Lotus/Liaison application in another DESQview window. Table 10.2 lists the prices of these products.

1. See the foreword.

Table 10.2 Ratliff Software Productions Products and Prices

Price	Product
$195	Emerald Bay, up to 4 users.
$395	Emerald Bay, up to 8 users.
$595	Emerald Bay, more than 8 users.
$395	Vulcan
$159	Liaison
$395	C Toolkit
$199	PASCAL Toolkit

dBASE Dialects from Gen Soft Development Corporation

This Bellevue, Washington, company (near Microsoft headquarters) produces dBFast/PLUS, an MS-DOS compiler with an operating environment claimed to be similar to that of MS-Windows. dBFast/PLUS/Windows is a development environment and compiler for MS-Windows. dBFast/PLUS/Mac is the Macintosh implementation. The DOS versions sell for $249.

dBMAN V from Versasoft Corporation

The dBMAN V dialect has been around for many years. It has never had much recognition, but it has survived to port its DOS version to AIX, XENIX, UNIX, Atari ST, Commodore Amiga, LANs, and several mainframes. This dialect includes windows, arrays, user-defined functions, SAVE/RESTORE SCREEN, a relational report writer, and a compiler. An optional unlimited distribution runtime is sold separately.

The FORCE Compiler from Sophco

The FORCE compiler from Sophco, Inc., like Vulcan, does not have a large market share, but it is important due to the concepts which are promoted in its implementation.

FORCE requires you to declare the type of identifiers; the type of a FORCE identifier cannot change during execution. In other dBASE dialects, the type of an identifier cannot be declared and is determined during execution by the type of data assigned to it. For example, the following code is quite legal in most dialects:

```
X = DATE()
X =  "a character string"
X = 3
X = .T.
```

In a FORCE program, at most one of these assignment statements would be syntactically legal, because X would always have the same type. I personally feel that it is better to restrict variables as FORCE does, because there are many programmer bugs which the compiler can identify that otherwise must be found by testing — and testing can take years.

By enforcing extra structure on your dBASE code, FORCE is able to produce very small .EXE files, like the ones C and PASCAL programmers are accustomed to. Clipper compiles the one-line program

```
? "Hello, World!"
```

into an .EXE file of about 150K, whereas FORCE produces a 2K .EXE file.

With C, PASCAL, or FORCE, the size of the .EXE file produced depends on the amount of source code, with a minimum size of 2K or less. In contrast, FoxBASE+, FoxPro, and dBASE III PLUS applications all require the entire runtime package to be present and loaded; Clipper produces .EXE files whose minimum size is approximately 150K.

It is frustrating not to be able to produce small executable files with the typical dBASE dialect. At last dBASE dialect programmers have this benefit in the FORCE compiler. At the time of writing, FORCE 2.1 was listed at $199, down from a price of $695 for earlier versions.

Chapter 11

dBASE Information Sources

Millions of people are involved with dBASE dialects at either the programmer level or the end-user level. As a consequence, there are many different kinds of sources for information on dBASE dialects and related products.

dBASE-Related Books

There is a standard reference called *Books in Print,* which lists all currently known American books in print. The electronic form of this directory is published by R. R. Bowker and is available on the DIALOG electronic information service, which may be accessed directly or through CompuServe.

Appendix F, which starts on page 435, lists titles from *Books in Print* which contain one of the following terms: Clipper, dBASE, dBXL, FoxBASE, FoxPro, or Quicksilver.

Titles are listed alphabetically in each category. There are also lists of selected software engineering and systems analysis titles from Yourdon Press and Addison-Wesley.

Truly advanced books on dBASE programming are rare. The presence of the word *advanced* in a title does not necessarily mean very much.

Recommendation on buying dBASE books. Persons who write dBASE books have primary competence either in writing or in computer science and computer programming, but professional programmers will not get much benefit from books written by the first type of author. When you evaluate a computer book for possible purchase, use the understanding of the canonical approach which you gained from Chapter 2 to ascertain the category to which the author belongs.

For example, when you read the following text at the beginning of Arthur Fuller's book *Dynamics of Clipper,* you know that he has a canonical viewpoint and that his book has the potential to influence your productivity — and fun!

> *Professionals approach software development much differently than hackers, crackers, weekend hobbyists and most nine-to-fivers in corporate information centers and MIS departments. They know that with the right tools, application development can be a piece of cake. Therefore professionals write or buy the tools required to do the job — not just a particular application, but all applications.* (Fuller 1989: xxvi)

The dBASE Language Handbook

The dBASE Language Handbook, written by long-time *Data Based Advisor* editor-in-chief David M. Kalman[1] (Kalman 1989), is a unique reference for dBASE dialect programmers who work with the dialects covered by his book: Clipper, dBASE III, dBASE III PLUS, dBASE IV, dBXL, FoxBASE+, and Quicksilver. This book lists each command and function in the supported dialects and explains the variations. *The dBASE Language Handbook* is published by MicroTrend Books and is sold in bookstores and through *Data Based Advisor.*

> **Recommendation on *The dBASE Language Handbook*.** This book is a recommended purchase if you use at least two of the dialects which the book supports. The *Handbook* is a natural companion to *dBASE Dialects Software Engineering.*
>
> *However:* please bear in mind that writers like Kalman and myself make mistakes! While we will in some cases clarify misinformation or provide information missing from vendor manuals, your ultimate reference on any computer product is the vendor manual and the vendor.
>
> *Furthermore:* for many reasons, reference works which attempt to be comprehensive virtually always exclude relevant information. If you find a feature described for a particular dialect in *The dBASE Language Handbook* or in *dBASE Dialects Software Engineering,* then you can be fairly confident that the feature exists in that dialect; an omission may mean that a feature doesn't exist, or just that it wasn't described. These reference works are the *first* place to look, not the last; they do not necessarily give you cross-references to all other relevant commands, functions, and features.

Periodicals

There are two dBASE-oriented publications of large circulation, in addition to several specialty journals of limited circulation. The oldest and most prominent of the magazines is *Data Based Advisor,* which comes from San Diego, California, near the hotbed of dBASE activity in the Los Angeles area. Its January 1990 issue was Volume 8, Number 1.

This magazine covers all of the major dialects, with periodic reports and reviews of other dialects and dBASE programmer productivity products. There is also regular coverage of Paradox and emerging technologies like SQL. Each issue contains information sources including user group listings and the Express Lane advertisements.

A subscription to 12 issues (one year) costs about $20 in the United States. The January 1990 issue was accompanied by the *Data Based Advisor Database Directory 1990,* printed in magazine format on 130 8 ½-by-11-inch pages. This *Directory* covers hundreds of products and services in 28 categories, and will be published again in 1991.

---

1. After several years in this position, Kalman was replaced by John L. Hawkins in September 1990.

The January 1990 issue of *DBMS* was Volume 3, Number 1. This magazine offers some important coverage for dBASE dialect programmers, but is not as focused on dBASE dialects as is *Data Based Advisor*. There is a secondary orientation to mini-computer database products and database servers, which are admittedly technologies that are starting to merge with dBASE dialects.

A subscription to 12 issues (one year) costs about $20 in the United States. Unlike *Data Based Advisor, DBMS* offers a reader response card, on which you circle small numbers corresponding to vendors. You then mail the card to *DBMS,* which forwards your information request to the specified vendors.

Dialect-Specific Periodicals

Pinnacle Publishing publishes the monthly journals *FoxTalk,* for programming-level users of Fox Software dBASE dialects, and *Reference(Clipper),* for Clipper users. You may find these journals to be rather expensive at $99 per year for 24 8 ½-by-11-inch pages per issue. However, there is no advertising in these publications, so they are all meat. For an additional $60 per year, you receive the source code from these publications on diskette.

The Reference Pages of Idaho publishes the monthly *Compass* for Clipper developers. Each issue consists of 40 to 50 loose-leaf pages — free of advertising — which are stored in a binder provided with your first issue. You also receive the information on diskette, and a copy of the Norton Instant Access program is included to permit you to retrieve Compass information on disk. At the time of writing, subscriptions are $149 in the United States, $169 in Canada, and $199 elsewhere.

Gary Beam and Stephen Straley publish newsletters for Clipper developers. **See the heading "dBASE-Related Periodicals" on page 449 for more information on these and other dBASE-related periodicals.**

In many cases, the vendors have their own publications. Ashton-Tate has the *Ashton-Tate Quarterly,* Nantucket has *Nantucket News,* and Fox Software has *FoxTrax.*

Directories

Table 11.1 lists several directories which provide various kinds of information for dBASE end-users and programmers. **Also see the heading "dBASE-Related Directories" on page 450 for more information.**

Online Information

In this section we'll look at the CompuServe information service and BBSs operated by dBASE dialect vendors. The CompuServe competitors, Genie and The Source, are not recommended and are not discussed.

Table 11.1 Directories of dBASE-Related Products and Services

1. *Ashton-Tate Developer Registry* (Ashton-Tate 1989). This large book from Ashton-Tate lists thousands of products for end-users and programmers. See Table 13.2 on page 206, Table 13.3 on page 207, and Table 14.1 on page 209 for a listing of its categories.
2. *Books in Print*. The online form of this comprehensive database is published by R. R. Bowker and is available on the DIALOG information service, which can be accessed through IQuest on CompuServe.
3. *Clipper Third Party Products Directory* (Nantucket Corporation 1988). This directory from Nantucket lists products for Clipper developers.
4. *Data Based Advisor Database Directory*. This directory is published annually by the premier dBASE magazine, *Data Based Advisor*.
5. *dBASE Programmer's Index*. This quarterly index from Poder Associates provides keyword access to over 1,200 dBASE-related articles.
6. *dBUtility Directory*. This directory of dBASE utilities from EMS consists of 100 pages in print form and 1,400 records in .DBF.
7. *The Programmer's Shop Catalog*. This very comprehensive catalog lists many categories of products for programmers who use a number of microcomputer languages, including dBASE dialects. The Spring 1990 catalog cover proclaims "over 1,750 software tools."

How Does It Work?

Computerized online services are accessed over the telephone lines, using a modem and a communications program on your PC. When your modem calls the telephone number of an online service, and communications with the remote computer are properly established, a series of prompts and menus guides you in your use of the service.

Online services come in two varieties. A service such as DIALOG offers a library of online information which is retrieved with the vendor's software or generic communications software. You cannot give this type of service any of your information; you can only receive.

In contrast, electronic bulletin boards, called BBSs, usually permit you to provide information as well as to receive it. In the United States, every city of any size at all has a number of free BBSs operated by individuals as a hobby and community service. Local and regional computer newspapers and magazines typically list the telephone numbers and other basic information about area BBSs, such as theme and member requirements. Computer clubs often operate their own BBSs — such clubs can be an excellent way to meet other users and programmers and to exchange computer information, industry news, sales leads, and so on.

Some BBSs are open to any caller, while others may require a password from you before you can access the service. In some cases, you may apply for the password by mail at no charge. In other cases, the service is not free, and the password is used to prevent unauthorized access to your account.

CompuServe

If your time usage and your programs have a significant financial impact on youself and others, you must subscribe to the CompuServe online service, which is available 24 hours a day, every day of the year. The dBASE dialects are difficult to use wisely. It takes a long time to develop foolproof canonical techniques and supporting tools and procedures.

In addition, advanced books on dBASE dialect programming are quite difficult to find. When you find a substantial book, it takes a long time to read it, and an even longer time to absorb it.

So there is no substitute for access to experts and fellow practitioners in your professional area. Since we are all so specialized today, other experts may not exist or be available in our communities. Online services such as CompuServe link like minds literally all over the world.

CompuServe Costs

At the time of writing (Summer 1990), CompuServe costs $12/hour while you are connected at 1200 or 2400 baud, plus any long-distance telephone charges, plus any surcharges for special services. Fortunately, most cities in the United States (and several in Puerto Rico and Canada) have local telephone numbers which you can call in order to be connected to CompuServe without long-distance charges. In addition to the vendor information areas and forums for user interactions, CompuServe offers many databases of information provided by information vendors other than CompuServe. There are often additional costs associated with retrieving information from these databases.

What Does CompuServe Offer to dBASE Dialect Programmers?

CompuServe is divided into special interest areas called *forums*. Some of the forums of interest to dBASE dialect programmers are listed in Table 11.2, and Table 11.3 summarizes some of the major benefits of CompuServe membership.

Recommendation on CompuServe membership. If you use CompuServe wisely, you will save far more money than you spend. For this reason, CompuServe membership is mandatory for most dBASE dialect programmers!

Remark on *CompuServe Almanac*. The information in Table 11.2 comes from the *CompuServe Almanac*, which is an inexpensive and mandatory purchase for the wisest use of the CompuServe resource. Please remember that forums and databases come and go; some of those listed in Table 11.2 may not be available when you read this. Furthermore, other new and relevant CompuServe services may be available by the time you read this which were not available at the time of writing.

Table 11.2 CompuServe Forums for dBASE Dialect Programmers

1. **Ashton-Tate Support Library.** At any "!" prompt, enter GO ASHTON or GO ASHFORUM to go directly to the Ashton-Tate Forum.
2. **The Computer Consultant's Forum.** At any "!" prompt, enter GO CONSULT.
3. **Computer Database Plus.** At any "!" prompt, enter GO COMPDB to access this database, with over 61,000 abstracts and full text articles from 130 periodicals, including *PC Week, PC Magazine, Byte,* and *Communications of the ACM.* The database is updated weekly. There are nine search methods; in addition to regular charges you pay a per-minute surcharge, and a charge for each search.
4. **The Data Based Advisor Forum.** *Data Based Advisor* magazine, the premier magazine for dBASE dialect programmers, went online in October 1990. At any "!" prompt, enter GO DBADVISOR to access what is arguably the most provocative forum of all those listed here.
5. **Dr. Dobb's Journal.** At any "!" prompt, enter GO DDJ.
6. **The Fox Software Area.** Fox Software did not have a dedicated forum until March 8, 1990. Formerly, you entered GO PCVENA at any "!" prompt; Fox Software was one of the areas in PCVENA. Now you enter GO FOXFORUM.
7. **IBM Software Forums.** At any "!" prompt, enter GO IBMSW to access thousands of public domain and shareware programs, in addition to other IBM PC users.
8. **Microsoft Systems Forum.** At any "!" prompt, enter GO MSSYS.
9. **Nantucket Forum.** At any "!" prompt, enter GO NANFOR. Serves single-user and multiple-user Clipper programmers and McMax users.
10. **PC Expert Database.** At any "!" prompt, enter GO PCEXPERT to access a keyword-searchable database of the "best messages from the IBM Forums," according to the *CompuServe Almanac.*
11. **Programmers Forum.** At any "!" prompt, enter GO PROSIG.
12. **Safeware Computer Insurance.** At any "!" prompt, enter GO SAF to get information on specialty insurance for personal computers.
13. **The SOFTEX Software Catalog.** At any "!" prompt, enter GO SOFTEX to order a variety of software which is downloaded to you through your modem and charged to your CompuServe account.
14. **The WordTech Forum.** WordTech Systems opened a CompuServe forum in September 1990. Enter GO IBMNET at any "!" prompt to reach the PC Vendor C area and choose menu item 12.

Ashton-Tate BBS

Although Ashton-Tate operates one of the most important CompuServe forums, it also has its own BBS, which can be accessed at (213) 324-2188 using 2400 baud, 8 data bits, no parity, and 1 stop bit. However, in the summer of 1990, Ashton-Tate inaugurated a new access method to its BBS which will be toll-free for most residents of the United States. You can now dial the Ashton-Tate BBS using the same

Table 11.3 Major Benefits of CompuServe Membership

1. **Access to experts in your professional area.** If you are an expert in your area, you can share tips and information with other experts. If you are learning, the experts will help you.
2. **Access to vendor personnel.** Vendor personnel monitor many of the forums, in particular, the forum run by their company, so any message sent to "All" on a forum may influence a vendor's decision. You may unexpectedly receive responses from vendor personnel, or, alternatively, you may direct your messages to specific vendor representatives. As with any other vendor contact, you may receive or give technical advice, and communicate your desires for product changes and enhancements.
3. **Access to vendor information.** The computer industry moves very rapidly indeed, and it is difficult to keep informed about the pace of product development by your favorite vendors. CompuServe will give you both new information and background information, such as product lists, news of new and upcoming releases, bug fixes, and prices.
4. **Free software.** Many thousands of public domain and shareware programs are available for downloading. The cost of downloading these programs to your computer is connect time plus any telephone charges — the electronic mail equivalent of shipping charges. The programs themselves are free to you; in the case of shareware, as opposed to public domain, you are supposed to send a registration fee to the shareware publisher if you continue to use the shareware program. Sending the registration fee is your option, since the publisher has no way of knowing that you are using the software.
5. **Uploading.** If you have written a program which you'd like to place in the public domain, you can upload it to the appropriate CompuServe library. You may also upload your shareware programs and demo programs for your commercial software!

local-access telephone numbers which give toll-free access to CompuServe. At the "Host:" prompt, enter ATBBS.

Data Based Advisor and *DBMS* BBSs

Data Based Advisor magazine operated a private BBS for many years, but at the time of writing, this BBS was scheduled to be discontinued in November 1990 as a result of the new CompuServe forum: at any "!" prompt, GO DBADVISOR. (It seems that CompuServe membership becomes more compelling for dBASE dialect programmers every month!) *DBMS* magazine offers the TelePath service on TymNet; see the magazine for more information.

WordTech BBS

In September 1990, WordTech became vendor 12 in CompuServe's PC Vendor C area; see Table 11.2. WordTech also offers its own BBS at (415) 254-1141. This BBS uses the standard communications protocol of 8 data bits, 1 stop bit, and no parity.

Further Information

For more information, see the heading "dBASE-Related Electronic Bulletin Boards" on page 450.

dBASE-Oriented Consulting Services for Programmers

There are two kinds of consulting services available to you, *voice* and *online*. We looked at online consulting in the previous section.

Sometimes online conversations are just too slow, and you need to talk to an expert on the telephone. One source of expertise across the dBASE dialects is the California company Database Specialties, which can be contacted at the address and phone number given in Appendix I on page 457. This company does dBASE consulting to the business community, but it also sells selected dBASE and network products.

If you buy products from this company, it offers you unlimited free support in using the products. Note that although you do not pay the consultants at Database Specialties for their consulting time, you still pay your long-distance carrier for the call.

Magazine writers who list their telephone numbers are a second source of expert advice by telephone. If the writer didn't want to be called, the telephone number would not appear. (However, the publication of the telephone number does not mean that the writer can necessarily engage in formal consulting by telephone. The writer may only be interested in brief conversations to get feedback from readers. In many parts of the country, it is difficult or impossible for a writer to arrange to receive credit card payments. Without this ability, the writer may not have any feasible way to handle the financial part of the consulting transaction.)

People who write and publish software for dBASE programmers are another source of expert help by telephone. Again, you can't *assume* that software authors are available for telephone consultation, but many *are* available.

Do you need advice on a user interface? Call a company that has a superior user interface product. Do you need help with your multiple-user dBASE dialect programming? Then approach a company with a multiple-user product. (Database Software Consultants publishes the unique *dMILL Network Kit for Clipper*, a *docu-software*™ product whose educational component teaches you what you need to know to convert single-user applications to share resources on networks via the software component of the *Kit*. Kits are also available for other dialects.)

Another possibility for help is organizations which offer training for programming-level users of dBASE dialects. See page 451 for a list of such companies; some of the dBASE directories also list companies which offer training.

Chapter 12

Public Domain dBASE Software and dBASE Shareware

Over the years a great many dBASE-oriented files have been placed into freeware (public domain) or shareware distribution, primarily through electronic bulletin boards. You can find such files in several of the CompuServe special-interest sections, and if you live in a large city, you can probably find several local BBSs that feature a dBASE focus or that have a dBASE special-interest area.

Recommendation on freeware and shareware. The object of this book is to tell you how to write ever-better applications in ever-shorter amounts of time. You could easily spend 40 hours per week evaluating dBASE-oriented freeware and shareware files, but that wouldn't leave much time for developing applications. I recommend that you do not spend time investigating freeware and shareware programs — unless someone recommends a specific program for you or unless you know exactly what you are looking for.

For example, I use a wonderful printing utility for my HP LaserJet II. I read about this utility in the CompuServe subscribers' magazine, downloaded it, and installed it in perhaps 10 minutes. This utility prints two pages of code, side by side, on one piece of paper — I love it!

Evaluating freeware and shareware programs can be a career — literally. Over the years, a second important source of freeware and shareware has developed, consisting of companies that select and sell freeware and shareware titles. These companies generally charge around $5 per diskette, so they make their money on a volume shipping and handling business. The companies do not sell the software itself; rather, they charge you for their labor and materials in selecting the programs, producing the diskettes, and mailing the diskettes and their catalogs.

Ordering freeware and shareware products by catalog is a very, very different activity from searching through the BBSs yourself, looking for the occasional tidbit. When you order a specific program which is advertised in a catalog, other people have already done the evaluation work for you. Of course, some of these catalogs will sell you a large set of diskettes full of programs, which puts you back in the position of evaluating and selecting.

Recommendation on ordering from freeware and shareware catalogs. When you order a specific program with a separate description in a catalog, then (1) you have a fairly specific idea about what you will receive, and (2) a professional evaluator has selected the product and described it for the catalog. I recommend that you order a specific program with its own catalog description if the description suggests the product's potential to save you time. I recommend that you do not order large collections of freeware or shareware programs.

One freeware/shareware distribution company which specializes in dBASE-oriented files is EMS, whose contact information is given in Appendix I, "Alphabetic List of dBASE-Related Vendors." See that same appendix for contact information for Public Brand Software, a distributor which offers an exceptionally handsome and comprehensive freeware/shareware catalog. This catalog covers perhaps 150 categories of software, including several dBASE-oriented categories.

Chapter 13

dBASE Software for End-Users: Benefits and Scope

Since dBASE dialects are powerful and in wide use, thousands of commercial applications have been developed in the dBASE environment. For example, Table 13.2 on page 206 lists dozens of categories of end-user software from the *Ashton-Tate Developer Registry* (Ashton-Tate 1989). (The next chapter covers third-party software for programmers from the *Ashton-Tate Developer Registry* and other software directories.)

This chapter introduces the motivation for programming in dBASE dialects and for purchasing products which have been developed using dBASE dialects. We also look at customizable accounting software, vertical market software, and the various information resources available in the uniquely comprehensive *Ashton-Tate Developer Registry*.

Advantages of Commercial Software Written with a dBASE Dialect

Commercial software written with a dBASE dialect offers many special advantages over software written with general-purpose languages like C and PASCAL, unless the C and PASCAL programs use dBASE file formats, which is increasingly common. These advantages are very important for the manager, end-user, and programmer to understand.

In this section, we'll look at several factors: the availability of dBASE programmers, the growth path to future operating systems and hardware platforms, the ability of the software to be modified or extended, the universality of dBASE file formats, and the availability of dBASE software for both end-users and programmers.

Availability of dBASE Programmers

The availability of dBASE programmers is of concern to anyone who (1) buys commercial software written with a dBASE dialect, (2) uses a dBASE consultant, or (3) hires or manages a full-time dBASE programmer. For example, after software is installed, who will keep it going? Who will recover the databases and indexes when there is a hardware problem or a power failure when the files are open? Who will explain its arcane workings? Who understands the long-range consequences of database growth?

The excellent news is that there are undoubtedly more microcomputer programmers working with dBASE dialects than with any other programming language. Not only are dBASE dialects here to stay — they are growing like wildfire and are proliferating to ever-larger numbers of operating systems and hardware platforms. I feel safe in predicting that by 1995, at least one dBASE dialect will be available on every "major" computer from PCs to mainframes. The growth of the dBASE world means that more and more programmers have primary or secondary competence in dBASE dialects.

The Growth Path of dBASE Dialects and Applications

The rapid advancement of dBASE dialects and their proliferation to a variety of operating systems and hardware platforms means that dBASE applications ride a kind of technological wave. For example, when a programmer moves a Clipper or dBASE III PLUS application to FoxPro, the user suddenly has a full windowing environment with mature windowing paradigms, although the programmer did very little work to make the application blossom with its new features and intelligence.

It is the fate of most databases to grow continuously over the time that they are used. In some cases, old data can be removed to archive storage like diskettes in order to minimize the size of the databases on the hard disk. In other cases, the database may grow too large to handle comfortably on a PC.

One growth path for applications with constantly growing databases is a LAN with a very big server disk. For example, at the time of writing, 330 MB disks are a common large size. The arrival of client-server architecture for dBASE dialects makes this path more and more attractive.

The traditional alternative is to move the dBASE application to a minicomputer or mainframe when its databases grow too large for the PC environment. Formerly, this meant rewriting the application. At the time of writing, dBMAN V and Recital offer dBASE dialects for minicomputers and mainframes, and more dialects are being ported to these environments every day.

Indeed, more and more *applications* are being ported to larger computers. It is no longer necessary to rewrite a dBASE application to move it to a larger computer. (See page 183 for a related field report.)

Modifying or Extending dBASE Applications

Over and over again, we hear end-users say, "This software would be perfect if it just did so-and-so." Sometimes we can show them a technique or feature which grants their wish, but many times we see that satisfying their wish would require modification of the application's source code.

Well, first of all, many dBASE applications *are* sold with source code. Source code may be either a standard or extra-cost option.

Second, it is always possible to modify or extend the functionality of a dBASE application. For example, one of the most frequent requests from users of database applications is for more reports, more reports! If the application is indeed a dBASE application, then its data is stored in .DBF files and .DBT files; index files with the extensions .NDX, .NTX, .IDX, and .MDX; and report and label form files with the extensions .FRM and .LBL.

Consequently, you can write reports on the .DBF and .DBT files using almost any dialect. With the right dialect or R&R Relational Report Writer, you can even use the application's index files.

You can modify any .FRM or .LBL files included, as necessary. You can also make additional .FRM and .LBL files available to the application's users, but this usually requires you to write one or more menu interfaces.

When you extend the functionality of an existing application, you won't be able to modify the existing menus unless you have the application's source code. If you do not have the source code, then you may put your own menu before the application's main menu. Your menu might look like the following:

```
Press  N  to get the new functions for the Personnel System.
Press  R  to get the regular functions for the Personnel System.
```

When users press "R", they get the commercial application just as they did before. When they press "N", they get your menu of extended functions — for the Personnel Department, in this example.

This method works both when you add functions and when you modify them. For example, assume that the Hire submenu of the Personnel System above contains functions which have been replaced by your code. This means that users must know that they no longer access the Hire submenu in the commercial product; you probably cannot prevent access to the Hire submenu unless you can determine how to patch the binary-format distribution file. In the new scenario, users first press "N" to get the new functions, and then they access the replacement Hire submenu.

Universal Data File Format

The ability to extend dBASE software which was discussed in the previous subsection is of course based on the storage of an application's data in standard dBASE file formats. This storage has many benefits, including data exchange, data recovery, ad hoc operations, and easy reporting.

Data Exchange

It is very often the case that I would like to exchange word processing document files with you. If you and I both use brand X and have our document files in the X-format, then sharing files is simple. If you use brand Y and your files are in the different Y-format, then we must convert our files back and forth between the X-format and Y-format in order to share them. This conversion process is known to be full of pitfalls.

While there are several standard formats for files which hold spreadsheet data (DIF, SYLK, WKS, WK1), there is really only one standard format for database data — the .DBF file format. If you have a text editor which will read and edit all of the bytes in any file, then you can — perhaps laboriously — edit the document format of one word processor by hand to make it look like the document format of another word processor.

Conversions of data files from one format to another are generally too complex to be handled except by software. Conversion software which flawlessly handles all cases is rare. Furthermore, if you bring me a file made by product X, and the file format is unpublished, then I may not be able to figure out the X-format in a reasonable amount of time. If I can't figure out the X-format, then I can't convert its data.

Life is so simple when you and I have .DBF files to exchange. There are a few possible problems, such as the different number of database fields supported by different dialects, but these are easy to solve.

Data Recovery

All data files are subject to damage. Enlightened users make frequent backups in order to have a safety net when data files are damaged. You may need to help people recover dBASE files for which there is no backup. If the files are in the X-format, you may not be able to recover the data in the file at a reasonable cost, even if the X-format is published.

Fortunately, there are tools and books to assist you in the repair of damaged dBASE files. Paul Heiser of ComTech Publishing has been publishing recovery aids for years, including the book *Salvaging Damaged dBASE Files,* now in its second edition, and the software product dSALVAGE Professional.

> **Recommendation on *Salvaging Damaged dBASE Files.*** Every programming-level user of dBASE dialects should acquire this book. When you need it, you will need it badly and without delay. For a cost of around $20, there is no way to argue against its purchase. If you can afford it, also acquire recovery software.

Heiser publishes recovery software which has gone through a number of versions over the years. The current product, called dSALVAGE Professional, includes the powerful sector editor DiskMinder from Westlake Software and the book *Salvaging Damaged dBASE Files,* all for $199.

In 1989, Ashton-Tate released a product called dBASE FILE RECOVERY. This product sells for $99.95 and offers help with the recovery of dBASE IV SQL tables, as well as dBASE III, dBASE III PLUS, and dBASE IV databases.

> **Warning on hidden damage in large databases.** Large databases can have damaged sections which go undetected for long periods of time. These sections can look all right to the operating system, and the database files may be properly handled by the DOS COPY command and by backup and restore software. However, the data can be damaged without the file format being damaged. For ex-

ample, you may find 1,024 "%" characters in the middle of your data records. The last backup in which the records were undamaged may be one week old, one month old, one year old, or older!

On-Demand Answers and Ad Hoc Operations in Interpreter Mode

The dBASE file format empowers end-users by permitting them to use a dBASE interpreter to browse and otherwise query databases for ad hoc answers that would otherwise require programming. When users access databases from the dot prompt, anything can happen. A user might inadvertently change a crucial field, ZAP the production database instead of the temporary database, and so on.

In this situation, the users need a dialect whose BROWSE command supports the NOMODIFY clause, which protects the database from alteration during browsing. If your users will access your production databases at the dot prompt, you may want to mark all of your databases "read-only" (with, for example, the DOS 3.3 ATTRIB command) as part of your application's termination process. On entry, your application would mark these databases as "read-write."

Full-Featured, Easy Reports from R&R Relational Report Writer

Data in .DBF format can be reported on with the splendid Concentric Data Systems product, R&R Relational Report Writer, which permits report designers to work at or near the design level. In my experience, end-users with modest technical competence are able to successfully make simple changes to existing report definitions. End-users with slightly more technical competence can develop R&R report definitions of moderate complexity without assistance.

Remark on R&R alternatives. The report facilities in dBASE IV and FoxPro have obviously been heavily influenced by R&R Relational Report Writer and sometimes go beyond it. R&R also has several competitors, although none of them are nearly as well known as R&R.

Customizable Accounting Software

In the beginning of this chapter we saw some lists of categories of commercial dBASE applications. We saw that if a product uses the dBASE file formats, we can extend it with our own dBASE code. If the dBASE source code is available for our dialect, we can modify the application's menus and internal features.

Accounting software deserves special mention, due to its importance in general, and its prominent role in the dBASE world. Most companies see little need to modify their word processors or spreadsheets, but it seems that unless a company is built around the limitations of a particular accounting package, there is always something different about the way the company operates and the view of company operations taken by the accounting software.

Sometimes a company can change its procedures to accommodate the software. Sometimes the software is lied to in a systematic way that causes bottom line totals to be correct, even though transactions were not accurately modeled in all cases. These kinds of accommodations range from somewhat unpleasant to repugnant, depending on the situation.

You of course want the software to adjust to *you* and not the other way around. For this reason, many companies which publish accounting software written in a dBASE dialect sell the software's source code.

The SBT Corporation has a major presence in the dBASE market. It has an entire line of accounting and support products for which dBASE source code is available. Champion Business Systems is also well known; it has been selling dBASE-based accounting software since 1981.

Vertical Market Software

A vertical market consists of an industry or specific industry segment, such as rental agencies, law offices, or grocery stores. Software which serves a particular vertical market is called *vertical market software.*

In many cases, the marketing materials of a company do not indicate the implementation language, or, more to the point, whether data is stored in the .DBF format. However, if the application handles a great deal of data, the use of .DBF files is a definite possibility. Call the vendor if necessary to discover if the product uses .DBF files and whether dBASE source code is available.

In my view, *your first responsibility to a client who needs extensive custom software to automate a segment of his or her business is to investigate whether an existing commercial product might fill the needs.* The route of commercial software is often eliminated from consideration because it is obvious to you and/or your client that no off-the-shelf product will fit your client's particular data processing situation. It is true that the source code of a product may not be available or may not be useful even if it is available, due to its complexity and dependence on commercial and proprietary tools. (This tends to be particularly true for C-based applications.)

However, reasonably priced dBASE source code is often available for a package which performs a substantial part of your client's required information processing. Furthermore, dBASE applications structure data in standard ways, and the code has at least a minimum of internal structure which is imposed by the menu tree of the application, so the code is relatively easy to modify. In that case, the least-cost solution is probably for the client to purchase the package and have you modify and/or extend it, rather than to have you develop all the code from specifications.

To the uninitiated, locating such a program might seem to be difficult or impossible. However, the following table shows a variety of tactics.

Table 13.1 Information Sources for Vertical Market Software

1. **CompuServe.** Log onto CompuServe and leave messages to "All" in the appropriate areas. Ask for leads to specific vendors or to information sources.
2. ***Ashton-Tate Developer Registry*** (Ashton-Tate 1989). Check this reference. Call Ashton-Tate to ask if they have a more recent edition of the *Registry* than the one that you have seen. Ask to talk to the people who maintain the *Registry*. Do they know of any packages in your vertical market which do not appear in the *Registry?* Look in the Industry Index of the *Registry* for vertical markets which are related to your client's line of business.
3. **EMS.** Consult the dBASE software directory published by shareware distributor EMS, whose contact information is given in Appendix I, "Alphabetic List of dBASE-Related Vendors."
4. **Client contacts.** Ask your client to contact his or her fellow professionals to ask about vertical market software.
5. **Client journals.** Publications for persons in the client's line of work may contain articles and/or advertisements about software for your client's type of business. The staff at such publications may know of one or more programs in the vertical market you seek.
6. **Professional associations.** Contact professional associations in your client's line of business and ask for references and referrals.

Recommendation on Automating a Business Segment

If the automation is extensive, investigate to see if vertical market software exists which will meet the client's needs. If no existing package will meet all of the client's needs, but (1) a particular package will meet many needs and (2) the package's dBASE source code is available, then consider if purchasing that product and modifying or extending it will be a better investment for the client than having you write the entire application.

If your client is in-house, remember to include overhead in your estimate of the cost of independent development. For example, if you estimate 1,000 hours of your time, and you receive $20/hour, don't calculate the labor cost at $20,000, because that calculation ignores overhead such as equipment and your benefits. As a rule of thumb, calculate your cost to your employer at at least twice your hourly compensation; in this example, calculate a labor cost of at least $40,000.

Remember also to consider the impact of earlier completion on your client's net income. If your software enters service three months earlier when you modify an existing commercial application, and the client saves or earns $10,000/month with the new system, then an additional $30,000 will be saved or earned with an earlier delivery.

The *Ashton-Tate Developer Registry*

The *Ashton-Tate Developer Registry* is published by Ashton-Tate and is updated regularly. The 1989 edition is 744 pages long and contains a wealth of information for end-users and programmers. While the main focus is products and services related to Ashton-Tate dialects, the *Registry* contains much information which is also relevant to users of other dialects.

Table 13.2 lists the product and service categories and subcategories which are relevant to end-users and Table 14.1 (page 209) lists those which are relevant to programmers. The subcategories appear in parentheses after each category name.

Table 13.2
***Ashton-Tate Developer Registry* End-User Software Categories**

Accounting (general, accounts payable, accounts receivable, general ledger, integrated, inventory control, invoicing, payroll, purchase order processing, time management and billing, other)

Communications and Data Transfer (see Table 14.1)

Data Retrieval (see Table 14.1)

Hardware Products (see Table 14.1)

Manufacturing/Distribution (general, communications, equipment maintenance/history, freight management/dispatching, job costing/quotations, manufacturing resource planning, plant and equipment, production planning, quality control, scheduling/job tracking, other)

Marketing and Promotion (general, advertising, desktop publishing, direct mail, fund raising, public relations, research and analysis, telemarketing, other)

Office and Departmental (general, calendering, filing/document control, finance, legal, list management, messaging/electronic mail, management information systems, project management, scheduling, other)

Personnel and Human Resource Management (general, benefits and compensation, pension planning/reporting, personnel file management, salary administration, staffing analysis and tracking, other)

Sales and Service Management (general, customer/client write-up, mail order, market research/reporting, order entry, point of sale, sales lead tracking, sales tracking, statistical analysis, other)

Training and User Aids (general, audio tape, books, classroom instruction, computer based training, custom training development, software/hardware service and support, user documentation, videotape, workbook/disk, other)

Index Aids

The *Registry* contains seven indexes: Geographic, Area Code, Company Name, Product Name, Function, Industry, and Ashton-Tate Product Compatibility. The Geographic Index lists firms by city in each state or Canadian province. The Area

Code Index lists firms by telephone area code. The categories and subcategories which appear in the Function Index are listed in Tables 13.2 and 14.1, according to their relevance to end-users and programmers, respectively. Table 13.3 lists the categories and subcategories from the Industry Index.

Table 13.3 *Ashton-Tate Developer Registry* Industry Index Categories

Business Services (general, accounting, advertising, architecture, construction, EDP, engineering, import/export, legal, membership, news, nonprofit, packaging, personnel, property management, publishing, real estate, religious institutions, rentals, transportation, other)

Distribution (general, retail, wholesale, other)

Education (general, colleges/universities, libraries, primary/secondary schools, trade schools, other)

Finance (general, banking, brokerage, credit union, investments/financial planning, lending credit, tax planning, trust, other)

Government (general, city, county, military, national, state, other)

Health (general, clinics, dental, home health care, hospitals, laboratory, nursing homes, pharmacy, private practice, veterinary, other)

Insurance (general, agents and brokers, carriers, casualty, medical, property, other)

Manufacturing (general, aerospace, electrical, printing, textile, tools and machinery, other)

Natural Resources (general, agriculture, forestry, marine, mining, petroleum)

Personal Services (general, hotels, restaurants, sports, theaters, other)

Processing (general, chemicals, food)

Utilities (general, broadcasting, communications, electric, telephone, water)

Cross Industry (general)

Chapter 14

Third-Party Software for Programmers

Ashton-Tate has a slogan, "With dBASE, you get more than what's in the box." This quote refers to the vast world of dBASE products and services for the end-user and programmer. Alternative database environments like Paradox, Smart Software, and Magic PC might be preferable to a selected dBASE dialect without supplemental dBASE products and services, but the range of products and services which support users and programmers of such alternative databases is tiny in comparison to the offerings in the dBASE world.

In the last chapter we looked at dBASE software for end-users, and in Part VIII in Volume 2 of this book we will take a very comprehensive look at the collection of published software aids for dBASE dialect programmers. In this chapter, I want to introduce you to this collection in order to make you aware of the *types* of productivity products which are available; the individual products will be covered in Part VIII.

The three tables in this chapter list categories of products and services for dBASE dialect programmers from the following sources: the *Ashton-Tate Developer Registry* (Ashton-Tate 1989), the *Data Based Advisor Database Directory 1990* (Data Based Solutions 1990), and the *Clipper Third Party Products Directory* (Nantucket Corporation 1988). Table 14.1 lists the subcategories for each major division from the Function Index in the *Ashton-Tate Developer Registry*. The subcategories appear in parentheses after each division name.

Table 14.1
***Ashton-Tate Developer Registry* Programmer Software Categories**

Communications/Data Transfer Utilities (general, data format conversion, electronic mail/document transfer, file/data transfer, local area network, micro-mainframe link/data extractor, voice messaging, other)

Data Retrieval (general, catalog systems, mapping systems, research, stock/commodity systems, video image retrieval, other)

Design/Development (general, computer aided design, custom programming, design, scientific software, other)

Development Utilities (general, application generator, database repair and recovery, debugging aid, documentation aid, encryption and security, graphics generator/interface, memory resident application development, program generator, query system, report generator, text editor, other)

Hardware Products (general, bar code reader, communications/I/O boards, expanded/extended memory, local area network board, pointing device, other)

Table 14.2
***Data Based Advisor Database Directory 1990* Product and Service Categories**

Database management systems	Miscellaneous user tools
Flat file programs	File recovery tools
Text based data managers	File conversion tools
Function/code libraries	Accounting products
Graphics tools	Program editors
Communications tools	Publications/books
Query/search tools	Distributors
Report writers	Training
User interface/screen design tools	Hardware/storage media
Documenting tools	Bar code products
Application generators	Miscellaneous
Help systems	Vertical markets
Network/multiuser/connectivity tools	Consultants
Miscellaneous developer tools	

Table 14.3
***Clipper Third Party Products Directory* Product and Service Categories**

Application and code generators
Communication libraries
File repair
General purpose libraries
Online help systems
Print utilities
Program analyzers, debuggers, and documentors
Report writers
Search utilities
Special-purpose libraries
Special-purpose utilities
Translators
Publications

Each block is a simple stone,
yet piled to the sky, a permanent home,
eternally housing Pharoah's bones.
T. D. M.

[My library] functions are programmed on the assumption that whatever you always *have to do, you should* never *have to do. Because of their careful design, they are flexible enough to accommodate even highly complex and sophisticated demands.*
Arthur Fuller, *Dynamics of Clipper*, 1989, p. xxx

Most of the very basic cooking materials ... go
into ninety-nine out of a hundred recipes. ... Success
in cooking depends largely on one's becoming fully aware
of how both common and uncommon ingredients react.
Irma S. Rombauer and Marion Rombauer Becker, *Joy of Cooking*, 1975

Rich the treasure,
Sweet the pleasure, —
Sweet is pleasure after pain.
John Dryden, 1631–1700

Part III

Building Blocks for Standard and Custom dBASE Applications

In this part of the book we move into some of the technology transfer that you read about on the back cover and in the Preface. We will see that there is a standard form to dBASE applications. Armed with that insight, we will in essence reduce the design and implementation of the menu interfaces of a dBASE application to a checklist process.

We will then immerse ourselves in what you might think of as a *chemical* view of dBASE software engineering. In the twentieth century, we know that all of the incredibly varied substances that exist are composed of different arrangements of about 100 fundamental elements. Now you will see how a library of a dozen or more software elements called *templates*, combined with an appropriate subroutine library, can be used to build an unlimited variety of stable and efficient dBASE applications.

Many of the productivity gains that you can obtain from this book are to be found in adopting this library technology, which is not to be underestimated. As you grasp and begin to apply these building block concepts, you will see how to extend them to reap their full benefits for your specific situations.

Chapter 15

The Beautiful Benefits of Standardization

In engineering and commercial design work of all varieties, the use of standard tools and methods is associated with advances in the state of the art and efficiencies in the whole design and implementation process. The absence of standard tools and methods creates the engineering equivalent of the Tower of Babel.

Consider the English language. Although it has many variations the world over, there is an agreed-upon syntax and a common vocabulary which is shared by all educated speakers of English. This shared language allows people to conduct their personal and private business in an easy way which would be quite difficult or impossible without the shared language. Imagine what your life would be like if you had a colleague who sent you memos in Swahili. You couldn't even read his or her communications until you had them sent out for translation.

While the analogy of the Tower of Babel might seem extreme, it is, if anything, too weak. From one viewpoint, an engineering design or product consists of a collection of concepts. The chaos of nonstandard components is more multidimensional than the communication obstruction of different languages, because it is the *ideas themselves* which are incompatible.

In hardware engineering, designers are often constrained, for a variety of mostly economic reasons, to use standard hardware components in design and manufacturing or construction. However, software engineers typically have no external discipline whatsoever to steer them to standard software components.

> **Remark on exploiting standard software components.** One of the many distinctions that can be made between software engineering and programming per se is that the software engineer exploits proven engineering techniques like the use of standard components. In exchange for the discipline of establishing and maintaining standards, there are many benefits, some of which are shown in Table 15.1.

In the section "Canonical Information Structures," starting on page 21 in Chapter 2, we saw some examples which suggested that using canonical structured techniques may make you 10, 100, or even 1,000 times more efficient on a given project. The three benefits listed in Table 15.1 give some insight into these astronomical differences in efficiency; also see Appendix D on page 429.

Table 15.1 Benefits of Standard Software Components

1. A standard software component exists because it does a typical job. A prime example would be code that links menu choices to routines. Without a standard component, you must write the interface each time you put another menu in the application. This is extremely time consuming and very often results in inconsistencies between menus.

   With standard menu components, programmer time is kept to a minimum. Furthermore, the user always sees a consistent interface. *The benefits of minimum programmer time and internal and external consistency accompany this and every other standard component.*

2. Applications can be modified and extended with a minimum of work and with predictable results. Applications which lack standardization are difficult or impossible to modify with predictable results.

3. Applications which are initially developed by more than one individual, or which are maintained over time by more than one individual, retain a standard structure. This eliminates communication and coordination difficulties that would otherwise exist.

Building Blocks: Templates and Subroutines

By using a very small number of different kinds of *standard* parts, a house builder can construct homes with a great variety of external and internal appearances. However, building *custom* features which cannot be constructed from standard parts increases the construction cost and often increases the cost of maintenance also.

In the same way, *standard dBASE applications, which serve the vast majority of dBASE users, can be constructed from a small number of different kinds of components.* In Chapter 2 we met the macro concept, the subroutine concept, and the library concept. In Part III we will see that well-documented libraries of macros and subroutines comprise the standard parts for a state-of-the-art builder of software applications.

In this chapter, the word *macro* refers to the macro concept as explained in Chapter 2. Macros which fully implement the macro concept of Chapter 2 can be *parameterized* and can be used to generate any arbitrary contiguous section of source code. In contrast, dBASE macros can be used to generate at most one command and no parameters may be passed to the macro.

We will shortly see in detail how we can implement information structures which are very similar to parameterized, multiple-line macros. *We will use the term* template *for these structures throughout the book.*

The Relationship of Template Libraries to Subroutine Libraries

Templates and subroutines represent two different but complementary applications of canonical thinking to the software engineering problem: how do we produce the best application at the least cost? Templates and subroutines from libraries can be contrasted by their impact on program size, program speed, and programmer productivity during initial development and maintenance.

Every subroutine can be implemented as a template, but the converse is false, since templates can generate pieces of code that could not be implemented as subroutines. But for the moment, let's think only about templates which *could* be implemented as subroutines.

When code in a subroutine is executed, the system must perform certain housekeeping tasks both before and after the code in the subroutine is executed. Since there is no overhead associated with executing the code in a template, templates lead to faster applications, *but this speed advantage is typically negligible.* One possible exception would be in the case of compiled applications with overlays, because calling a subroutine might cause an overlay to be loaded.

"Speed versus size" is one of the most classic trade-offs in computer programs, and while the templates under discussion implement so-called *in-line subroutines* for a speed advantage, they also inflate the size of source and object code. When a given section of code is implemented as a template and used 10 times in an application, the code appears 10 times. When the same code is implemented as a subroutine, then there are 10 references to the subroutine, but the code appears only once.[1]

If you were using a template to implement an in-line subroutine without parameters, you would use your text editor to insert the text of the subroutine, and you would be done.[2] With the subroutine approach, you would insert a reference of the form "DO NoParms" or "NoParms()". With no-parameter routines, it is the same amount of work for the programmer to create the initial source code with either method.

However, there is a big difference when NoParms must be updated! In that case, you alter one copy or many copies, depending on whether you used the subroutine or template approach.[3]

If a subroutine with parameters is implemented with the template approach, (1) you insert the template text, and (2) at well-marked places in the inserted text, you enter the expressions or identifier names that you would otherwise pass as

1. Depending on its implementation, a dBASE subroutine named MENU might be referenced as "DO MENU", "DO MENU WITH <parameter list>", or "MENU(<parameter list>)". (Note that the second two references might require some assignment statements to initialize parameters.)
2. Alternatively, you could use a preprocessor to implement a multiple-line macro facility. Remember, though, that the overhead of using a preprocessor can be justified only when the benefits are significant.
3. If you used a preprocessor, you would alter the macro definition and then use the preprocessor to generate new source code.

arguments. When you reference the equivalent subroutine, you fill out an argument list, as in "DO ParmProc WITH Parm1,Parm2" or "ParmProc(Parm1,Parm2)".

The subroutine approach might seem to be faster for the programmer who is writing source code. After all, instead of just filling out the argument list, the programmer must search through the template and replace exactly the right text. However, a well-designed template shows you very clearly the places where text must be replaced or inserted.

See the listing of MainScrn.TEM on page 263 for an example. In addition to showing *where* text should be inserted, the well-constructed template also *documents the purpose* of the text which you insert. If the places where text is inserted are clearly indicated, then it is typically faster to use the template than to fill out the argument list, for the following reason.

Unless you are extremely familiar with a library routine, you will need to consult the printed or online documentation for it to see which arguments to specify and in what order. With a good template, you are unlikely to make a mistake in inserting replaceable text. When you build the argument list, you may mistakenly omit arguments, give them the wrong type, or list them in the wrong order.[4]

Clipper permits you to pass 0 to n arguments to a routine with n identifiers in its PARAMETERS statement. FoxPro permits you to pass 1 to n arguments to a routine with n identifiers in its PARAMETERS statement. Thus, if you intend to pass all 5 arguments to a routine with 5 parameters, but you only pass 4 arguments, then some dialects do not complain.

However, for the purposes of illustration, let's assume — for the moment — that you are equally likely to enter a template's replaceable text correctly and to construct the equivalent argument list correctly. In this case, you can generate the first version of the source code in about the same amount of your time with either method.

Under this assumption, creating the source code for the first time is not a differentiating factor. However, if there are any changes to the routine, the subroutine implementation is dramatically superior to the template approach. Again, under our assumption, *the implication is that templates should only be used to generate code whose structure is unlikely to change as the application evolves.*

We will see shortly how to use the template technology to generate the argument lists for subroutine calls in a way which is as reliable as entering replaceable text in subroutine-like templates. Therefore, we can make a recommendation to cover all cases.

---

4. However, we can exploit the template idea to help us fill out the argument list correctly. This approach is explored under the heading "The Millican Interface" later in the chapter.

Table 15.2 Subroutine-Type Templates versus Subroutines

Measurement	Comparison
Program size	Template use generates more code than subroutine use.
Program speed	Template-generated code is faster in theory, but is typically equivalent in practice. The exception is when a subroutine call causes an overlay to be loaded, in which case template-generated code is definitely faster.
Initial development	Using subroutine-type templates takes about the same amount of programmer time as using subroutines.
Maintenance	Templates have the following disadvantages. If a procedure structure that was implemented with a template must be changed, and the template is used more than once, then using templates takes *much* more programmer time than using subroutines, because the alternatives are updating *one* occurrence of a procedure structure versus updating *many* occurrences of a procedure structure. This strongly implies that templates which are used more than once in an application should be used for procedure structures which are unlikely to change over the lifetime of the application.
	Templates have the following advantages. Template-generated source code becomes part of the application, whereas library subroutines are usually documented and maintained separately. The source and object code of the library may be lost, even if the application's source code is not lost. (See the subsection "Maintenance Pitfalls of Subroutine Libraries" on page 218 for more information.)
	Differences in array handling and subroutine calling may favor subroutine-type templates over subroutines when an application has to run under more than one dialect. In many cases, you can implement the in-line form of the subroutine in a dialect-independent fashion, even though you could not write a dialect-independent subroutine to perform the same task.

Let's summarize the results of our analysis in two tables. Table 15.2 contrasts the two approaches, and Table 15.3 presents some recommendations. *Remember that for now we are talking* only *about templates which can be implemented as subroutines.*

Table 15.3 Recommendations on Subroutines and Subroutine-Like Templates

Recommendation on templates as in-line subroutines. Templates should be used to generate in-line subroutines only when (1) the code structure is unlikely to change during the lifetime of the application, (2) the replaceable text is difficult or impractical to pass in arguments, or (3) the subroutine is only used once in the application.

Recommendation on constructing argument lists for library subroutines. For each subroutine, construct a template to set up a call to it. When you need to call this subroutine, insert its "calling" template and enter its replaceable text.

Maintenance Pitfalls of Subroutine Libraries

Cost-effective programming depends critically on the use of subroutine libraries. For that reason, it is all the more important to understand that there are several significant maintenance pitfalls in using subroutine libraries.

Libraries have an evolutionary path that is independent of the applications which use library subroutines. As a library evolves, subroutines may disappear, input specifications may change, or output specifications may change. If the maintenance programmer gets an old application and the new library, they may not be compatible.

An even more serious problem occurs when the maintenance programmer cannot find either the source or object code for the library. Perhaps only undocumented object code is available for the library, which makes its continued use difficult or impossible. And even if the object code is documented, the library cannot be updated unless the source code is also available.

Two common maintenance challenges faced by Clipper consultants illustrate these pitfalls. In the first situation, an application must be maintained which depends on a private library which the original programmer considers to be proprietary. If the library's source code is not available, it will eventually be necessary to rewrite the application. Even if the source code is available, it may still be more cost effective to rewrite the application.

In the second situation, the application depends on one or more unidentified commercial libraries. If you are familiar with the most popular libraries, you will frequently be able to identify the ones in use. In order to maintain such an application, you must (1) own or otherwise have access to all of the libraries used, or (2) rewrite the application.

As subroutine libraries become popular for dialects other than Clipper, all dBASE dialect programmers and consultants will become familiar with these issues. *If you use one or more subroutine libraries in an application, be sure to identify them in source code comments in the main routine!*

Three Non-Subroutine Uses for Templates

Templates constitute a very powerful and general technology. In this subsection we'll see three important uses for fill-in-the-blanks templates other than as forms to generate in-line subroutines.

The Millican Interface

On page 216 we made a temporary assumption about the likelihood of filling in argument lists correctly. We said that it is easier to provide the variable information to the information structure when we fill in a properly labeled template than when we simply fill in an argument list.

However, we can extend the template technology by using a well-labeled, fill-in-the-blanks template to help us get the argument list correctly filled out. For example, say that the routine DispLin2 provides the services of (1) displaying a string at specified screen coordinates in given colors, and (2) setting specified colors after the string is displayed. We may be able to remember the name of the routine and that there are arguments to specify the coordinates, the string, and the two color sets, but in which order should they be specified?

To correspond to our library subroutine DispLin2, we might have a template DispLin2.TEM, which looks like the following:

Listing 15.1 DispLin2.TEM—A Sample Fill-in-the-Blanks Template

```
* Parameters: <Row>,<Column>,<String Color>,<String>,<Reset Color>
DO DispLin2 WITH
```

When you needed to call DispLin2 in your code, you would insert the template, fill in the argument list after "WITH", and then optionally delete the comment line that documents the arguments. (More complex argument lists would require several comment lines of explanation, which again could be erased when they were no longer needed.) This method of generating the source code reference to a library routine is probably even more fail-safe than replacing text in a well-documented subroutine-type template. (This observation also shows that our previous assumption about the rough equivalence of the amount of programmer time used to generate source code the first time with templates versus subroutines is valid in a broad context.)

Remark on Millican interfaces. I define *Millican interface* as a template which is used to construct a call to a subroutine. The Millican interface to a subroutine library is the set of templates which are used to construct calls to the subroutines in the library.

Recommendation on Millican interfaces. Construct a Millican interface for each subroutine that you use on a regular basis. If you publish a subroutine library, include a Millican interface with it.

Templates for Procedures Which Cannot Be Parameterized

A second important use of templates is to implement procedure structures with replaceable text when the text is impossible or inconvenient to pass as an argument. For example, in the menu screen templates we'll see in Chapter 18, part of the replaceable text is the screen text of the menu.

This text is displayed between TEXT/ENDTEXT keywords. In dialects with array support, the screen lines could be passed in one argument as an array of character strings. In any case, it will be more work to get the text into an argument than to simply type it between TEXT and ENDTEXT.

The following trade-off occurs when the replaceable text in a procedure structure is complex and possibly difficult to pass as one or more arguments. If we decide to use the subroutine approach (with its requirement to prepare complex argument lists), then we have the benefits of using a standard library subroutine: the subroutine source code is stored in one place only, it is standard, it can be reused, and so on. (We are also subject to the maintenance pitfalls of subroutine libraries, as explained in the previous subsection.)

Otherwise, we insert the template into our source code and enter the replaceable text. When this text must change, we edit it "in context" instead of only in an argument list. *This method may be more dialect-independent than passing arguments.* For example, many procedure structures can be implemented as subroutines only with the use of array parameters, but it is not possible to write a dialect-independent subroutine with an array parameter. However, such a procedure structure may often be implemented as a dialect-independent in-line subroutine.

Templates for Frequently Used Procedure Structures

A third important use of templates is to minimize your typing of common text patterns. Prime examples are loops and if/then/else structures.

For example, the template library presented in this book implements three standard formats for dBASE loops. Source code which is implemented with the assistance of these templates might have 100 *occurrences* of the standard loops, but each occurrence would have been generated with one of the three loop templates in the template library.

Much of Part III of this book is devoted to enumerating and demonstrating a basic set of template building blocks for dBASE dialects. This template technology requires nothing beyond a text editor with an "insert file" command. Despite its simplicity, this technology is very powerful.

Applications developed with template building blocks are not dependent on extra products like code generators, yet they offer many of the same benefits. *Building block code which is handed over to a programmer who has not seen the building block library will simply seem to be very well structured.* The benefits of this approach are discussed in detail in the first pages of Chapter 18.

At this time, let's officially meet the book's template concept. Then we'll look at some of the usage issues connected with this template technology and learn about some related software engineering principles.

Fill-in-the-Blanks Source Code Templates

These software building blocks are implemented as code structures which are literally data-entry forms. I call these forms *templates*.

Our templates have two types of text, fixed and replaceable. Fixed text is in a fixed position relative to the other parts of the template and is not modified by the programmer. Replaceable text refers to the dBASE code which must replace the description.

Here is perhaps the simplest useful example, an IF statement with no ELSE part. The fixed text is the IF and ENDIF. The replaceable text is the condition tested and the body of the IF. The condition is replaced by a dBASE expression with type Logical. The body of the IF template is replaced by one or more dBASE statements.

Listing 15.2 Template for IF—A Sample

```
IF (<logical expression>)
   <one or more statements>
ENDIF
```

Templates, Readability, and Coding Standards

One of the most important software engineering concepts is that source code should be as readable as possible. To facilitate readability, the components of canonically structured source code are arranged according to the following two principles:

Principle A. The *differences* between components are as obvious as feasible.
Principle B. The *relationships* between components are as obvious as feasible.

To follow Principle A, we write the IF and ENDIF keywords at the same level of indentation, we write the body at the next level of indentation, and we place the logical condition in parentheses, even though the parentheses aren't required. A typical choice for levels of indentation is 3 columns or characters per level. With this scheme, an IF keyword would be in one of the columns 0, 3, 6, ..., and so on.

In addition, programmer-created elements like the logical condition are written in a mixture of uppercase and lowercase letters to facilitate reading, just as you find in ordinary text. Try printing one of your documents in all uppercase letters and you will notice that it is harder to read.

To follow Principle B, we write the keywords in uppercase and also place them at the same level of indentation. This standard technique for all programming languages tells us by inspection the identity of the procedure structure which we examine. Remember that a canonical representation shows us *on inspection* some of the characteristics of the structure it represents.

Remark. I personally choose to violate Principle B when I feel that readability is improved by the violation. For example, I write the commonly used built-in functions RECNO() and RECCOUNT() as RecNo() and RecCount(). Since these functions are used very often, my successors and I won't forget that these functions are built in. Generally speaking, I prefer "SET Display ON" to "SET DISPLAY ON"; again, it is obvious that "Display" is a keyword.

Most well-thought-out conventions for using uppercase and lowercase letters in source code are probably roughly equivalent in benefit. A more important point to remember is the importance of consistency. Choose any convention you can justify, but then *follow it religiously!* (For more information on coding standards, see Appendix E, "Coding Standards for dBASE Dialects," on page 431, and *Building Source Code Libraries* (Yellick 1989a).)

Editing Procedures for Templates

If you use an editor with macro capabilities or a TSR with macro capabilities, like SuperKey or one of its brethren, you have the option of storing templates as macros which are invoked by a single keystroke. However, our fill-in-the-blanks template technology can be implemented using nothing more than an editor with an "insert file" command.

When this command is invoked, the editor prompts you for a filename and inserts the contents of the named file at the cursor. Most editors have such a command; in particular, the typical dBASE dialect's built-in editor has this command.

Throughout this book, I refer to the recommended directory structure which is shown in Appendix C on page 427. With this structure, dBASE files which may be used by any application are stored in \DB\Util. I recommend that you give your template files the extension .TEM and store them in \DB\Util.

Handling Pathnames

Some text editors will not allow you to specify a pathname for an inserted file, but you can virtually always specify a disk drive for the file. MS-DOS versions 3.1 and higher give you the SUBST command, which permits you to assign an unused drive letter as an abbreviation for a pathname.

Assuming that you have the SUBST command in your DOS, I recommend that you include the line

LastDrive=Z

in your CONFIG.SYS file. This gives you the use of all 26 drive letters from A: to Z:. Then have a list of SUBST commands in your AutoExec.BAT file. For example:

```
SUBST F: C:\Batch
SUBST U: C:\DB\Util
```

These two SUBST commands permit you to type "F:12CPI.LJ2" or "U:IF.TEM" as abbreviations for "C:\Batch\12CPI.LJ2" or "C:\DB\Util\IF.TEM". Notice that this solves the file insertion problem for editors which do not support pathnames. When you want the IF template, ask for "U:IF.TEM".

However, you'll want to use this abbreviation technique even if your editor *does* support pathnames. You will save a lot of typing by entering the form "U:IF.TEM" instead of the much longer "C:\DB\Util\IF.TEM".

Column Alignment

There is one other implementation problem with fill-in-the-blanks templates. When the cursor is in column 0 and you insert a file, its contents appear onscreen with an indentation of 0. However, template files must be displayed with the proper indentation, which often is not 0.

If the cursor is in column 3 and you insert a template file, then the first line of the template will have an indentation of 3, but subsequent lines probably will have an indentation of 0. Thus, putting the cursor in column 3 is usually not enough to cause the template to be aligned to column 3.

Many editors have column commands or left margin commands which you can apply to a block of contiguous lines to shift the lines to the right or left onscreen — that is, to alter the indentation of the block. In my editor, the text which is inserted with the Insert File command is already marked as a block, so all I need to do to get a template to the proper column is to insert it at column 0 and then give the command to shift a block to the right by the appropriate number of columns.

A second approach is to store each combination of template and indentation in its own template file. For example, in the first approach we have IF.TEM, which is inserted at column 0, 3, 6, ..., or inserted at column 0 and then moved to column 3, 6, 9, ... However, we could have IF0.TEM, IF3.TEM, IF6.TEM, ..., which would all be inserted at column 0. With this method, you would get an IF template at an indentation of 3 by inserting IF3.TEM at column 0.

Now that I have introduced the concepts and issues of fill-in-the-blanks source code templates, I want to turn in the next two chapters to the related topics of the standard top-level procedure structures in dBASE applications on MS-DOS computers. Then we'll finish Part III by listing and discussing the templates in our library of dBASE templates.

Code Generators versus Our Templates

Code generators for dBASE dialects are typically based on template files which are conceptually very similar to our templates. Like our templates, those used with code generators have both fixed and replaceable text. The code generator solicits information from you which is used to substitute for the replaceable text when the code generator produces executable source code.

The most advanced dBASE dialect code generators have a benefit which is difficult to duplicate with templates, which is the ability to generate code for all of the major dialects from the same template. To get the equivalent benefit from template libraries, you must maintain a separate version of the library for each supported dialect.

Syntax-Directed Editing versus Automatic Code Generation

When we humans type procedure structures with our text editors, we are subject to mistakes like misspelling keywords (NEDIF appears instead of ENDIF) and forgetting to terminate multiple-command structures (missing ELSE, ENDIF, ENDDO). Templates help us avoid such clerical-level errors.

Templates facilitate code generation in an automatic or semiautomatic fashion. When we use code generators, they solicit replaceable text for the templates from us and automatically produce source code that is a combination of the fixed text of the templates and the replaceable text which we provide. When templates are used during the conventional editing process that produces source code manually, you insert the text of the template and enter replaceable text at locations which you manually identify and to which you move the cursor.

The most obvious advantage of the editor-level use of templates is the saving of keystrokes, but there is a more subtle benefit of equal importance, which is syntax support. Syntax support helps us avoid the purely clerical errors which may reflect more on our typing ability or the number of phone calls we got when we were entering the source code than on our programming ability.

At the time of writing, I am not aware of a syntax-directed editor for any dBASE dialect. A syntax-directed editor works like any other editor, except that it imposes structure requirements on the text which is entered, so that some arrangements of text can be produced and others cannot be produced.

In such an editor, when you need to enter an IF statement, you tell the editor, which then inserts an IF statement template at the proper indentation in your source code file. While you are building the IF statement, you may enter text either in the logical-condition part of the template, or in the IF-clause part of the template. Such an editor will *not* let you move the cursor to the IF or ENDIF keywords, which prevents accidental alteration or deletion of properly spelled keywords.

Similarly, you will not be able to move the cursor into the left margin of the lines in the IF/ENDIF structure. This means that the indentation of your source code will continuously reflect its logical structure, according to the quite sensible standard of our industry.

The template technology in this book allows you to make any editor look something like a syntax-directed editor. A highly programmable editor, like Brief, can be set up to act even more like a real syntax-directed editor.

The only true syntax-directed editor which I have ever seen was created for PASCAL by a California university. Please write to me at the address in Appendix A if you know of — or if you develop (!) — a true syntax-directed editor for one or more dBASE dialects. I will put this information in a news file on the companion diskettes for Volumes 1 and 2 and incorporate it in the next edition of the book.

Compiled Code versus Interpreted Code

If your code will be compiled after it is prepared, the compiler will (presumably) detect any syntax errors of the type that the Millican templates are designed to prevent. However, interpreters (such as dBASE III PLUS) might not be able to detect problems like missing ENDIF and ENDDO statements, or misspellings like NEDIF and ENDO, until the code is exercised in a certain way. When FoxBASE+ produces .FOX files from .PRG files, a structure defect like a missing ENDIF is passed into the .FOX file without complaint; tokenization is a much lower level of translation than compilation.

The obvious implication is that syntax support via templates is more important for interpreter users than for compiler users. Compilers will usually detect all of the syntax errors which templates help you avoid after each change in source code. Interpreters detect some syntax errors only under some conditions, if at all. (Beware: so-called debuggers may not find as many errors as compilers, and compilers will not necessarily find all errors.)

Ode to a Blockhead

Beautiful blocks canonically measured
Lead to a love eternally treasured,
Giving the gift of your constant pleasure;
Enriching your work and easing the pressure.

Chapter 16

A Standard DOS Menu for a dBASE PC

Maximum user productivity results from an information processing system which is as automatic as possible. In particular, operations which are performed often should be invoked from a menu. In the next chapter we will look at menu issues for a dBASE application, but applications are of course run on top of the OS (operating system). Therefore, at least one menu is needed at the OS level, and this chapter presents a sample for MS-DOS. The syntax of the example is specific to MS-DOS, but the technique is the same on any OS.

A Menu for the Operating System Level

Let's assume that you are setting up an MS-DOS computer to run dBASE and other applications. The user needs an OS-level menu to choose dBASE, other applications, and basic operations needed by all users. Listing 16.1 presents a sample DOS menu.

Listing 16.1 Sample DOS Menu

```
                         The ACME Brick Company
                           ***  DOS  Menu  ***

          D      Database Processing
          S      Spreadsheet Processing
          W      Word Processing
          B      Backup the databases to diskettes
          R      Remote operations by the programmer
          P      Prepare hard disk for turning the computer off
          T      Reset the time and/or date if incorrect as displayed
  Your choice of D,  S,  W,  B,  R,  P,  or  T ?
```

There are two typical methods for displaying a DOS menu from a batch file. In the first method, you use a series of ECHO statements to display the lines of the menu onscreen. This keeps all of the information in the batch file, but the menu is rather difficult to construct and edit.

The usual technique is to place the menu in a file by itself and display that file with the TYPE command. I recommend the following nomenclature. If the batch file is DOSmenu.BAT, then call the file which contains the first menu to be displayed DOSmenu.I1. The "I" stands for "Insert" and the "1" represents insert number 1. Somewhere in DOSmenu.BAT, there is a line which reads

TYPE DOSmenu.I1

Subsequent files containing text to be TYPEd are named DOSmenu.I2, DOSmenu.I3, and so on. The next listing shows a batch file which would clear the screen and display the menu stored in the text file DOSmenu.I1.

Listing 16.2 A Batch File to Display a Menu

```
ECHO OFF
REM File = DOSmenu.BAT.
CLS
TYPE DOSmenu.I1
```

After the menu is displayed, control returns to DOS, which displays the default DOS prompt or the prompt defined with the DOS PROMPT command. The cursor blinks immediately to the right of the last character of the prompt, awaiting user input. In this example, batch files named D.BAT, S.BAT, W.BAT, B.BAT, R.BAT, P.BAT, and T.BAT must be found in the current DOS directory or in directories listed in the DOS PATH.

Each batch file must return to the DOS directory which was current when the batch file was invoked. For example, if the batch file started on drive C: and switched to drive D:, then it must change back to C:. If it started in C:\Cats and switched (with CD) to C:\Dogs, then it must CD back to C:\Cats at the end of the batch file.

Each of the batch files D.BAT, S.BAT, and so on must end with the command "DOSmenu", which causes the DOS Menu to be displayed again. Without this command, the user would be dumped at the DOS level without a menu. Here is an example of the batch file associated with the "T" choice.

Listing 16.3 A Batch File Associated with a DOS Menu Choice

```
REM File = T.BAT  — helps user reset time and date.
Time
Date
DOSmenu
```

A Smarter DOS Menu

In the absence of a special utility, like ASK.COM in the Norton Utilities, you link menu choices to actions with batch files whose filenames consist of one letter. For example, if "P" is the label for the choice "Park the hard disk", then a file called P.BAT would contain a PARK command or commands.

Unfortunately, this approach gives you very little control over use of the menu. For example, if the user types "G" when aiming for the "T" key, DOS says "file not found" or worse, DOS finds and executes a file which is invoked by mistake!

A tool like ASK.COM permits you to branch to batch files with any names you like. Alternatively, you can branch to sections of the same batch file, so that you can keep all of the code in one batch file. You can also reject choices which aren't on the menu, in order to restrict your user to supported options.

If you use MS-DOS 3.3 or higher, you have the CALL command to invoke batch files as subroutines. Consider this batch file:

```
ShowMenu.BAT
Park.COM
```

When the MS-DOS command processor sees the ShowMenu.BAT command, it starts executing ShowMenu.BAT without saving a return address. Unlike the case with the usual called procedure, control does not return to the caller. This means that Park.COM will never be executed by the batch file.

MS-DOS 3.3 introduces the CALL verb. If you execute the following batch file in MS-DOS 3.3 or higher, then the Park program is run after ShowMenu.BAT:

```
CALL ShowMenu.BAT
Park.COM
```

Listing 16.4 shows a "smart" batch file for menu display which uses the ASK command from the Norton Utilities and the CALL command from DOS 3.3; the menu text is in the file DOSmenu.I1. (Public domain or shareware equivalents to Norton's ASK.COM should be available on electronic bulletin boards.)

Listing 16.4 A Smart Batch File to Display a Menu

```
@ECHO OFF
REM File = DOSmenu.BAT.  For MS-DOS 3.3 or higher.
:Start
CLS
TYPE DOSmenu.I1
ASK  "", DSWBRPT
IF ERRORLEVEL 7 CALL T
GOTO Start
IF ERRORLEVEL 6 CALL P
GOTO Start
IF ERRORLEVEL 5 CALL R
GOTO Start
IF ERRORLEVEL 4 CALL B
GOTO Start
IF ERRORLEVEL 3 CALL W
GOTO Start
IF ERRORLEVEL 2 CALL S
GOTO Start
IF ERRORLEVEL 1 CALL D
GOTO Start
```

The batch files T.BAT, P.BAT, and so on no longer need the last line of "DOSmenu". As an additional benefit, menu choices which are not on the list will be rejected. (DOS versions 3.3 and higher permit the form "@ECHO OFF", which suppresses the onscreen message "ECHO OFF" which otherwise appears.)

This batch file will work as shown only if ASK.COM and the batch files T.BAT, P.BAT, and so on are in the current DOS directory or can be found on the DOS PATH. You must also have the ASK.COM utility from the Norton Utilities, or an equivalent utility.

PC Magazine DOS Power Tools

PC Magazine has published a must-have book called *PC Magazine DOS Power Tools* (Somerson 1988). This massive book has 1,275 pages, includes a diskette, and covers DOS versions through 4.0. *PC Magazine* is famous for its constantly growing collection of utilities — each issue includes a presentation of at least one utility. This book presents a wealth of information which is crucial for programmers who develop DOS-based applications and includes over 200 documented utilities.

For example, Where.COM searches your hard disk for the directory or directories which include files matching a filespec. Test1980.COM tests to see if the system date is 1980, which means that your user did not set the system time. RenDir.COM renames directories. Sweep.COM executes a command in every directory on a disk.

KeyPress.COM is very similar to the Norton Utilities' ASK.COM. The differences are that (1) keystrokes not on the specified list cause KeyPress.COM to return a DOS ERRORLEVEL of 0 (ASK.COM sounds the bell and waits for a valid keystroke) and (2) KeyPress.COM does not support a prompt; you must use a command such as ECHO or TYPE instead.

The High-Fashion DOS Menu

You can make your menus more visually appealing by using the line drawing characters in the 8-bit IBM ASCII character set. Although these characters may not print on some printers, they should display properly on any MS-DOS computer.[1] With more work, we could present our Acme Brick client or employer with the DOS menu shown in Listing 16.5.

Listing 16.5 A High-Fashion DOS Menu

```
                    The ACME Brick Company

                         DOS    MENU

        D       Database Processing
        S       Spreadsheet Processing
        W       Word Processing

        R       Remote operations by the programmer

        B       Backup the databases to diskettes
        P       Prepare hard disk for turning the computer off
        T       Reset the time and/or date if incorrect as displayed

  Your choice of  D,  S,  W,  R,  B,  P,  or  T ?
```

1. The file Boxes.REF on the companion diskette includes a large variety of boxes drawn with different combinations of line-drawing characters; you can cut and paste from this file into your applications.

A menu like this can be constructed in less time than you might think by using the screen part of the screen templates in Chapter 18. It does not, however, change the way in which the user selects options.

You may offer your user a colorful point-and-shoot menu with a moving-bar cursor by using a commercial or shareware menu product for DOS. Note, however, that this benefit for the user means added complexity for the initial programmer and the maintenance programmer. For example, *you* may have an anecdotal familiarity with the ZYU54BC.COM public domain DOS menu program, but how about your successor? Will the maintenance programmer know how to operate this program? Will the documentation for it be stored with the documentation of the application which uses it?

Will ZYU54BC.COM continue to work with later DOS versions? Will the maintenance programmer know how to get updates of ZYU54BC.COM? Will there *be* any upgrades?

Let's rank the DOS menu options available to us and then study some recommendations.

A Hierarchy of DOS Menu Methods: Costs and Benefits

You can implement a basic DOS menu in very little time, but it won't stun and amaze the user (should this be important). Furthermore, such DOS-only menus don't let you reject the user keystrokes which don't correspond to menu choices.

With increasing effort and reliance on utilities which are not included with DOS, you can filter keystrokes and make the DOS-level menus fancier in appearance and more elegant in usage. Here is a summary of the costs and benefits of each approach; Table 16.1 lists recommendations.

1. **The no-frills DOS menu.** *Benefits:* very quick to implement, uses only DOS facilities, and doesn't cause problems with users who type carefully. *Costs:* does not trap unsupported keystrokes, does not look or act "fancy," and does not support popup help screens.
2. **The no-frills DOS menu with line-drawing characters.** *Benefit:* much more visually appealing than the no-frills menu. *Cost:* only a little more work than the no-frills menu.
3. **The DOS menu with error trapping.** *Benefit:* filters user keystrokes so that those which do not correspond to menu choices are ignored. *Costs:* a DOS-level utility which is not included with MS-DOS must be available to all initial and maintenance programmers, the utility must be understood by all the programmers, the utility must be installed properly on each computer which executes the main application, the utility must be updated as its vendor eliminates bugs, the utility must be compatible with all DOS versions which are to be used during the lifetime of the application, and the utility must be compatible with the *combination* of DOS and all drivers and TSRs which might be loaded when the utility is invoked, during the entire lifetime of the application.

4. **The high-fashion DOS menu.** *Benefit:* offers your users colorful point-and-shoot interfaces. *Costs:* the same as with the error-trapping menu, except that the ASK.COM type of utility is easy to understand and can probably be figured out from an example, even if the programmer has no documentation. In contrast, a menu utility is far more complex and might be unusable without its documentation. Furthermore, to a much greater extent than with a very simple utility like ASK.COM, a menu utility is subject to bugs and incompatibilities with drivers, TSRs, and future DOS versions.

Table 16.1 Recommendations for DOS Menus

Identifying minimum cost. Determine which of the DOS menu methods will be acceptable to the user. Then implement the acceptable method which takes the least amount of money and programmer time.

There is no further consideration when you are serving other employees at your company. When you market your services to clients, you may wish to provide a fancier DOS menu than they would require, in an attempt to increase the likelihood of further work. If you sell a program on the open market, you may want to use point-and-shoot menus throughout, both at the DOS level and inside your application.

Trapping user keystrokes. If it is possible and feasible, use a utility like ASK.COM to filter user keystrokes. Such a utility is so simple in its operation and implementation that it should be relatively immune to changes in DOS. The main cost is making sure that ASK.COM (or its equivalent) stays installed and available to the batch files that reference it during the lifetimes of the batch files.

Determining cost versus benefit. Use the menu method whose benefits balance its cost. If you use a non-DOS menu utility, pick one which is well supported by a vendor who has been in business for a period of time, and make sure that all needed information about the menu utility will be available to the maintenance programmer.

A Checklist for Implementing OS-Level Menus

Several operations are needed on all personal computers, such as parking the hard disk heads and backing up data files. For this reason, the set of selections for a MS-DOS menu is standard, as shown in Table 16.2. If appropriate, you could also add other choices such as “W” for word processing, “S” for spreadsheet processing, and so on.

Table 16.2 Standard OS-Level Menu Choices

1. A choice “B” to back up data files.
2. A choice “P” to park the hard disk heads prior to turning the computer off.
3. A choice “T” to reset the time and/or date, if they do not display correctly.

4. A choice "U" to unfragment the disk, if an unfragment utility is installed. (Example: OPTune from Gazelle Systems.)
5. A choice "R" to prepare the computer for remote operations by the programmer. (Example: PCanywhere from Dynamic Microprocessor Associates.)

The Format of .BAT Subroutines for the DOS-Level Menu

Now say that T.BAT contains the DOS commands TIME and DATE. If you use the ASK utility, you will "CALL T.BAT" when the user strokes "T". In that case, T.BAT only needs the two lines

```
REM T.BAT.
REM This form is OK when you CALL T.BAT.
TIME
DATE
```

Otherwise, the last line in T.BAT should be "DOSmenu" or "DOSmenu.BAT". Such a line runs the menu-display batch file after the chosen action has been performed; without it, the user would choose "T", correct the time and/or date, and then be greeted with the naked DOS prompt, without menu guidance!

```
REM T.BAT.
REM This form is required when the user strokes T to run T.BAT.
TIME
DATE
DOSmenu
```

Chapter 17

The Standard Model of a dBASE Application

The top-level procedures of a dBASE application display a main menu and associate choices with actions. Some of the actions may be to display submenus. This chapter explains the structure of templates which can be used to construct the main menu and submenus of an application *in minimum programmer time.*

In the next chapter, we'll take a detailed look at each template in the template library, including the main menu and submenu templates. *For now, our objective is to conceptually understand how to build the user interface with menu templates.*

The Psychology and Economics of Menu Interfaces

Issues of menu interfaces can become quite emotional for both programmers and end-users. Both parties are sometimes more focused on the look and feel of menu interfaces than on the services which are invoked by the menu selections! In addition, programmers who do not have menu-building tools such as code generators, menu templates, or a menu interface library sometimes spend huge amounts of time developing their menus, at the expense of the quality and quantity of the services which the menu choices invoke.

There is no question that many PC users have come to expect point-and-shoot interfaces in all programs, both commercial and custom. The only way to communicate the distinction between commercial and custom programming to some users is to say, "Your fancy menu interface will cost an extra X dollars," or "Your fancy menu interface will take an extra X days."

Fancy menu interfaces are typically dialect-dependent. If you master a technique in one dialect and must port your application to another dialect, you may find yourself rewriting a great deal of code. If you have to develop code for another dialect, you will have to research menu methods in that dialect.

Generally speaking, two conflicting goals challenge programmers. On the one hand, users want very high quality in their applications; furthermore, their expectations are constantly being elevated as the state of the art advances. On the other hand, the demand for applications exceeds any supply rate that is achievable in our lifetimes.

Remark on the object of software engineering. One can say that the object of software engineering is to simultaneously increase the quality and quantity of applications. This can be done by developing better tools and techniques.

In Chapter 22 we will address the range of menu options which is available in the different dialects. In this chapter, we look at a menu technology for dBASE dialects which is dialect-independent, highly functional, very fast for the initial programmer to create, and very easy for the maintenance programmer to update.

The menu screens are colorful and attractive, so there is no loss of visual appeal in this minimum-cost implementation method. However, while keystrokes which do not correspond to menu choices do generate an error message, the interface is look-and-type instead of the state-of-the-art point-and-shoot. Table 17.1 gives some recommendations.

Table 17.1 Recommendations on Minimum-Cost dBASE Menus

Calculating menu costs. When you calculate the cost of using a particular menu interface, consider the implications for the maintenance programmer, in addition to the implications for you as the initial developer. How difficult is it to add, delete, and rearrange menu choices? Will your code have to be ported, and if so, at what cost? Will the maintenance programmer understand your special techniques well enough to duplicate them? Will you need to write documentation for your menu techniques which the maintenance programmer wouldn't need for a simpler technique (like the one in this chapter)?

Selecting menu templates. If your users do not require point-and-shoot menu interfaces, use the dialect-independent menu templates in this book to develop your menu interface.

Using point-and-shoot menu interfaces. If you decide to use point-and-shoot menus in your application, think about the likelihood that the application will be ported to another dialect during the lifetime of the application. If porting seems likely, design your code so as to isolate the dialect-dependent parts into well-identified subroutines. If you have to port the code later, you will just replace the dialect-dependent subroutines (and possibly modify their calling sequences). Alternatively, if you know in advance the specific dialect to which the code will be ported, then — if feasible — design menu code which works under both dialects!

The Main Procedure

The top-level procedure (or command file) has three parts: a first part for initialization; a second part which calls the main menu-displaying routine in a loop; and a third part, generically called an *epilogue*, which is executed to close down the application.

Initialization of the Main Procedure

In any computer language, applications must perform actions such as the initialization of top-level variables when the application begins. A well-structured application isolates these start-up actions in code which I'll call the *initialization segment.* The initialization segment may perform one or more of the actions in Table 17.2.

Table 17.2 Initialization for the Main Procedure

1. Establish the default states for one or more of the SET commands. (Here, the word *default* applies to the application. If EXACT ON is the application default, any routine which executes SET EXACT OFF should execute SET EXACT ON at or before exit.)
2. Set the current DOS drive and DOS directory. (The current dBASE directory is the same as the current DOS directory, but dBASE has its own default drive, controlled by SET DEFAULT TO <drive letter>.)
3. CLOSE ALL to close any open files, except currently active command files, which stay open.
4. CLEAR ALL to release any currently defined memory variables.
5. Perform dialect-specific initializations, such as CLEAR PROGRAM for Fox-BASE+.
6. Define function keys. (For example, have F9 type out today's date, followed by a carriage return.)
7. Create PUBLIC and PRIVATE variables and assign values to them.

The Main Menu Loop

The routine which displays the main menu is enclosed in a loop which is executed until the user exits from the application. The first action inside the loop is to call a routine to display the menu onscreen and solicit a menu choice from the user in the form of a single keystroke. This keystroke is passed back to the caller in a character parameter called MenuChoice.

Back in the caller, MenuChoice is used in a DO CASE structure to associate the menu choices with actions. The menu templates in this book use the <period> keystroke to return to the caller. Inside the loop, this value of MenuChoice triggers loop exit.

Epilogue Code

When the loop is exited, the commands between the last ENDDO and the end of the file are called the *epilogue* in generic jargon. This code performs the final actions necessary before returning to the interpreter prompt. For example, when returning to the interpreter mode, you will normally want to set SAFETY, STATUS, and TALK ON; presumably you turned them OFF in the initialization part of the application.

Main Menus and Submenus

Submenus differ from main menus in several ways. First, they usually do not need to do much initialization; certainly they do not need to set up variables and settings for the entire application, as does the main menu routine.

Second, the main menu template has standard entries to return to DOS or to the interpreter level. These options are not needed by submenus.

Third, no epilogue code is usually required. Occasionally, a special setting is used in a portion of an application which is associated with a specific submenu. In that case, the setting is established in the initialization part of the submenu routine, and the setting is returned to its usual *application default* value in the epilogue.

Menu Screens and Exit Keystrokes

The main screen template that is used with the main menu template has the choice <period> to return to the interpreter, where the period is usually used as the default prompt. In dBASE, this default prompt is called the *dot prompt*. The user can easily remember the natural rule, "Enter a dot to get the dot prompt."

There is an unexpected advantage in using the period as the exit character, because it ends sentences and thus is associated with ending one activity and starting another. By analogy, the right angle bracket ">" is used on the main menu to return to DOS, where the right angle bracket is often the default prompt.

Although there is no problem in theory with giving users a choice to exit to DOS on each menu, I believe that it is poor design. It certainly adds to the size of the source code and to the amount of information which the user sees onscreen. Accordingly, the submenu templates in this book do not have an "exit to DOS" choice.

However, each submenu *does* need an exit to return to the previous menu. Following the same reasoning as before, we use the period as the exit character. Use of the period as the exit character for submenus also maintains compatibility with the use of the period as an exit character on the main menu!

Sample Menu Screens from the Millican Templates

The sample screens in Listings 17.1 and 17.2 were generated by code produced from the four menu templates in the next chapter. Underlined text in the listings appears onscreen in the currently defined alternate colors. These colors are typically used only for the editing windows in which data is entered or updated. However, with the use of CLEAR GETS, we can display the status line at the top of the screen and the list of keystroke choices in an alternate color without using any SET COLOR TO commands.

For example, unless my users request otherwise, I give them primary colors of yellow on blue and alternate colors of blue on green. With these colors, the status line and the list of keystroke choices are in blue on green; the solid lines are yellow.

(On a black-and-white monitor, the status line and keystroke choices are in inverse video (black on white) and the solid lines are white.)

Listing 17.1 Sample Main Menu from Template-Generated Code

```
Million $ Version 3.4.        2,951,168 bytes free.        Sunday, 10/22/89 05:24:52

                  Main Menu for The ACME Brick Company

   D    Data Base Management
   A    Accounting Functions

   W    Word Processing with Microsoft Word
   S    Spreadsheet Processing

   Q    Quick-DOS (look & select replacement for MS-DOS commands)
   R    Run an MS-DOS command

   >    Return to the ACME DOS Menu and the DOS prompt

   .    Run dBASE III from the . prompt (requires some dBASE III knowledge)

   Your Pleasure of D, A, W, S, Q, R, >, .? A
   Change your choice or stroke a carriage return to confirm it:  A
```

Listing 17.2 Sample Submenu from Template-Generated Code

```
Million $ Version 3.4.        2,949,120 bytes free.        Sunday, 10/22/89 05:36:36

              Database Submenu for The ACME Brick Company

   A    Add a person or organization to the People database.
   E    Edit or display a record in the People database.

   M    Mailing labels Submenu.

   Q    Query the PEOPLE database with ad hoc questions.
   R    Reports Submenu.

   C    Conferences & Seminars Submenu.
   S    Maintenance Submenu.

   .    Return to the Main Menu.

   Your Pleasure of A, E, M, Q, R, C, S, .? S
   Change your choice or stroke a carriage return to confirm it:  _
```

The solid lines are created using IBM ASCII characters 219 to 223, and the double horizontal rule character is 205. (See ASCII.REF and Boxes.REF on the companion diskette to this book for a table of all 256 ASCII characters and a large collection of boxes of different types.) Using character 223 for the box top and character 220 for the box bottom gives a larger box interior than using the character 219 for all sides of the box.[1] Line-drawing characters in code generated from the Millican templates always appear in the currently defined foreground color.

The first sample is a main menu and the second sample is the database submenu invoked with choice "D" on the main menu. The PUBLIC memvar Version is set to "Million $ Version 3.4" in the code that made these menus.

How Canonical?

Some of the dialects offer a variety of selection options for menus, such as pull-down and moving-bar menus. In some cases, you will definitely want to use these "fancy" interfaces. However, I urge you not to use a dialect-specific interface just because it is flashy. If you develop applications for a client or employer, it is very likely that someone other than yourself will maintain the code in the long run. Even if your application does not have a long life, parts of it may move into other applications. Your menu implementation decisions may have implications for many years.

The menus implemented by the Millican templates are extremely functional for the user and are very easy for the programmer to construct and maintain. Even so, they involve no technology beyond that available in the dBASE dialect you use.

The source code is highly structured and easy to understand. This means that a less experienced programmer can understand it without much effort. As far as I know, the code will operate in all dBASE dialects (although the graphics characters used in the screen template may not be available on all computers). This means that a programmer who is versed in a different dBASE dialect than the one you use will not be obstructed by encountering dialect-specific commands. So not only will any dBASE dialect programmer understand menu code built from these templates, so will any dBASE dialect!

Remark on circumstances which force a change of dialect. A host of predictable and unpredictable circumstances can cause you to have to use a different dBASE dialect than the one you started with. Sometimes you abandon the original dialect for a better one, and sometimes the code must be made to work under two or more dialects. The Millican-template menus will work with all dialects, so no modification is required for them to run under several dialects at once, or under a "new and improved" dialect!

Programmer Effort

As much as feasible, all Millican templates, and not just the menu ones, limit the programmer's typing to the bare minimum of information which must be provided. A small exception is the screen templates, whose menu choices must be entered

1. This book was typeset using the PostScript page description language. Due to a limitation in a PostScript workaround to provide line-drawing characters which are not normally available in PostScript fonts, characters 220 to 223 appear as character 219.

both in the TEXT ... ENDTEXT section of the template and in a character constant. Note that the template provides the space for a small number of menu choices.

My intent is that you will use the copy-and-paste facilities of your editor to duplicate template components as needed. For example, if you need five occurrences of the pattern

```
CASE (<expL>)
   DO <routine>
```

then you can copy one occurrence and duplicate it as many times as needed.

In the case of menu screens, I intend that you use copy-and-paste facilities to make new sections of choices in the menu, if the screen template has an insufficient number of lines. The same principle applies to the box which holds the menu title. To adjust the size of the box, you will need to insert some of the special characters used to draw the thick and thin lines which enclose the menu text. Again, use the cut-and-paste facility of your editor to create copies of these special characters. In this way, you don't have to know how to enter those characters directly!

If you are familiar with your editor and the templates, you can fill out the menu and screen templates for one menu in 5 to 15 minutes, depending on the size of the menus and the level of detail in the specification. For example, you may or may not have to develop the 1-character menu choices and their 70-character descriptions; sometimes a specification shows those choices and descriptions.

In making the estimate of 5 to 15 minutes, I assume that you fill in the cases in the menu template with one line of the form "DO <routine>". Of course, if you write out the code for the case instead of putting it in a procedure to DO, you will need more than 5 minutes to replace the replaceable text in the menu template.

User Benefits

The menu templates give you and your users some benefits that reduce programming, because the beneficial features are implemented in fixed (nonreplaceable) text in the templates. Unlike menu systems which use numbers to label choices, this system permits you to use any ASCII character you like to label your choices. The choices are validated and the user is told when an incorrect choice has been made.

The list of characters which are possible choices for the menu is displayed on the line where the menu choice is solicited, to make explicit the nature of the choices available to the user. **Note the crucial safety-net feature: the user must confirm or change his or her menu choice with a second keystroke.**

Menus generally offer the user either a two-step point and shoot or a one-step shoot, according to the service provided by the selection. For example, if you press the PageDown key while using a word processor, you want instant service; you would never want the word processor to ask you: "Are you sure you want to page down? (Y/N)".

Now consider a state-of-the-art implementation of a pick list. You may point at an item by entering its first letter, which causes a bar cursor to highlight the item. If there are multiple choices which begin with the same letter, pressing the key corresponding to that first letter causes the bar cursor to advance through the items with the same first letter. You may also use the arrow keys to move the bar cursor. When the bar cursor points to the desired item, the selection takes an additional keystroke (quite often the ENTER key is stroked).

In menus implemented from the Millican templates, the first keystroke points to the desired menu option, assuming that the user has typed correctly. If this option is not desired, another option may be chosen with another keystroke. The user strokes keys corresponding to menu options until the desired option is selected.

These keystrokes are the "point" part of point-and-shoot. If the first keystroke is correct, then only one keystroke is used to point at the desired menu option. Subsequently, a final keystroke (ENTER) invokes the service which is labeled by the selected menu option. The ENTER keystroke is the "shoot" part of point-and-shoot.

Some programmers believe that a one-step "shoot" menu is always best, but I feel that the safety-net feature is required for menus in database applications. In many cases, menu choices will trigger processes which use a great deal of time or paper, or which alter an application's databases. Once they begin, it is not always possible to conveniently escape from these processes.

In practice, my users and I have found this interface to work as follows. When you are learning the menus, you will stop to verify your choices before stroking the ENTER key. Later, when you have learned the application, and you are sure of your choices and your typing, you will stroke the ENTER key without pausing, with two exceptions.

When you are using submenus which you visit with insufficient frequency to maintain familiarity, or, more importantly, when you are selecting services which have great consequence or which use large amounts of time and computer resources, then you will pause quite deliberately to verify your choices before stroking ENTER! More than once this safety-net feature has kept me from inadvertently starting long indexing operations. At first, I am irritated at myself because I pressed the wrong key, but then I am relieved and grateful that the software's safety net saved me!

Point-and-Shoot Moving-Bar Menus

Moving-bar menu methods have the advantage for the user that the menu choice and the bar cursor are in the same place. However, in most implementations, moving-bar menus have the disadvantage of rather short labels for choices.[2] The Millican templates allow approximately 70 characters for a description of a menu choice. Some moving-bar systems overcome this limitation by displaying a description of the menu choice somewhere onscreen when the bar cursor is on the label for the choice, but this causes two problems.

2. We'll look at nonstandard bar cursor menus with long choices in Chapter 22.

First, the user must search for the display area in which the description appears — there is no standard way to display this description, and the user must learn the location of the display areas on an application-by-application basis. Second, the user's eyes must move back and forth between the menu choice and the menu description. *Our templates have the choice and the description in the same place, which avoids this problem.*

The user of our menus looks at a line with a menu choice and label, selects the choice by typing it, and then looks at the bottom of the screen to see if there was a typing error or if a second thought has developed after the single keystroke was made. Usually, the user won't look back and forth between two screen locations, as happens with the variety of moving-bar menu that we have been discussing.

For example, a user named Diana sees a menu line like

R Report on the Accounts database.

She strokes "R", looks at the bottom of the screen to confirm that she entered "R" and not another character, and then she strokes ENTER to confirm the choice, *or* she strokes "R" and ENTER to correct a typing mistake.

We can see that the interface provided by moving-bar menus is satisfactory for the user when the menu choices are obvious and when the two-step point-and-shoot is used in preference to the one-step "shoot" — as in "shoot first and ask questions later." But we know that fancy menus are usually dialect-dependent and that they typically involve more skill and more work or much more work to construct and maintain over the lifetime of the application. Can we construct a functional, easy-to-understand, dialect-independent menu method?

As you know by now, the answer is yes — such a method is implemented by the Millican menu templates. Sometimes this menu interface just isn't fancy enough, but the menu style of these templates is very, very common, and the user has seen or will see this menu style in other products.

Table 17.3 summarizes the benefits for the programmer and for the user from the Millican menu templates. *You can see how canonical thinking was used to maximize the number and power of features for the programmer and the end-user while minimizing the programmer time taken to produce working source code.*

Table 17.3 Canonical Benefits of the Millican Menu Templates

1. *The source code generated from the templates can be understood by programmers with experience in any dBASE dialect.*
2. *The source code generated from the templates can be executed by any dBASE dialect.* (Some menus use dialect-specific methods, assembly language code, or the TSR technology, and are consequently not nearly as portable as applications which consist of only source code.)
3. The application can be maintained by a programmer who does not know about the template library. (Often, when tool T is used to implement application A, then A and T must go together from then on.)
4. The application can be maintained by a programmer who knows about the template library but who does not have access to it. (The menu templates can be fairly easily reconstructed from the source code made from the templates.)
5. By using standard editor insert-file and cut-and-paste commands, the programmer types virtually nothing beyond the minimum text which must be provided to define the menus and associated actions.
6. When you neglect to provide for one of the options on a menu screen in your menu routine, then this error is announced onscreen. The user is directed to print the screen and the printout tells you what choice was requested and in which procedure.
7. If the user enters an incorrect menu choice, this error is explained onscreen and the user is given another chance.
8. *The user can change his or her mind after selecting a menu choice, but before confirming it.* (This is a critical safety-net feature for high-level menus.)
9. *The user can correct a typing error made in selecting a menu choice.* (This is a critical safety-net feature for high-level menus.)
10. The menu templates implement a standard interface across the entire application in which they are used.
11. The menu templates implement an interface which is standard and common (except for the safety-net feature) and which is found in many products such as electronic bulletin board software.
12. The user typically does not move his or her eyes back and forth between two areas of the screen when making menu selections.
13. Any ASCII character can be used as the keystroke for a menu choice.

Chapter 18

Speed Programming through Building Block Templates

I now conclude Part III by showing you the templates for a library which includes virtually all of the most common procedure structures used by dBASE programmers. These templates constitute a speed-programming technology which serves users of all dialects; in fact, this generic approach can be applied to any programming language.

Remark on templates and the companion diskette. These templates are available on the book's companion diskette. See Appendix A for order information and see Appendix B for a listing of source code files from the book which appear on the diskette.

Customize the Templates for Yourself!

Before I show you the Millican templates, I want to promote a customization concept. These templates are not meant to be "one size fits all." Rather, they are *seed forms* for you to grow.

> **The exact form of the templates is not nearly as important as the concept of fill-in-the-blanks templates. Please adjust these templates to fit your preferences and requirements.**[1]

For example, in the beginning you might like a fully commented IF/ELSE template like the following.

Listing 18.1 Template for IF/ELSE (Learning Form)

```
IF (<logical expression>)
   <if statement(s)>
ELSE
   <else statement(s)>
ENDIF
```

1. Or, as comedian Henny Youngman might say, "Take my templates — PLEASE!"

To use the first form, you must delete the characters "<logical expression>" before replacing them. Similarly, you must delete and replace the text "<if statement(s)>" and "<else statement(s)>" in the body of the IF statement.

Once you gain familiarity with the template approach, you'll probably prefer the next form. It doesn't require you to erase any text.

The lowercase "b" is used to show where a blank appears in the template. Here, the indentation of three blanks is already provided under the assumption that the programmer uses the recommended indentation of three character columns.

Listing 18.2 Template for IF/ELSE (Familiar Form)

```
IF (
)
bbb
ELSE
bbb
ENDIF
```

To use the second form, place the cursor after the "(" (using the editor's end-of-line command), enter a logical expression, stroke the Delete key to move the ")" up to the first line of the template, and stroke the DownArrow key to move to the end of the second line of the template, which is already indented with three blanks. At that place you enter one or more dBASE statements. Next you enter one or more statements after the ELSE and you are done changing the IF/ELSE template into an IF/ELSE statement!

> **Remark.** When you enter more than one line in the IF or ELSE part, remember that most text editors have a way for you to start a new line at the same indentation as the current line. By using such a facility, you can start typing at a given level of indentation and all new lines will start at this indentation until you change the indentation.

Survey of the Millican Templates

In the rest of the chapter we'll see templates which handle procedure structures in the following categories:

1. Command file templates.
2. Alternatives (branching).
3. Loops.
4. Main menus and submenus.
5. Simple dialogs.
6. Interface to R&R Relational Report Writer.
7. Custom templates.

The interface to R&R is included here because R&R is such a widely used report writer. Furthermore, this template illustrates the concept of combining library routines with corresponding templates which facilitate the use of the library routines. The advantage is especially great here, since a large amount of information must be gathered from the user to pass in arguments to the routine.

The last category on the list is custom templates, which perhaps should not even appear there, since this section of the chapter does not contain any templates. Rather, you are reminded that the Millican templates are *seed forms* for you to change and extend. *You* are the best judge of your own needs.

Command File Templates

In the philosophy of standard software components, you establish habits and procedures which, for one thing, give your source code a common format for all routines. For example, if a command file named Accounts.PRG is called by MainMenu.PRG, then I recommend the first and last lines of Accounts.PRG to be

```
* File = Accounts.PRG.  Called by MainMenu.PRG.
* End of Accounts.PRG.
```

A template to support that format appears in the following listing (PRG.TEM on the companion diskette).

Listing 18.3 Template for an Unspecialized Command File

```
* File = /.PRG.  Called from \.PRG.


* End of /.PRG.
```

To use the template, insert it into an empty file. Then substitute all occurrences of "/" with the command file name, which is a single command in most editors. Last, substitute "\" with "various " if the command file is a utility; otherwise substitute "\" with the name of the caller or callers.

A Template for a Non-Menu Top-Level Command File

Later in the chapter you'll see a complex template used for the top-level routine in an application. Use the template in Listing 18.4 (DotPrg.TEM on the companion diskette) to generate simple command files which don't need initialization or menus.

Alternatives

The dBASE programming language gives you three structures for alternatives, which are the IF, the IF/ELSE, and the DO CASE statements. For the sake of completeness, I list both the learning form and the familiar form of the IF and IF/ELSE templates in Listings 18.5, 18.6, 18.7, and 18.8 (IF1.TEM, IF.TEM, ELSE1.TEM, and ELSE.TEM, respectively, on the companion diskette).

Listing 18.4 Template for a Non-Menu Top-Level Command File

```
* File = /.PRG.  Called from the dot prompt.
CLOSE ALL
SET Safety OFF
SET Status OFF
SET Talk   OFF

CLOSE ALL
SET Safety ON
SET Status ON
SET Talk   ON
* End of /.PRG.
```

Listing 18.5 Template for IF (Learning Form)

```
IF (<Logical Condition>
)
   <if case code>
ENDIF
```

Listing 18.6 Template for IF (Familiar Form)

```
IF (
)
ENDIF
```

Listing 18.7 Template for IF/ELSE (Learning Form)

```
IF (<Logical Condition>
)
   <if case code>
ELSE
   <else case code>
ENDIF
```

Listing 18.8 Template for IF/ELSE (Familiar Form)

```
IF (
)
ELSE
ENDIF
```

You may wish to use the learning forms of these templates before you switch to the familiar forms. The IF template is arguably too much work to use as an alternative to typing the template yourself. This argument becomes weaker for the IF/ELSE statement — remember that we seek not only to save keystrokes, but also to reduce the number of syntax errors, as was explained in the material on syntax-directed editing on page 224.

The DO CASE template (CASE.TEM on the companion diskette) is more interesting:

Listing 18.9 Template for DO CASE

```
DO CASE
   CASE ()
      DO <name of command or procedure file>

   CASE ()
      DO  <name of command or procedure file>

   OTHERWISE
      ?  "
<name of prg>
.PRG: Case statement error: case not found."
      ?  "Print or copy screen for programmer."
      DO WaitOnC
ENDCASE
```

Recommendation on parentheses in source code. The parentheses that I show in these templates for alternatives are not required, but parentheses are strongly recommended in order to improve the readability of the source code. Sometimes the OTHERWISE clause is needed for default processing, in which case you must replace all of the text between the keywords OTHERWISE and ENDCASE.

However, if all of the permitted cases are treated explicitly, then the form of the OTHERWISE clause in the template provides your application with an easily implemented safety feature. In the absence of such a safety feature, subtle and nasty problems may result — if there is no OTHERWISE clause and none of the CASE conditions are satisfied, dBASE will continue execution with the statement following the ENDCASE.

In some dialects, a built-in function can identify the name of the current procedure. When you use such a dialect exclusively, you might want to change the template to invoke that built-in function as an alternative to entering the procedure name manually. Such a measure will unfortunately reduce the portability of your code.

Loops

The standard dBASE dialect has only the DO WHILE command for looping. Our template library uses three dialect-independent loop templates to perform three standard looping tasks. These tasks are to read through a database file, iterate on a loop counter variable in character form, or iterate on a loop counter variable in numeric form. We will also see more powerful, but dialect-dependent, ways to implement the same loops.

A File-Processing Loop

Here is the file-processing loop template (While.TEM on the companion diskette). If a filter is required which is not already active, then the first line is erased and replaced by a SET FILTER TO statement. Next, the text "<insert first code line>" is erased and the first statement of the loop body is inserted there.

Listing 18.10 Template for a Database File-Processing Loop

```
* <set filter if necessary>
GOTO TOP
DO WHILE (.NOT. EOF())
   <insert first code line>
   SKIP
ENDDO && (.NOT. EOF())
```

The loop is not executed if any of the following conditions apply:

1. The database is empty.
2. No records meet the filter.
3. SET DELETED ON is the last SET DELETED statement to be executed, and all records which meet the filter are marked for deletion.

Otherwise, qualifying records are processed, one by one, until they have all been processed. Remember that the records are processed in storage order if no index is active, or else the records are accessed in the order specified by the master index.

Recommendation on eliminating DO WHILE loops. The dBASE language offers many commands which process an entire database, such as COUNT, SUM, and LIST. Many dBASE commands that process database files or records have the scope option, which permits you to apply the command to a group of database records. Whenever possible, use single commands (with or without the scope option) to replace DO WHILE loops.

A Dialect-Independent Iterative Loop with a Numeric Counter

One of the most startling omissions of the dBASE programming language as implemented in dBASE III PLUS and dBASE IV is the lack of an iterative loop, such as the DO loop of FORTRAN or the FOR/NEXT loop of BASIC, Clipper, and dBXL. Moreover, dBASE III PLUS does not support arrays, although most other dialects have array support. So we must discover how to simulate arrays and iteration (1) when these facilities are not available, or (2) when we must write dialect-independent code.

In this subsection we'll see how iteration is done in dBASE dialects which lack an iterative loop, and in the next subsection we'll see how to simulate arrays with a technique that works with all dialects. Here is the template for iterating on a numeric variable in a dialect-independent way (LoopNum.TEM on the companion diskette).

Listing 18.11
Template for a Dialect-Independent Iterative Numeric Variable Loop

```
* Template File: LoopNum.TEM. Dialect-independent iterative loop, numeric index.
PRIVATE Ndex_N
Ndex_N = <initial value for first time through loop =========================>
DO WHILE (Ndex_N <= <value of Ndex_N last time through loop =================>
)
   <insert first code line of loop body here>
   Ndex_N = Ndex_N + 1
ENDDO && WHILE (Ndex_N <= UPPER BOUND)
```

This template assumes that you usually want to increment the iteration variable by 1 each time through the loop. In general, you would have

Ndex = Ndex + <increment>

If the increment is positive, then the condition in the DO WHILE statement must contain "<=" (as shown); if the increment is negative, then the condition in the DO WHILE statement must contain ">=".

Notice that we need a PRIVATE memory variable for our iteration. It is important to declare this variable to be PRIVATE, because there may be many variables named "Ndex" in the application, and they must be isolated from each other in order to avoid chaos.

> **Remark.** There is a pitfall in using an identifier called "Index" for an iteration variable. INDEX is a dBASE keyword, and "Index = Index + 1" is illegal syntax. Instead, you must use "STORE Index + 1 TO Index" — or else use an identifier which is not a dBASE verb!

Normally, you will move the PRIVATE Ndex statement to the top of the command file in which you have inserted this template or add Ndex to an existing PRIVATE statement. Next, you fill in the starting and ending values of the iteration variable where indicated and supply one or more statements for the loop body. That's it!

Dialect-Dependent Iterative Loops with Numeric Counters

Some dBASE dialects offer an iterative loop. Here is an iterative loop template for Clipper, dBXL, and Quicksilver (LoopNext.TEM on the companion diskette).

Listing 18.12 An Iterative Loop Template for Clipper and dBXL/Quicksilver

```
* Template File: LoopNext.TEM.  Iterative loop for Clipper, dBXL, Quicksilver.
PRIVATE Ndex_N
Ndex_N = <initial value for first time through loop ========================>
FOR Ndex_N = <start value> TO <end of range> STEP <increment>
   <insert code lines of loop body here>
NEXT && Ndex_N
```

FoxPro uses the ENDFOR keyword instead of the NEXT keyword. Its iterative loop template (LoopNpro.TEM on the companion diskette) follows. (dBASE IV has no iterative loop like FOR/ENDFOR.)

Listing 18.13 An Iterative Loop Template for FoxPro

```
* Template File: LoopNpro.TEM.  Iterative loop for FoxPro.
PRIVATE Ndex_N
Ndex_N = <initial value for first time through loop =========================>
FOR Ndex_N = <start value> TO <end of range> STEP <increment>
   <insert code lines of loop body here>
ENDFOR && Ndex_N
```

If the increment is positive, then the end of range must be greater than the start value. If the increment is negative, then the end of range must be less than the start value. The loop is executed until the iteration variable is no longer between the start value and the end of range. If you use macros for the start value or the end of range, then they are evaluated exactly once, before the loop is executed the first time.

An Iterative Loop with a Character Counter

The loop for iterating on a numeric variable in character form is very similar to the dialect-independent loop for iterating on a numeric variable. Note that you enter the final value of the iteration variable as before, but the initial value is enclosed in quotes. (The template is LoopChr.TEM on the companion diskette.)

Listing 18.14 Template for an Iterative Character Variable Loop

```
* Template File: LoopChr.TEM.
* Dialect-independent iterative loop on a character index.  Use when execution
* speed is not a factor.
PRIVATE Ndex_C
Ndex_C =  "<value of index first time through the loop>"
DO WHILE (VAL(Ndex_C) <= <value of index last time through the loop>
)
   <insert code lines of loop body here>
   Ndex_C = LTRIM( STR( VAL(Ndex_C)+1 ) ) && Increment the character-format index.
ENDDO && (VAL(Ndex_C) <= UPPER BOUND)
```

In contrast to the previous loop, the iteration variable is available in character form inside the loop. This is the form which is required when accessing the elements of a simulated array. In listing 18.16, we'll see some source code generated from this template.

A Faster Variant

Usually speed is not a factor for loops with character counters because the number of iterations is small. However, when speed is important, the following variant (LoopChr1.TEM on the companion diskette) may execute significantly faster, because the VAL() function is only called once per iteration, instead of twice, as in the first form.

Listing 18.15 Template for a Faster Iterative Character Variable Loop

```
* Template File: LoopChr1.TEM.
* Dialect-independent iterative loop on a character index.  Use when rapid
* execution speed is required.
PRIVATE Ndex_C,Ndex_N
Ndex_N = <value of index first time through the loop>
DO WHILE (Ndex_N <= <value of index last time through the loop>
)
   Ndex_C = LTRIM( STR(Ndex_N) ) && Convert to character form of index memvar.
   <insert code lines of loop body here>
   Ndex_N = Ndex_N + 1
ENDDO && (VAL(Ndex_C) <= UPPER BOUND)
```

Simulating Arrays

You can simulate an array in the dBASE programming language via the macro facility. Say that your application needs an array called "Month", which is indexed from 0 to 2. The initial values of the array elements are to be 0. Assuming that the array elements are to be PRIVATE to some procedure, the simulated array would be set up as follows:

```
PRIVATE Month0, Month1, Month2
STORE 0 TO Month0, Month1, Month2
```

When you process the simulated Month array with the following template, you refer to its elements with the syntax "Month&Ndex". We use three built-in functions to increment the iteration variable when it is in character form. The function VAL() converts the character form to a numeric form so that the arithmetic of adding 1 can be performed. Then STR() takes it back to a character form with leading blanks, which are removed by LTRIM().

Listing 18.16 shows an example of how this template would be used to store the sum of the elements in a variable called MonthSum.

Listing 18.16 Sum of a Dialect-Independent Simulated Array

```
PRIVATE Month0,Month1,Month2,MonthSum,Ndex
<Get values for Month0, Month1, and Month2.>
MonthSum = 0
Ndex     =  "0"   && Lining up the equal signs makes for greater readability.
DO WHILE (VAL(Ndex) <= 2)
   MonthSum = MonthSum + Month&Ndex
   Ndex = LTRIM( STR( VAL(Ndex)+1 ) )
ENDDO && (VAL(Ndex) <= UPPER BOUND)
```

Using Built-In Arrays

Since built-in arrays are unity indexed (subscripts run from 1 to n), we cannot directly mimic the code in the previous example of the simulated one-dimensional array, whose subscripts run from 0 to 2.[2] For simplicity, let's assume that the problem is redefined so that a unity-indexed array can be used, as shown in Listing 18.17.

Listing 18.17 Sum of a Built-In Array in Clipper or Quicksilver

```
PRIVATE Month,MonthSum,Ndex
DECLARE Month[3]
<Get values for Month[1], Month[2], and Month[3].>
MonthSum = 0
FOR Ndex = 1 TO 3
   MonthSum = MonthSum + Month[Ndex]
NEXT && Ndex
```

This code is immensely more pleasurable to read and is certainly easier to understand than the code which simulates the array. *However, there are at least two problems with this prettier code.*

First, we cannot get the zero-indexing that we got with the simulated array. As always, a limitation in the language which causes us to think about our problem in a limited way may reduce the degree to which our solution is canonical. Second, the array-based approach above may be difficult to port to other dBASE dialects which support arrays, should this be necessary.

For example, to convert the Clipper code above to run under FoxBASE+, you'd have to change the pairs "[]" to "()" in all array references and declarations (and change the FOR/NEXT loop to DO WHILE). In a large application with many array references, this could take a great deal of time![3]

2. It is unfortunate that dBASE dialect arrays are unity indexed, because zero-indexed arrays are often required in canonical algorithms.
3. Code translators that translate source code from one dialect to another provide an alternative to manual recoding. Buzzwords International offers translator products which handle various dialect combinations. See Appendix I for Buzzwords' address and phone number.

In some cases, source code must run under dialects which use either the parentheses convention or the square bracket convention, such as FoxBASE+, which requires parentheses, and Clipper, which requires square brackets.[4] The following table shows some of your alternatives for array handling in these situations.

Table 18.1 Array Alternatives for Multiple-Dialect Code

1. Don't use arrays.
2. Simulate arrays with the macro technique shown above.
3. Use IF statements to isolate array declarations and references from incompatible dialects. For example, if code must run under Clipper and FoxPro, you can use "IF CLIPPER" statements to isolate declarations of Clipper arrays and references to them from declarations of FoxPro arrays and references to *them*. (The PUBLIC memvar Clipper will have the value .T. when the code is executed under Clipper and the value .F. otherwise.)
4. Maintain the code for one dialect and use a source code translator to generate the source code for the other dialect as necessary.

Subroutines Used by the Menu Templates

The menu templates reference two subroutines, WaitOnC and HeadLine, which we'll look at here before we look at the menu templates.

Subroutine WaitOnC, A WAIT Command Substitute

The dBASE verb WAIT pauses until the user enters a character. Therefore, this verb is frequently used when the programmer wants the user to read something onscreen before proceeding.

Unfortunately, this technique is defeated by the type-ahead feature, which permits the user to enter keystrokes into a temporary buffer, where they are stored by the operating system until they are requested by the application. The WAIT statement will not have the effect you want if the user has typed ahead before the WAIT was executed; the next character will be removed from the type-ahead buffer and there will be no pause.

The CLEAR TYPEAHEAD command will solve part of the problem. This command can be placed before each WAIT, so that the characters that the user typed before the WAIT was executed will not be used to bypass the WAIT.

However, if the user is typing ahead when the WAIT is executed, then the type-ahead buffer is being filled both before and after the WAIT. This again defeats the intended effect of the WAIT statement.

The following command file solves these problems. It clears the type-ahead buffer before soliciting the keystroke. Furthermore, it requires a specific keystroke to end the pause.

---

4. FoxPro permits you to use either convention interchangeably.

The technique is not foolproof, because the user could be typing ahead and stuff a "C" or "c" into the type-ahead buffer after the CLEAR TYPEAHEAD is executed. However, in practice, it is nearly foolproof.

Listing 18.18 A Service Subroutine to Replace the Wait Command

```
* File = WaitOnC.PRG.  Service routine to pause until user strokes  "C".
***************************************************************************
* Dialects: All.
***************************************************************************
PRIVATE WaitOnKey
WaitOnKey =  "?"

?
DO WHILE .NOT. (WaitOnKey $  "cC")
   CLEAR TYPEAHEAD

   WAIT  "   When you are ready to CONTINUE, press the   C   key.  " to WaitOnKey
   ?

   IF .NOT. (WaitOnKey $  "cC")
      @ ROW()-2,0 SAY  ""
   ENDIF

ENDDO

* End of WaitOnC.PRG.
```

Subroutine HeadLine

Code generated from the template calls the command file HeadLine.PRG, which is shown in Listing 18.19. This command file displays a status line at the top of the screen in the currently defined alternate colors. This status line shows the version of the application, the day of the week, the date, and the time.

Listing 18.19 HeadLine.PRG

```
* File = Headline.PRG.  Called from .PRG generated from MainScrn.TEM or
* SubScrn.TEM in the Millican templates to display a status line at
* the top of menu screens.  This status line is of the form
* <version>  <bytes free>  <time/date>
* where the version label is taken from the PUBLIC memvar Version.
***************************************************************************
* Dialects: All.
***************************************************************************
PUBLIC Version
PRIVATE Piece1,Piece2,Spacing,TopLine

Piece1  = LTRIM(Transform( DiskSpace() ,  "999,999,999" )) +  " bytes free."
Piece2  = Cdow(Date()) +  ",  " + DtoC(Date()) +  "   " + Time()
Spacing = MAX( 40 - (LEN(Version) + LEN(Piece1) + LEN(Piece2))/2, 1)
TopLine = Version + SPACE(Spacing) + Piece1 + SPACE(Spacing) + Piece2
TopLine = Left( TopLine + SPACE(80), 80 )

@ 0,0 GET TopLine
CLEAR GETS
@ 0,0 SAY  ""

* End of Headline.PRG.
```

Recommendation on manual verification of system time and date. For database work, it is particularly important that the date and time be set correctly in the computer. Encourage end-users to look at the top line to verify the correctness of the time and date.

Main Menu Templates

The templates I have designed for menus are used in pairs. Main menus are implemented with MainMenu.TEM and MainScrn.TEM.

In the previous chapter, you read about the design concepts of these templates. Let's look at the main menu template now to see how these concepts are implemented. After we understand the main menu template, we'll look at the main screen template and its associated presentation issues.

The main menu template is shown in Listing 18.20. It begins by clearing the screen and closing all data files. Then it fixes application defaults for several SET commands. Under FoxBASE+, the PUBLIC memvar FOX has a value of logical true, and in this dialect, we CLEAR PROGRAM to force an update of RAM copies of command files. In other dialects, FOX is false, and CLEAR PROGRAM is not executed. (However, Clipper will not compile such a line, and you must remove this code to use this template with Clipper.)

Listing 18.20 Template for the Main Menu

```
* Replace  "????" with your choice of name throughout this file; then erase
* these first two lines.  =====================================================>
* File = ????Menu.PRG.
**************************************   Establish standard starting point :
CLEAR
* Later,  CLEAR ALL  or not according to value of InstalledQ set below.
CLOSE ALL
SET Bell OFF
SET Deleted OFF
SET Exact OFF
SET Safety OFF
SET Status OFF
SET Talk OFF
*************************** Declare and initialize all PUBLIC variables here.
* Remove the following four lines to use this template with Clipper:
PUBLIC Fox
IF Fox
   CLEAR PROGRAM  && make sure we execute current versions of .PRG files.
ENDIF
DO MainInit  && Handle the rest of the PUBLIC variables.
************************************************ Log into drive & subdirectory
RUN C:
RUN CD &ProgSubdir
SET Path to C:\DB\Util  && Set path to find dBASE utility files.
*******************************************************  Set Function Keys
SET FUNCTION 2 TO  'DO <fill in name of this .PRG here ======================>
* In CONFIG.DB or equivalent, PROMPT can be set to  "F1:Help; F2:Menu  "
****************************************************************************
PRIVATE Exit_L,MenuChoice
Exit_L = .F.
DO WHILE (.NOT. Exit_L)
```

```
    MenuChoice =  "  "
    DO ????Scrn with MenuChoice
    DO CASE
       CASE (MenuChoice =  "<uppercase letter from menu screen ==============>
 ")
      <lines of code for this menu choice ================================>
       CASE (MenuChoice =  "<uppercase letter from menu screen ==============>
 ")
      <lines of code for this menu choice ================================>
       CASE (MenuChoice =  "<uppercase letter from menu screen ==============>
 ")
      <lines of code for this menu choice ================================>
       CASE (MenuChoice =  ".")
      Exit_L = .T.
       CASE (MenuChoice =  ">")  && Exit to the operating system.
      QUIT
       OTHERWISE
      ?  "
<.PRG filename=============================================================>
: Case selector var out of list.  Illegal value:",MenuChoice
      ?  "Print this screen and notify the programmer."
      DO WaitOnC
    ENDCASE
ENDDO
SET Safety ON
SET Status ON
SET Talk ON
* End of ????Menu.PRG.  THIS IS THE ONLY EXIT POINT (except QUIT).
*************************************************************************
*************************************************************************
* REMEMBER TO SAVE THE FOLLOWING CODE IN A SEPARATE FILE CALLED MainInit.PRG.
*************************************************************************
*************************************************************************
* File = MainInit.PRG.  Called from <insert name ============================>
* Initializes PUBLIC vars for application.
PUBLIC InstalledQ,ProgSubDir,Version
*************************************************************************
InstalledQ = (GetEnv("Computer") #  "Develop")
*************************************************************************
IF InstalledQ
   CLEAR ALL
   <Insert code for SET commands and to initialize PUBLIC variables ========>
ELSE
   * Don't CLEAR ALL in order to preserve any PUBLIC variables which already
   * exist.
   <Insert code for SET commands and to initialize PUBLIC variables ========>
ENDIF
ProgSubDir =  "<insert the name of the directory holding the .PRG files =====>
 "
Version    =  "Version <insert the version number ===========================>
 "
* End of MainInit.PRG.
```

Even a small application tends to have some "global" variables which are known to all of the application's routines. Defining these variables may take many lines, and these lines would clutter the main routine to an unacceptable extent. Therefore, these variables are defined in the helper routine MainInit.PRG, which is also provided in template form.

The template for MainInit.PRG follows the main menu template in Main-Menu.TEM. However, before we can discuss it, *we must cope with a distinction between interpreted and compiled dBASE dialects.*

Returns to the dBASE Environment versus Returns to the DOS Environment

Variables which are defined PRIVATE in MainMenu.PRG are known in all routines of the application, assuming that MainMenu.PRG is the top-level routine and that the variables have unique names. (If "PRIVATE X" appears in Main-Menu.PRG and in a procedure called by MainMenu.PRG, then the occurrence in the called procedure establishes a second memvar that is also called "X". References to "X" in the called procedure are to the second memvar.) PRIVATE memvars are placed in the symbol table when the PRIVATE statement is executed; they are removed from the symbol table and their storage space is returned to the free pool when the procedure in which they are declared PRIVATE is exited.

Let's assume that you call MainMenu.PRG from the dot prompt by entering "DO MainMenu". Interpreted applications generally have the CLEAR ALL command as part of their initialization, because any memvars which were defined at the dot prompt are PUBLIC and are therefore known to the application if they are not removed from the symbol table with the CLEAR command.

When you return to the dot prompt, any variables declared PRIVATE in Main-Menu are *automatically* released. However, any memvars declared PUBLIC are *not* automatically released.

This distinction is not significant either for compiled applications, which always return to DOS, or for interpreted applications, which always terminate with QUIT (to the DOS prompt) instead of RETURN (to the dot prompt). Otherwise, there is the issue of whether there are any PUBLIC memvars which must exist both before and after the application is executed.

In some cases, information about the interpreter environment is held in PUBLIC memvars. For example, in my FoxBASE+/FoxPro environment, I maintain a PUBLIC memvar which records the DOS directory which was current when the application was started. If this PUBLIC memvar survives the application's execution, then I can access it and return to the original directory.

Recommendation on PUBLIC memvars and returning to the dot prompt. If your application returns to the dot prompt, and you want the symbol table to be empty when the application finishes (no memvars defined), then put the CLEAR ALL command in your application's epilogue.[5] Otherwise, use one of the following three strategies:

1. In your application's epilogue, use RELEASE statements to release some PUBLIC memvars and not others.

5. The epilogue for applications built with MainMenu.TEM is the code following the ENDDO.

2. Declare "global" variables, that is, memvars which must be known in all routines of your application, in PRIVATE statements in MainMenu.PRG. (The usual practice is to define global variables with PUBLIC statements in MainInit.PRG, so as not to clutter MainMenu.PRG. Remember that variables defined PRIVATE in MainInit.PRG are released when MainInit returns to MainMenu.)
3. Save all PUBLIC variables defined when the application begins. This is done by placing a "SAVE TO <filename>" statement before the CLEAR ALL in the prologue of the main routine. Then you restore these memvars in the epilogue of the main routine with a "RESTORE FROM <filename>" statement. (If you do not wish to retain any of the PUBLIC memvars created by the application, then precede the RESTORE FROM statement with CLEAR ALL.)

Initialization for the Main Procedure

When you implement your main menu with MainMenu.TEM, you will remove the template for MainInit.PRG to a file named MainInit.PRG. You then edit MainInit.PRG and replace its replaceable text.

Notice the three PUBLIC variables defined at the beginning of MainInit. These variables are needed in virtually all applications. InstalledQ is used by the application to tell whether it is running in the environment of the developer on the developer's PC or LAN. If InstalledQ is true, the application is running on the end-user's computer.

The maintenance of dBASE applications over their lifetimes is greatly facilitated by a data-driven approach to specifying the location of data and program files. In the "hard-coded" approach, you write "USE C:\Data\Receipts", whereas in the data-driven approach, you define PUBLIC DataDir in MainInit.PRG and assign it the value "C:\Data\" (or whatever). Then you write "USE &DataDir.Receipts" whenever you need to open Receipts.DBF.

With this technique, you can

1. Store different versions of your application in different directories. This permits you to work two systems in parallel when you move from one version to its replacement. If there are problems with the replacement, you can shift back to the earlier version.
2. Install the new version with little or no disruption to existing operations. When all is ready, you make a simple change to cause the users to execute the new version; there is no time lag or downtime between versions.
3. Store different versions of your data files in different directories. By changing the value of DataDir in this example, you can process Receipts databases in directories \JAN, \FEB, \MAR, and so on, *with the same code*, as long as each Receipts database has the same structure.[6]

6. Actually, the requirement is even less stringent than that: it is only necessary that all the databases have all of the fields that the code references.

MainInit supports this concept with the memvar ProgSubDir, which stores the name of the DOS directory in which MainMenu.PRG resides. Then this memvar is used in MainMenu to set the correct DOS directory:

RUN CD &ProgSubdir

Note that a compiled application must be found in the current DOS directory or on the DOS path, but that an interpreted application must be found in the current DOS directory or on the dBASE path. Generally speaking, you'll want the directory holding MainMenu.PRG to be the current DOS directory while MainMenu.PRG is being executed.

The third "global" PUBLIC memvar is "Version". This memvar is used to coordinate the version of the software with the version of the documentation. This variable is referenced by the menu screen routine to show the current version of the application on the top line of the screen. If the user has documentation marked "Version 1.0" and "Version 2.0" and the screen shows version 2.1, then the user knows to use the later documentation.

If the user telephones you with a particular problem which you thought you fixed in version 2.1, then ask him or her to look at the top line of any menu to see the version number. If the version number is earlier than 2.1, then the fix is to update the user to the new version.

The InstalledQ memvar is initialized with a built-in function which retrieves MS-DOS environment variables. The GetEnv()[7] function is specific to MS-DOS, so its equivalent may or may not be available for dialects running on other operating systems. In your MS-DOS AutoExec.BAT file, add the line

SET Computer=Develop

That way, InstalledQ is true on the user's PC and false on your PC. If your files are in differently named directories, you can use InstalledQ with the IF/ELSE statement to set your file directory macros accordingly.

For example, Receipts.DBF may be stored in C:\DB\TestData\ on your PC, and in M:\ISD\Accounts\ on the user's PC. You set DataDir = "C:\DB\TestData\" if InstalledQ is false and you set DataDir = "M:\ISD\Accounts\" if InstalledQ is true. Then, throughout your application, you refer to Receipts.DBF as

&DataDir.Receipts.DBF

Remark on using MS-DOS environment variables with dBASE applications. Note that the use of MS-DOS environment variables with dBASE applications is an excellent way to gain easy control over the application's behavior without altering its code. This is a particularly important consideration for compiled applications.

There is a possible snag in that the default amount of RAM which MS-DOS allocates to hold environment variables is rather small and is easily exceeded with several MS-DOS SET statements. The remedy for this limitation is to load COM-

7. GetE() in Clipper 4.0.

MAND.COM in CONFIG.SYS with the SHELL option. The /E parameter of COMMAND.COM can be used to set the amount of RAM for environment variables. See your MS-DOS manual for details and remember that not all MS-DOS versions have this option.

The Main Menu Loop

The main menu loop uses the variables Exit_Q and MenuChoice. The former memvar controls the loop and the latter controls the option which is executed, based on the user's menu selection.

For example, say that there is a main menu choice "A" for accounting functions, and that those functions are contained in Accounts.PRG. If this is the first choice on the menu, then the first occurrence of

```
 CASE (MenuChoice =  "<uppercase letter from menu screen ==============>
")
    <lines of code for this menu choice ================================>
```

in the template would be changed to

```
CASE (MenuChoice =  "A")
   DO Accounts
```

There are three preprogrammed alternatives for the main menu:

1. Execute the Assistant for dBASE III and dBASE III PLUS, the Control Center for dBASE IV, or any equivalent in other dialects. (Remove this option from main menus for users who should not have unstructured access to data.)
2. Return to the dot prompt, that is, the interpreter.
3. Return to the DOS prompt, that is, the operating system level.

Choices for these alternatives appear on the main menu screen.

The Main Menu Epilogue

In the epilogue for the main menu, SAFETY, STATUS, and TALK are restored to the settings which are appropriate for the interpreter. Note that the epilogue code is reached only for the period keystroke. All files will be closed and other housekeeping performed as necessary when the application quits to DOS, so no programmer-provided epilogue is needed.

When the application returns to the dot prompt, you may wish to add the statement CLOSE ALL to your epilogue, or perhaps

```
IF InstalledQ
   CLOSE ALL
ENDIF
```

When you use the IF statement shown and you execute the application in *your* environment with an interpretive dialect, databases will be open for your inspection after the application returns to the dot prompt. On the user's PC, all files will be closed when the user reaches the dot prompt.

Although all of the dialects are supposed to close all files when the application quits to the operating system, bugs may prevent this in some situations. Placing the CLOSE ALL statement in the main routine's epilogue doesn't hurt anything (assuming that you do want to close all the files), and it may conceivably help to keep files intact.

> **Remark on database file damage.** File damage frequently occurs when an application terminates without closing all of its files which are open for read/write access.

The Main Menu Screen

The main menu screen is displayed with MainScrn.PRG, which is implemented with MainScrn.TEM, as shown in Listing 18.21.

Listing 18.21 Template for the Main Screen

```
* File = MainScrn.PRG.  T. D. Millican.  Called from  <name of caller =======>
* Called from a .PRG made from MainMenu.TEM.
* Calls: WaitOnC.PRG and HeadLine.PRG.

PARAMETERS MenuChoice
PUBLIC Version
PRIVATE Choices,Correct_Q,Line,LineSpace1,LineSpace2
Choices =  "< add the letters of the remaining choices ======================>
.>"
Correct_Q = .F.

* LineSpace1 blank lines separate the top of the menu from the bottom
* status line.  LineSpace2 blank lines separate the bottom of the menu from
* the prompt line.
LineSpace1 = 1  && Decrease to 0 if you need more menu lines.
LineSpace2 = 1  && Decrease to 0 if you need more menu lines.

MenuChoice =  "  "
SET Scoreboard OFF
DO WHILE (.NOT. Correct_Q)

   CLEAR
   DO HeadLine
   @ LineSpace1,0 SAY  ""

   TEXT
                           Main Menu Name






    .   Quit to the dot prompt.   (Press F2 to get this menu.)
    >   Quit to the operating system.
```

```
    EndText

    Line = Row() + LineSpace2 + 1
    * GET Choices to put in inverse video only:
    @ Line,4 SAY  "Your Pleasure of" GET Choices ;
     PICTURE  "@R X, X, X, X, X, X, X, X, X, X, X, X, X, X, X, X, X, X, X,"
    CLEAR GETS  && cancel GET on Choices
    @ ROW(),COL() SAY  "?" GET MenuChoice PICTURE  "!"

    SET Confirm OFF
    READ

    @ Line+1,4 SAY ;
     "Change your choice or stroke a carriage return to confirm it:";
    GET MenuChoice PICTURE  "!"

    SET Confirm ON
    READ

    Correct_Q = (MenuChoice $ Choices)
    IF (.NOT. Correct_Q)
       ?
       ?  "   Regret to say that your choice was not one of  " + Choices
       ?
       DO WaitOnC
    ENDIF
ENDDO WHILE (.NOT. Correct_Q)

SET Scoreboard ON
CLEAR && Needed by Clipper, but not dBASE III Plus or FoxBASE+.

* End of MainScrn.PRG.
```

Instructions

Edit a new file called MainScrn.PRG and insert MainScrn.TEM. *Your text editor must be able to display ASCII characters above 200 in order to process MainScrn.TEM.* The built-in dBASE editors should all be able to display such codes (on 256-character ASCII computers).

Note that the replaceable text in the template is shown in angle brackets. At the line which begins

Choices = "

delete the characters following the double quote, enter the list of one-character choices that you used on your menu to label the choices, and delete the carriage return which separates this line from the line following it. For example, if your menu choices are D, A, and W, then the two lines

```
Choices =  "< add the letters of the remaining choices =======================>
*.>"
```

become

```
Choices =  "DAW*.>"
```

The corresponding menu lines might appear as follows:

```
D    Data Base Management
A    Accounting Functions

W    Word Processing with Microsoft Word
```

Typical values for LineSpace1 and LineSpace2 are 1. These values are then set to 0 if you need more menu lines later.

Next, replace the text "Main Menu Name" with the actual name you have chosen for this menu. For example, you might label the menu as "Ordering Department Main Menu". Then enter the menu choices and descriptions in the boxed areas below the title.

Note that you can use the "type-over mode" of your editor, as contrasted with its "insert mode," in which text to the right of the cursor is pushed right as you type new characters. In type-over mode, you can insert the title in the title area and the text for the menu choices in the large blank areas without changing the positions of the graphics characters onscreen.

However, you may need to create space for more menu choices and descriptions. I assume that your editor can make a copy of a portion of the template like

Any editor which can display these graphics characters can probably copy and paste text which contains the characters. (Note: the file Boxes.REF on the companion diskette contains a large variety of boxes which you can cut and paste into your program files.)

Note the long character constant following the PICTURE keyword after the text part of the menu. This PICTURE causes the list of choices in the memvar Choices to be displayed with a comma and blank between each choice. For example, if Choices = "DAW*.>", the prompt is

Your pleasure of D, A, W, *, ., >?

When you use the trick of CLEAR GETS, the prompt is shown in the currently defined alternate colors, which are the same colors that are used for the one-character window into which the menu choice is entered.

Safety Nets: Principles and Features

In database operations, menu choices may start processes which are difficult to cancel or undo. For this reason, the menu screen templates for main screens and subscreens prompt for confirmation of the choice. If the first prompt is

Your Pleasure of D, A, W, *, ., >?

and you stroke the "A" key, the second prompt will be

Change your choice or stroke a carriage return to confirm it:

followed by a one-character editing window which displays "A" in the currently defined alternate colors. If "A" is the choice you want, you stroke the ENTER key; otherwise you enter the choice you want.

Note that no ENTER keystroke is required following the first keystroke; the second prompt appears on the basis of a single keystroke because CONFIRM is OFF when this GET is READ. The second prompt stays onscreen, accepting keystrokes until a keystroke like ENTER or PageDown is made.

> **Recommendation on user training for safety-net menus.** Train your users to make one keystroke which indicates their menu selection, and then pause to look at the screen to see their choice echoed back in the second prompt. Next, train them to visually confirm the choice, and only then to stroke the ENTER key.

This way of choosing menu selections is really quite easy and natural, even if this explanation is not! You will find that when you are sure you have made the correct keystroke, you will follow it immediately with the ENTER keystroke. (In that case, you use two keystrokes, just as you would with the usual two-keystroke point-and-shoot method.)

At other times, when you are distracted or uncertain, or when the services selected will take a long time to perform, you will automatically pause to see if you got the keystroke you wanted. All this quickly becomes second nature: go fast when you are sure; go slow when you are unsure.

Submenu Templates

Now that we have seen the main menu and screen templates, the submenu and subscreen templates will be easy to understand. The latter are simply stripped-down versions of the former, as shown in Listing 18.22.

The first thing you notice about the submenu template is its solicitation for you to select a four-character name for this menu-handling procedure; actually a name which is one, two, or three characters in length is also fine. If the menu handles the mailing labels part of your application, you might replace "????" with "Mail". In that case, your mailing labels menu and functions would be handled by MailMenu.PRG and MailScrn.PRG, with the latter called by the former.

The subscreen template in Listing 18.23 is again simpler than the main screen template. In SubScrn.TEM, replace "????" with the same string you used to replace "????" in SubMenu.TEM. For example, if you are creating MailMenu.PRG and MailScrn.PRG, you (1) edit a new file called MailMenu.PRG and insert SubMenu.TEM, (2) edit a new file called MailScrn.PRG and insert SubScrn.TEM, and (3) replace the replaceable text in MailMenu.PRG and MailScrn.PRG.

As with the main screen template, you pick single-character labels for your menu choices, enter these choices in the Choices memvar, enter the characters and their choices on the menu form, and pick values for LineSpace1 and LineSpace2.

Listing 18.22 Template for the Submenu

```
* Replace  "????" with your choice of name throughout this file; then erase
* these first two lines.  =====================================================>
* File = ????Menu.PRG.  Called from  <name of caller =========================>
PRIVATE Exit_L,MenuChoice
Exit_L = .F.
DO WHILE (.NOT. Exit_L)
   MenuChoice =  "  "
   DO ????scrn with MenuChoice
   DO CASE
      CASE (MenuChoice =  "<uppercase letter from menu screen ==============>
 ")
     <lines of code for this menu choice ===============================>
      CASE (MenuChoice =  "<uppercase letter from menu screen ==============>
 ")
     <lines of code for this menu choice ===============================>
      CASE (MenuChoice =  ".")
     Exit_L = .T.
      OTHERWISE
     ?  "????Menu.PRG: Case selector variable not in list.   "
     ??  "Illegal value:",MenuChoice
     ?  "Print screen and notify programmer."
     DO WaitOnC
   ENDCASE
ENDDO
* End of ????Menu.PRG.  ONLY EXIT POINT IS HERE.
```

Listing 18.23 Template for the Subscreen

```
* Replace  "????" with your choice of name throughout this file; then erase
* these first two lines.  =====================================================>
* File = ????Scrn.PRG.  Called from ????Menu.PRG.
* This file started from SubScrn.TEM; called from a .PRG made from SubMenu.TEM.
* SubScrn.TEM by T. David Millican.
* Calls HeadLine.PRG.
* Makes a call to WaitOnC when incorrect menu choice is made.
PARAMETERS MenuChoice
PUBLIC Version
PRIVATE Choices,Correct_Q,Line,LineSpace1,LineSpace2
Choices =  "<list all menu choice letters with no spaces between =============>
."
Correct_Q = .F.
* LineSpace1 blank lines separate the top of the menu from the bottom
* status line.  LineSpace2 blank lines separate the bottom of the menu from
* the prompt line.
LineSpace1 = 1  && Decrease to 0 if you need more menu lines.
LineSpace2 = 1  && Decrease to 0 if you need more menu lines.
MenuChoice =  "  "
SET Scoreboard OFF
DO WHILE (.NOT. Correct_Q)
   CLEAR
   DO HeadLine
   @ LineSpace1,0 SAY  ""
   TEXT
                              Submenu Name
```

```
   .   Return to the previous menu.
   EndText

   Line = Row()
   * GET Choices to put in inverse video only:
   @ Line+LineSpace2+1,4 SAY  "Your Pleasure of" GET Choices ;
    PICTURE  "@R X, X, X, X, X, X, X, X, X, X, X, X, X, X, X, X, X, X, X, X,"
   CLEAR GETS  && cancel GET on Choices
   @ ROW(),COL() SAY  "?" GET MenuChoice PICTURE  "!"
   SET Confirm OFF
   READ
   @ Line+LineSpace2+2,4 SAY ;
    "Change your choice or stroke a carriage return to confirm it:";
   GET MenuChoice PICTURE  "!"
   SET Confirm ON
   READ
   Correct_Q = (MenuChoice $ Choices)
   IF (.NOT. Correct_Q)
      ?
      ?  "    Regret to say that your choice was not one of  " + Choices
      ?
      DO WaitOnC
   ENDIF
ENDDO WHILE (.NOT. Correct_Q)
SET Scoreboard ON
CLEAR && Needed by Clipper, but not dBASE III Plus or FoxBASE+.
* End of ????Scrn.PRG.
```

A Simple Question/Answer Template and Subroutine

A standard programming task is to solicit a one-keystroke response from a user for a specific question. In this section we look at both template and subroutine approaches to this task.

Reply.PRG

Listing 18.24 shows a subroutine implementation of a simple question/answer dialog with the user. The code is dialect-independent.

This subroutine is typically used in combination with the IF, IF/ELSE, or CASE templates; once you solicit the keystroke from the user, you generally select an alternative based on its value. The typical usage pattern would be: (1) call the Reply subroutine; (2) insert one of the "alternative" templates, IF, IF/ELSE, or CASE; and (3) code the alternatives. Listing 18.25 shows an example of calling the Reply subroutine before an IF statement.

Listing 18.24 Reply.PRG for Simple Replies (Dialect-Independent)

```
* File = Reply.PRG.  Solicit simple replies from a user.
*****************************************************************************
* Dialects: All.
*****************************************************************************
* Input parameters:
*    Choices      Character; holds the keystrokes which are permitted as
*                 answers to the prompt.
*    Prompt       Character; holds the question to which reply is solicited.
*****************************************************************************
* Output parameters:
*    Reply        Character, length 1.  Holds the one-character answer to the
*                 question in the prompt.
* Entry conditions assumed:
* 1. The arguments to Choices and Prompt are type character.
* 2. LEN(Choices) > 0.
* 3. At least one character in Choices can be entered at the keyboard into a
*    memvar through the WAIT command.
* 4. The argument to Reply is a memvar or parameter derived from a memvar; it
*    is not a constant.
*****************************************************************************
* Entry conditions verified: NONE.
* Exit conditions guaranteed if entry conditions are true:
* 1. Reply is of type character, length 1.
* 2. Reply is one of the characters in the Prompt parameter.
*****************************************************************************

PARAMETERS Choices,Prompt,Reply

Reply =  "?"
DO WHILE (.NOT. Reply $ Choices)

   WAIT Prompt TO Reply
   Reply = UPPER(Reply)

ENDDO

* End of Reply.PRG.
```

Listing 18.25 Sample Use of Reply.PRG

```
FeedC =  ""
DO Reply WITH  "FL",;
   "Enter  F  for a formfeed, or  L  to leave the paper where it is:", FeedC

IF (FeedC =  "F")
   EJECT
ENDIF
```

Reply.TEM

If we prefer, we can implement this procedure structure as a template, as shown in Listing 18.26. Notice how much lower the intellectual complexity of the template is than that of the subroutine equivalent. When we enter the replaceable text as indicated, the code we produce is syntactically legal. In contrast, the proper working of the code in the subroutine is dependent on qualities of the actual parameters which are not verified.

This template is typically used in combination with the IF, IF/ELSE, or CASE templates; once you solicit the keystroke from the user, you generally select an alternative based on its value. The typical usage pattern would be: (1) insert the Reply template; (2) insert one of the "alternative" templates, IF, IF/ELSE, or CASE;

and (3) code the alternatives. Listing 18.27 shows an example of using the Reply template followed by an IF statement.

Listing 18.26 Template for Simple Replies

```
* Template File: Reply.TEM.
* A template for soliciting simple replies from a user.
PRIVATE Reply
Reply =  "?"
DO WHILE (.NOT. Reply $  "<upper case list of allowable letters ===========>
 ")
   WAIT  "<prompt ==================================================>
 " TO Reply
   Reply = UPPER(Reply)
ENDDO
```

Listing 18.27 Code Sample from the Reply Template

```
PRIVATE Reply
Reply =  "?"
DO WHILE (.NOT. Reply $  "FL")
   WAIT  "Enter  F  for a formfeed, or  L  to leave the paper where it is:  ";
    TO Reply
   ?
   Reply = UPPER(Reply)
ENDDO
IF (Reply =  "F")
   EJECT
ENDIF
```

Notice what a small amount of typing you would have to do in order to convert the Reply and IF templates to the working source code in Listing 18.27. If you are building your own subroutine library, this code (or something like it) may be a good candidate for inclusion; otherwise, it is easy to construct when needed from the templates. (This sort of service will not be available in the usual commercial library, which tends to have a different philosophy in its collection of routines than one which would provide such a service.)

We have already noted the increased flexibility of library templates over library subroutines: the subroutine's service is fixed until we modify it, whereas we can customize the template as we wish, as shown in the next example.

A Non-Subroutine Template Example

Although we could limit the dialog prompt to one line, as shown in the WAIT command in Listing 18.27, we could also use the TEXT/ENDTEXT facility to display a multiple-line menu of choices. Listing 18.28 shows a dialog generated with little effort from Reply.TEM — this dialog could not be implemented with a subroutine in a simple way.

Listing 18.28 A Non-Subroutine Code Sample from a Template

```
PRIVATE Reply
Reply =  "?"
DO WHILE (.NOT. Reply $  "NBA2")
   TEXT
   Choice   Meaning
     N      No eject before or after printing the report.
     B      Eject the paper before printing the report, but not afterwards.
     A      Eject the paper after printing the report, but not before.
     2      Eject the paper before and after printing the report.
   ENDTEXT
   WAIT  "Your choice?  " TO Reply
   Reply = UPPER(Reply)
ENDDO
```

A Template for R&R Relational Report Writer

R&R Relational Report Writer from Concentric Data Systems is arguably the most important dBASE add-on product. It provides a dialect-independent way of producing reports from optionally indexed .DBF files; the indexes of dBASE III PLUS, Clipper, and FoxBASE+ are supported. Data can be reported in storage order or R&R can build its own indexes.

The big advantage of R&R, besides its portability across dialects, is that it permits you to work at the design level. The reporting facilities in dBASE IV and FoxPro were obviously strongly influenced by R&R.

I will treat R&R in detail in Part VIII, but for now I want to show you a template to build an interface to R&R. The template in Listing 18.29 is fairly complete in the sense that very little of the text has to be replaced. You may need to comment out or remove some lines, or to add code, depending on which features of R&R you need for your users.

Listing 18.29 Template for R&R Relational Report Writer

```
* File = RR3.TEM.  Template for setting call to R&R Version 3 Runtime.
*******************************************************************************
* Dialects: All.
*******************************************************************************
PARAMETERS MenuChoice
PRIVATE Dummy,Eject_L,Exit_C,EndPage,Finished_L,Message_L,;
    mPrinter,nCopies,OnScreen_L,RR3_1,RR3_2,RR3_3,StartPage
Eject_L     = .T.
EndPage     = 9999
StartPage   = 1
*******************************************************************************
IF FILE("RR3.MEM")
   RESTORE FROM RR3.MEM ADDITIVE
   mPrinter   = RR3_1
   OnScreen_L = RR3_2
   mFilter    = RR3_3
ELSE
   mPrinter = 0
   OnScreen_L = .F.
   mFilter = SPACE(254)
ENDIF
```

```
Dummy   =  "  "
Exit_C  =  "  "
nCopies = 1
CLEAR
@ ROW()+2,3 SAY  "Enter 0 for the default printer, else printer 1 to 8:"
            GET mPrinter PICTURE  "9" RANGE 0,8
@ ROW()+2,3 SAY  "Enter  True  to see the report onscreen, else  False:" ;
            GET OnScreen_L PICTURE  "L"
@ ROW()+2,3 SAY  "Enter your query expression, if any:"
@ ROW()+1,3 GET mFilter
@ ROW()+2,3 SAY  "Enter the number of copies to print:" ;
            GET nCopies PICTURE  "999" RANGE 1,999
@ ROW()+2,3 SAY  "Enter . to return to the previous menu:" GET Exit_C
@ Row()+2,0 SAY;
  "Review and correct your entries as necessary.  Then press enter.";
 GET Dummy
READ
RR3_1 = mPrinter
RR3_2 = OnScreen_L
RR3_3 = mFilter
SAVE ALL LIKE RR3* to RR3.MEM
******************************************************************************
Finished_L = (Exit_C =  ".")
DO WHILE (.NOT. Finished_L)
***   In this block of code, set needed parameters in the R&R jobfile, called
***   RRunIn.DBF by default.  If you add the fields ReportTime,C,8, and
***   ReportDate,D, to RRunIn.DBF, use the code lines here that record the time
***   and date the report was requested.
   USE RRunIn


   REPLACE RI_Library with <R&R library name.  Usually a .RP1 file.>>>>>>>>>>>>
   REPLACE RI_Master  with <a .DBF filename which usually depends on the >>>>>>
                           <parameter MenuChoice, but which may be constant.>>>
   REPLACE RI_Report  with <a report name in RI_Master which depends on the >>>
                           <parameter MenuChoice. >>>>>>>>>>>>>>>>>>>>>>>>>>>>



   REPLACE RI_Printer with IIF(OnScreen_L,"D",STR(mPrinter,1) ),;
           RI_Filter with mFilter, RI_Query with IIF(""=TRIM(mFilter),"S","O");
          ,RI_Copies with nCopies
***REPLACE ReportDate with Date(), ReportTime with Time()
   REPLACE RI_ChkTime with  "P", RI_BegPage with StartPage, ;
              RI_EndPage with EndPage
   REPLACE RI_Query with IIF("" = TRIM(RI_Filter),"S","O"), RI_DispErr with .T.
   CLOSE DATABASES
   RUN RRunTime RRunIn 1
   USE RRunOut
   Finished_L = (RO_Ecode #  "C")
   Message_L  = (.NOT. (RO_Ecode $  "NC") )
   * If the code is  "C" the user canceled and the message says same, which
   * user already knows.  Therefore only report messages for abnormal aborts
   * other than the user pressing ESCAPE.
   IF Message_L
      ? TRIM(RO_Emsg)
      ?  "Please print screen for programmer.   R&R Error message in name>>>>>>
.PRG."
      DO WaitOnC
   ENDIF
   IF (.NOT. Finished_L)
      CLEAR
      @ 6,0 SAY  "Report canceled.  Last page to print was  " +  ;
           LTRIM(STR(RO_Pages))
      StartPage = RO_Pages
      @ Row()+2,0 SAY ;
```

```
        "To restart the report, enter the page to start with or 0 for the menu  ";
         GET StartPage PICTURE  "9999"
      Line = Row()
      READ
      IF (StartPage = 0)
         RETURN
      ELSE
         @ Line+2,0 SAY  "Enter the page to end with  " ;
          GET EndPage PICTURE  "9999" RANGE StartPage,9999
         READ
      ENDIF
   ENDIF

   USE
ENDDO

IF Eject_L .AND. (Exit_C #  ".")
   EJECT
ENDIF

* End of RR3.TEM.
```

This template is for version 3 of R&R. It gives you control over the following features of the interface to the R&R runtime.

1. You can permit the user to select the printer to be used if the report does not go to the screen.
2. You can permit the user to optionally direct the report to the screen. R&R then displays the report onscreen at a pace which is controlled by the user.
3. You can permit the user to enter a logical expression which references the fields of the databases which are reported. Records are reported if the logical expression is true for the data in the record. (Your nontechnical end-users will need a possibly lengthy list of sample expressions in order to use this feature.)
4. You can permit the user to select the number of copies to print, ranging from 1 to 999.

The following features of the R&R, version 3, interface are *not* accessed in this template:

1. The ability to output the report to a file named at print time.
2. The ability to append the report to a file named at print time.
3. The ability to specify a beginning or ending page number on the first screen. (Note that if the user cancels the report, he or she is given a chance to restart it on a specified page number.)
4. The ability to have label samples printed for alignment purposes.
5. The ability to specify the starting and ending values of the index key for the report's index. For example, on a ZIP code index, you would specify "50000" to "99999" to print out ZIP codes of 50000 or higher from your database.

You can give users access to the above features by soliciting more information from them. The fields needed are always present in RRunIn.DBF, so once the information is solicited, it is just a matter of using the REPLACE command to store the solicited values into the appropriate fields.

When you set up RRunIn.DBF, you may be able to give RI_Library a value which is always used for the application. In that case, you do not need to REPLACE RI_Library, as shown in the template. Similarly, you can assign a value to RI_Master when you set up RRunIn.DBF, if the master database to be reported on is always the same for the application.

The master database will often vary with the report which is chosen. The choice is reflected in the parameter MenuChoice. You may use the submenu/subscreen templates to present the user with a menu of reports, so that the selection is recorded in the memvar MenuChoice.

You must then perform the association between the menu choice for a particular report and the name of that report. This can be done either inside or outside the command file RR3.PRG, which is made from the R&R template file.

For example, MenuChoice might be "1", corresponding to an R&R report named "Receipts by Date Entered". In this case, code in RR3.PRG would map choice "1" to this name, so that RI_Report would receive the value "Receipts by Date Entered".

Alternatively, if the master database is always the same, then this association could be made before RR3.PRG is called. In that case, the parameter would contain the report name and you would code

```
REPLACE RI_Report with MenuChoice
```

Recording Request History

As written, code generated from the R&R template will use record 1 of RRunIn over and over, so that no history of previous report requests is retained. You can APPEND BLANK after the USE RRunIn statement in order to record each report request in its own record.

In that case, you will want to add the fields ReportDate (type D) and ReportTime (Character, length 8) to RRunIn and remove the asterisks at the beginning of the "REPLACE ReportDate" statement. If your software records the user's identity in a PUBLIC memvar called UserID, add a field called UserID to the RRunIn database and store the current M->UserID in the database with the time and date.

I have found the recording of this historical information to be extremely useful for user training and support. These issues will be treated in depth later in the book.

A Sample Subroutine from a Commercial Library

Now let's look at an example of a routine from a commercial library which takes the idea which we started to develop in the discussion for Reply.PRG on page 268 and pushes it to its logical conclusion. The routine is ASK_FOR() from Arthur

Fuller's ArtFul.LIB Clipper library, as explained in his book *Dynamics of Clipper* (Fuller 1989: 40–43).

ASK_FOR() takes up to five arguments and returns the user's response, which may be of type character, date, or numeric. Its basic service is to popup a dialog box with a prompt and an @ GET statement with a PICTURE and a VALID clause. The value read is returned to the caller.

There are many sophistications in this subroutine, which is only 34 lines long, although it does call four other subroutines in the library. This subroutine is implemented in a way which is designed to reduce your work to a minimum; that is, after all, the core idea of a subroutine library.

There are definite costs associated with using a subroutine library, so its benefits must be substantial in order to justify its use.

The first two arguments are required in order for the routine to do anything sensible. These arguments supply the prompt and the initial value for the memvar which is to receive the reply in the @ GET statement.

The optional third argument supplies the picture to be used in the PICTURE clause of the @ GET statement. If you pass only two arguments, or if the type of the third argument is not character, ASK_FOR() will supply an appropriate PICTURE clause for you.

The fourth argument passes an optional validation condition. For example, if you are soliciting a member code which must be in the list A, B, N, or X, you might pass a validation condition such as

Memvar $ "ABNX"

ASK_FOR() uses an identifier called "Memvar" in its @ GET statement, so you must use this same identifier in your validation expression. Here is a sample call to ASK_FOR() to solicit a member code from a user:

```
MembCode = ;
 ASK_FOR("Please enter a member code of A, B, N, or X:",;
         "  ",  "!",  'Memvar $  "ABNX"')
```

The initial value of the response is blank, so the user must enter an alphabetic code in order to complete the dialog. We could have used "A" as the second argument, in which case the initial value of the response would be a legal member code and the user could stroke ENTER to accept the default. The PICTURE clause passed in the third argument causes lowercase keystrokes to be converted to uppercase on input.

The optional fifth argument of ASK_FOR() controls whether a character response has its blanks trimmed before being returned. This argument would be useful when the allowed responses would have varying lengths when trimmed, and you require trailing blanks in the response:

```
MembCode = ;
 ASK_FOR("Please enter a member code of A1, A2, N, or X:",;
         "   ",  "@! A9",;
        '"/" + Memvar +  "/" $  "/A1/A2/N /X /"', .T.)
```

In this example, the member codes are numeric:

```
MembCode = ;
 ASK_FOR("Please enter a member code of 1, 2, 8, or 9:",;
        1,  "9",  'STR(Memvar,1) $  "1289"')
```

Here is an example where date data is solicited. Notice that we didn't bother to specify a PICTURE for the date data; ASK_FOR() will supply it for us. The default entry is today's date. The date which is entered must be sometime this year.

```
BirthDay = ;
 ASK_FOR("Enter the member's birthday this year:",
        DATE(),  "",   "YEAR(Memvar) = YEAR(DATE())" )
```

Custom Building Blocks

By now, you have fully grasped the concept of fill-in-the-blanks templates and have seen how templates and subroutines relate to each other. Now you are in a position to develop and/or acquire some templates and subroutines to serve your particular situation.

Subroutine or Template?

When you notice a pattern in your code, it may be obvious whether the pattern is suitable for partial automation as a template or as a subroutine. For example, if you see the same pattern each time that you prepare the calling sequence for subroutine DoIt, then you would want to write a template DoIt.TEM to automate the production of your calling sequence.

In the case of a simple dialog, we saw that we might appropriately implement the dialog code as Reply.TEM, Reply.PRG, or the procedure form of Reply.PRG, according to the situation. In still other cases, the decision to implement a particular pattern as a subroutine or a template may be less clear or more complex. See the discussion starting on page 214 for more information.

Commercial Libraries

Commercial libraries are treated in their own chapter in Part VIII. For now, let's look at a few sources of information about these libraries.

A comprehensive index to the world of dBASE programmer aids is provided by EMS of Olney, Maryland, which publishes *dBUtility Directory*; at the time of writing this directory listed over 1,000 public domain or shareware programs and over 600 commercial programs, as well as dBASE magazines, BBSs, and discount distributors. By the time you read this, EMS should have released its *Dbase Source Code Applications Directory*, which lists dBASE programs whose source code can be purchased.

EMS also publishes the rather daunting *dBUtility Library*, "a comprehensive collection of all known public domain and shareware utilities produced specifically for dBASE programmers." According to EMS, "It contains over 1,000 programs (in compressed format) on over 48 diskettes." (See Appendix I, "Alphabetic List of dBASE-Related Vendors," on page 457, for contact information for EMS and the other vendors listed in this book.)

The pages of *Data Based Advisor* and *DBMS* magazines are filled with advertisements for commercial libraries. Unfortunately, most of the libraries are only for the Clipper dialect, *so we need to lobby the Clipper library vendors to support more dialects!!!*

You can find Clipper library information in the *Clipper Third Party Products Directory* (Nantucket Corporation 1988), the vendor of Clipper, and you can find support products for dBASE III PLUS and dBASE IV development in the *Ashton-Tate Developer Registry* (Ashton-Tate 1989). At the time of writing, Fox Software was developing its first directory of Fox-related products; unfortunately, this directory is unlikely to be as useful as other directories because of the substantial fees which Fox is charging for entries — the industry convention is to provide listings free to vendors in order to maximize the number of listings.

Several of the library providers have written books or shorter monographs on libraries. See *Dynamics of Clipper* (Fuller 1989) and *Building Source Code Libraries* (Yellick 1989a).

Recommended Exploitation of Library Technology

Table 18.2 lists some recommendations on exploiting this technology for yourself, your users, your clients, and your employers.

Table 18.2
Recommendations on Exploiting Template and Subroutine Libraries

1. Examine the templates in this book. Type those templates onto your hard disk (or order the companion diskette for the book according to the procedures in Appendix A). Modify and extend these templates as appropriate to your situation.
2. Investigate commercial subroutine libraries if that is an option for you. (If you use a subroutine library with code which executes under two different dialects, you must use a version of the library that is specific to each dialect, or else the library must consist of dialect-independent code, which is unlikely to be the case in a horizontal-market library.)
3. If you use library subroutines, construct a template for each routine that minimizes the number of keystrokes you need in order to generate a syntactically legal reference to the routine. Use the macro features of your editor to implement the template, or else put it in a file with the .TEM which is stored in your dBASE dialect utilities directory (\DB\UTIL in the recommended structure used in this book). The filename of the template file should be the same as the name of the subroutine whose calling sequence it models. For example, DoIt.TEM

would automate the calling sequence for subroutine DoIt (which could be a command file, function, or procedure).

4. If you implement a code pattern as both a subroutine and a template, as in the Reply.PRG and Reply.TEM files in this chapter, then document the calling sequence for the subroutine in comments in the beginning of the template.
5. Look at the standard kinds of coding tasks you face. Which of the repetitive tasks are not covered by the templates and subroutines in the libraries that you use? Write your own templates and subroutines to fill the gaps so that you can get ever closer to the true building block construction of your applications!

When in doubt, make in general.
Subroutine-design aphorism of Professor W. Wesley Peterson,
Department of Information and Computer Sciences, University of Hawaii

The process of preparing programs for a digital computer is especially attractive, not only because it can be economically and scientifically rewarding, but also because it can be an aesthetic experience much like composing poetry or music.
Donald E. Knuth, Preface to *The Art of Computer Programming*,
Volume 1, 1973a, p. v

There is an asymmetry in the relationship between amateur and professional programmers, because the one cannot appreciate the complexities that the other faces.
Gerald M. Weinberg, *The Psychology of Computer Programming*,
1971, p. 126

The time spent on careful planning is almost always less than time spent fixing mistakes that result from rushing through the coding for an application.
Stephen J. Straley, *Programming in Clipper*, 1988, p. 720

Part IV

dBASE Software Engineering Techniques of General Application

As of this point, you know how to use the Millican templates or modifications of them to rapidly construct the top-level structure and dialect-independent menus for an application. Now you will learn what to put behind the menus, and how to program user interfaces with a wide range of sophistication.

Several of the chapters in Parts IV and V could be expanded to book length, so there is much more to say than you will read here and in Volume 2. Relative to space constraints, however, these two parts of the book try to give you as many solutions as possible to intermediate and advanced single-user dBASE programming problems. (With suitable effort, you can exploit the canonical approach promoted in this book to develop elegant solutions for the problems the book doesn't treat!)

Part IV presents ideas and techniques which you will probably use in most of your programs. In Volume 2, Part V, "dBASE Software Engineering Techniques of Specific Application," presents techniques to handle data processing problems which are restricted to certain kinds of applications. For example, the techniques for handling mailing addresses will be used in programs which process mailing addresses, and not otherwise.

Chapter 19

Standard Limitations and Pitfalls with Countermeasures

This chapter tells you about missing features which you might expect dBASE dialects to possess, depending on your background, such as tables of databases. As part of the treatment, I also describe any tools and/or techniques that I know of which can help to reduce the impact of the missing features.

As experienced dBASE programmers know so well, there are a number of pitfalls in the programming use of dBASE dialects. You must know about these pitfalls and their countermeasures in order to produce stable applications in reasonable amounts of time.

The mission of this chapter is to present some of the major limitations and pitfalls in the dBASE programming language and to show you how to protect yourself and your users from the consequences of low productivity and unstable applications. In some cases, the problem exists in some dialects and not in others, and these dialects will be clearly identified.

No Data Dictionary

Mainframe database programmers are accustomed to having a *data dictionary* facility in their database programming environment, commonly called a *DBMS*, for *Data Base Management System*. The data dictionary records a variety of information about the attributes of the data objects in a given application. In DBMSs with active data dictionaries, the attributes of data objects are enforced by the DBMS, but among the dBASE dialects, only Recital has an active data dictionary. However, any dBASE dialect will support a passive data dictionary wherein data object attributes are stored for the reference purposes of programmers.

In dBASE terms, a data dictionary could contain the information listed in Table 19.1 about the database fields it uses. The first four items of information in the table are contained in the headers for dBASE .DBF database files; these items are implemented by all dBASE dialects. The Recital dialect also permits you to enter a short description for each field.

The other attributes must be controlled by your programming code. For example, if you wish to edit the PhoneNum field with a PICTURE of "@R 999-9999", then you must code

```
@ GET PhoneNum PICTURE "@R 999-9999"
```

With a fuller implementation of the data dictionary approach, you would be able to specify "@R 999-9999" as the default PICTURE for the field PhoneNum and to code "@ GET PhoneNum" when the default PICTURE would be satisfactory.

Table 19.1 Data Dictionary Sample Contents

1. Field name.
2. Field type.
3. Field length.
4. Field decimals (for numeric types).
5. PICTURE specification to use for editing and display.
6. A range for character, date, and numeric data.
7. A logical expression or UDF to use to validate the field's data.
8. Default colors to use for display.
9. Default colors to use for editing.
10. A description of what the field is used for.

Countermeasures

Our options for working around the data dictionary limitations of current dBASE dialects are rather limited. When the use of uniform colors, PICTUREs, ranges, and so on is not enforced by the programming language, our applications tend to display data in an inconsistent fashion, and we programmers may not apply the same validation criteria to the same data in all instances.

For example, we may use the same PICTURE to display a field throughout an application that we write this month, but is this PICTURE the same as the one we used in previous applications? Is this PICTURE the same PICTURE which was used by other programmers who access that same field? Is this PICTURE the same PICTURE which will be used in the future? A built-in data dictionary can enforce field attributes across *all* of the applications which use a given field!

In theory, one effective countermeasure to the lack of a built-in data dictionary (except for elementary attributes such as field name and type) is the use of a code generator with a full-featured data dictionary. If the field PhoneNum were assigned the PICTURE "@R 999-9999" in the data dictionary used by the code generator, then when you needed to GET the value of PhoneNum, the generator would generate the code

```
@ GET PhoneNum PICTURE "@R 999-9999"
```

and when you displayed this field, the generator would code

```
TRANSFORM(PhoneNum,"@R 999-9999")
```

and include the PICTURE automatically.

In practice, code generators are not an option for most of us. Powerful code generators take time to learn and involve significant procedural complexities which are not otherwise involved. A fundamental prohibition in many cases is the necessity for the application's code to be maintained by any dBASE dialect programmer in the future; you certainly cannot assume that every dBASE dialect programmer knows even one code generator, much less the particular generator that you favor.

Recommendation on exploiting passive data dictionaries. Build a data dictionary in a .DBF file to store various field attributes. Store this attribute information in a single .DBF file which holds all of the field information for all of your applications, or use a separate data dictionary for each .DBF file. Consult the data dictionary information when you are coding in order to use the correct display formats, validation, and so on for field I/O. The data dictionary file or files become part of the programmer documentation for your applications.

Use the same field names and attributes for the first four fields in your data dictionary database that are used in structure extended files. This permits you to use the "CREATE <new database> FROM <structure extended file>" command in the form "CREATE <new database> FROM <data dictionary database>" to create your databases with the field structures defined in the data dictionary. See the presentation on structure extended files starting on page 290 for more information.

Execution Time Use of Data Dictionaries

One of the most problematic deficits of current dBASE dialects is their failure to support the "->" construct in macro expansions. In many cases, it would be extremely convenient to expand an expression such as "M->X" or "DataDict->Picture" as a macro, but we cannot write &DataDict->Picture or even &(DataDict->Picture) to expand DataDict->Picture as a macro. This deficit eliminates some of the more obvious approaches to using data dictionaries at execution time.

However, it is sometimes possible to use cleverly designed UDFs to access data dictionaries at execution time. Consider the following code to enter and later report a customer's identification code:

```
@ 1,1 SAY  "Enter the customer ID:" GET Customer->ID PICTURE  "A999"
READ
<other statements>
? TRANSFORM(Customer->ID,  "A999")
```

How can we use the data-driven concept to access the PICTURE specification from a data dictionary at execution time? Imagine that we have a UDF called FieldPicts() that takes two arguments: the database name and field name. This UDF would open the appropriate data dictionary file, search for specifications for the desired field, and return the PICTURE for this field. In the current example, FieldPicts("Customer","ID") would return the PICTURE "A999". If we had such a UDF, we could rewrite the above code as follows:

```
PRIVATE ID_Pict
ID_Pict = FieldPicts("Customer","ID")
@ I,1 SAY  "Enter the customer ID:" GET Customer->ID PICTURE &ID_Pict
READ
<other statements>
? TRANSFORM(Customer->ID, FieldPicts("Customer","ID"))
```

Notice that we can directly reference the UDF in the TRANSFORM function, but we must create a temporary memvar (which must be declared PRIVATE for safety's sake) for PICTURE specification in the GET statement. This example shows that there are significant problems in the execution time use of data dictionaries in current dBASE dialects, with of course the exception of Recital.

For more information, see the following: "Data Driven Systems: A Fresh Approach to Application Generation" (Oliver 1990); the manual for QuickTek's Schooner product; Chapter 3, "Data Dictionary," in *Developing FoxPro Applications* (Olympia and Cea 1990: 43–58) and the heading "Performing Data Validation" (Olympia and Cea 1990: 65–72); and "The Data Dictionary" (Olympia 1990).

No Tables of Databases

Users of full-featured DBMSs are accustomed to setting up the file-based data structures of an application in one large data structure called either a *table* or a *database*, depending on the product. In dBASE terms, such a large data structure consists of a set of databases.

In a fully implemented data dictionary approach, you can define relationships between databases which are automatically managed by the system. In the last section, we saw how the data dictionary approach could permit you to code "@ GET <fieldname>" as an alternative to

@ GET <fieldname> PICTURE <default PICTURE for field>

and "? <fieldname>" as an alternative to

? TRANSFORM(<fieldname>,"<default PICTURE for field>")

Similarly, the data dictionary approach could eliminate the need for you to code SET RELATION TO and SET SKIP TO commands. The dBASE programming language uses these two commands to assist you in managing related databases, but you must manage related files using commands in source code.

Countermeasures

I recommend that you build a subroutine to open your databases. Rather than code "USE <database>", you will code

DO <open routine> WITH "<database>" [,<options>]

You can hide the SET RELATION TO and SET SKIP TO commands in your <open routine>. For example,

```
DO OpenDBF WITH "Members",5
```

might open Members.DBF and its related files, with SET RELATION TO and SET SKIP TO issued as needed to establish which files are related and whether the relations are many-to-one or many-to-many.

This data-driven concept is explored in detail in Chapter 23. See the discussion which begins on page 395.

No Arrays or User-Defined Functions in Some Dialects

If you are new to dBASE dialects, you may be surprised to discover that some dialects do not implement arrays or user-defined functions. Furthermore, those dialects which implement UDFs usually place restrictions on commands which may appear in UDFs and on where UDF references may appear.

These issues are discussed in the language-survey chapter, Chapter 3, where arrays and UDFs are presented. See pages 83 and following for a presentation of arrays, and see pages 49 and following for a presentation of dBASE subroutine types, including UDFs, and argument and parameter issues.

No Nested Records

The data which our programs use and process often has a tree structure. For example, we might wish to store the information shown in Table 19.2 for a printer driver facility in our program.

In languages such as PASCAL, COBOL, and PL/I, you are able to set up data structures in your program which exactly reflect the tree structure of data like that in the example. To reference the character variable which holds the start string for boldface, you might code a reference like "Printer.Attribute_Data.Boldface.On". To pass the four items of attribute data to a subroutine, you might call a subroutine with an argument list like "Text,'B',Attribute_Data"; the third parameter for the subroutine would echo the structure of Attribute_Data as shown.

With the exception of Clipper 5.0, which permits arrays as array elements, there is no equivalent facility in the dBASE programming language. In dBASE, you must represent such a structure as a simple list of fields. Moreover, the field names are limited to 10 characters in the dBASE standard, so you can't have a descriptive field name like "Attribute_Data_Boldface_On".

Table 19.2 Example of Nested Records

- **Printer**
  - **Communications_Data**
    - Parallel (Logical)
    - **Serial_Data**
      - Baud_Rate (Numeric, 300 to 56000)
      - Data_Bits (Numeric, 7 or 8)
      - Stop_Bits (Numeric, 0 or 1)
      - Parity (Logical)
  - **Setup_Data**
    - Setup_String (Character, length 70)
    - Reset_String (Character, length 70)
  - **Attribute_Data**
    - **Boldface**
      - On (Character, length 70)
      - Off (Character, length 70)
    - **Italics**
      - On (Character, length 70)
      - Off (Character, length 70)

Countermeasures

One of the beauties of nested data structures is that a group of memvars can be passed as a single argument to a subroutine, whereas "standard" dBASE requires you to pass each memvar as a separate argument. However, in dialects which implement arrays, you can group related memvars into an array which can be passed as one argument.

Database files implement one-dimensional sets of records numbered 1, 2, ..., and dBASE arrays with one subscript implement one-dimensional sets of memvars numbered 1, 2, ... You have a limited nesting capability when you use memvar arrays with more than one subscript, which are supported in some dialects.

Your countermeasure to short variable names is a preprocessor. A preprocessor adds a layer of functionality to your source code. You can have the preprocessor translate your long identifiers to short ones which will be accepted by the dialect.

Remark. We will cover preprocessors and other productivity aids for dBASE dialect programmers in great detail in Volume 2. For now, I mention PRE/DB from Pinnacle Publishing, a preprocessor specifically designed for dBASE dialects. In addition, Clipper 5.0 offers a built-in preprocessor.

No Named Constants

Many applications have identifiers which by design are assigned data only once. If you use a variable for such a purpose, it is possible that the variable's value will change when you don't want the value to change.

Many languages other than dBASE provide a special class of identifier, often called a *constant* or a *named constant*, for this purpose. You can add this feature to your dBASE source code with a preprocessor, as explained in the previous subsection. (Note: Clipper 5.0 has a built-in preprocessor.)

No Type Declarations

A language such as PASCAL is said to be *strongly typed* because each identifier has one and only one type associated with it. In such a language, you must declare the type of an identifier before you can reference the identifier. Identifiers which represent dBASE fields are strongly typed because they can only hold one type of data, but dBASE memvars take their type from the data they hold.

For example, you could have a memvar named PageNumber which was alternately numeric or character, according to your need in the program: PageNumber = LTRIM(STR(PageNumber)) converts PageNumber from its numeric form to its character form (without leading spaces or zeroes), and PageNumber = VAL(PageNumber) converts PageNumber from its character form to its numeric form (leading spaces and zeroes ignored).

Type declarations are a limitation in a language which provide the benefit of certain kinds of automatic error checking. Strongly typed languages such as PASCAL do not permit you to make some of the errors that are possible in dBASE dialects.

I personally feel that the dBASE programming language loses more than it gains by not having each memvar restricted to hold one type of data. Evidently, I am not alone, as Clipper 5.0 and Sophco's FORCE compiler introduce some typing into their respective dialects.

Countermeasures

If you wish to use an identifier in your application whose type is guaranteed not to change, make the identifier into a database field. For example, you could create a database named System.DBF, which would have such identifiers as its fields.

This database would have only one record. You would assign values to those identifiers with the REPLACE command and reference them with the syntax "System-> <identifier>".

Bad Bedfellows

In a canonical information structure, as many as possible of our questions can be answered by looking at the structure: the concept is *exposure* versus *camouflage.* A practice which goes very much against the canonical approach is that of controlling two features with one switch.

Imagine how difficult it would be to drive your automobile if the throttle were controlled by the steering wheel: turn left to slow down, turn right to speed up. The dBASE programming language has at least two instances where two features are controlled by one switch: SET BELL and SET EXACT.

SET BELL

In some (probably rare) full-screen editing situations, a user will want an audible alarm to sound when a character has been entered into the last available character position in each onscreen editing window. This feature is controlled with SET BELL ON/OFF. In a much more typical situation, the user will want an audible alarm to sound when illegal data is entered in a field, such as an invalid date in a date field. Unfortunately, this feature is *also* controlled by SET BELL ON/OFF, so to get a feature that you usually want, you must have a feature which you almost never want.

Countermeasures

Computers which use the ASCII character set generally recognize character number 7, CHR(7) in dBASE syntax, as the "bell" character. When this character is sent to terminals equipped with a speaker, the terminal will usually emit a short sound. In MS-DOS dialects, you code "?? CHR(7)" (but remember to SET PRINT OFF first, or else the CHR(7) will also be sent to the printer, which may or may not ignore it).

In dialects which support the VALID clause of the @ GET command and UDFs, you can code a UDF to check the data entered for validity and to sound an alarm if the data is invalid. You can also have this facility for fields with the FoxPro BROWSE command, which permits your UDF to validate field data entered while you browse.

Note that the custom programming approach permits you to control the audible alarm feature for selected items. SET BELL ON/OFF controls the feature for all items.

SET EXACT

In most programming languages, two character strings will compare as equal if and only if the strings have the same length and the characters are the same in each position. The dBASE programming language compares two strings to each other in two different situations where the length of the strings may be different, yet the strings will be considered to be the same!

The first kind of comparison is in logical expressions of the form "A = B" or "A # B", where A and B are of type character. If you SET EXACT ON, then A and B must have the same length in order for "A = B" to be a true expression. I have not encountered or heard of any situation where a programmer would want "A = B" to be a true expression if the lengths of A and B were different, but this can happen in dBASE if you SET EXACT OFF.

The obvious solution is to SET EXACT ON all the time, but unfortunately, SET EXACT controls *another* feature which typically requires you to SET EXACT OFF in order to obtain the desired functionality! When you attempt to retrieve a record in an indexed database by its key value in the master index, you often want to know if there was a key with a partial match to the key you seek.

For example, say that you want to find the first ZIP code in your database which starts with "5" and that the first such ZIP code is "50534". In this case, you are interested in getting a match between the first character of the key you seek ("5") and the first character of the key in the database ("50534"). If you SET EXACT OFF, then SEEK "5" will move the record pointer to the record with ZIP code "50534"; if you SET EXACT ON, then SEEK "5" will move the record pointer to the end of file!

Countermeasure

Some dialects give you the "==" operator. If A and B are strings, the expression "(A == B)" can be true in such dialects only if both strings have the same length. The "==" operator works in a way which does not depend on SET EXACT.

> **Recommendation on the "==" operator.** In dialects which support the "==" operator, compare strings A and B with the syntax "(A == B)" or "(.NOT. (A == B))" as alternatives to "(A = B)" and "(A # B)".
>
> **Recommendation on SET EXACT when == is not available.** When the == operator is not available, have your application SET EXACT ON at entry. When you need to SEEK, and your search key is shorter than your index keys, have your application SET EXACT OFF, SEEK, and SET EXACT ON in three consecutive statements.

Work Areas, SELECT, and USE

If your applications only open one database at a time, then you don't even need to understand what a work area is and you have no need for the SELECT command. If, however, your applications require more than one database to be open simultaneously, then (1) you must understand the definition of *work area* and how to use the SELECT and USE commands, and (2) you must understand how to use these commands in the proper combination in order to create stable applications.

Here is the first problem. If you need an unused work area in order to open a database file, you might code "SELECT 4" with the belief that work area 4 will be available when the "SELECT 4" statement is encountered. This approach produces fragile applications.

Here is the second problem. You may code "SELECT 4" when you need to select the database which you believe is open in work area 4. This again tends to make your applications unstable.

Countermeasures

Here are two recommendations for handling work areas.

Recommendation on selecting an unused work area. Do not code a number greater than 0 in "SELECT <number>". If your dialect supports SELECT 0 or the equivalent, such as SELECT SELECT() in dBASE IV, then use SELECT 0 or the equivalent whenever you need to select a work area in which no database is open. If your dialect does *not* support SELECT 0 or the equivalent, as is the case with dBASE III PLUS, then use Select0.PRG on page 73.

Recommendation on selecting a database by work area number. Do not use the form "SELECT <number>" to select the work area in which the database you want is open. Use the form "SELECT <alias>".

Creating a .DBF Database File Programmatically

In many cases it is convenient to create a .DBF file by command. Some dialects, such as Clipper, have a command for this purpose. Other dialects permit you to create databases in indirect but quite acceptable ways, providing you know the tricks. The purpose of this section is to show you how your major-dialect programs can create an empty database with specified file name, field names, and field attributes. In order to understand how programs can create database files, we must first know about structure extended files.

Structure Extended Files

A *structure extended file* is a special .DBF file which is used to store the names and attributes of the fields of a .DBF database. The fields and attributes of a structure extended file are shown in Table 19.3.

Table 19.3 Fields of a Structure Extended File

1. **Field_Name.** Character, length 10. Holds a left-justified string which conforms to the dBASE rules for programmer-defined identifiers.
2. **Field_Type.** Character, length 1. Holds the first letter of the field type: C for Character, D for Date, F for Float, L for Logical, M for Memo, and N for Numeric.
3. **Field_Len.** Numeric, length 3 or 5. Holds the length of a field.
4. **Field_Dec.** Numeric, length 2. Holds the number of decimal places to the right of the decimal point, if Field_Type = "N".
5. **Field_Ndx.** Logical. dBASE IV only: If true, this field is a TAG for the associated .MDX file.

If you have a structure extended file, you can create a database whose structure matches the field specifications in the structure extended file by using the syntax "CREATE <database> FROM <structure extended file>". You can make a structure extended file whose data matches the fields in the currently selected database with the command "COPY STRUCTURE EXTENDED TO <structure extended file>".

Notice that if your program can find one .DBF file, then it can USE this file and COPY STRUCTURE EXTENDED in order to create a structure extended file with data in it. However, you can ZAP the structure extended file and store the database structure of your choice in it.

What if your program cannot assume that it can find a .DBF file?

Creating a .DBF from No .DBF

The Clipper and Quicksilver dialects use the "CREATE <structure extended file>" command to make an empty structure extended file. The file is opened in the current work area after it is made.

In dBASE III PLUS and dBASE IV, you can create a structure extended file with the subroutine in Listing 19.1. This form requires you to pass arguments to inform the subroutine of the settings of TITLE and SAFETY on entry, so that these settings may be restored on exit. However, the lovely SET() function in dBASE IV permits you to eliminate the last two parameters for a routine which is much simpler to use, as shown in Listing 19.2.

Listing 19.1
MakeSEF3.PRG—Create a Structure Extended File for dBASE III PLUS

```
* File = MakeSEF3.PRG for dBASE III PLUS.  Called from several .PRG.
* Make a structure extended file in the currently selected work area.
********************************************************************************
* Dialect: dBASE III PLUS.
********************************************************************************
* Input parameters:
* First parameter: name of structure extended file to create.
* Second parameter:.T./.F. to SET SAFETY ON/OFF on exit.
* Third parameter:  .T./.F. to SET TITLE  ON/OFF on exit.
********************************************************************************
PARAMETERS SEF_Name,Safety_L,Title_L

SET Safety OFF
SET Title OFF
SET CATALOG TO           && Close any catalog file now open.
SET CATALOG TO EraseMe   && Create the catalog file EraseMe.CAT.
SET CATALOG TO           && Close EraseMe.CAT.

USE EraseMe.CAT
COPY STRUCTURE EXTENDED TO &SEF_Name
USE &SEF_Name

ERASE EraseMe.CAT

IF Safety_L
   SET SAFETY ON
ENDIF

IF Title_L
   SET TITLE ON
ENDIF

* End of MakeSEF3.PRG.
```

Listing 19.2 MakeSEF4.PRG—Create a Structure Extended File for dBASE IV

```
* File = MakeSEF4.PRG for dBASE IV.  Called from several .PRG.
* Make a structure extended file in the currently selected work area.
**************************************************************************
* Dialect: dBASE IV.
**************************************************************************
* Input parameter:
* First parameter: name of structure extended file to create.
**************************************************************************
PARAMETERS SEF_Name
PRIVATE Catalog_C,Safety_C,Title_C
Catalog_C= SET("Catalog")
Safety_C = SET("Safety")
Title_C  = SET("Title")
SET Safety OFF
SET Title OFF
SET CATALOG TO              && Close any catalog file now open.
SET CATALOG TO EraseMe      && Create the catalog file EraseMe.CAT.
SET CATALOG TO              && Close EraseMe.CAT.
USE EraseMe.CAT
COPY STRUCTURE EXTENDED TO &SEF_Name
USE &SEF_Name
ERASE EraseMe.CAT
SET CATALOG TO &Catalog_C
SET SAFETY &Safety_C
SET TITLE &Title_C
* End of MakeSEF4.PRG.
```

In FoxBASE+, we can use the KEYBOARD command to create the structure of a database file in a program with the "CREATE <database>" command, which is an interactive command that requires keyboard input. The subroutine in Listing 19.3 is based on GenDBF2.PRG by Carlos Berguido and John Bauman (Berguido and Bauman 1989). Also see the reply to the letter "DBFs on the Fly and dBMAN" (Bauman 1989c).

Listing 19.3 MakeSeFB.PRG—Create a Structure Extended File for FoxBASE+

```
* File = MakeSeFB.PRG for FoxBASE+ 2.0.  Called from several .PRG.
* Make a structure extended file in the currently selected work area.
**************************************************************************
* Dialect: FoxBASE+ 2.0 or 2.1.
**************************************************************************
* Input parameters:
* First parameter: name of structure extended file to create.
* Second parameter:.T./.F. to SET SAFETY ON/OFF on exit.
**************************************************************************
PARAMETERS SEF_Name,Safety_L
PRIVATE SEF
SEF = IIF("." $ SEF_Name, SEF_Name, SEF_Name +  ".DBF")
IF (.NOT. FILE(SEF))
   PRIVATE ScreenImag
   SAVE SCREEN TO ScreenImag
   CLEAR
   ?  "Please wait."
   KEYBOARD  "FIELD1" + CR + CR +  "10" + CR + CR + CR +  "N"
   SET SAFETY OFF
   CREATE EraseMe.$$$
   COPY STRUCTURE EXTENDED TO &SEF
```

```
   USE &SEF
   ZAP
   RESTORE SCREEN FROM ScreenImag
   IF Safety_L
      SET SAFETY ON
   ENDIF
ENDIF
* End of MakeSEF3.PRG.
```

In FoxPro, we can write the bytes of an empty structure extended file directly to disk with the SET PRINTER TO command. See the comments in Listing 19.4 that explain why SET ALTERNATE TO does not work for this application.

Listing 19.4 MakeSeFP.PRG—Create a Structure Extended File for FoxPro

```
* File = MakeSEFp.PRG for FoxPro.  Called from several .PRG.
* Make a structure extended file in the currently selected work area.
********************************************************************************
* Dialect: FoxPro.
********************************************************************************
* Input parameters:
* First parameter: name of structure extended file to create.
********************************************************************************
********************************************************************************
* Note: The ALTERNATE file facility does not work for this purpose due to
* undocumented text-file formatting:
* In FoxPro 1.0,  "?? CHR(10)" had the same effect as  "?? CHR(13) + CHR(10)"
* That is,  "?? <line feed>" was interpreted as  "?? <carriage return> +
* <line feed>"
* Also note that CHR(26) is automatically appended to the alternate file as its
* last character.
PARAMETERS SEF_Name
PRIVATE SEF
SEF = IIF("." $ SEF_Name, SEF_Name, SEF_Name +  ".DBF")
IF (.NOT. FILE(SEF))
   PRIVATE Console_C,Null,Safety_C
   Console_C = SET("Console")
   Null      = CHR(0)
   Safety_C  = SET("Safety")
   SET Console OFF
   SET Safety  OFF
   SET PRINTER TO &SEF
   SET PRINTER ON
   ?? CHR(3) +  "Z" + CHR(3) + CHR(23) + REPLICATE(Null,4) + CHR(161)
   ?? Null + CHR(18) + REPLICATE(Null,21)
   ??  "FIELD_NAME" + Null +  "C" + CHR(1) + REPLICATE(Null,3)
   ?? CHR(10) + REPLICATE(Null,15)
   ??  "FIELD_TYPE" + Null +  "C" + CHR(11) + REPLICATE(Null,3)
   ?? CHR(1) + REPLICATE(Null,15)
   ??  "FIELD_LEN" + Null + Null +  "N" + CHR(12) + REPLICATE(Null,3)
   ?? CHR(3) + REPLICATE(Null,15)
   ??  "FIELD_DEC" + Null + Null +  "N" + CHR(15) + REPLICATE(Null,3)
   ?? CHR(3) + REPLICATE(Null,15)
   ?? CHR(13) + CHR(26)
   SET PRINTER TO
   SET PRINTER OFF
   SET Safety  &Safety_C
   SET Console &Console_C
ENDIF
* End of MakeSEFp.PRG.
```

Persistency of FOUND()

The FOUND() built-in function determines the success of the previous LOCATE, FIND, or SEEK command. A natural assumption on the part of a programmer is that following a LOCATE, FIND, or SEEK command, FOUND() would continue to return the same value until a subsequent LOCATE, FIND, or SEEK command. Unfortunately, this assumption cannot be made for all dialects.

Countermeasures

Here is a recommendation on how to use FOUND().

Recommendation on FOUND(). Determine the success of a LOCATE, FIND, or SEEK command using one of these two options. Option 1: reference FOUND() in an IF statement which is executed immediately after the LOCATE, FIND, or SEEK command. Option 2: assign FOUND() to a memvar immediately after the LOCATE, FIND, or SEEK command, and test the value of the memvar later, rather than FOUND().

David Kalman reports that "FOUND() does not always work properly in dBASE III PLUS and FoxBASE+. Instead, you should use EOF() to test for the end-of-file. If EOF() is true, the FIND did not succeed" (Kalman 1989: 217).

Appending Many Records to a Database with Indexes

There are two options for appending a large number of records programmatically to an indexed database. Option 1 is to USE the database with its indexes and append while the indexes are open. Option 2 is to USE the database without its indexes, append while the indexes are closed, and then build the indexes again.

When the number of records to append is very large in absolute terms, or the number of records to append is very large relative to the size of the database, then option 2 is likely to be faster than option 1. In some cases the difference will be dramatic.

Number of Passes

A "pass" of a database processes the database records in index or storage order. In many instances, it is convenient to think of making one pass to get each needed summary piece of information, or to update each field.

When databases are small, the difference between the amount of time taken for one pass and the time taken for several passes may not be significant. However, when databases are large, the difference is *very* significant. When you implement your passes, try to combine them so as to use the minimum possible number of passes.

Memvar Names Which Must Be Assigned with STORE

You can use dBASE keywords as dBASE memvar names, but you must use the STORE form of the assignment statement to give values to such memvars. For example, if you code "Index = 1", dBASE will think that you are beginning an INDEX ON command, and an error will occur when this statement is executed or compiled.

Countermeasures

To assign a value to a memvar whose name is the same as the first token of a command, use the syntax "STORE <value> TO <memvar>" or "STORE <value> TO <memvar list>".

Chapter 20

Design of dBASE Dialect Subroutines

There are two contexts for the design of dBASE dialect subroutines. The first context is subroutines which are part of an application and which will not be used in other applications, or will not be reused in any formal way. The second context is subroutines which will be added to a library of subroutines for use in many applications.

Many design issues are common to both contexts, as we will see in this chapter. There is, however, an additional set of considerations which exist for the design of library subroutines.

In order to really exploit dBASE dialect subroutines, you must understand the basic material presented in Chapter 3 on subroutine types, arguments, and parameters. This presentation starts on page 49.

You must also understand the advanced material in this chapter on the scope of dBASE variables, and the concepts of environment detection and preservation. In this chapter, we'll look first at scope issues, then at issues of environment detection and preservation, and finally at some principles of library subroutine design.

Scope of Variables

The scope of variables is a fundamental aspect of any computer language, because the variables of an application are typically known to some procedure structures and not to others.

Goals and Issues

In order to program dBASE applications with predictable behavior, you must understand how scope works in dBASE dialects. You must understand each class of identifier; when identifiers can be declared, cannot be declared, or must be declared; and when an identifier is defined, hidden, and released.

The dBASE language has four classes of identifiers for data objects: PUBLIC memory variables ("memvars" for short), PRIVATE memvars, database fields, and parameters. Although vendor manuals do not generally distinguish memvars and parameters, we will see that this distinction is important.

The same name can be used for objects in different classes, just as you might have several friends, all named Jim Jones. When you refer to Jim Jones in a conversation with your spouse, you have to find a way to distinguish one Jim Jones from the others, in order to have an unambiguous reference. A dBASE program might have a PUBLIC memvar named X, a PRIVATE memvar named X, a database field named X, and a parameter named X.

In dBASE dialects, the scope and disambiguation rules are used to determine which identifier is picked in the event that your application has several identifiers with the same name. In theory, we can avoid dealing with the issue of having two or more data objects with the same name by giving each named object in our applications a unique name, but this is not always practicable.

For example, we typically want to use many different temporary variables which share a limited set of names like Ndex, I, and Temp. Furthermore, in some conditions we deliberately use a memvar with the same name as a field. In other conditions, we may not know which memvars, fields, and parameters may be defined when a particular piece of code is executed.

Let's see if we can develop a really comprehensive understanding of what can go wrong and what can work right with dBASE identifiers. Such an understanding will permit us to design stable applications and modify unstable ones so that they become stable!

Defining dBASE Identifiers for Data

When an identifier appears in a PUBLIC statement for the first time, it is placed into the symbol table with an initial value of .F. It is known in all subroutines from the time it first appears in a PUBLIC statement until the time that it is removed from the symbol table with CLEAR ALL or RELEASE.

Once a PUBLIC statement in which an identifier appears is executed, the identifier may subsequently appear in other PUBLIC statements. In all cases, the identifier refers to the same PUBLIC memvar.

When "PUBLIC X" is first executed, a variable named X is entered into the symbol table. No changes in the symbol table occur when "PUBLIC X" is executed again.

It is standard software engineering practice to declare all variables which are used in program units like dBASE command files, procedures, and user-defined functions (UDFs). In dBASE, this principle means that each memvar or parameter whose value is referenced in a subroutine also appears in a PUBLIC, PRIVATE, or PARAMETERS statement in that subroutine.

Memvars and parameters are created during execution. In contrast, fields are part of the structure of database files and are created when the database structure is created or modified. Field names are added to the symbol table when the database is opened with the USE command.

Each parameter *must* appear in a PARAMETERS statement, as there is no other way to define a parameter. On the other hand, memvars can be defined in procedures other than the procedures in which the variables are referenced.

If ProgA defines memvar X with "PRIVATE X" and subsequently calls ProgB, and if ProgB must reference the same X as in ProgA, then ProgB cannot contain another "PRIVATE X" statement. In contrast, If ProgA defines memvar X with

"PUBLIC X" and calls ProgB, then ProgB can and should contain the statement "PUBLIC X", ideally with a comment indicating that the value of X is set elsewhere.

Tree-Structured Scope of Memory Variables

This brings us to the topic of the tree-structured scope of variables in the dBASE programming language. The language *does* permit both a subroutine and its caller to have the statement PRIVATE X, but this creates different variables.

Say that procedure ProgA calls ProgB, ProgB calls ProgC, and no CLEAR ALL or RELEASE statements appear in these procedures or any procedures which they call. (Remember that CLEAR ALL removes all symbols from the symbol table, and RELEASE removes named variables.) Then if a PRIVATE memvar named "X" is defined when ProgB is called, X will be defined in ProgB and ProgC.

If PRIVATE memvar Y is defined in ProgB, then it will be defined in ProgC but not in ProgA. PRIVATE memvars are released when control returns from the procedure in which the memvars are defined. PUBLIC variables are only released by the RELEASE verb or CLEAR ALL.

These principles are demonstrated by Scope.PRG. Let's look at this command file's code (Listing 20.1 and Scope.PRG on the companion diskette to this book) and its output (Listing 20.2 and Scope.I1 on the companion diskette to this book).

Listing 20.2 shows the FoxBASE+ version of the output from Scope.PRG. This output is virtually the same as the output from dBASE III PLUS, except that dBASE III PLUS identifies all the variables as being defined in Scope.PRG, instead of in the procedures ProgA and ProgB.

The LIST MEMORY command reports the contents of the symbol table and shows the value of each variable in the table. After the CLEAR ALL command in Scope.PRG, the first LIST MEMORY command shows an empty table, but the second LIST MEMORY command in Scope.PRG shows the PUBLIC variable A, which was defined in ProgA and remains defined.

Notice that the first LIST MEMORY command in ProgB shows the same symbol table as the LIST MEMORY command in ProgA. When the identifier X is declared PRIVATE in ProgB, the existing X from ProgA becomes "hidden," which means that it is still in the symbol table, but it is not available. References to X now access the second X in the symbol table.

When we return from ProgB, the symbol table has lost the X and Y which were defined in ProgB. When we return from ProgA, the symbol table has lost the X which was defined in ProgA, but the PUBLIC memvar A stays in the symbol table until it is RELEASEd before the last LIST MEMORY statement to be executed.

Converting Code Sections to Subroutines

A major software engineering consequence of dBASE's tree-structured scope of variables is that — quite unlike most other languages — it is trivial to convert a section of a procedure into a subroutine of that procedure. For example, say that the first statement in command file ProgA.PRG is DO CASE. You can create an

Listing 20.1 Scope.PRG, a Command File to Demonstrate dBASE Scope Rules

```
* File = Scope.PRG.  Called from the dot prompt.
********************************************************************************
* Dialects: dBASE III PLUS, dBASE IV, dBXL, FoxBASE+, FoxPro.
********************************************************************************
SET Safety OFF
SET Status OFF
SET Talk OFF

SET PROCEDURE TO Scope

SET ALTERNATE TO Scope.I1
SET ALTERNATE ON

CLEAR ALL
? VERSION()
LIST MEMORY

DO ProgA

LIST MEMORY

RELEASE A

LIST MEMORY
CLOSE ALTERNATE

SET Safety ON
SET Status ON
SET Talk ON
************************************************************************  ProgA
PROCEDURE ProgA

PUBLIC  A
PRIVATE X

X =  "The PRIVATE memvar X in ProgA"
A =  "The PUBLIC memvar A"
LIST MEMORY

DO ProgB

LIST MEMORY
********************************************************************************

************************************************************************  ProgB
PROCEDURE ProgB

LIST MEMORY

PUBLIC  A
PRIVATE X,Y

X =  "The PRIVATE memvar X in ProgB"
Y =  "The PRIVATE memvar Y in ProgB"

LIST MEMORY
********************************************************************************

* End of Scope.PRG.
```

empty file called ProgB.PRG and move the lines in ProgA.PRG from DO CASE to the matching ENDCASE into ProgB.PRG. In place of the DO CASE in ProgA.PRG, you code "DO ProgB". Let's call this *Alternative A.*

Now, standard software engineering conventions, when applied to dBASE, require data identifiers other than fields to be declared in PARAMETERS, PUBLIC, or PRIVATE statements at the beginning of the procedure in which they are referenced. When this is done, all parameters and PRIVATE variables in ProgA which are needed in ProgB must be passed as arguments to ProgB's parameters. Let's call this *Alternative B.*

Listing 20.2 Output from Scope.PRG

```
FoxBASE+ Rev 2.00
    0 variables defined,          0 bytes used
  256 variables available,     3000 bytes available

A            Pub   C    "The PUBLIC memvar A"
X            Priv  C    "The PRIVATE memvar X in ProgA"          C:PROGA.PRG
    2 variables defined,         62 bytes used
  254 variables available,     2938 bytes available

A            Pub   C    "The PUBLIC memvar A"
X            Priv  C    "The PRIVATE memvar X in ProgA"          C:PROGA
    2 variables defined,         62 bytes used
  254 variables available,     2938 bytes available

A            Pub   C    "The PUBLIC memvar A"
X            Priv  (hidden)  C    "The PRIVATE memvar X in Prog
                                      A"                              C:PROGA
X            Priv  C    "The PRIVATE memvar X in ProgB"          C:PROGB.PRG
Y            Priv  C    "The PRIVATE memvar Y in ProgB"          C:PROGB.PRG
    4 variables defined,        134 bytes used
  252 variables available,     2866 bytes available

A            Pub   C    "The PUBLIC memvar A"
X            Priv  C    "The PRIVATE memvar X in ProgA"          C:PROGA.PRG
    2 variables defined,         62 bytes used
  254 variables available,     2938 bytes available

A            Pub   C    "The PUBLIC memvar A"
    1 variables defined,         26 bytes used
  255 variables available,     2974 bytes available

    0 variables defined,          0 bytes used
  256 variables available,     3000 bytes available
```

Alternative A is recommended when your code is experimental or is to be used for only a short time. Alternative B is recommended when the application must be really solid or when it is to be used for a long period of time.

Remark on passing subroutine data only in parameters. When your subroutines receive all data in the form of parameters (versus receiving data in PUBLIC memvars or a combination of memvars and parameters), the subroutines can be tested and debugged *separately* before they are integrated into your applications! This approach is critically important in large applications and in projects with more than one programmer.

Resolving Name Conflicts

We have just seen that dBASE uses the most recently defined PRIVATE memvar X when there are two or more PRIVATE memvars named X in the symbol table. If a PUBLIC X and a PRIVATE X are both defined, then dBASE uses the PRIVATE X.

If a field named X is defined at the same time as a memvar named X, then some references are ambiguous and others are not. For example, the syntax to assign a value to a field is

REPLACE <field name> WITH <value>

whereas memvars are assigned with

STORE <value> TO <memvar>

or

<memvar> = <value>

But a read-only reference such as

? X

is ambiguous and dBASE accesses the field in such cases, with the exception of Clipper programs compiled with the "-V" switch, which access the memvar in this situation.

dBASE gives you a way to qualify fields and memvars, so that you can specify a reference to either the field or the memvar, as needed. Let's say that the field X comes from a database called "Observed", which is open in work area 2. Then you can reference the field in these four ways:

1. Observed->X
2. 2->X
3. B->X
4. X

The first form is preferred, because in following the techniques recommended in this book, you generally won't know the area in which a particular database will be opened. The first form of reference would only need to be changed if you renamed Observed.DBF. Even then, you can use the ALIAS clause of the USE statement to keep the same ALIAS.

For example, say that you renamed Observed.DBF to Gathered.DBF. You could change "USE Observed <options>" to "USE Gathered <options> ALIAS Observed".

Avoid the second form, because it will confuse some dialects and tools in some situations. It may also be somewhat confusing for humans to read. If for some reason you cannot reference a work area by ALIAS, then use the letter and not the number of the area, as in "B->X", not "2->X".

The fourth form isn't as clear as the first three forms. Furthermore, this form requires the database in which X is a field to be the currently selected database. In contrast, the first three forms work independently of the current work area.

There is a de facto standard among dBASE programmers for naming memvars which temporarily hold field values. The convention is to prefix the memvar name with a lowercase "m". For example, if a field is named Amount, then its associated memvar is named mAmount.

If you must reference the memory variable X when the field X is defined, then dBASE gives you the "M->" prefix, which is analogous to the database prefixes discussed above. Note that the letter codes for the 10 work areas are A, B, ..., J, so the prefixes "A->", "B->", ..., "J->" refer to databases, but the prefix "M->" always refers to memvars.

Clipper supports up to 254 work areas. Areas 11 to 254 must be referenced by number or ALIAS. FoxPro supports up to 25 work areas. Areas 11 to 25 must be referenced by number or ALIAS. (Referencing by ALIAS is recommended over referencing by number.)

The following syntax would print the value of a field named X in a database named Observed, followed by the value of a memvar named X:

```
? Observed->X, M->X
```

An Option for Clipper Programmers

The Clipper compiler offers the "-V" switch to reverse the default resolution of references to identifiers which represent both memvars and fields. When an application is compiled with this switch, and a memvar name is the same as a field name in the current database, then the memvar is used.

Recommendation on Clipper's "-V" switch. If you work exclusively in the Clipper environment, I recommend that you always compile with the "-V" switch. If you choose to give a field and a memvar the same name, then refer to the field using its ALIAS, as in "Members->JoinDate".

Parameters versus Memory Variables

It is a programming error to define a memvar and a parameter with the same name in the same procedure. The dBASE language does *not* have a syntax like "P->X" to distinguish the parameter X from the memvar X. In fact, the resolution of this ambiguity depends on the dialect.

I believe that it is pointless to enumerate the ways in which the different dialects resolve this ambiguity, because you should never deliberately introduce such ambiguities into your applications. Unfortunately, you may do so inadvertently.

In a typical situation of this kind, you have a memvar named X, which you later decide should really be a parameter. You add X to the PARAMETERS statement, but you forget to remove it from the PRIVATE statement where it was formerly declared!

When you discover such ambiguities, resolve them by changing the name of either the parameter or the memvar, or by eliminating either the parameter or the memvar.

Memvar Arguments versus Field Arguments

If a memvar and a field are both defined with the same name, then the interpretation of this name as an argument depends on the dialect. Consider the reference to Name in "DO Proc1 WITH Name" or "Proc2(Name)", where Name is currently defined both as a memvar and as a field in Customer.DBF. Does "DO Proc1 WITH Name" mean "DO Proc1 WITH Customer->Name" or "DO Proc1 WITH M->Name"? There is a related question: "Is M->Name passed by reference or value?" (Fields such as Customer->Name are always passed by value.)

These questions are answered in Table 20.1. The big surprise is what happens when you pass "M->Name" as an argument. Some of the dialects think that this reference is an expression, which is always passed by value, of course. This means that "DO Proc1 WITH M->Name" is *not* dialect-independent when M->Name is passed to an input/output or an output parameter!

Table 20.1 Memvar Arguments versus Field Arguments

Statement	Resolution	Passed by	Dialects
DO Proc1 WITH Name	Customer->Name	Reference	C+4FPQX
DO Proc1 WITH Name	M->Name	Reference	V
Proc2(Name)	Customer->Name	Value	C4QX
Proc2(Name)	Customer->Name	Reference	FP
Proc2(@Name)	Customer->Name	Reference	C
Proc2(Name)	M->Name	Value	V
Proc2(@Name)	M->Name	Reference	V
DO Proc1 WITH M->Name	N/A	Reference	C4FP
DO Proc1 WITH M->Name	N/A	Value	+QX
DO Proc1 WITH Customer->Name	N/A	Value	All
Proc2(Customer->Name)	N/A	Value	All

Legend:
C = Clipper without "-V", + = dBASE III PLUS, 4 = dBASE IV,
F = FoxBASE+ 2.1, P = FoxPro, Q = Quicksilver,
V = Clipper with "-V", X = dBXL.

How do we code a library subroutine which is to be used in several dialects? We cannot use the form "DO Proc1 WITH Name" because there may be a field called "Name". When Name is passed to an input/output or output parameter, we cannot use the form "DO Proc1 WITH M->Name", because some dialects pass "M->Name" by value.

The solution lies in recognizing the dialect and setting up the appropriate IF/ELSE statement. The "recognize the dialect" routine on page 307 has a PUBLIC memvar called PassNoM_L which is true for the dialects that pass "M->Name" by value. Now we can safely code the call to Proc1, as shown in Listing 20.3.

Listing 20.3 Dialect-Independent Argument Lists

```
PUBLIC PassNoM_L
DO RecogEnv  && Set PassNoM_L.
IF PassNoM_L
   * This form passes the memvar Name for dBASE III PLUS, dBXL, & Quicksilver.
   DO Proc1 WITH Name
ELSE
   * This form passes the memvar Name for Clipper, dBASE IV, FoxBASE+, & FoxPro.
   DO Proc1 WITH M->Name
ENDIF
```

Rules and Recommendations

In order to create stable dBASE applications, you *must* understand and properly observe the scope and ambiguity-resolving rules of dBASE. Accordingly, I have organized the rules and recommendations from the preceding discussion in Table 20.2.

Table 20.2
dBASE Identifiers' Scope and Disambiguation Rules and Recommendations

1. Recommendation: Avoid creating identifiers with the same name when this creates ambiguity in references.
2. Recommendation: Write "<ALIAS> -> <field name>" instead of "<field name>" in your source code. This is particularly important for multiple-user applications.
3. Recommendation: Declare each memvar used in a procedure, command file, or user-defined function to be either PUBLIC or PRIVATE.
4. A memory variable may be declared PUBLIC as many times as desired.
5. A memory variable may be declared PRIVATE only once in each procedure, unless the variable is removed from the symbol table with CLEAR ALL or RELEASE.
6. Memory variables which are defined PRIVATE in different procedures are distinct variables.
7. When a memory variable is defined PRIVATE, you may not define an identifier with the same name to be PUBLIC.
8. When a memory variable is defined PUBLIC, you may define an identifier with the same name to be PRIVATE, in which case the PUBLIC memvar becomes hidden until the PRIVATE memvar is removed from the symbol table.
9. PUBLIC variables are defined until CLEAR ALL is executed or the variable appears in the memory variable list of a RELEASE statement. (In particular, PUBLIC memvars created by an application are still defined if the application returns to the dot prompt.)
10. Memory variables created at the dot prompt are PUBLIC in scope.
11. PRIVATE variables are defined until CLEAR ALL is executed, until the variable appears in the memory variable list of a RELEASE statement, or until control returns from the procedure in which the variable was declared.
12. When an identifier may refer to either a field or a memory variable, dBASE accesses the field.
13. An identifier preceded by "m->" or "M->" is a memory variable.
14. An identifier preceded by "<work area number>->" or "<work area letter>->" is a field in the database which is open in the specified work area.
15. An identifier preceded by "<database ALIAS>->" is a field in the database with the specified ALIAS. (Remember that the database name is used as the ALIAS unless there is an ALIAS clause in the USE statement that opens the database.)

16. When a parameter and a memory variable have the same name (which is a bug), the reference is dialect-dependent. Recommendation: Do not use the same names for parameters and memory variables.
17. When a routine is to be used in circumstances where unknown field names may be defined when the routine is executed, then (1) you must use "M->" to prefix all memvar references, except arguments, or (2) you must compile using Clipper and its "-V" switch. (Otherwise, a field may be defined with the same name as a memory variable; without the "M->", the field will be used in that case and not the memvar, as you expect and require.)
18. When a dBASE III PLUS, dBXL, or Quicksilver routine is to be used in circumstances where unknown field names may be defined when the routine is executed, then (1) you must *not* use "M->" to prefix memvar arguments passed to input/output or output parameters, and (2) you *must* qualify field names passed as arguments with "<ALIAS>->" when the field has the same name as a memvar. For example, use the form "DO Proc1 WITH Name" to pass the memvar to an input/output parameter and use the form "DO Proc1 WITH Customer->Name" to pass the field to an input parameter.
19. When a Clipper (no "-V" switch), dBASE IV, FoxBASE+, or FoxPro routine is to be used in circumstances where unknown field names may be defined when the routine is executed, then (1) you *must* use "M->" to prefix memvar arguments, and (2) you *may* qualify field names passed as arguments with "<ALIAS>->" when the field has the same name as a memvar. For example, use the form "DO Proc1 WITH M->Name" to pass the memvar to any kind of parameter and use the form "DO Proc1 WITH Customer->Name" or "DO Proc1 WITH Name" to pass the field to an input parameter.
20. When a Clipper ("-V" switch) routine is to be used in circumstances where unknown field names may be defined when the routine is executed, then (1) you *may* use "M->" to prefix memvar arguments, and (2) you *must* qualify field names passed as arguments with "<ALIAS>->" when the field has the same name as a memvar. For example, use the form "DO Proc1 WITH Name" or "DO Proc1 WITH M->Name" to pass the memvar and use the form "DO Proc1 WITH Customer->Name" to pass the field.

This table can be a quality control tool for you. When you have written a unit of source code, you can use the table as a checklist to see if you have followed all of these rules and recommendations for identifiers.

This concludes the presentation of scope of variables. Now let's see how to code applications which automatically recognize the dialect under which they execute.

Recognizing the Dialect

When you write code which is to execute under more than one dialect, you usually need some way of recognizing the dialect under which the code will execute. The Clipper dialect sets the memvar CLIPPER to .T. when you code PUBLIC CLIPPER; the Fox Software dialects set FOX to .T. when you code PUBLIC FOX. Dialects other than Clipper offer the built-in function VERSION(), which you can test to discover not only the name, but also the version number of a dialect.

The "Recognize Environment" routine RecogEnv.PRG in Listing 20.4 sets several logical PUBLIC memvars which show the dialect in use and which indicate the memvar versus field disambiguation rule used for arguments. The PUBLIC memvar PassNoM_L is used for this purpose. (It is possible, although unlikely, that another identifier in your application will have the name PassNoM_L, in which case one of the names must be changed.) In dialects where PassNoM_L is true, you must pass input/output and output memvar arguments *without* the "M->" qualification; otherwise "M->" is permitted for disambiguation purposes.

Listing 20.4
RecogEnv.PRG—A Routine to Recognize the Dialect at Execution Time

```
* File = RecogEnv.PRG.  Called from several .PRG to detect dBASE dialact.
* Sets the PUBLIC memvars below according to the dialect in use.
**************************************************************************
* Dialects: All, but see the end of the routine for special instructions for
* Clipper usage.
**************************************************************************
* PUBLIC memvars CLIPPER and FOX are set by Clipper and FoxBASE+/FoxPro, resp.
**************************************************************************
* Some dialects do not support the following usage:
* DO Proc with M->InOut,M->Out
* where InOut is an input/output parameter and Out is an output parameter.
* For these dialects, PassNoM_L is true, and M->InOut and M->Out are passed by
* value, not reference, as you might expect.  To make your calls
* dialect-independent, use the following form AFTER A CALL TO RecogEnv TO SET
* THE VALUE OF PassNoM_L.
*     IF PassNoM_L
*        DO Proc WITH InOut,Out
*     ELSE
*        DO Proc WITH M->InOut,M->Out
*     ENDIF
* In the dialects in which PassNoM_L is true, if there are fields named
* InOut and Out in the currently selected database, memvars InOut and Out are
* passed by reference in DO Proc WITH InOut,Out.  To pass field data with such
* dialects, you must code DO Proc WITH <ALIAS>->InOut,<ALIAS>->Out as in
* DO Proc WITH Members->InOut,Members->Out.
* In the dialects in which PassNoM_L is false, if there are fields named InOut
* and Out in the currently selected database, then InOut and Out are passed by
* reference in DO Proc WITH M->InOut,M->Out and field values are passed by
* value in DO Proc WITH InOut,Out.
PUBLIC Clipper,dBASE3P,dBASE4,dBXL,FOX,FOXPRO,PassNoM_L,Quicksilvr
DO CASE
   CASE ("dBASE III PLUS" $ VERSION())
      dBASE3P = .T.
   CASE ("dBASE IV" $ VERSION())
      dBASE4 = .T.
   CASE ("dBXL" $ VERSION())
      dBXL = .T.
   CASE FOX
      FoxPro_L = ("FoxPro" $ VERSION())
   CASE ("QUICKSILVER" $ UPPER(VERSION()))
      Quicksilvr = .T.
   OTHERWISE
      ?  "RecogEnv.PRG: Case statement error: case not found."
      ?  "Print or copy screen for programmer."
      DO WaitOnC
ENDCASE
PassNoM_L = dBASE3P .OR. dBXL .OR. Quicksilvr
```

```
* In Clipper, you must link Extend.LIB or uncomment the following function:
* FUNCTION Version
* RETURN  "Clipper"
* End of RecogEnv.PRG.
```

Recognizing the Environment

It is often the case that a subroutine will need to execute a particular SET command. For example, if the subroutine must examine all of the records in a database, whether or not the records are marked for deletion, then it must execute SET DELETED OFF. However, the previous setting may have been SET DELETED ON. In order to work properly, the subroutine must SET DELETED ON at exit if this was the setting on entry.

There are two ways for a subroutine to handle the restoration of the environment which it changes. The first way is for you to pass an argument that indicates the state of the part of the environment which the subroutine will change. For an example, see the listing of MakeSEF3.PRG on page 291. The second and third parameters represent the settings of SET SAFETY and SET TITLE when the subroutine is called.

This first method is inordinately difficult to use in a consistent fashion. It makes you, the programmer, work too hard to keep track of information which the system should maintain.

The second method is shown in the listing of MakeSEF4.PRG on page 292. The dBASE IV version of subroutine MakeSEF3.PRG only needs one argument, because the SET() function of dBASE IV permits you to get system settings on demand. This method is strongly recommended over the first method.

A question naturally arises about what kinds of system information can be detected by each dialect. The following material considers the features which are available without facilities external to the dialect, such as commercial subroutine libraries. For example, the Clipper Tools One library product from Nantucket enables you to recover system information as you do in dBASE IV by using SET().

Saving and Restoring the Environment

Dialects which implement the CREATE VIEW <view file> FROM ENVIRONMENT command (CREATE VIEW <view file> in FoxBASE+ 2.1 and FoxPro) give you a way to save the status of many aspects of the dBASE environment upon entry to a subroutine. You use the companion command, SET VIEW TO <view file>, on exit to restore the environment settings saved in the view file.

The dialects vary somewhat in the amount of information which they save in view files, as shown in Table 20.3. In particular, note that ON/OFF settings are handled only by the Fox Software dialects.

Table 20.3 View File Contents by Dialect

Dialect	System Information
34FPX	All database and index files and their work areas.
34	Any currently open FORMAT file.
FP	All filters and all alternate files currently open and their work areas.
FPX	FORMAT files currently open and their work areas.
4X	The active filter.
34FPX	All relations between the database files.
34	The currently selected work area.
34FPX	The fields from the most recent SET FIELDS TO statement.
FP	The DEFAULT and PATH settings.
FP	The procedure file setting.
P	The current help file.
P	The current resource file.
F	All ON/OFF settings.
F	The current function key settings.
F	ON ESCAPE and ON KEY settings.

Legend:
C = Clipper 4.0, 3 = dBASE III, + = dBASE III PLUS, 4 = dBASE IV,
F = FoxBASE+ 2.1, P = FoxPro, Q = Quicksilver, X = dBXL.

FoxBASE+ 2.0 does not implement view files. The documentation for FoxPro 1.01 does not indicate that FoxPro view files contain all of the same information that is in FoxBASE+ 2.1 view files, but testing indicates that at least some of the ON/OFF settings are saved in FoxPro view files, and presumably all ON/OFF settings are saved if some settings are saved.

If the number of files and relationships is large, then saving and restoring the environment with view files may take quite a bit of time. This means that view files may be too slow to use for saving and restoring the environment in frequently called subroutines.

Tests to Determine ON/OFF Settings

While dBASE IV and FoxPro offer the SET() function to recover ON/OFF settings and other system information, other dialects do not. Fortunately, the following special tests can simulate SET() for some settings.

SET CENTURY

SET CENTURY ON or SET CENTURY OFF is in effect, according to whether the following logical expression is true or false, respectively:

LEN(DtoC(DATE())) = 10

SET DELETED

The subroutine in Listing 20.5 has one output parameter which is "ON" if SET DELETED ON is in effect and "OFF" otherwise. For simplicity, the subroutine assumes that a database is open in the current work area. If there are no records in the database, a test record is appended and deleted. Otherwise, the record pointer is positioned to a record which is used as a test record.

Listing 20.5 Deleted.PRG—Determine the SET DELETED Setting

```
* File = Deleted.PRG.  Called from several .PRG to determine status of
* SET DELETED as ON or OFF.  Could be implemented as UDF if dialect has UDFs.
* This routine will execute significantly faster if there are no indexes
* for the currently selected database, or if you SET ORDER TO 0 before calling
* Deleted.PRG.
********************************************************************************
* Dialects: All.
********************************************************************************
* Input Assumptions:
* There is a database open in the current work area.
********************************************************************************
* Parameters:
*  Deleted_C, Output, Character.  Value is  "ON" or  "OFF",
*                                 as DELETED is SET ON or OFF.
********************************************************************************
PARAMETERS Deleted_C
PRIVATE K,mRecNo
IF (RecCount() = 0)
   APPEND BLANK
   DELETE
   COUNT TO K
   Deleted_C = IIF(K = 0,  "ON",  "OFF")
   PACK
ELSE
   mRecNo = RecNo()
   GOTO 1
   IF DELETED()
      COUNT TO K
      Deleted_C = IIF(K < RecCount(),  "ON",  "OFF")
   ELSE
      DELETE      && Temporarily delete record 1.
      COUNT TO K
      Deleted_C = IIF(K < RecCount(),  "ON",  "OFF")
      GOTO 1
      RECALL      && Un-delete record 1.
   ENDIF
   DO CASE
      CASE (mRecNo < 1)
     GOTO TOP
     SKIP -1

      CASE (mRecNo > RecCount())
     GOTO BOTTOM
     SKIP +1

      OTHERWISE
     GOTO mRecNo

   ENDCASE
ENDIF
* End of Deleted.PRG.
```

Note that this subroutine will execute quite slowly if you call it while you have a large database open. To get a quick return, call this subroutine from a work area where a small database is open. The fastest return is provided by databases with one record.

SET EXACT

Either SET EXACT ON or SET EXACT OFF is in effect, according to whether the following logical expression is false or true, respectively: ("AA" = "A"). An expression which evaluates to "ON" or "OFF", according to the setting of SET EXACT, is IIF("AA" = "A", "OFF", "ON").

Retrieving System Information from LIST STATUS

All of the major dialects except Clipper and Quicksilver offer the LIST STATUS command, which lists a great deal of information about the current operating environment, including the names and uses of open files and the ON/OFF settings. You can use the SET ALTERNATE TO and SET ALTERNATE ON/OFF commands to capture the output from LIST STATUS to a file. You can then parse (search) that file for the environmental information that you need.

FoxPro gives you the ability to read the LIST STATUS report which you captured in a file one line at a time with its low-level file functions. In the other dialects, define a database file like that shown in Table 20.4.

Table 20.4 TextData.DBF, a Database File for Parsing Text Files

Field	Field Name	Type	Width	Dec
1	Rec	Character	150	

The length of the field Rec is set to 150 under the assumption that the longest line in a text file to be processed with TextData.DBF is at most 150 characters in length. The length of Rec must be greater than or equal to the maximum length of a text file line that you will process.

Use the APPEND FROM command to read the data from a text file into TextData.DBF. For example, assume that TextData.DBF is open in the current work area. Then the following command reads the data in the text file Status.DOC into TextData.DBF: "APPEND FROM Status.DOC TYPE SDF".

Built-In Techniques for Retrieving System Information

Each dialect offers several built-in functions to retrieve system information of various types. Table 20.5 lists built-in functions, the dialects that implement them, and a short description of each function.

Note that SECONDS() is an integer measurement under Clipper, but FoxPro returns the measurement to the resolution of milliseconds — for example, 152 seconds versus 152.186 seconds.

UPDATED() has the same value as the logical expression (ReadKey() >= 256). Many of the functions in the table have equivalents in the SYS() function options of FoxBASE+ and FoxPro (see page 132).

Table 20.5 Built-In Functions for Retrieving System Information

Function	Dialects	Description
ACCESS()	+4	Accesses the level of last network user to log in.
ALIAS()	C4FP	ALIAS of current database.
BAR()	4P	Number of option chosen from popup menu.
CAPSLOCK()	P	Current state of Caps Lock.
CHRSAW()	P	Is character in keyboard buffer during specified wait?
COMPLETED()	4	Did transaction complete?
CURDIR()	CP	Current DOS directory.
CURWIN()	Q	Number of currently selected window.
DATE()	All	Today's date in date form.
DBF()	+4FPQX	Database file name.
DBF()	C	Database ALIAS.
DBFILTER()	C	Active filter expression.
DBRELATION()	C	Relation expressions.
DBRSELECT()	C	Target database of a SET RELATION TO command.
DISKSPACE()	All	Bytes free on current DOS drive or SET DEFAULT drive.
DOSERROR()	C	Number of execution time DOS error.
ERROR()	+4FPQX	Number of last dBASE error.
ERRORLEVEL()	C	Current DOS error level.
FERROR()	CP	Last DOS file error number.
FILE()	All	Does named file exist?
FKLABEL()	All	Name of first available programmable function key.
FKMAX()	All	Number of programmable function keys on keyboard.
FULLPATH()	P	Fully qualified DOS path for the given file.
GETE()	C	Value of named DOS environment variable.
GETENV()	+4FPQX	Value of named DOS environment variable.
HEADER()	CP	Number of bytes in database file header.
IN()	QX	Gets byte from specified port.
INDEXEXT()	C	"NTX" or "NDX", according to type of index in use.
INDEXKEY()	C	Key expression of open index file.
INDEXORD()	C	Ordinal of master index in index list: 1 = first.
INKEY()	All	Numeric code for next key in keyboard buffer.
INKEY()	C4P	Waits for keypress for up to a specified amount of time.

INSMODE()	P	Insert or overwrite mode?
ISCOLOR()	All	True if color adapter card used, else false.
ISPRINTER()	C	Is the printer ready?
KEY()	4P	Key expression of active index.
LASTKEY()	C4P	Last key to be fetched from keyboard buffer.
LINENO()	4P	Line number in source file of statement currently executing.
LKSYS()	4	Returns time, date, and log-in name for a locked file.
LUPDATE()	All	Date on which database was last updated.
MDX()	4	Name of open .MDX index file.
MEMORY()	C4QX	Amount of free RAM.
MENU()	4P	Name of most recently activated menu.
MESSAGE()	+4FPQX	Message text for last dBASE error.
NDX()	+4FPQX	Name of index file specified by ordinal in list.
NETERR()	C	Was the requested network resource delivered?
NETNAME()	C	Workstation ID for the IBM PC Network.
NETWORK()	4	Is the application running on a network?
NEXTKEY()	C	Reads the next key from the keyboard buffer, leaving key in buffer.
NUMLOCK()	P	Is Num Lock on or off?
ORDER()	4	Which TAG is the controlling TAG?
ORDER()	P	File name of master index.
OS()	+4FPQX	Name and version of operating system loaded.
OS()	C	The string "MS/PC-DOS".
PAD()	4P	Name of the most recently selected PAD.
PARAMETERS()	P	Number of arguments passed to subroutine.
PCOL()	All	Column position of print head while SET PRINT is ON.
PCOUNT()	C	Number of arguments passed to subroutine.
POPUP()	4	Name of current popup menu.
PRINTER()	QX	Is the printer ready?
PRINTSTATUS()	4P	Is the printer ready?
PROCLINE()	C	Source code line of statement currently executing.
PROCNAME()	C	Source code file name/procedure name of statement currently executing subroutine.
PROGRAM()	4	Name of currently executing subroutine.
PROMPT()	4P	PROMPT string of current popup or bar menu.
PROW()	All	Count of lines printed since last EJECT.
READINSERT()	C	Current insert mode setting.
READKEY()	All	Keypress used to exit full-screen editing.
READVAR()	C	Name of current GET or MENU variable.
RECSIZE()	All	Size of record in current database file.
RELATION()	P	Relational expression for relation specified by ordinal.
ROLLBACK()	4	Was the last rollback successful?
ROW()	All	Current row of onscreen cursor.

SCHEME()	P	Information about a color scheme.
SCOLS()	P	Number of text columns for current display mode.
SECONDS()	CP	Number of seconds since midnight.
SELECT()	C+FPQX	Number of currently selected work area.
SELECT()	4P	Number of unused work area with highest number.
SET()	**4P**	**Current settings of SET ON/OFF and SET TO commands.**
SETCOLOR()	C	Current color settings.
SINKEY()	Q	Like INKEY(), but returns 1 or 2 bytes; doesn't wait.
SROWS()	P	Number of text rows in current video mode.
SYS()	FP	Offers options to return a great variety of system information. See the table on page 132.
SYS(2001)	**FP**	**Current settings of SET ON/OFF and SET TO commands.**
TAG()	4	Name of TAG or index file, specified by ordinal.
TARGET()	P	Target file of relation specified by ordinal.
TIME()	All	System time, in format HH:MM:SS.
TYPE()	All	Type of identifier or expression.
UPDATED()	CFP	Was data changed during last READ?
USED()	CP	Is this work area in use?
USER()	4	Name of current user under PROTECT system.
USERNO()	Q	Current workstation number on network.
VARREAD()	4P	Name of memvar or field in current GET or PROMPT.
VERSION()	All	Version name of the dBASE dialect.
WACTIVE()	QX	Is the current window area in use?
WCOLS()	P	Number of text columns in current or named window.
WEXIST()	P	Does window exist?
WOUTPUT()	P	Is the named window currently used for output?
WOUTPUT()	P	Window currently used for output.
WROWS()	P	Number of text rows in current or named window.
WSELECT()	QX	Number of current window area.
WVISIBLE()	P	Is the named window visible?

Legend:
C = Clipper 4.0, + = dBASE III PLUS, 4 = dBASE IV,
F = FoxBASE+ 2.1, P = FoxPro, Q = Quicksilver, X = dBXL.

Design Considerations

The factors which you might take into consideration when designing subroutines are numerous and the issues are profound in their breadth and depth, so here we must confine our attention to a few dBASE dialect specifics. For more information, you can see virtually any general book on software engineering, such as those listed in Appendix F. For dBASE dialect information, look at *Building Source Code Libraries* (Yellick 1989a) and *Dynamics of Clipper* (Fuller 1989).

Subroutines Which Are Used in One Application

Pretend for a moment that your current application was written without subroutines. This would mean that large sections of your code would be identical or similar, and by introducing subroutines, you could reduce the total size of the code.

Some subroutine uses are extremely obvious. For example, I use the WaitOnC subroutine introduced on page 255 whenever I want the user to react to something on the screen before continuing to the next step. If you saw one of my applications written out without subroutines, it would be easy to identify the segments of code that correspond to WaitOnC.PRG as subroutine candidates.

Other subroutine candidates are not so obvious. For example, look at the character string functions which have been added to the dialects as they have evolved. Over time, people realized that certain functions could reduce both the size and the complexity of their character-processing source code — that is, the right set of functions would support canonical programs whose operation could be understood easily by reading the code.

There is a certain subroutine design for a given application which will minimize its number of source code statements. There is also a design which will tend to maximize the comprehensibility of the source code, which will tend to minimize the amount of time spent to develop the application.

Fortunately, these two subroutine designs are not very different for medium-sized or large applications. As a generally applicable design principle, I believe that the number of statements taken by a design which is easy for an experienced programmer to understand is not too much greater than the number of statements in the shortest implementation.

With a canonical set of subroutines, you can add a layer of functionality to your dBASE dialect to make it act like a programming language which is tailored for your particular application. With such a set of subroutines, you can work very close to the design level.

Information Hiding and Modularity

One of the maxims of subroutine design is that a subroutine should not have any more information than is necessary for it to do its job. The "cleanest" dBASE subroutines use only information in fields, variables declared PRIVATE in the subroutine, and parameters. Such subroutines do not use PUBLIC or PRIVATE memvars created in other subroutines. Any changes are made only to field data, variables declared PRIVATE in the subroutine, and parameters. The identifiers which appear in such subroutines are fields, variables declared PRIVATE in the subroutine, or parameters.

Recommendation on declaring memvars. Declare every memvar in a PUBLIC or PRIVATE statement before you assign a value to the memvar. Declare every PUBLIC variable in every subroutine which references the variable.

Recommendation on field references. Use the reference form "<ALIAS> -> <field name>" instead of just "<field name>". This convention is extremely useful for multiple-user applications. If you anticipate your application becoming multiple-user at a later time, give special consideration to this recommendation.

You can think of modularity in the same way that a mason thinks of brick size. Bricks of the standard size can be used to make a large variety of shapes in a structured and stable fashion. If the bricks were larger, they would limit the variety of shapes which could be built. If the bricks were smaller, they would require too much mortar and labor to achieve the final result.

Your subroutines have an optimal amount of capability. If you put too many different kinds of services into a subroutine, it may be needlessly complex to use and difficult to maintain. If you put too little functionality into your service subroutines, you may have an inordinate number of subroutine calls in your applications, which makes the applications hard to understand and modify.

Designing dBASE Subroutines for Libraries

When you consider the design of a subroutine which will be used in many applications, you are led to think of a standard service which would be frequently needed. When you have thought of a standard service, such as displaying a prompt and getting a response, the canonical approach leads you to make the service routine as powerful as is feasible in providing its focused service.

For example, see the presentation on subroutine Reply.PRG starting on page 268. This subroutine provides a basic level of prompting service with two input parameters and one output parameter. An advanced level of prompting service is provided by Arthur Fuller's ASK_FOR(), whose presentation begins on page 274. Fuller's subroutine takes up to five arguments and supports a more complex dialog than Reply.PRG.

These two subroutines show you the trade-off between power and complexity. You get a higher level of service from ASK_FOR(), but you must know more about this subroutine than about Reply.PRG, and you must provide up to five arguments to ASK_FOR().

Variable-Length Argument Lists

Clipper permits you to pass 0 to N arguments to a subroutine whose PARAMETERS statement contains N identifiers; you must test for the number of arguments passed with PCOUNT(). FoxPro permits you to pass 1 to N arguments to a subroutine whose PARAMETERS statement contains N identifiers; here, you test for the number of arguments passed with PARAMETERS().

This facility is very useful in the design of library routines, because it permits them to perform a standard set of services with great flexibility. For example, consider the dBASE built-in function MIN(), which returns the minimum of two values. It would be convenient in some cases if MIN() could take more than two arguments and return the smallest of the list. In fact, FoxPro does permit you to list as many arguments as you like in a call to MIN(); it will return the value of the smallest argument.

Variable-Type Arguments

All dBASE dialects support variable-type arguments. This flexibility is exploited in Fuller's ASK_FOR() function, where the argument which holds the initial value of the user's response may be of type character, date, or numeric.

Inside the subroutine, you use the built-in TYPE() function to determine the type of data which was passed to a parameter. Let's think about the MIN() function once again. In dBASE, data of type character, date, and numeric is ordered, so we would ideally like to be able to code MIN("A","B"), MIN(DATE(), Members-> ExpireDate), and MIN(10, Count), where Members->ExpireDate is of type date and Count is numeric. Let's say further that you wish to order logical data, and that you will define .F. < .T. Then you could code a version of MIN(A,B) to handle character, date, logical, and numeric data, as shown in Listing 20.6.

In the Clipper dialect, you can check the assumption that the third argument is passed by verifying that PCOUNT() = 3. In the FoxPro dialect, you can check the assumption that the third argument is passed by verifying that PARAMETERS() = 3. Dialects which do not permit a variable number of arguments to be passed to a given subroutine will themselves require three arguments to be passed to MinType.PRG.

Note that references to parameters A and B are coded as "M->A" and "M->B". It is possible that fields named A and B may be defined when MinType is called. Without this coding precaution, TYPE(A) could refer to a *field* named A and not the parameter.

In contrast, if Smaller is a defined field, you must change its value with a command of the form "REPLACE Smaller WITH <value>". The form "Smaller = <value>" refers to the memvar Smaller.[1]

Subroutine Documentation for the Programmer

If you are to use a library subroutine properly and efficiently, its documentation must include certain items of information. Before we examine these items, let's pause to think about what a subroutine does.

---

1. Unless Smaller is declared FIELD in Clipper 5.0! Sorry.

Listing 20.6 MinType.PRG—Calculate the Minimum of Two Values of Any Type

```
* File = MinType.PRG.  Called from several .PRG.
* Return the smaller of two values of type character, date, logical, or
* numeric.  Logical data is ordered by .F. < .T.
*****************************************************************************
* Dialects: All.  Can be implemented as a UDF in dialects which support UDFs.
*****************************************************************************
* Input parameters:
* First parameter: Type character, date, logical, or numeric.
* Second parameter:Type character, date, logical, or numeric.
*****************************************************************************
* Output parameters:
* First parameter: same type as input parameters.
*****************************************************************************
* Input assumptions verified:
* 1. TYPE(A) = TYPE(B)
* 2. TYPE(A) = C, D, L or N.
* Input assumptions NOT verified:
* 1. A third argument is passed.
*****************************************************************************
PARAMETERS A,B,Smaller
DO CASE
   CASE (TYPE(M->A) # TYPE(M->B))
      ?  "Notify programmer: In subroutine MinType, arguments passed of types  "
      ?? TYPE(M->A) +  " and  " + TYPE(M->B) +  ", but types must be the same."
      WAIT
      CANCEL
   ************************************** Types are the same: are they legal?
   CASE (TYPE(M->A) $  "CDN")
      Smaller = IIF(M->A < M->B, M->A, M->B)
   CASE (TYPE(M->A) =  "L")
      Smaller = (M->A .OR. M->B)
   OTHERWISE
      ?  "Notify programmer: In subroutine MinType, arguments passed of type  "
      ?? TYPE(M->A)
      ??  ", but the type must be character, date, logical, or numeric."
      WAIT
      CANCEL
ENDCASE
* End of MinType.PRG.
```

Generally speaking, the system and our data are in one state when the subroutine is entered and they are in another state when the subroutine is exited. What can change? Data in files and memvars may be different, system attributes such as settings of SET commands may have changed, and system-controlled data objects such as windows may have been opened, modified, or closed.

A properly designed subroutine permits you to *control* these changes with the arguments which are passed to the subroutine. A carefully designed subroutine offers this guarantee: if entry assumptions are true, then the exit conditions will be true after the call.

Now we are in a position to enumerate the minimum documentation for a library subroutine, as shown in Table 20.6.

Table 20.6 The Minimum Documentation for a Library Subroutine

1. **Description.** Begin the documentation with the name and a description of the services of the subroutine.
2. **Dialects.** List the dBASE dialects under which the subroutine will properly execute.
3. **Entry assumptions.** These assumptions, sometimes called "input assumptions," are the conditions which the subroutine needs at entry in order to do its job.
4. **Verification of entry assumptions.** Each entry assumption may or may not be verified or partially verified. The documentation lists the assumptions which are verified.
5. **Input arguments.** The arguments which are used only for input are listed first in the PARAMETERS list and in the documentation. The corresponding parameters receive values from the arguments and these values do not change while the parameters exist. Input arguments can be passed by *value* or by *reference*.
6. **Input/output arguments.** The arguments which are used for both input and output are listed second in the PARAMETERS list and in the documentation. The corresponding parameters receive values from the arguments and these values are subsequently changed. Input/output arguments must be passed by *reference*.
7. **Output arguments.** With the exception of returned UDF values, dBASE dialects do not support output-only arguments, because fields and constants are always passed by value, and all memvar arguments must be assigned a value before they are passed. However, we can define output arguments for dBASE as input/output arguments whose initial value is not significant. List such identifiers last in the PARAMETERS statement and document them last.
8. **Function value returned.** Document the type and value of data returned from a UDF. Remember that, unlike UDFs in other programming languages, a dBASE UDF can return data of any type.
9. **Exit conditions.** These conditions, sometimes called "output conditions," are the conditions which the subroutine claims to produce if the entry assumptions are true. Describe here any changes to PUBLIC memvars, fields, files, SET command settings, and system-controlled data objects such as windows and filters.

A Template for the Call

In Chapter 15, which starts on page 213, I recommended that you use a fill-in-the-blanks source code template to construct the calls to your library routines; I called such a template a *Millican interface* to the subroutine. Listing 20.7 gives an example of a template which could be used to set up a call to subroutine MinType, which was discussed earlier in this chapter.

Listing 20.7 Sample Template for a Call to a Library Subroutine

```
* MinType: given two arguments of type C, D, L, or N, third argument gets
* smaller of two values, with convention that .F. < .T.
* <Memvar to receive return value> = ""
* DO MinType WITH <value 1>, <value 2>, <smaller of two values>
```

To use MinType in your code, you would first insert this text, which might be stored in a file named MinType.TEM in the directory where you keep your source code templates. You would construct the call to MinType with this information, and then delete the comment lines.

Memvars versus Fields

Remember that under some conditions your subroutines will not execute properly unless memvar references are preceded with M->, with the exception of memvar arguments passed to input/output or output parameters. In that case, the M-> qualification is either required or prohibited, according to the rules listed in Table 20.2 on page 305.

Chapter 21

Full-Screen I/O

Until recently, conventional programming languages had no concept of screen coordinates. Output devices accepted one line of data at a time, which meant that CRTs and hard-copy terminals were controlled with the identical code.

In contrast, the dBASE programming language supports the concept of a screen as a data-entry (or report) form. This chapter builds on the material in Chapter 3 to give you a more detailed presentation of full-screen techniques. Then the advanced but extremely important topics of menus and pick lists will be treated in Chapter 22.

Goals and Issues

Our goal is to be able to present the user with intelligent electronic equivalents of ordinary paper-based data-entry forms. This means that we must be able to control the color and use of each portion of the screen.

You will see that two different kinds of elements may be located at specified screen coordinates. The first kind of element is read-only text, which can be viewed but not changed, and the second kind of element is read-write text, which can be viewed and changed.

You will learn how to set screen colors, to clear specified portions of the screen, to draw boxes, and to edit database records in the EDIT and BROWSE modes. You will be able to go beyond simple data-entry screens by exploiting facilities in the dBASE language which support certain kinds of validation when data elements are entered or edited.

Finally, you will learn efficient and powerful solutions for some of the most common and important applications of full-screen editing, other than providing menu interfaces, which are covered in detail in Part III and in Chapter 22. Software engineering remarks and discussions throughout the chapter point you toward the best implementation options and away from weak techniques and pitfalls.

Screen Color Commands

In dialects which precede dBASE IV and FoxPro, color control is straightforward. You may specify two combinations of foreground/background colors and a border color. The first combination of a foreground color on a background color applies to most text displayed onscreen. The second combination is used for the edit windows of data-entry screens and for the STATUS line of the interpreter.

The syntax follows. See your dBASE dialect manual for a listing of colors and color codes.

SET COLOR TO <default colors>,<alternate colors>,<border color>

Color control in dBASE IV and FoxPro is more complex because you may optionally set many more than two color combinations. However, the usual SET COLOR TO command is still supported, so you need not understand the advanced facilities in order to code colors for these dialects.

Screen-Clearing Commands

You can clear the entire screen with the CLEAR command — which also issues a CLEAR GETS! To clear the portion between and including two coordinates, use the syntax

@ <row1>,<column1> CLEAR TO <row2>,<column2>

You can abbreviate

@ <row1>,<column1> CLEAR TO <last row>,<last column>

to

@ <row1>,<column1> CLEAR

To clear the screen but not the pending GETS, code "@ 0,0 CLEAR".

Box-Drawing Commands

You can draw boxes with either single or double lines around any rectangular area onscreen. The syntax is

@ <row1>,<column1> TO <row2>,<column2> [DOUBLE]

A single line is used unless the DOUBLE keyword appears. Use SET COLOR to control the colors of the box border.

You can also construct boxes line-by-line in strings which are displayed with the @ SAY command, or blocks of text which are displayed with TEXT/ENDTEXT, or files which are displayed with the TYPE command. (Be sure to SET HEADING OFF when using TYPE this way in dBASE IV or FoxPro.) You can consult the files ASCII.REF and Boxes.REF on the companion diskette to this book for a list of all 256 ASCII characters and a collection of many types of boxes which you can display with TEXT/ENDTEXT or TYPE.

The @ SAY GET Command with READ

Read-only elements are displayed with @ SAY statements. Read-write elements are displayed with @ GET or @ SAY GET statements. When a READ is executed, the cursor moves to the coordinates of the first GET item and the user moves the cursor through the items in the sequence in which the GET statements were executed. In addition, you can display read-only text with the ?, ??, and TEXT/ENDTEXT facilities.

Read-write elements are usually displayed in onscreen areas which have different colors or video attributes from other onscreen elements. In window terminology, these onscreen areas are windows without borders. During full-screen editing, the cursor moves from edit window to edit window.

Editing windows are usually one line by K characters, where the value of K depends on the data item being edited and any PICTURE or FUNCTION clause in the @ GET or @ SAY GET statement. Without a PICTURE clause, the value of K is the length of the data item being edited. When the K characters cannot be displayed on one screen line, they are wrapped to as many screen lines as are required to display all K characters.

Let's look at the full syntax of the @ statement for dBASE III PLUS:

```
@ <row>,<column>
     [SAY <exp_C> [PICTURE <exp_C>]]
     [GET <exp_C> [PICTURE <exp_C>]]
     [ [RANGE <exp_N>,<exp_N>] | [RANGE <exp_D>,<exp_D>] ]
```

In the following subsections, we'll look at the clauses of this command.

The PICTURE Clause

The PICTURE clause is used to control the display format of the character expression it modifies. The complete syntax of the PICTURE clause is

PICTURE "[@<PICTURE function><blank>]<PICTURE template>"

Remark. Note that these PICTURE templates are a different kind of template from the fill-in-the-blanks source code templates presented in Part III of this book!

Table 21.1 shows some examples of how data would appear when displayed according to various PICTURE formats. See the @ command description in your dBASE dialect manual for a listing and explanation of PICTURE functions and templates.

Note that the PICTURE specification is not accessed once the data has been displayed. Therefore, the "b" in the second line is not followed by a comma, despite the fact that there is a comma in the PICTURE. In contrast, the last example has two leading blanks in the displayed result.

Table 21.1 PICTURE-Formatted Data Examples

Data	PICTURE	Appearance
"abc"	@!	ABC
"ab"	@R X, X, X	a, b
"abc"	@R X, X, X	a, b, c
"abc"	@R !, !, !	A, B, C
–123.45	@CX	123.45DB
123.45	@CX	123.45CR
–123.45	@(	(123.45)
1234.5	999,999.99	1,234.50

Editing versus Display

PICTURE specifications used for editing have different purposes than those used for display. When PICTURE specifications are used for display, they modify the appearance of the displayed data. When they are used for editing, they can

1. Accept or reject certain keystrokes for each character of the edited item.
2. Translate character input into uppercase as it is entered.
3. Implement horizontal scrolling when the item is wider than the editing window.

The TRANSFORM() Built-In Function

The TRANSFORM() built-in function (of type character) permits you to access the power of PICTURE templates in any expression. For example,

LTRIM(TRANSFORM(1234.5, "999,999.99"))

evaluates to "1,234.50"; without the LTRIM(), there would be two leading blanks. The syntax of TRANSFORM() is

TRANSFORM(<exp>, <expC containing PICTURE>)

The FUNCTION Clause

Some dialects support the additional clause "[FUNCTION <function codes>]", which allows you to write

PICTURE "@R! X, X, X"

as

FUNCTION "R!" PICTURE "X, X, X"

I recommend that you do not use the second option, even when it is available. It might not be understood by some dBASE tools, by the programmers who come after you, or by a dialect to which you might port your code.

The RANGE and VALID Clauses

Some dialects support the additional clause "[VALID <exp_L>]", and all dialects after dBASE III support "[RANGE <exp_N>,<exp_N>]".

These two clauses provide very important quality control facilities to the dBASE programmer. For example, when an application prompts the user to enter a number whose valid range is 1 to 5, use the clause "RANGE 1,5". Attempts to enter a value outside this range cause a message such as "Range is 1 to 5. Press space" to appear on the top line of the screen. The user must press the space bar before getting another chance to enter a value.

In most dialects, the RANGE clause can also be applied to date data. FoxBASE+ supports the variation "RANGE <exp>," to enforce only a lower limit and the variation "RANGE ,<exp>" to enforce only an upper limit. If the dialect does not support these variations, you can implement them with "RANGE <exp>,<a very large number or late date>" and "RANGE <a very large negative number or very early date>,<exp>".

The VALID clause, supported by most dialects after dBASE III PLUS, causes the specified logical expression to be evaluated after the data item is edited or entered. If the expression is false, the user is directed to try again.

This clause becomes very powerful when the logical expression is a reference to a user-defined function. In this case, you can interact with your user as necessary in order to obtain a correct entry. A typical use of this technique would be to display a pick list or an error message with suggested remedies.

A FoxPro Extension

FoxPro permits a VALID clause to have an integer value as well as a logical value. If the value is false or 0, the item is edited again; the cursor will not move to the next item. If the value is true or +1, the cursor moves to the next item. If the value is a positive number N, the cursor moves to the Nth item following the item with the VALID clause. If the value is a negative number –N, the cursor moves to the Nth item preceding the item with the VALID clause.

The WHEN Clause

You can control whether an @ GET item is edited or not with the WHEN clause in dBASE IV and FoxPro. A false value causes the item to be skipped, and a true value causes the item to be edited as usual.

The EDIT Command and FORMAT Files

The CHANGE verb can be used interchangeably with the EDIT verb. The syntax of the EDIT command is

```
EDIT [<scope>] [FIELDS <field list>]
     [WHILE <expL>] [FOR <expL>]
```

The EDIT command lies at the very heart of the dBASE language. This command permits you to edit all fields or selected fields of one record at a time, where the records are taken from the entire database or from a set of records specified by the scope.

The fields are displayed on one or more screens, as necessary. The PageUp and PageDown keys are used to navigate between the screens. These keys also move the record pointer to the previous or next record, respectively.

The default data-entry form for EDIT lists field names in column 0 and starts the edit window for the field's data in column 10 in the same line. In the case of character fields longer than 70 characters, the edit window is displayed on two to four lines; otherwise, the edit window for a field is displayed only on the line containing the field name.

Memo fields are shown as if they were character fields with the contents "memo". When the cursor is on a memo field and the user strokes CONTROL-PageDown, dBASE executes the text editor which is defined in CONFIG.DB (or its equivalent). Then a new memo is created, or an existing memo is edited, after which the former appearance of the screen is restored. (FoxPro is able to show memo contents in a separate user-defined window during BROWSE or EDIT.)

In many situations, the default data-entry form is perfectly adequate. Sometimes, however, you must program a custom data-entry form for a database's records.

There are two basic approaches, both using @ SAY GET commands with READ or EDIT. In the first approach, you develop a procedure that contains the @ SAY GET commands (with a READ) to position and label the edit or display windows for each field to be edited or displayed. If the procedure is called EditRec, then you use it as follows:

1. Position the record pointer to an existing record.
2. DO EditRec.

If more than one screen is required to display the database records, then collect the @ SAY GET commands into groups which display together onscreen and separate the groups with READ statements. This approach preserves only part of the interface of the EDIT command; you can PageDown to the next screen, but you cannot PageUp to return to the previous screen. (Later in the chapter, we'll see how to get around this problem.)

On the other hand, you can include any dBASE commands you like in EditRec, such as SET COLOR TO commands to "paint" the screen any way you want, and IF statements to control options.

If EditRec contains only @ and READ statements, then you can make it into a FORMAT file for dialects with the EDIT command, which excludes the Clipper and Quicksilver dialects. FORMAT files normally have an extension of .FMT; the command "SET FORMAT TO EditRec" specifies EditRec.FMT as the FORMAT file. The usage pattern is as follows:

1. Position the record pointer to an existing record.
2. SET FORMAT TO <FORMAT file>.
3. APPEND, EDIT, INSERT, or READ.
4. SET FORMAT TO.

The dBASE language has a nasty pitfall: an open FORMAT file is invoked by READ as well as by APPEND, EDIT, and INSERT. This is of course disastrous for the uninformed, which is why you must open the FORMAT file, use it, and then close it with SET FORMAT TO.

The PageUp and PageDown keys work with FORMAT files as they do with the default data-entry form. If there are two screens per record, PageUp moves from screen 2 to screen 1 and PageDown moves from screen 1 to screen 2.

When you use the first approach, your user can edit *only* the selected record. When you use FORMAT files with the EDIT command, your user can edit one or more records in the database, depending on the scope clause of the EDIT command, the filter, and the setting of SET DELETED.

Limiting EDIT to One Record

There is a very useful technique which preserves the ability of the user to move between data screens for one selected record, with or without a FORMAT file, but which blocks the user from viewing or editing the other records in the database. The technique is "EDIT NEXT 1".

The EDIT command supports a scope, a WHILE condition, and a FOR condition, so you can limit the set of records to be edited in any way which is supported by these clauses. In particular, the scope of "NEXT 1" specifies only the current record.

Sometimes you need to offer the user the option of saving or discarding changes made to a record. In that case, the following technique works more cleanly than the typical solution based on the SCATTER and GATHER commands, which are not found in all dialects.

1. Position the record pointer to an existing record.
2. COPY NEXT 1 TO EraseMe.DBF.
3. Select an available area with "SELECT 0" or "DO Select0" (Select0.PRG is listed on page 73).
4. Select EraseMe.
5. SET FORMAT TO <FORMAT file>.
6. EDIT.
7. USE.
8. If appropriate, query the user "Save changes? (Y/N)".

9. SELECT <original area>.
10. If changes are to be saved, copy changed fields from EraseMe.DBF, using the FIELD() function, as shown after the listing of Select0.PRG.

You can use the FIELD() built-in function (FieldName() in Clipper) to access the field names of an open database. The following code replaces the contents of each field in the currently selected record in the currently selected database with the corresponding field contents from EraseMe.DBF.

Listing 21.1 Copy Selected Records between Databases

```
PRIVATE I
I = 1
DO WHILE ("" # TRIM(FIELD(I)))  && FieldName() in Clipper.
   F1 = FIELD(I)
   REPLACE &F1 WITH EraseMe->&F1
   I = I + 1
ENDDO && WHILE (I <= upper bound)
```

There is a second technique which is very quick for the programmer to implement, although it uses more disk space. Simply mark the original record for deletion and APPEND FROM EraseMe.DBF! This alternative will probably be faster, perhaps much faster, than updating the fields one by one. If the database is packed every night in batch mode, then the extra space taken by the deleted records is probably no problem.

Relative versus Absolute Addressing in Full-Screen I/O

FORMAT files which are generated by CREATE/MODIFY SCREEN or equivalent utilities typically have the screen coordinates as numeric constants, which is fine when you always have the utility to help you maintain the FORMAT file. However, when you have no utility, it is better to use relative addressing, except for the first @ SAY, @ GET, or @ SAY GET command.

For example, the code in the following two listings does the same work. However, you can insert or delete statements in the second form, and the other screen elements will move up or down automatically. When you insert or delete statements in the first form, you must renumber the row coordinates.

Listing 21.2 Example of Absolute Screen Coordinates

```
@ 1,0 SAY  "ACME Brick Company"
@ 2,0 SAY  "Current time:   " + TIME()
@ 3,0 SAY  "Current date:   " + DtoC(Date())
```

Listing 21.3 Example of Relative Screen Coordinates

```
@ 1,0 SAY  "ACME Brick Company"
@ ROW()+1,0 SAY  "Current time:   " + TIME()
@ ROW()+1,0 SAY  "Current date:   " + DtoC(Date())
```

Simulating Multiple-Screen FORMAT Files

Let's say that you have a database whose records require three screens to display for editing. You have written Screen1.PRG, Screen2.PRG, and Screen3.PRG to handle each of the three screens. If you code

```
DO Screen1
DO Screen2
DO Screen3
```

then the user can PageDown but not PageUp. You want the user to be able to PageUp as well.

We'll assume that you can't use a multiple-page FORMAT file because your dialect doesn't support such files *or* because you need to have commands other than @ commands and READ in Screen1.PRG, Screen2.PRG, and/or Screen3.PRG. The following technique has been explained in explicit detail, with a long code example, by John Bauman (1989a).

The heart of the technique is a loop which calls the Screen<n> routines and a routine to check on the exit keystroke from each Screen<n> routine. Let's call our checking routine KeyCheck and give it one parameter, ScreenNo_C, to specify the number of the screen to edit next; "0" means stop editing. Listing 21.4 shows a loop to simulate a multiple-page FORMAT file.

Listing 21.4 Simulating Multiple-Page FORMAT Files

```
ScreenNo_C =  "1"
DO WHILE (ScreenNo_C #  "0")
   DO Screen&ScreenNo_C
   DO KeyCheck with ScreenNo_C
ENDDO
```

Our canonical type of thinking leads us to use the screen pointer in its character form. The "_C" suffix is a convention to remind us that this variable is used in its character form.

The KeyCheck routine uses the ReadKey() function (LastKey() in Clipper) to retrieve the keystroke used to exit the READ command at the end of each Screen<n> routine. Unfortunately, the ReadKey() and LastKey() values are dialect-dependent, so no generic KeyCheck routine can be written, unless it were to detect the dialect under which it was executed and act accordingly.

Recommendation on simulating multiple-page FORMAT files. Use this technique if you need more functionality than just @ commands in your screen-handling routines, or if your dialect does not support multiple-page FORMAT files.

Validation

Some validations are impossible or inconvenient to make during a READ statement's execution. The Screen1 routine might be written so that the user has to keep editing the screen until all of its data is correct, or the record is abandoned. In this regard, the validation technique involving the READ SAVE and CLEAR GETS commands, whose presentation starts on page 89, may be very useful.

Automatic Time-Date Stamps for Records

In many cases, it is convenient, useful, or mandatory to have fields in a database which store the time and/or date on which the record was last updated. This facility would be the record-level equivalent of LUPDATE(), a built-in function which returns the date of last update for the currently selected database.

An appropriate way to implement record-level time stamping is not obvious. You can easily keep track of when a user examines a record, but was the record changed when examined?

The design of the ReadKey() built-in function makes this question very easy to answer when the FORMAT file only has one screen. If ReadKey() >= 256 after an APPEND, EDIT, INSERT, or READ command invokes the FORMAT file, then the record was changed.

Notice that this test will only tell you if a record's data has changed on the last screen of a multiple-screen FORMAT file. However, the multiple-page FORMAT simulation technique can tell you whether a record was updated on a particular screen. This is very easy to do in KeyCheck.

To implement this technique, introduce two additional KeyCheck parameters named DateField and TimeField to hold the names of the date and character fields of length 8 in the database which hold the time/date stamp. If these names are "Update" and "Uptime", the call would be

```
DO KeyCheck with ScreenNo_C,"Update","Uptime"
```

In KeyCheck you update these fields (when necessary) with the code

```
REPLACE &DateField WITH DATE(), &TimeField WITH TIME()
```

Software Engineering Aids for Constructing FORMAT Files

The Ashton-Tate dialects dBASE III PLUS and dBASE IV provide the CREATE SCREEN and MODIFY SCREEN commands, which give you an interactive tool to create and update definitions of FORMAT files. The definitions are held in .SCR files; .FMT files are made from .SCR files on demand while CREATE SCREEN or MODIFY SCREEN executes.

Clipper, dbXL, and Quicksilver lack this command or its equivalent. FoxBASE+ and FoxPro have code generators which can handle screen I/O, but these products have an extensive learning curve and cannot be recommended as substitutes for the CREATE SCREEN command.

Remark. The absence of CREATE SCREEN or its equivalent in some dialects need not be a problem, because screen design tools are the most highly populated category of dBASE programmer productivity products. These tools are covered in detail in Part VIII.

For now, let me direct you to the advertisements in *Data Based Advisor* and *DBMS* magazines. You can also find freeware and shareware screen design tools on BBSs.

Objections to EDIT and BROWSE

There are a number of dBASE myths, and one of them is that using the EDIT or BROWSE commands in a program is equivalent to giving your user a sledgehammer or flamethrower to use on his or her data. This myth has been propagated by WordTech relative to its Quicksilver compiler and by Nantucket relative to its Clipper compiler, which do not implement the EDIT and BROWSE commands found in dBASE III PLUS, dBASE IV, FoxBASE+, FoxPro, and dBXL.

Users *must* be able to view and/or modify their database data, and the BROWSE and EDIT commands, with or without FORMAT files, work admirably for this purpose. Let's look at the objections one by one.

Modify Any Record

Objection. EDIT and BROWSE permit the user to modify any record.

Countermeasure 1. Use a scope clause to restrict editing to the records in the scope. For example, code "EDIT NEXT 1" or "EDIT RECORD RecNo()" to edit only the current record. Code "BROWSE REST" to permit the user access to the records from the current record to the last record.

Countermeasure 2. For EDIT, use the FOR and/or WHILE clauses to restrict the set of records which may be edited.

Countermeasure 3. Use the SET FILTER facility to limit the set of records which may be edited.

Countermeasures 4 and 5. Under the heading "Limiting EDIT to One Record" on page 327, there are two techniques with EraseMe.DBF which restrict the user to editing the selected record.

Modify Any Field

Objection. EDIT permits the user to modify any field.

Countermeasure. Use a FIELDS clause to restrict editing to the desired fields. For example, code "EDIT FIELDS FirstName,LastName" to edit only the name fields in the current database. Alternatively, code "SET FIELDS TO FirstName, LastName" and then EDIT.

Modify Read-Only Data

Objection. EDIT and BROWSE permit the user to modify data even if you just want the user to view data without updating it.

Countermeasure 1. In dialects later than dBASE III PLUS which implement the BROWSE and EDIT commands, use the NOMODIFY clause to enable viewing and disable modification. dBASE IV and FoxPro permit you to enable or disable modification for specified fields!

Countermeasure 2. If there isn't very much data to view, copy it to EraseMe.DBF and let the user EDIT or BROWSE this file. (As a last resort, you can mark a database file as read-only at the operating system level, but this is not recommended if there are alternatives.)

Enter Unvalidated Data

Objection. Users will enter invalid data if they have a chance, and EDIT and BROWSE cannot help with validation.

Countermeasure 1. Dialects which support the VALID clause of the @ GET statement have the validation services of this clause whether or not the @ GET statement is in a FORMAT file. Therefore, you may validate fields during EDIT by using FORMAT files whose @ GET statements contain VALID clauses.

Countermeasure 2. The FoxPro dialect supports field-by-field validation in BROWSE.

Countermeasure 3. All dialects support the method of validating a record's data after the record is edited.

Inappropriate Interactive Commands

Objection. Interactive commands are not appropriate for compiled applications.

Observation 1. Clipper 4.0 includes the DBedit() built-in function, which is a programmable BROWSE-like command whose provision refutes the vendor's claim that EDIT-type commands do not belong in compiled applications. The Extend.LIB library file also includes BROWSE(), another BROWSE-like command.

Observation 2. dBXL programs may contain EDIT and BROWSE, but you cannot use Quicksilver to compile these programs. However, the extra-cost WorkFast utility product from WordTech contains simulations of EDIT and BROWSE which you can incorporate into your applications so that they will execute under both dBXL and Quicksilver.

Simulating EDIT in Dialects Which Lack It

If you need to compile applications which contain EDIT commands, you can use the subroutine in Listing 21.5 to simulate the EDIT command in Clipper — it is *not* necessary to develop custom data-entry screens, which can take a great deal of time. Note that we can simulate EDIT (without a FORMAT file) with the @ commands, the FIELD() built-in function (called FieldName() in Clipper), and the ReadKey() built-in function (called LastKey() in Clipper). (With minor modifications, this routine should work with any dialect, in particular, with Quicksilver.)

Listing 21.5 EditCl.PRG, a Clipper Procedure to Simulate the EDIT Command

```
* File = \DB\Util\EditCL.PRG.  EDIT implementation for Clipper.
* Entry conditions :
*     dBASE III database is open.
*     1 <= Recno() <= LastRec()
*     DB is passed as a character string
*     DB = <name of open database>
*     ConfirmVal is passed as  "On" or  "Off" (case insensitive)
*****************************************************************************
* Exit conditions :
*     dBASE III database is open.
*     1 <= Recno() <= LastRec()
*     Parameters have their original types and values.
*     Some field values of some records may be changed.
*     The delete mark may be different for some records.
*     SET CONFIRM &ConfirmVal in effect
*****************************************************************************
* Editing may be terminated on one screen by PageDown, PageUp, ENTER, ESCAPE,
* CONTROL-End or CONTROL-W.
* Confirm is SET ON unconditionally inside the .PRG file.  On exit,
* CONFIRM is SET to the value ConfirmVal.
* Confirm must be ON when READ is executed because otherwise we fall out of
* the EDIT when we fill up the last field of the record with data.  This way
* we force the exiting keystroke to be CONTROL-M.

PARAMETERS DB,ConfirmVal
PRIVATE FieldNum,ScreenNum,DeleteFlag,BlankField,Fname,DBscrLines

DBscrLines = 23
BlankField = Space(10)
DeleteFlag = Deleted()
FieldNum = 1
DO WHILE (BlankField # FieldName(FieldNum))

   CLEAR
   ScreenNum = Int(FieldNum/DBscrLines) + 1
   @ 0,0  SAY  "Database:  " + DB
   @ 0,38 SAY  " Record" + Str(Recno(),6) +  " of" + Str(Lastrec(),6)
   @ 0,71 SAY  "Screen:" + Str(ScreenNum,2)

   @ 1,0  SAY  "Delete record later? (Y = yes; N = no)"
   @ 1,Col()+1 GET DeleteFlag PICTURE  "Y"
   @ 1,56 SAY Cdow(Date())
   @ 1,66 SAY DtoC(Date()) +  "   " + Substr(Time(),1,5)
   @ 1,0 SAY  ""

   DO WHILE (FieldNum # ScreenNum*DBscrLines + 1) .AND. ;
            (BlankField # FieldName(FieldNum))

      Fname = FieldName(FieldNum)
      @ Row()+1,0 SAY FieldName(FieldNum)
      @ Row(),11 GET &Fname

      FieldNum = FieldNum + 1
   ENDDO

   * Set the confirm value for READing this screen of GETs.
```

```
   SET Confirm ON
   READ
   ***************************** Set the value that CONFIRM will have on exit.
   SET Confirm &ConfirmVal
   ************************************** Handle deletion/recall of records :
   DO CASE
      CASE (Deleted() .AND. (.NOT. DeleteFlag))
         RECALL
      CASE ( (.NOT. Deleted()) .AND. DeleteFlag )
         DELETE
   ENDCASE
   DO CASE
      CASE (LastKey() = 3) .OR. (LastKey() = 13)
         * PageDown or ENTER was pressed.  FieldNum is the ordinal of the field
         * next to display :
         IF (BlankField = FieldName(FieldNum))
            IF (Recno() = LastRec())
               * Attempt to PageDown past last record :
               ***********************************************************RETURN
               RETURN
            ELSE
               SKIP +1
               FieldNum = 1
               DeleteFlag = Deleted()
            ENDIF
         ENDIF
      CASE (LastKey() = 18)
         * PageUp was pressed.
         IF (ScreenNum > 1)
            FieldNum = (ScreenNum - 2)*DBscrLines + 1
         ELSE
            IF (Recno() = 1)
               * Attempt to PageUp past First record :
               ***********************************************************RETURN
               RETURN
            ELSE
               SKIP -1
               DeleteFlag = Deleted()
               FieldNum   = 1
            ENDIF
         ENDIF
      CASE (LastKey() = 27) .OR. (LastKey() = 23)
         * Escape or CONTROL-End or CONTROL-W has been pressed; do not edit
         * further:
         ****************************************************************RETURN
         RETURN
   ENDCASE
ENDDO WHILE (BlankField # FieldName(FieldNum))
* End of EditCL.PRG.
```

Note that the top line shows the database, the record number, and the screen number. The highest-quality database applications show status in the form "Screen: 1 of 3" instead of the form "Screen: 1".

The dBASE standard is that users can stroke CONTROL-U when editing a database record to toggle the delete byte. This feature is invisible and is probably better replaced with an explicit, labeled entry, as you see in EditCl.PRG:

Delete record later? (Y = yes; N = no)

The CASE statement uses the LastKey() built-in function to detect user keystrokes and explicitly code the actions which are part of the EDIT command. The dialects are notoriously incompatible with the LastKey() function, which is called ReadKey() in other dialects. Thus, the code shown will probably work in any dialect, but you may have to adjust the LastKey() or ReadKey() test values and rename the FieldName() function to FIELD().

The BROWSE Command

The BROWSE command is a companion to EDIT. The EDIT command shows you fields from one record at a time, using as many screens as necessary to display the fields. As we have seen, you can use FORMAT files to customize the appearance of these screens.

The contrasting view of database data from the BROWSE command displays fields from many records on one screen. The records are accessed in storage order if no index is in effect, or in the order specified by the master index otherwise. You can select the fields to display, and you can specify the maximum width of a displayed field. There is really no analog of FORMAT files for BROWSE, which has a tabular presentation format: each row corresponds to a record, and each column of data corresponds to a field.

The EDIT command uses vertical scrolling (via PageUp and PageDown), but it does not have the concept of horizontal scrolling. In contrast, BROWSE uses vertical scrolling to display other records, as does EDIT, but BROWSE also uses CONTROL-RightArrow and CONTROL-LeftArrow for horizontal scrolling.

The BROWSE in dBASE III PLUS displays 13 or 17 records, depending on whether HELP is SET ON or OFF. When HELP is SET ON, a four-line chart of editing keystrokes is shown at the top of the screen. The keystroke CONTROL-Home brings up a top-line, moving-bar menu which permits you to move to the top or bottom of the database or to a selected record. Other options permit you to fix fields onscreen during horizontal scrolling.

dBASE IV and FoxPro support more than 25 lines per screen for EGA and VGA monitors. In some cases, up to 45 records can be shown on the same screen by BROWSE!

A partial syntax of BROWSE for the dialects which support it is

```
BROWSE [WIDTH <number of characters>]
       [FIELDS <field list>]
```

By using WIDTH in combination with FIELDS, you can quickly inspect the values of critical fields in your databases. For example, BROWSE WIDTH 10 shows at least seven fields on each screen.

Recommendation on a programmed interface to BROWSE. The three most critical kinds of control to give users of a programmed interface to the BROWSE command are the ability to specify

1. The starting record.

2. The index, if any, to be used.
3. The maximum displayed width of a field.

BROWSE in Programmed Applications

Some users can be trusted to use a BROWSE command without corrupting data, whereas other users cannot be trusted with unrestricted edit access to database field data. Remember that both EDIT and BROWSE normally give the user the ability to update any displayed field.

Nevertheless, BROWSE is extremely useful for many purposes, and some dialects permit us to block changes to database data by using the NOMODIFY clause of the BROWSE command. Without such a clause, you can have the operating system mark a database as read-only before you permit a user to EDIT or BROWSE it. Any changes to the database will be rejected by the operating system, which may or may not cause insurmountable problems. (The ON ERROR command may help you to handle the conditions generated when the user tries to modify the read-only database.)

A second data-protection possibility which is feasible for small databases and infeasible for large ones consists of copying the data to a temporary file. The user BROWSEs the temporary file, which is erased after use. However, much better solutions for data protection are supported by BROWSE options offered in various dialects.

The clause NOAPPEND, found in dBASE III PLUS, dBASE IV, dbXL, FoxBASE+, and FoxPro, prevents the user from appending records. When the last record is current and the user strokes DownArrow, a prompt like "Add records? (Y/N)" appears unless NOAPPEND is specified.

FoxBASE+ and FoxPro give us the NOMODIFY clause for BROWSE. In these dialects, BROWSE NOMODIFY lets the user have all the numerous benefits of BROWSE, *except* the ability to modify data. dBASE IV has this capability but calls its clause NOEDIT instead of NOMODIFY. (FoxPro recognizes either NOEDIT or NOMODIFY.)

Remark. The BROWSE command works splendidly as an easily implemented pick list, particularly with NOMODIFY or NOEDIT. If there are any records to BROWSE, then one of them is current when BROWSE is exited. It is very convenient that the ESCAPE keystroke can be used to exit the BROWSE command. The user points with the arrow keys and selects with ESCAPE.

For example, say that a client uses only 20 to 30 suppliers. The supplier information is stored in Supplier.DBF, which has the field "Name" to hold the name of the supplier. To let your client select a supplier record to edit:

```
USE Supplier
BROWSE FIELDS Name NOMODIFY

* Use EDIT NEXT 1, or perform fancier editing
* with FORMAT files, validation, and so on.
EDIT NEXT 1
```

dBASE IV and FoxPro give the user a keystroke to bounce back and forth between the EDIT and BROWSE views of a database record. All dialects support the SET FIELDS TO and SET FIELDS ON/OFF commands, which control a default field list for the EDIT and BROWSE commands. For example, "SET FIELDS TO Name" followed by "EDIT" is the same as "EDIT FIELDS Name".

dBASE IV and FoxPro also permit you to set any displayed field to be read-only and permit you to define calculated fields. FoxPro gives you a robust set of display and validation facilities on the field level; see George Goley's column, "The Power of BROWSE," in the September 1990 *Data Based Advisor* (Goley 1990).

Elegant menus,
a marvelous mode:
Optimal sinews
from users to code!

Chapter 22

Onscreen Menus and Pick Lists

In many applications, the vast majority of the code performs services which are accessed through an interface provided by a small percentage of the total amount of code. Nonetheless, the user interacts with your application through its interface, which consequently has an importance to the user that may be very much out of proportion to its percentage of source code.

This chapter presents some of the facilities and issues associated with building the user interface in your dBASE applications. In particular, we will focus on the implementation of pick lists and menus to assist users (1) in picking choices from lists, and (2) in adding, deleting, and modifying database records.

In Volume 2 we will look at many products which help you produce the user interface in your programs. In this chapter, we restrict ourselves to facilities available in the dialects themselves.

Basics: How to Detect User Keystrokes

Let's begin the presentation of menus and pick lists by reviewing the dBASE facilities for keyboard input. We'll start with the dialect-independent facilities and then go on to the dialect-dependent facilities.

Dialect-Independent Facilities

The ACCEPT and INPUT commands can be used to transfer values to memvars, but their use is not recommended. The WAIT command accepts a single keystroke as input in its variation "WAIT [<message>] TO <memvar>"; this command is acceptable when you need only one keystroke from the user and you do not need the services of @ GET with READ.

However, when you use the @ GET command with READ instead of WAIT TO, there are many more ways for you to control the interaction with the user. In the case of a single-keystroke response, you can create a one-character editing window into which the keystroke is entered. You can control the colors in this window, and you can use a specification in a PICTURE clause to force the keystroke into uppercase or to reject certain keystrokes. You can provide an initial value for the @ GET statement which defines a default response for the user, and you can use the RANGE and VALID clauses to further control the interaction.

Notice that the WAIT TO command processes a single keystroke, whereas @ GET solicits the entry of information which may comprise several keystrokes. Furthermore, even when the item of information being solicited consists of a single character, @ GET with READ starts a *dialog* with the user in which individual keystrokes might be ignored, and in which submitted values may be rejected with the requirement for the user to enter another value.

There are also several built-in functions which support keyboard input. The user's keystrokes are entered into a buffer by the operating system and are subsequently processed by your application. The INKEY() function returns the next-to-be-processed character in the keyboard buffer,[1] and removes that character from the buffer.

The INKEY() function can be referenced anywhere, but the READKEY() function is designed to report the keystroke used to exit a READ command. In dialects other than Clipper, READKEY() values of 256 or greater indicate that data was changed during the READ; otherwise data was not changed. Clipper and FoxPro users have the UPDATED() built-in function to determine if data changed during the GET.

Warning on READKEY() with multiple-page FORMAT files. If you edit a record with a multiple-screen FORMAT file, the READKEY() function cannot reliably tell you if the record's data has changed. Remember that each screen in the FORMAT file, except the last, is followed by a READ command; the READKEY() function will tell you if any fields that appear on the last screen were changed.

The major dialects other than Clipper have ON KEY, and Clipper has SET KEY. These facilities permit you to associate a keystroke with the execution of a subroutine. (See Chapter 3 for more information.) These commands are concerned with *processing* keystrokes rather than *obtaining* them, which is the focus of this chapter, so the ON KEY and SET KEY commands won't be mentioned again in this chapter.

Dialect-Dependent Facilities

The dialects which implement window objects permit you to solicit keystrokes through a dialog conducted in a window. There are also a number of dialect-dependent features to assist your programming of menus and pick lists.

One of the most elegant and easy-to-use facilities is provided by the MENU TO command in Clipper, FoxBASE+, and FoxPro. This command is used in connection with the SET MESSAGE TO command and the @ PROMPT ... MESSAGE command, as shown in Listings 22.9 (page 360) and 22.10 (page 361) later in this chapter.

The MENU TO facility can be used to generate simple boxed pick lists or Lotus-style moving-bar menus. The Clipper ACHOICE() function implements a simple unboxed pick list, which permits the user to choose from an array of items.

1. Called the *type-ahead* buffer in dBASE terminology.

dBASE IV implements several new information structures to support the programming of pick lists and menus. With the DEFINE POPUP facility, you can easily code pick lists for lists defined by database fields, files matching a file specification like "*.DBF", and field values from an open database! The DEFINE MENU facility creates an information structure which can be used to implement horizontal moving-bar menus, vertical moving-bar menus, and Macintosh-style menus with a top menu bar presenting choices that activate drop-down menus.

The DEFINE POPUP and DEFINE MENU facilities of dBASE IV are present in FoxPro, but FoxPro also offers an extension of the MENU TO facility to support the Macintosh-style menu. The FoxPro MENU BAR facility is much easier to use than the DEFINE MENU facility when you want to implement a Macintosh-style menu in an application, as we shall see below.

The User Interface for Updating Database Records

In this section, we'll look at some ways to implement the part of your applications that helps the user to update data in database records. This may involve appending or deleting records as well as altering the contents of existing records.

When the user has selected a database to view and/or update, you will typically want to offer at least the two choices of "Edit or view an existing record" and "Add a new record". In some situations, appending records is handled by a separate process, and the only choice to offer is "Edit or view an existing record".

It is also often appropriate to offer some kind of browsing capability to permit the user to see data from more than one record onscreen. Remember to use the NOMODIFY clause of the BROWSE command if you use the BROWSE command and you don't want the user to change data during BROWSE. Clipper users achieve browsing capability through the powerful and flexible DBEDIT().

It is also easy to code a read-only browsing facility which has a fixed field list (no horizontal scrolling) and only the ability to page up or page down through the database data. In brief, you display the first screen of data, consisting of the first N records, and on the bottom line of the screen (for example), you present the prompt "Enter U to page up, D to page down, or E to exit". You adjust the record pointer as appropriate and list data from N records on N lines, replacing the previous onscreen data.

Retrieving Existing Database Records

To assist retrieval, offer your users a screen on which they may enter a record number, key value, or search specification. The search specification may match more than one record, and your application ideally will anticipate this possibility.

For databases which store names in first-name and last-name fields (called FirstName and LastName), you will probably use @ GET with READ to solicit a name specification, as shown in DupKeys.TEM:

Listing 22.1 Template for Retrieval of Duplicate Keys

```
* File = DupKeys.TEM.
* A template for retrieval of records in databases with duplicate keys.
*************************************************************************
* Dialects: dBXL, FoxBASE+, FoxPro.
* Remarks:  To run in dBASE III PLUS, you must delete the NOMODIFY clause from
* the BROWSE command, with the consequence that the user can modify data which
* should not be modified.  To run in dBASE IV, change the NOMODIFY clause to
* NOEDIT.
*************************************************************************
* The key for the Name index is UPPER(LastName + FirstName):
USE <database> INDEX Name

* SET FILTER and SET DELETED as appropriate.

mFirstName = SPACE( LEN(FirstName) )
mLastName  = SPACE( LEN(LastName) )

CLEAR
@ 5,0 SAY  ""
TEXT
   Enter (1) some or all of the characters of the last name, OR
     (2) ALL of the characters of the last name and
         some or all of the characters of the first name.
ENDTEXT

@ ROW()+2,5 SAY  "First Name   " GET mFirstName
@ ROW()+1,5 SAY  "Last  Name   " GET mLastName
READ

SearchKey = UPPER(TRIM(mLastName + mFirstName))
Nmatches  = 0

SET EXACT OFF
SEEK SearchKey
IF (.NOT. EOF())
   FirstMatch = RecNo()
   * The longer string must be on the left in the WHILE clause.
   COUNT WHILE (UPPER(LastName + FirstName) = SearchKey) TO Nmatches
   GOTO FirstMatch
   IF (Nmatches > 1)
      ?  "More than one name matches your specification, as follows."
      ?  "Please use the arrow keys to make your selection and press ESCAPE."
      DO WaitOnC
      BROWSE NEXT Nmatches FIELDS FirstName, LastName NOMODIFY
   ENDIF
ENDIF
SET EXACT ON  && This example assumes that the application default is EXACT ON.

* End of DupKeys.TEM.
```

It may be that more than one record matches the name specification entered by the user. In that case, display a list of the names using the BROWSE command to create a pick list from the actual fields in the record to be selected. You can protect the name fields from modification with the NOMODIFY clause (except in dBASE III PLUS, which lacks this clause). Clipper and Quicksilver lack the BROWSE command, but Clipper has the DBEDIT() function, which can duplicate the services of the BROWSE command in the example. Quicksilver users can access a BROWSE routine on the optional WorkFast diskette from WordTech.

Deleting Records

When you edit a database record via the EDIT or BROWSE command without specifying a read-only option, you can stroke CONTROL-U to toggle the status of the delete byte, but you can make your applications more friendly by handling the delete status of records more explicitly. When you use a FORMAT file or a custom data-entry screen, I recommend that you include a statement like the following @ GET at or near the top of the form:

@ <row>,<column> SAY "Mark this record for later deletion?"
GET Delete_L

After the READ you execute code like the following:

```
IF Delete_L
   DELETE
ELSE
   RECALL
ENDIF
```

Appending Records

If records with duplicate keys are permitted, then the user's request to add a new record can be followed immediately by a data-entry form for the new record. This form may be blank or some fields may have initial values. If duplicate keys are not permitted, present the same screen for edit requests and append requests. When the user wishes to append a new record whose key should be unique, you can verify the uniqueness of the key for the new data by soliciting the data for the fields in the key expression *before* you APPEND BLANK.

In retrieval code generated from the duplicate-keys template above, the user who wishes to add "Jeb Long" to the database enters "Jeb" and "Long" as the first name and last name, respectively. If there is no record with a key whose first M + 7 characters match "LONG" + SPACE(M) + "JEB" (where M = LEN(LastName) – 4), then you code

```
APPEND BLANK
REPLACE FirstName WITH mFirstName, LastName WITH mLastName
<edit the new record>
```

Otherwise, you take the appropriate action for the application. Here are some possibilities:

1. Deny the request to append the record.
2. Tell the user he or she is about to create a record with a duplicate key. Ask the user if he or she really wants to create such a record, and, if so, create it.
3. If there is just one record matching the search key, assume that the user wants to edit this record and display the record's data onscreen.
4. If there is just one record matching the search key, ask if the user wants to edit this record and, if so, display the record's data onscreen.

5. If more than one record matches the search key, display a list of identification information for each record in a pick list. Then edit the selected record.
6. If more than one record matches the search key, ask the user if he or she wants to edit any of the matching records. If so, display a list of identification information for each record in a pick list, and edit the selected record.

For example, you might need to store two individuals with the same name in your database. Although an attempt to add a record for "Sam Smith" is probably in error if a record for "Sam Smith" already exists, one Sam may live in Phoenix and the other in Chicago. To accommodate such events, a name-storing database may need to permit duplicate name keys.

The Append Cycle

In some applications, you will always want to append a single record and then return to the menu with the "Add a record" option. However, users frequently need to add several records at a time. In that case, here are two possible ways to handle the append cycle:

1. After each record is appended, you present the screen on which the key data for the next new record is entered. If the user enters no key data, control returns to the menu with the "Add a record" option.
2. After each record is appended, you present a small menu offering these choices: "Append a blank record", "Copy the last record to a new record", and "Return to the previous menu".

A Full-Screen Submenu for Editing

In some cases, the most appropriate service returns the user to the menu offering the "Edit a record" choice following the viewing or editing of a record. However, in other cases you may wish to return the user to a special editing submenu, such as the one shown in Listing 22.2.

Text which is underlined in the listing appears onscreen in alternate colors. This sample menu is available as EditIndS.TEM on the companion diskette.

You can use the trick of @ GET followed by CLEAR GETS to display the name, serial number, and organization onscreen in the currently defined enhanced colors without the SET COLOR TO command and without the necessity of keeping track of color specifications.

Listing 22.2 A Menu for Editing Individual Database Records

```
        Edit Submenu for Processing Individual People Database Records

 Serial Number 1345
          Name Sam Smith
  Organization Smith and Sons, Limited

  E   Edit this record.
  S   Show this record on the screen in summary form.
  P   Print this record in summary form.

  N   Edit another record.
  A   Add a new record.

  \   Move to previous record in surname order.
  /   Move to next record in surname order.

  .   Return to previous menu.

  Your Pleasure of E, S, P, N, A, \, /, . █
```

A Bottom-Line Editing Submenu

There is an alternate approach to the one in the preceding section which has achieved a certain amount of popularity among dBASE dialect programmers. In this approach, we collapse the menu part of the screen in the preceding listing to a single line, such as:

Append/Edit/Beginning/Last/Next/Previous/Copy/Delete/Help/Quit █

This line is displayed at the bottom of the screen, and the user's one-keystroke choice is solicited. For example, the user strokes "A" to add a blank record, "C" to add a record with the same data as the current record, "E" to edit the current record, and so on.

The rest of the screen is used to show record data. In the approach used in the last section, the screen only shows three lines of identification information for the current record. Here, all but one line of the screen is available to show record information.

Design of dBASE Pick Lists

For our current purposes, a *pick list* is a list of text items called *picks*, which are displayed onscreen, one below the other, in the same column. For example, if the first pick is displayed at screen coordinates (1,10), then the second pick is at (2,10), the third pick at (3,10), and so on.

There are mechanisms which allow the user to point at a pick and select it. Here, we distinguish between a pick list and a menu with a numbered list of items. With the menu approach, the user enters the number of a pick, and with the pick list approach, the user has a visual means of pointing to a pick.

There are two dBASE contexts in which you may want to present a pick list to a user. The first context is outside of a READ and the second is in an @ GET statement activated by a READ statement. The first context is covered in this chapter, and the second context is covered in Volume 2.

However, before we can discuss the *programming* of dBASE pick lists, we need to know how to *design* a pick list.

The Look of a Pick List

Pick lists are usually presented to the user in a window or in a box with a single-line or double-line border. If the number of picks exceeds the number of lines on which picks can be displayed (inside the box or border), a scrolling mechanism is provided to enable the user to view all possible picks.

The "look" of a pick list is determined by whether it is in a window or a box and by the use of video attributes. When pick lists are displayed on color monitors, you set foreground/background colors for several components: the window or box border, the interior of the window or box where the picks are displayed, and the bar cursor, if any. On monochrome monitors, the video attributes of inverse, underline, and blinking are at your disposal. (In fact, blinking is available for both color and monochrome, but I recommend that you do *not* use blinking characters in pick lists and menus.)

Some pick list implementations also provide you with the ability to assign a letter in each pick which is used to point to a pick. For example, you might list a pick in your program as "Edi~t" instead of "Edit" in order to indicate that the user presses "t" or "T" to point to the Edit pick. Onscreen, the "t" in "Edit" would be in its own color combination, or the "t" would be underlined on a monochrome monitor. Without such a mechanism, the first letters of the picks are used for pointing, unless pointing is limited to the use of arrow keys.

With a window implementation, you would specify the presence or absence of a border shadow. You might also specify a title for the list, to be displayed at the top of the window; such titles are typically embedded in the top border.

The Feel of a Pick List

The "feel" of a pick list is determined by the actions which the user takes to point to picks and to select the current pick. The feel of a pick list also includes the default selection.

There are at least two popular methods for visually indicating the currently selected pick. The first method uses one or two special characters to point to or mark the pick as selected. In the following example, the graphic for the CHR(26) character in the IBM ASCII character set gives the small right-pointing arrow, and the other pointing characters are just the left and right angle brackets.

```
 Smoking
→Nonsmoking
 Don't care
```

```
 Smoking
>Nonsmoking<
 Don't care
```

Notice the width of the box interior in the two variations. The first variation, which has one pointing character, uses three characters plus the number of characters in the widest pick, which is "Nonsmoking" in this example. The second variation has two pointing characters and uses four characters plus the number of characters in the widest pick, which again is "Nonsmoking".

A second way of showing the current pick uses video attributes instead of a pointing character or characters. On monochrome monitors, you indicate the current pick by showing it underlined or in inverse video. On color monitors, you show the current pick with a special color combination.

Pointing

The default pick is pointed to when the pick list is first presented. One or both of two common methods may be implemented to point at a different pick.

The first method uses arrow keys. Pressing DownArrow points at the next pick and pressing UpArrow points to the previous pick.

A fully implemented pick list permits you to point at the picks as if they were arranged in a circle instead of a vertical stack. In these pick lists, pressing DownArrow when the last pick is pointed to will point to the first item; pressing UpArrow when the first pick is pointed to will point to the last item.

A second method uses one character from each pick as a label for that pick. In the first variation of this scheme, the first character in each pick is chosen. In the second variation, the programmer specifies which character in each pick is its label.

The user points to a pick with a given one-character label by stroking the key corresponding to the label. If there are multiple picks with the same label, the user may have to stroke the key corresponding to the label more than once to point at the desired item.

Combined Point and Select

In some cases, you may want to collapse the pointing and selection actions into a single keystroke. In this case, when the user strokes "A", the first choice that starts with "A" is selected; if a second choice starts with "A", the user must move to this choice with the arrow keys and select it with a specified keystroke. One-keystroke point-and-select pick lists tend to be awkward for the user when more than one pick starts with the same letter.

The one-keystroke implementation deprives users of the "pause for reflection." Therefore, it can be appropriate when the actions taken are small in impact and great in frequency, but it is probably not appropriate when the consequences of the actions are large.

For example, when you select record 100 to edit, but you intended to select record 101, you can simply ESCAPE from record 100 and select record 101 instead; little time is lost. In contrast, if a choice triggers the production of a massive report, or an index operation which takes hours, you need a pause for reflection to guard against the unintentional selection of such expensive and/or time-consuming services.

A Dialect-Independent Boxed Pick List

Several dialects have commands or features which support the implementation of pick lists in your programs. For example, dBASE IV has its POPUP facility; Clipper has ACHOICE(); and FoxPro users can use a read-only BROWSE on a field, where the BROWSE table appears in either a system-defined or programmer-defined window.

However, it is possible to write a fairly powerful dialect-independent pick list routine which relies on the InKey() built-in function as its only command whose operation is not necessarily identical across dialects. The action of InKey() is not always reproducible under different dialects, because InKey() simulates multi-tasking under single-tasking operating systems. For this reason, applications which perform complex activities while InKey() is active may respond to keystrokes in an unpredictable way.

On the other hand, this command is implemented in all of the major dialects. Furthermore, it can be used in a conservative and predictable fashion, as shown in Pick.PRG in Listing 22.3 on page 350. This routine waits in the tight loop, DO WHILE (M->KeyPress_N = 0), until a key is pressed and detected with InKey(); then the loop is exited and the keystroke is processed.

Pick.PRG demonstrates a dialect-independent pick list. Due to its reliance on canonical techniques, this routine is easy for programmers and simple for end-users.

Limitations

There are, however, a few limitations. The pick list is passed in a character memvar, which means that you are limited to 254 characters of pick text in dialects with a limit of 254 characters per memvar. In contrast, you can pass an arbitrarily long pick list in the long strings of Clipper and FoxPro.

This pick list does not support scrolling; the size of the box in which the list is displayed is determined by the number of items in the list. You must therefore display the pick list onscreen at a location where all of the items can be listed, and where there is enough room to display the widest item.

Performance

Depending on the dialect, the hardware, and the amount of text in the list, you may encounter performance problems, particularly with larger lists and/or slower dialects. You can speed up the code considerably by using arrays in dialects which support them, although this modification will make the code dialect-dependent.

A dialect-independent modification to increase execution speed at the expense of greater memory usage and more programmer time is to pass the choices as fixed-length elements of a list of character picks, packed into a character memvar. Currently, Pick.PRG accepts a list of variable-length picks in the parameter PackedList, and the list must be parsed in order to extract the pick text between delimiters.

Note that the current implementation of Pick.PRG requires you to pass the pick list in the format "/Cats/Dogs/Birds/". One option is to modify the routine to support the format "Cats Dogs Birds", where each choice is the same length (five characters in this case).

In this modified scheme, you would use an additional parameter, say, ElemWidth, to pass the element width. Inside Pick.PRG, you would refer to element N as SUBSTR(PackedList, ElemWidth*(N – 1) + 1, ElemWidth). Thus, in the current example

"Cats" = TRIM(SUBSTR(PackedList, 1, 5))
"Dogs" = TRIM(SUBSTR(PackedList, 6, 5))
"Birds" = SUBSTR(PackedList, 11, 5)

Computer Speed versus Code Efficiency

There are two ways to speed up a program which runs too slowly — get a faster computer, or make the code more efficient. In the days of multimillion-dollar mainframes with only a few kilobytes of RAM memory, it was almost always more economical to upgrade the code than to upgrade the computer. In today's world, $5,000 might pay for only one month of a programmer's salary and overhead costs, yet $5,000 buys a PC which is at least 10 times or 1,000% faster than an IBM XT, which was state of the art in the rather recent past.

For example, I am currently using a CompuAdd 325 with 2 MB RAM, a 4 MB hardware cache on a 150 MB disk, and 16-bit color VGA, which is a configuration that costs less than $5,000 (Millican 1990). This PC runs FoxBASE+ programs so fast that there is no reason to pseudocompile them!

There are two major software methods for increasing the speed of dBASE dialect applications. The first is to replace the current dialect with a faster dialect, and the second is to replace the current algorithms with faster ones.

There are two kinds of hardware speed-ups available. While you can replace a slow PC with a fast PC, you can also upgrade the components of the slow PC. The cheapest option is to install enough extended RAM to support a large software disk cache; more expensive options are to upgrade the processor with an accelerator card, and to upgrade the disk with a faster model.

Recommendation on speeding up a slow dBASE dialect application. Under the assumption that you are already using one of the faster dialects — see "The dBASE Shootout" (Goley 1989a) and "The Benchmarks Revisited" (Streich and Kalman 1990) — make an estimate of how much time it would take you to convert an application's slow algorithms to fast ones. Convert this time estimate to a money estimate; remember to add the so-called *opportunity costs* of *not* programming new applications which could bring extra income to you, your employers, or your clients. For example, you might compute $10,000 in direct costs and $15,000 in opportunity costs, for a total cost estimate of $25,000.

Then compare this cost estimate to the cost of upgrading the hardware on which the slow application executes. In some cases, the most cost-effective solution will be to upgrade the hardware and leave the code as it is!

The Listings

Here is the listing for Pick.PRG, which displays an unboxed pick list onscreen. Pick.PRG calls the utility routines RecogEnv.PRG and Tokens.PRG, which are called by many routines, and the service subroutine PickNext.PRG, which is specific to Pick.PRG. RecogEnv.PRG is listed on page 307 and Tokens.PRG and PickNext.PRG are listed after Pick.PRG.

After we understand how Pick.PRG and its subroutines provide an unboxed pick list, we will implement a boxed pick list with PickBox.PRG, which calls Pick.PRG.

Listing 22.3 Pick.PRG—A Dialect-Independent Pick List Routine

```
* File = Pick.PRG.  Called from several .PRG.

* Pick.PRG implements a dialect-independent pick list.  The picks are displayed
* onscreen in a vertical list, with each pick starting in column StartCol; the
* first pick is on row StartRow.  The selected item is indicated by the
* IBM ASCII character with an onscreen representation of a right arrow,
* CHR(26), which is always displayed in column StartCol-1.  The pick which is
* first pointed to when the list is displayed is specified by the parameter
* FirstChoic.

* There is no scrolling.  You must pass a list of picks which can be
* displayed onscreen between StartRow and the bottom of the screen.

* The pick items are passed in a character argument to PackedList, with the
* first character of PackedList taken as the delimiter character.  PackedList
* is of the form <delimiter><pick text><delimiter><pick text> ... <delimiter>
* Example: /Accounts/Database/Word Processing/

* The user points to an item by entering the first character of the pick:
* in the example, "A" for "Accounts", "D" for "Database", and so on.  A single
* keystroke is made: "A", not "A" followed by ENTER.

* The list is circular.  For example, if all the items start with "K", then
* stroking "K" repeatedly moves the onscreen pointer from the first item to the
* second item, third item, ..., to the last item and back to the first.

* Pointing is not case-sensitive.  For example, if you have two choices on the
* list named "Accounts 1" and "accounts 2", then stroking "A" the requisite
* number of times will point to either pick.

* The user selects an item by entering a character in parameter ExitList.
* For example, to allow selection by the space bar or ESCAPE, pass
* SPACE(1)+CHR(27) to ExitList.

* The pick is returned in the form of the pick text itself, passed in output
```

```
* parameter PickText.
* Example.  The following call displays a 3-item list in the form
*    Smoking
*    Nonsmoking
*    Don't Care
* where the "S" in "Smoking" is at row 10 and column 40.  The user points to
* the choices by stroking "S" or "s", "N" or "n", or "D" or "d", and selects
* the current pick by stroking the ESCAPE key.
*-----------------------------------------------------------------------------
* Option_C = ""
* DO Pick WITH "/Smoking/Nonsmoking/Don't Care/",10,40,CHR(27),Option_C
*-----------------------------------------------------------------------------
******************************************************************************
* Input parameters:
* PackedList, character.  Delimiter-separated list of picks.
* FirstChoic, numeric.    Ordinal of pick which is default selection.
* StartRow, numeric.      Row of box top.
* StartCol, numeric.      Column of left edge of box.
* ExitList, character.    Characters permitted as selection keystrokes.
* Output parameter:
* PickText, character.  The text of the pick selected by the user.
******************************************************************************
* Input assumptions:
* 1. PackedList is of the format given in the comments above.
* 2. StartRow represents a row which is available in the current video mode.
* 3. StartCol represents a column which is available in the current video mode.
* 4. ExitList is of type character.
* 5. LEN(ExitList) > 0.
* 6. The number of items in PackedList can be displayed in available space.
* 7. The following routines are available as command files or procedures:
*    RecogEnv, Tokens, PickNext.
* Output conditions:
* 1. PickText contains the text of the selected list item.
******************************************************************************
PARAMETERS PackedList,FirstChoic,StartRow,StartCol,ExitList,PickText
******************************************************************************
* Determine whether we pass input/output memvar arguments as M->OutParm or
* OutParm:
PUBLIC PassNoM_L  && True if we must "DO Proc WITH OutParm"
DO RecogEnv  && Set value for PUBLIC memvar PassNoM_L.
******************************************************************************
PRIVATE ArrowChar,Delimiter,DownArrowN,KeyPress_C,KeyPress_N,KeyPressUC,;
    ListLength,Loop_L,mRow,mCol,Ndex_C,Ordinal,P1,P2,Token,UpArrow_N
ArrowChar  = CHR(26)
Delimiter  = SUBSTR(M->PackedList,1,1)
DownArrowN = 24
ListLength = 0
Ordinal    = 0
UpArrow_N  = 5
************************************ Unpack list into simulated PRIVATE array:
Ndex_C = "0"
P1     = 1
P2     = 1
Token  = ""
DO WHILE (M->P2 < LEN(M->PackedList))
   IF PassNoM_L
      DO Tokens WITH M->PackedList,M->Delimiter,P2,Token
   ELSE
      DO Tokens WITH M->PackedList,M->Delimiter,M->P2,M->Token
   ENDIF
   Ndex_C = LTRIM( STR( VAL(M->Ndex_C)+1 ) ) && Increment the character index.
   PRIVATE Token&Ndex_C
   *   STORE M->Token TO M->Token&Ndex_C
   Token&Ndex_C = M->Token
ENDDO
```

```
************ Now display the list vertically, starting at the specified screen
* coordinates:
ListLength = VAL(M->Ndex_C)
mRow       = M->StartRow
mCol       = M->StartCol
Ndex_C     = "1"
DO WHILE (VAL(M->Ndex_C) <= M->ListLength)
   @ M->mRow,M->StartCol SAY M->Token&Ndex_C
   mRow   = M->mRow + 1
   Ndex_C = LTRIM( STR( VAL(M->Ndex_C)+1 ) ) && Increment the character index.
ENDDO
****************************************************** Point to first choice.
Ordinal = FirstChoic
@ M->StartRow-1 + M->Ordinal,M->StartCol-1 SAY M->ArrowChar

*****************************************************************************
* Execute this loop once for each user keystroke.  Action: either select
* current pick with a character in ExitList, or point to a pick (DO PickNext).
Loop_L = .T.
DO WHILE (M->Loop_L)

   KeyPress_N = 0
   DO WHILE (M->KeyPress_N = 0)
      KeyPress_N = InKey()
   ENDDO
   KeyPress_C = CHR(  M->KeyPress_N)
   KeyPressUC = UPPER(M->KeyPress_C)

   * Have received keystroke code.
   IF (M->KeyPress_C $ M->ExitList)
      Loop_L   = .F.
      Ndex_C   = LTRIM(STR( M->Ordinal ))
      PickText = M->Token&Ndex_C
   ELSE
      DO CASE
     CASE (M->KeyPress_N = M->DownArrowN)
        Ordinal = IIF(M->Ordinal = 1, M->ListLength, M->Ordinal - 1)

     CASE (M->KeyPress_N = M->UpArrow_N)
        Ordinal = IIF(M->Ordinal = M->ListLength, 1, M->Ordinal + 1)

     CASE (M->Delimiter + M->KeyPress_C $ M->PackedList) .OR. ;
          (M->Delimiter + M->KeyPressUC $ M->PackedList)
        * If keystroke does not correspond to pick first letter, leave
        * pointer where it is.  Else move pointer to next-in-circular-sense
        * pick with first letter of pick = keypress.

        @ M->StartRow-1 + M->Ordinal,M->StartCol-1 SAY SPACE(1)

        IF PassNoM_L
           DO PickNext WITH M->ListLength,M->KeyPress_C,Ordinal
        ELSE
           DO PickNext WITH M->ListLength,M->KeyPress_C,M->Ordinal
        ENDIF

        @ M->StartRow-1 + M->Ordinal,M->StartCol-1 SAY M->ArrowChar

      ENDCASE
   ENDIF
ENDDO

* End of Pick.PRG.
```

Listing 22.4 Tokens.PRG—A Dialect-Independent Token Extractor Routine

```
* File = Tokens.PRG.  Called from several .PRG.
******************************************************************************
* Dialects: All.
******************************************************************************
* This subroutine is used to parse tokens from a stream of characters.  A token
* is defined as a string which lies between two delimiter characters and which
* does not contain a delimiter character.  For the purposes of this
* definition, a delimiter character is assumed to start and end the data
* stream.  This subroutine does in fact require a delimiter at the end of
* the data stream passed in the character parameter DataStream, but no
* delimiter character is required at the start of the data.  The parameter
* Delimiters is a character string which contains all of the delimiter
* characters for your parsing situation.
*   The input/output parameter P2 is used to keep track of how much of the
* data stream has been processed; it points to the beginning of the data
* stream, or to a delimiter character immediately following a token.  The
* output parameter Token returns the token whose terminal delimiter is
* SubStr(DataStream,P2,1).
*   This subroutine is called in a loop in order to get the tokens from the
* data stream; one token is delivered with each call.  The caller uses a loop
* of the following form.
*    P2 = 1
*    Token =  ""
*    DO WHILE (P2 < LEN(DataStream))
*       DO Tokens WITH DataStream,<delimiter string>,P2,Token
*       <process Token>
*    ENDDO
******************************************************************************
* Input parameters:
* DataStream, character.  Holds character strings from which tokens to be
*                         extracted.
* Delimiters, character.  Holds set of delimiters for tokens.
******************************************************************************
* Input/output parameter:
* P2, numeric.  Set to 1 to start; thereafter, set to first delimiter following
*               previous token.
******************************************************************************
* Output parameter:
* Token, character.  Call n to Tokens returns the nth token in DataStream.
******************************************************************************
* Input assumptions not verified:
* 1. IF (P2 > 1) THEN SubStr(DataStream,P2,1) $ Delimiters
* 2. SubStr(DataStream,Len(DataStream),1) $ Delimiters
* 3. IF (there is at least one token) THEN
*       SubStr(DataStream,Len(DataStream)-1,1) not $ Delimiters

* Output conditions:
* 1. IF (P2 < LEN(DataStream)) THEN Token = SubStr(DataStream,P1,P2-1)
* 2. IF (P2 > 1) THEN SubStr(DataStream,P2,1) $ Delimiters
******************************************************************************

PARAMETERS DataStream,Delimiters,P2,Token
PRIVATE P1

IF (M->P2 < LEN(M->DataStream))
   * Initial position of P2 is 1 or on delimiter character between tokens.
   * Find start of next token.  Remember that DataStream ends with exactly
   * one delimiter character.  If P2 points to that character, the IF
   * statement doesn't let us execute the following loop.
   DO WHILE (SubStr(M->DataStream,M->P2,1) $ Delimiters)
      P2 = M->P2 + 1
   ENDDO

   P1 = M->P2
   DO WHILE (.NOT. (SubStr(M->DataStream,M->P2,1) $ M->Delimiters) )
      P2 = M->P2 + 1
   ENDDO
```

```
   Token = SubStr(M->DataStream, M->P1, M->P2 - M->P1)
ELSE
   Token =  ""
ENDIF
* End of Tokens.PRG.
```

Listing 22.5 PickNext.PRG—An Auxiliary Routine for Pick.PRG

```
* File = PickNext.PRG.  Called from Pick.PRG to move pointer to the next pick,
* if any, that has the keystroke as its first character.  The MOD function is
* used to make the list "circular" so that the first item follows the last
* item.  The list items are defined in Pick.PRG as Token1, Token2, ...,
* Token&ListLength.
*   The search is case-insensitive as coded; use the alternate form of the IF
* shown below to make the search case-sensitive.
******************************************************************************
* Input parameters:
* ListLength, numeric.  Length of list of picks.
* KeyPress_C, Character, length 1.  Letter entered by user for next pick.
******************************************************************************
* Input/Output parameter:
* Ordinal, numeric.  At entry: Ordinal in list of current pick.
*                    At  exit: Ordinal in list of new pick.
******************************************************************************
PARAMETERS ListLength,KeyPress_C,Ordinal
PRIVATE Loop_L,Ndex_C,Ntries
* Do not select current selection the first time.
Loop_L  = .T.
Ntries  = 0
DO WHILE (M->Ntries < M->ListLength) .AND. M->Loop_L
   Ordinal = MOD(M->Ordinal, M->ListLength) + 1
   Ndex_C  = LTRIM(STR(M->Ordinal))
   * To make pointing case-sensitive, use
   *IF (M->KeyPress_C = SubStr(M->Token&Ndex_C,1,1))
   IF (UPPER(M->KeyPress_C) = UPPER(SubStr(M->Token&Ndex_C,1,1)) )
      Loop_L = .F.
   ELSE
      Ntries = M->Ntries + 1
   ENDIF
ENDDO
* End of PickNext.PRG.
```

When Pick.PRG is entered, the first task is to determine which dialect is executing the code. Subroutine RecogEnv is called to set a PUBLIC memvar which determines the use of "M->" in arguments. This subroutine is listed on page 307.

The next task is to store the text for the picks into memvars which simulate array elements, namely, Token1, Token2, and so on. Note the technique of declaring the memvars inside the loop. Without this PRIVATE Token&Ndex_C statement, Token1 might refer to a variable which was defined in another routine. (Alternatively, you could list Token1, Token2, ..., in a series of PRIVATE statements until you had declared the maximum number of Token<n> memvars which you think might ever be needed. This approach limits the subroutine and fills the symbol table with usually useless entries. It also clutters the subroutine listing and is not recommended.)

Then Pick.PRG shows the picks at the specified location and positions the onscreen pointing character at the specified default pick. The remaining action is to process keystrokes to move the pointer or to select the current pick.

The utility routine Tokens.PRG is used to extract the picks from the packed list in which they are passed, and PickNext is used to process pointing keystrokes. See the programmer documentation in the code listings for more information.

Now enter the code for Pick and its subroutines into files on your hard disk, or copy these routines from the book's companion diskette (see Appendix A). You may test the routine with a code sequence as simple as the following one. This sequence should display a list with three choices, starting at row 1 and listing each choice starting in column 10. You stroke "C" or "c" for Cat, "D" or "d" for Dog, and "H" or "h" for Horse; stroke the space bar to select the current pick.

```
PickText =  ""
DO Pick WITH  "/Cat/Dog/Horse/",3,1,10,SPACE(1),PickText
? PickText
```

Putting the Picks in a Box

Now that we understand how the pick list works, we can add the cosmetic but nontrivial details of setting colors and drawing a box around the pick list. We do this with the command file, PickBox.PRG, which appears in Listing 22.6.

Listing 22.6 PickBox.PRG—A Dialect-Independent Boxed Pick List

```
* File = PickBox.PRG.  Called from several .PRG to make boxed pick list,
* using the dialect-independent Pick.PRG.
******************************************************************************
* This subroutine adds the ability to draw boxes around the pick lists
* which are generated with Pick.PRG.  See that subroutine for an explanation
* of all of the parameters of PickBox except BoxTitle, ColorsBox, ColorsIn,
* and ColorsOut.  Color specifications are only used if non-null.
******************************************************************************
* Subroutines called:
* Pick.PRG, dialect-independent; handles interior of box and selection details.
* RecogEnv, dialect-independent; to recognize the dialect.
******************************************************************************
* Input parameters:
* PackedList, Character.  See Pick.PRG.
* FirstChoic, numeric.    Ordinal of pick which is default selection.
* StartRow, numeric.      Row of box top.
* StartCol, numeric.      Column of left side of box.
* BoxTitle, character.    Title placed at top of box.
* ColorsBox, character.   Color specification for border.
* ColorsIn, character.    Color specification for interior of box.
* ColorsOut, character.   Color specification set at exit.
* ExitList, character.    See Pick.PRG.

* Output parameter:
* PickText, character.  See Pick.PRG.
******************************************************************************

PARAMETERS ; && Write the parameters on one line in dBASE III PLUS.
PackedList,FirstChoic,StartRow,StartCol,BoxTitle,;
ColorsBox,ColorsIn,ColorsOut,ExitList,PickText

******************************************************************************
* Determine whether we pass input/output parameters as M->OutParm or OutParm:
PUBLIC PassNoM_L  && True if we DO Proc WITH OutParm
DO RecogEnv  && Set value for PUBLIC memvar PassNoM_L.

******************************************************************************
PRIVATE Delimiter,Gap,ListLength,MaxWidth,P,P1

******************************************************************************
* Determine length of list.  There are N+1 delimiters in a list with N
```

```
* items, so we use  "<" and not  "<=" in the loop and don't count the last
* delimiter.
Delimiter  = SubStr(M->PackedList,1,1)
ListLength = 0  && First character assumed to be delimiter.
P          = 2  && Assume that list is not empty.
P1         = 1  && Point to first delimiter.
MaxWidth   = 0
DO WHILE (M->P <= LEN(M->PackedList))
   IF (SubStr(M->PackedList,M->P,1) = M->Delimiter)
      MaxWidth   = MAX(M->MaxWidth, M->P - M->P1 - 1)
      P1         = M->P  && Advance P1 to the current delimiter.
      ListLength = M->ListLength + 1
   ENDIF
   P = M->P + 1
ENDDO
*******************************************************************************
* Set any specified box border colors and draw the double-line border.
IF (LEN(M->ColorsBox) > 0)
   SET COLOR TO &ColorsBox
ENDIF
@ M->StartRow, M->StartCol TO ;
  M->StartRow+M->ListLength+1, M->StartCol+M->MaxWidth+2 DOUBLE
*******************************************************************************
* Display the box title centered on the top border:
Gap = 3 + M->MaxWidth - LEN(M->BoxTitle)
IF (M->Gap <= 0)
   @ M->StartRow, M->StartCol SAY SubStr(M->BoxTitle, 1, 3 + M->MaxWidth)
ELSE
   @ M->StartRow, M->StartCol + INT( M->Gap/2 ) SAY M->BoxTitle
ENDIF
*******************************************************************************
* Color the inside of the box if interior colors are specified:
IF (LEN(M->ColorsIn) > 0)
   SET COLOR TO &ColorsIn
   @ M->StartRow+1, M->StartCol+1 CLEAR TO ;
     M->StartRow+M->ListLength, M->StartCol+M->MaxWidth+1
ENDIF
*******************************************************************************
* Display the pick list now:
IF PassNoM_L
   DO Pick WITH ;
   M->PackedList,M->FirstChoic,M->StartRow+1,M->StartCol+2,M->ExitList,PickText
ELSE
   DO Pick WITH ;
      M->PackedList,M->FirstChoic,M->StartRow+1,M->StartCol+2,M->ExitList,;
      M->PickText
ENDIF
*******************************************************************************
* Reset the colors, if a reset color string is specified:
IF (LEN(M->ColorsOut) > 0)
   SET COLOR TO &ColorsOut
ENDIF
* End of PickBox.PRG.
```

When PickBox.PRG is entered, the first task is to determine which dialect is executing the code. Subroutine RecogEnv is called to set a PUBLIC memvar which determines the use of "M->" in arguments.

Then a loop determines the number of picks and the widest pick in the list; this information is needed to set the box dimensions. The @ TO command is used to draw a double-lined box around the area where the picks will be displayed, and then Pick is called to display the picks and get the user's choice.

Note the technique to control color. If you are in a hurry, leave the color strings null. Color combinations will stay the same before, during, and after the pick list.

If you pass a color specification for the box border (ColorsBox), you only need to pass the first color combination, as in "R/N", but not "R/N,G/B" or "R/N,G/B,BG" — assuming that you pass enhanced colors and a border color in at least one of ColorsIn or ColorsOut. If you pass "" to both ColorsIn and ColorsOut, then the colors after the pick list will be those set with ColorsBox.

The colors which are set after the pick list are those in the last of the parameters ColorsBox, ColorsIn, and ColorsOut which are not empty. ColorsIn, if not empty, sets the colors in the interior of the box, and ColorsOut, if not empty, sets the colors to be used after the pick list is displayed. As with ColorsBox, you need only specify the first color pair for ColorsIn, but you should specify the standard colors, enhanced colors, and border color in ColorsOut, if one or both of ColorsBox and ColorsIn are not empty.

The other arguments are passed as documented in the listing for PickBox.PRG. To test this routine, you can type the driver in Listing 22.7 or load it from the companion diskette for Volume 1. This driver displays a four-item pick list, starting on row 1 at column 10, with a red-on-black double-line border; bright-green-on-white picks; and, on exit, yellow-on-blue standard colors, blue-on-green enhanced colors, and a cyan border. The initial pick is "Nonsmoking" and the final pick is shown onscreen at row 20 following return from Pick.PRG.

Listing 22.7 PickTest.PRG

```
* File = PickTest.PRG.  Called from the dot prompt to test Pick & PickBox.
*****************************************************************************
* Dialects: dBASE III PLUS, dBASE IV, dBXL, FoxBASE+, FoxPro.
* Make modification indicated below for Clipper and Quicksilver.
*****************************************************************************

SET Safety OFF
SET Talk OFF

PUBLIC FOX
* To compile in Clipper or Quicksilver, remove or comment out this IF statement:
IF FOX
   ClearCmd =  'CLEAR PROGRAM'
   &ClearCmd
ENDIF

CLEAR

PL =  "/Smoking/Nonsmoking/Don't Care/Don't know/"
Picktext =  ""
DO PickBox WITH PL,2,1,10,"Smoke?","R/N","G+/W","GR+/B,B/G,BG",SPACE(1),PickText
@ 20, 0 SAY  "User selection:" + PickText

SET Safety ON
SET Talk ON

* End of PickTest.PRG.
```

Dialect-Independent Menus

The Millican main menu and submenu templates in Part III (see page 257 and following) help you to implement dialect-independent menus using @ GET with READ. The pick list we looked at earlier in this chapter is also dialect-independent; it depends on the INKEY() function which is implemented in all the major dialects.

With more effort, the dialect-independent pick list routine we developed could be upgraded to support a moving-bar pointing method, the use of arrow keys, and a scrolling feature to support more picks than can be displayed at once in the box. In the case of arrow keys, we might have to introduce a CASE statement based on the dialect memvars set in RecogEnv.PRG in order to recognize the keystrokes from the INKEY() code.

There is no barrier in the dBASE programming language to constructing dialect-independent routines to offer the services of some of the menu-oriented, dialect-specific commands that we'll look at in the rest of this chapter. *However, dialect-independent routines may perform with problematically slow speed.*

Controlling Colors in Menus

All dialects offer the ISCOLOR() built-in function and the SET COLOR TO command for basic control of video attributes on monochrome and color monitors. dBASE IV and FoxPro implement additional color-control commands.

In these dialects, you can use the following routine (or one like it) to control the colors of parts of user-defined menus. The actual colors specified are for example only; you may change them as appropriate. You may wish to modify ColorSet to receive arguments, so that you can pass the individual colors to this routine. (ColorSet is used in some of the examples below.)

Listing 22.8 ColorSet.PRG—Control Colors of User-Defined Menus

```
* File = ColorSet.PRG.  Called from several .PRG to control colors for
* user-defined menu objects in dBASE IV and FoxPro.
PUBLIC FoxPro_L  && initialize this memvar to ("FOXPRO" $ UPPER(VERSION()) )
PRIVATE Command
* FoxPro permits you to control the colors of parts of user-defined menus with
* SET COLOR OF SCHEME 2 TO ,<unselected options>,<border>,,<message>,
* <selected option>
IF FoxPro_L
   IF IsColor()
      Command =  "SET COLOR OF SCHEME 2 TO ,B+/BG,B/G,,W+/G,BG+/B"
      &Command   && Done this way to avoid dBASE IV compilation error.
   ENDIF
ELSE
   IF IsColor()
      SET COLOR OF BOX        TO B/G     && Border colors.
      SET COLOR OF HIGHLIGHT  TO BG+/B   && Selected option.
      SET COLOR OF MESSAGES   TO B+/BG   && Top-line menu bar color;
                                       && unselected options; MESSAGEs.
   ENDIF
   SET MESSAGE TO  && Otherwise, any already-defined message is NOT replaced!
ENDIF
* End of ColorSet.PRG.
```

Point-and-Shoot Menus

The dialect-independent pick list we saw earlier in this chapter implements a point-and-shoot menu to pick one choice from a list of choices. If the picks are in database fields, then BROWSE FIELDS <field name> NOMODIFY works as an unboxed pick list, with pointing by arrow keys and selection by ESCAPE.

The MENU TO Facility: Menus

Clipper, FoxBASE+, and FoxPro offer the very nice MENU TO facility, which is used to implement menus and pick lists. This facility consists of three commands that are used in combination: SET MESSAGE TO, @ PROMPT ... MESSAGE, and MENU TO.

The @ PROMPT and MENU TO commands are analogous to the @ GET and READ commands. A set of @ PROMPT commands displays the choices onscreen, and the choices are "activated" with MENU TO.

The menu method supported, often used for commercial software, is sometimes called the "Lotus-style" menu method, in reference to the leading 1-2-3 spreadsheet product from Lotus Corporation. The Lotus-style menu displays one or more rows of choices which are selected with a bar cursor; that is, a special color combination is used to indicate the item currently pointed to. A nearby area onscreen optionally displays a description of the item being pointed to.

MENU TO supports single-line descriptions of choices. These choices are displayed starting in column 0 of the row specified in "SET MESSAGE TO <screen row>". The optional descriptive text for each prompt is specified in the MESSAGE clause of the @ PROMPT command.

Listing 22.9 shows an example of the first type of usage. In this example, the choices are displayed on screen line 0. Lines 1 and 3 display a double rule, and line 2 displays the MESSAGE for each PROMPT.

The use of relative addressing in the prompts causes them to be displayed with a space between each prompt. To have an equal amount of screen space for each choice, pad the choices with blanks so that they are of the same length.

The MENU TO Facility: Pick Lists

The second way of using the MENU TO facility allows you to implement a boxed pick list. In contrast to PickBox.PRG above, pick lists implemented with MENU TO appear onscreen without appreciable delay.

The operation of MENU TO is somewhat different from that of PickBox.PRG and Pick.PRG. First, MENU TO supports the arrow keys, whereas Pick.PRG only permits you to point by entering the first letters of the picks. When you use a pick list implemented with Pick.PRG, you make at least one keystroke to point at a pick, and you make a second keystroke to select the pick at which you point.

Listing 22.9 MenuTo2.PRG—A Lotus-Style Moving-Bar Menu with MENU TO

```
* File = MenuTo2.PRG.  Called from the dot prompt to demonstrate the MENU TO
* facility in Clipper, FoxBASE+, and FoxPro.  This demo shows how to implement
* a Lotus-style top-line moving-bar menu with short explanations on one screen
* line.

SET Safety OFF
SET Talk OFF
CLEAR

PRIVATE Choice_N,Code

SET MESSAGE TO 2
@ 1,0 SAY REPLICATE(CHR(205),80)
@ 3,0 SAY REPLICATE(CHR(205),80)

@ 0    , 0      PROMPT "Smoking"    MESSAGE "Smoking section"
@ Row(), COL()+1 PROMPT "Nonsmoking" MESSAGE "Nonsmoking section"
@ Row(), COL()+1 PROMPT "Don't care" MESSAGE "Smoking or Nonsmoking section"
@ Row(), COL()+1 PROMPT "Don't know" MESSAGE "To be determined later"

MENU TO Choice_N

DO CASE
   CASE (Choice_N = 1)
      Code = "S"

   CASE (Choice_N = 2)
      Code = "N"

   CASE (Choice_N = 3)
      Code = "DC"

   CASE (Choice_N = 4)
      Code = "DK"

   OTHERWISE
      Code = "undefined"
ENDCASE

@ 5, 0 SAY "Code = " + Code
? "Choice_N = ", Choice_N

SET Safety ON
SET Talk ON

* End of MenuTo2.PRG.
```

MENU TO collapses the point-and-select process to a single keystroke. If two picks begin with "A", pressing "A" always selects the first of the two picks. If you want the second pick beginning with "A", you must use the arrow keys to point to it and then stroke ENTER to select it. With Pick.PRG, you may stroke "A" repeatedly to point at the choices beginning with "A" in a cycle from first to last and back to first. Listing 22.10 presents a pick list implemented with MENU TO.

The DEFINE POPUP Facility

The multiple-personality DEFINE POPUP facility in dBASE IV and FoxPro gives you three kinds of pick lists and a general menu facility comparable to that of MENU TO. Items are pointed to with a bar cursor; you may point by entering the first character of a choice or by using the arrow keys. You select the current choice with ENTER and you may exit the POPUP without making a choice by stroking ESCAPE.

Listing 22.10 MenuTo.PRG—A Pick List with MENU TO

```
* File = MenuTo.PRG.  Called from the dot prompt to demonstrate the MENU TO
* command in Clipper, FoxBASE+, and FoxPro.  This program shows how to use
* MENU TO to implement pick lists.

SET Safety OFF
SET Talk OFF
CLEAR

PRIVATE Choice_N,Code

SET MESSAGE TO 9
@ 4,9 TO 9,21 DOUBLE

@ 4       , 12 SAY     "Smoke?"
@ Row()+1, 10 PROMPT "Smoking"
@ Row()+1, 10 PROMPT "Nonsmoking"
@ Row()+1, 10 PROMPT "Don't care"
@ Row()+1, 10 PROMPT "Don't know"

MENU TO Choice_N

DO CASE
   CASE (Choice_N = 1)
      Code = "S"

   CASE (Choice_N = 2)
      Code = "N"

   CASE (Choice_N = 3)
      Code = "DC"

   CASE (Choice_N = 4)
      Code = "DK"

   OTHERWISE
      Code = "undefined"
ENDCASE

@ 10, 0 SAY "Code = " + Code
? "Choice_N = ", Choice_N

SET Safety ON
SET Talk ON

* End of MenuTo.PRG.
```

Instructions

The DEFINE POPUP facility consists of the following commands and functions: ACTIVATE POPUP, BAR(), CLEAR POPUPS, DEACTIVATE POPUP, DEFINE BAR, DEFINE POPUP, ON SELECTION POPUP, POPUP(), PROMPT(), RELEASE POPUPS, SET BORDER TO with the COLOR commands, and SET MESSAGE TO. The ways in which these commands and functions are combined to produce pick lists are shown below in POPUP1.PRG (page 363); menu functionality is demonstrated below with POPUP2.PRG (page 366).

The color commands are also involved in controlling the colors or other video attributes of onscreen menu components. All of the dialects give you the "SET COLOR TO <standard>, <enhanced>, <screen border>" command. FoxPro and dBASE IV give you the SET COLOR OF BOX, SET COLOR OF HIGHLIGHT, and SET COLOR OF MESSAGES commands, which are explained in the following list. FoxPro also offers you the SET COLOR OF SCHEME facility to control onscreen colors with very fine granularity.

To make a pick list with the POPUP facility, do the following:

1. If the default border is not satisfactory, use the SET BORDER TO command to set the border to a single line, a double line, a solid bar, or a custom box using your specified characters.
2. If the default or current colors are not satisfactory, specify colors for parts of the menu, as follows. In dBASE IV, use the commands SET COLOR OF BOX, SET COLOR OF HIGHLIGHT, and SET COLOR OF MESSAGES to control the colors of the border, selected option, and unselected options, respectively. In FoxPro, use the command "SET COLOR OF SCHEME 2 TO , <unselected options>, <border>,, <message>, <selected option>". (See the listing of ColorSet.PRG on page 358 for more information.)
3. Use the DEFINE POPUP command to name the POPUP object and define its placement onscreen. Use the PROMPT clause to define the kind of pick list you want.
4. If you want a message to appear when the pick list is displayed, then use the MESSAGE clause in DEFINE POPUP. This message (of up to 79 characters) will display on the line specified in SET MESSAGE TO <screen row>.
5. Code an ON SELECTION command to process the user's pick after the POPUP is displayed. This command is usually DO <subroutine>, where the subroutine contains a DEACTIVATE POPUP command immediately preceding the RETURN command.
6. You may now initiate the pick list dialog with the user by executing the "ACTIVATE POPUP <POPUP name>" command.
7. When the pick list has been displayed and the user has stroked ENTER or ESCAPE, use the DEACTIVATE POPUP command to remove the pick list from the screen; any text which was hidden by the pick list is again visible.
8. The function BAR() returns the ordinal of the pick. The function PROMPT() returns the text of the pick. The function POPUP() returns the name of the active POPUP.
9. POPUPs are data structures which use memory. Use RELEASE POPUPS <POPUP name> to remove a POPUP definition from memory; use RELEASE POPUPS to release all POPUP definitions.
10. Alternatively, leave the POPUP defined and ACTIVATE it again with the same or a new ON SELECTION command.

The usage pattern for POPUPs which are used as menus is quite similar.

1. Use the SET BORDER TO and COLOR commands as desired.
2. Use the DEFINE POPUP command without the PROMPT clause and optionally with the MESSAGE clause.
3. If you use the MESSAGE clause, set the line on which the message is displayed with the SET MESSAGE TO command.
4. Follow the DEFINE POPUP command with one DEFINE BAR command for each option in the POPUP menu. Use the screen coordinates in the DEFINE BAR command to place each option anywhere onscreen that you

like. You may have the options appear in a horizontal row or rows, in a vertical row or rows, or in any other arrangement you like. There is no scrolling: the position of each option must be explicitly specified by available onscreen coordinates.

5. Code an ON SELECTION command to process the user's pick after the POPUP menu is shown.
6. Display the menu to the user with the "ACTIVATE POPUP <POPUP name>" command.
7. When the menu has been displayed and the user has stroked ENTER or ESCAPE, use the DEACTIVATE POPUP command to remove the menu from the screen; any text which was hidden by the menu is again visible.
8. The function BAR() returns the bar number of the menu choice. The function PROMPT() returns the text of the pick. The function POPUP() returns the name of the POPUP.
9. If you don't need the POPUP after its use, release its memory with "RELEASE POPUPS <POPUP name>". Otherwise, you may optionally code another ON SELECTION command before using the POPUP menu again with ACTIVATE POPUP.

Creating Pick Lists with the DEFINE POPUP Facility

We look now at the three types of pick lists which are supported by the DEFINE POPUP facility: lists of file names in specified directories, lists of field names in the current database, and lists of field values in the current database.

Examples

The program POPUP1.PRG in Listing 22.11 demonstrates POPUP pick lists in dBASE IV and FoxPro. Execute POPUP1 to see four pick lists displayed using three POPUPs.

Listing 22.11 POPUP1.PRG—Pick Lists for Files and Fields with POPUPs

```
* File = POPUP1.PRG.  Called from the dot prompt to demonstrate the pick
* list features of the POPUP facility in dBASE IV and FoxPro.

CLEAR
SET Safety OFF
SET Talk OFF

SET BORDER TO PANEL && Default border is single line without SET BORDER.
DEFINE POPUP  FileList FROM 5,5 PROMPT FILES LIKE *.DBF
SET BORDER TO DOUBLE
DEFINE POPUP  Fields   FROM 5,5 PROMPT STRUCTURE
SET BORDER TO CHR(31),CHR(30),CHR(16),CHR(17),CHR(1),CHR(2),CHR(11),CHR(12)
DEFINE POPUP  Names    FROM 5,5 PROMPT FIELD Customer->Name
SET BORDER TO && Restore default border.
*****************************************************************************
?  "Press <ENTER> to select an item."
?  "Press <ESCAPE> to close the POPUP window."
ON SELECTION POPUP FileList ?  "The selected file is  " + PROMPT()
```

```
ACTIVATE   POPUP FileList
DEACTIVATE POPUP && Erase the POPUP window.
WAIT
******************************************************************************
Fname =  ""
ON SELECTION POPUP FileList   DO PoppedUp WITH Fname
ACTIVATE POPUP FileList
?  "The selected file is  " + Fname
?  "Notice that the POPUP window closed after you selected a file."
RELEASE POPUPS FileList  && Release the memory occupied by the POPUP definition.
WAIT
******************************************************************************
USE Customer
?  "Now let's see what fields we have in the Customer database:"
FieldName =  ""
ON SELECTION POPUP Fields   DO PoppedUp WITH FieldName
ACTIVATE POPUP Fields
?  "The selected field is  " + FieldName
RELEASE POPUPS Fields  && Release the memory occupied by the POPUP definition.
WAIT
******************************************************************************
?  "Now let's see what names we have in the Customer database:"
Cname =  ""
ON SELECTION POPUP Names   DO PoppedUp WITH Cname
ACTIVATE POPUP Names
?  "Selected customer is  " + Cname
WAIT
******************************************************************************
RELEASE POPUPS  && Release all currently defined POPUPs.
CLOSE ALL
SET Safety ON
SET Talk ON
******************************************************************************
* This FUNCTION cannot be used in dBASE IV 1.0 and FoxPro 1.0, because the
* DEACTIVATE POPUP command causes immediate return with  "" returned.
* Thus, you cannot use the command
* ON SELECTION POPUP FileList   Fname = PoppedUp()
*  FUNCTION PoppedUp
*  PRIVATE P
*  P = PROMPT()
*  DEACTIVATE POPUP
*  RETURN P
******************************************************************************
PROCEDURE PoppedUp
PARAMETERS ReturnVal
ReturnVal = PROMPT()
DEACTIVATE POPUP
RETURN
******************************************************************************
* End of POPUP1.PRG.
```

The first POPUP is used in two ways. The first "ON SELECTION POPUP FileList" command does *not* call a subroutine to close the POPUP window with DEACTIVATE POPUP. Consequently, the user must stroke ESCAPE to close the POPUP. The second "ON SELECTION POPUP FileList" command *does* call a subroutine to close the POPUP window with DEACTIVATE POPUP, so the user sees the POPUP close after stroking ENTER to select the current pick.

The FileList window is defined with a solid-bar (PANEL) border, but the second POPUP, Fields, is defined with a double-line border. The fields in CUSTOMER.DBF are displayed in a double-line box.

Finally, a custom border is specified for POPUP Names. The names in the Customer database are displayed in a pick list by this POPUP.

Picking a File Name from a List

The first form of DEFINE POPUP which is used to generate a pick list is

DEFINE POPUP <POPUP name> FROM <row>,<column> PROMPT FILES

This form presents a boxed pick list whose upper left hand corner is at the specified coordinates and whose contents consist in part of the files in the current directory. Additional contents of the list provide full support for tree-structured directories!

You may limit the files to be displayed by adding a file specification to the PROMPT FILES clause, as in "PROMPT FILES LIKE *.DBF". Listing 22.12 is an example of the list generated by a POPUP with the "PROMPT FILES LIKE *.DBF" clause for the directory C:\Writing\DBbook\, which has the subdirectories BusLtrs and PickList.

Listing 22.12 dBASE IV and FoxPro Pick Lists from DEFINE POPUP ... PROMPT FILES

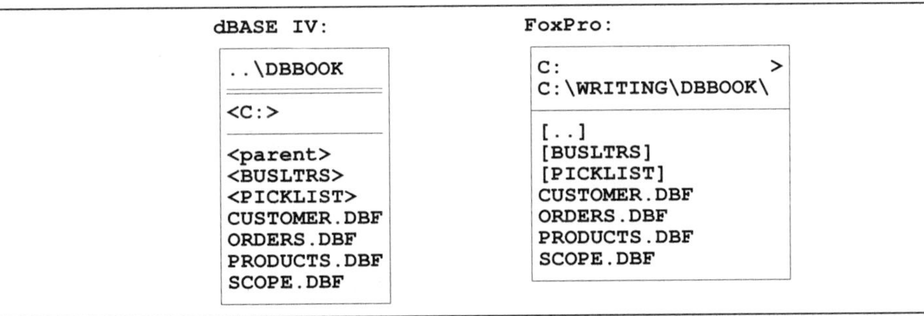

```
dBASE IV:              FoxPro:

..\DBBOOK              C:                    >
                       C:\WRITING\DBBOOK\
<C:>
                       [..]
<parent>               [BUSLTRS]
<BUSLTRS>              [PICKLIST]
<PICKLIST>             CUSTOMER.DBF
CUSTOMER.DBF           ORDERS.DBF
ORDERS.DBF             PRODUCTS.DBF
PRODUCTS.DBF           SCOPE.DBF
SCOPE.DBF
```

This command was executed from the directory C:\Writing\DBbook\. Notice the differences in the ways in which file and directory information are presented. In particular, dBASE IV shows only the last directory name in the path, and not the full path. The bar cursor cannot be moved to a separator line or to the line containing the directory name.

You may choose a file by moving the bar cursor to the file and pressing ENTER. You may select another drive by moving the bar cursor to the line containing the drive specification and pressing ENTER. A second POPUP appears to the right with a list of available drive names.

You may move toward or away from the root directory in the directory tree by selecting named subdirectories or the parent directory. In the example here, the user can select any .DBF file in any directory on any drive.

Picking a Field Name or Value from the Current Database

You may offer the user a pick list with which to choose a field from the current database with the syntax

DEFINE POPUP <POPUP name> FROM <row>,<column> PROMPT FIELD

You may offer the user a pick list with which to choose a field *value* from a record in the current database with the syntax

DEFINE POPUP <POPUP name> FROM <row>,<column>
PROMPT FIELD <field name>

Creating Menus with the DEFINE POPUP Facility

Imagine that a program's specification calls for the following onscreen menu:

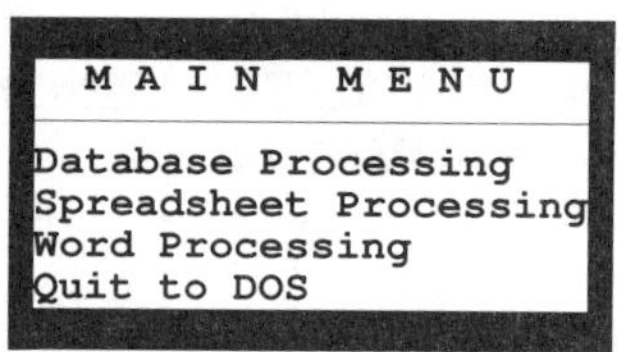

The demonstration program POPUP2.PRG in Listing 22.13 generates this menu by using the menu-making facility of DEFINE POPUP. The SKIP clause in the first two DEFINE BAR statements prevents the user from moving the bar cursor to these items, which therefore are for display only!

Listing 22.13 POPUP2.PRG—Menus with POPUPs

```
* File = POPUP2.PRG.  Called from the dot prompt to demonstrate menu-building
* with the POPUP facility in dBASE IV and FoxPro.
CLEAR
SET ESCAPE ON
SET Safety OFF
SET Talk OFF
PRIVATE BarNum,Exit_L,MenuChoice
*****************************************************************************
* Define POPUP for the Main Menu:
SET BORDER TO PANEL && Without SET BORDER, default border is single line.
DEFINE POPUP  MainMenu FROM 1,1
* Implement the following choices: Database Processing, Spreadsheet
* Processing, Word Processing, Quit to DOS.
BarNum = 0
BarNum = BarNum+1
DEFINE BAR BarNum OF MainMenu PROMPT  "  M A I N   M E N U"     SKIP
```

```
BarNum = BarNum+1
DEFINE BAR BarNum OF MainMenu PROMPT  "──────────────────"  SKIP
BarNum = BarNum+1
DEFINE BAR BarNum OF MainMenu PROMPT  "Database Processing"
BarNum = BarNum+1
DEFINE BAR BarNum OF MainMenu PROMPT  "Spreadsheet Processing"
BarNum = BarNum+1
DEFINE BAR BarNum OF MainMenu PROMPT  "Word Processing"
BarNum = BarNum+1
DEFINE BAR BarNum OF MainMenu PROMPT  "Quit to DOS"
*****************************************************************************
Exit_L = .F.
ON SELECTION POPUP MainMenu DO MenuScrn
DO WHILE (.NOT. Exit_L)
   * Display the Main Menu and get the user's selection in memvar MenuChoice.
   * Set MenuChoice to default selected when user strokes ESCAPE.
   MenuChoice =  "D"        && Default menu choice is  "Database processing".
   ACTIVATE POPUP MainMenu  && Replaces: DO MainScrn with MenuChoice
   @ 20, 0 SAY  ""
   DO CASE
      CASE (MenuChoice =  "D")
     ?  "Show database menu."
     WAIT
      CASE (MenuChoice =  "S")
     ?  "RUN spreadsheet."
     WAIT
      CASE (MenuChoice =  "W")
     ?  "RUN word processor."
     WAIT
      CASE (MenuChoice =  "Q")  && Exit to DOS
     ?  "QUIT here."
     WAIT
     Exit_L = .T.
   ENDCASE
ENDDO
*****************************************************************************
RELEASE POPUPS  && Release all currently defined POPUPs.
CLOSE ALL
SET Safety ON
SET Talk ON
*****************************************************************************
PROCEDURE MenuScrn
MenuChoice = LEFT(PROMPT(),1)
DEACTIVATE POPUP   && Erase the POPUP window.
* End of POPUP2.PRG.
```

Notice the use of relative bar numbering in the DEFINE BAR statements. This helps you avoid renumbering the BARs when options are added or deleted. For example, you can add the choice "Graphics Processing" by inserting two commands:

```
DEFINE BAR BarNum OF MainMenu PROMPT  "Database Processing"
BarNum = BarNum+1
DEFINE BAR BarNum OF MainMenu PROMPT  "Graphics Processing"
BarNum = BarNum+1
DEFINE BAR BarNum OF MainMenu PROMPT  "Spreadsheet Processing"
```

You can remove the spreadsheet option from the menu by simply deleting these two lines:

```
BarNum = BarNum+1
DEFINE BAR BarNum OF MainMenu PROMPT  "Spreadsheet Processing"
```

Notice that we only need the first character of each option for the CASE statement because all first characters are unique for this list. Otherwise, we would have to use a more complex CASE statement.

Creating Macintosh-Style Menus with DEFINE MENU and MENU BAR

Both dBASE IV and FoxPro offer the DEFINE MENU facility, analogous to the DEFINE POPUP facility, to support the programming of Macintosh-style interfaces. In this interface, a list of choices is displayed on the top screen line.

A bar cursor marks the current choice. Upon its selection, a pick list appears beneath the choice. dBASE IV users must employ the arrow keys to highlight choices with the bar cursor. FoxPro users can stroke the arrow keys or the first letter of the choice.

FoxPro also supports the Macintosh-style interface with the MENU BAR facility, which is analogous to MENU TO. Just as the MENU TO facility is much simpler to code than DEFINE POPUP, MENU BAR is much simpler to code than DEFINE MENU.

The DEFINE MENU Facility

The DEFINE MENU facility is available in both dBASE IV and FoxPro to support the programming of Macintosh-style interfaces. In dBASE IV and FoxPro terminology, the choices on the top line are called PADs. When a PAD is selected, any dBASE command may be executed; the Macintosh-style interface is realized when a pick list is displayed, usually with a POPUP.

Usage Patterns

The DEFINE MENU facility consists of the following commands and functions: ACTIVATE MENU, CLEAR MENUS, DEACTIVATE MENU, DEFINE MENU, DEFINE PAD, ON SELECTION PAD, MENU(), PAD(), PROMPT(), RELEASE MENUS, SET BORDER TO with the COLOR commands, and SET MESSAGE TO. The ways in which these commands and functions are combined to produce pick lists are shown in DefMenu1.PRG (Listing 22.14 on page 371); menu functionality is demonstrated with DefMenu2.PRG (Listing 22.15 on page 373).

To create a menu with the DEFINE MENU facility, do the following:

1. If the default border is not satisfactory, use the SET BORDER TO command to set the border to a single line, a double line, a solid bar, or a custom box using your specified characters.
2. If the default or current colors are not satisfactory, specify colors for parts of the menu, as follows. In dBASE IV, use the commands SET COLOR OF BOX, SET COLOR OF HIGHLIGHT, and SET COLOR OF MESSAGES to control the colors of the border, selected option, and unselected options, respectively. In FoxPro, use the command "SET COLOR OF SCHEME 2 TO , <unselected options>, <border>,, <message>, <selected option>". (See the listing of ColorSet.PRG on page 358 for more information.)
3. Use the "DEFINE MENU <menu name>" command with the optional MESSAGE clause.
4. If you use the MESSAGE clause in FoxPro, set the line on which the message is displayed with the SET MESSAGE TO command. (dBASE IV always displays the message on the last screen line.) If you use the MESSAGE clause in dBASE IV, give the command "SET MESSAGE TO" to cancel any message which was previously defined with "SET MESSAGE TO <string>"; otherwise, this message will stay onscreen and no MESSAGEs defined in the menu commands will appear when the menus are activated.
5. Follow the DEFINE MENU command with one DEFINE PAD command for each option in the POPUP menu. If you do not want the default positioning of options across the top screen line, use the screen coordinates in the DEFINE PAD command to place each option anywhere onscreen that you like. You may have the options appear in a horizontal row or rows, in a vertical row or rows, or in any other arrangement you like. There is no scrolling: the position of each option must be explicitly specified with available onscreen coordinates.
6. To automatically display a drop-down menu for each highlighted option in the top-line menu bar, you must do two things: (1) code an ON PAD command for each PAD to associate a POPUP with the PAD, and (2) specify coordinates in the DEFINE POPUP command which defines the POPUP for the given pad so that the POPUP will appear beneath the pad.
7. To execute an arbitrary command (typically "DO <subroutine>") for each highlighted and selected menu PAD, code an ON SELECTION PAD command for each PAD. In contrast to the ON PAD command, the ON SELECTION PAD command may be used to execute any dBASE command when a PAD is selected. Also, note that with ON SELECTION PAD, the associated command is performed only when the user selects the currently highlighted PAD by typing ENTER. POPUPs referenced in ON PAD commands are displayed just by highlighting the PAD.
8. Display the menu to the user with the "ACTIVATE MENU <menu name>" command.

9. When the menu has been displayed and the user has stroked ENTER or ESCAPE, you use the DEACTIVATE MENU command to remove the menu from the screen; any text which had been hidden by the menu is again visible.
10. The function MENU() returns the name of the menu. The function PAD() returns the PAD name of the menu choice. The function PROMPT() returns the text of the menu choice.
11. If you don't need the menu after its use, release its memory with "RELEASE MENUS <POPUP name>" or "CLEAR MENUS". Otherwise you may optionally code another ON SELECTION command before using the menu again with ACTIVATE MENU.

Rules and Remarks

The DEACTIVATE POPUP and DEACTIVATE MENU commands possess an extremely unusual feature: they cause immediate return from procedures and functions in which they are used. dBASE IV will tell you that code which follows DEACTIVATE MENU is unreachable! This means that these commands must be the final ones in the procedures and functions in which they are used, except possibly for optional RETURN statements.

If you intend to use the built-in functions BAR(), MENU(), POPUP(), or PROMPT() to detect user responses to ACTIVATE POPUP or ACTIVATE MENU commands, you must use these functions before DEACTIVATE POPUP or DEACTIVATE MENU is executed.

An ON SELECTION PAD or ON SELECTION POPUP command generally calls a subroutine which performs at least two actions: (1) an expression which references PROMPT() or BAR() is stored into a memvar or output parameter, and (2) DEACTIVATE MENU or DEACTIVATE POPUP is executed (as the last command before RETURN). We will call these subroutines "ON SELECTION" subroutines.

Despite the examples in the vendor manuals, it is not necessary to pass BAR(), MENU(), POPUP(), or PROMPT() as arguments to ON SELECTION subroutines. You may reference these functions in such subroutines prior to any DEACTIVATE command.

If you do not DEACTIVATE in the ON SELECTION subroutine, the user must select a choice by stroking ENTER followed by ESCAPE instead of ENTER alone.

Do not try to keep a menu onscreen by executing ACTIVATE MENU once at the beginning of your application and DEACTIVATE MENU once at the end. Instead, place ACTIVATE MENU in a WHILE loop, as shown in the sample routines.

Creating a Simple Moving-Bar Menu with DEFINE MENU

The program DefMenu1.PRG in Listing 22.14 uses the DEFINE MENU facility to demonstrate a moving-bar menu in dBASE IV and FoxPro. The menu's top line displays the choices: Database Processing, Spreadsheet Processing, Word Processing, and Quit to DOS. A POPUP with a "PROMPT FILES LIKE *.DBF" clause is associated with the first choice; the other choices simply display a message.

Listing 22.14 DefMenu1.PRG—A Simple Moving-Bar Menu with DEFINE MENU

```
* File = DEFMENU1.PRG.  Called from the dot prompt to demonstrate menu-building
* with the DEFINE MENU facility in dBASE IV and FoxPro.

SET Escape ON
SET Safety OFF
SET Status ON
SET Talk   OFF
****************************************************************************
PUBLIC FoxPro_L
PRIVATE BarNum,Exit_L,MenuChoice
****************************************************************************
FoxPro_L = ("FOXPRO" $ UPPER(VERSION()) )
****************************************************************************
* Define colors for user-defined menu objects in dBASE IV and FoxPro:
DO ColorSet

* Define style of borders to be used:
SET BORDER TO SINGLE  && Single-line border.
****************************************************************************
* Define MENU for the Main Menu:
DEFINE MENU  MainMenu  MESSAGE ;
"Main Menu for dBASE Dialects Software Engineering Example"
****************************************************************************
* Implement PADs for the following choices: Use a database, Use a spreadsheet,
* Edit a text file, Quit to DOS.

DEFINE PAD        Database OF MainMenu PROMPT "Database" ;
                                      MESSAGE "Use a database."
ON SELECTION PAD Database OF MainMenu DO MenuScrn WITH MenuChoice

DEFINE PAD        Spread   OF MainMenu PROMPT "Spreadsheet" ;
                                      MESSAGE "Use a spreadsheet."
ON SELECTION PAD Spread   OF MainMenu DO MenuScrn WITH MenuChoice

DEFINE PAD        Word     OF MainMenu PROMPT "Word Processing" ;
                                      MESSAGE "Edit a text file."
ON SELECTION PAD Word     OF MainMenu DO MenuScrn WITH MenuChoice

DEFINE PAD        Quit     OF MainMenu PROMPT "QUIT" ;
                                      MESSAGE "Quit to DOS."
ON SELECTION PAD Quit     OF MainMenu DO MenuScrn WITH MenuChoice
****************************************************************************
DEFINE       POPUP FileList FROM 1,0 PROMPT FILES LIKE *.DBF
ON SELECTION POPUP FileList DO ClosePOP
****************************************************************************
Exit_L = .F.
DO WHILE (.NOT. Exit_L)

   CLEAR
   DO ScrnMess
   * Display the Main Menu and get the user's selection in memvar MenuChoice:
   MenuChoice = "D"  && Default if user presses <ESCAPE>.
   ACTIVATE MENU MainMenu && Replaces: DO MainScrn with MenuChoice

   DO CASE
      CASE (MenuChoice = "D")
     ACTIVATE POPUP FileList
     WAIT

      CASE (MenuChoice = "S")
     @ 18,0 SAY "RUN spreadsheet."
     WAIT

      CASE (MenuChoice = "W")
     @ 18,0 SAY "RUN word processor."
```

```
      WAIT
       CASE (MenuChoice = "Q")  && Exit to DOS
      @ 18,0 SAY "QUIT here."
      WAIT
      Exit_L = .T.
   ENDCASE
ENDDO
******************************************************************************
RELEASE MENUS  && Release all currently defined MENUs.
CLOSE ALL
SET Safety ON
SET Status ON
SET Talk   ON
******************************** End of DEFMENU1.PRG code.  Procedures follow.
******************************************************************************
******************************************************************************
******************************************************************************
**************************************************************** ClosePOP
PROCEDURE ClosePOP
@ 17,0 SAY "Prompt = " + PROMPT()
DEACTIVATE POPUP
RETURN
******************************************************************************
**************************************************************** MenuScrn
PROCEDURE MenuScrn
PARAMETERS MenuChoice
MenuChoice = LEFT(PAD(),1)
DEACTIVATE MENU
RETURN
******************************************************************************
**************************************************************** ScrnMess
PROCEDURE ScrnMess
* dBASE IV displays MESSAGEs at the bottom of the screen.
* FoxPro lets you set the line where MESSAGEs are to appear.
PUBLIC FoxPro_L
IF FoxPro_L
   SET MESSAGE TO 20
   @ 19,0 SAY REPLICATE(CHR(205),80)
   @ 21,0 SAY REPLICATE(CHR(205),80)
ELSE
   SET MESSAGE TO && dBASE IV will not replace any defined message.
ENDIF
RETURN
******************************************************************************
* End of DEFMENU1.PRG.
```

Notice that the POPUP does not appear automatically; the database choice must be highlighted first, and then you must stroke ENTER. This is because ON SELECTION PAD commands are used in DefMenu1.PRG. In contrast, DefMenu2.PRG in Listing 22.15 uses ON PAD commands for automatic display of drop-down menus as top-line choices are highlighted with the bar cursor.

Creating a Macintosh-Style Menu with DEFINE MENU

The command file DefMenu2.PRG in Listing 22.15 extends the functionality of the command file DefMenu1.PRG in Listing 22.14 by associating a list of options with each choice on the top-line menu. The database choice offers the options

"Open database" and "Close database"; the spreadsheet choice offers the options "Lotus 1-2-3" and "Quattro"; the word processing choice offers the options "MS-Word", "Sprint", and "WordPerfect"; and the QUIT choice offers the options "Quit" and "Don't quit".

Listing 22.15 DefMenu2.PRG—Macintosh-Style Menus with DEFINE MENU

```
* File = DEFMENU2.PRG.  Called from the dot prompt to demonstrate the building
* of a top-line menu bar with automatic drop-down submenus using the DEFINE
* MENU facility in dBASE IV and FoxPro.

SET Escape ON
SET Safety OFF
SET Status ON
SET Talk   OFF

*************************************************************************
PUBLIC FoxPro_L
PRIVATE Exit_L,PAD_ID,PROMPT_ID

*************************************************************************
FoxPro_L = ("FOXPRO" $ UPPER(VERSION()) )
STORE "" TO PAD_ID,PROMPT_ID

*************************************************************************
* Define colors for user-defined menu objects in dBASE IV and FoxPro:
DO ColorSet

* Define style of borders to be used:
SET BORDER TO SINGLE  && Single-line border.

********************************************* DEFINE MENU for the Main Menu:
DEFINE MENU  MainMenu  MESSAGE ;
"Main Menu for dBASE Dialects Software Engineering Example"

**************************************************************************
* Implement PADs for the following choices: Use a database, Use a spreadsheet,
* Edit a text file, Quit to DOS.

DEFINE PAD        Database OF MainMenu PROMPT   "Database" ;
                                       MESSAGE "Use a database."

ON SELECTION PAD Database OF MainMenu ACTIVATE POPUP FileList

DEFINE PAD        Spread   OF MainMenu PROMPT   "Spreadsheet" ;
                                       MESSAGE "Use a spreadsheet."

ON SELECTION PAD Spread   OF MainMenu ACTIVATE POPUP Spread

DEFINE PAD        Word     OF MainMenu PROMPT   "Word Processing" ;
                                       MESSAGE "Edit a text file."

ON SELECTION PAD Word     OF MainMenu ACTIVATE POPUP Word

DEFINE PAD        Quit     OF MainMenu PROMPT   "QUIT" ;
                                       MESSAGE "Quit to DOS."

ON SELECTION PAD Quit     OF MainMenu ACTIVATE POPUP Quit

******************************************* Define POPUPs for the Main Menu:
DEFINE       POPUP FileList FROM 1,0
DEFINE BAR 1 OF    FileList PROMPT "Open database"
DEFINE BAR 2 OF    FileList PROMPT "Close database"
ON SELECTION POPUP FileList DO MenuData WITH PAD_ID,PROMPT_ID

DEFINE       POPUP Spread   FROM 1,10
DEFINE BAR 1 OF    Spread   PROMPT "Lotus 1-2-3"
DEFINE BAR 2 OF    Spread   PROMPT "Quattro"
ON SELECTION POPUP Spread   DO MenuData WITH PAD_ID,PROMPT_ID

DEFINE       POPUP Word     FROM 1,25
DEFINE BAR 1 OF    Word     PROMPT "MS-Word"
DEFINE BAR 2 OF    Word     PROMPT "Sprint"
DEFINE BAR 3 OF    Word     PROMPT "WordPerfect"
ON SELECTION POPUP Word     DO MenuData WITH PAD_ID,PROMPT_ID

DEFINE       POPUP QUIT     FROM 1,43
DEFINE BAR 1 OF    QUIT     PROMPT "Quit"
DEFINE BAR 2 OF    QUIT     PROMPT "Don't quit"
```

```
ON SELECTION POPUP QUIT     DO MenuData WITH PAD_ID,PROMPT_ID
*************************************************************  Main Menu loop:
Exit_L = .F.
DO WHILE (.NOT. Exit_L)

   DO ScrnMess

   * Display the Main Menu and get the user's selection in memvar MenuChoice:
   ACTIVATE MENU MainMenu && Replaces: DO MainScrn with MenuChoice
   PAD_ID1 = LEFT(PAD_ID,1)
   DO CASE
      CASE (PAD_ID1 $ "DSW")
    DO MENU_&PAD_ID1 WITH LEFT(PROMPT_ID,1)

      CASE (PAD_ID1 = "Q")
    DO MENU_Q WITH LEFT(PROMPT_ID,1),Exit_L

      OTHERWISE  && Default choice is QUIT when user strokes ESCAPE.
    DO MENU_Q WITH "Q",Exit_L
   ENDCASE

ENDDO
******************************************************************************
RELEASE MENUS  && Release all currently defined MENUs.
CLOSE ALL
SET Safety ON
SET Status ON
SET Talk   ON
RETURN
******************************** End of DEFMENU2.PRG code.  Procedures follow.
******************************************************************************
******************************************************************************
******************************************************************************


********************************************************************  MenuData
PROCEDURE MenuData
PARAMETERS PAD_ID,PROMPT_ID

PAD_ID    = PAD()
PROMPT_ID = PROMPT()

@ 16,0 SAY "PAD = " + PAD_ID
@ 17,0 SAY "PROMPT = " + PROMPT_ID

DEACTIVATE MENU
RETURN
******************************************************************************
**********************************************************************  MENU_D
PROCEDURE MENU_D
PARAMETERS MenuChoice

DO CASE
   CASE (MenuChoice = "O")
      @ 18,0 SAY "Open a database file."

   CASE (MenuChoice = "C")
      @ 18,0 SAY "Close a database file."
ENDCASE

WAIT
RETURN
******************************************************************************
**********************************************************************  MENU_S
PROCEDURE MENU_S
PARAMETERS MenuChoice

DO CASE
   CASE (MenuChoice = "L")
      @ 18,0 SAY "RUN Lotus 1-2-3."

   CASE (MenuChoice = "Q")
      @ 18,0 SAY "RUN Quattro."
ENDCASE
```

```
WAIT
RETURN
**************************************************************************
******************************************************************  MENU_Q
PROCEDURE MENU_Q
PARAMETERS MenuChoice,Exit_L

DO CASE
   CASE (MenuChoice = "Q")
      @ 18,0 SAY "Quit to MS-DOS."
      Exit_L = .T.

   CASE (MenuChoice = "D")
      @ 18,0 SAY "OOPS!  Returning to application."
ENDCASE

WAIT
RETURN
**************************************************************************
******************************************************************  MENU_W
PROCEDURE MENU_W
PARAMETERS MenuChoice

DO CASE
   CASE (MenuChoice = "M")
      @ 18,0 SAY "RUN MS-Word."

   CASE (MenuChoice = "S")
      @ 18,0 SAY "RUN Sprint."

   CASE (MenuChoice = "W")
      @ 18,0 SAY "RUN WordPerfect."
ENDCASE

WAIT
RETURN
**************************************************************************
****************************************************************  ScrnMess
PROCEDURE ScrnMess
* dBASE IV displays MESSAGEs at the bottom of the screen.
* FoxPro lets you set the line where MESSAGEs are to appear.
PUBLIC FoxPro_L

CLEAR

IF FoxPro_L
   SET MESSAGE TO 20
   @ 19,0 SAY REPLICATE(CHR(205),80)
   @ 21,0 SAY REPLICATE(CHR(205),80)
ELSE
   SET MESSAGE TO && dBASE IV will not replace any defined MESSAGE.
ENDIF
RETURN
**************************************************************************

* End of DEFMENU2.PRG.
```

Notice how the WHILE loop and PROCEDURE MENU_Q are structured to implement a single exit at the end of DefMenu2.PRG, based on the value of memvar Exit_L. The macro facility is used to collapse the following three cases into the first case in DefMenu2.PRG.

```
CASE (PAD_ID1 =  "D")
   DO MENU_D WITH LEFT(PROMPT_ID,1)

CASE (PAD_ID1 =  "S")
   DO MENU_S WITH LEFT(PROMPT_ID,1)

CASE (PAD_ID1 =  "W")
   DO MENU_W WITH LEFT(PROMPT_ID,1)
```

In an application of any size at all, you would probably want to implement MENU_D, MENU_S, and so on as command files instead of procedures. These routines to process menu choices can easily be of a size to justify separate handling.

FoxPro's MENU BAR Facility

The MENU BAR facility of FoxPro can be used to implement a Macintosh-style interface with much less effort than by using the DEFINE MENU and DEFINE POPUP facilities. There are, however, a number of trade-offs, including the fact that no other dialect currently implements the MENU BAR facility.

In order to understand these trade-offs, let's contrast the two approaches. In MenuBar.PRG, we'll code the same interface with the MENU BAR facility that we did with the DEFINE MENU facility in DefMenu2.PRG.

Let's first notice the similarities in DefMenu2.PRG and MenuBar.PRG. Both command files call these procedures in the same way: ColorSet, MENU_D, MENU_Q, MENU_S, MENU_W, and ScrnMess. The structure of the WHILE loop is the same: the main menu is displayed repeatedly until the logical memvar Exit_L becomes true. Inside the WHILE loop, very similar DO CASE statements process the user's menu choices.

There are also a number of differences. When you study the code for MenuBar.PRG in Listing 22.16, you'll notice that this kind of menu is *not* a named data object in your application. Therefore, its name, scope, and storage do not have to be managed, unlike the case with POPUPs and MENUs created with DEFINE POPUP and DEFINE MENU.

One reflection of reduced complexity in the second approach is that PROCEDURE MenuData does not occur in MenuBar.PRG. However, in one way the second approach is *more* complex than the first approach.

The advantage of the second approach is reduced by the fact that there is no analog of the PROMPT() built-in function for the MENU BAR facility. There is an analog of the BAR() facility, which can then be used to recover the prompt text, as shown in the CASE statement in MenuBar.PRG. The consequence of this extra complexity is the fact that we use three CASE statements (the cases PAD_Num = 1, 2, and 3) to do what took one CASE statement before (the case (PAD_ID1 $ "DSW")).

Notice a technique used to avoid data duplication in MenuBar.PRG. The dimensions of the arrays must be referenced both in the DIMENSION statement and in the MENU statements in the WHILE loop. Rather than using constants, which is a classic programming pitfall, this technique defines memvars to control the sizes of the arrays and to inform other parts of the program what those sizes are. (FoxPro does not have any built-in function to determine the size of an array.)

When PAD_Num and Option_Num are initialized outside the WHILE loop, the previously selected pad and option are highlighted when the menu is displayed again. To always select the same initial choices, initialize PAD_Num and Option_Num immediately before the READ MENU BAR statement.

Listing 22.16 MenuBar.PRG—A Macintosh-Style Menu via the MENU BAR Facility

```
* File = MenuBar.PRG.  Called from the dot prompt to demonstrate the FoxPro
* MENU BAR facility.

SET Safety OFF
SET Talk OFF

PUBLIC FoxPro_L
PRIVATE DataDim,MainDim,QuitDim,SpreadDim,WordDim
DataDim   = 4
MainDim   = 4
FoxPro_L  = ("FOXPRO" $ UPPER(VERSION()) )
QuitDim   = 3
SpreadDim = 2
WordDim   = 3
*****************************************************************************
* Define the arrays to hold the text of the top-line and drop-down menus:
DIMENSION Database[DataDim], MainMenu[MainDim,2], QuitApp[QuitDim],;
      Spread[SpreadDim], Word[WordDim]

MainMenu[1,1] =  "Database"
MainMenu[1,2] =  "Use a database."
MainMenu[2,1] =  "Spreadsheet"
MainMenu[2,2] =  "Use a spreadsheet."
MainMenu[3,1] =  "Word Processing"
MainMenu[3,2] =  "Edit a text file."
MainMenu[4,1] =  "QUIT"
MainMenu[4,2] =  "Quit to DOS"

Database[1] =  "Open database"
Database[2] =  "Close database"
Database[3] =  "\-"
Database[4] =  "\To be coded"

Spread[1] =  "Lotus 1-2-3"
Spread[2] =  "Quattro"

Word[1] =  "MS-Word"
Word[2] =  "Sprint"
Word[3] =  "WordPerfect"

QuitApp[1] =  "Quit"
QuitApp[2] =  "\-"
QuitApp[3] =  "Don't quit"


*****************************************************************************
* Define colors for user-defined menu objects in dBASE IV and FoxPro:
DO ColorSet

* Define style of borders to be used:
SET BORDER TO SINGLE
*************************************************************  Main Menu loop:
Exit_L     = .F.
Option_Num = 1
Pad_Num    = 1
DO WHILE (.NOT. Exit_L)

   DO ScrnMess

   * Display the Main Menu and get the user's selection in memvars
   * PAD_Num and Option_Num.  Replaces: ACTIVATE MENU MainMenu.

   MENU BAR MainMenu,MainDim  && Display the menu bar.

   * Install the 4 PAD-analogs:
   MENU 1, Database, DataDim
   MENU 2, Spread  , SpreadDim
   MENU 3, Word    , WordDim
   MENU 4, QuitApp , QuitDim

   READ MENU BAR TO Pad_Num,Option_Num

   @ 15,0 SAY  "Pad_Num ="
   ?? Pad_Num
```

```
    ?  "Option_Num =  ", Option_Num
    DO CASE
       CASE (Pad_Num = 1)
      DO MENU_D WITH LEFT(Database[Option_Num],1)
       CASE (Pad_Num = 2)
      DO MENU_S WITH LEFT(Spread[Option_Num],1)
       CASE (Pad_Num = 3)
      DO MENU_W WITH LEFT(Word[Option_Num],1)
       CASE (Pad_Num = 4)
      DO MENU_Q WITH LEFT(QuitApp[Option_Num],1),Exit_L
       OTHERWISE  && Default choice is QUIT when user strokes ESCAPE.
      DO MENU_Q WITH  "Q",Exit_L
    ENDCASE
ENDDO
******************************************************************************
RELEASE MENUS  && Release all currently defined MENUs.
CLOSE ALL
SET Safety ON
SET Status ON
SET Talk   ON
RETURN
******************************** End of MenuBar.PRG code.  Procedures follow.
******************************************************************************
******************************************************************************
******************************************************************************

********************************************************************** MENU_D
PROCEDURE MENU_D
PARAMETERS MenuChoice
DO CASE
   CASE (MenuChoice =  "O")
      @ 18,0 SAY  "Open a database file."
   CASE (MenuChoice =  "C")
      @ 18,0 SAY  "Close a database file."
ENDCASE
WAIT
RETURN
******************************************************************************
********************************************************************** MENU_S
PROCEDURE MENU_S
PARAMETERS MenuChoice
DO CASE
   CASE (MenuChoice =  "L")
      @ 18,0 SAY  "RUN Lotus 1-2-3."
   CASE (MenuChoice =  "Q")
      @ 18,0 SAY  "RUN Quattro."
ENDCASE
WAIT
RETURN
******************************************************************************
********************************************************************** MENU_Q
PROCEDURE MENU_Q
PARAMETERS MenuChoice,Exit_L
DO CASE
   CASE (MenuChoice =  "Q")
      @ 18,0 SAY  "Quit to MS-DOS."
      Exit_L = .T.
   CASE (MenuChoice =  "D")
      @ 18,0 SAY  "OOPS!  Returning to application."
ENDCASE
```

```
WAIT
RETURN
****************************************************************************

*******************************************************************   MENU_W
PROCEDURE MENU_W
PARAMETERS MenuChoice

DO CASE
   CASE (MenuChoice =  "M")
      @ 18,0 SAY  "RUN MS-Word."

   CASE (MenuChoice =  "S")
      @ 18,0 SAY  "RUN Sprint."

   CASE (MenuChoice =  "W")
      @ 18,0 SAY  "RUN WordPerfect."
ENDCASE

WAIT
RETURN
****************************************************************************

*******************************************************************   ScrnMess
PROCEDURE ScrnMess
* dBASE IV displays MESSAGEs at the bottom of the screen.
* FoxPro lets you set the line where MESSAGEs are to appear.

PUBLIC FoxPro

CLEAR
IF FoxPro
   SET MESSAGE TO 20
   @ 19,0 SAY REPLICATE(CHR(205),80)
   @ 21,0 SAY REPLICATE(CHR(205),80)
ELSE
   SET MESSAGE TO && dBASE IV will not replace any defined MESSAGE.
ENDIF
RETURN
****************************************************************************

* End of MenuBar.PRG.
```

MENU BAR Features

When the bar cursor is in a pull-down menu, the RightArrow and LeftArrow keys move the bar cursor to the pull-down menu on the right or left, respectively. This feature is not supported by DEFINE MENU.

The number of choices on the menu bar is not limited to those which can appear onscreen at one time. If more choices exist than can be displayed at once, horizontal scrolling may be used to access all choices. Again, this feature is not supported by DEFINE MENU.

Messages can appear on the MESSAGE line which correspond to highlighted menu bar choices, but you cannot show messages which correspond to highlighted options on pull-down menus. In contrast, pull-down menus implemented with DEFINE MENU and DEFINE POPUP can display messages for options both on the top line and in the pull-down menus.

You may add the SAVE keyword to the end of a READ MENU BAR command, in which case the menu will remain onscreen after the user selects a choice. If a menu is created with the DEFINE MENU and/or DEFINE POPUP facilities, it is not feasible to try to keep it onscreen after the user has selected a choice.

While in most respects the MENU BAR facility is much easier to use than the DEFINE MENU facility, there is one very major drawback to its use. The MENU BAR facility is not currently supported by any other dialect. If your FoxPro application encounters a FoxPro bug which you cannot work around by recoding to get the same result in a different way, it could be very important to you to be able to execute that application under dBASE IV (or another dialect).

When you code your Macintosh-style menus with the DEFINE MENU facility, the code will work under both dBASE IV and FoxPro. For less programmer effort and even greater program portability, you can use dialect-independent menu routines implemented with the Millican menu templates presented in Part III.

Recommendations

Depending on your dialect, you may have several menu-building possibilities available to you. When you choose a menu-building method, consider these factors:

1. Do you feel safe in programming an application to work with only one dialect?
2. If not, under which dialects will the application (potentially) execute?
3. Will the maintenance programmers be able to understand everything you code, or is it possible that you would use a simpler menu-making method if you anticipated the possibility of a maintenance programmer with limited dBASE skills?
4. How difficult is it to add, change, and remove menu choices with each method you are considering?
5. Is the simple-to-create-and-maintain menu style provided by the Millican menu templates satisfactory?

After answering these and related questions which may occur to you, you will have a list of acceptable menu-making methods. Choose the one that minimizes the amount of time taken to create and maintain the menu-making part of your code.

Chapter 23

Indexing, Sorting, and Retrieving Data

This chapter covers one of the most fundamental areas in dBASE programming — indexing, sorting, and retrieving data in .DBF databases. There are two approaches to putting the data we have into the order we want: sorting and indexing. We use sorted or indexed databases to report data in a desirable order or to rapidly retrieve selected records.

Before you read this chapter, read the text in Chapter 3 under the headings "Indexes" (page 78) and "Filtered Indexes" (page 80). Now let's examine our indexing and sorting options and determine how to exploit them.

Keys: Fields versus Expressions

The INDEX ON command permits you to specify an order which is determined by a field in a database (or an expression involving database fields). For example, if Members.DBF has a field called Name, then the command "INDEX ON Name TO MembName" builds an index file called "MembName". When you "USE Members INDEX MembName", your view of Members is as if its records were in alphabetic order by member name.

Now assume that the member names are stored in *two* fields called FirstName and LastName. In that case, a member's name is not Members->Name, but rather Members->FirstName + Members->LastName. To index on member name with this database structure, we use the command "INDEX ON FirstName + LastName TO MembName". If we had stored the names in Members->Name using the last-name-first format, then the equivalent indexing would be "INDEX ON LastName + FirstName TO MembName" to place the names in order by last name instead of by first name.

To reduce the size of the index file, you might decide to use all of the characters of the last name, but only four characters of the first name. In that case, you would use the command "INDEX ON LastName + LEFT(FirstName,4) TO MembName".

The SORT command is both more and less limited in its ordering options. If Members.DBF has one field for names, called Name, then the command "SORT TO MembSort ON Name" creates a database called MembSort.DBF in which the records are in alphabetic order by name, starting with "A". You can have the names stored in reverse alphabetic order with the command "SORT TO MembSort ON Name /D".

You could get the same effect if the names were in two fields, FirstName and LastName, with the command "SORT TO MembSort ON FirstName, LastName" for first-name-first order, or "SORT TO MembSort ON LastName, FirstName" for lastname-first order. However, you cannot order by part of a field, as when our INDEX expression included "LEFT(FirstName,4)".

Keys: Random Retrieval versus Sequential Retrieval

Once data is sorted or indexed, there are two ways in which programmers commonly exploit the ordering: random and sequential retrieval. An example of sequential retrieval is "USE Members INDEX MembName" followed by LIST, which causes field values of the member records to be listed in name order. (The Clipper dialect requires the form "LIST <field list>".)

In random retrieval, the index to a database is used to retrieve records by using their keys. For example, if we store a member's name (as it is spelled in our database) in the memvar mName, then "USE Members INDEX MembName" followed by "SEEK mName" will cause the record pointer to move to the first record where Members->Name = mName, assuming for the moment that LEN(Members->Name) = LEN(mName), SET EXACT is ON, SET DELETED is OFF, and no filter is in place.

FIND, SEEK, and LOCATE

The dBASE programming language offers two commands that retrieve records from indexed databases: FIND and SEEK. The FIND command has an orientation toward interactive use; you can enter

```
FIND Jones
```

at the dot prompt, but you would be unlikely to place a line reading "FIND Jones" in your program.

> **Recommendation on FIND and SEEK.** Use FIND at your option at the dot prompt, but use SEEK in program code. The syntax for SEEK is "SEEK <search expression>", where the search expression is of the same form as the key expression for the current master index.

You may use the LOCATE command to retrieve data from unindexed databases, using the syntax

```
LOCATE [<scope>] FOR <Condition1> [WHILE <Condition2>]
```

<Condition1> must reference at least one of the fields in the current database, and <condition2>, if used, typically also references one or more fields in the current database. For example, the equivalent of "FIND Jones" is

```
LOCATE FOR Name = "Jones"
```

The LOCATE command has a companion command called CONTINUE, which moves the record pointer to the end-of-file position or to the next record meeting the scope and conditions, whichever comes first.

Retrieval and the Record Pointer

When you retrieve sequentially from a database produced by the SORT command, the record pointer moves through the database in storage order. If a filter is in place, or SET DELETED is ON, then some records may be skipped, but the records which are selected have the same order as they do in the sorted database.

When you retrieve sequentially from an indexed database, the record pointer moves through the database in index order. If a filter is in place, or SET DELETED is ON, then some records may be skipped, but the records which are selected have the same order as they do in the index.

When you attempt to retrieve a record with the SEEK or FIND commands, the attempt may succeed, in which case the record pointer moves to the first record in the database whose INDEX key matches the SEEK or FIND expression and any SET DELETED or SET FILTER conditions in place. If the attempted retrieval is unsuccessful, then the record pointer may move to the end-of-file position, or it may move to the first record whose INDEX key is greater than the SEEK or FIND expression, depending on the dialect and a dialect-dependent SET command.

When a retrieval is unsuccessful in dBASE III PLUS, dbXL, or FoxBASE+, the record pointer moves to the end-of-file position and EOF() is true. In Clipper, record pointer movement is controlled by SET SOFTSEEK, and in dBASE IV and FoxPro, the movement is controlled by SET NEAR. In a Clipper, dBXL, or FoxPro application, when SET SOFTSEEK or SET NEAR is OFF, and the retrieval is unsuccessful, the record pointer moves to the end-of-file position and EOF() is true. When SET SOFTSEEK or SET NEAR is ON, and the retrieval is unsuccessful, the record pointer moves to the first record whose INDEX key is greater than the SEEK or FIND expression, and FOUND() is false.

See the section “Persistency of FOUND()” on page 294 for a recommendation on the proper use of FOUND() in any dialect. See page 113 for a caution on using FOUND() instead of EOF() in dBASE III PLUS.

An Example of “Soft” Seeking

Consider the following reporting requirement. You must generate two reports from a database which is indexed on a ZIP code field; the first report lists the addresses with ZIP codes between “00000” and “49999” and the second reports lists the addresses with ZIP codes between “50000” and “99999”.

The first report is easy to code: open the file with its index and list records WHILE (ZIP < "49999"). To produce the second report, you must move the record pointer to the first record whose ZIP code is greater than or equal to “50000”. This is easy in Clipper: SET SOFTSEEK ON, SEEK "50000", and list the remaining records. Similarly, in dBASE IV or FoxPro, you would SET NEAR ON, SEEK "50000", and list the remaining records.

Keys: Primary versus Secondary

In the examples above, when we split the name into two fields and formed a key expression like LastName + FirstName, we were using LastName as the *primary key* and FirstName as the *secondary key*. The concept of primary versus secondary keys is, at the first level, only a definition. At the second level, the concept is profound, essential, and surprisingly easy to grasp.

Let's look at our name problem from a different perspective now. Again, we'll assume that we store the names in Members.DBF in a FirstName field and a LastName field. We want to either index or sort the database so that (1) the records are ordered by LastName, and (2) within a group of records with the same LastName, the records are ordered by FirstName.

The SORT command gives us this ability explicitly. We tell it to sort first on the LastName field and subsequently on the FirstName field.

At first examination, it is not clear whether the same result could be achieved with the INDEX ON command. If we "INDEX ON LastName TO MembSort", then the records are ordered by LastName, but the first names could occur in any order among the Jones records, Smith records, and so on. How can we index the sets of records with the same primary key so that they will be in order by secondary key?

The answer to that question expresses a theorem or principle about information structures which in my view is extreme in its serendipity and beauty. *If you want to order on one or more secondary keys in addition to the primary key, index on the concatenation of the primary and secondary keys!*

Listing 23.1 shows two ways to produce an alphabetized list of names from Members.DBF. The first way uses the SORT command and the second way uses the INDEX ON command.

Listing 23.1
Equivalent Actions with SORT and INDEX ON—One Secondary Key

```
* Method 1, using SORT:
USE Members
SORT TO MembSort ON LastName, FirstName
USE MembSort
LIST FirstName, LastName

* Method 2, using INDEX ON:
USE Members
INDEX ON LastName + FirstName to MembName
LIST FirstName, LastName
```

This principle extends to any number of secondary keys. Let's say that we have a field MiddleName to hold the middle name or initial of members. When a group of records has the same first and last name, we want those records ordered by the MiddleName field. Listing 23.2 gives a version of the previous example with two secondary keys.

Listing 23.2
Equivalent Actions with SORT and INDEX ON—Two Secondary Keys

```
* Method 1, using SORT:
USE Members
SORT TO MembSort ON LastName, FirstName, MiddleName
USE MembSort
LIST FirstName, MiddleName, LastName

* Method 2, using INDEX ON:
USE Members
INDEX ON LastName + FirstName + MiddleName to MembName
LIST FirstName, MiddleName, LastName
```

Keys: Character, Date, and Numeric

When you index using the syntax "INDEX ON <key expression> TO <file>", you may use any key expression which conforms to these rules:

1. The key expression references at least one field from the currently open database.
2. The key expression has one type for all records in the database.
3. The type of the key expression is character, date, or numeric.
4. Values of key expressions of type character must not exceed the dialect's limit on key length, which is 100 characters for most dialects. (See Table 3.18 on page 79 for the details.)
5. The source code which represents a key expression must not exceed the dialect's limit on key expression length.

Retrieval of Character Keys

There are two issues which affect the matching of SEEK expressions and character-typed INDEX keys: key case (uppercase versus lowercase) and key length. When you SEEK and SET EXACT is ON, then the length of the search expression and the INDEX key must be the same in order for a match to be possible.

For example, say that the length of the LastName field in your database is 10, the database is indexed on the LastName field, and you wish to retrieve a record whose LastName field contains "Fulton" followed by four blanks. If you SET EXACT ON and SEEK "Fulton", then the search will fail; you must SEEK "Fulton" + SPACE(4). If you SET DELETED OFF, SET FILTER TO, SET EXACT OFF, and SEEK "Fulton", then the record pointer will move to the first record whose LastName field contains "Fulton" + SPACE(4).

In practice, programmers usually INDEX ON UPPER(LastName) in preference to INDEX ON LastName. Then they SEEK UPPER(<search key>) in order to remove case distinctions from the matching process. For example, a data-entry operator may have entered "fulton", "Fulton", or "FULTON". If case distinctions are not removed, then you must SEEK "fulton" to match "fulton", "Fulton" to match "Fulton", and so on.

Recommendation on indexing character data. Unless you know that the case of character data is significant in an application, use the INDEX and SEEK commands in the forms INDEX ON UPPER(<character key>) TO <filename> and SEEK UPPER(<seek expression>).

Minimizing Key Length

When you index a database on a LastName field of length 30, each key in the index file will be of length 30. If you increase the LastName field to 40 characters, then the index file will contain length 40 keys and this file will be much larger than a file with length 30 keys. Similarly, if you decrease the LastName field to length 20, the index file will contain length 20 keys, and the index file will be much smaller than a file with length 30 keys.

Let's assume that the LastName field in your database is of length 30; typically, each field will have many blanks following the name which is entered in the field. If you INDEX ON TRIM(UPPER(LastName)), and the average length of the last names in your database is 10, then you might think that your index file would be of the same size as when you INDEX ON UPPER(LastName) with a LastName field of length 10, but this is false. If the LastName field is length 30, then the keys in the index file will all be of length 30, even if you INDEX ON TRIM(UPPER(LastName)).

Recommendation on variable-length INDEX keys. Always use INDEX keys which have the same length for each record in the database to be indexed. Use SET EXACT OFF to support variable-length SEEK expressions.

In a typical application which stores names, the names are split into a FirstName field and a LastName field, and your name index is built with the command INDEX ON UPPER(LastName + FirstName) TO <filename>. Let's assume that the LastName field is length 30 and the FirstName field is length 20, so that the INDEX key is length 50.

There is a way for you to save space in this index file which has little effect on your ability to retrieve records with name keys. In the typical application, an INDEX expression like UPPER(LastName + LEFT(FirstName,5)) will produce unique keys. This expression produces keys of length 35; your SEEK expression is also of the form UPPER(LastName + LEFT(FirstName,5)) (if you SEEK with EXACT ON).

In order to avoid the problems caused by data duplication, you can use a memvar to specify the number of characters of FirstName to be used in the keys, leading to INDEX and SEEK expressions of the form UPPER(LastName + LEFT(FirstName,FnamKeyLen)). Note, however, that there are pitfalls with this approach.

First, FnamKeyLen must be defined when you use the index file. For example, if your database is called Names.DBF and you index to a file with filename Name, then the command "USE Names INDEX Name" will lead to a error message like "variable not found" if FnamKeyLen is not defined. Second, if you want to "USE Names INDEX Name" at the dot prompt or in a program, you must first assign a numeric value to FnamKeyLen. Third, this value must be the same value as was used when the INDEX ON command built the Name index. Fourth, you cannot recover the original value of FnamKeyLen from the index file; you must keep track of this original value in some other way.

Retrieval of Date Keys

When you SEEK a date key using a date expression, dates are compared in an internal format which reduces each day to an integer representation. This internal representation is independent of SET CENTURY, because the century is always stored internally. There is a match only if a SEEK expression and an INDEX key represent the same date.

Blank Keys in Date Indexes

Let's say that Orders.DBF has a date field called Order_Date, as is the case with the Orders.DBF file on the companion diskette. If we "USE Orders" and "INDEX ON Order_Date to O_Date", then the records with nonblank dates will be in chronological order in the index, with the earliest date first. The blank dates are grouped together at the end or beginning of the index, according to the dialect, as shown in Table 23.1.

Table 23.1 Position of Blank Dates in Date Indexes

Position	Dialects
Start	Clipper, FoxBASE+, FoxPro
End	dBASE III PLUS, dBASE IV, dBXL, Quicksilver

Retrieval of Numeric Keys

dBASE dialects use three different representations for numbers: a character form, a binary internal representation, and a decimal internal representation, as explained in Chapter 3. Numeric fields are stored in .DBF files and in program files in character form, but computations and comparisons use either the binary or the decimal internal form.

Say that you have a database called Stock.DBF with a numeric field, Cost, of length 6 with two decimal places. If you wish to retrieve a record whose cost is "101.25", and you SEEK "101.25", then the search should always be successful (assuming that the record meets any SET FILTER or SET DELETED conditions in effect). However, if you SEEK X, where X is computed, say, as 100 + 1.25, then the match may fail, due to the problems of converting between the character and internal forms of numbers.

You can avoid the pitfalls of these conversions with the STR() function. In this example, you can INDEX ON STR(Cost,6,2) TO Cost, and SEEK STR(X,6,2).

Note that there are no problems with sequential retrieval. The records will always be retrieved in the correct order from databases which are indexed on numeric fields using numeric INDEX keys. For example, if you USE Stock, INDEX ON Cost to Cost, and LIST, the records will be listed in order of lowest to highest Cost.

Combining Differently Typed Data in Key Expressions

It is sometimes the case that primary and secondary keys have different data types; you must then combine the key components with the type-conversion functions to produce an expression of type character, date, or numeric. It is usually most convenient to produce an expression of type character.

You can convert numbers to their character form with the STR() built-in function. For example, if Orders has the numeric field Totals of length 7 and decimals 2, then "INDEX ON Cust_ID + STR(Totals,7,2)" is an alternative to "SORT ... ON Cust_ID, Totals", and "INDEX ON STR(Totals,7,2) + Cust_ID" is an alternative to "SORT ... ON Totals, Cust_ID".

You can convert dates to their character form with the built-in function DtoC(), but the result depends on the setting of SET DATE. In particular, some forms produce chronological order and other forms do not.

Say that you must produce a report on the Orders database which lists the customer code and the order date; customer code is to be the primary key and the order date is to be the secondary key. If you SET DATE ANSI at all times, then you may use the INDEX expression "Cust_ID + DtoC(Order_Date)"; otherwise this key expression orders groups of records with the same Cust_ID by the month of the order date, instead of the year of the order date. To obtain chronological ordering when you SET DATE AMERICAN at all times, the following very long INDEX expression is often recommended:

```
Cust_ID + SUBSTR(DTOC(Order_Date,7,2)) +
SUBSTR(DTOC(Order_Date,1,2)) + SUBSTR(DTOC(Order_Date,4,2))
```

You can use an even simpler approach in Clipper, dBASE IV, dBXL, and Quicksilver by using the DtoS() function. This function returns a date in the character form YYYYMMDD, where YYYY is a 4-digit year, MM is the month (01, 02, ..., 12), and DD is the day (01, 02, ..., 31). FoxBASE+ has an equivalent function, DtoC(<date>,1). The corresponding dialect-dependent expressions are

```
Cust_ID + DtoS(Order_Date)
```

and

```
Cust_ID + CtoD(Order_Date,1)
```

However, the dBASE language supports date arithmetic, so you can code the much shorter expression

```
Cust_ID + STR(Order_Date - CtoD("1/1/1800"), 6)
```

which works correctly for all dates in the range 1/1/1800 to 1/1/1800 plus 999,999 days, which is 1800 A.D. to approximately 4537 A.D. *This form is recommended for any application which must execute under more than one dialect.* Note that all of the above INDEX expressions with Cust_ID and Order_Date produce an order equivalent to that obtained with "SORT ... ON Cust_ID, Order_Date".

Logical Keys

You cannot use a logical field as a primary or secondary key, but you can use the IIF() function to convert it to a character or numeric value, which *can* be used as a key. For example, if Members.DBF contains the character field Name and a logical field Members_L, then you can "INDEX ON IIF(Members_L, "M", "N") + UPPER(Name) TO Members". When you "USE Members INDEX Members" and "LIST Name", the alphabetized member names appear first, followed by the alphabetized names of nonmembers.

Indexing in Descending Order

Indexing in descending order is an optional convenience for your custom code. For example, consider the following example. The first loop reports names in alphabetic order, and the second loop reports names in reverse alphabetic order, using the same index file.

```
USE Members INDEX MembName
* Report names in alphabetic order:
DO WHILE (.NOT. EOF())
   ? <data>
   SKIP
ENDDO
* Report names in reverse alphabetic order:
GO BOTTOM
DO WHILE (.NOT. TOF())
   ? <data>
   SKIP -1
ENDDO
```

However, note that we can replace the first loop by "LIST <data>". Without the appropriate index, we cannot obtain reverse-order listing with commands like LIST and REPORT FORM, and with external tools like R&R Relational Report Writer, which sometimes use dBASE indexes.

Descending Order for Character Keys

When you sort with the SORT command, you can use the "/D" option to cause descending ordering on the specified field. Some dialects provide the DESCEND() function to support the easy programming of descending indexes. In Clipper, dBXL, and Quicksilver, you can code "INDEX ON DESCEND(Name) TO MembName". Then, when you "USE Members INDEX MembName", the built-in commands LIST, REPORT FORM, and so on will list your data in reverse alphabetic order. Correspondingly, the form of the SEEK command for such an index is "SEEK DESCEND(mName)".

In FoxBASE+ and FoxPro, you can use the SYS(15) built-in function to emulate the DESCEND() function. Construct a character memvar of length 254, called, say, DescTable, as follows: SUBSTR(DescTable,I,1) = CHR(255 – I), for I = 1, 2, …, 254. Then DESCEND(S) = SYS(15, DescTable, S), for all strings S which do not contain CHR(0) or CHR(255).

All dialects permit you to construct a procedure to compute the result of DESCEND() in an output parameter. Therefore, if you absolutely must have a descending character key index in a dialect which does not have DESCEND() or any character translation functions, you can create a character field called, say, ReverseKey which holds what would be the result of DESCEND(<INDEX key>); you then INDEX ON ReverseKey and SEEK on an expression of the same form. Listing 23.3 shows a command file implementation of such a function.

Listing 23.3 A Command File Equivalent of DESCEND()

```
* File = DescendC.PRG.  Called from several .PRG.
* Simulates the DESCEND() function of Clipper and dBXL.
*************************************************************************
* Dialects: All.
*************************************************************************
* Input arguments:
* InString, Character.  String to be translated.
*************************************************************************
* Output arguments:
* OutString, Character.  Translated string.
*************************************************************************
* Input assumptions:
* 1. TYPE(InString) = character.
*************************************************************************
PARAMETERS InString, Outstring
PRIVATE I,Last

I         = 1
Last      = LEN(InString)
Outstring =  ""
DO WHILE (I <= Last)
   OutString = OutString + CHR( 255 - ASC( SubStr(InString,I,1) ) )
   I = I + 1
ENDDO

* End of DescendC.PRG.
```

Descending Order for Numeric Keys

To index on numeric fields in reverse order, simply put a minus sign in front of the key expression. For example, say that Members.DBF has a numeric field called Age to hold the members' ages. To get ages in the order 1, 2, 3, …, "INDEX ON Age TO <file>"; to get descending order, "INDEX ON –Age TO <file>". If you SEEK, remember to SEEK –<value> if the INDEX expression is –Age.

Descending Order for Date Keys

We can use the technique of indexing negative numbers to index in reverse chronological order. First, remember that you can subtract two dates to get an integer.

To index on date fields in reverse order, create a PUBLIC memvar of type date which holds a date that is greater than any date in your database; for example, HighDate = CtoD("1/1/2100"). Then use an INDEX key expression of the form "HighDate – <date expression>", where <date expression> refers to at least one date field in your database. Remember to also use a SEEK expression of this same form.

Descending Order for Secondary Date Keys

To get an order equivalent to that obtained with "SORT ... ON Cust_ID, Order_Date/D", use the INDEX expression: Cust_ID + STR(100000 – (Order_Date – CtoD("1/1/1800")), 5). The power of 10 used after "STR(" has five zeroes to match the five characters produced by the STR() reference. This expression is valid for dates in the range 1800 A.D. to approximately 4537 A.D.

Descending Order for Secondary Numeric Keys

If Orders.DBF has a numeric field called Totals of width 5 and 2 decimals, then you can report the records from the highest total to the lowest with "INDEX ON –Totals ...". You might think that you can get the ordering equivalent to that achieved by "SORT ... ON Cust_ID, Totals /D" with "INDEX ON Cust_ID + STR(–Totals, 6, 2)", but this approach does not work.

Instead, use an INDEX expression of the form "Cust_ID + STR(Top – Totals, W, D)", where Totals is a numeric field of width W and D decimals, and

Top >= VAL("1" + REPLICATE("0", W))

Indexing a Subset of the Database

Sometimes it is incredibly useful to be able to index a subset of a database. For example, say that Members.DBF contains an Org field to hold the company name of corporate members, who comprise 1% of the database; in 99% of the records, the Org field is blank. To report the corporate members in alphabetic order by organization, you need an index on the Org field. If you build an unfiltered index for the Org field, 99% of it will be wasted; you want a filtered index for the Org field which only contains nonblank keys! See page 80 for a detailed presentation of filtered indexes.

Implementation of dBASE Indexes

dBASE dialects use two methods of storing index information. The traditional approach is the INDEX ON command, which creates one index file for each INDEX key. dBASE IV introduces the .MDX format, which can contain key data for several indexes.

.MDX Index Files

The analog of the index filename for .MDX files is the TAG name; the .MDX form of the INDEX ON command gives a name called a TAG to each index which is stored in the .MDX file. The syntax for adding an index to an .MDX file is "INDEX ON <key expression> TAG <TAG name> [OF <.MDX filename>] [UNIQUE] [DESCENDING]". If a named .MDX file does not exist, it is created and the index identified by <TAG name> is the first and only index in the .MDX file.

If the "OF <.MDX filename>" clause does not appear, and there is no .MDX file with the same filename as the current database, then such a file is created. If this file already exists, then the index is added to the .MDX file.

The .MDX file is called a *production* index; it is opened automatically by the USE command, unlike ordinary index files, which must be opened by name in a USE or SET INDEX statement. For example, if the header of dBASE IV database Members.DBF indicates the existence of a production index, then "USE Members" causes Members.MDX to be opened.

You may also establish .MDX index files for your dBASE IV databases which are not production indexes and which consequently are not opened automatically. You open such indexes like the old indexes: reference them by name in the USE command or SET INDEX TO command. For example, if you have built a multiple-index file called Members1.MDX, you can open it with "USE Members INDEX Members1".

You can mix .MDX and .NDX files in the index file lists. For example, if MembName.NDX and Members1.MDX exist, you can open both of them with "USE Members INDEX Members1, MembName" or "USE Members INDEX Members1, MembName".

Random and Sequential Retrieval from Sorted Databases

There is no equivalent of SEEK which works for sorted databases, but we can use the subroutine shown in Listing 23.4 to do the same job. This subroutine uses the binary search method to find a match on the submitted field name. In this elegant method, we ask: Is the match in the first half of the database? According to our answer, the new database to search is either the first half or last half of the original database. We repeat the process of halving until we have reached the answer.

Listing 23.4
SeekSDBF.PRG—A SEEK Equivalent for Unfiltered Sorted Databases

```
* File = SeekSDBF.PRG.  Called from several .PRG and library routine SekSDBFD.
*****************************************************************************
* Dialects: All.
*****************************************************************************
* Implements the SEEK command for sorted databases.  The database may be sorted
* in ascending order or descending order.  The record found may or may not
* match any SET DELETE or SET FILTER conditions.

* This routine responds to SET EXACT ON/OFF in the same way as SEEK.  For
* example, with SET EXACT ON, a search key of  "BAB" will not match a record
* key of  "BABS"; with SET EXACT OFF, there will be a match.

* If there are several records with the key value which matches the search key,
* one of them will be found.  This record may be the first, last, or a middle
* record in the set of matching records.
*****************************************************************************

* This routine has been generalized from the binary search routine on page 407,
*   "The Art of Computer Programming," Vol. 3, by D. Knuth, to handle lists
* which are sorted in either increasing or decreasing order.

*****************************************************************************
* Input arguments:
* SearchKey, Character.  The key value to search for.
* KeyExpr, Character.  The key expression on which the database is sorted.
*****************************************************************************
* Output arguments:
* Found_L, Logical.  True if a record with the specified key is found, else .F.
* RecordNum, Numeric, no decimals.
*****************************************************************************
* Input assumptions:
* 1. A database is open in the current area.
* 2. RecCount() > 1.
* 3. No indexes in use for the database are open in current work area.
* 4. The database is sorted on the key expression &KeyExpr.
* 5. LEN(SearchKey) <= Len(&KeyExpr).
* 6. The SORT is either ascending for all fields, or descending for all fields.
*****************************************************************************
* Exit conditions:
* 1. If Found_L is true, RecordNum contains record number where match found.
* 2. If Found_L is false, RecordNum contains record number of a near match, OR
*    0, if the database has no records.
* 3. No indexes are open for the current database.
*****************************************************************************

PARAMETERS SearchKey,KeyExpr,Found_L,RecordNum

PRIVATE End,Start,Trial,TrialValue,UpOrder_L
Found_L = .F.

IF (RecCount() > 0)
   SET INDEX TO

   * Determine if sort order is ascending or descending:
   GOTO RecCount()
   EndKey = &KeyExpr

   GOTO 1
   UpOrder_L = (M->EndKey > &KeyExpr)

   Start = RecNo()
   End   = RecCount()
   DO WHILE (M->End >= M->Start) .AND. (.NOT. M->Found_L)
      Trial = INT( (M->Start + M->End)/2 )
      GOTO M->Trial
      TrialValue = &KeyExpr
      DO CASE
     CASE (M->TrialValue < M->SearchKey)
        IF UpOrder_L
           Start = M->Trial + 1
        ELSE
```

```
            End   = M->Trial - 1
         ENDIF
      CASE (M->TrialValue > M->SearchKey)
         IF UpOrder_L
            End   = M->Trial - 1
         ELSE
            Start = M->Trial + 1
         ENDIF
      * For character keys, we assume LEN(SearchKey) <= LEN(TrialValue)
      CASE (M->TrialValue = M->SearchKey)
         Found_L = .T.
       ENDCASE
   ENDDO
   RecordNum = RecNo()
ELSE
   RecordNum = 0
ENDIF
* End of SeekSDBF.PRG.
```

If a matching record is found, it may or may not match any SET DELETED or SET FILTER conditions which you have set. As a second complication, there may be more than one matching record. To find the matching record with the lowest record number which also meets any SET DELETED or SET FILTER conditions, use SekSDBFD.PRG, shown in Listing 23.5, which adds a layer of functionality to SeekSDBF.PRG.

Listing 23.5
SekSDBFD.PRG—A SEEK Equivalent for Filtered Sorted Databases

```
* File = SekSDBFD.PRG.  Called from several .PRG.
*****************************************************************************
* Dialects: All.
*****************************************************************************
* This routine implements the SEEK command for sorted databases.  See the
* documentation for SeekSDBF.PRG, which it calls.  SekSDBFD and SeekSDBF are
* identical except for their output conditions.
*****************************************************************************
* Output conditions:
* 1. Found_L is true if there is at least one record which meets any SET
*    DELETED and SET FILTER conditions, and for which the key value matches the
*    search key.
* 2. If Found_L is true, Record RecordNum is the record with the lowest record
*    number which meets any SET DELETED and SET FILTER conditions, and for
*    which the key value matches the search key.
* 3. If Found_L is false, RecordNum contains the record number of a near
*    match, or 0, if the database is empty.
* 4. No indexes are open for the current database.
*****************************************************************************
PARAMETERS SearchKey,KeyExpr,Found_L,RecordNum
RecordNum = 0
PRIVATE RecFound,RecNumber
DO SeekSDBF WITH SearchKey,KeyExpr,Found_L,RecordNum
IF M->Found_L
   RecFound = RecNo()
   DO WHILE (&KeyExpr = M->Searchkey)
      RecNumber = RecNo()
      SKIP -1
   ENDDO
   GOTO M->RecNumber
   * If RecFound # RecNo(), then the current record satisfies
   * &KeyExpr = M->SearchKey, and also the SET DELETED and SET FILTER
```

```
   * conditions.  Otherwise, the current record satisfies &KeyExpr =
   * M->SearchKey, but perhaps not the SET DELETED and SET FILTER conditions.
   IF (M->RecFound = RecNo())
      * GOTO the first preceding record which meets SET DELETED and SET FILTER
      SKIP -1

      * GOTO the first following record which meets SET DELETED and SET FILTER
      SKIP +1

      IF (&KeyExpr = M->Searchkey)
     * Current record is record of lowest record number which satisfies the
     * SET DELETED and SET FILTER conditions and which also is a match,
     * with &KeyExpr = M->SearchKey
     RecordNum = RecNo()
      ELSE
     * There is at least one record with &KeyExpr = M->SearchKey, but no
     * record meets &KeyExpr = M->SearchKey and the SET DELETED and SET
     * FILTER conditions.
     Found_L = .F.
      ENDIF
   ENDIF
ENDIF
* End of SekSDBFD.PRG.
```

Reporting on a Subset of a Sorted Database

Sequential retrieval from sorted databases is linked to random retrieval when you start reporting with a record other than the first record. In that case, you can use the SeekSDBF subroutine in Listing 23.4 to move the record pointer to the starting record for your report.

Recommendation: Use LOCATE with Small Databases

Many times dBASE programmers use small databases to hold data which might be stored in arrays in other programming languages. A typical use for such databases is to store codes of one kind or another. You might have a database of the two-character state abbreviations used in mailing addresses, or a list of member codes and their corresponding category titles to support the member codes used in the MemberCode field in Members.DBF.

It is not usually necessary or appropriate to index such small code files. In addition to the programming overhead involved in having one or more indexes for each small database, you suffer the performance penalty of more open files.

Recommendation on LOCATE versus SEEK for small databases. Use the LOCATE command instead of SEEK to retrieve data from small databases, which are defined here as those whose data can be recovered faster with LOCATE than with SEEK, or in equivalent time (such as both in less than 1 second). Use the SORT command or other methods to keep the databases in any required order.

Recommendation: Hide All USE Commands in One Procedure

You can control the database and index files in your application much better if you have a central routine which you always call to open these databases and their associated indexes. With such a routine, you follow the rules in Table 23.2. (For convenience, let's call this subroutine OpenDBF. See "Referential Integrity in Clipper" (Spence 1989) for a Clipper implementation of such a routine.)

Table 23.2 Rules for Using an Open-File Subroutine

1. To open a database file, call OpenDBF.
2. To close a database file, use the USE command with no options, or the CLOSE DATABASES or CLOSE ALL command.
3. To select the work area in which a database is open, use the syntax "SELECT <alias>".
4. To select an unused area, use SELECT 0 in dialects which support it. Use SELECT SELECT() in dBASE IV. In dialects which offer no equivalent to SELECT 0, use Select0.PRG, which is listed on page 73.

Structure of Subroutine OpenDBF

The structure of subroutine OpenDBF will vary according to the application; typically such a subroutine would take arguments for the database file to open, and one or more arguments to control USE options such as index files. When you update a database, you usually want all of the index files to be open so that they can be updated to reflect changes in the database. In contrast, when you report from a database, you usually want at most one index file to be open (assuming that you open the database just to report from it).

The second and any subsequent parameters are used to control which indexes are opened for an indexed file. These parameters can also control options such as which index is the master index, and whether the database is opened in exclusive mode. (Note that dBASE IV supports "USE <database> READONLY" for a read-only opening mode.)

You can also use OpenDBF to transparently handle any relations via SET RELATION and SET SKIP commands. With this approach, a single call to OpenDBF could open a set of related databases and indexes!

For further reading, see "The Data Dictionary" (Olympia 1990), "Data Driven Systems: A Fresh Approach to Application Generation" (Oliver 1990), and the manual to the Schooner product from the Quicktek Corporation. This manual is available separately for $50.

Chapter 24

Reporting with REPORT FORM, LABEL FORM, and Custom Programming

There are three main database activities: get the data, maintain the data, and report on the data. In this chapter we look at some issues and techniques associated with reporting data in .DBF files. We will concentrate mainly on *printed* reports, in contrast to reports which are displayed onscreen.

Page Size

There are two interacting factors in report design: the selection and formatting of data to report, and the amount of space on the printed page. Database reports are typically written in fixed spacing fonts, so the amount of space on a page can be described in terms of the maximum number of characters printed per line and the number of lines printed per page. For example, when you print 8 ½-by-11-inch pages using 10 pitch (characters per horizontal inch) on a printer with an 8-inch carriage, and you use 6 lines per inch, then your printed page is a character matrix of 80 characters across by 66 lines down.

The best report layout in the world won't help you very much if you need to put more on a page than your printer will allow. There are several ways to print more data on a page with dot-matrix and laser printers.

Options for More Characters per Line

Dot-matrix printers for personal computers usually offer a "standard" pitch of 10 CPI (characters per inch) and a "compressed" pitch of 15 CPI or 16.66 CPI. By changing to compressed print, you can increase the amount of print data per line by 50% to 66.6%. At pitches of 10, 12, 15, and 16.66, you can print 80, 96, 120, or 133 characters per 8-inch line.

In many cases, printing 80 characters at 10 pitch on a printer with an 8-inch carriage causes an automatic line feed after the 80th character is printed. If each line you printed were 80 characters in length, you would receive a double-spaced report instead of a single-spaced report. Therefore, you must often print no more than the maximum permitted number of characters per line, minus one character. If you use a printer with an 8-inch carriage and this type of automatic line feed, you will limit yourself to printing 79, 95, 119, or 132 characters per line at 10, 12, 15, and 16.66 CPI.

Recommendation on 12 CPI. Many dot-matrix printers offer 12 CPI, which is typically the most readable of the print pitches. I recommend that you use 12 CPI if it offers you enough characters per line.

Wide-Carriage Printers

Dot-matrix printers come in two standard carriage widths. One width accommodates 8 1/2-inch-wide paper, and the other width, supported by the so-called *wide-carriage* models, is 15 inches, which accepts mainframe-size 8 1/2-by-14 7/8-inch paper with a print width of 14 inches. At pitches of 10, 12, 15, and 16.66 CPI, you can print 140, 168, 210, or 233 characters per 14-inch line.

Rotated Print on Dot-Matrix Printers: Sideways

The famous Sideways printing utility from Funk Software introduced to many people the concept of rotated print on dot-matrix printers. Rotated text prints in lines which run along the *length* of the paper, instead of across its *width*.

Using the graphics modes of such printers, Sideways prints files with long lines using continuous forms. For example, if you had a report which was 250 columns by 40 lines, Sideways would print it on two successive sheets of 8 1/2-by-11-inch paper, for a report size of 8 1/2 inches down by 22 inches across.

You may now buy programs from several vendors for this service. Perhaps even better, you can get freeware and shareware versions of such programs from BBSs.

Landscape Printing on Laser Printers

The new generation of printers based on laser technology typically offers a choice of *portrait* or *landscape* print modes. Portrait printing puts lines across the short dimension of the paper, as usual. The alternative is landscape printing, in which the text lines are printed along the long dimension of the paper, as with Sideways.

For example, the factory default settings for the industry-standard HP LaserJet Series II are as follows: 60 lines of 8 inches across in portrait, or 45 lines of 10.5 inches across in landscape. The LaserJet II has built-in Courier fonts of 10 pitch and 16.66 pitch. In portrait mode you would print either 80 or 133 characters per line with these fonts; in landscape mode you would print either 105 or 174 characters per line.

There are three important differences between the output from Sideways on a dot-matrix printer and the output from a laser printer in landscape mode. First, laser printers deliver individual sheets of paper, in contrast to the continuous forms of the dot-matrix printer. Second, laser printers usually cannot print to the edges of the paper; they certainly cannot print part of a character on one page and the rest of it on the next page, as Sideways does when it prints lines across page perforations. Third, if the number of characters you can print on a line in landscape mode is limited to X, then without a Sideways-type program, you are limited to printing reports with lines no longer than X characters.

Mechanisms for Printer Control

Sometimes programmers generate reports which print acceptably in a given printer's default mode for fonts, margins, page length, and so on. In this case, the application doesn't need to know how to control the printer; no printer control data is sent to the printer other than the generic carriage return, linefeed, and formfeed characters.

More commonly, attributes of the printer must be changed from their default values. For example, the printer may print 10 characters per inch and 6 lines per inch by default, but your reports may require 12 characters per inch and 8 lines per inch. In this case, your application must know which control strings to send to the printer to set the desired attributes, or how to access those control strings.

Applications which control printers deal with two dimensions of printer data. The first dimension is the printer to which control and print data are sent. For example, if a user must print to either a dot-matrix printer or a laser printer, then the application must solicit the printer in use from the user and send the appropriate control strings for that printer.

The second dimension of printer control data is the attribute set of each supported printer. Minimum attribute sets usually include 10, 12, and 15 or 16.66 characters per inch, line spacing of 6 and 8 lines per inch, boldface, underlining, and sometimes italics.

Some attributes are associated with two data items, instead of one. For example, to set the attribute of 12 characters per inch, you send a single character string; to start boldface printing, you send one string, and to stop boldface printing, you send a second string.

Table 24.1 lists some information which your application may want for each supported printer. These items could be implemented as fields in a database, but other implementations are possible, as we shall see.

Start and stop strings for print attributes such as boldface or italics can be specified as null for printers which do not support those attributes. In this way, the same code can produce a report with boldface for a printer which supports boldface, or produce the same report without boldface for a printer which does not offer boldface.

For maximum flexibility, set up your printer drivers to support either a setup string or data contained in a specified file. Dot-matrix printers seldom need more than 5 or 10 characters of setup or reset control data, but laser printers may need dozens!

Table 24.1 Sample Data Needed for a Printer Driver

1. Name or other identification of the printer.
2. Parallel or serial.
3. Serial speed.
4. Serial data bits.
5. Serial stop bits.
6. Serial parity.
7. Setup string or file name.
8. Reset string or file name.
9. Control string for 10 characters per inch.
10. Control string for 12 characters per inch.
11. Control string for 15 or 16.66 characters per inch (commonly called *compressed* print).
12. Control string for 6 lines per inch.
13. Control string for 8 lines per inch.
14. Start boldface.
15. Stop boldface.
16. Start underlining.
17. Stop underlining.
18. Start italics.
19. Stop italics.

A File-Based Printer Control Mechanism

One obvious way to store the printer driver information listed in Table 24.1 is in a .DBF file, where there would be one record for each printer, and one field for each item of control data. However, there is another approach which is much more general in that it makes this control data available to batch files and programs that are not able to read .DBF files.

In this approach, you store in files the information that otherwise would be stored in fields. In MS-DOS, you use the filename to represent the attribute and the extension to represent the printer. For example, .LJ2 might represent the HP LaserJet Series II printer, .o92 an Okidata 92, and so on. Table 24.2 lists some possible filenames and their associated attributes. The first group of choices is suggested for any printer and the second group of choices is suggested for laser printers.

Implementation

In the context of the recommended directory structure given in Appendix C on page 427, I recommend that you store these files in \Batch. For example, say that your application needs to print a report in landscape mode on a LaserJet II. It would copy \Batch\LandOn.LJ2 to the printer before sending print data and copy \Batch\Default.LJ2 to the printer afterward.

If your application prints to more than one printer, it presents a menu of printer choices to the user. Your application has a look-up table or its equivalent to associate a printer's three-letter code with its name in the menu. Store this code in a PUBLIC memvar called, say, PrintrCode. If the printers are always attached to the same printer port, then your application copies \Batch\Default.&PrintrCode to this port upon receiving the user's selection of printer. The usual command is "RUN COPY \Batch\Default.&PrintrCode PRN:".

If printers are attached to different ports, then you first execute the appropriate MODE command to tell MS-DOS which port is associated with the standard print device PRN: and to specify the communication parameters for serial ports. Then you copy the file \Batch\Default.&PrintrCode to the PRN: device.

Table 24.2 Filenames and Printer Attributes for File-Based Printer Control

Filename	Attribute
Default	The default set of attributes for the printer.
6LPI	6 lines per inch.
8LPI	8 lines per inch.
10CPI	10 characters per inch (10 pitch).
12CPI	10 characters per inch (12 pitch).
15CPI	15 characters per inch (15 pitch).
17CPI	16.66 characters per inch (16.66 pitch).
BoldOn	Start boldface.
BoldOff	Stop boldface.
UnderOn	Start underlining.
UnderOff	Stop underlining.
ItalOn	Start italics.
ItalOff	Stop italics.
PortOn	Set or return to portrait mode.
LandOn	Set or return to landscape mode.
EnvOn	Set or return printer to envelope-printing mode.
Label1	Set up printer for the first type of laser labels you use.
Label2	Set up printer for the second type of laser labels you use.
Courier0	Select Courier 10 pitch.
Courier2	Select Courier 12 pitch.
TmsRmn10	Select Times Roman 10 point.
TmsRmn12	Select Times Roman 12 point.
Helv10	Select Helvetica 10 point.
Helv12	Select Helvetica 12 point.
Helv14	Select Helvetica 14 point.

When your application needs a particular printer attribute, it copies a file to the printer whose file name is of the form

<drive>:\Batch\<attribute>.&PrintrCode

If a computer is always attached to an Okidata 92, then the AutoExec.BAT file can contain the command "COPY C:\Batch\Default.o92 PRN:", assuming that the setup strings for an Okidata 92 printer are stored in the specified file. If the computer's parallel printer cable may be attached to either an Okidata 92 or a LaserJet II, then the AutoExec.BAT file can ask the user which printer is connected.

This query can be performed by a utility like ASK.COM in the Norton Utilities. Then the batch file copies C:\Batch\Default.LJ2 or C:\Batch\Default.o92 to device PRN:, as appropriate. This action sets up the printer to support screen printing via the Print-Screen key and console logging (CONTROL-P at the MS-DOS prompt or dot prompt or SET PRINT ON at the dot prompt).

The REPORT FORM Facility

Database reports are classified as *detail* or *summary*, according to the level of information reported. For example, a detail report from a sales orders database might report the descriptions and amounts of individual orders grouped by month, with total sales shown for each month. The summary version of this report lists only the monthly sales totals.

At its simplest, a database detail report lists some or all fields for some or all of the database records. The records to be reported can be selected using SET DELETED; SET FILTER TO; the WHILE and FOR clauses of database commands, as applicable; and the scope facility.

You can list the contents of selected fields to the screen with the syntax "LIST OFF <field list>".[1] If you SET PRINT ON before you LIST, then the information is also sent to the printer; when you are done printing, you must SET PRINT OFF. Alternatively, you can code "LIST OFF <field list> TO PRINT".

The columnar reports produced by the LIST command have no pages, just a list of field data for selected records, line after line. By defining a dBASE data structure called a *report form,* stored in a .FRM file, you can generate simple columnar reports which have a standard page header. In dBASE III PLUS and its clones, report forms can also accommodate a limited amount of grouping and subtotaling.

The dBASE IV and FoxPro dialects offer full-featured report generators which have evidently been strongly influenced by R&R Relational Report Writer, which is covered in its own section later in this chapter. The reporting facilities offered by dBASE IV and FoxPro are not comparable to the limited report forms available in earlier dBASE dialects, to which my current remarks apply.

---

1. The OFF keyword suppresses the listing of record numbers.

Report forms are used to print data from specific databases by "USE <database> [INDEX <index file>]" followed by a REPORT FORM command. Table 24.3 shows the syntax of the REPORT FORM command for dBASE III PLUS; other dialects may have additional options.

Table 24.3 REPORT FORM Syntax

```
REPORT FORM <.FRM filename> [<scope>]
            [WHILE <condition>] [FOR <condition>]
            [PLAIN] [HEADING <header string>]
            [NOEJECT] [TO PRINT]
            [TO FILE <file name>] [SUMMARY]
```

When to Use REPORT FORM

Here is a recommendation on the REPORT FORM facility.

Recommendation on when to use REPORT FORM with the earlier dialects. Simple columnar reports are very easy to generate with the REPORT FORM facility in the earlier dialects, but such forms may not accommodate all the reports needed by an application. Readers will tend to be confused if the reports do not have a consistent page format. Therefore, I recommend that you use REPORT FORM to generate an application's reports only if you can generate *all* of the reports with this facility. Since the page format of REPORT FORM reports is quite limited, I recommend that you use a more attractive format with your custom reports.

In contrast to the earlier dialects, the reporting facilities of dBASE IV and FoxPro are sophisticated and can probably generate all of your reports.

Recommended Page Formats for Reports

The most attractive reports have a page format with a page header, a page footer, and ample margins around the edges of the paper. It is conventional to use a 0.5-inch top margin, above a page header[2] of one or more lines, and to separate the last line of the page header from the first line of the report on the page by 0.5 inch or more. Similarly, it is conventional to use a 0.5-inch bottom margin, below the page footer of one or more lines, and to separate the first line of the page footer from the last line of the report on the page by 0.5 inch or more. It is conventional to use about 1 inch of left and right margins.

Recommendation on a format for a one-line page header on a report. Print the company or organization name left justified in the page header, and print the report name right justified in the page header. If it is available, use boldface for

2. I use the terms *page header* and *page heading* as synonyms; similarly for *page footer* and *page footing.*

the header. Use a second line to show especially long report names which do not fit on the top line. (You may wish to indicate special filter conditions in the header.)

Recommendation on a format for a one-line page footer on a report. Print any department or group name left justified in the page footer, with the date and time of the report centered, and the page number right justified. If it is available, use boldface for the footer. Consider whether you wish to print a time-date stamp on each page that reflects either the time and date when the page was sent to the printer (or spooler) or the time and date when the report was requested.

The LABEL FORM Facility

The mission of LABEL FORM is to support the printing of mailing labels. It differs in several ways from REPORT FORM. First, label forms report a record's data *down* the page, instead of *across* the page. Second, label forms do not have a page orientation, so there is no page heading or page margins. Third, since mailing addresses do not need to be labeled like columnar reports, there are no headings for columns of data.

A fourth major difference is the ability to print data records on a page in a columnar format. This is possible because mailing labels come in forms which are 1-across, 2-across, 3-across, and so on.

You will obviously use LABEL FORM to print mailing labels, but you may also find it convenient for reports that extract only a small number of characters of data for each reported record. In this case, you can print data for several records across the page, and possibly print data for a great many records on one page.

The LABEL FORM command and its options are very similar to the REPORT FORM command and its options, but the LABEL FORM command offers the SAMPLE keyword to assist the user in aligning the label forms properly in the printer. When this option is coded, a sample row of labels is printed, using asterisks for sample data. Then a prompt appears which is similar to "Print another sample? (Y/N)". A "no" response causes the label data to be printed.

Printing Labels with Laser Printers

When a program prints labels on continuous forms, there is no concept of pages; there is just a continuous stream of blank labels upon which to print. In contrast, laser labels come in 8 ½-by-11-inch pages, so on first examination it would appear that you need a facility other than LABEL FORM to print such labels.

Fortunately, this is false, but you must have a good grasp of the margin commands for your laser printer. Let's assume that you use Avery 5162 Laser Printer Labels, which come in 8 ½-by-11-inch sheets. Then the labels on the laser sheets upon which you will print have ⅚-inch margins top and bottom and ¼-inch left and right margins. Within the remaining space on each 8 ½-by-11-inch page there are 14 labels of size 1 ⅓-by-4-inch, 7 down and 2 across.

When you set up the label form (using CREATE LABEL or MODIFY LABEL or the equivalent utility), you define your labels as 7 lines in length, 2 across, with one line between labels, assuming that you print 6 lines per inch. Then you set the margins used by the laser printer to conform to the margins on the laser label forms. If the left and right margins for the forms differ from the the default left and right margins used by the printer, you'll need to send the control strings to the printer to set the left and right margins. Then send control strings to the laser printer to tell it to use top and bottom margins of 5/6 inch (0.83 inch).

Assuming that you print 6 lines per inch with top and bottom margins of 0.83 inch, you will print 56 lines per page; this is 8 lines per label, or 7*8 = 56 lines per laser label page. When you print using the LABEL FORM command, label data is written onto the first page one line at a time until 56 lines of blanks and data have been sent, which fills up the print area on the first page.

When line 57 is sent to the printer, the printer does a form feed automatically and line 57 is then printed as the first line of the first two labels on the second page. This technique enables the LABEL FORM command to drive the laser printer as if the printer had continuous forms instead of separate sheets.

A LABEL FORM Pitfall

There is a pitfall associated with printing laser labels with LABEL FORM which will cause us to sometimes prefer custom programming. The LABEL FORM command has a really dreadful attribute, which is that one blank line is sent to the printer before the first line of label data. When you print to dot-matrix or daisy wheel printers, you cannot align the printer ribbon with the top of the first label, which is natural and fairly easy; you must align the printer ribbon with the top of the first label *minus one print line.* When you print to a laser printer, there is no such manual countermeasure.

Listing 24.1 contrasts correct and incorrect ways to code a label-printing program. Notice that in the first algorithm, a line-feed character is sent to the printer before the first line of data for the first label — this is the problem with LABEL FORM. In the second algorithm, the first line of label data is printed at the margin set by the user or program; a line-feed character is sent *after* the label data to position the print head to the next label.

When you print laser labels with LABEL FORM, you will obtain acceptable results only if the last line of each label, as defined, is always blank. Consider the case of our example with Avery 5162 labels. The first line of the first label on the first page is blank due to the unwanted initial line-feed sent by LABEL FORM; since you have a page length of 56 lines, you print the first 55 lines of label data on the first page and you print line 56 of the label data at the top of the second page of laser labels. Similarly, you print line 56 + 56 at the top of the third page, and so on. If you print 6 lines per inch, you have 8 lines per label; if line 8 of each label is always blank, then the nonblank label data will print in the label spaces. If line 8 is not always blank, then LABEL FORM will *not* produce acceptable results.

Listing 24.1 Correct and Incorrect Label Printing Code

```
USE <database>
* <set filter if necessary>
GOTO TOP
***************************  An Incorrect Method   ***************************
DO WHILE (.NOT. EOF())
   ? <first label line>  && This method is unfortunately used by LABEL FORM.
   ? <second label line>
   ...
   ? <last label line>
   SKIP
ENDDO && (.NOT. EOF())

****************************  A Correct Method   *****************************
GOTO TOP
DO WHILE (.NOT. EOF())
   ?? <first label line>  && Always use this method for custom programs.
   ? <second label line>
   ...
   ? <last label line>
   ?
   SKIP
ENDDO && (.NOT. EOF())
```

Work-Arounds for LABEL FORM with Laser Labels

If you wish to print N lines per laser page, one countermeasure is to set the page length to N lines and print N – 1 lines on a page before executing LASER FORM <form> TO PRINT. The initial linefeed of LABEL FORM will complete the page, and the first data for the first label will print on the first line of the first label. If PRINT is SET ON, you can send N – 1 line-feed characters to the printer with the dBASE command REPLICATE(CHR(10), N – 1).

A second countermeasure is to define label data to consist of L printing lines with one blank line between labels. For example, if you had to print 8 lines of data on Avery 5162 labels, you would define the labels as having 8 lines, set the "lines between labels" to 1, and set the page length to 7*(8 + 1) lines to print 9 lines per each 4/3 inches.

Here is a third and somewhat awkward countermeasure for this problem. Print the labels to a file, import the file into TextData.DBF as described in subsection "Text File Input" on page 85, GOTO 2, SET PRINT ON, and LIST OFF REST TO PRINT. If there are a large number of mailing labels to print, then TextData.DBF will be very large, and this method will be very slow. However, the technique is easy to program and is acceptable when the amount of print data is small.

As a fourth countermeasure, write a program called LaserCpy.EXE in, say, PASCAL or C, which receives a filename as a command-line argument. Then print to file with LABEL FORM, as in "LABEL FORM <form> TO Erase.Me", and then "RUN LaserCpy Erase.Me". LaserCpy.EXE sends every line of Erase.Me to PRN:, except the first.

When to Use LABEL FORM

Use LABEL FORM when you print pressure-sensitive labels on dot-matrix or laser printers. Label forms can also be useful when you print only a small amount of information from each record, and you must get the maximum possible amount of information on a printed page. In this case, you would print more than one label across the page.

Reporting from Normalized versus Unnormalized Databases

We will not investigate the topic of normalized databases in a formal or comprehensive way here, but we must touch on the differences between reporting from normalized versus unnormalized data. For a comprehensive, formal approach, see, for example, *An Introduction to Database Systems, Volume 1* (Date 1990), *Fundamentals of Database Systems* (Elmasri and Navathe 1989), or *Fundamentals of Data Normalization* (Dutka and Hanson 1989).

For the current purposes, let's informally define a normalized set of databases as a set of related databases in which there is no duplication of data beyond that required to relate the databases. Here is a typical example.

Imagine that we have a business which processes customer orders using Orders.DBF. We need to record the items ordered for each sale, plus the name, address, and phone number of the customer who is buying the items. If we never get any repeat business, then a customer will only appear once in Orders.DBF, but if there is repeat business, the name, address, and phone number of a customer will be stored in every record of an order from that customer.

This way of storing the data is said to be unnormalized — data on a customer may be stored in several places. Table 24.4 lists some of the consequences of duplicate data.

Table 24.4 Consequences of Duplicate Data

1. It takes more storage to record data several times than to record it once. (However, normalizing your databases may not necessarily reduce your total storage, due to the need for indexes to link each pair of related databases.)
2. When there is more than one copy of data, it is difficult to update all occurrences in all conditions.
3. When there is more than one copy of data, and the versions differ, it is difficult to know which version to use.

To *normalize* this data, we create a second database, Customer.DBF, which holds the name, address, and related information for each customer. Data on each customer is stored in one record in Customer.DBF.

For simplicity, let's say that a Customer field called ID holds a unique identification code for each customer. Then in Orders.DBF, instead of fields to hold customer data like name, address, and phone number, you have one field called, say, Cust_ID, which holds the identification code for each customer who places an order.

The data in Orders->Cust_ID is used to *relate* each order record to a customer in the Customer database on the basis of the value of the field Customer->ID; when the values in Orders->Cust_ID and Customer->ID are the same, then the records are related. Records in Orders.DBF are related in a many-to-one fashion to records in Customer.DBF in that many Orders records may have the same customer code in their Cust_ID field.

In theory, no additional data structure is needed to relate Orders.DBF and Customer.DBF: when we need customer data for an order, we search Customer.DBF until we find a match between Orders->Cust_ID and Customer->ID. However, if Customer.DBF is large, a sequential search will be too slow and we will need an index on ID for Customer.DBF. With such an index, we can relate a customer record to a given Orders record in a negligible amount of time.

Database systems, including dBASE, usually require such an index. The dBASE SET RELATION TO command has two forms, one which requires an index and retrieves based on key values, and a second form where the record number of a child database record is specified in the parent database.

While normalized data often has an irresistible appeal, it is unfortunately more difficult to report than unnormalized data. Consider the unnormalized form of Orders.DBF, where the various customer fields are stored in each Orders record. It is quite simple to report a list of orders with the names of customers. Index files and filters can be used to report on a particular set of products or customers in any desired order.

When you report on the normalized Orders.DBF, related to Customer.DBF on the fields Orders->Cust_ID and Customer->ID, you have two databases to synchronize and you must manage the index file which relates the databases, as well as any index that determines the report order of Orders.DBF. In this case, you will conceptually perform the normalization process in reverse: at the design level, you will pretend that the data is arranged in a single unnormalized database. Then you have to write code to support your conceptual view.

In the rest of this chapter, we will see two convenient ways to report data from related databases. We can use either a reporting tool like R&R Relational Report Writer or the SET RELATION TO and SET SKIP TO commands in dBASE custom reporting code. (At the time of writing, dBASE IV is the only major dialect which supports SET SKIP TO, although I expect to see it in Arago dBXL and FoxPro 2.0.)

In R&R terminology, the unnormalized database forms the *composite* record; your R&R report definitions may refer to any field in the composite record. With custom code, we can use the SET RELATION TO and SET SKIP TO commands to implement the equivalent of a composite record for reports from several related databases.

R&R Relational Report Writer

R&R Relational Report Writer is a powerful and dialect-independent tool for generating reports from .DBF databases that can save you up to half or more of the time you would spend to program reports with custom dBASE code (Millican 1987). If a report specification requires data from .DBF files to be arranged on pages, then R&R can probably produce the report. R&R also supports mailing labels, and, starting with version 3, form letters are directly supported.

R&R cannot write data into .DBF files; it can only read data *from* .DBF files. Consequently, it cannot produce any report which requires more than one pass through your databases. Although R&R is not a statistics product, it is able to calculate counts, sums, and averages of expressions involving fields and system information like time and date. In addition to the usual dBASE functions like SUBSTR() and STR(), R&R offers UDFs which reference fields in the composite record.

R&R can generate its own indexes or use the .NDX indexes of dBASE III PLUS and other dialects which use the .NDX format. An extra-cost module permits R&R to use Clipper's native .NTX indexes and the FoxBASE+ .IDX indexes.

The power of R&R lies in permitting you to work primarily at the design level. When you develop a reporting program written with custom dBASE code, you work first on the design of the report, and second on code that gathers and prints data according to the report's specification. Changes in report design may cause many lines of code to be discarded or modified.

When you work with R&R, you develop a *report definition,* which is the specification for a report in R&R terms. You can display the report definition in a form which is suitable for use in programmer documentation. All R&R output can be directed to the screen, a file, or a printer, including report definitions as well as the reports themselves.

As you develop the report, you can check its appearance against your expectations by applying the existing report definition to your databases. At this stage, you typically direct the report to the screen for preview without the delay of printing.

R&R is a fully engineered reporting tool for the programmer and end-user. End-users can construct reports on single files or simple relational reports by imitating examples from the R&R manual and elsewhere. Your more computer-literate users can also make simple modifications to your R&R reports, such as altering page headings or footings, or placing an additional field on the report.

When you direct R&R output to a printer, you have a choice of up to eight installed printers. When you direct output to a file, you can store the report either with or without the printer codes for boldface, underlining, and so on. If you select output to a file with printer codes, you also identify which of the eight sets of printer codes will be used.

Interactive versus Batch Reporting

R&R can be used interactively, or its runtime can be used from your dBASE dialect programs. When R&R is used interactively, it is a replacement for the CREATE REPORT and MODIFY REPORT commands. You use R&R in this mode to develop report definitions.

When R&R is used in batch mode, you control it with data passed in .DBF files and on the command line, as in "RUN RRunTime RRunIn 1". This RUN command tells DOS to execute a file whose filename is "RRunTime" (the R&R runtime file), and to use record 1 of RRunIn.DBF to determine which report definition is to be applied to which database with which reporting options. You can generate several reports with a command like "RUN RRunTime RRunIn 1 5 3", which produces three reports, using the instructions in records 1, 5, and 3 of RRunIn.DBF.

If appropriate, your R&R interface should give the user a choice of sending output to the screen, to a file, or to any printer to which the user is connected. In practice, the user often has a single printer and no need to ever send output to a file. In this case, offer your user a choice to see the report onscreen or to print the file.

Onscreen reporting is performed in an ergonomic fashion. A top-line menu permits you to see the next line or screen of the report; to list the report continuously; or to pan, restart, or cancel the report!

Information on the success or failure of reporting is contained in RRunOut.DBF, which your dBASE dialect program can check after the RUN RRunTime command. Part of this information is the page number on which output stopped, which permits you to restart the report from the middle rather than the beginning following a printer problem like a paper or labels jam.

These control options are implemented in the Millican template file RR3.TEM, which you can use to quickly generate an interface to the R&R runtime in your dBASE dialect applications. The presentation for this template begins on page 271.

When to Use R&R Relational Report Writer

R&R is recommended when your application requires reports which are too complex for the REPORT FORM and LABEL FORM facilities in your dBASE dialect. In this case, produce all of the reports with R&R for a consistent look.

R&R is also recommended when your application executes under more than one dBASE dialect, and the reports are too complex to be programmed with the REPORT FORM and LABEL FORM facilities which are common to all of the dialects under which your application executes.

Remark. The reporting facilities of dBASE IV and FoxPro are not comparable to those available through the REPORT FORM command of dBASE III PLUS, dBXL 1.3, Clipper 4.0, and FoxBASE+. These facilities are strongly influenced by R&R and in some cases are superior.

Graph Forms

Graphics are, of course, a very important reporting modality. Although we will see in Volume 2 that there are many products which add graphics services to dBASE applications, only WordTech dialects (dBXL and Quicksilver) support graphics directly, without the need for third-party software.

dBXL and Quicksilver offer you GRAPH FORM, the graphics analog of REPORT FORM. See page 172 for a presentation of this facility.

Form Letters

R&R Relational Report Writer and the report writers in dBASE IV and FoxPro support form letters to one degree or another. Generally speaking, a word processor is the right tool for a word processing job like producing attractive letters, and you frequently won't be able to reproduce the look of letters printed by your word processing software with your database report writer.

However, most word processing software has built-in support for form letters, using two files: a document file with references to database fields, and a data file, which lists the data to be merged into the letter form to produce each form letter. With the "COPY TO ... TYPE SDF" command, you can usually create the format required for the data file.

This approach is the standard process for interfacing .DBF data to the form letter facilities of a word processing program. You can use a database program to manage your data and a word processor to manage your text, thus getting the best features of each product.

Custom Programming

Under many circumstances we programmers must write custom code to generate the reports needed by our users. The reports available through REPORT FORM are often not sufficiently powerful or convenient, and we may not be able to use a reporting tool like R&R. The reporting facilities in dBASE IV and FoxPro are very powerful, but we may use another dialect.

First, we'll discuss the case of printing reports on pages with optional page headers and footers. Then we'll discuss labels and form letters.

Reports on Pages

Let's assume that you have coded a report which works just fine, except that it has no page orientation — it's just a stream of data, one line after another, from the start to the end, whether that's 10 lines or 1,000 lines. You now wish to modify the reporting code to print headings and footings at the top of each page to give the report a nice "word-processed" look.

You need the following information, which doesn't change during the report:

1. The number of printed lines per page.
2. The number of blank lines to print before the page heading.
3. The number of lines in the page heading.
4. The number of blank lines to print below the page heading.
5. The number of blank lines to print before the page footing.
6. The number of lines in the page footing.
7. The number of blank lines to print below the page footing.

While the report is being produced, memvars count the number of lines printed on a page and the number of pages printed. Let's call these counters LinesOnPag and PageNumber, respectively. The basic format of a custom report on one database — without pagination — is as follows:

```
* <open database>
* <set filter if necessary>
DO WHILE (.NOT. EOF())
   <list of ? and/or ?? statements referring to fields>
   SKIP
ENDDO && (.NOT. EOF())
```

When we add pagination, we need a routine to print the page header, say, PageHead, and a routine to print the page footer, say, PageFoot, which accepts the page counter as an argument in order to print the page number at the bottom of each page. We print the page header to start the report; we enter a loop to print the data and increment the line counter LinesOnPag; when the line counter reaches a certain value in the loop, we print the page footer, eject, and print the page header; and after the loop we space to the bottom of the page and print the page footer, as shown in Listing 24.2.

Listing 24.2 Template for a Custom Report with Page Headings and Footings

```
* A template for a custom report with page headings and footings:
* <open database>
* <SET FILTER and SET DELETED as necessary>
PageNumber = 1
DO PageHead WITH LinesOnPag
* LinesOnPag = <number of lines above header, in header, and below header>
DO WHILE (.NOT. EOF())
   IF (LinesOnPag > <trigger value>)
      * Print blank lines and the page footer; increment the page counter.
      DO PageFoot with LinesOnPag,PageNumber
      EJECT
      DO PageHead WITH LinesOnPag
   ENDIF
   <list of ? and/or ?? statements referring to fields which prints N lines>
   LinesOnPag = LinesOnPag + N && N = <number of lines printed with each loop>
   SKIP
ENDDO && (.NOT. EOF())
DO PageFoot with LinesOnPag,PageNumber
EJECT
```

The trigger value is computed so that the N lines of data for one record will always print on the same page. If there is not room to print N lines and the page footer with its preceding and following blank lines, then PageFoot is called to do the following: the page is finished out with blank lines, the page footer is printed, and the page number is incremented. Then a new page is started (EJECT) and the PageHead routine is called to print the header and to initialize the LinesOnPag counter to the number of lines in the header, plus the number of blank lines printed above and below the header.

For illustration, the EJECT command is listed after each reference to PageFoot. In practice, we would place EJECT inside the PageFoot routine.

Multiple-File Reporting

All dialects implement the SET RELATION TO command, which is the command that gives dBASE dialects the claim of being "relational." The SET RELATION TO command supports the programming of one-to-one or many-to-one relationships. The dBASE IV dialect also implements the SET SKIP TO command, which extends SET RELATION to support many-to-many relationships!

Many-to-One Relationships

Let's return to the example earlier in the chapter about Orders.DBF and Customer.DBF. Our first task is to print the amount of each order, Orders->Total, and the name of the customer making the order, Customer->Name. First we'll code the report without the SET RELATION TO command, and then we'll use SET RELATION TO in a second version in order to see its benefit, as shown in Listing 24.3 (Relate0.PRG on the companion diskette to this book).

Both versions of the code give the following result in dBASE III PLUS, dBASE IV, FoxBASE+, FoxPro, and dBXL, assuming that the databases have the contents listed. The customer ID "nono" is not found in Customer.DBF, so order record 7 has no customer name.

```
. USE Customer
. LIST
Record#  NAME        ID
      1  Abbott      ABB
      2  Babcock     BAB
      3  Babson      BABS
      4  Carson      CAR
      5  Pauper      PAU
. USE Orders
. LIST
Record#  CUST_ID TOTAL
      1  ABB        10
      2  BAB        20
      3  BABS       30
      4  CAR        40
      5  ABB        50
      6  ABB        60
      7  nono       70
```

```
 DO RELATE1
10 Abbott
20 Babcock
30 Babson
40 Carson
50 Abbott
60 Abbott
70
```

Listing 24.3 Reporting with and without the SET RELATION Command

```
* File = Relate0.PRG.  Compiled or called from the dot prompt to demonstrate
* the SET RELATION command.
*******************************************************************************
* Dialects: All.
*******************************************************************************
SET Safety OFF
SET Talk OFF
************************************************ Version without SET RELATION.
CLOSE ALL
SELECT 0
USE Customer
INDEX ON ID TO ID
SELECT 0
USE Orders
DO WHILE (.NOT. EOF())
   ? Orders->Total
   SELECT Customer
   SEEK Orders->Cust_ID
   IF (.NOT. EOF())
      ??  "  " + Customer->Name
   ENDIF
   SELECT Orders
   SKIP
ENDDO && (.NOT. EOF())
*************************************************** Version with SET RELATION.
CLOSE ALL
SELECT 0
USE Customer
INDEX ON ID TO ID
SELECT 0
USE Orders
SET RELATION TO Cust_ID INTO Customer
DO WHILE (.NOT. EOF())
   ? Orders->Total, Customer->Name
   SKIP
ENDDO && (.NOT. EOF())

SET Safety ON
SET Talk ON
* End of Relate0.PRG.
```

One-to-Many Relationships

The last example used Orders as the parent database and Customer as the child, in a many-to-one relation: in general, there could be many order records with a given customer code. Now let's look at the report requirement of listing the customers and their orders, if any.

This time, the parent and child database roles will be reversed, and the relation will be one-to-many: in general, there can be many order records with the same customer code. As with the SET RELATION example, I show the versions with and without the SET SKIP TO command (Listing 24.4).

Listing 24.4 Reporting with and without the SET SKIP Command

```
* File = Skip.PRG.  Called from dot prompt to demonstrate the SET SKIP command
* of dBASE IV.  The first version of the report coded below works in any
* dBASE dialect but the second version requires dBASE IV.
******************************************** Generic version without SET SKIP.
CLOSE ALL
SELECT 1
USE Orders
INDEX ON Cust_ID to Cust_ID
SELECT 2
USE Customer
INDEX ON UPPER(Name) TO Name
DO WHILE (.NOT. EOF())
   SELECT Orders
   SEEK Orders->Cust_ID
   IF (.NOT. EOF())
      DO WHILE (Orders->Cust_ID = Customer->ID)
     ? Customer->Name,Orders->Total
     SKIP
      ENDDO
   ELSE
      ? Customer->Name, 0
   ENDIF
   SELECT Customer
   SKIP
ENDDO && (.NOT. EOF())
*********************************************** dBASE IV version with SET SKIP.
CLOSE ALL
SELECT 1
USE Orders
INDEX ON Cust_ID to Cust_ID
SELECT 2
USE Customer
INDEX ON UPPER(Name) TO Name

SET RELATION TO ID INTO Orders
SET SKIP TO Orders                  && Here's the magic command!

SCAN
   ? Customer->Name,Orders->Total
ENDSCAN
* The above SCAN/ENDSCAN loop abbreviates
* DO WHILE (.NOT. EOF())
*     ? Customer->Name,Orders->Total
*     SKIP
* ENDDO && (.NOT. EOF())
* End of /.PRG.
```

The first version can be used in any major dialect to get the same result as with the second version under dBASE IV. Using the same database contents as above, the output generated by either version of the code in Listing 24.4 is shown in Listing 24.5.

Listing 24.5 Results from SET SKIP Code

```
Abbott      10
Abbott      50
Abbott      60
Babcock     20
Babson      30
Carson      40
Pauper       0
```

As you can see, SET SKIP is a *very* powerful command. When you are relating several databases with many-to-many relationships, the savings in initial coding time and debugging time may be enormous.

Appendix A

How to Order the Companion Products for This Book

This appendix tells you how to order the companion products for this book, which include the companion diskette and the semiannual supplements. See Appendix B on page 423 for a listing of the files on the companion diskette.

Note that the companion diskette contains a list of identified errors in the book. At the time of writing, the companion diskette has 87 files comprising 186,368 bytes.

How to Order the Companion Diskette for This Book

You may order the companion diskette for the book either by phone or by mail from Database Software Consultants, POB 8380, Austin, TX 78713, U.S.A., (512) 477-3423, according to the procedures explained below. The companion diskette contains the command files and templates listed in this book, as well as some small test databases which exercise the book's demonstration programs. The companion diskette also has several text files generated by the demonstration programs running under various dialects, and it lists all known errors in the book. Appendix B on page 423 contains an annotated directory of the source code files listed in this book which are also on the companion diskette.

The cost of the diskette is $19.95 plus shipping and handling and sales tax in Texas. Shipping and handling is $5 for shipping to addresses in the United States (U.S.), Canada, and Mexico, and $7 otherwise. We ship to addresses in the United States using first class mail, and we ship to all other addresses using international air mail. The total cost to customers in different places is given in the following table.

Table A.1 Cost of the Companion Diskette

Total Cost in $ U.S.	Shipping Address
$24.95	Outside Texas, but inside the United States, Canada, or Mexico.
$26.40	Inside Texas, but outside of Austin, assuming a tax rate of 7.25%.
$26.55	Austin, Texas, assuming a tax rate of 8%.
$26.95	Outside the United States, Canada, and Mexico.

How to Order the Semiannual Supplements for This Book

You may order the supplements for the book either by phone or by mail from Database Software Consultants, POB 8380, Austin, TX 78713, U.S.A., (512) 477-3423, according to the procedures explained below. These supplements will be published every six months, starting six months after the publication of the book. Each *Supplement* will (1) be typeset and printed on Classic Laid Baronial Ivory paper in the 8 1/2-by-11-inch size, (2) consist of an estimated 40–80 pages, and (3) list corrections for all known errors in the book.

The cost of each supplement is $29.95 plus shipping and handling and sales tax in Texas. Shipping and handling is $6 for shipping addresses in the United States, Canada, or Mexico, and $11 otherwise. We ship to addresses in the United States using first class mail, and we ship to all other addresses using international air mail. The total cost to customers in different places is given in the following table.

Table A.2 Cost of a Semiannual Supplement

Total Cost in $ U.S.	Shipping Address
$35.95	Outside Texas, but inside the United States, Canada, or Mexico.
$38.12	Inside Texas, but outside of Austin, assuming a tax rate of 7.25%.
$38.35	Austin, Texas, assuming a tax rate of 8%.
$41.95	Outside the United States, Canada, and Mexico.

Phone Orders

To order by phone, call (512) 477-3423. Please have your MasterCard or VISA ready. We normally ship within one business day. We will charge your card according to Tables A.1 and A.2, except that the tax charges will reflect current rates, if these rates differ from those used to calculate the numbers in the tables.

Mail Orders

To order by mail, send a check or money order for U.S. dollars drawn on a U.S. bank in the amount given in Tables A.1 and A.2, according to your shipping address. Alternatively, you may pay by MasterCard or VISA.

When you order by mail, you must give us your shipping address and tell us which of our products you are ordering. You must also supply additional information if you are paying with MasterCard or VISA. The most convenient way to do this is to photocopy or cut out one of the order forms which is printed at the back of this book, fill it out, and mail it to the indicated address. Otherwise, please provide the following information with your payment.

Table A.3 Required Information for Mail Orders

1. The date.
2. Your name.
3. Your title.
4. Your company name.
5. The address we will ship to:
   a. Street address or post office box.
   b. City.
   c. U.S. state or Canadian province.
   d. U.S. ZIP code or other postal code.
   e. Country.
6. Daytime phone number. This is important — we won't bother you with sales calls at this number, but we *will* use it to help resolve any problem with your order in the fastest way possible.
7. Payment options:
   a. You may pay by check or money order in U.S. dollars. Checks must be drawn on U.S. banks.
   b. You may pay by MasterCard or VISA. In that case, do the following.
      i. Print your credit card type as MasterCard or VISA.
      ii. Print the number on the card.
      iii. Print the expiration date on the card.
      iv. Print the exact name on the card.
      v. Print your name.
      vi. Sign your name as a legitimate user of the card.
8. Product options:
   a. Specify whether you want a companion diskette for Volume 1 or Volume 2.
   b. Specify whether you want a supplement for Volume 1 or Volume 2. Then specify the supplement number, as in number 1, number 2, and so on.
9. Mail your payment and completed order form to:

   Database Software Consultants
   POB 8380
   Austin, TX 78713-8380
   U.S.A.

Companion Products
for dBASE Dialects Software Engineering, Volume 1
Mail Order Form

Date: ______________________________

Circle payment method: Check Money Order MasterCard VISA

Credit card number:

__________-__________-__________-__________

Expiration date: month/year: _____/_____

Exact name on card: ______________________________

Your name: (enter "same" if same) ______________________________

If names are different, which name should we mail to?

Circle: first second

Your company name: ______________________________

Your title: ______________________________

To what street address or Post Office Box do you want us to mail?

____

____

City, State: ______________________________

ZIP code or COUNTRY: ______________________________

Daytime phone number, area code first:

(_____)________-________X________

Circle the products desired:

Volume 1 Companion Diskette: 5¼ inch size 3½ inch size

Volume 1 Supplement: #1 #2 #3 #4 #5 #6 #7

Mail to:

Database Software Consultants, POB 8380, Austin, TX 78713-8380, U.S.A.

Appendix B

Names and Descriptions of Templates and Listings

Here is an annotated directory of the source code files listed in this book which are also on the companion diskette. See the Index for the page numbers on which these listings appear. The diskette also contains some small databases which are used by the demonstration programs and some text file reports generated from some of the demonstration programs.

Note in particular the routines RecogEnv.PRG and Select0.PRG. The first of these especially valuable routines recognizes the dBASE dialect under which code executes and the second implements SELECT 0 for dBASE III PLUS.

The text file Errors.TXT lists all of the errors in the book which were discovered after the book was printed — please report any errors you discover to me at the address in Appendix A. The text file ReadMe.TXT reports any news which is relevant to readers of this book, such as the date of publication of the next supplement to the book.

Table B.1 Annotated Contents for the Companion Diskette

ASCII.REF	A table of IBM (8-bit) ASCII listing the decimal and character form of each character.
Boxes.REF	A text file containing a large number of different box forms, using both the line-drawing characters in the lower half of the IBM (8-bit) ASCII character set (which will print on any printer) and the line-drawing characters in the upper half of the IBM (8-bit) ASCII character set, which will print on some printers and which will display properly on any IBM-compatible PC. Use this file to cut and paste box forms into your documentation and program files.
CASE.TEM	Template for DO CASE.
ColorSet.PRG	Demonstration color-setting routine for dBASE IV and FoxPro; used in some examples in this book.
DefMenu1.PRG	Demonstrates the building of a top-line menu bar with arbitrary actions taken when menu choices are selected; uses the DEFINE MENU facility in dBASE IV and FoxPro.

DefMenu2.PRG	Demonstrates the building of a top-line menu bar with automatic drop-down submenus using the DEFINE MENU facility in dBASE IV and FoxPro.
Deleted.PRG	Routine to determine setting of SET DELETE.
DescendC.PRG	Emulates the DESCEND() function of Clipper, dBXL, FoxPro, and Quicksilver as a procedure.
DOSmenu.BAT	Demonstration BATCH file to implement a DOS-level menu.
DotPrg.TEM	Template for command file called from the dot prompt.
DupKeys.TEM	Template for retrieval of records in databases with duplicate keys.
EditCL.PRG	A simulation of the EDIT command for Clipper.
EditIndS.TEM	A screen template for editing individual database records.
ELSE.TEM	Template for ELSE, nonbeginner's form.
ELSE1.TEM	Template for ELSE, beginner's form.
Errors.TXT	**Errata for the book.**
HeadLine.PRG	Called from routines built from MainScrn.TEM or SubScrn.TEM to display status information on the top screen line.
IF.TEM	Template for IF, nonbeginner's form.
IF1.TEM	Template for IF, beginner's form.
LoopChr.TEM	Template for dialect-independent iterative loop with character index.
LoopChr1.TEM	Template for dialect-independent iterative loop with character index to be used (instead of LoopChr.TEM) when rapid execution is a consideration.
LoopNext.TEM	Template for FOR/NEXT iterative loop with numeric index, for Clipper, dBXL, and Quicksilver.
LoopNpro.TEM	Template for FOR/ENDFOR iterative loop for FoxPro.
LoopNum.TEM	Template for dialect-independent iterative loop with numeric index.
MainMenu.TEM	Template for top-level routine of an application.
MainScrn.TEM	Companion template to MainMenu.TEM; displays the main menu screen for the top-level routine of an application.
MakeSEF3.PRG	Makes empty structure extended file for dBASE III PLUS.
MakeSEF4.PRG	Makes empty structure extended file for dBASE IV.
MakeSeFB.PRG	Makes empty structure extended file for FoxBASE+.
MakeSeFP.PRG	Makes empty structure extended file for FoxPro.
MenuBar.PRG	Demonstrates the implementation of Macintosh-style menus using the MENU BAR facility in FoxPro.

MenuTo.PRG	Demonstrates the implementation of pick lists using the MENU TO command in Clipper, FoxBASE+, and FoxPro.
MenuTo2.PRG	Demonstrates the implementation of Lotus-style top-line moving-bar menus using the MENU TO command in Clipper, FoxBASE+, and FoxPro.
MinType.PRG	Dialect-independent demonstration of passing parameters of different types to the same routine.
Pick.PRG	Dialect-independent unboxed pick list routine.
PickBox.PRG	Dialect-independent boxed pick list routine; calls Pick.PRG.
PickNext.PRG	Subroutine for Pick.PRG.
PickTest.PRG	Demonstration subroutine for Pick.PRG and PickBox.PRG.
POPUP1.PRG	Demonstrates the three pick list options of the POPUP facility in dBASE IV and FoxPro.
POPUP2.PRG	Demonstrates the menu-building feature of the POPUP facility in dBASE IV and FoxPro.
PRG.TEM	Template for a command file which is not called from the dot prompt.
ReadMe.TXT	**News for readers of this book.**
RecogEnv.PRG	**Recognizes the dialect at execution time.**
Relate*.PRG	Demonstrates the SET RELATION command.
Reply.PRG	Routine for simple dialogs with user: displays a one-line prompt and gets a one-keystroke response.
Reply.TEM	Template for simple dialogs with user: displays a multiple-line prompt and gets a one-keystroke response.
ReportPg.TEM	Template for custom report with page headings and footings.
RR3.TEM	Template for routine to interface your application with R&R Relational Report Writer.
Save_ABC.PRG	Demonstrates scope of variables.
Scope*.*	Routines (and the text files they produce) to demonstrate scope of variables.
SeekSDBF.PRG	Emulation of SEEK for sorted databases; will match a record even if the record does not match the current filter or SET DELETED conditions. In the case of duplicate keys, any record in the set of records with the same key may be selected.
SekSDBFD.PRG	Emulation of SEEK for sorted databases; will select a record which meets the current filter or SET DELETED conditions. In the case of duplicate keys, the first record in the set of records with the same key will be selected.
Select0.PRG	**Emulates SELECT 0 in dBASE III PLUS.**
Skip.PRG	Demonstrates the SET SKIP command of dBASE IV.

SubMenu.TEM	Template for top-level routine of an application.
SubScrn.TEM	Companion template to SubMenu.TEM; displays the submenu screen.
TextBrow.PRG	Browse a text file in Clipper.
Tokens.PRG	Routine to extract tokens of arbitrary definition from a string.
UDF_Test.PRG	Called from the dot prompt to test the SET UDFPARMS command of FoxPro 1.01.
WaitOnC.PRG	Ergonomically safe alternative to WAIT.
WHILE.TEM	Template for DO WHILE (.NOT. EOF())

Appendix C

A Recommended Directory Structure

The following directory structure is recommended for MS-DOS computers which are used for developing or executing dBASE applications. Variants on this structure will be appropriate for other operating systems.

Recommended Directories

The following directories are recommended.

1. **\Batch.** This directory holds all of the .BAT files which are executed on your computer. Batch files which you develop for execution on other computers may be kept in other directories. This directory must be on the DOS PATH.
2. **\DB\Data.** This directory holds miscellaneous .DBF files and their associated indexes.
3. **\DB\R&R.** This directory holds the R&R Relational Report Writer files.
4. **\DB\Software.** This directory holds the executable files of the primary dBASE dialect which you use. This directory must be on the dBASE PATH.
5. **\DB\Util.** This directory holds the command and procedure files which you use across applications. Therefore, this directory must be on the dBASE PATH.
6. **\DOS.** This directory holds all of the files that you use from the MS-DOS system diskettes. This directory must be on the DOS PATH.
7. **\Temp.** This directory is used to store files which are only needed for a short time and whose loss has little consequence. You can always erase any files which you find in this directory, because you only store files there with that principle in mind.
8. **\Util.** This directory holds all of the executable files, that is, *utilities*, which supplement DOS. These files may be executed from any directory, so this directory must be on the DOS PATH.

Path Requirements

Among the recommended directories, the following must be on the list in a DOS PATH statement, as in

```
PATH=\Batch;\DOS;\Util
```

or

PATH=C:\Batch;C:\DOS;C:\Util

Among the recommended directories, the following must be on the list in a dBASE PATH statement, as in

SET PATH TO \DB\Software;\DB\Util

or

SET PATH TO C:\DB\Software;C:\DB\Util

Directory Abbreviations

MS-DOS versions 3.1 and higher permit you to abbreviate directory names with the SUBST command. The SUBST command is used to assign a drive letter to a directory. For example, the DOS command "SUBST F: C:\Batch" would permit you to reference the file "C:\Batch\12CPI.LJ2" as "F:12CPI.LJ2". For more information, see page 222.

Appendix D

Productivity Gains and Skill Levels

This appendix presents three scenarios to show the book's possible impact on the productivity of programmers at different skill levels. We look at two entry-level programmers, an intermediate programmer, and an experienced programmer.

Two Entry-Level Programmers

Identical twins Jeb and Ed take introductory programming courses in PASCAL and dBASE III PLUS, where they get the same grade, as usual. Then they go to different corporations for 10-week summer internships, where each of them is asked to modify an application produced with the menu templates in this book.

We'll assume that the applications have the same characteristics in terms of size, complexity, and number of menus. Each application's reports are generated with R&R Relational Report Writer. Jeb is given a copy of this book, but Ed is not.

The changes requested are to add flashing colors to the menus and to make minor changes in two reports. Jeb reads the material on the canonical approach in Chapter 2 and then writes a subroutine which is called at strategic places in the existing menu code to produce the requested flashing colors. From the book's mention of R&R, he realizes that this product is easy to learn. In three hours, he has learned R&R well enough to make the desired report changes.

Ed has every advantage that Jeb has, except this book. Unlike Jeb, he doesn't read about the canonical approach, the subroutine concept, the template concept, and the library concept in Chapter 2. He assumes that R&R is like the dBASE language itself: very difficult and slow to learn.

Consequently, Ed totally rewrites the code of each menu routine, using slightly different methods in each routine. He doesn't write any subroutines to help him paint screens, but instead laboriously writes out hundreds of lines of SET COLOR TO and @ SAY GET statements. Because he assumes that R&R takes years to learn, he rewrites the two reports from scratch.

Ed uses all 10 weeks of his internship to do what Jeb does *in his first week!* In that week, Jeb is 10 times, or 1,000%, more productive than Ed. He then goes on to develop three simple, but useful applications for marketing and sales personnel that help them add another $10 million to annual revenues.

This tale is not literally true, but it is based on common events. In practice, programmers like Jeb discover pieces of the canonical approach on their own or in other books. But we all "stand on the shoulders of giants," as Isaac Newton said, and a book like this one offers both Ed and Jeb the distilled benefits of hundreds of lifetimes of thought and experience.

An Intermediate-Level Programmer

Janet tried a code generator once, and it seemed to take a lot more time than it saved, so she went back to writing all of her code herself. She has a few favorite subroutines, but nothing like a real library. After reading this book, she expands her subroutine library, buys a commercial subroutine library and a template library, and extends the template library to partially automate the construction of calling sequences to library subroutines. She also eliminates some misconceptions which led to code that sometimes crashed "mysteriously."

With a set of standard building blocks, Janet develops a standard approach to applications development that cuts her production times in half. Not only is she 200% faster than before in developing the initial code, resulting in a 100% boost in coding productivity, but she now finds that her applications are much more stable and much easier to modify than before.

An Experienced Programmer

Amy is a consultant who supports clients who use a variety of dBASE dialects. Although she is very efficient, she does not use dialect-specific commercial subroutine libraries, because she supports too many dialects, and because code with references to commercial library routines may be difficult or impossible for her clients to maintain without her.

After studying all of the material in this book, Amy makes a comprehensive reorganization of her development environment. She extends her template library, writes a dialect-independent subroutine library, develops and institutes documentation and quality control procedures, and makes some judicious selections of dialect-independent development tools for report generation, graphics production, multiple-user code insertion, and so on.

The net result is that, when she programs from specifications, she is able to deliver the debugged application about 50% faster than formerly, on the average. Like Janet, she finds that her more standard applications are easier to develop, modify, maintain, and move between dialects. Because she works for herself and is in heavy demand, Amy finds that a 50% productivity increase leads to similar increases in her compensation!

Appendix E

Coding Standards for dBASE Dialects

Generally speaking, there are many design principles, such as those governing the use of uppercase and lowercase in variable names, which are associated with the appearance and structure of "good" source code. These design principles are often grouped into coding standards or conventions.

Following is a coding standard which covers many aspects of the appearance and structure of dBASE dialect source code. The patterns described below appear in code examples throughout this book, so they will be more or less familiar to book readers.

Table E.1 A Coding Standard for dBASE Dialects

1. **Use of uppercase and lowercase.** Use a mixture of uppercase and lowercase text to make the meaning of identifiers more clear. For example, write "PageNumber" and not "PAGENUMBER" or "pagenumber". Use uppercase for keywords, with the first exception of very common keywords, such as ReadKey(), which are compounds that are more easily comprehended when their components are indicated with capitalization. The second exception is the second keyword in lists of consecutive SET statements, where capitalization is recommended.
2. **Use self-describing identifiers.** Choose identifiers which describe themselves as much as possible within the 10-character limit of dBASE dialect identifiers. For example, write "PageNumber" and not "PN" or "X".
3. **Use a type suffix if feasible.** If your code would be easier to understand when one or more identifiers have a type suffix, then use the suffix. For example, PageCountN is the numeric form of the page count, and PageCountC is the character form of the page count.
4. **Comment carefully.** If the action of the code is not obvious, include a comment to explain the code. If the action *is* obvious, do *not* include a comment.
5. **Use blanks to improve readability.** Always surround relational operators with blanks. If the insertion of a blank will make the code easier to read, then insert the blank.

```
* Use this form:
IF (mPage >= System->Page)

* Don't use this form:
IF mPage>=System->Page
```

6. **Use blank lines to improve readability.** Surround segments of your code which are logically grouped with blank lines and/or lines of asterisks. By presenting your code in clearly indicated segments, you will make it much easier to understand (i.e., more canonical!).
7. **Alphabetize.** In lists of identifiers, assignment statements, or SET statements, impose alphabetic order if no other ordering is required: for example, "PRIVATE A,B,C" and not "PRIVATE B,A,C".

```
* Use this form:
A = 1
B = 2
C = 3

* Don't use this form:
B = 2
A = 1
C = 3
```

8. **Align equal-signs in lists of assignments.** In consecutive assignment statements which use the "=" form (as opposed to the STORE form), follow the longest identifier with one blank and the equal-sign. Then put all the equal-signs in that group of assignment statements in the same column.

```
* Use this form:
Page       = "YES"
Page_L     = .F.
PageNumber = 0

* Don't use this form:
Page = "YES"
Page_L = .F.
PageNumber = 0
```

9. **Align successive && comments.** If feasible, align && comments on successive lines so that the && characters are in the same character columns.

```
* Use this form:
Page       = "PAGE" && This string precedes the page number.
Page_L     = .F.    && Becomes true when a new page is needed.
PageNumber = 0      && Stores the number of the current page.

* Don't use this form:
Page       = "YES" && This string precedes the page number.
Page_L     = .F. && Becomes true when a new page is needed.
PageNumber = 0 && Stores the number of the current page.
```

10. **Put logical expressions inside parentheses.** A logical memvar does not need to be in parentheses: code "IF Loop_L" and not "IF (Loop_L)". A logical expression is most readable when it is enclosed in parentheses. For example, code "Loop_L = (PageNumber > 0)" and not "Loop_L = PageNumber > 0".
11. **Force the order of evaluation for logical expressions.** A logical expression with two clauses does not depend on the order in which the clauses are listed: (A .AND. B) always equals (B .AND. A); (A .OR. B) always equals (B .OR. A). However, the value of (A .AND. B .OR. C) may be either (A .AND. (B .OR. C)) or ((A .AND. B) .OR. C), which in general are different. If you use a logical expression with three or more clauses, use parentheses to force the expression to be evaluated the way you want.

12. **Parameter ordering.** List parameters in the order of input, input/output, and output in PARAMETERS statements.
13. **Indentation.** Indent control structures as shown in the control structure templates and code examples. See IF.TEM, CASE.TEM, ELSE.TEM, and WHILE.TEM in Chapter 18.
14. **Command file structure.** Use the structure shown in PRG.TEM and DotPrg.TEM for command files in Chapter 18.
15. **Procedure structure.** Precede the PROCEDURE statement with a line consisting of asterisks, two blanks, and the name of the procedure; the last character of the procedure name should be in the 78th column. Follow the last statement of the procedure with a line of asterisks.
16. **Application subroutine structure.** Use the structure shown in MainMenu.TEM for the top-level routine of an application. Note that this structure can be used for any menu method.
17. **Subroutine documentation.** Document your subroutines as specified in the table "The Minimum Documentation for a Library Subroutine" on page 318.
18. **Use subroutines.** Sometimes dBASE III PLUS programmers who worked under DOS 2 would write very long command files — DOS 2 would only permit dBASE to have 15 open files, and using a subroutine could cause the application to crash with too many open files. It is extremely important to use DOS 3 or a dialect which permits at least 30 open files. In this case, you can usually nest subroutines as deeply as you need to without exceeding the limit of the maximum number of open files allowed. Under the assumption that your application can open as many files as it needs, I recommend that you limit your subroutines to 100 lines and that you use an additional subroutine whenever it improves the readability of your code. (You may also increase the number of subroutines in your application without increasing the number of open files by placing the subroutines into a procedure file!)
19. **Balance power and complexity in subroutine design.** When you wonder if a subroutine should have a certain capability which might very well be needed, include the capability. Adding capability to a subroutine usually means adding one or more parameters to the list of parameters. When you expand the list of parameters, consider whether the subroutine is becoming too complex. If so, split it into two subroutines: a moderately general subroutine with a modest parameter list, and a more general version with a longer list of parameters.
20. **Use memvars as named constants.** If a constant appears more than once with the same meaning in your application, replace the constants with a memvar. For example, if you find yourself writing "6" in two places in your application to indicate the number of lines per inch, then invent a memvar like LPI, declare the memvar in a PUBLIC or PRIVATE statement, assign 6 to LPI, and replace the references to "6" with references to LPI.
21. **Use "M->" qualification in subroutines.** When a subroutine does not know what fields may be defined, and you are *not* using Clipper with the "-V" switch, then precede each memvar reference with "M->", with these exceptions: (1) code "A = 1" instead of "M->A = 1", and (2) use the "M->" prefix for arguments or not, as described under the heading "Memvar Arguments versus Field Arguments" on page 303.

Other Coding Standards

The coding standard in this book does not treat all issues, and it reflects the perspective of one school of thought. However, you can consult the following sources to see alternative approaches.

Table E.2 Other Coding Standards

1. "A Word on Coding Style," in *Dynamics of Clipper* (Fuller 1989: xxx). This two-paragraph note defines a little of the coding standard that Fuller follows. It addresses the use of uppercase and lowercase in identifiers and the use of indentation in source code.
2. Section 2.1, "Style," in *Professional Database Development Using dBASE III PLUS, Clipper, and FoxBASE+* (Steele 1989: 15–26). Steele has advice on variable names, capitalization and procedure use, indentation, command usage, comments, constants for InKey(), and general coding techniques.
3. "Eleven Rules for Success in Programming," in *Programming in Clipper* (Straley 1988: 720–722). This collection of rules is not an explicit standard which details conventions such as the use of uppercase and lowercase. However, it does establish coding principles to follow.
4. "Source Code Conventions," in *User Interface and Screen Control Library* (Yellick 1989b: 7–9). Expert Panelist Yellick presents a substantial set of conventions in the manual for his library product.
5. "Suggested Standards for Coding in COBOL" (Yourdon 1979a: 237–249) and "Suggested Standards for Coding in PL/I" (Yourdon 1979a: 251–259) in *Managing the Structured Techniques* give you examples from the old master himself, Edward Yourdon, for COBOL and PL/I.

Appendix F

dBASE-Related Books in Print

This first part of this appendix lists dBASE-related books from R. R. Bowker's *Books in Print* by permission. The titles were downloaded in May of 1990 from the electronic form of this publication on the DIALOG information service. The dialects are covered in the order of Clipper, dBASE II, dBASE III, dBASE III PLUS, dBASE IV, FoxBASE+, FoxPro, Macintosh-related titles, miscellaneous titles, and dBXL/Quicksilver titles.

The information listed below has been extensively reformatted. However, no changes were made to alphabetization, capitalization, or spelling.

The second part of this appendix lists some representative systems analysis and software engineering titles from the literature. While this information is sometimes incomplete, in virtually all cases it should be enough for a bookstore to order the title for you.

dBASE-Related Books

The publisher codes used below are usually self-explanatory, but in a few cases, they are highly abbreviated or refer to specialty publishers who are not generally known. Here is a list of codes and full names for publishers in the second group.

Codes for Selected Publishers

Digit Consult MA. Digital Consulting. (508) 470-3880.

HarBraceJ. Harcourt Brace Jovanovitch.

P H. Prentice-Hall.

P-H. Prentice-Hall.

Scott F. Scott, Foresman.

Slawson Comm. Slawson Communications. See the company listings in Appendix I, which starts on page 457.

Tate Pub. Tate Publishing; order Tate Publishing titles directly from Ashton-Tate or your Ashton-Tate dealer.

Van Nos Reinhold. Van Nostrand Reinhold, the publisher of this and other fine books.

Clipper Books

Advanced Clipper dBASE Compiler. 03/1988. Beam, Gary. TAB Bks. 0-8306-9307-6.

Advanced Clipper dBASE Compiler Applications. 02/1988. Beam, Gary. TAB Bks. 304p. 0-317-67260-6.

Advanced Programming in Clipper: With C. 09/1989. Straley, Stephen J. Addison-Wesley. 0-201-51735-3.

Clipper 5.0. 05/1990. Mueller, John. Wordware Pub. 384p. 1-55622-162-2.

Clipper Connection to dBASE III. 03/1988. Goldenthal, Nathan. Weber Systems. 515p. 0-938862-96-0.
Clipper Programming Guide. 02/1989. Spence, Rick. Slawson Comm. 700p. 0-915391-31-7.
Clipper: A Programmer's Guide. Date not set. Beam, Gary. TAB Bks. 240p. 0-8306-3207-7.
Clipper: dBASE Compiler Applictions. 09/1987. Beam, Gary. Tab Bks. 190p. 0-8306-2917-3.
Dynamics of Clipper. 11/1988. Fuller, Arthur. Dow Jones-Irwin. 1-55623-131-8.
Programming in Clipper. 08/1988. Straley, Stephen J. Addison-Wesley. 752p. 0-201-14583-9.
Programming in Clipper. 10/1988. Zinky, Margaret; Werner, Justin; Donaldson, Bruce. Scott F. 0-673-38361-X.
Programming in Clipper: The Definitive Guide to the Clipper dBASE Compiler. 01/1988. Straley, Stephen J. Addison-Wesley. 0-201-11993-5.
Sixty-Four Clipper User-Defined Functions. 10/1988. Steele, Philip. TAB Bks. 256p. 0 8306-3126-7.
Tom Rettigs Clipper Encyclopedia. 07/1989. Rettig, Tom. Bantam. 0-553-34798-5.
Using Clipper. 10/1988. Tiley, W. Edward. Que Corp. 500p. 0-88022-379-0.

dBASE II Books

Application Junction: A Catalog of dBase II Software Applications. Ashton-Tate Staff. McGraw. 0-07-912649-9.
Creative Business Applications with dBASE II: A Beginner's Introduction. 05/1984. Dinerstein, Nelson T. Scott F. 160p. 0-673-15957-4.
Data Base Management System Design Using dBASE II. 08/1984. McNichols, Charles W. P-H. 0-8359-1222-1.
Designing Education Information Systems Using dBASE II & the Apple II: A Systems Guide to the Apple & dBase II. 01/1986. Bruno, James E. Blackwell Sci. 250p. 0-86542-314-8.
Essential dBASE II. 04/1985. Brown, Carl. Brooks-Cole. 128p. 0-534-05070-0.
Everyman's Database Primer Featuring dBASE II. 1985. Byers, R. A. McGraw. N/A.
Everyman's Database Primer: Featuring dBASE II. 1982. Byers, Robert A.; Barre, Virginia-Editor. Tate Pub. 295p. 0-912677-00-7.
Information Management with dBASE II. Florence, Alan. P-H. 320p. 0-317-13065-X.
Introducing dBASE II. 02/1985. Barnes, Lan. McGraw. 380p. 0-07-041807-1.
Measured Doses of dBASE II. 01/1985. Blake, Robert M. Macmillan. 0-02-948690-4.
Programming with dBASE II. 1984. Prague, Cary N.; Hammitt, James E. TAB Bks. 288p. 0-8306-0776-5.
Quick & Easy dBASE II. 1984. Reymann, Joseph. Manusoft. 64p. 0-88284-291-9.
Report Writing in dBASE II. McMahon, Marilyn; Hoover, Sarah; Popp, William. P-H. 0-317-06186-0.
Simply dBASE II. 02/1984. Chirlian, Barbara S. Dilithium Pr. 300p. 0-88056-138-6.
Simply dBASE II. Chirlian, Barbara S. Crown. 255p. 0-517-56384-3.
The DBASE II. 09/1985. Tate Pub. 0-912677-60-0.
The DBASE II Cash Manager. 04/1985. Heiser, Paul W.; Pickney, Inge D. P H. 230p. 0-13-196023-7.
The DBASE II for Beginners. 01/1985. Lima, Anthony K. P-H. 160p. 0-13-196080-6.
The dBASE II for Every Business. 1983. Byers, Robert A.; Thomson, Monet-Editor; Lincoln, Mary-Editor. Tate Pub. 339p. 0-912677-03-1.
The DBASE II for the First Time User. 05/1984. Freedman, Alan. Tate Pub. 174p. 0-912677-08-2.
The DBASE II for the IBM PC. 02/1986. Ingalsbe, Ron. Merrill. 0-675-20612-X.
The DBASE II for the Programmer: A How-to-Do-It Book. 1984. Dinerstein, Nelson T. Scott F. 176p. 0-673-15956-6.
The DBASE II in English I. Eng Comp Tut. 234p. 0-915869-00-4.
The DBASE II Programmer's Companion. 01/1985. Calmus, Lawrence; Perelman, Bruce. Tate Pub. 0-912677-30-9.
The DBASE II Simplified for the IBM Personal Computer. 01/1985. Cassel, Don. P-H. 176p. 0-13-195934-4.

The DBASE II Techniques & Reference Manual. Lohman, Jack E. Technique Assoc. 133p. 0-9614034-0-3.

The DBASE II: A Comprehensive User's Manual. 02/1985. Bharucha, Kerman D. TAB Bks. 304p. 0-8306-0884-2.

The IBM-PC & Business Software: VisiCalc, dBASE II & WordStar Explained. 09/1983. Kelley, James E.,Jr. Putnam Pub Group. 352p. 0-88693-000-6.

The Illustrated dBASE II Book. 1983. Stultz, Russell A. Tate Pub. 300p. 0-912677-10-4.

The Illustrated dBASE II Book. 02/1984. Stultz, Russell A. Wordware Pub. 312p. 0-915381-55-9.

The Software Primer for dBASE II. Harper, Larry D. JNZ. N/A; N/A.

The Software Primer: dBASE II-Level 1. 12/1983. Harper, Larry D. JNZ. 172p. 0-913871-06-0.

The Software Primer: dBASE II-Level 2. 11/1983. Harper, Larry D. JNZ. 166p. 0-913871-05-2.

Understanding dBASE II. 01/1984. Simpson, Alan. SYBEX. 260p. 0-89588-147-0.

Using dBASE II. 11/1983. Townsend, Carl. Osborne-McGraw. 250p. 0-07-881108-2.

Using Small Business Computers with Lotus 1-2-3, dBASE II & WordStar. 04/1985. Dologite, Dorothy G. P-H. 0-13-940230-6.

Working with dBase II. 1985. De Pace, M. Sheridan. 174p. 0-00-383251-1.

dBASE III Books

Advanced dBASE III Applications. 08/1985. Baker, Richard H. Tab Bks. 448p. 0-8306-0418-9.

Advanced dBASE III: Programming & Techniques. 02/1986. Liskin, Miriam. Osborne-McGraw. 630p. 0-07-881196-1.

Advanced Programmer's Guide Featuring dBASE III & dBASE II. 07/1984. Hanson, Jay; Rettig, Tom; Castro, Luis. Tate Pub. 664p. 0-912677-05-8.

Building Expert System for 1-2-3 & DBASE III & Using Insight. 04/1988. Lipton, Russell C. Bantam. 352p. 0-553-34495-1.

Computers Today & International Educations Lab Manual: Using Wordperfect 4.2, VP Planner & dBase III. 01/1988. Intentional Educations Staff; Sanders, Donald H. McGraw. N/A.

DBASE II & dBASE III: An Introduction for Information Services. 1984. Palmer, Roger C. ALA. 90p. 0-8389-2037-3.

DBASE III - Programmer's Reference Guide. 03/1988. Goldenthal, Nathan. Weber Systems. 538p. 0-938862-95-2.

DBASE III Tips & Tricks. 08/1987. Jenkins, David. Wiley. 160p. 0-471-62577-9.

DBASE III: A Practical Guide for Professional & Business Users. 11/1985. DePace, M. Van Nos Reinhold. 192p. 0-442-22296-3.

Dbase III: Procedures Manual. 06/1989. Curtin. P-H. 0-13-198862-X.

DBASE Programmer's Field Guide. 09/1987. Boies, Robert; Dickler, Howard. Tate Pub. 175p. 1-55519-022-7.

Essential dBASE III. Brown, Carl. Brooks-Cole. 0-534-05082-4.

Expert dBASE: An Advanced Textbook for dBASE Programmers. 07/1985. Robbins, Judd; Braly, Ken. Comp Options. 264p. 0-9614937-0-4.

Four Software Tools with DOS, WordStar, VP-Planner, & dBASE III. 1987. Duffy, Tim. Wadsworth Pub. 522p. 0-534-07962-8.

Learning to Use dBASE III. 09/1986. Metzelaar; Fox. Benjamin Cummings. 0-8053-6716-0.

Learning to Use dBASE III: An Introduction. 05/1986. Shelly, Gary B.; Cashman, Thomas J. Boyd & Fraser. 210p. 0-87835-210-4.

Learning to Use SUPERCALC3, dBASE III & WordStar 3.3: An Introduction. 03/1986. Shelly, Gary B.; Cashman, Thomas J. Boyd & Fraser. 450p. 0-87835-208-2.

M. A. S. H. 101: Software Notes for dBase III. Date not set. MASH. N/A.

Mastering dBASE III in Less Than a Day. 01/1986. Lima, Anthony K. P-H. 160p. 0-13-559816-8.

Mastering dBASE III: A Structured Approach. 08/1985. Townsend, Carl. Sybex. 338p. 0-89588-301-5.

MS-DOS, Lotus 1-2-3, & DBASE. 1987. Massey, Joseph G. Forest Res Syst. 158p. N/A.

One Hundred & One Questions about dBASE III: Software Application Guide. P-H. N/A.

One Hundred One Questions about dBASE III. Date not set. Green, Adam B.; Fletcher, William; Ing, Julie. S&S. N/A.

Personal Productivity Using dBASE III. 03/1987. Gorham, Ken. Wm C Brown. 144p. 0-697-05551-5.

Programming the dBase III & User Interface. 06/1987. Rubel, Malcolm C. Bantam. 0-553-34408-0.
Programming with dBASE II & dBASE III. 01/1986. Rob, Peter. Wadsworth Pub. 380p. 0-534-06186-9.
Sales Management with dBASE III. 03/1986. Berry, Timothy. M&T Pub Inc. 150p. 0-934375-15-1.
The Complete Guide to dBASE III: A Self-Teaching Guide. 06/1986. Greenberg, Philip; Greenberg, Rita. Wiley. 378p. 0-471-81041-X.
The DBASE II & dBASE III: An Introduction for Information Services. 09/1984. Palmer, Roger C. Pacific Info. 94p. 0-913203-09-2.
The DBASE II & III in English I. Eng Comp Tut. 312p. 0-915869-02-0.
The DBASE III for the Programmer: A How-to-Do-It-Book. 04/1985. Dinerstein, Nelson T. Scott F. 320p. 0-673-18180-4.
The DBASE III Programming Handbook. 02/1986. Prague, Cary N.; Hammitt, James E. TAB Bks. 240p. 0-8306-0676-9.
The DBASE III Tips & Traps. 03/1986. Andersen, Dick; Cooper, Cynthia; Dempsey, Bill. Osborne-McGraw. 300p. 0-07-881195-3.
The DBASE III User's Handbook. 06/1985. Weber Systems, Inc. Staff. Ballantine. 0-345-32378-5.
The dBASE III: Applications & Subroutines. 06/1985. Lee, Sang C.; Lee, Minja P. Wiley. 320p. 0-471-80225-5.
The DBASE Programming Language. 12/1986. De Pace, M. Sheridan. 192p. 0-00-383267-8.
The Programmer Library. 12/1985. Cooper, Jeffrey. Tate Pub. 0-912677-79-1.
Time & Task Management with dBASE III. 02/1986. Berry, Timothy. M&I Pub Inc. 75p. 0-934375-09-7.
Understanding & Using Data Base III: Including D Base II. 11/1985. Ross, Steven C. West Pub. 196p. 0-314-96211-5.
Understanding & Using dBASE II & III. 1985. Krumm, Rob. Brady Bks. 320p. N/A.
Understanding & Using dBASE III: A Guide for Business & Professional Users. 08/1985. Christie, Linda G.; Bullard, Gary. P-H. 224p. 0-13-937087-0.
Understanding dBASE III. 01/1985. Simpson, Alan. SYBEX. 300p. 0-89588-267-1.
Using dBASE III. 03/1985. Jones, Edward. Osborne-McGraw. 200p. 0-07-881162-7.
Using dBASE III on the IBM PC. Davisson, Darrell. S&S. N/A.
Using WordPerfect 4.2, VP Planner & dBase III. 01/1988. Intentional Educations Staff. McGraw. 288p. 0-07-031511-6.

dBASE III PLUS Books

ABC's of dBASE III PLUS. 08/1986. Cowart, Robert. Sybex. 264p. 0-89588-379-1.
Advanced dBASE III Plus. 09/1987. Knecht, Ken. Scott F. 0-673-18777-2.
Advanced dBASE III PLUS: Programming & Techniques. 09/1986. Liskin, Miriam. Osborne-McGraw. 885p. 0-07-881249-6.
Advanced Programming with dBASE III PLUS. 08/1987. Prague, Cary N.; Hammitt, James E. Tab Bks. 0-8306-0176-7.
Advanced Techniques in dBASE III PLUS. 08/1986. Simpson, Alan. Sybex. 454p. 0-89588-369-4.
Applications Exercises Using Lotus 1-2-3, dBASE III-III Plus & Wordstar. 03/1987. Neely, Alex. Merrill. 150p. 0-675-20902-1.
Applications Exercises Using VP-Planner, dBASE III-III Plus & Wordstar with VP Planner, dBASE III-III Plus & Wordstar Student Software. 01/1987. Neely, Alex. Merrill. 150p. 0-675-20844-0.
Business Applications for the IBM PC with Lotus, dBASE III-III Plus & Wordperfect. 01/1988. Ingalsbe, Lon. Merrill. 0-675-21042-9.
Business Applications for the IBM PC with VP-Planner, dBASE III-III Plus & Wordperfect with Software. 01/1988. Ingalsbe, Lon. Merrill. 0-675-21035-6.
Business Applications for the IBM-PC with VP-Planner, dBASE III & III Plus & WordPerfect. 01/1988. Ingalsbe, Lon. Merrill. 0-675-21000-3.
Cases & Applications in dBASE III Plus. 01/1988. Smith, David G. Irwin. 0-256-05923-3.
Command Performance, dBASE III PLUS: The Microsoft Reference Guide to All Commands, Functions & Features. 06/1987. Hergert, Douglas. Microsoft. 656p. 1-55615-024-5.
Como Usar dBase III Plus: Understanding dBase III Plus. 03/1988. Simpson, Alan; Macrobit Corporation Staff-Editor;

Tamayo, Jorge- Translator; Suckoo, Orville-Illustrator; Tamayo, Jorge-Intro. by. Macrobit Corp. 401p. 0-939573-04-0.
Compute! 's Quick & Easy Guide to dBASE III Plus. 07/1987. Doherty, Chuck. Compute Pubns. 259p. 0-87455-107-2.
Computing Fundamentals: dBase III Plus. 08/1989. Davis, William S.; Schreiner, Paul. Addison-Wesley. 192p. 0-201-19825-8.
Computing Fundamentals: Productivity Tools PC & MS-DOS, Wordperfect 5.0, Lotus 1-2-3, dBase III PLUS. 02/1990. Davis, William S. Addison-Wesley. 608p. 0-201-19820-7.
DBASE Demystified: dBASE II-III-III Plus R Applications & Solutions to Real Problems. 09/1986. Barnes, Lan. McGraw. 320p. 0-07-003844-9.
DBASE III & III Plus for the IBM-PC. 03/1987. Ingalsbe, Lon. Merrill. 148p. 0-675-20901-3.
DBASE III Plus. 12/1987. De Pace, Mario. Sheridan. 215p. 0-00-383378-X.
DBASE III Plus. 02/1987. Stultz, Russell A. Scott F. 0-673-18790-X.
DBASE III Plus Multiuser Applications. 1987. Baker, Richard H. TAB Bks. 450p. 0-8306-2908-4.
DBASE III Plus Networking & Multiuser Systems. 05/1987. Carrabis, Joseph. MIS Press. 270p. 0-943518-26-1.
Dbase III Plus Procedures Manual. 05/1989. Curtin, Dennis. P-H. 128p. N/A.
DBase III Plus Programmer Field Guide. 06/1989. Doies, R. P-H. 0-13-199365-8.
DBASE III Plus Programmer's Library. 03/1987. Carrabis, Joseph-David. Sams. 536p. 0-672-22579-4.
DBASE III Plus Programmer's Reference Guide. 10/1986. Jones, Edward C. Sams. 448p. 0-672-22509-3.
DBASE III Plus Programming Tips & Techniques. 07/1986. Prague, Cary N.; Hammitt, James E. Tate Pub. 275p. 0-912677-91-0.
DBase III Plus Programming: Tips & Techniques. 09/1986. Prague; Hammitt. P-H. 0-13-198698-8.
DBASE III Plus Tips, Tricks, & Traps. 06/1987. Chou, George T. Que Corp. 350p. 0-88022-286-7.
DBASE III Plus: A Comprehensive User's Manual. 1986. Bharucha, Kerman D. TAB Bks. 380p. 0-8306-9454-4.
DBase III Plus: Concepts, Exercises, & Applications 5.25" IBM Version & 3.5" IBM Version. 03/1989. Arnston, Joyce L. SW Pub. 336p. 0-538-70301-6.
Dbase III Plus: Educational Version Manual. 05/1987. Christie, Linda G. Wiley. 0-471-85511-1.
DBase III Plus: Quick Reference Handbook. 04/1988. CPCE (Center for Professional Computer Education) Staff. Wiley. 0-317-66883-8.
DBASE III PLUS: The Complete Reference. 12/1986. Carrabis, Joseph D. Osborne-McGraw. 768p. 0-07-881012-4.
DBase III Plus: Things the Manual Didn't Tell You. 01/1987. Dunlop, Neil. Weber Systems. 200p. 0-938862-72-3.
DBASE III-Plus Program Reference Guide. 09/1987. Abacus Soft. 128p. 1-557550-04-2.
DBASE Instant Reference. 12/1987. Simpson, Alan. Sybex. 471p. 0-89588-484-4.
Decision Support Software for the IBM Personal Computer: Featuring Lotus Version 2.01, dBASE III plus, WordPerfect. 1988. McLeod, Raymond. SRA. N/A.
Decision Support Software: Featuring dBase III Plus, Lotus 1-2-3, & WordPerfect. 1988. McLeod, Raymond. SRA. 496p. 0-574-18695-6.
Easy dBase: Taming the Dot. 04/1989. Beatty, Greg. Shamrock CA. 113p. 0-913351-07-5.
Essential Guide to dBASE III-plus in Libraries. 12/1986. Beiser, Karl. Meckler Corp. 0-88736-064-5.
Everyman's Data Base Primer Featuring dBASE III Plus. 12/1985. Byers, Robert A. Tate Pub. 250p. 0-912677-85-6.
Expert Advisor: dBASE III Plus. 04/1988. Rettig, Tom; Moody, Debby. Addison-Wesley. 400p. 0-201-17197-X.
Fast Access-dBASE III Plus. 07/1988. McClure, Rhyder; Rizzo, Tony. Brady Bks. 256p. 0-13-307554-0.
Four Software Tools with DOS, WordPerfect, Lotus 1-2-3-, & dBASE III Plus (Green). 03/1988. Duffy, Tim. Wadsworth Pub. 601p. 0-534-09210-1.
Four Software Tools with DOS, WordPerfect, VP-Planner, & dBASE III Plus. (Orange). 1988. Duffy, Tim. Wadsworth Pub. 613p. 0-534-08820-1.
Four Software Tools with DOS, WordStar, Lotus 1-2-3, & dBASE III Plus (Blue). 1990. Duffy, Tim. Wadsworth Pub. 0-534-11670-1.
Hands on Using MS DOS, WordPerfect, dBase III Plus & Lotus 1-2-3. 05/1988. Metzelaar, Larry. Benjamin-Cummings. 150p. 0-8053-2052-0.

Hands-on dBase III Plus. 02/1990. Duffy, Tim. Wadsworth Pub. 0-534-13356-8.

How to Use dBASE III Plus. 07/1986. Menges, Patricia A.; Rinehart, Janice S.-Editor. FlipTrack. 108p. 0-917792-36-X.

Introduction to Application Software Using VP-Planner, dBase III Plus & WordPerfect with Student Software. 1988. Zollos; Szymanski; Morris; Pulschen; Zollos. Merrill. 0-675-21051-8.

Learning dBase Three Plus. 1989. Thomason, Annette. HM. 0-395-35732-2.

Learning to Use dBase III Plus. 02/1989. Gary, Shelly; Cashman, Thomas J. SW Pub. N/A.

Learning to Use WordPerfect: Lotus 1-2-3, & dBase III Plus. 01/1989. Shelly, Gary; Cashman, Thomas. SW Pub. 0-538-91124-7.

Learning to Use WordPerfect: VP-Planner Plus, & dBase III Plus. 02/1989. Shelly, Gary; Cashman, Thomas. SW Pub. 0-538-91100-X.

Mastering dBASE III PLUS: A Structured Approach. 07/1986. Townsend, Carl. Sybex. 342p. 0-89588-372-4.

Microcomputer Applications Using Wordperfect, Lotus 1-2-3, dBASE III Plus. 08/1988. Grupe, Fritz H. Wm C Brown. 416p. 0-697-05930-8.

Microcomputer Database Management Using dBase III Plus. 1988. Pratt, Philip J. Boyd & Fraser. 448p. 0-87835-303-8.

Microcomputer Use: Software Applications & Problem Solving with WordPerfect 4.2 & 5.0, WordStar, Lotus 1-2-3, dBase III Plus. 02/1989. Alberte-Hallam, Teresa; Hallam, Stephen F. HarBraceJ. 608p. 0-15-558394-8.

Microcomputer Use: Software Applications & Problem Solving with Wordperfect 4.2 & 5.0, Wordstar, Lotus 1-2-3, DBase III Plus. 04/1989. Alberte-Hallam, Teresa; Hallam, Stephen F. HarBraceJ. 256p. 0-15-558395-6.

Microref For dbase III Plus. 12/1987. Educ Systs IL. 0-913365-11-4.

Personal Productivity with dBASE III Plus. 06/1988. Gorham, Kenneth. Wm C Brown. 36p. 0-697-06390-9.

Personal Productivity with dBASE III Plus. 08/1988. Gorham, Kenneth. Wm C Brown. 228p. 0-697-05898-0.

Programming the dBASE III Plus User Interface. 1987. Rubel, Malcolm C. Bantam. 0-317-61488-6.

Programming with dBASE III Plus. 05/1986. Prague, Cary N.; Hammitt, James E. TAB Bks. 384p. 0-8306-0326-3.

Quick Reference Guide to dBASE III PLUS: A Handy, Alphabetic Guide to dBASE III PLUS Commands & Functions. 06/1987. Microsoft. 72p. 1-55615-040-7.

Teach Yourself dBASE III Plus. Charra, Pierre-Jean; Moys, Marie-Jose; EDIDACOM Staff-Translator. Tutorland. 171p. N/A.

The dBASE III Plus Applications Library. 12/1986. Carlton, Thomas W. Que Corp. 622p. 0-88022-228-X.

The dBASE III Plus Concepts, Exercises & Applications. 03/1988. Arntson, L. Joyce. Tate Pub. 400p. 1-55519-051-0.

The DBASE III Plus for Every Business. 12/1985. Byers, Robert. Tate Pub. 0-912677-86-4.

The dBASE III Plus for the Programmer. 06/1987. Dinerstein, Nelson T. Scott F. 0-673-18835-3.

The DBASE III Plus Handbook. 10/1986. Chou, George T. Que Corp. 517p. 0-88022-269-7.

The dBASE III Plus Made Easy. 01/1988. Liskin, Miriam. Osborne-McGraw. 350p. 0-07-881294-1.

The dBase III Plus Programming. 02/1988. Wray, Robert. Boyd & Fraser. 432p. 0-87835-293-7.

The DBASE III PLUS Programming Handbook. 03/1987. Prague, Cary N.; Hammitt, James E. Tab Bks. 0-8306-0256-9.

The dBase III Plus to Go. 09/1987. Bennett, Steven; Randall, Peter. Brady Bks. 300p. 0-13-196214-0.

The dBase III Plus Workbook & Disk. 04/1988. Clifford, Michael J. Que Corp. 125p. 0-88022-338-3.

The dBASE III Plus, Educational Version. Date not set. Christie, Linda G. Wiley. 0-471-62220-6.

The dBase III Plus: Power User's Guide. 01/1988. Jones, Edward. Osborne McGraw. 750p. 0-07-881317-4.

The dBASE III Plus: The Complete Reference. 08/1987. Carrabis, Joseph-David. Osborne McGraw. 768p. 0-07-881315-8.

The dBASE III Plus: The Pocket Reference. 10/1987. Liskin, Miriam. Osborne-McGraw. 120p. 0-07-881305-0.

The dBase III Plus? ut? um: Quick Reference Handbook. 05/1988. Center for Professional Computer Education Staff. Wiley. 0-471-63646-0.

The Illustrated dBASE III PLUS Book. 12/1986. Stultz, Russell A. Wordware Pub. 373p. 0-915381-92-3.
Understanding & Using dBASE III Plus. 07/1987. Krumm, Rob. Brady Bks. 400p. 0-13-935859-5.
Understanding & Using dBASE III Plus. 05/1987. Ross, Steven C. West Pub. 283p. 0-314-34744-5.
Understanding dBASE III PLUS. 03/1986. Simpson, Alan. Sybex. 415p. 0-89588-349-X.
Using Computers & Applications Software Featuring Lotus, dBASE III-III Plus. 01/1989. Ingalsbe. Merrill. 800p. 0-675-21179-4.
Using Computers & Applications Software Featuring VP Planner, dBASE III-III Plus & WordPerfect. 05/1989. Ingalsbe, Lon. Merrill. 800p. 0-675-21097-6.
Using dBASE III Plus. 05/1987. Intentional Educations Staff. McGraw. 128p. 0-07-031504-3.
Using dBASE III Plus. 09/1986. Jones, Edward. Osborne-McGraw. 530p. 0-07-881252-6.
Using dBASE III Plus: Limited Use Version & Manual. 1987. Metzelaar, Larry; Fox, Marianne. Benjamin-Cummings. 210p. 0-8053-6742-X.
Using Lotus 1-2-3, Supercalc 4, WordPerfect, WordStar & dBASE III Plus. 02/1988. Warrner, D. Michael; Werner, Thomas W. Scott F. 0-673-38131-5.
Using Lotus 1-2-3, WordStar & dBASE III Plus. 01/1987. Warrner, Thomas W.; Werner, D. M. Scott F. 0-673-18761-6.
Using VP-Planner, Word Perfect, WordStar, & dBASE III Plus. 1988. Warrner, Thomas W.; Werner, D. Michael. Scott F. 0-673-38325-3.
Using WordStar 3.3 VP Planner & dBase III Plus. 04/1987. Intentional Educations Staff. McGraw. 304p. 0-07-031502-7.
Wordstar, Lotus 1-2-3 & dBase III Plus: Student Software Manual. 1987. Colantonio, Ernest S. Heath. 219p. 0-669-14114-3.

dBASE IV Books

Advanced dBase IV. 1989. Ratliff, Wayne; Heimendinger, Larry; Byers, Robert A. Brady Bks. 256p. 0-13-307562-1.
Advanced dBase IV for Business Users. 06/1989. Brownstein, Mark. Wiley. 0-471-61748-2.
Advanced dBase IV Programming. 06/1989. Prague, Cary N.; Hammitt, James E. TAB Bks. 0-8306-9376-9.
Advanced Training for dBASE IV. 09/1989. Jonas, Jacqueline. FlipTrack. 80p. 0-917792-66-1.
Building Systems with dBASE IV. 01/1990. Dinerstein, Nelson. Scott F. 600p. 0-673-46077-0.
Computing Fundamentals: dBase IV. 01/1990. Davis, William S.; Schreiner, Paul. Addison-Wesley. 192p. 0-201-19829-0.
DBase for Professionals with dBase IV. 12/1989. Dunlop, Neil. Van Nos Reinhold. 0-442-20741-7.
DBase III Plus to dBase IV: The Language Bridge Book. 09/1988. Green, Adam. P-H. 400p. 0-13-198680-5.
DBase IV Advanced Programmer's Guide. 01/1989. Davis, Ralph; Freeland, Russell; Olympia, Peter. P-H. 450p. 0-13-198722-4.
DBase IV Applications Library. 04/1989. Carlton, Thomas W. Que Corp. 675p. 0-88022-357-X.
DBase IV Business Applications Programming. 11/1988. Dickler, Howard. P-H. 0-13-198730-5.
dBASE IV: complete reference for programmers. 1989. Hergert, Douglas. Microsoft Press. 1-55615-165-9. 629 p.
DBase IV Essentials. 1988. Hursch, Jack L.; Hursch, Carolyn J. TAB Bks. 0-8306-9616-4.
DBase IV for the First-Time User. 09/1988. Dickler, Howard; Ledbetter, Cathy. P-H. 300p. N/A.
DBASE IV Guidebook. Davis, Steve. S Davis Pub. 200p. 0-911061-18-5.
DBASE IV Handbook. 04/1988. Carrabis, Joseph-David. Bantam. 768p. 0-553-34494-3.
DBase IV Handbook. 02/1989. Chou, George T. Que Corp. 600p. 0-88022-380-4.
DBASE IV Problem Solver. 10/1989. Steele, Philip. Scott F. 0-673-46144-0.
DBASE IV Programmer's Reference Guide. 02/1989. Jones, Edward C. Sams. 448p. 0-672-22654-5.
Dbase IV Programmers Library. 11/1989. Carrabis, Joseph-david. SAMS. 0-672-22653-7.
DBase IV Programming. 02/1989. Prague, Cary N.; Hammitt, James E. TAB Bks. 0-8306-9466-8.

DBase IV Quick Reference. 02/1989. Que Corporation Staff. Que Corp. 160p. 0-88022-371-5.

DBase IV QuickStart. 04/1989. Que Corporation Staff. Que Corp. 350p. 0-88022-389-8.

DBase IV SQL User's Guide. 09/1988. Hursch, Jack; Hursch, Carolyn. P-H. 400p. N/A.

DBase IV Tips, Tricks, & Traps. 03/1989. Chou, George T. Que Corp. 450p. 0-88022-359-6.

DBASE IV User's Instant Reference. 05/1989. Simpson, Alan. Sybex. 349p. 0-89588-605-7.

DBase IV Workbook & Disk. 03/1989. Bauman, James. Que Corp. 300p. 0-88022-424-X.

DBase IV: A Ready Reference Manual. 01/1990. Garrison, Catherine; McGowen, Mercedes. Addison-Wesley. 176p. 0-201-19714-6.

Dbase IV: Programmers Quick Reference. 01/1990. Viescas, John. Microsoft. 1-55615-237-X.

Dbase IV: Quick Reference Handbook. 05/1990. Cuneo, Karen. Wiley. 0-471-51677-5.

Developing dBASE IV Applications: Programming with the dBASE Template Language. 05/1989. Lima, Tony. Addison-Wesley. 400p. 0-201-19798-7.

Eighty-Five dBASE IV User-Defined Functions & Procedures. Date not set. Steele, Philip. TAB Bks. 256p. 0-8306-3236-0.

Encyclopedia of dBASE IV: The Master Reference. 09/1989. Stark, Robin. TAB Bks. 496p. 0-8306-8332-1.

Everyman's Database Primer Featuring dBASE IV. 06/1988. Byers, Robert A.; Prague, Cary. Tate Pub. 350p. 1-55519-056-1.

Everyman's Database Primer Featuring dBASE IV. Date not set. Byers, Robert A.; Prague, Cary N. P-H. 426p. 0-13-198763-1.

Everyman's Database Primer Featuring dBase IV. 09/1988. Byers, Robert; Prague, Cary. P-H. 400p. 0-13-292798-5.

Expert Advisor: dBase IV. 02/1990. Krumn, Rob; Miller, Laurie. Addison-Wesley. 700p. 0-201-51736-1.

Fast Access - dBASE IV. 06/1989. McClure, Rhyder. P-H. 320p. 0-13-307570-2.

Guide to SQL under dBASE IV. 09/1989. Baker, Richard. Scott F. 352p. 0-673-38826-3.

Hands on Computing Using Wordperfect 5.0, Lotus 1-2-3 & dBASE IV with 5.25 Inch Disk. 1990. Hobart. Merrill. 480p. 0-675-21110-7.

How to Use dBASE IV. 03/1989. Jonas, Jacqueline. FlipTrack. 80p. 0-917792-65-3.

Illustrated dBase IV. 1989. Stultz, Russell A. Wordware Pub. 448p. 1-55622-116-9.

Inside dBASE IV. 12/1988. Lima, Tony. Addison-Wesley. 400p. 0-201-16683-6.

Inside dBASE IV. 02/1989. Lima, Tony. Addison-Wesley. 0-201-16638-0.

Introduction to dBase IV. 07/1989. Taylor, Allen G. Compute Pubns. 352p. 0-87455-160-9.

Liskin's dbase Iv Programming Book. 12/1989. Liskin, Miriam. McGraw. 0-07-881530-4.

Mary Campbell's Dbase IV Handbook. 07/1989. Campbell, Mary. Bantam. 0-553-34776-4.

Mastering dBASE IV Programming. 03/1989. Townsend, Carl. Sybex. 496p. 0-89588-540-9.

PC Applications for Business, Using Lotus 1-2-3 (Version 2.2), WordPerfect 5.0 & dBase IV. 1990. Werner, D. Michael; Warrner, Thomas W. Scott F. 0-673-46256-0.

Peter Norton's dBase IV On-Line Guide. 01/1990. Norton, Peter. Brady Bks. 0-13-662362-X.

Professional dBase IV Programming. Date not set. Steele, Philip; Heydt, Robert. Wiley. 0-471-50985-X.

Quick & Easy Guide to dBASE IV. 02/1990. Davis, Steve. Compute Pubns. 224p. 0-87455-206-0.

Quick Guide to dBASE: The Visual Approach. 05/1989. Kolodney, David. Sybex. 350p. 0-89588-596-4.

SQL for dBASE IV. 03/1989. Sayles, Jonathan. QED Info Sci. 262p. 0-89435-289-X.

SQL for dBase Programmers. 06/1989. Dowgiallo, Edward. M&T Pub Inc. 1-55851-034-6.

Teach Yourself dBase IV. 03/1989. Campbell, Mary. McGraw. 0-07-881502-9.

The ABC's of dBASE IV. 12/1988. Cowart, Robert. Sybex. 338p. 0-89588-531-X.

The Best Book of: dBASE IV. 05/1989. Carrabis, Joseph-David. Sams. 700p. 0-672-22652-9.

The dBASE III Plus to dBASE IV: The Language Bridge Book. 06/1988. Green, Adam. Tate Pub. 350p. 1-55519-063-4.

The dBase III Plus to dBase IV: The Language Bridge Book. 09/1988. Green, Adam. Tate Pub. N/A.

The dBASE IV Advanced Developers Guide. 10/1989. Braunstein, Bruce. Bantam. 0-553-34753-5.

The dBASE IV Developer's Reference Guide. Date not set. Phillip, Clifford. MIS Press. 1-55828-010-3.

The dBASE IV for Beginners. 08/1989. Abacus Soft. 220p. 1-55755-069-7.

The dBASE IV for Everyone. 12/1989. Ratliff, Wayne; Heimendinger, Larry; Byers, Robert. Brady Bks. 400p. 0-13-942814-3.

The dBASE IV for the First-Time User. 06/1988. Dickler, Howard. Tate Pub. 200p. 1-55519-068-5.

The dBASE IV for the First-Time User. 01/1989. Dickler, Howard. Tate Pub. 250p. N/A.

The dBASE IV Functions. 10/1989. Rubel, Malcolm C. Bantam. 0-553-34768-3.

The dBase IV Made Easy. 03/1989. Liskin, Miriam. Osborne-McGraw. 800p. 0-07-881464-2.

The dBASE IV Programmers Instant Reference. 07/1989. Simpson, Alan. Sybex. 544p. 0-89588-538-7.

The dBASE IV Programming Language. Date not set. Long, Jeb J.; Dallas, Alastair W. P-H. 550p. 0-13-199647-9.

The dBase IV Programming Language. 1989. Long, Jeb J.; Dallas, Alastair W. Tate Pub. 550p. N/A.

The dBASE IV Programming: Tips & Techniques. 08/1989. Prague, Cary N.; Hammitt, James E. P-H. 350p. 0-13-199050-0.

The dBase IV QueCards. 05/1988. Que Corporation Staff. Que Corp. 200p. 0-88022-274-3.

The dBase IV SQL User's Guide. 09/1988. Hursch, Jack; Hursch, Carolyn. Brady Bks. 0-13-198755-0.

The dBASE IV SQL User's Guide. 01/1989. Hursch, Jack L.; Hursch, Carolyn. Tate Pub. 400p. 1-55519-052-9.

The dBASE IV Systems Development Handbook. 07/1989. Boston System Group, Inc. Staff-Editor; Galdieri, Beth-Editor; Klein, Theodore-Editor; Ryan, Daniel-Editor; Walsh, Robert-Editor. Tate Pub. 600p. 1-55519-050-2.

The dBASE IV Template Language Reference. 09/1989. Aspenwall, Dan. P-H. 0-13-197278-2.

The dBASE IV to Go. 09/1989. Randall, Peter; Bennett, Steven. P-H. 254p. 0-13-197229-4.

The dBASE IV User's Desktop Companion. 09/1989. Simpson, Alan. Sybex. 940p. 0-89588-523-9.

The dBASE IV, Vol. 1: User's Reference. 09/1989. Gardner, Anstol. P-H. 300p. 0-13-200338-4.

The dBASE IV, Vol. 2: Programmer's Reference. 09/1989. Gardner, Anatol. P-H. 300p. 0-13-200353-8.

The dBASE IV: A Comprehensive User's Manual for Nonprogrammers. Date not set. Bharucha, Kerman D. TAB Bks. 512p. 0-8306-1324-2.

The dBASE IV: Advanced Applications for Nonprogrammers. Date not set. Hartman, Patricia A. TAB Bks. 304p. 0-8306-9168-5.

The dBASE IV: Complete Reference for Programmers. 09/1989. Hergert, Douglas. Microsoft. 600p. 1-55615-165-9.

The dBase IV: Secrets, Solutions, Shortcuts. 06/1989. Biow, Lisa. McGraw. 0-07-881515-0.

The dBase IV: The Complete Reference. 04/1989. LeBlond Group. McGraw. 0-07-881503-7.

The dBase IV: The Pocket Refernce. 06/1989. Liskin, Miriam. McGraw. 0-07-881511-8.

Tom Rettigs Dbase IV Encyclopedia. 11/1989. Rettig, Tom. Bantam. 0-553-34772-1.

Understanding & Using dBASE IV. 05/1989. Krumm, Rob. P-H. 600p. 0-13-945056-4.

Understanding & Using dBASE IV. 09/1989. Ross, Steven C.; Leyh-Editor. West Pub. 200p. 0-314-47364-5.

Understanding dBASE IV. 05/1989. Robbins, Judd. Sams. 300p. 0-672-27284-9.

Understanding dBASE IV. 11/1988. Simpson, Alan. Sybex. 880p. 0-89588-509-3.

Understanding dBASE IV Programming. 09/1989. Robbins, Judd. Sams. 300p. 0-672-27286-5.

Using dBase IV. 12/1988. Jones, Edward. Osborne-McGraw. 700p. 0-07-881475-8.

Using dBASE IV. 1990. Que Corporation Staff. Que Corp. 750p. 0-88022-551-3.

Using DBase IV. Date not set. Taylor, R.; Kanai, June; Hurtado, J.-Editor; Fischbuch, L.- Illustrator. M-USA Busn Systs. 0-929978-22-6.

Using Dbase IV. 1990. Werner, D. Michael; Warrner, Thomas W. Scott F. 0-673-38982-0.

Using dBase IV SQL & SQL Server. 11/1989. Stephenson, Peter; Rash, Wayne,Jr. Wiley. 0-471-51263-X.
Using dBASE IV: Basics for Business. 01/1989. Brownstein, Mark. Wiley. 0-471-61749-0.
Using IBM Microcomputers: Word Perfect, dBase III Plus & IV, & Lotus. 02/1989. Pitter, Keiko. Mitchell Pub. 300p. 0-394-39449-6.

dBXL Books

See the heading "Quicksilver Books" below.

FoxBASE Books

Dynamics of FoxBASE Plus Programming. 03/1988. Goley, George F.,IV. Dow Jones-Irwin. 150p. 1-55623-096-6.
FoxBASE Plus 2.10. 05/1990. Granillo, Bob. Wordware Pub. 352p. 1-55622-168-1.
Sixty-Six FoxBASE User-Defined Functions. 12/1988. Steele, Philip. TAB Bks. 256p. 0-8306-3136-4.

FoxPro Books

Best Book of Foxpro. 04/1990. Philip, Clifford. Macmillan. 0-672-48487-0.
Foxpro Made Easy. 12/1989. Jones, Edward. McGraw. 0-07-881609-2.
Foxpro Programming. 05/1990. Pinter, Les. TAB Bks. 0-8306-3525-4.
FoxPro Simplified for the IBM PC. 02/1989. Masterson, Michael P. TAB Bks. 304p. 0-8306-3286-7.
Programming in Foxpro. 05/1990. Knecht, Ken. Bantam. 0-553-34936-8.
Tom Rettings Foxpro Handbook. 04/1990. Retting, Tom. Bantam. 0-553-34937-6.
Using FoxPro. 1990. Que Corporation Staff. Que Corp. 650p. 0-88022-514-9.

Macintosh-Related dBASE Books

DBASE MAC Advanced Techniques & Applications. 06/1988. Loggins, Richard. Bantam. 0-553-34392-0.
DBASE Mac in Business. 09/1987. Heid, Jim. Tate Pub. 250p. 0-912677-90-2.
Dbase Mac in Business. 12/1987. Heid, Jim. P-H. 0-13-198797-6.
Dynamics of Foxbase Programming: Macintosh Edition. 11/1989. Goley, George F.,IV. Dow Jones-Irwin. 1-55623-272-1.
Introduction to dBase Mac. 04/1988. Ashton Tate Staff. McGraw. 0-07-912732-0.
Introduction to dBase Mac: Application Development Workbook. 11/1987. McGraw. 0-07-912735-5.
The Complete Guide to dBASE Mac. 08/1988. Shafer, Dan; Huntington, Don. Scott F. 0-673-18732-2.
Using dBase Mac. 05/1988. Springer, Paul; DeFranco, Ralph. Que Corp. 400p. 0-88022-337-5.
Working with dBASE MAC: A User's Guide & Reference. 02/1988. DeMaria, Rusel; Fontaine, George. Prentice Hall Pr. 400p. N/A.
Working with dBase Mac: Pushing Productivity to the Limit. 07/1988. Demaria, Rusel; Fontaine, George R. Brady Bks. 500p. 0-13-939760-4.

Miscellaneous dBASE Books

Clipper - dBase III Plus - Foxbase. 09/1989. Huber, B. P-H. 350p. 0-13-137886-4.

Database Management Through dBase. 09/1988. Grauer, Robert T.; Maryann, Barber. McGraw. 416p. 0-07-834780-7.

DBASE Compilers: A Programmer's Resource Book. 1988. Knecht, Ken. Tab Bks. 290p. 0-8306-2943-2.

Dbase Power: Building & Using Programming Tools. 10/1988. Olympia, P. L. P-H. 0-13-198805-0.

DBASE Power: Building & Using Programming Tools. 10/1987. Olympia, P. L.; Freeland, Russell; Wallin, Randy. Tate Pub. 350p. 1-55519-021-9.

DBase Systems Development Handbook. 01/1989. Boston Systems Group Staff. P-H. 450p. N/A.

DBASE Tools: Pascal Programmer's Library. 10/1986. Jeff Cooper & Company. Tate Pub. 0-912677-93-7.

Introduction to Application Software Using VP-Planner, dBase, WordPerfect Worksheet with Site License. 01/1989. Zollos; Szymanski; Morris; Pulschen; Zollos. Merrill. 0-675-21036-4.

Professional dBASE Development. 09/1988. Steele, Philip. Scott F. 0-673-38359-8.

Salvaging Damaged dBASE Files. 02/1987. Heiser, Paul W. Comtech Pub. 200p. 0-9616370-0-5.

Salvaging Damaged dBASE Files. 05/1989. Heiser, Paul W. Slawson Comm. 0-915391-33-3.

Secrets of dBase. 11/1988. White, C. P-H. 0-13-798380-8.

Secrets of dBase. 02/1988. White, Christopher. McGraw. 0-07-912742-8.

Secrets of the dBASE Programming Language. 10/1987. White, Christopher. Tate Pub. 350p. 1-55519-024-3.

SQL for dBASE Programmers. 09/1989. Dowgiallo, Edward. M&T Pub Inc. 350p. 1-55851-035-4.

The dBASE Handbook for the Real Estate Associate. Date not set. Lord, Joseph M.; Young, James A.-Intro. by. Cambridge Assocs. 0-935351-04-3.

The dBase Language Handbook. 03/1988. Kalman, David M.; Levanthal, Lance A.-Editor. Slawson Comm. 800p. 0-915391-30-9.

The dBase Power: Building & Using Programming Tools. 04/1988. Olympia, P. L. McGraw. 0-07-912743-6.

The DBase Symposium Proceedings: Fall, 1988. 1988. Digit Consult MA. N/A.

The dBASE Systems Development Handbook. 08/1989. Boston Systems Group, Inc. Staff; Galdieri, Beth; Klein, Theodore; Ryan, Daniel B.; Walsh, Robert D. P-H. 900p. 0-13-198771-2.

The Graphics Handbook & Salvaging DBASE Files. Brady Bks. N/A.

Quicksilver and dBXL Books

DBXL & Quicksilver Programming: Beyond dBASE. 10/1988. Stephenson, Peter; Clifford, Barbara. Que Corp. 450p. 0-88022-374-X.

Using Oracle dBXL & Quicksilver. 11/1989. Stephenson, Peter; Gupta, Rakesh-Intro. by. P-H. 450p. 0-13-939950-X.

Software Engineering and Systems Analysis Books

This section contains a short list of recommended books on database theory, systems analysis, and software engineering and some representative titles from Yourdon Press and Addison-Wesley. *Managing the Structured Techniques* and *Structured Walkthroughs*, both by Edward Yourdon, are highly accessible and especially recommended.

Miscellaneous Publishers — Recommended Titles

Fundamentals of Database Systems. 1989. Elmasri, Ramez; Navanthe, Shamkant. Benjamin/Cummings Publishing. 802p.
An Introduction to Database Systems, Fifth Edition. 1990. Date, C. J. Addison-Wesley. 854p.
Managing the Structured Techniques, Second Edition. 1979. Yourdon, Edward. Prentice-Hall. 266 pages. (Fourth edition by Yourdon Press.)
The Mythical Man-Month: Essays on Software Engineering. 1975. Brooks, Frederick P. Addison-Wesley. 206p. Paperback.
The Psychology of Computer Programming. Weinberg, Gerald M. Van Nostrand Reinhold. 288p. Paperback.
Software Engineering. 1990. Ince, D. Van Nostrand Reinhold. 208p. Paperback.
Software Testing Techniques, Second Edition. 1990. Beizer, Boris. Van Nostrand Reinhold. 508p.
Structured Walkthroughs. 1977. Yourdon, Edward. Prentice-Hall.

Yourdon Press Books: Software Engineering

Classics in Software Engineering.
Concise Notes on Software Engineering.
Controlling Software Projects.
Crunch Mode.
Current Practices in Software Development.
Information Engineering for the Practitioner.
People and Project Management.
The Politics of Projects.
Principles of Visual Programming Systems.
Software Conflict.
Software Design.
Techniques of EDP Project Management.
Writings of the Revolution.

Yourdon Press Books: Systems Analysis and Design

Agents of Change.
Building Controls into Structured Systems.
Creating Effective Software.
Developing Structured Systems.
Essential Systems Analysis.
Fundamental Concepts of Information Modeling.
Intuition to Implementation.
Managing the System Life Cycle.
Object-Oriented Analysis.
Practical Guide to Structured Systems Design.
The Practice of Structured Analysis: Exploding Myths.
Structured Analysis.
Structured Analysis and System Specification.
Structured Design.
Structured Systems Development.
Structured Systems Development Manual.
Structured Walkthroughs.
Using the Structured Techniques.

Addison-Wesley Books

The Art of Computer Programming, Volumes I, II, and III.
The Art of Human-Computer Interface Design.
CASE*METHOD: Entity Relationship Modelling.
CASE*METHOD: Tasks and Deliverables.
The Craft of Software Engineering.
Cost Estimation for Software Development.
The Design and Analysis of Computer Algorithms.
Fundamentals of Database Normalization.
Fundamentals of Database Systems.
Human Factors in Computing Systems.
Information Engineering: Basic Principles.
Japanese Perspectives in Software Engineering.
Managing the Software Process.
The Mythical Man-Month: Essays on Software Engineering.
Performance Engineering of Software Systems.

Principles of Software Engineering Management.
Professional Software Themes and Thickets: Software Engineering Principles.
Program Derivation: The Development of Programs from Specifications.
The Program Development Process.
Program Verification.
The Programmer's Apprentice.
Relational Database: Selected Writings.
Software Analysis and Software Tools.
Software Configuration Management: Coordination for Team Productivity.
Software Engineering, Third Edition.
Software Engineering: Metrics and Models.
Software Engineering with Abstractions.
Software Perspectives: The System is the Message.
Software Reusability.
Software Specification Techniques (anthology).
Software Testing and Evaluation.
Software Tools.
The Specification of Computer Programs.
Structured Programming: Theory and Practice.
Systems Analysis and Design: A Structured Approach.
Tools and Techniques for Structured Systems Analysis and Design.

Appendix G

dBASE-Related Information Sources by Category

This appendix lists information on user groups, dBASE-related periodicals, BBSs (electronic bulletin boards), consulting services for programming-level users of dBASE dialects, training directories, and courseware. Contact information for publishers is listed in Appendix I on page 457.

dBASE-Related User Groups

In the world of computers, user groups are clubs or organizations with a focus on certain types of software and/or hardware. For example, my community offers the River City Apple Corps for users of Apple computers and the Central Texas PC Users' Group, which is oriented to users of IBM PC-compatible computers.

Data Based Advisor publishes lists of user groups in the issues where there is sufficient space for the lists. However, note that according to the editorial response to the letter titled "User Group Gripe" on page 16 of the October 1990 *Data Based Advisor*, the lists are incomplete when they do appear.

In some cases, the vendors can provide you with information on user groups dedicated to the vendor's dBASE dialects. For example, I recently received a printout from Nantucket which listed Clipper-related user groups in the United States and other countries. (In addition, you should be aware that the major vendors offer conferences with increasing frequency: contact your vendor for more information.)

One may argue that the special-interest areas on various BBSs constitute user groups; see the BBS section below. Apart from BBSs, a user group called IDBUG (International Dbase Users' Group) is open to everyone. The IDBUG BBS can be reached at the phone number shown in the BBS section below; you can also write to 70 A Greenwich Avenue #101, New York, NY 10011, U.S.A.

dBASE-Related Periodicals

Here is some basic information on all of the dBASE-related periodicals which I have been able to identify.

Ashton-Tate Quarterly. Published quarterly by dBASE dialect vendor Ashton-Tate.

Compass. Published monthly by The Reference Pages. Contains 40–50 pages of Clipper information in each issue.

Data Based Advisor. Published monthly by Data Based Solutions. The premier magazine for dBASE dialect programmers. A mandatory subscription for most readers of this book.

DBMS. Published monthly (twice in June) by M&T Publishing. The number-two magazine for dBASE dialect programmers.

Extensions. A newsletter for Clipper developers by Gary Beam, 21175 Tomball Parkway #137, Houston, TX 77070, (713) 251-3319.

FoxTalk. Published monthly by Pinnacle Publishing.

FoxTrax. Published by dBASE dialect vendor Fox Software.

From the Desk of Steve Straley. (Also called *From D.O.S.S.*) A biweekly newsletter for Clipper developers from the Four Seasons Publishing Company.

Nantucket News. Published by dBASE dialect vendor Nantucket.

Pinter FoxBASE/FoxPRO Letter. Published monthly by Pinter Consulting.

Reference(Clipper). Published monthly by Pinnacle Publishing.

Supplement to dBASE Dialects Software Engineering, Volume 1. Published twice a year by Database Software Consultants.

Tech Notes. Published by dBASE dialect vendor Ashton-Tate.

dBASE-Related Directories

Here is a list of directories and indexes which are partly or completely devoted to dBASE-related products and services.

Ashton-Tate Developer Registry. Ashton-Tate. Third Edition, 1989.

Books in Print. R. R. Bowker. Updated continuously on the DIALOG information service. Also available in print form in many bookstores and libraries.

Clipper Third Party Products Directory. Nantucket Corporation. First edition, 1988.

Data Based Advisor Database Directory 1990. Data Based Solutions. January 1990.

dBASE Programmer's Index. Poder Associates. Updated quarterly to provide keyword access to over 1,200 dBASE-related articles.

Dbase Source Code Applications Directory. EMS. To be published in 1990 for the first time.

dBUtility Directory. EMS. Updated quarterly.

dBUtility Library. EMS. Updated quarterly.

Fox Software Developers Directory, 1990-91. Fox Software. To be published in 1990 for the first time.

Programmer's Shop Catalog. The Programmer's Shop. Published several times per year. A fairly comprehensive listing of tools and products for programmers who use dBASE dialects and other programming languages.

dBASE-Related Electronic Bulletin Boards

dBASE dialects are in such wide use now that you will probably find other dBASE programmers on programming-oriented local BBSs. If your community is larger than a few hundred thousand people, then there are probably one or more local BBSs devoted in whole or part to programming-level users of dBASE dialects.

Here are some nationally known BBS opportunities for dBASE dialect programmers. See page 193 for more information on CompuServe opportunities.

The Ashton-Tate BBS. See the heading "Ashton-Tate BBS" on page 194.

The Ashton-Tate Forum on CompuServe. Access this forum with GO ASHTON. The forum gives you the opportunity to download numerous dBASE utilities and information files, and to interact with other dBASE users. You can find information and assistance with any Ashton-Tate product in this forum.

The *Data Based Advisor* Readers Exchange BBS, (619) 481-5928, 1200/2400 baud, 8 data bits, 1 stop bit, and no parity bit. This BBS was formerly only for *Data Based Advisor* subscribers, but in early 1990 it was opened to all callers. However, at the time of writing, this BBS was scheduled to be discontinued in November 1990 as a result of the *Data Based Advisor* forum which opened on CompuServe in October 1990: at any "!" prompt, GO DBADVISOR.

***DBMS* magazine BBS.** *DBMS* offers the TelePath service on TymNet; see the magazine for more information. On Telepath you can join technical conferences, download source code and software, and send E-mail to *DBMS* editors and other TelePath users.

The Fox Software Forum on CompuServe. Access this forum with GO FOXFORUM. The forum gives you the opportunity to download numerous FoxBASE and FoxPro utilities and information files, and to interact with other Fox Software users. You can find information and assistance for any Fox Software product in this forum.

The IDBUG BBS. The BBS of the International Dbase Users' Group, (212) 869-3932.

The M&T Publishing BBS. M&T, the publisher of *DBMS* magazine, has discontinued this service and replaced it with TelePath, which is listed just above under "*DBMS*."

The Nantucket Forum on CompuServe. Access this forum with GO NANFOR. The forum gives you the opportunity to download numerous Clipper utilities and information files, and to interact with other Clipper users. You can find information and assistance for any Nantucket product in this forum.

BBS Support for WordTech Systems Dialects. WordTech Systems opened a CompuServe forum in September 1990. Enter GO IBMNET at any "!" prompt to reach the PC Vendor C area and choose menu item 12. WordTech also offers a private BBS: call (415) 254-1141; use 300/1200/2400 baud, 8 data bits, 1 stop bit, and no parity bit.

dBASE-Related Consulting Services for Programming-Level Users

Many of the persons who write magazine articles and books are available for telephone or other consulting to assist you with your dBASE programming problems. If the writer lists a telephone number, you may assume that inquiries are solicited.

The vendors' telephone support staff can also help you. Some vendors offer free telephone support; others charge, but offer extended support plans to handle payment.

Last, Database Specialties of Oakland, California, provides consulting for dBASE programmers and end-users. This firm also sells selected dBASE dialect and network products. If you purchase a copy of a dBASE dialect from them, you are entitled to unlimited free technical support, although the call is not toll-free.

dBASE-Related Training Services for Programming-Level Users

The following companies offer seminars and classes for dBASE dialect programmers. In some cases, the seminars and classes are offered only in the community where the company is located, whereas in other cases, the seminars and classes are offered at your site, or in selected cities as part of periodic tours.

The companies are listed in ZIP code order to help you locate a company in your area; for your convenience, the ZIP codes appear in boldface. The first two entries are from Brazil and Australia, the last two entries are from Canada, and the other entries are in the United States. In some cases, the dBASE dialect vendors can direct you to training organizations in your area, but be sure to ask for programmer-level training.

Megatron A. Treinamento. Rua Do Arouche 49-CJ 300, Sao Paulo, SP 01219, BRAZIL, Clipper, dBASE IV. Phone: 55 11 220-6148.

Mr. Aleks Ozolins, Database Advisors. 68 Dundas Court, Phillip, ACT 2606, AUSTRALIA, (062) 852-097 . Authorized Nantucket training.

Mr. Adam Green, Adam Green Seminars, Incorporated. 1 Faneuil Hall, Boston, MA **02109,** U.S.A., (617) 227-8541. dBASE IV, FoxPro, Alpha Four; multiple-user programming for FoxPro/LAN. Adam Green is *the* pre-eminent dBASE dialect trainer.

Mr. Richard Heffernan, Heffernan Consulting. 132 Highland Avenue, Wakefield, RI **02879,** U.S.A., (401) 789-8941. On-site training for dBASE III PLUS, dBASE IV, and Clipper.

Software Training Center. RR#4, Box 6340, Troop RD, Gardiner, ME **04345,** U.S.A., (207) 582-5444. dBASE.

Joseph White Associates. 36 Locust Street, Greenwich, CT **06830,** U.S.A., (203) 661-5337. dBASE, SBT accounting.

Wellington Systems, Incorporated. 40 Richards Avenue, Norwalk, CT **06854,** U.S.A., (203) 866-4900. FoxBASE+, FoxPro, and FoxBASE+/MAC for the end-user and computer professional or programmer.

Mr. Steve Straley, The Steve Straley Seminars, Four Seasons Publishing Company, Incorporated. POB 20025, New York, NY **10017-0001,** U.S.A., (212) 599-2141. Single-user and multiple-user Clipper programming for beginning, intermediate, and advanced levels.

Mr. Neil Weicher, President, Communication Horizons. Suite 900, 701 Seventh Avenue, New York, NY **10036,** U.S.A., (212) 724-0150. Authorized Nantucket training; single-user and multiple-user programming.

Mr. Marc Schnapp, Micro Business Services, Incorporated. 75-22 182nd Street, Flushing, NY **11366,** U.S.A., (718) 380-6175. Arago dBXL/Quicksilver, Clipper, DESQview API, dBASE IV, FoxPro, Framework, UI2 and Luis Castro's Stage; single-user and multiple-user programming.

Marta Fien, MicroTrek. 19 West 44th Street, Second Floor, New York, NY **11375,** U.S.A., (212) 398-6410. Authorized Nantucket training, multiple-user programming, and FoxBASE+, FoxPro, Paradox, R:BASE training at all levels.

Mr. David Lobel, President, Barrow York Associates, Limited. 50 Charles Lindbergh Blvd., Suite 400, Uniondale, NY **11553,** U.S.A., (516) 229-2220, (800) 292-8050. Authorized training for Clipper, R&R Relational Report Writer, dLESKO'S FUNCky library for Clipper, including both single-user and multiple-user programming.

Mr. George F. Goley, IV, President, MicroEndeavors, Incorporated. 3150 Township Line Road, Upper Darby, PA **19026,** U.S.A., (215) 449-4757. Single-user and multiple-user training for FoxBASE+ and FoxPro by author and columnist Goley. Contact: Ed Martini.

Mr. Scott Hanson, Applied Technology Associates, Incorporated. 1612 "K" Street N.W., Suite 802, Washington, DC **20006,** U.S.A., (202) 293-0909. Authorized Nantucket training.

Mr. Michael Horwith, Financial Dynamics. 5201 Leesburg Pike, Suite 209, Falls Church, VA **22041,** U.S.A., (703) 671-3003, (800) 486-5201. Toolkit/engine-oriented single-user and multiple-user programming for Clipper professionals. Recommended.

Mr. Al Soskin, Computer Essentials. Suite 110, 6 Executive Park Drive, Atlanta, GA **30329,** U.S.A., (404) 633-3046. Clipper, DataEase, dBASE III PLUS, FoxBASE+, FoxPro, Paradox/PAL; single-user and multiple-user. Company President Michael J. Clifford has written several dBASE dialect books.

Mr. Mike Schinkel, The DSW Group, Limited. Suite 640, 1175 The Exchange, Atlanta, GA **30339,** U.S.A., (404) 953-0393, (800) 356-9644. Single-user and multiple-user Clipper training.

Mr. Ed Weber, Partner, The DSW Group, Limited. Suite 640, 1175 The Exchange, Atlanta, GA **30339,** U.S.A., (800) 356-9644. Single-user and multiple-user Clipper training.

Mr. Michael Prudhom, MAD Software. 3613 Kinzie Avenue, Racine, WI **53405,** U.S.A., (419) 632-4394. Novell Netware, dBXL, Quicksilver; single-user and multiple-user programming.

Mr. Craig Yellick, Senior Analyst/Partner, Alto Microcomputer, Incorporated. 7107 Ohms Lane, Edina, MN **55435,** U.S.A., (612) 835-1080. Toolkit-oriented single-user and multiple-user Clipper training. See the "Courseware" heading in this appendix.

Mr. Bill Kwan, Advanced F1. 2021 Midwest Road, Suite 300, Oak Brook, IL **60521,** U.S.A., (708) 953-8651. Authorized Nantucket training.

Mr. Paul Ransom, Advanced Business Solutions, Incorporated. 1401 E. Washington Street, Pittsfield, IL **62363,** U.S.A., (217) 285-2482. FoxPro single-user and multiple-user programming.

Kelly Goodrich, Chrina Corporation. 414160 Dallas Parkway, Suite 120, Dallas, TX **75240,** U.S.A., (214) 404-8292. Authorized Nantucket training.

Gary Arnett or Marty Monk, Vision Labs Information Systems, Incorporated. Suite 390, 4544 Post Oak Place, Houston, TX **77027,** U.S.A., (713) 623-0595. Classes in FoxBASE/MAC and FoxPRO for end-users and programmers.

Mr. Peter J. Squier, President, Squier Computer Services/PPI. 7800 Shoal Creek Blvd., Suite 160-E, Austin, TX **78757,** U.S.A., (512) 452-1200. dBASE III PLUS, dBASE IV, FoxPro, and authorized Nantucket training. Contact: Joe Temborius.

Systems Design Corporation. 3615 South Huron Street, Suite 203, Englewood, CO **80110,** U.S.A., (303) 781-5081. FoxPro, FoxPro/LAN, and R&R Relational Report Writer.

Getty Information Systems. 1919 14th Street, Boulder, CO **80302,** U.S.A., (303) 449-1099. Clipper, dBXL/Quicksilver, dBASE III PLUS, dBASE IV, FoxBASE+, FoxPro.

Mr. Rick Spence and Mr. Jack Tollefson, Island Publishing. POB 2347, Coeur d'Alene, ID **83814,** U.S.A., (208) 667-3727. Single-user and multiple-user Clipper 5.0 seminars presented in cities throughout the U.S. and Canada.

Ms. Margaret Zinky, Margaret Zinky. 926 West Montecito Avenue, Phoenix, AZ **85013,** U.S.A., (602) 279-5864. Authorized Nantucket training.

Mitchelle Chi, MicroSage Computer Group. 1247 Central Avenue, Los Alamos, NM **87544,** U.S.A., (505) 662-7244. Authorized Nantucket training.

Mr. Tom Williams, Lexcel Systems, Incorporated. 5522 Keniston Avenue, Los Angeles, CA **90043,** U.S.A., (213) 674-8505. Authorized Clipper training for single-user and multiple-user programming.

Systems Integration Group. Suite 19, 501 North Commonwealth Avenue, Fullerton, CA **92631,** U.S.A., (714) 393-1052. dBASE, Lotus, WordPerfect.

Dr. Tony Lima, Ph.D., President, Pacific System Design Workshop, Incorporated. 1328 Magnolia Avenue, San Carlos, CA **94070,** U.S.A., (415) 593-6431. dBASE II, dBASE IV, and Clipper 4.0; multiple-user programming; customized on-site presentations.

Mr. Chick Bornheim, MicroMega Systems. 834 Baker Street, San Francisco, CA **94115,** U.S.A., (415) 346-4445. Systems analysis, applications design, programmer productivity, training for trainers, LAN issues for FoxPro/LAN and FoxBASE+/MAC, and toolkit/engine-based programming — highly recommended.

Ms. Jennifer Alton, Director of Sales, Computer Utilization, Incorporated. 9851 Horn Road, Suite 250, Sacramento, CA **95827,** U.S.A., (916) 364-0203. Single-user and multiple-user programming for Clipper, dBASE III PLUS, dBASE IV, and FoxBASE+.

Mr. Sam Perrin, Perrin Data Consulting. 7 Barnes Crescent, Nepean, ON **K2H 7C1,** CANADA, (613) 829-3495. Classroom training or on-site training in dBASE II, dBASE III PLUS, dBASE IV, FoxBASE+, and FoxPro.

Mr. Bill Wilson, Delcom International Institute of Office Automation. 294 Albert Street, Suite 300, Ottawa, ON **K2P 6E6,** CANADA, (613) 230-3815. Authorized Nantucket training.

dBASE-Related Courseware for Programming-Level Users

Several companies offer text-only or software-and-text products with an explicitly educational orientation; these products are generically called *courseware* and some of them are listed below. In addition, some of the training organizations in the preceding section may sell their course materials. Also see Appendix F, starting on page 435, which lists hundreds of dBASE-related books.

Ashton-Tate offers a variety of training aids for dBASE III PLUS and dBASE IV. Contact Ashton-Tate for information on their current offerings.

Database Software Consultants offers a line of *docusoftware*™ products (written by your author) in which documentation and software are given equal weight in design and implementation as an expression of the canonical approach promoted in this book. These products include *dMILL Network Kit for Clipper* (formerly *dCL-Net Library* — see Kinney 1990), *dMILL Network Kit for dBXL/Quicksilver*, *dMILL Network Kit for dBASE III PLUS/dBASE IV*, and *dMILL Network Kit for FoxBASE+/FoxPro*. Each *dMILL Network Kit* includes an elegant subroutine library for handling resource contention; an extensive tutorial covers multiple-user design and reduces the implementation of networked applications to a checklist process. The *Kits* are appropriate for self-study or seminars.

Robert Self at the IBEX Company has written a 250-page training manual called "Learning dBXL." It is designed to take a DOS-literate programmer to 80% of the capability of a seasoned dBXL programmer in 40 hours of study. At the time of writing, Self was investigating several distribution possibilities; he said that interested parties should contact WordTech Systems to discover how they can acquire the manual.

Expert Panelist Craig Yellick has written a set of Clipper tutorials that are distributed through Alto Microcomputer. Titles for Clipper 4.0 include *Arrays, Building Source Code Libraries, DOS <-> Clipper, Introduction to Clipper for dBASE Programmers, Low-Level File Functions, Printer Control Methods, Symbols & Tokens, User Interface & Screen Control,* and *Wonderful Differences: dBASE and Clipper.* Related products include *bugArry, The Array Debugger; Printer Control Function Library;* and *User Interface and Screen Control Library.* Similar titles will be available for Clipper 5.0. A text and software product called *DBFtrieve* gives access to the Btrieve record manager from Clipper 4.0 and 5.0, FoxBASE+, and FoxPro applications.

Appendix H

Alphabetic List of dBASE-Related Products

Here is a list of most of the products mentioned in this book. The product name is followed by the vendor name. Vendors are listed in Appendix I on page 457.

Ashton-Tate Developer Registry, Third Edition, 1989. Ashton-Tate.
Ashton-Tate/Microsoft SQLserver. Ashton-Tate and Microsoft Corporation.
Books in Print. R. R. Bowker.
C Toolkit. Ratliff Software Productions.
Clipper. Nantucket Corporation.
Clipper Third Party Products Directory, First Edition, 1988. Nantucket Corporation.
Clipper Tools One. Nantucket Corporation.
Data Based Advisor Database Directory 1990. Data Based Solutions.
dBASE II. Ashton-Tate.
dBASE III. Ashton-Tate.
dBASE III PLUS. Ashton-Tate.
dBASE IV. Ashton-Tate.
dBASE Direct/36, dBASE Direct/38. Ashton-Tate.
dBASE File Recovery. Ashton-Tate.
dBASE Programmer's Index. Poder Associates.
dBFast/PLUS. Gen Soft Development Corporation.
dBFast/PLUS/Mac. Gen Soft Development Corporation.
dBFast/PLUS/Windows. Gen Soft Development Corporation.
dBMAN V. Versasoft Corporation.
dBXL, dBXL/SQL, dBXL/Kanji. WordTech Systems.
dBUtility Directory. EMS.
dBUtility Library. EMS.
dCLIP. Donnay Software Designs.
dCL-Net Library. Database Software Consultants.
DESQview. QuarterDeck Corporation.
dMILL Network Kit for Clipper. Database Software Consultants.
dMILL Network Kit for dBASE III PLUS/dBASE IV. Database Software Consultants.
dMILL Network Kit for dBXL/Quicksilver. Database Software Consultants.
dMILL Network Kit for FoxBASE+/FoxPro. Database Software Consultants.
Emerald Bay. Ratliff Software Productions.
FORCE. Sophco.
Fox Software Developers Directory, 1990-91. Fox Software.
FoxBASE Multi-User. SCO (The Santa Cruz Operation).
FoxBASE+. Fox Software.
FoxBASE+/386. Fox Software.
FoxBASE+/LAN (formerly called FoxBASE+ Multi-User). Fox Software.
FoxBASE+/MAC, FoxBASE+/Mac Multi-User. Fox Software.
FoxPro. Fox Software.
FoxPro/LAN. Fox Software.
Gupta SQLBase. Gupta Technologies.
IBM OS/2 EE. IBM Corporation.
Invisible Network. Invisible Software.
LANtastic Network. ArtiSoft Corporation.
Liaison. Ratliff Software Productions.
McMax. Nantucket Corporation.
Microsoft linker LINK.EXE (with MS-DOS). Microsoft Corporation.
MS-DOS. Microsoft Corporation.
MS-Windows. Microsoft Corporation.
Networker Plus. Wordtech Systems.
NoLink. Next Wave Software and Sunbelt Computing.
Norton Utilities. Peter Norton Computing.
Novell Netware SQL. Novell, Inc.
Oracle RDBMS. Oracle Corporation.
OPTune. Gazelle Systems.
PageMaker. Aldus Coporation.
PASCAL Toolkit. Ratliff Software Productions.
PC Paintbrush. Zsoft.
PCanywhere. Dynamic MicroProcessor Associates.
Plink86. POLYTRON Corporation.
Printer Control Function Library. Alto Microcomputer.

The Programmer's Shop Catalog. The Programmer's Shop.
Quicksilver, Quicksilver/UNIX, Quicksilver/Kanji. WordTech Systems.
R&R Relational Report Writer. Concentric Data Systems.
Recital/4GL. Recital Corporation.
Salvaging Damaged dBASE Files. ComTech Publishing.
SCO FoxBASE. SCO (The Santa Cruz Operation).
User Interface and Screen Control Library. Alto Microcomputer.
Ventura Publisher. Ventura Software Incorporated.
Vulcan. Ratliff Software Productions.

Appendix I

Alphabetic List of dBASE-Related Vendors

Here is contact information for most of the vendors mentioned in this book. A strong effort has been made to ensure the accuracy of this information. However, please remember that I may have committed transcription errors, I may have copied from incorrect data, and phone numbers and addresses change over a period of time.

It may be most prudent to call a company listed below in order to solicit their current mailing address before writing to them. This would be a one-minute call; just say, "I need your current mailing address" to the person who answers.

Many companies have toll-free numbers which you can discover by calling (800) 555-1212; if there is no toll-free number, call 555-1212 in the telephone area code for the city where the company is located. CompuServe subscribers can GO ATT to get toll-free numbers, which at the time of writing was a service free of connect charges.

Addison-Wesley Publishing Company. Route 128, Reading, MA 01867, (800) 333-0088.

Aldus Corporation. (206) 628-2320.

Alto Microcomputer, Inc. 7107 Ohms Ln., Edina, MN 55439, (612) 835-1080.

ArtiSoft Corporation. 575 East River Rd., Tucson, AZ 85704, (602) 293-6363.

Ashton-Tate. 20101 Hamilton Ave., Torrance, CA 90502, (213) 329-8000.

The Benjamin/Cummings Publishing Co. 390 Bridge Pkwy., Redwood City, CA 94065-9984, (800) 950-BOOK.

R. R. Bowker Electronic Publishing, 245 West 17th Street, New York, NY 10011, (212) 645-9700.

Bumblebee Software, Inc. 1715 114th Ave. S.E., Bellevue, WA 98004, (206) 462-0130.

Buzzwords International, Inc. 2879 Hopper Rd., Cape Girardeau, MO 63701, (314) 334-6317.

Champion Business Systems. 17301 West Colfax, Suite 250, Golden, CO 80401, (800) 243-2626.

COB System Designs. 206 South Hampton Dr., Jupiter, FL 33458, (407) 744-9835.

CompuServe Information Services, Inc. 5000 Arlington Centre Blvd., POB 20212, Columbus, OH 43220, (800) 848-8199 or (614) 457-0802.

ComTech Publishing, Ltd. POB 456, Pittsford, NY 14534. Orders: (800) 456-7005. Information and support: (716) 586-3365.

Concentric Data Systems. 18 Lyman St., POB 4063, Westborough, MA 01581-4063, (617) 366-1122.

Creative Software. POB 14203, Santa Rosa, CA 95401, (707) 576-1265.

Data Based Solutions. 4010 Morena Blvd., Suite 200, San Diego, CA 92117, (800) 336-6060.

Database Software Consultants. POB 8380, Austin, TX 78713-8380, (512) 477-3423. Publisher and Chief Software Designer: T. David Millican.

Database Specialties. POB 2975, Oakland, CA 94618. Orders: (800) 322-7375. Consulting: (415) 652-3630.

Digital Consulting. (508) 470-3880.

Donnay Software Designs. 4000 Park Newport, #401, Newport Beach, CA 92660, (714) 721-6720.

Dynamic MicroProcessor Associates. 60 East 42nd St., New York, NY 10165, (212) 687-7115.
EMS. 4505 Buckhurst Ct., Olney, MD 20832, (301) 924-3594. In France: dBFirst, 14 7763872. In Australia: Data Base Advisors, 62 852097.
Four Seasons Publishing Co., Incorporated. POB 20025, New York, NY 10017-0001, (212) 599-2141, FAX: (212) 599-3226.
Fox Software. 118 West South Boundary, Perrysburg, OH 43551, (419) 874-0162.
Funk Software. 222 Third St., Cambridge, MA 02142, (617) 497-6339.
Gazelle Systems. 42 North University Ave., Suite 10, Provo, UT 84601, (800) 733-0383.
Gen Soft Development Corporation. 4122 128th Ave. S.E., Suite 200, Bellevue, WA 98006, (206) 562-1157.
Gibson Research Corporation. POB 6024, Irvine, CA 92716.
OmniQuest Software, Incorporated. 8716 Mopac North, Suite 200, Austin, TX 78759, (512) 794-8858.
Gupta Technologies, Inc. Suite 200, 1040 Marsh Rd., Menlo Park, CA 94025, (415) 321-9500.
IBEX Company. 13658 O'Connor Rd., Suite 501, San Antonio, TX 78233, (512) 653-6164.
International Business Machines (IBM). See your telephone directory for local IBM offices.
Invisible Software. 1165 Chess Dr., Suite D, Foster City, CA 94404, (415) 570-5967.
M&T Publishing. Editorial: 501 Galveston Dr., Redwood City, CA 94063. Subscriptions: write *DBMS*, POB 57511, Boulder, CO 80322-7511, or call (800) 456-1859 or (303) 447-9330.
Microsoft Corporation. 1 Microsoft Way, Redmond, WA 98052, (206) 882-8080, or (800) 541-1261.
MicroTrend Books. 165 Vallecitos de Oro, San Marcos, CA 92069.
Nantucket Corporation. 12555 West Jefferson Blvd., Los Angeles, CA 90066, (213) 390-7923.
Next Wave Software. 1800 Water Pl., Suite 280, Atlanta, GA 30339, (404) 422-8255.
Novell, Inc. Development Products Division. #917, POB 9802, Austin, TX 78766, (512) 346-8380.
Oracle Corporation. 20 Davis Dr., Belmont, CA 94002, (415) 598-8000.
Peter Norton Computing. 100 Wilshire Blvd., 9th Floor, Santa Monica, CA 90401, (213) 319-2000.
Pinnacle Publishing, POB 8099, Federal Way, WA 98003, (800) 231-1293 or (206) 941-2300.
Pinter Consulting, POB 1324, Menlo Park, CA 94026-1324, (415) 325-7953.
Poder Associates. 248 Ashland Ave., Santa Monica, CA 90405. Orders: (800) 448-3888. Support: (213) 829-1982.
POLYTRON Corporation. 1700 NW 167th Pl., Beaverton, OR 97006, (503) 645-1150.
The Programmer's Shop. Five Pond Park Rd., Hingham, MA 02043-9837. Call (800) 421-8006 in the United States, (800) 446-3846 in Canada, or (617) 740-2510 locally.
Public Brand Software. POB 51315, Indianapolis, IN 46251. 24-hour order lines: (800) 426-3475 outside Indiana, (800) 727-3476 inside Indiana, or 856-7571 in Indianapolis. Business offices: (317) 856-4144.
QuarterDeck Corporation. 150 Pico Blvd., Santa Monica, CA 90405, (213) 392-9851.
Quicktek Corporation. 224 Whiteside Pl., Thousand Oaks, CA 91362, (805) 498-5853.
Ratliff Software Productions, 2155 Verdugo Blvd., #20, Montrose, CA 91020, (818) 248-2605.
Recital Corporation. 85 Constitution Ln., Danvers, MA 01923, (508) 750-1066.
The Reference Pages, POB 1436, Coeur d'Alene, ID 83814, (800) 678-7331 or (208) 667-7331.
The Santa Cruz Operation. 400 Encinal, Santa Cruz, CA 95060, (408) 425-7222.
SBT Corporation. One Harbor Dr., Suite 300, Sausalito, CA 94965, (800) 331-8998 or (415) 331-9900.
SCO. See The Santa Cruz Operation.
Scott, Foresman & Company. 1900 East Lake Ave., Glenview, IL 60025.
Slawson Communications. C/O MicroTrend Books, 165 Vallecitos de Oro, San Marcos, CA 92069.
Sophco, Inc. POB 7430, Boulder, CO 80306, (800) 922-3001 or (303) 444-1542.
Sunbelt Computing. 11210 Wilshire Chase Dr., Atlanta, GA 30136.
Van Nostrand Reinhold. VNR Order Processing, POB 668, Florence, KY 41022, (800) 926-2665 or (606) 525-6600.
Ventura Software Incorporated. 15175 Innovation Dr., San Diego, CA 92128, (800) 822-8221 or (619) 673-0172.
Versasoft Corporation. 4340 Almaden Expressway, #250, San Jose, CA 95118, (408) 723-9044.

WordTech Systems. 21 Altarinda, Orinda, CA 94563, (415) 254-0900.

Yellick Computing. Has merged with Alto Microcomputer, Inc.

Zsoft. 450 Franklin Rd., Suite 100, Marietta, GA 30067, (404) 428-0008.

Glossary

actual parameters. The identifiers or expressions in the list that follows the WITH keyword in some DO statements are actual parameters. When functions are referenced, the identifiers or expressions inside the parentheses are the actual parameters. A synonym for *actual parameter* is *argument*.

application. When you *apply* software tools and hardware to the solution of an information processing problem, you create a set of executable files and their supporting files and documentation, which is called an *application*. (Contrast *program*, which refers to a single executable file and its support files, and *software*, which is a generic term for binary data that represents instructions for computer hardware.)

application programming. The process of producing applications. (Contrast *systems programming*, an activity which produces the software on which applications depend, such as the operating system and programmer tools such as linkers.)

argument. See *actual parameters*.

assignment. The action of giving a value to a data variable.

assignment statement. A statement in which one or more data variables are assigned values.

BBS. Electronic bulletin board; accessed with a modem and communications software. Generally speaking, you can send files to the BBS (uploading), receive files from the BBS (downloading), and leave and receive messages.

bug update. A release of a software program which does not contain significant numbers of enhancements with respect to its predecessor, but which does fix known bugs with the predecessor version.

call (a routine). To reference a subroutine, as in "DO MainMenu", which references a procedure or command file named MainMenu, or "? TIME()", which references a function named TIME.

calling sequence. 1. The order in which arguments are specified in a call. 2. The sequence of commands which must be executed before a call in order to produce the conditions which are required by the called subroutine.

cardinal number. An integer which refers to the count of items in a set, such as 1 item, 2 items, and so on. See the related entry *ordinal number*.

client-server. A software architecture for DBMSs in which the server performs some of the database functions which would otherwise be performed on the workstation. For example, when a workstation requests the sum of a numeric field in a database stored on a server, and client-server architecture is not used, then every record of the database is passed across the network to the workstation; if client-server architecture is used, then the server performs the additions and passes the answer only across the network to the workstation.

command file. A file containing dBASE source code statements, usually with a .PRG extension.

compile. 1. In strongly typed languages (such as PASCAL), a process that translates source code to machine code. 2. In weakly typed languages (such as dBASE), a process that translates source code to intermediate code and that combines the intermediate code with an interpreter in the same file, which will have a .EXE or .COM extension in MS-DOS.

concurrent. Overlapping in time. (See the related entry *simultaneous*.)

data-driven. 1. A style of source code in which identifiers with descriptive names are used in preference to constants. For example, if the data-driven approach is *not* used, then references to the constant 6 might appear in several places in a program. In the data-driven approach, an identifier like LinesPerIn is assigned the value 6 and LinesPerIn appears where the constant 6 formerly appeared to represent 6 lines per inch. 2. A style of application implementation in which the data that controls the application's behavior is stored in one or more data files. Such a dBASE application would not contain a statement such as "LinesPerIn = 6". Rather, LinesPerIn would be a database field, or its value would be assigned with a RESTORE FROM statement.

data structure. A set of individual data items and/or data structures with the following attributes: (1) the items or structures are related, (2) an order of storage is specified, and (3) a binary representation of the data structure is either implicit or explicit.

DBMS. Data Base Management System.

disambiguation. The process of resolving ambiguity.

docusoftware™. A product in which text and software is given equal weight in design and implementation; a trademark of Database Software Consultants.

dot prompt. The interactive prompt of dBASE interpreters.

download. To transfer a copy of a file from a second computer to your computer.

epilogue. One or more "housekeeping" statements which are executed at the end of a subroutine. For example, the epilogue for a menu subroutine might include the CLEAR statement.

extension, DOS file name. MS-DOS file names have a mandatory first component called a *filename* (of up to eight characters) and an optional second component called an *extension* (of up to three characters). The file name for a file with an extension is written in the form "<filename>.<extension>", as in "Accounts.DBF".

feature update. A release of a software program which contains a significant number of enhancements with respect to its predecessor.

fields. A dBASE database record consists of N bytes, where N is the same for all records belonging to the same database. The first byte is the delete byte field, which is always present and which is controlled with the DELETE and UPDATE statements (or CONTROL-U in EDIT/BROWSE). The next K1 bytes store the first field, the next K2 bytes store the second field, and so on. All fields have the attributes of *name, type,* and *length*; numeric fields have the additional attribute of *decimals*.

file name. See *extension, DOS file name.*

filename. See *extension, DOS file name.*

fully qualified file name, MS-DOS. A file reference of the form <filename>.<extension> may be ambiguous because (1) no drive is specified, and (2) no directory is specified. A fully qualified MS-DOS file reference is not ambiguous because it specifies the drive and path, as in

<drive>:<path><filename>.<extension>

formal parameters. In dBASE dialects, the identifiers which appear in the PARAMETERS statement.

FORMAT file. A file used in connection with a .DBF file that defines the data-entry form which is to be used when database records are edited with the EDIT command. The FORMAT file is not used automatically; it must be opened with the SET FORMAT TO statement.

freeware. Software which has been placed into the public domain. Freeware may be used without payment to the creator.

index key. An expression which references the fields of a database and which is used to build an index to the database. The index contains the number of each record and the value of the expression for the fields of the record. When a *search key* is provided, the index is rapidly searched for an index key whose value matches that of the search key. If a match is found, the index gives the number of the matching record.

information structure. Either a *procedure structure* or a *data structure.*

integer. A number whose fractional part is 0. For example, 1 and 1.00 are both integers.

I/O. Input/Output.

iteration variable. The variable in an iterative loop which controls the number of times that the loop is executed. For example, the identifier in the syntax "FOR <identifier> = …" is an iteration variable.

iterative variable. Synonym for *iteration variable.*

key. 1. Either a *search key* or an *index key.* 2. A key on the keyboard.

keyword. An identifier whose meaning is defined as part of the language.

life cycle. The period of time during which an application is used.

macro. 1. In the dBASE programming language, the macro is a character memvar which holds part or all of a command. Macros are referenced by preceding a memvar with an ampersand, as in &EditBrowse. If the memvar EditBrowse has the value "EDIT", then executing the statement &EditBrowse is the same as executing the EDIT statement, with the exception that more time is required to interpret &EditBrowse than to interpret the EDIT command. 2. In dBASE IV and FoxPro, a sequence of keystrokes which is assigned to a single keystroke; for example, pressing ALT-E would be equivalent to typing EJECT followed by an ENTER keystroke if that keystroke sequence were made the macro for ALT-E.

main menu. The top-level menu of a routine; usually the first menu seen by the user when the application is executed.

main procedure. The procedure or command file which displays the main menu and processes its choices.

main routine. Synonym for *main procedure.*

maintenance. The process of fixing bugs which are identified during the lifetime of a program, after the initial testing period. Also, the process of modifying or adding features to a working program.

maintenance documentation. Documentation written by the maintenance programmer.

maintenance programmer. A programmer who performs maintenance.

master index. The index which controls the order of access when more than one index is open.

memo fields. Fields that hold variable-length character strings, which are stored in a .DBT file with the same filename as its corresponding .DBF file.

memory variables. Identifiers which are created and assigned while an application is executing. PRIVATE memvars created by a program do not exist after the program finishes. PUBLIC memvars do not exist after the termination of compiled programs, but PUBLIC memvars do exist after the termination of interpreted programs. (See the related entry *fields.*)

memvars. Synonym for *memory variables.*

null character. The first character in ASCII, represented as ASC(0).

null string. A string of length 0, represented as "".

OEM. Original equipment manufacturer.

ordinal number. An integer which refers to the position of an item in an ordered list. For example, the ordinal number 1 refers to the first item, the ordinal number 2 refers to the second item, and so on. (See the related entry *cardinal number.*)

paradigm. A standard way of solving or viewing a given problem.

parameter. A pointer to data which is used to communicate information between a routine and the subroutine which it calls.

parameterized information structure. An information structure which has fixed portions and replaceable portions whose content is determined by parameters.

parameters, actual versus formal. See *actual parameters* and *formal parameters.*

PC/MS-DOS. The generic Intel-architecture microcomputer operating system from Microsoft, and/or its implementation for IBM microcomputers.

procedure. One of the three types of dBASE subroutine. Procedure code is preceded with the PROCEDURE keyword and is followed by another PROCEDURE statement or the end-of-file. Procedures are grouped in special command files called *procedure files.*

procedure structure. A set of consecutive programming statements (and the routines which they call) that performs a specific task.

product life cycle. The period of time during which a product is used.

pseudocompilation. The process of translating source code to intermediate code.

pseudocompile. To perform the activity of pseudocompilation.

reference a routine. To call a routine.

routine. Generically, a subroutine. In dBASE dialects, a command file, procedure, or function.

runtime. A product produced by removing the dot-prompt support from a dBASE interpreter; a runtime executes programs in their intermediate code form.

search key. See *index key.*

semantics. The meaning of a command, that is, what changes in the state of the computer are made by the action of the command.

shareware. Software which you may legally use for a limited period of time without payment to the creator. Following a trial period, you are to stop using the software or else follow the registration procedures specified by the creator, which will involve making a payment.

simultaneous. At the same time. (See the related entry *concurrent.* For example, when you and I sit down at the dinner table, we may eat simultaneously, but we use the salt shaker concurrently.)

software. Bit patterns which control the hardware of a digital computer.

software engineering. The application of engineering principles to the production of software.

submenu. A menu other than the main menu of an application.

subroutine. In dBASE dialects, a command file, procedure, or function.

symbol table. A table that stores the name and other attributes of named data objects while your application executes.

syntax. The way in which you must sequence characters in source code in order to construct commands which are recognized by your dBASE dialect.

systems programming. An activity which produces the software on which applications depend, such as the operating system and programmer tools such as linkers. (See the related entry *application programming,* which is the process of producing applications.)

template. A text file (or the equivalent) containing fixed and replaceable text. When the replaceable text is replaced with code of the kind which the replaceable text describes, the template becomes syntactically legal source code. In this book, templates are used as aids to the manual construction of source code. Code generators use templates for the automatic construction of source code.

token. A syntactic element in a programming language, such as a keyword, a relational or mathematical operator, or a user-defined identifier.

tokenize. To separate the characters which comprise source code into a sequence of tokens.

TSR. Terminate and Stay Resident. A kind of MS-DOS program which stays loaded in RAM after you exit from it.

UDF. User-defined function. (Contrast *built-in function,* which is provided by the vendor of a computer language product.)

unity-indexed arrays. Arrays whose subscripts start with 1. (See the related entry *zero-indexed arrays.*)

upload. To transfer a copy of a file to a second computer from your computer.

zero-indexed arrays. Arrays whose subscripts start with 0. (See the related entry *unity-indexed arrays.*)

References

Adams, Pat. 1989. "Recital Revealed." *DBMS* (May): 52 ff.

Ashton-Tate. 1989. *Ashton-Tate Developer Registry.* 3rd ed. Torrance, California: Ashton-Tate. 743 pp.

Bauman, John. 1989a. "SuperFMT: A Better Format File." *Data Based Advisor* (June): 125–131.

Bauman, John. 1989b. "DBFs on the Fly." *Data Based Advisor* (August): 128–134.

Bauman, John. 1989c. Reply to letter "DBFs on the Fly and dBMAN." *Data Based Advisor* (October): 144.

Berguido, Carlos, and John Bauman. 1989. Letter "DBFs on the Fly and dBMAN." *Data Based Advisor* (October): 144.

Bohm, C., and G. Jacopini. 1966. "Flow Diagrams, Turing Machines and Languages with Only Two Formation Rules." *Communications of the ACM* (May).

Castro, L., J. Hanson, and T. Rettig. 1985. *Advanced Programmer's Guide Featuring dBASE III and dBASE II with dBASE III PLUS Update.* Torrance, California: Ashton-Tate. 679 pp.

Data Based Solutions. 1990. *Data Based Advisor Database Directory 1990.* San Diego, California: Data Based Solutions.

Date, C. J. 1990. *An Introduction to Database Systems, Volume 1.* 5th ed. Reading, Massachusetts: Addison-Wesley Publishing Co. 800 pp.

Dunlop, Neil. 1989. *dBASE for Professionals, with dBASE IV.* New York: Van Nostrand Reinhold. 382 pp.

Dutka, Alan F., and Howard H. Hanson. 1989. *Fundamentals of Data Normalization.* Reading, Massachusetts: Addison-Wesley Publishing Co. 196 pp.

Elmasri, R., and S. B. Navathe. 1989. *Fundamentals of Database Systems.* Redwood City, California: Benjamin/Cummings Publishing Co. 802 pp.

Feldheim, Shar. 1990. "Between Friends." *Data Based Advisor* (November): 142–146.

Fuller, Arthur. 1989. *Dynamics of Clipper.* Homewood, Illinois: Dow Jones-Irwin. 511 pp.

Goley, George F. 1989a. "The dBASE Shootout." *Data Based Advisor* (April): 52–89.

Goley, George F. 1989b. "Macintosh Speed Tests." *Data Based Advisor* (April): 114–120.

Goley, George F. 1990. "The Power of BROWSE." *Data Based Advisor* (September): 56–60.

Green, Adam. 1990. *DBMS* (October): 37.

Heiser, Paul. 1985. *Salvaging Damaged dBASE Files*. Pittsford, New York: ComTech Publishing, Ltd.

Heiser, Paul. 1989. *Salvaging Damaged dBASE Files*. 2nd ed. San Marcos, California: MicroTrend Books. Sold in bookstores and through *Data Based Advisor* magazine.

Kalman, David M. 1989. *The dBASE Language Handbook*. San Marcos, California: MicroTrend Books. 992 pp. Sold in bookstores and through *Data Based Advisor* magazine.

Kinney, John M. 1990. "dCL-Net Library." *Data Based Advisor* (June): 112.

Knuth, Donald E. 1973a. *The Art of Computer Programming, Volume 1*. Reading, Massachusetts: Addison-Wesley Publishing Co.

Knuth, Donald E. 1973b. *The Art of Computer Programming, Volume 3*. Reading, Massachusetts: Addison-Wesley Publishing Co.

Millican, T. David. 1987. "Database Writer Makes Dbase III Reporting Easy." *InfoWorld* (May 25): 55–61.

Millican, T. David. 1990. "What Can You Get for $5,000?" *Computer Shopper* (November): 322 ff.

Nantucket Corporation. 1988. *Clipper Third Party Products Directory*. Los Angeles, California: Nantucket Corporation.

Oliver, Brett. 1990. "Data Driven Systems: A Fresh Approach to Application Generation." *Ashton-Tate Update Developer* (Summer/Fall): 8–9.

Olympia, P. L. 1990. "The Data Dictionary." *DBMS* (May): 78–81.

Olympia, P. L., and Cathy Cea. 1990. *Developing FoxPro Applications*. Reading, Massachusetts: Addison-Wesley Publishing Co. 434 pp.

Olympia, P. L., R. Russell Freeland, and Randy Wallin. 1988. *dBASE Power: Building and Using Programming Tools*. Torrance, California: Ashton-Tate.

Price, Candy. 1990. "That Makes Two of You," letter to *Data Based Advisor* (January): 126 ff.

Rettig, Tom. 1990a. "FoxPro for Clipperheads, Part 1." *DBMS* (February): 61–71.

Rettig, Tom. 1990b. "FoxPro for Clipperheads, Part 2." *DBMS* (March): 53–63.

Rettig, Tom. 1990c. "FoxPro for Clipperheads, Part 3." *DBMS* (April): 46–58.

Sackman, Harold, et al. 1968. "Exploratory Experimental Studies Comparing Online and Offline Programming Performance." *Communications of the ACM* 11, no. 1 (January): 3–11.

Software Digest. 1984. *Software Digest Ratings Newsletter* (December). Wynnewood, Pennsylvania: Software Digest, Inc.

Somerson, Paul. 1988. *PC Magazine DOS Power Tools*. New York: Bantam. 1,275 pp.; includes diskette.

Spence, Rick. 1989. "Referential Integrity in Clipper." *Reference(Clipper)* 3, no. 12 (December).

Spence, Rick. 1990. "Nested READS the Smart Way." *Data Based Advisor* (September): 52–55.

Steele, Philip. 1989. *Professional Database Development Using dBASE III Plus, Clipper, and FoxBASE+*. Glenview, Illinois: Scott, Foresman & Company. 284 pp.

Straley, Stephen J. 1988. *Programming in Clipper*. 2nd ed. Reading, Massachusetts: Addison-Wesley Publishing Co. 960 pp.

Streich, Mark, and David Kalman. 1990. "The Benchmarks Revisited." *Data Based Advisor* (April): 100–101.

Strickler, David. 1989. "Recital: dBASE III+ Clone for VAXs — And Much More." *Digital News* (January 23).

Wallace, B., D. Wallenchinsky, A. Wallace, and S. Wallace. 1980. *The Book of Lists #2*. New York: William Morrow & Co.

Weinberg, Gerald M. 1971. *The Psychology of Computer Programming.* New York: Van Nostrand Reinhold. 288 pp.

Yellick, Craig. 1989a. *Building Source Code Libraries*. Edina, Minnesota: Alto Microcomputer. 30 pp.

Yellick, Craig. 1989b. *User Interface and Screen Control Library*. Edina, Minnesota: Alto Microcomputer. The manual for this software/text product has approximately 150 pages.

Yellick, Craig. 1990. *Wonderful Differences: dBASE & Clipper*. Edina, Minnesota: Alto Microcomputer. 64 pp.

Yourdon, Edward. 1976, 1979a. *Managing the Structured Techniques*. 2nd ed. Englewood Cliffs, New Jersey: Prentice-Hall. 266 pp. 4th ed., Englewood Cliffs, New Jersey: Yourdon Press.

Yourdon, Edward. 1977, 1978, 1979b. *Structured Walkthroughs.* 2nd ed. Englewood Cliffs, New Jersey: Prentice-Hall. 137 pp. 4th ed. Englewood Cliffs, New Jersey: Yourdon Press.

Index

Terms which are italicized refer to the glossary entry for that term or to the names of publications.

B

C

D

E

F

G

H

I

J

K

L

M

N

Q

R

T

U

V

W

X

Y

Z

Companion Products
for dBASE Dialects Software Engineering, Volume 1
Mail Order Form

Date: ______________________________

Circle payment method: Check Money Order MasterCard VISA

Credit card number:

__________-__________-__________-__________

Expiration date: month/year: ______/______

Exact name on card: ______________________________

Your name: (enter "same" if same) ______________________________

If names are different, which name should we mail to?

Circle: first second

Your company name: ______________________________

Your title: ______________________________

To what street address or Post Office Box do you want us to mail?

____

____

City, State: ______________________________

ZIP code or COUNTRY: ______________________________

Daytime phone number, area code first:

(______)________-________X________

Circle the products desired:

Volume 1 Companion Diskette: 5¼ inch size 3½ inch size

Volume 1 Supplement: #1 #2 #3 #4 #5 #6 #7

Mail to:

Database Software Consultants, POB 8380, Austin, TX 78713-8380, U.S.A.

Companion Products
for dBASE Dialects Software Engineering, Volume 1
Mail Order Form

Date: ______________________________

Circle payment method: Check Money Order MasterCard VISA

Credit card number:

__________-__________-__________-__________

Expiration date: month/year: ______/______

Exact name on card: ______________________________

Your name: (enter "same" if same) ______________________________

If names are different, which name should we mail to?

Circle: first second

Your company name: ______________________________

Your title: ______________________________

To what street address or Post Office Box do you want us to mail?

____

____

City, State: ______________________________

ZIP code or COUNTRY: ______________________________

Daytime phone number, area code first:

(______)________-________X_______

Circle the products desired:

Volume 1 Companion Diskette: $5^1/_4$ inch size $3^1/_2$ inch size

Volume 1 Supplement: #1 #2 #3 #4 #5 #6 #7

Mail to:

Database Software Consultants, POB 8380, Austin, TX 78713-8380, U.S.A.

Companion Products
for dBASE Dialects Software Engineering, Volume 1
Mail Order Form

Date: ____

Circle payment method: Check Money Order MasterCard VISA

Credit card number:

__________-__________-__________-__________

Expiration date: month/year: ______/_______

Exact name on card: ______________________________________

Your name: (enter "same" if same) ____________________________

If names are different, which name should we mail to?

Circle: first second

Your company name: _______________________________________

Your title: ____

To what street address or Post Office Box do you want us to mail?

____

____

City, State: ____

ZIP code or COUNTRY: _____________________________________

Daytime phone number, area code first:

(______)________-________X_______

Circle the products desired:

Volume 1 Companion Diskette: 5¼ inch size 3½ inch size

Volume 1 Supplement: #1 #2 #3 #4 #5 #6 #7

Mail to:

Database Software Consultants, POB 8380, Austin, TX 78713-8380, U.S.A.
